# The Monetarists

# The Monetarists

*The Making of the Chicago Monetary Tradition, 1927–1960*

GEORGE S. TAVLAS

THE UNIVERSITY OF CHICAGO PRESS      CHICAGO AND LONDON

The University of Chicago Press, Chicago 60637
The University of Chicago Press, Ltd., London
© 2023 by The University of Chicago
All rights reserved. No part of this book may be used or reproduced in any manner what-
soever without written permission, except in the case of brief quotations in critical articles
and reviews. For more information, contact the University of Chicago Press, 1427 E. 60th St.,
Chicago, IL 60637.
Published 2023
Printed in the United States of America

32 31 30 29 28 27 26 25 24 23     1 2 3 4 5

ISBN-13: 978-0-226-82318-8 (cloth)
ISBN-13: 978-0-226-82319-5 (e-book)
DOI: https://doi.org/10.7208/chicago/9780226823195.001.0001

Library of Congress Cataloging-in-Publication Data

Names: Tavlas, George S., author.
Title: The monetarists : the making of the Chicago monetary tradition, 1927–1960 /
    George S. Tavlas.
Description: Chicago : The University of Chicago Press, 2023. | Includes bibliographical
    references and index.
Identifiers: LCCN 2022026743 | ISBN 9780226823188 (cloth) | ISBN 9780226823195 (ebook)
Subjects: LCSH: Chicago school of economics—History. | Monetary policy—
    United States—History—20th century. | Quantity theory of money.
Classification: LCC HB98.3 .T38 2023 | DDC 330.15/53—dc23/eng/20220718
LC record available at https://lccn.loc.gov/2022026743

Give me a place to stand and I will move the earth. But first, I need to have a place to stand—a foundation.   ARCHIMEDES

To the women who gave me the foundation to write this book:
my late mother, Louisa Tavlas
my wife, Sophia Tavlas
my daughters, Louisa Tavlas Atkinson and Julia Tavlas

# Contents

# Preface

This book tells the story of a small group of University of Chicago economists who preserved the importance of the quantity theory of money and defended the free-market system. They did so at a time when the American economics community discredited the role of monetary forces in the economy, viewed fiscal policy as the only game in town, and embraced a greatly expanded role for government in economic affairs. The members of "The Group"—as the Chicagoans referred to themselves in the 1930s—included Henry Simons, Lloyd Mints, Paul Douglas, Frank Knight, Aaron Director, and Garfield Cox. The Group used the quantity theory of money to formulate an unconventional and original policy agenda that included (1) money-financed fiscal deficits to combat depressions with the provision that the budget should be balanced over the business cycle; (2) monetary rules to reduce uncertainty; (3) 100 percent reserve requirements on demand deposits to ensure the safety of deposits, control the quantity of money better, reduce the frequency and the intensity of the business cycle, and make seigniorage from money creation the exclusive privilege of the government; and (4) flexible exchange rates to provide space for domestic economic policies.

Jacob Viner, who, along with Knight, was the most renowned of the Chicagoans in the 1930s, mostly dissented from The Group's policy platform although Viner's interpretation of Federal Reserve policies during the Great Depression found its way, via Mints, into Milton Friedman's work. Douglas, who agreed with and helped create the policy platform, mainly dissented from The Group's free-market principles, but his dissension softened after the early 1930s.

Using the quantity theory of money, the Chicagoans advocated increasing the money supply to combat the Great Depression. They believed that fiscal deficits were the most effective way to generate increases in the money supply, thereby linking fiscal deficits with the quantity theory. Thus, the Chicagoans were well placed to reject the central policy message of John Maynard Keynes's 1936 book *The General Theory of Employment, Interest and Money*, a main purpose of which was to provide a theory to rationalize fiscal deficits. In the late 1940s, the ideas of these economists found a cohort in Friedman, who, after joining the Chicago economics faculty in 1946, adopted and pushed forward their policy agenda.

The period chronicled in this book begins in 1927, a year that saw the arrival of Knight, Simons, and Director at Chicago, and the initial sprouts of ideas that would become hallmarks of Chicago monetary economics over the ensuing several decades. The period ends in 1960, the year in which Friedman published the book *A Program for Monetary Stability*, which summarized the policy conclusions, including his monetary-growth rule, that sprang from his research in monetary economics during the previous decade. Several years after the publication of that book, Friedman's research findings, emphasizing the important role played by money in the economy and the policy conclusions of those findings, came to be characterized as "monetarism." This book tells the story of the emergence and development of what came to be known as the Chicago monetary tradition.

The notion of a Chicago monetary tradition became the focus of professional interest with Friedman's essay "The Quantity Theory of Money: A Restatement," in 1956. In that essay, Friedman, who had been a graduate student at Chicago in the early 1930s, claimed that his monetary economics derived from a 1930s and 1940s oral Chicago quantity-theory tradition developed by his mentors—singling out Simons, Mints, Knight, and Viner. The next fifty years saw an outpouring of publications that examined the validity of Friedman's claim. The doctrinal literature called an assortment of monetary economists who wrote in the 1930s and 1940s—Chicagoans and non-Chicagoans alike—to the stage to shed light on the following question: Did Friedman's monetarist framework more closely resemble what had been produced earlier at Chicago, or did it more closely resemble what had originated outside of Chicago? The predominance of the doctrinal historical evidence concluded that Friedman's monetary framework, in terms of its (1) emphasis on the efficacy of monetary policy conducted through open-market operations, (2) empirical orientation, (3) monetary interpretation of the origins of the Great Depression, and (4) espousal of a money-supply-growth rule, had numerous forerunners at American institutions outside of Chicago in the 1930s and 1940s but few forerunners at Chicago. Thus, the evidence concluded that, contrary to Friedman's claim, the Chicago Economics Department of the 1930s and 1940s had not been an isolated center that used the quantity theory to stress the importance of money. Indeed, a conclusion that emerged from the debate over the existence of a Chicago monetary tradition was that Friedman's 1956 "Restatement" of the quantity theory resembled more closely the Keynesian theory of liquidity preference than any version of the quantity theory used, either at Chicago or at any other American institutions, in the 1930s and 1940s.

In light of the evidence produced up to that time, notably by Don Patinkin, in his 1970 Richard T. Ely Lecture before the American Economic Association, Harry Johnson, Friedman's Chicago colleague, accused Friedman of having "invented" a Chicago monetary tradition. Friedman, Johnson charged, attempted to manufacture a counter-revolution in macroeconomics to show that his monetary framework had pre–*General Theory* roots and, thus, could be considered a valid counter-revolutionary challenge to the prevailing Keynesian orthodoxy. Other researchers joined Johnson in the accusation that Friedman had invented a Chicago monetary tradition. The doctrinal evidence produced over the years was sufficiently compelling against Friedman's position that, in the early 2000s, Friedman, who did not have expertise in doctrinal history, backtracked on his earlier claim of a Chicago monetary tradition that was related to his monetary framework.

This book provides a very different view of the matter. I provide evidence that challenges—and, I believe abrogates—the prevailing consensus that Friedman invented an earlier Chicago monetary tradition. I also challenge the related contention that, even if such a tradition existed, it was not unique in a way that directly influenced Friedman's monetarist views. In particular, I show that (1) there *was* a 1930s and 1940s Chicago quantity-theory tradition; (2) the quantity-theory framework developed and used at Chicago was very different from that used at other institutions; (3) at the time (in the late 1940s) that Friedman made monetary economics the main focus of his research, his views fully reflected that tradition; and (4) the Chicago version of the quantity theory provided a platform for Friedman to launch the monetarist counter-revolution. Without that particular platform, any other challenge to the Keynesian orthodoxy of the 1950s and 1960s would likely have taken a very different form. I provide contemporaneous evidence from the 1940s and early

1950s that the Chicago Economics Department was considered by other economists at the time to have been an iconoclastic fortress that defended the importance of money in the economy and the advantages of the free-market system.

Why do the results contained in this study differ so fundamentally from the prevailing consensus about the absence of a Chicago monetary tradition that cultivated Friedman's monetarism? There are several reasons. The first relates to the rules of engagement followed in previous research on the relationship between Friedman's monetarist economics and the monetary economics of his quantity-theory predecessors. The objective of that research strategy has been to search for forerunners of Friedman's views in the 1930s and 1940s—an approach that is comparative static in essence. In contrast, my approach is to analyze *the evolution* of Chicago monetary economics. In other words, although the comparative-static approach can yield *anticipations* of Friedman's monetarist framework in the 1930s and 1940s literature, it does not necessarily provide evidence of an *influence* on Friedman's monetarism. The approach I take is to trace the development of monetary economics at Chicago. This development explains the way Friedman's views on monetary economics were shaped shortly after he began teaching at Chicago in 1946. Second, in addition to Chicagoans Simons and Viner, whose work in the 1930s and 1940s had been the primary focus in previous doctrinal studies, my cross section of Chicagoans includes the works of Mints, Director, Douglas, Knight, and Cox. Each of them has previously been thought to have had marginal or peripheral influences on the development of Friedman's monetary thought. By broadening the cross section of Chicago economists considered in the data sample, I show that—far from having been marginal figures—those economists appreciably and fundamentally helped shape Friedman's monetarist framework. Thus, I trace direct lines of influence on Friedman's initial thinking on monetary economics from the Chicago monetary framework as it existed in the early 1930s to its embellishment from the mid-1930s to the late 1940s by Simons, Mints, Knight, and Director. I also show that the work of a non-Chicagoan, Clark Warburton, intrudes into this Chicago story; Warburton's work in the 1940s and early 1950s played a pivotal role in helping shape Friedman's emerging monetarism.

Third, unlike previous research on the doctrinal foundations of Friedman's monetarist economics—which typically focused on the differences in the theoretical frameworks between the 1930s and 1940s Chicagoans and Friedman's version of the quantity theory (and, as I document, any differences in monetary theory were relatively minor at the time that Friedman began working in the field of monetary economics)—I focus on the policies advocated by the earlier Chicagoans and Friedman. I show that, with minor modifications, Friedman espoused the earlier Chicago policy agenda at the time that he made monetary economics his primary field of interest in the late 1940s, and incorporated much of that policy agenda into his monetarist framework of the late 1950s. Fourth, my data set includes both published and unpublished works by the economists in question. The unpublished material, some of it presented for the first time in the literature, provides additional evidence on the influence of other economists, especially Director and Warburton, on Friedman's thinking. Finally, at the time (in the late 1940s) that he moved into monetary economics as his primary field of interest, Friedman brought to the table a skill set that his Chicago predecessors did not have—a cutting-edge knowledge of applied and theoretical statistics. I show the way Friedman applied that skill set to the monetary framework that he had inherited from his Chicago mentors to develop, from the late 1940s to the late 1950s, what became known as monetarism. In this way, he launched a successful counter-revolutionary challenge to the Keynesian orthodoxy. I also show that, in the 1950s, Friedman and Director moved the Chicago framework in the direction of reduced government involvement in economic affairs compared with the involvement advocated, notably by Simons, at Chicago in the 1930s and the 1940s.

# Acknowledgments

The origins of this book are to be found in my graduate studies at New York University (NYU) in the 1970s and, in particular, Bill Silber's outstanding course on monetary economics. That course introduced me to, and cultivated a lifetime affair with, monetary economics in general, and doctrinal monetary history in particular. Bill and the late James Becker, who taught me the history of economic thought, supervised my PhD dissertation, "Essays on the Doctrinal Foundations of Milton Friedman's Monetary Economics," completed at NYU in 1977. Since then, Bill has remained a friend. One of the reading assignments in Bill's course was an article on the development of the quantity theory of money by Tom Humphrey, who had worked at the Federal Reserve Bank of Richmond before retiring. Through that article, I was introduced to the work of one of the foremost scholars in the area of doctrinal monetary history. I started reading Tom's articles, and I have never stopped. Tom, who remains active in retirement, read earlier drafts of this book and made corrections and invaluable comments.

My biggest debt for this project is to the people at the two institutions with which I am associated—the Bank of Greece and the Hoover Institution at Stanford University. At the Bank of Greece, I want to express my deeply felt gratitude to Yannis Stournaras, the governor of the bank, for his encouragement and support throughout the course of writing this book, and for stimulating discussions and leadership on monetary policy during challenging times. I also want to express my sincere appreciation to George Provopoulos, the previous governor of the bank, for his encouragement and generosity, and for astute management during a crisis. Since I joined the Bank of Greece in 2001, I have had the benefit of working under two other governors, Nicholas Garganas and Lucas Papademos, each of whom provided an environment conducive to economic analysis and research.

At the Hoover Institution, I owe special thanks to the director, Condoleezza Rice, and the previous director, Thomas Gilligan. I have had the privilege of working with a stimulating group of colleagues at Hoover. I wish to single out John Taylor, the intellectual heir to the tradition concerning monetary rules discussed in this book, along with John Cochrane and the late George Shultz. Each backed and encouraged this project from its inception, and each helped shape the direction of this book. Finally, at Hoover, I have had the good fortune to have had Mike Bordo as a colleague. Mike, whose knowledge of monetary history is unsurpassed, has provided me with insight into Chicago monetary economics and has staunchly supported my work.

Although I maintained an interest in the history of monetary doctrine over the years, research for this particular project began in 2013, when I was a visiting scholar at the Becker Friedman Institute for Economics at the University of Chicago. Since that time, I have visited the Becker Friedman Institute on several occasions. I am indebted to Lars Peter Hansen, Michael Greenstone, James Heckman, Bob Lucas, Kevin Murphy, and the late Gary Becker, for their encouragement and support. I also conducted research for this book while a visiting scholar at both Drexel University's LeBow School of Business and the Center for the History of Political Economy at Duke University. I owe special gratitude to LeBow's George Tsetsekos and the center's Kevin Hoover, Bruce Caldwell, E. Roy Weintraub, and the late Craufurd Goodwin.

At the start of my career, and for many years after, I had the good fortune of having two distinguished macroeconomists as mentors and collaborators: the late Joseph Aschheim and the late Martin J. Bailey. I learned a lot from those two individuals. At the IMF, Ed Brau and Peter B. Clark played pivotal roles in advancing my career. To go back further in time, I am grateful to my undergraduate teachers at Babson College, especially the late Joseph Alexander, who steered me into a career in economics, and Bill Casey, who taught my first course in economics and has remained a friend.

Several people read drafts of the entire book and provided valuable and constructive comments and criticism. I owe Harris Dellas an enormous debt. Without his constant encouragement and stimulating commentary, the book would never have been completed. David Laidler pushed me to travel down roads that were not on my initial intellectual roadmap. I have learned a great deal from David, both while working on this book and through his many publications in monetary economics. Michael Ulan read multiple drafts of each chapter, making corrections, providing suggestions, and improving the presentation. Ever since we worked together in the US State Department in the 1980s, Mike has been an invaluable colleague. Ed Nelson, who recently published the definitive study on the development of Milton Friedman's economics, has been an exceptional source of advice, information, and inspiration. Ed has provided me with numerous comments that have improved the book. I have benefited from discussions with Samuel Demeulemeester about the history of banking reform. Samuel also made extremely valuable and detailed written comments on all the chapters. Ronnie Phillips, whose work on the Chicago banking proposal has become highly influential, also provided valuable comments.

I have benefited from comments from, and discussions with, a number of other individuals. These include Michael Bernstam, Rebeca Gomez Betancourt, Jennifer Burns, Tom Cate, Robert Dimand, Jim Dorn, Pedro Duarte, Paul Dudenhefer, Sebastian Edwards, Ross Emmett, David Friedman, Paul Gregory, Daniel Hammond, Robert Hetzel, Peter Ireland, Douglas Irwin, Otmar Issing, George Kouretas, Robert Leeson, Steven Medema, David Mitch, Athanasios Orphanides, Athanasios Papadopoulos, Sam Peltzman, Sylvie Rivot, Hugh Rockoff, Allen Sanderson, Roger Sandilands, George Selgin, Stephen Stigler, George Stubos, the late Donald Moggridge, and the late Richard Timberlake. I also want to express gratitude to my professional collaborators: Ralph Bryant, Deborah Gefang, Heather Gibson, Stephen Hall, George Hondroyiannis, Harry Kelejian, Jim Lothian, Pavlos Petroulas, and P. A. V. B. Swamy. In addition, the book has benefited from comments received at seminars that I gave at the Hoover Institution, the University of Chicago, and Duke University.

At the Bank of Greece, I am fortunate to have been working with what has to be the best policy staff in the central banking community: Dafni Papadopoulou, Vassilis Spiliotopoulos, Ifigeneia Skotida, Eleni Argiri, Angeliki Momtsia, Pinelopi Tsalaporta, and Christina Tsochatzi.

The personnel at the University of Chicago Press have been consummate professionals. I give special thanks to Chad Zimmerman, executive editor at the University of Chicago Press, and Erika Barrios for their support. I am indebted to Kathleen Kageff for exceptional copyediting and to Tamara Ghattas for superb manuscript and production advice. I am also grateful to Joe Jackson, a former editor at the University of Chicago Press, who commissioned this book. Morris Goldings, a retired First Amendment attorney, provided exceptional legal advice on copyright matters.

I have been especially fortunate to have had superb office support at the Bank of Greece in the persons of Elisavet Bosdelekidou and Maria Monopoli. The outstanding quality of their work has been equaled only by their patience in retyping draft after draft. Maria provided superlative research assistance. Among her many contributions, she proofread the entire manuscript for accuracy of the quotations and completed the references section, working all day and often into the night. At the Hoover Institution, I wish to thank Kathy Campitelli for her logistical support, always ensuring, in the kindest way, that changes in my travel schedule are accommodated fully and efficiently. Also at the Hoover Institution, I want to acknowledge the excellent support of David Sun and the other staff at the library archives. At the Bank of Greece, I wish to thank Eva Semertzaki, Anna Nadali, and the other library staff for excellent support. Much of the research for this book was conducted at the University of Chicago's Regenstein Library. I thank Christine Colburn and the rest of the staff at that library for assistance.

## CHAPTER ONE

# The Light in the Secret Shrine

In 1956, Milton Friedman wrote an essay, "The Quantity Theory of Money: A Restatement," as an introduction to a collection of doctoral essays written by his students in the University of Chicago's Workshop in Money and Banking, and published under the title *Studies in the Quantity Theory of Money* (Friedman 1956b).[1] Both the title and the timing of Friedman's essay were audacious. Friedman had begun teaching at Chicago in 1946 and, within a few years, had embarked on a research program studying the role of monetary forces on the US economy. The period from the mid-1940s to the mid-1960s marked the high tide of Keynesian influence on the economics profession. Fiscal policies were viewed by both academicians and policy makers as the only game in town. Monetary forces were considered to be—at best—of second-order importance; the quantity theory of money was relegated to the dustbin of history. Amid this Keynesian dominance, the aim of Friedman's 1956 "Restatement" and the accompanying essays was to restore the importance of the quantity theory and the role of monetary forces to academic and policy thinking. The decade that followed the publication of Friedman's essay saw the accumulation of a large amount of empirical evidence, much of it produced by Friedman and his associates, demonstrating the important role played by monetary factors in the economy, with the result that a monetarist counter-revolution, which underlined that role, emerged as a strong challenge to the then-existing Keynesian orthodoxy. In retrospect, Friedman's 1956 "Restatement" came to be viewed as the initial shot fired in that counter-revolution.[2]

The launch of the counter-revolution, however, was accompanied by a controversy that persists more than sixty years after the publication of Friedman's 1956 essay. In that essay, Friedman, who had undertaken graduate studies at Chicago during the 1932–33 academic year and had returned to that institution to serve as a research assistant during the 1934–35 academic year,[3] claimed that his monetary framework was a direct outgrowth of a 1930s and 1940s oral quantity-theory tradition at Chicago that differed markedly from the "atrophied and rigid" versions of the quantity theory espoused at other institutions during those years. At Chicago, Friedman (1956a, 3) asserted, his mentors, "Henry Simons and Lloyd Mints directly, and Frank Knight and Jacob Viner at one remove, taught and developed a more subtle and relevant version [of the quantity theory], one in which the quantity theory was connected and integrated with general price theory and became a flexible and sensitive tool for interpreting movements in aggregate economic activity and for developing relevant policy prescriptions." Then, after stating that, to the best of his knowledge, "no systematic statement of this theory as developed at Chicago exists," Friedman set down "a particular 'model' of a quantity theory in attempt to convey to the flavor of the oral [Chicago] tradition" (Friedman 1956a, 3–4). In so doing, he presented the quantity theory as a portfolio theory of the demand for money, one in which the analysis of money demand was made formally identical with that of the demand for a consumption good or service. As in the usual theory of consumer choice, the demand for money was shown to depend on three major sets of factors: (1) total wealth—"the analogue of the budget constraint"; (2) the price of, and rate of return on, money and other forms of wealth; and (3) the tastes and preferences of the wealth-owning units (1956a, 4). From these and other considerations, Friedman derived a demand function for money of the form:

$$M = g\left(P, r_b, r_e, \frac{1}{P}\frac{dP}{dt}, w, Y, u\right) \tag{1.1}$$

where $M$ is the nominal quantity of money; $P$ is the price level; $r_b$ is the interest rate on bonds; $r_e$ is the rate of return on equities; $(1/P)\,(dP/dt)$ is the inflation rate—and, hence, the negative of the rate of return on money balances; $w$ is the ratio of nonhuman-to-human wealth; $Y$ is nominal income; and $u$ is a vector of residual influences—variables that can be expected to affect tastes and preferences (Friedman 1956a, 9).[4]

Friedman noted that it would be possible to approach perfect stability in the demand-for-money function by adding more and more variables to the function. Doing so, however, would empty the function of its empirical power. Friedman maintained that a quantity theorist accepts the precepts that the demand for money is (1) a stable function of a limited number of variables, as in equation (1.1), (2) relatively independent of the supply of money, and (3) less than infinitely elastic at all interest rates.

Several points about Friedman's "Restatement" are important. First, Friedman (1956a, 9) distinguished between nominal rates of return and real rates of return. For example, he stated that the nominal interest rate on bonds is "equal to the 'real' rate plus the percentage rate of change of prices," where the latter effect "must be interpreted as an 'expected' rate of change." Nobay and Johnson (1977, 478) noted that Friedman's formulation of the demand for money, therefore, "incorporates the important Fisherine distinction between real and nominal interest rates, and the influence of anticipated inflation, a feature that distinguishes Friedman's analytical derivation of the demand for money from that of alternative formulations, especially Keynes's." Second, Lothian (2009, 1088) pointed out that "by including a range of alternatives to holding money, Friedman in effect widened the monetary-transmission mechanism from the narrow money-to-bonds channel of the then reigning IS-LM approach to channels linking monetary changes and spending on a much broader scale—goods and services as well as other financial assets."[5] Third, in his empirical implementation of the demand for money in his 1959 article "The Demand for Money: Some Theoretical and Empirical Results"—discussed in chapter 8 of this study—Friedman used permanent income as the empirical surrogate for wealth. As in his 1957 monograph *A Theory of the Consumption Function*, Friedman constructed permanent income as a weighted average of current and past income. The incorporation of permanent income in the empirical specification of money demand allowed Friedman to reconcile the apparently conflicting secular and cyclical behavior of the velocity of circulation of money (see chapter 8 of this study).

Friedman's reformulation of the quantity theory went unchallenged for more than ten years. But with the emergence of monetarism as a counterrevolutionary force against the Keynesian orthodoxy in the late 1960s, the reformulation—especially the claim of a particular Chicago version of the quantity theory—came under fire. Don Patinkin was the first to challenge Friedman's exegesis of a Chicago monetary tradition. Patinkin had undertaken both his undergraduate and his graduate studies at Chicago in the early 1940s, completing his PhD in 1947. He had been a student of the four individuals singled out in Friedman's 1956 essay—Henry Simons, Lloyd Mints, Frank Knight, and Jacob Viner. Patinkin was also a member of the Cowles Commission, which was situated at the University of Chicago, from May 1946 to June 1948.[6] Patinkin taught in Chicago's Economics Department in the 1947–48 academic year.[7] Overlapping at Chicago with each other during those years, Patinkin and Friedman became friends.[8] After Patinkin emigrated to Israel in 1949, he and Friedman carried on a correspondence over many years.[9]

In 1956, the year during which Friedman's "Restatement" appeared, Patinkin published the book *Money, Interest, and Prices*, in which he sought to fill in the basic chapter that he viewed as missing in classical monetary theory: the presentation of a dynamic analysis of the determination of the absolute level of prices through the working of the real balance effect. The book became an important part of the neoclassical synthesis of macro theory that emerged after the publication of John Maynard Keynes's *General Theory* in 1936. Under the neoclassical synthesis, in the long run prices and quantities were determined at full employment by the theory of general competitive equilibrium, after wages and prices had sufficient time to adjust to clear markets—thus, confirming the self-regulatory property of the market system; the Keynesian model, which assumed that prices and wages did not have sufficient time to adjust between shocks, was used to explain the short-run effects of disturbances to the economy and to justify policy interventions (Woodford 1999, 9–10). Patinkin demonstrated that, in the presence of declining aggregate demand and falling output, a fall in the price level in the short run worked by raising the level of real money balances and, through the effect of rising real cash balances on consumption, countered the fall in aggregate demand.[10] In the long run prices would change in proportion to a change in the nominal money stock, ensuring monetary neutrality as postulated under classical monetary theory. The empirical significance of the real balance effect became an active area of economic research and debate in the late 1950s and early 1960s.[11] By the late 1960s, however, interest in the real balance effect had waned, and the focus in macro had shifted on all fronts—empirical, theoretical, and policy—to the Phillips curve relationship.[12]

Patinkin's initial reaction to Friedman's "Restatement" was unfavorable, although that reaction was limited to his personal communication with Friedman. In a letter from Patinkin to Friedman dated November 16, 1959, Patinkin criticized Friedman's "Restatement" because, in Patinkin's view, the model presented in that essay was heavily influenced by Keynesian liquidity-preference theory and bore no relationship to what both Friedman and Patinkin had been taught as students about the quantity theory at Chicago. Specifically, Patinkin objected to Friedman's "refusal to recognise the strongly Keynesian flavour of the analysis it [the essay] presents." "To me it seems that . . . an exposition with the contents and spirit of yours could not have been written (and was not written) before Keynes [of the *General Theory* (1936a)]. I find it particularly difficult to accept your implication that your essay represents the kind of thing that was taught at Chicago by Knight, Viner, Simons and Mints. My own recollections are different" (letter, Patinkin to Friedman, November 16, 1959, quoted from Leeson 2003a, 8).

For the next ten years, Patinkin's critical assessment of the "Restatement" remained confined to what he wrote in his 1959 letter to Friedman. But, in 1968, Friedman published an entry on the quantity theory in the *International Encyclopedia of the Social Sciences*, an event that Patinkin viewed as an opportunity for public criticism. In the *International Encyclopedia* piece, Friedman (1968c) made two concessions—one direct and the other indirect—to the criticisms made by Patinkin in the latter's 1959 letter without, however, explicitly referring to those criticisms. These criticisms concerned the Keynesian orientation of Friedman's theoretical framework and the absence of a connection of that framework to what was taught at Chicago in the 1930s and 1940s. In a direct concession to Patinkin, although Friedman continued to represent the quantity theory as a portfolio theory of the demand for money similar to equation (1.1) above,[13] he stated that his version of the quantity theory had been strongly influenced by the Keynesian theory of liquidity preference.[14] In an indirect concession to Patinkin, Friedman no longer claimed that his monetary framework emanated from a Chicago quantity-theory tradition. In fact, there was no mention of a possible influence of such a tradition in the 1968 *International Encyclopedia* entry, nor did Friedman mention the names of his Chicago mentors—Simons, Mints, Knight, and Viner.

The concessions failed to appease Patinkin. In 1969 he published what would become a highly influential paper, "The Chicago Tradition, the Quantity Theory and Friedman," in the inaugural issue of the *Journal of Money, Credit and Banking (JMCB)*. The paper amounted to a belated attack on the intellectual integrity of the presentation of the quantity of theory in Friedman's 1956 "Restatement" of that theory. Patinkin began his paper with "an apology for having been a decade late" in responding to the "Restatement." He wrote, however, that "the recent appearance of Friedman's *International Encyclopedia* article on the quantity theory . . . provides an appropriate, if tardy, occasion to raise some basic questions—from the viewpoint of the history of monetary doctrine—about the validity of Friedman's interpretation of the quantity theory of money, and of its Chicago version in particular" (Patinkin 1969, 46). Patinkin continued:

> The main purpose of this paper ... is to describe ... the *true* nature of the Chicago monetary tradition. In this way I shall also demonstrate the invalidity of Friedman's contention (in his 1956 essay) that this tradition is represented by his "reformulation of the quantity theory." As a minimum statement let me say that though I shared with Friedman—albeit, almost a decade later—the teachers at Chicago (namely, Knight, Viner, Simons, and Mints), his representation of the "flavor of the oral tradition" which they were supposed to have imparted strikes no responsive chord in my memory. (emphasis added, 1969, 47)[15]

Patinkin went on to write that "I would like finally to emphasize that my concern in this paper is with the analytical framework of the Chicago monetary tradition, and not with its policy proposals as such" (1969, 47). Using evidence contained in the writings of the earlier Chicagoans— Simons, Mints, Knight, and Viner—as well as lecture notes he took during his graduate studies in the years 1943–45, Patinkin described a Chicago monetary tradition that consisted of five "summary propositions," three of which were theoretically oriented and two of which were policy related— even though he had stated that his concern would be with the analytical aspects of the Chicago monetary tradition (Patinkin 1969, 50–51). Patinkin's propositions may be restated in abridged form as follows:

*Summary proposition, no. 1.* The basic theoretical framework used by the earlier Chicagoans was Irving Fisher's (1911b) equation of exchange:

$$MV + M'V' = PT. \qquad (1.2)$$

where $M$ is the quantity of money, $V$ is the velocity of circulation of money, $M'$ is the quantity of demand deposits (or near moneys), $V'$ is the velocity of circulation of demand deposits, $P$ is the average price level of the considerations traded for money, and $T$ is the physical volume of these considerations.[16]

*Summary proposition, no. 2.* The economic system is inherently unstable. Economic fluctuations are caused by sharp, autonomous variations in $V$, which affect prices initially and then, via sticky wages, affect profits and output. Variations in $V$ are cumulative in nature—and there is no limit to how far velocity can fall—because of effects of changes in price expectations and in the state of business confidence on $V$; the fall of $V$—or alternatively, the act of hoarding—

will cause prices to fall even further, thus, leading to a greater fall of $V$, and so on. In this way, a cumulative process of economic contraction that has no natural limit is set into motion. That is, once prices and, therefore, profits and output start to fall, they will continue to do so.

*Summary proposition, no. 3.* The effects of cumulative changes in $V$ are greatly exacerbated by the "perverse" behavior of a fractional-reserve banking system, which expands credit, and, thus, demand deposits, or $M'$, in economic expansions and contracts lending, and, thus, demand deposits, in economic downturns. As a result, the quantity of money $(M)$, near moneys $(M')$, and their velocities $(V$ and $V'$, respectively) increase in booms and contract in depressions.

*Summary proposition, no. 4.* To smooth the business cycle, the government has an obligation to undertake countercyclical policy. The "guiding principle" of government policy is to effectuate countercyclical changes in $M$ in order to restore full-employment.

*Summary proposition, no. 5.* The necessary variations in $M$ can be generated by either open-market operations or money-financed budget deficits. In turn, budget deficits can be generated by varying either government expenditure or tax receipts. From the viewpoint of limiting the role of government in economic life, the variation of tax receipts is definitely preferable. Therefore, a tax system that relies heavily on the income tax is desirable from both the point of view of distributive justice and that of automatic countercyclical variations in tax receipts.

In his 1969 article, Patinkin contrasted the monetary-theoretic approaches of Keynes both in his 1930 book *A Treatise on Money* and in his 1936 book *General Theory*, and of Friedman in his "Restatement," with pre-Keynesian treatments of the quantity theory, including the earlier Chicago version of that theory.[17] Patinkin made the following arguments. First, both Keynes in the *Treatise* and the *General Theory*, and Friedman in his "Restatement," were concerned primarily with the optimal relationship between the stock of money and the stock of other assets, whereas the earlier quantity theorists were concerned primarily with the direct relationship between the stock of money and the flow of spending on goods and services. For both Keynes and Friedman, wealth (in the case of Friedman, permanent income) constituted the total budget constraint on the holdings of assets, including money. Therefore, an increase in wealth generally increases the holdings of all assets whereas an increase in income increases the demand for money at the expense of other assets. Moreover, Keynesian theory analyzes the initial impact of an increase in the quantity of money on the economy through the effect of the increase on the balance sheet of an individual. Specifically, in order to persuade an individual to hold more money under the Keynesian portfolio-balance model, the rates of return on other assets in the portfolio must decline. This decline in the rates of return on other assets increases the demand for the flow of consumption and investment goods, thus disturbing equilibrium in the commodity-flow markets. Second, for Keynes and Friedman, the rate of interest on bonds represented the opportunity cost of holding wealth in the form of money whereas pre–*General Theory* quantity theorists paid little, if any, attention to the effects of the rate of interest on the demand for money or its reciprocal, the velocity of circulation of money; Chicago quantity theorists, in particular, paid *no* attention to the effects of the interest rate on velocity or on money demand (or hoarding). Third, Patinkin argued that, whereas Friedman had presented the demand for money as a stable functional relationship between money balances and other variables, the Chicagoans of the 1930s and 1940s considered the velocity of circulation unstable (i.e., Patinkin's "summary proposition, no. 2").

Patinkin's (1) contrast between the emphasis of the earlier Chicago quantity theorists on an unstable velocity of circulation of money within the context of the Fisherine equation of exchange, $MV + M'V' = PT$, and Friedman's presentation of the quantity theory in terms of a portfolio theory of the demand for money, and (2) Patinkin's textual evidence of a Chicago monetary framework that appeared to be completely unrelated to that of Friedman, had an immediate—and devastating—impact on professional opinion of Friedman's scholarly integrity. In 1969, Harry Johnson, who made major contributions to both the monetary and the trade literature in the 1950s and 1960s, and who was Friedman's colleague at Chicago, wrote to Patinkin about the latter's 1969 *JMCB* paper as follows: "I've just read your [*JMCB*] hatchet job on Milton. . . . You have shown him to be a crook" (letter, Johnson to Patinkin, September 29, 1969, quoted from Leeson 2000, 736).

The following year, Johnson delivered the prestigious Richard T. Ely Lecture before the American Economic Association, using the occasion to attack Friedman's veracity publicly.[18] In his lecture, titled "The Keynesian Revolution and the Monetarist Counter-Revolution," Johnson enumerated the conditions that he believed are needed to produce a successful counter-revolution in economics.[19] One of those conditions, Johnson

(1971, 10) argued, was the "problem of establishing some sort of continuity with the orthodoxy of the past. . . . The problem in the case of [the monetarist] counter-revolution was to establish a plausible linkage with pre-Keynesian orthodoxy." In that connection, Johnson accused Friedman of having contrived "the invention of a University of Chicago oral tradition that was alleged to have preserved understanding of the fundamental truth among a small band of the initiated through the dark years of the Keynesian despotism" (Johnson 1971, 10–11). Criticizing Friedman for having used "the techniques of scholarly chicanery . . . to promote a revolution or counter-revolution in economic theory," Johnson stated:

> The Chicago quantity theorists—Simons and Mints—were no different from their quantity theory colleagues elsewhere. . . . There was no lonely light constantly burning in a secret shrine on the Midway, encouraging the faithful to assemble in waiting for the day when the truth could safely be revealed to the masses; that candle was made, and not merely lit, only when its light had a chance of penetrating far and wide and attracting new converts to the old-time religion. (Johnson 1971, 11)

The idea that Patinkin had conclusively demonstrated that Friedman had invented a Chicago monetary tradition to promote the monetarist counter-revolution became quickly and widely accepted in the 1970s. Donald Moggridge and Susan Howson, prominent monetary historians, wrote that "the . . . famous oral tradition, of Chicago, has been shown by Patinkin to be a mythical invention" (1974, 227n3). Ronald Teigen, a well-known monetary economist in the 1970s, wrote that Friedman's "Restatement" of the quantity theory had been shown to be "a sophisticated version of Keynes' liquidity preference theory rather than the up-to-date statement of an alleged Chicago oral tradition that monetarists take it to be" (1972, 10). Joan Robinson expressed the view that "there is an unearthly, mystical element in Friedman's [monetary] thought." Relying on Patinkin's (1969) article, Robinson added: "In so far as Friedman offers an intelligible [monetary] theory, it is made up of elements borrowed from Keynes" (Robinson 1972, 86–87). In a review of a 1972 book, *Studies in Monetary Economics*, edited by Patinkin (1972d), reprinting a collection of his articles (including the 1969 *JMCB* article), David Laidler, who had been Friedman's student at Chicago in the early 1960s, suggested that Patinkin's at-one-time influential theoretical work, as reflected in Patinkin's book *Money, Interest, and Prices*, seemed to have fallen out of favor in light of the inundation of the monetarist counter-revolution. In that connection, Laidler (1973, 263) expressed the view: "Perhaps indeed he [Patinkin] was the principal victim of Friedman's myth about the Chicago tradition, a myth which he himself so decisively explodes in this volume."

Friedman was troubled by what he regarded as attacks on his veracity by Patinkin and Johnson. He responded in print in the September/October 1972 issue of the *Journal of Political Economy* (*JPE*). The events leading up to that occasion were as follows. Following the publication of his 1956 "Restatement" and subsequent empirical studies by Friedman, including *A Monetary History of the United States*, co-authored with Schwartz in 1963, there was widespread interest in the profession in a more formal presentation of his theoretical framework by Friedman, a presentation in which he would, among other things, spell out in some detail the channels of influence of monetary policy and compare his quantity-theory framework with the Keynesian doctrines that dominated academic thinking in the 1960s. Friedman responded with two articles — "A Theoretical Framework for Monetary Analysis," published in the *JPE* in 1970, and "A Monetary Theory of Nominal Income," published in the *JPE* in 1971.[20] Robert Gordon, the editor of the *JPE*, solicited critical reviews of Friedman's two *JPE* papers from several prominent monetary economists, one of whom was Patinkin.[21] All the reviews were finished in the summer of 1971, submitted to Gordon, and sent to Friedman; the latter's draft replies were written later that year. Following a round of revisions in the winter 1971–72, a symposium based on the reviews and Friedman's responses appeared in print in the September/October 1972 issue of the *JPE*.

In his paper for the symposium, Patinkin pressed ahead with the two themes contained in his 1969 *JMCB* paper — namely, that Friedman's analytic framework was more in the tradition of Keynes than in the tradition of the quantity theory and that Friedman's framework bore no relation to the 1930s and 1940s Chicago quantity-theory approach. In particular, Patinkin pointed out that in Friedman's 1970 and 1971 *JPE* papers and his earlier *International Encyclopedia* entry, Friedman "does not mention either the Chicago school or its individual members" — and Patinkin again described Friedman's framework as "a reformulation of the quantity theory that has been strongly affected by the Keynesian analysis of liquidity preference." Patinkin also expressed the view, however, that "Friedman has not yet faced up to the implications" of the fact that his monetary framework differed fundamentally from that of the earlier

Chicago monetary tradition: "the basic assumption of the Chicago school analysis was that the velocity of circulation is unstable . . . [and] sharp changes in this velocity [were considered] to be a major source of instability in the economy" (Patinkin 1972a, 887). In not facing up to the fact that his analytic framework was unrelated to that of the earlier Chicago monetary tradition, Friedman, Patinkin argued, had effectively misled the profession:

> My criticism of Friedman is . . . that on many occasions he has not provided . . . [relevant] evidence; that, indeed on some occasions, he has ignored the detailed evidence which has been adduced against the views he expresses; and that on other occasions he has indulged in casual empiricism in the attempt to support his doctrinal interpretations. (Patinkin 1972a, 884)

As mentioned, Friedman completed his initial response to Patinkin's review (as well as to the other reviews) in late 1971. An initial draft of his response to Patinkin's review conveyed the depth of his agitation with both Patinkin and Johnson. Friedman (1971b) wrote the following:

> Though I leave Patinkin to last, that is the reply which most deeply and passionately concerns me. This is only one of three articles [i.e., Patinkin (1969; 1972a; 1972b)] in which Patinkin has, as I see it, seriously misrepresented not only my work but more important, the Chicago tradition that inspired that work. Moreover, Patinkin's incredibly narrow-minded interpretation of the Chicago tradition has provided the occasion for Harry Johnson's recent libels on the Chicago tradition and on me. Accordingly, I have taken this opportunity to document a Chicago tradition that is more distinctive, more important, and more generous than any reader of Patinkin could envision. (1971b, 2)

In his initial draft response, Friedman attacked Patinkin's "neutrality myopia" and called Patinkin a "heartstruck swain" (1971b, 5), the implication being that the macroeconomic analysis in Patinkin's 1956 book was not worth the time invested.

On January 12, 1972, shortly after completing his draft reply to Patinkin, Friedman sent a letter (without attaching his draft response for the *JPE*) to Patinkin in which he wrote: "I am sorry to say that you will be disturbed and unhappy about my reply which is in some respects brutal, even though I believe it is entirely justified." Friedman went on to say that, following the publication of *Money, Interest, and Prices* in 1956, Patinkin had wasted his career away by having become excessively preoccupied with that book. Here is what Friedman wrote:

> As background for my [*JPE*] reply, let me recall to you a conversation we had quite a number of years ago when I told you that I once knew a young man of enormous intellectual promise, ability and originality who had written a first-rate important book and then was in the process of frittering away the rest of his professional life by trying to defend, improve, and revise every jot and tittle of that book. My biggest regret on reading your articles carefully for the purpose of being able to write a reply was to discover that story is, unfortunately, as applicable today as it was when we talked about it. I respect you too much not to be frank about this. It continues to seem to me a shame that your extraordinary abilities should not yield more extensive fruit. I do hope you will accept my comments in the spirit of personal friendship and intellectual sympathy in which I intend them. (letter, Friedman to Patinkin, January 12, 1972, Milton Friedman Papers, Hoover Institution Library and Archives, Stanford University)

After receiving a copy of Friedman's draft reply from Gordon, Patinkin wrote to Gordon complaining about "Milton's inappropriately rude tone" (letter, Patinkin to Gordon, February 17, 1972, Milton Friedman Papers, Hoover Institution Library and Archives, Stanford University). Gordon agreed; he had Friedman tone down his rhetoric. Instead of writing that his reply to Patinkin "is the reply which most deeply and passionately concerns me," in the revised—and published—response Friedman wrote "that is the reply that concerns me most." He deleted the references to "heartstruck swain" and "neutrality myopia." Friedman also dropped the words "Patinkin's incredibly narrow-minded interpretation of the Chicago tradition." In place of "Harry Johnson's recent libels on the Chicago tradition," Friedman referred to "[the] misleading impression of that [Chicago] tradition by Harry Johnson" (Friedman 1972, 907). In the published version, Friedman continued:

> Grant for the sake of the argument—as I do not in fact grant—that my 1956 "Restatement" . . . which is the main object of criticism in Patinkin's 1969 article, had nothing whatsoever of the flavor of the Chicago tradition. That would indict my perception, or integrity, or scholarship, but it would in no way contradict the existence of an important Chicago tradition in the field of money that had a great influence on subsequent work in monetary economics and on

my own work in particular. Similarly, it might justify Johnson's charge that I engaged in "scholarly chicanery," but it would not justify his charge that the "University of Chicago oral tradition" was my "invention." Whether I conveyed the flavor of that tradition or not, there was such a tradition; it was significantly different from the quantity-theory tradition that prevailed at other institutions of learning. (Friedman 1972, 932)

In that published reply to Patinkin, Friedman drew a picture of an early 1930s Chicago monetary tradition that was policy activist and, thus, able to anticipate the Keynesian interpretation of the Great Depression and the expansionary fiscal policies that followed from that interpretation. Friedman contrasted Chicago's policy activism with the Austrian view of the business cycle, as taught at the London School of Economics in the early 1930s, which interpreted the Great Depression as an inevitable consequence of the prior boom and advised that the Depression should be allowed to run its course: "It was the London School (really Austrian) view that I referred to in my 'Restatement' when I spoke of 'the atrophied and rigid' " versions of the quantity theory used at other institutions (Friedman 1972, 936).

In depicting a policy-oriented Chicago monetary tradition, Friedman (1972, 937) stated: "The intellectual climate at Chicago had been wholly different." He presented three main arguments to make the case of "an important" Chicago quantity-theory tradition that influenced his work; in so doing, he drew on literature related to those arguments to support his position.

*Fiscal activism.* Friedman cited evidence presented earlier by J. Ronnie Davis in 1968, who showed that, during the early 1930s, Chicago economists—as well as some non-Chicago American economists—recommended the use of budget deficits to finance public works to combat the Great Depression. Citing writings by (among others) Chicagoans Knight, Simons, Viner, and Paul Douglas, J. R. Davis (1968, 481) concluded that "the policy proposals of Keynes and the Chicago economists were remarkably similar during the early 1930s." From Davis's evidence, Friedman drew the inference that the Chicagoans had been advocating Keynesian (fiscal) policies prior to the publication of the *General Theory*. Thus, Friedman inferred that the Keynesian policy message would not have provided novelty to the Chicagoans.

*Open-market operations and rediscounting operations.* At a January 1932 conference hosted by the University of Chicago, twelve Chicago faculty members were among a group of twenty-four conference participants who signed a telegram sent to President Herbert Hoover, advocating, among other measures, expansionary open-market operations, an easing of re-discounting requirements, and the maintenance of the government's pro-gram of public works at a level not lower than the level of 1930–31.[22] From the contents of this telegram, Friedman drew the inference that the early Chicagoans believed in the efficacy of monetary operations that worked through the banking system during the early 1930s, thus drawing a connec-tion between the policy views of those economists with his policy views. The 1932 Hoover telegram, which is discussed in some detail in chapter 2, would play a pivotal role in the ensuing debate about the relevance of an earlier Chicago monetary tradition.

*Monetary interpretation of the Great Depression.* In a lecture deliv-ered at the 1932 Chicago conference, Chicagoan Viner characterized the Federal Reserve's policy during the early 1930s as inept (Viner 1932a, 28), foreshadowing the Friedman and Schwartz (1963) monetary inter-pretation of the Great Depression under which those authors criticized the Federal Reserve for having both precipitated and exacerbated the Depression. In a lecture delivered in 1933 Viner again criticized Federal Reserve policy during the Great Depression and called for a policy of "inflation," by which he meant an increase in the money supply, to combat the Depression (Viner 1933a).[23] Using Viner's work as a reference, Fried-man (1972) drew the inference that the monetary interpretation of the Great Depression was part of the Chicago monetary tradition.

Thus, based on the foregoing sources, Friedman depicted a pre–*General Theory* Chicago quantity-theory tradition characterized by (1) a mone-tary interpretation of the Great Depression, and (2) the advocacy of both expansionary fiscal policy and expansionary monetary policy to combat the Great Depression. Friedman concluded his rebuttal to Patinkin and Johnson as follows:

> I shall not defend my "Restatement" as giving the "flavor of the oral tradition" at Chicago in the sense that details of my formal structure have precise coun-terparts in the teachings of Simons and Mints. After all, I am not unwilling to accept some credit for the theoretical analysis in that article. Patinkin has made a real contribution to the history of thought by examining and presenting the detailed theoretical teachings of Simons and Mints, and I have little quarrel with his presentation. But I certainly do defend my "Restatement" as giving the "flavor of the oral tradition" at Chicago in what seems to me the much more

important sense in which, as I said, the oral tradition "nurtured the remaining essays in" *Studies in the Quantity Theory of Money*, and my own subsequent work. And, in any event. It is clearly not a tradition that, as Johnson charges, I "invented" for some noble or nefarious purpose. (1972, 941)[24]

Three questions unrelated to monetary doctrine emerge from the allegations made by Patinkin and Johnson. These questions concern the motivations underlying the allegations. First, why did Patinkin wait for thirteen years, after Friedman had backtracked on the claim that his quantity-theory framework emanated from a Chicago monetary tradition, to challenge Friedman's exegesis of a Chicago quantity-theory tradition and the relationship of Friedman's analytic framework to the pre-Keynesian quantity theory publicly? Second, why did Patinkin stand on the sidelines after his criticisms of Friedman led to the charge by Johnson and others that Friedman had "invented" a 1930s and 1940s Chicago monetary tradition? After all, Patinkin had described key characteristics of that tradition; while arguing that it was unrelated to Friedman's analytic framework, Patinkin did not deny that a particular Chicago quantity-theory tradition existed.[25] Third, why was Johnson's criticism of Friedman's claim of an earlier Chicago monetary tradition so brutal, prompting Friedman to characterize that criticism as libelous?

Several interpretations of the rationales for the Patinkin and Johnson criticisms have been put forward. Leeson (2000) argued that, with the ascendancy of monetarism (and of Friedman's prominence in the profession) in the late 1960s, the attacks by both Patinkin and Johnson, whose professional reputations (especially that of Patinkin) had been essentially on a par with that of Friedman in the 1950s, but were no longer, were motivated by professional envy.[26] In the case of Patinkin, his delay in criticizing Friedman's presentation of a Chicago monetary tradition may have been related to the fact that he had been preoccupied with producing the second edition of his *Money, Interest, and Prices*, published in 1965.[27] Robert Clower attributed Johnson's criticism to the latter's desire to demonstrate independence from Friedman, Johnson's Chicago colleague; in a 1972 letter to Friedman, Clower characterized Johnson's argument as a "rather juvenile interpretation [that] might best be regarded as a bit of high spirits dictated by his desire to appear more independent of your influence than some of his friends suspect" (letter, Clower to Friedman, April 5, 1972, quoted from Moggridge 2008, 347). Clower's view is supported by statements made by Johnson in his 1969 "Autobiographical Notes," in which he referred to a Chicago economics department "pretty much dominated by Milton Friedman" and in which he characterized that department as "a tough environment, especially for someone accustomed to the English traditions of the reasonable compromise between conflicting points of view" (quoted from Moggridge 2008, 205).[28]

Additionally, it is likely to have been the case that Patinkin's rendition of earlier Chicago monetary thinking, and the contrast of that thinking with Friedman's monetarist views, persuaded Johnson that Friedman had indeed invented a 1930s and 1940s Chicago monetary tradition. Friedman had published a paper in 1949 on the Marshallian demand curve (see Friedman 1949b) and had spent the 1953–54 academic year as a visiting fellow at Cambridge University. Johnson believed that Friedman had become infatuated with Cambridge economics as a result of his work on Marshall and had conceived the idea of an oral Chicago monetary tradition from his encounter with a Cambridge oral tradition during his stay at Cambridge:

> My personal hypothesis is that, as a result of his studies of the Marshallian demand curve and his year as a visitor at Cambridge, Friedman became enamored of the "Cambridge oral tradition" as a concept permitting the attribution to an institution of a wisdom exceeding that displayed in its published work, and unconsciously stole a leaf from Cambridge's book for the benefit of his own institution. (Johnson 1970, 86; see also 107n48)[29]

In any case, Johnson's argument, that in 1956 Friedman had set in place a necessary condition for a counter-revolution by creating a linkage with the pre-Keynesian orthodoxy, is based on a false premise because, as Nelson (2020, chap. 5) pointed out, it assumes that Friedman's advocacy of the quantity theory began with the "Restatement" whereas, in fact, Friedman's monetarist views began to emerge in the late 1940s and early 1950s.

Why, then, did Patinkin, who had enumerated characteristics that marked the Chicago monetary tradition, stand on the sidelines after his criticisms of Friedman led Johnson and others to charge that Friedman had "invented" a 1930s and 1940s Chicago monetary tradition? There are several possible explanations. First, Patinkin's primary interest during the 1940s at Chicago was in the area of monetary theory.[30] Probably for that reason, Patinkin's delineation of that tradition emphasized its theoretical aspects while playing down its policy aspects. Consequently, Patinkin likely believed that Friedman had misrepresented history.[31] Second, and related to the former point. Patinkin's almost exclusive focus on theory caused *him* to misunderstand and misrepresent the nature of the Chicago monetary tradition. Third, Friedman's use of such language as "heartstruck swain" and "neutrality myopia" to characterize Patinkin in his initial draft response to the latter's 1969 *JMCB* article had to be personally insulting and hurtful, even if those characterizations did not make it into the published version of the response. Thus, Patinkin may have been happy to sit on the sidelines while Friedman was personally being reprimanded by other members of the profession, including Johnson.

## 1.1 The Aftermath

The dispute between Friedman and Patinkin and Johnson over the existence and nature of a 1930s and 1940s Chicago monetary tradition provoked a long-running debate on the relationship between Friedman's monetary framework and the monetary views of the Chicago school of the 1930s and 1940s and of other academic centers of that period. The rules of engagement had been set out both by Patinkin (1969; 1972a) and by Friedman in his reply (1972) to Patinkin: search for forerunners, both Chicagoan and non-Chicagoan, in the literature of the 1930s and 1940s, to establish links with characteristics that marked Friedman's monetarist views of the mid-1950s and after. By and large, the literature focused on the following characteristics of Friedman's framework: (1) the belief in the efficacy of monetary policy; (2) a monetary interpretation of the Great Depression; and (3) the advocacy of a money-supply growth-rate rule such as the 3 to 5 percent annual growth-rate rule prescribed by Friedman (1960); and (4) an empirically based research methodology as typified by Friedman's work. Patinkin (1973a; 1979; 1986) continued to be an active participant—and adversary to Friedman—in the debate after the publication of the 1972 *JPE* symposium.[32] Following his 1972 reply to Patinkin, Friedman, who, unlike Patinkin, was not a doctrinal historian, withdrew from the debate.[33] In fact, Friedman's 1972 reply was his only published engagement in debate with Patinkin over the existence of a Chicago monetary tradition.[34]

By the early 2000s, a large literature had accumulated; much it was assembled and reprinted in *Keynes, Chicago and Friedman* (two volumes), edited by Leeson (2003e). An assortment of monetary economists who wrote in the 1920s, 1930s, and 1940s was summoned to the stage. The evidence that emerged led to the conclusion that, with respect to Friedman's empirical orientation, his monetary interpretation of the Great Depression, his monetary-growth-rate rule, and his belief in the efficacy of open-market operations, there were numerous forerunners in the writings of non-Chicago economists. Here is a brief review of the findings.[35]

- Among the non-Chicago forerunners of Friedman, the works of Lauchlin Currie and Clark Warburton were singled out as having represented a clear and direct link to Friedman's monetarist framework—a much closer link than the works produced at Chicago in the 1930s and 1940s.
- Currie's contributions were described by Brunner (1968b), Humphrey (1971), Sandilands (1990), Laidler (1993; 1999), and Steindl (1995). Currie presented annual estimates of the money supply for the period 1921–32, the year-on-year changes of which were similar to those presented by Friedman and Schwartz (1963). Moreover, Currie argued along similar lines to the thesis subsequently developed by Friedman and Schwartz, namely, that the Fed's policy tended not to prevent—but rather to precipitate—the Great Depression. Finally, Currie's detailed construction and analysis of data anticipated the subsequent empirical approach followed by Friedman and Schwartz.
- The contributions of Warburton were assessed by Humphrey (1971; 1973), Patinkin (1973a), Bordo and Schwartz (1979; 1983), Cargill (1979; 1981), Yeager (1981), and Steindl (1995). Writing mainly in the 1940s and early 1950s, Warburton stressed the importance of empirical verification of competing theories. While accepting the validity of the quantity theory of the price level in the long run, he believed that what he called "erratic" money growth was largely responsible for economic instability. Based on the results of his empirical studies, during the late 1940s and early 1950s, Warburton concluded that a 3 to 5 percent annual rate of increase in the money supply would provide stable prices at full-employment output levels over the long run, mitigating extreme fluctuations in economic activity. Importantly, Warburton emphasized the role of monetary policy in both precipitating and deepening the Great Depression.
- Humphrey (1971), Garvey (1978), and Laidler (1999) showed that, in the 1920s, Carl Snyder offered an empirical reconciliation of Irving Fisher's long-run secular quantity theory with the short-run cyclical behavior of money and prices. Specifically, Snyder thought that the ratio $V/T$, though relatively stable in the short run, exhibited a downward secular trend because of the trend growth of $T$, which Snyder estimated to be 4 percent annually. To maintain price stability, Snyder recommended that the money supply should rise at an annual rate of 4 percent. Laidler (1999, 233) expressed the view that, in the mid-1930s, Snyder "hinted" at a monetary interpretation of the Great Depression.[36]

- Humphrey (1971; 1973) provided documentation showing that, during the 1930s, non-Chicagoans Lionel Edie, Harold Reed, and James Harvey Rogers also investigated the necessary growth rate of the money supply for stabilizing the price level and advocated the money-supply growth-rate rule while Friedman's Chicago forbearers were advocating a rule for stabilizing a price index. Humphrey demonstrated that—in contrast to Chicago economists in the 1930s and 1940s, but in common with Friedman—non-Chicago quantity theorists, including Edie and Snyder, offered detailed empirical verifications of their hypotheses. Patinkin (1973a) pointed out that Friedman's empirical orientation was also closer to the work of Fisher (1911b), who provided detailed statistical verification of his equation of exchange, than it was to the work of Friedman's Chicago mentors.

- Lee and Wellington (1984) furnished evidence showing that non-Chicagoan James Angell also advocated a stable money growth throughout the 1930s; again, the evidence implied that the antecedents of Friedman's monetary-growth rule were to be found at institutions other than Chicago in the 1930s.

- Steindl (1995) examined the money-supply mechanisms of nearly three dozen economists, including Chicagoans Douglas, Mints, Simons, and Viner, during the 1930s and 1940s to assess whether any of these economists anticipated what Steindl called the "core" elements of Friedman and Schwartz's monetary thesis of the Great Depression; those "core" elements, Steindl argued, consisted of: (1) a focus on the money supply, along with a documentation of its decline during the Depression; (2) the attribution of the decline in the money supply to Federal Reserve activities; and (3) the articulation of a framework to diagnose the main determinants—high-powered money, the currency ratio, and the reserve-deposit ratio—of the quantity of money. Steindl (1995) found that none of the Chicago economists anticipated the Friedman and Schwartz "core" elements; among the economists included in Steindl's study, only Warburton anticipated the Friedman and Schwartz's monetary thesis, suggesting that Friedman's monetarist views had more in common with views that had been held outside of Chicago than with views held in Chicago.

- Steindl (2004) assessed Friedman's handwritten lecture notes from a course on business cycles that Friedman taught at the University of Wisconsin in the fall semester of 1940 for evidence of an influence of an early 1930s Chicago quantity-theory tradition in those lectures. Steindl's examination of those lecture notes showed that they contained "no consideration of any money or credit variables" (2004, 524). Steindl (2004, 529) concluded that the lectures "fail to reveal any particular monetary orientation that . . . would be regarded as integral to the Friedman monetarist framework. . . . Whatever may have been the reminiscences [of Friedman], two decades later [i.e., in 1956], of monetary thought of Chicago in the early thirties, the evidence from the business cycles course indicates that those reminiscences do not reflect the practice as that decade [the 1930s] ended."

- Laidler (1993) showed that two key elements identified by Friedman (1972) as marking the Chicago monetary tradition—namely, (1) a monetary interpretation of economic fluctuations in general, and the Great Depression in particular, and (2) an optimistic view of the power of monetary policy—were contained in the writings of Harvard economist Currie, who, in turn, had been influenced by his Harvard teacher Allyn Young and British Treasury economist Ralph Hawtrey.

- Laidler and Sandilands (2002a; 2002b) uncovered a previously unknown—and unpublished—memorandum written in January 1932 by three young Harvard economists—Currie, Paul Ellsworth, and Harry Dexter White—the policy recommendations of which bore a strong resemblance to the policy recommendations of the Hoover telegram produced that same month at Chicago. On the basis of the Harvard memorandum, Laidler and Sandilands (2002a, 517) drew the following inference: "it is clear from the [Harvard-based] memorandum that there was nothing unique about the Chicago tradition as it stood in early 1932."

In contrast to the above findings, the literature on the Chicago monetary tradition uncovered relatively few connections between the views of earlier Chicago quantity theorists and Friedman's monetarist thinking.

- Davis contributed two important studies on the Chicago monetary tradition. In J. R. Davis (1968), he provided evidence showing that, in the early 1930s, Chicago economists had been in favor of fiscal deficits to combat the Great Depression. He also showed that in 1931 Viner proposed the idea of compensatory public finance, under which the government would execute budget deficits during depressions and budget surpluses during expansions; over the cycle, the budget would be balanced. This idea became an accepted part of the Chicago monetary tradition, Davis argued, and helped account for Chicago's unsympathetic reception of the *General Theory*, which advocated *secular* fiscal deficits.

- In his 1971 book *The New Economics and the Old Economists*, Davis provided evidence showing that a majority of US economists, including those at Chicago, favored fiscal deficits to combat the Depression. He singled out the contributions made by Chicago economists to the view that public-works spending should be used during the Depression. In doing so, Davis introduced the views of Chicagoan Douglas into the discussion about the Chicago monetary tradition. In light of Davis's finding that the *majority* of US economists—Chicagoans and non-Chicagoans alike—advocated fiscal deficits in the early 1930s, that finding did not support the idea that there was anything distinctive (in terms of policy) transpiring at Chicago.[37]

- In Tavlas (1977a; 1997), I provided evidence showing that Douglas advocated a money-supply growth-rate rule in the late 1920s and the early 1930s, thus anticipating Friedman's monetarist policy proposition.
- In Tavlas (1976), I argued that the earlier Chicagoans were distinguishable from other economists who advocated fiscal deficits to combat the Great Depression because, unlike economists at other institutions, the Chicagoans, using the $MV = PT$ theoretical framework, advocated such deficits to expand the money supply. Laidler and Sandilands (2002a; 2002b), however, showed that Currie, Ellsworth, and White (1932), in their January 1932 memorandum, also advocated money-financed fiscal deficits.
- Tavlas (1977b), McIvor (1983), and Steindl (1995) furnished documentation showing that, in the 1940s, Mints had criticized the Federal Reserve's policies during the Great Depression in a way that anticipated the criticisms subsequently made by Friedman and Schwartz (1963). However, it is not clear whether Mints's views on this issue were formed independently or had been influenced by those of non-Chicagoans Currie, or Warburton, or both.[38]
- In Tavlas (1981), I provided evidence showing that the 1930s and 1940s Chicagoans emphasized the relationship between hoarding, or velocity, and price expectations, thereby imparting a volitional character to velocity. I also documented that this behavioral interpretation of velocity differed from the treatment of velocity by Keynes's British disciples, who developed a purely mechanical interpretation of velocity following the publication of Keynes's *General Theory*.
- Parkin (1986) emphasized the continuity between the monetary-policy strategies of Simons and Friedman—namely, both were advocates of rules and opponents of discretionary policies. Patinkin (1986) countered, however, that Simons's price-level-stabilization policy was, viewed from the vantage at the mid-1980s, discretionary policy. Laidler (1999, chap. 9) argued that even if Simons did advocate a monetary rule in the 1930s, Simons was not alone in doing so; other economists, including Irving Fisher, proposed similar rules. Hence, the Chicago monetary tradition was not unique based on the rules criterion.
- As mentioned, Friedman (1972) had provided evidence that, in the early 1930s, Viner had been critical of the Federal Reserve's policies during the Great Depression. But the relationship of this evidence to an earlier Chicago monetary

tradition was assuaged by a letter that Viner had sent to Patinkin in 1969 in which Viner hammered a nail into the coffin of a Chicago monetary tradition:

It was not until after I left Chicago in 1946 that I began to hear rumors about a "Chicago School" which was engaged in *organized* battle for laissez faire and "quantity theory of money" and against "imperfect competition" theorizing and "Keynesianism." . . . But at no time was I consciously a member of it, and it is my vague impression that if there was such a school it did not regard me as a member, or at least as a loyal and qualified member. (letter, Viner to Patinkin, November 24, 1969, emphasis in original; quoted from Patinkin 1981b, 266)[39]

- Leeson (2003d) used Friedman's lecture notes, taken while Friedman attended Mints's 1932–33 lectures on money, to show that Mints devoted considerable attention to covering Keynes's portfolio-based treatment of the demand for money as presented in the *Treatise*.[40] Leeson drew the inference that there was validity in Friedman's (1956) assertion that his (Friedman's) portfolio-based monetary framework derived from Chicago. Nevertheless, Leeson's evidence did not dispel Patinkin's argument that Friedman's theoretical framework was based on Keynes's theory of liquidity preference as embedded in the *Treatise* (1930) since what Mints taught about money demand in his 1932–33 course was based on a theory developed at Cambridge, England—and not at Chicago.

The upshot of this evidence was stated early on by Patinkin (1973a, 457): "the picture of monetary economics in the 1930s that emerges . . . is one of widespread ferment with respect to questions of both monetary theory and policy. Thus contrary to Friedman's implication, the Chicago School of that time cannot be represented as an isolated center of monetary studies and of belief in the importance of money." Twenty years later, Laidler (1993, 1078), based, in part, on evidence he presented on the work of Harvard economists Young and Currie in the late 1920s and early 1930s, respectively, and Hawtrey in the 1920s, concluded that the monetary contributions emerging from Harvard were of a higher order than the contributions of Friedman's Chicago mentors: "as late as 1934, outstanding work in monetary economics was done at Harvard, the best of it at least as good as anything that would emanate from Chicago in the 1930s, and, indeed, if careful empirical analysis is valued far better."[41] The weight of the evidence led Friedman to backtrack from his earlier claim of a unique Chicago quantity-theory tradition. Thus, in the preface of Leeson's (2003e) two-volume collection of essays dealing with the debate about that tradition, Friedman (2001, x) wrote:

> I remain persuaded that I was the beneficiary of a Chicago oral tradition, but this evidence [assembled in Leeson's book] convinces me that I gave Chicago more credit for uniqueness than was justified. Were I writing the paper now, I would undoubtedly word those first four paragraphs [of his 1956 "Restatement," in which he claimed a connection between his monetary economics and the pre-Keynesian Chicago quantity theory] differently, but no change would be called for in the rest of the essay. The issue is entirely about the origin of ideas, not about the validity of content.

In light of Friedman's recantation, it is not surprising that the recent consensus among doctrinal historians is that the Chicago monetary tradition, to the extent that such a tradition existed, was not unique. Thus, in a review of the collection of essays on Chicago monetary economics of the 1930s and 1940s contained in Leeson (2003e), Howson (2005, 388) wrote: "Contrary to some of the claims, the overall impression from the accumulated evidence collected here on the issue of the Chicago oral tradition is that both it was not unique and that the most useful form of the quantity theory whether developed at Chicago or elsewhere was one which began from the demand for money function [instead of the Chicagoan velocity-based approach]." In another review of the Leeson (2003e) volume, Freedman (2006, 108) argued: "Patinkin had inflicted a grievous wound on Friedman's rhetorical strategy, but Johnson was worse. He showed how the wizard behind the curtain was manipulating the various levers to produce a desired result."[42] Dimand (2010, 77) expressed the view that Patinkin, Johnson, and Laidler had shown that the claim "about the immaculate conception of Chicago monetarism" was "heresy." Similarly, in a review of two books on the general nature of the Chicago School, Backhouse (2013, 346) asserted that "Milton Friedman's attempt to argue that there was a Chicago tradition in monetary economics" was "undermined by Harry Johnson (1971) and Don Patinkin (1969)."[43]

This book is a study of the development of Chicago monetary economics from the late 1920s to the late 1950s, by which time Friedman had set out the core elements of his monetarist economics. I provide evidence that challenges the prevailing consensus that the conception of an earlier Chicago monetary tradition was invented by Friedman, and the related contention that, even if such a tradition existed, it was not unique in a way that directly influenced Friedman's monetarist views. I document that the prevailing narrative is decidedly inaccurate. In particular, I demonstrate that (1) there *was* a 1930s and 1940s Chicago quantity-theory tradition; (2) the form of the quantity theory developed and used at Chicago *was* unique; (3) at the time (in the late 1940s) that he moved into monetary economics as the main focus of his research, Friedman's views fully reflected that tradition; (4) Chicago economists had come to refer to their quantity-theory-cum-free-market framework as that of a "Chicago tradition" years before the appearance of Friedman's 1956 "Restatement," and (5) the Chicago version of the quantity theory provided a launching pad for Friedman's monetarist counter-revolution. Without that specific launching pad, any other challenge to the Keynesian orthodoxy in the 1950s and 1960s would very likely have taken a different form.

It will be useful to clarify three issues from the outset. First, I follow the approach to the study of doctrinal history described by Patinkin in his 1969 *JMCB* critique of Friedman: "Questions about the history of economic doctrine are empirical questions. And the universe from which the relevant empirical evidence must be drawn is that of the writings and teachings of the economists in question" (1969, 47). Indeed, as Friedman (1970c, 318) stated, "The elementary cannons of scholarship call for [such] documentation." This study presents empirical evidence drawn from the relevant literature.

Second, in addition to Chicagoans Simons and Viner, whose work in the 1930s and 1940s had been the primary focus in previous doctrinal studies, my cross section of Chicagoans includes the works of Mints, Director, Douglas, and Knight, each of whom has previously been thought to have had marginal or peripheral influences on the development of Friedman's monetary thought. By broadening the cross section of Chicago economists considered in the data sample, I show that, far from having been marginal figures, those economists appreciably and fundamentally helped shape Friedman's monetarist framework.

Third, in contrast to the rules of engagement followed in most earlier studies on the relationship between Friedman's monetarist economics and the monetary economics of his quantity-theory predecessors, the aim of which, as mentioned, has been to search for forerunners of Friedman's views in the 1930s and 1940s literature—an approach that is comparative static in essence—the approach followed here is to delineate *the evolution* of Chicago monetary economics from the late 1920s to the late 1950s. In doing so, the evidence that I provide shows the following.

*The early consensus.* In the early 1930s a consensus had developed among Chicagoans Knight, Simons, Mints, Douglas, and Aaron Director on a core set of monetary beliefs. These beliefs correspond to: (1) the first four "summary propositions" set down by Patinkin to characterize the earlier Chicago quantity-theory tradition (listed above); (2) an amended— or corrected—version of Patinkin's fifth "summary proposition"; and (3) three additional propositions that were policy centric and essential for understanding the Chicago quantity-theory framework of the 1930s and 1940s and its relationship to Friedman's monetarist views.

Patinkin's "summary proposition, no. 5, corrected":[44]

*Summary proposition, no. 5a.* The belief that open-market operations and rediscounting operations are *ineffectual* policy instruments, especially during depressions, and, therefore, changes in $M$ need to be generated through the government's fiscal position.

Additional policy "summary propositions":

*Summary proposition, no. 6.* Long-run stabilization requires the use of monetary-policy rules, with the policy objective specified in terms of the price level. The ideal rule should be framed in terms of a policy instrument—either the level of the stock of money or its growth rate—to achieve the policy objective. The motivation for a rule was the aim of reducing *monetary-policy uncertainty*.

*Summary proposition, no. 7.* The advocacy of a 100 percent reserves scheme for demand deposits (1) to prevent the self-reinforcing nature of the business cycle that characterizes a fractional-reserve banking system, (2) to allow better control of the money supply, (3) to ensure the safety of deposits, and (4) to prevent the nationalization of the banking system.

*Summary proposition, no. 8.* The abandonment of the gold standard and the advocacy of a flexible exchange-rate system so that monetary policy could pursue domestic objectives.

I also show what the Chicago monetary tradition *was not*. For one thing, the telegram (referred to above) sent to President Hoover in 1932 advocating the use of expansionary open-market operations and rediscounting operations to combat the Great Depression was *not* representative of early 1930s Chicago thinking, despite the signatures of twelve Chicagoans on that telegram. For another thing, in the early 1930s, the Chicagoans, except for Viner, did *not* develop a monetary interpretation of the economic downturn that put the Federal Reserve's policies at the heart of the Depression; nor did they believe that monetary-policy measures that operated through the banking system would be effective in combating the Depression. As indicated in "summary proposition, no. 5a," above, they did, however, believe in the effectiveness of changes in the quantity of money that were generated through the government's fiscal position.

*Chicago uniqueness.* While other economists occasionally advocated some of the above-mentioned characteristics—Irving Fisher favored price-level stabilization in the 1920s and the 1930s, and Lauchlin Currie espoused the 100 percent reserve idea in 1934, the year after the Chicagoans proposed that scheme—I show that (1) there were crucial differences between the Chicagoans views on rules and Fisher's policy framework and (2) the notion, commonly accepted by doctrinal historians, of almost simultaneous discovery in 1933–34 of the 100 percent reserves scheme by the Chicagoans and by Currie, is mistaken.[45] Regarding the former issue, in advocating rules the Chicagoans wanted to *tie the hands* of the authorities in order to eliminate monetary-policy uncertainty; Fisher favored providing the authorities with a *free hand* in the use of policy instruments—that is, discretionary powers with regard to the selection and use of policy instruments—to achieve price-level stabilization; moreover, Fisher did not address the issue of monetary-policy uncertainty, an issue that figured prominently both in the earlier Chicago policy framework and in subsequent discussions of monetary-policy rules. Regarding the 100 percent reserves scheme, I show that Knight and Simons conceived the idea of 100 percent reserves in the 1920s, a decade before Currie proposed the idea in 1934. Finally, I show that while other American economists advocated the use of fiscal deficits to combat the Great Depression before the publication of Keynes's *General Theory*, the Chicagoans' use of the Fisherine equation of exchange to justify that policy set them apart from non-Chicago economists.

*Chicago perseverance.* The eight core beliefs continued to characterize the writings of Knight, Simons, Douglas, and Mints in the late 1930s and the first half of the 1940s, and of Mints and Friedman in the late 1940s and the early 1950s. These beliefs also characterized the views of Director, who had departed from the University of Chicago in the mid-1930s, after he returned to that institution in 1946; I show that in the 1950s Director continued to teach the Chicago "religion" on money, as he described it, developed by Simons in the 1930s.

The continuity in the thinking of Chicago quantity theorists from the early 1930s to the early 1950s in terms of their belief in the eight "summary propositions" listed above provides evidence of a unique Chicago monetary tradition directly tied to Friedman's views at the time that he started teaching at Chicago in 1946—that is, Friedman's early views on money corresponded to what had been the core beliefs at Chicago in the early 1930s. In the late 1940s and the early 1950s, two circumstances led Friedman to change his views into what emerged as monetarism. First, Friedman was influenced by the cross-fertilization of his thinking on monetary issues with his Chicago colleagues Mints and Director, and the criticisms of his ideas by Warburton. Second, Friedman's empirical work, including that connected with his research with Schwartz, convinced him of the important role played by changes in the quantity of money produced by discretionary policies in initiating and propagating the business cycle, and of the need of a money-supply-growth rule to prevent major policy mistakes, such as that of the Great Depression. Contrary to what Johnson had argued, there *was* a lonely light constantly burning in a secret shrine on the Midway.

Thus, I argue that the procedure of seeking analogies with Friedman's monetarist views in the literature of the 1930s and 1940s provides an incomplete and misleading account of the development of his monetarist thinking, and the relationship of Friedman's monetarist framework to the work of the 1930s and 1940s Chicago monetary tradition. The thesis of this book is that Friedman inherited a policy-centric monetary apparatus from the 1930s Chicagoans; Friedman espoused that apparatus in the late 1940s and early 1950s and then modified that apparatus as a result of his empirical research and the influences of Mints, Director, and Warburton. The equation between (1) Chicago of the 1930s, 1940s, and early 1950s, including Friedman of the late 1940s and early 1950s, and (2) Friedman's monetarism of the mid-1950s and after, was the belief in the importance of the quantity of money. Mints and Director, both of whom were holdovers from the early 1930s, carried forth the ideas from that period, especially the ideas of Simons, to the Chicago of the late 1940s and 1950s.

The economists making up the Chicago monetary tradition in the 1930s and 1940s were bound by a common analytic framework for studying the business cycle—namely, that of the quantity theory of money. Using that theory, they stressed the role played by money in the economy. In doing so, they advocated money-financed fiscal deficits to combat depressions, a monetary-policy rule as a long-term guide for action, 100 percent reserve requirements, and flexible exchange rates. Most of those Chicagoans— but, as we will see, not all—were strong proponents of the free market.

Who were those Chicagoans? I have already referred to the names Henry Simons, Lloyd Mints, Frank Knight, Paul Douglas, Aaron Director, and Jacob Viner. Another member was Garfield Cox, who taught in the School of Business. Although each of the Chicagoans did not agree to the full set of policy prescriptions developed by the Chicago group as a whole, except for Jacob Viner, a remarkable consensus developed in the early 1930s among the Chicagoans about the causes of, and policy responses to, the Great Depression.[46] This consensus was an outgrowth of regular departmental meetings and social gatherings during which those issues were discussed.[47] At those occasions, and in their written communications, the Chicagoans referred to themselves collectively as The Group. Let us take a closer look at its members.[48]

## 1.2 Dramatis Personae

*Garfield V. Cox (1893–1970).* Cox was born in Fairmount, Indiana, where he was reared on a farm. He graduated from Beloit College in Wisconsin in 1917 and completed his PhD at Chicago in 1929. Cox began teaching in Chicago's School of Business in 1920. He became a leading authority on forecasting and was promoted to professor of finance in 1930. Cox was acting dean of the School of Business from 1942 to 1944 and dean from 1945 to 1954. He was president of the American Finance Association in 1954.

Cox's name is typically not associated with the Chicago monetary tradition. Nevertheless, I include Cox as part of The Group for several reasons. First, as I will demonstrate, Cox was a proponent of monetary rules. Second, in the early 1930s, he signed the key policy memoranda that emanated from Chicago, and he participated in two important conferences held at the university. Third, Cox participated in a key 1951 Chicago-sponsored conference in which the notion of a "Chicago tradition" emerged in public discourse. Fourth, he taught (on occasion) courses in the Economics Department. For example, Cox taught the graduate course Research in Money and Banking (Econ 430), in the first semester of the 1932–33 academic year.[49] Finally, when asked about the members of the Chicago monetary tradition in a 1980 interview, Mints stated that he considered Cox to have been part of that tradition.[50]

*Aaron Director (1901–2004).* Director was born in Charterisk, Ukraine, where his father worked in a flour mill. In the early 1900s, the mill failed twice; his father emigrated to the United States following each failure. Shortly after the second time, his father sent for the rest of his family, which included Aaron's younger sister Rose, the future wife of Friedman. Along with fellow student Mark Rothkowitz, who would later become a famous abstract painter under the name of Mark Rothko, Director was admitted to Yale on a scholarship.[51] After graduating from Yale, Director worked in various jobs, including as a farm worker, coal miner, and teacher at the Newark Labor College. An interest in workers' education led him to Europe (on a cattle boat) to study adult workers' education. He returned to the United States to teach at Portland Labor College, run by the Oregon Federation of Labor.

In 1927, Director entered the University of Chicago as a graduate student to study labor economics with Douglas. Three years later, Director was made an instructor in the Economics Department, where he taught the courses Labor Problems (Econ 240) and Introduction to Statistics (Econ 211). During the early 1930s, his interest shifted from labor economics toward monetary economics. The shift was noted in a January 31, 1934, letter from Harry Millis, who was chair of the Economics Department, to Viner; Millis complained that in his course on labor problems, Director had "come to the conclusion that there was nothing worth the while to talk about except monetary theory and policy and business cycles" (quoted from Van Horn 2010a, 266). Paul Samuelson wrote of his experience as an undergraduate at Chicago in the early 1930s as follows: "I had learned my first economics from Aaron Director, who had a tremendous impact on me" (letter, Samuelson to Milton Friedman, December 8, 1995, Milton Friedman Papers, Hoover Institution Library and Archives, Stanford University). In the years leading up to 1934, Director had come increasingly under Knight's influence while his relationship with Douglas cooled. For reasons that will be explained in chapter 3, in 1934 Douglas refused to support the renewal of Director's teaching contract, with the result that the contract was terminated. During the next decade Director held positions with the Brookings Institution and the US Treasury, while unsuccessfully attempting to write a PhD dissertation at Chicago.[52] He returned to the University of Chicago—to the Law School—in 1946. As a member of the Law School faculty, Director founded the field of law and economics and has been credited with having "solved important problems in industrial organization such as the economics of tie-in sales, predatory competition, and patent licensing restrictions" (G. Stigler 1974, 3). Director retired from Chicago in 1965.

*Paul Douglas (1892–1975).* Douglas was born in Salem, Massachusetts, in 1892. His youth was spent in poverty. His mother died when he was four years old. His father remarried, but he was abusive. His wife left him, took

Paul and a second stepson with her, and reared them in Maine. Douglas graduated from Bowdoin College in 1913 and earned a PhD at Columbia University in 1921. He spent the 1915–16 academic year at Harvard, where he took a course with Frank Taussig, who had gained notoriety by "ruling by fear" in the classroom. Viewed as an outsider from Columbia, Douglas became Taussig's favorite classroom target. Douglas (1972, 33) recounted: "From the sounding of the first bell, [Taussig] set out to prove me ignorant, illogical, and intellectually ridiculous. . . . I left each session soaked with perspiration, and hurried back to my rooms to change my clothes and start studying for the next day."[53] He initially taught at the University of Illinois and then at Reed College in Portland, Oregon. While teaching at Reed College, he became absorbed in Quakerism, which Douglas described as a life-changing experience (Douglas 1972, 35–37), putting him on the road to social activism and reform.[54]

Douglas joined the University of Chicago faculty in 1920. He taught the courses Labor Problems (Econ 240) and Theory of Wages (Econ 306). Patinkin, who was Douglas's student in the early 1940s, described Douglas's classroom demeanor as follows: "For Douglas . . . (with his red cheeks and booming voice) the classroom meeting was a dramatic encounter, and the classroom itself a stage on which to pace back and forth, declaiming more than lecturing, and pausing on occasion to fend off premature student questions by slowly intoning, with a wave of his hand, 'lead kindly light, one step at a time'" (1981, 5). Douglas enlisted in the Marines in 1942—as a private—at the age of fifty! He saw combat in the Pacific region and was wounded at the Battle of Okinawa, with the result that his left arm was permanently disabled. He earned two Purple Hearts and a Bronze Star and rose to the rank of lieutenant colonel. He returned to Chicago in 1946.

As an academic, Douglas is best remembered for his pioneering work on production theory, including the co-discovery with Charles Cobb of the Cobb-Douglas production function, and the theory of wages and the supply of labor.[55] Samuelson (1979, 923) wrote: "If Nobel Prizes had been awarded in economics after 1901, as they were in physics, chemistry, medicine, peace, and literature, Paul H. Douglas would probably have received one before World War II for his pioneering econometric attempts to measure marginal productivities and quantify the demand for factor inputs." In 1947, Douglas served as president of the American Economic Association. Douglas demonstrated an interest in public issues throughout his academic career at Chicago. He established a reputation as a social reformer in support of left-wing causes and, beginning in the 1920s, became actively engaged in Chicago politics. In 1948, he was elected to the US Senate, where he served three terms (1949–67).

*Frank Knight (1885–1972)*. Knight was the first of eleven children born into a poor farming family in McLean County, Illinois. After studies at several colleges in Tennessee, he completed his PhD thesis, "A Theory of Business Profit," in 1916 at Cornell University under Allyn Young.[56] The thesis was published, with significant revision, under the title *Risk, Uncertainty and Profit* in 1921. The book established Knight's reputation as an elite economist. Knight distinguished between risk and uncertainty.[57] Risk was subject to quantification. For example, the probability of dying at a certain age can be calculated and shifted via insurance to others. Therefore, risk was governed by probability distributions and could be treated as an insurable cost, with the cost calculable from stable empirical regularities. Knight noted, however, that there are other uncertainties involving unprecedented situations in which both the outcomes and the probability models that govern them are unknown. In such situations, he argued, it is not possible to formulate uncertainty in terms of precise probabilities, and, thus, the risks are uninsurable. Knight maintained: "We live in a world full of contradiction and paradox, a fact of which perhaps the most fundamental illustration is this: that the existence of a problem of knowledge depends on the future being different than the past, while the possibility of the solution of the problem depends on the future being like the past" (1921, 313).[58] He argued that this uncertainty gave rise to economic profits. Specifically, Knight argued that, while profit is eliminated in a world of perfect competition by the assumption of perfect knowledge, in the real world profit exists because of uncertainty.

Knight taught at Cornell University for one academic year (1916–17), and at Chicago for two academic years (1917–18 and 1918–19), before moving to the University of Iowa, where he was an associate professor and then full professor. He returned to Chicago in 1927, where he remained part of the academic community for the remainder of his life although he formally retired in 1952. From the 1920s to the 1940s, Knight was the dominant intellectual influence on Chicago economics students (G. Stigler 1987).[59]

The main courses taught by Knight were Price and Distribution Theory (Econ 301), a course he often taught in alternate semesters with Viner, and the History of Economic Thought (Econ 302). As a colleague, he could be dogmatic, unreasonable, and inconsiderate. Reder (1982, 6n15), who had taken Knight's course on price theory, recalled the following classroom occurrence. Knight sold his students reprints of both Viner's 1931 article "Cost Curves and Supply Curves" (Viner 1931a) and Roy Harrod's 1934 article "Doctrines of Imperfect Competition." Knight then "urged us to read the latter carefully because 'it corrects all the errors' in Viner's article." Knight was president of the American Economic Association in 1950, having refused to be nominated in 1936 and 1937. He was awarded the Francis A. Walker medal in 1957.[60]

*Lloyd Winn Mints (1888–1989)*. Mints was born near Bushnell, South Dakota. He received his bachelor's degree in 1914 and his master's degree in 1915—both from the University of Colorado. After completing his master's degree, he worked for the federal government—first in Washington, DC, and then in Chicago. In 1919, he enrolled in the economics program at the University of Chicago but was assigned by the university's administration to teach without having formally applied for a teaching position.[61] He completed several graduate courses in economics but never completed the PhD program at Chicago. From 1919 until 1925 he taught courses, mainly in the area of financial organization, to undergraduates. During the 1925–26 academic year he was assigned to teach the graduate courses Money and Banking (Econ 330, 331) and Problems in Money and Banking (Econ 332).[62] The former course was devoted mainly to doctrinal issues related to the development of the quantity theory of money, as articulated in the works of such economists as Henry Thornton, Knut Wicksell, Alfred Marshall, Hawtrey, Fisher, and Keynes (of the *Treatise on Money*, 1930); after 1936 the course included a discussion of the impact of the Keynesian revolution on the quantity theory. Patinkin (1981a, 5) described Mints's classroom presentations as "clear, systematic, and very effective." Mints published two books on the subject of money—*A History of Banking Theory* in 1945 and *Monetary Policy for a Competitive Society* in 1950; the former book has become a minor classic in the area of monetary doctrine. Mints's highest position was that of associate professor.[63] He retired in 1953.

*Henry Simons (1899–1946)*. Simons was born into an upper-middle-class family in Virden, Illinois. After graduating from the University of Michigan in 1920, he taught economics at the University of Iowa while becoming a premier student of Knight. In 1927, he followed Knight to Chicago, where he was a lecturer and later an assistant professor (in 1928), mainly teaching graduate courses in public finance and undergraduate courses in price theory. George Stigler (1974) reported that Simons, although brilliant, had a capacity for boredom. Perhaps that characteristic helps explain the fact that, up to 1932, he had published nothing but three book reviews. That lack of publishing was the major reason that Douglas led a successful campaign in 1934 and 1935 to deny tenure to Simons. The advent of the Roosevelt administration, with its interventionist policies, in 1933, however, galvanized Simons into action. The prevalent view among intellectuals at the time was that the free-market system had failed, necessitating widespread government intervention in economic affairs. Through a series of philosophical tracts on economics—Simons was uninterested in empirical economics and formal modeling—he established himself as a leading defender of laissez-faire, albeit with strong emphasis on the government's responsibility to maintain appropriate monetary and competitive conditions, and to ensure income equality. His objective was to show that the free-market system had not failed but that the government had failed to discharge its role in ensuring the operation of that system (H. Stein 1987, 334). In addition to teaching in the Economics Department, Simons began teaching (part-time) in Chicago's Law School in 1939. He was not promoted to a full professorship until 1945 because of the opposition of a dean who was incensed by Simons's attacks on labor unions (G. Stigler 1974, 2).

Simons died in June 1946. In the months before he died, he led an effort to bring Director back to Chicago. The university administration turned down the proposal on June 18, 1946. That night, Simons died of an overdose of sleeping pills. In recent years, the consensus view, including among Chicagoans, is that Simons committed suicide—see, for example, Rose Friedman (Friedman and Friedman 1998, 155). Van Horn (2014) presented evidence supporting the view that Simons committed suicide.[64] In the event, the administration reversed its decision and decided to hire Director.

*Jacob Viner (1892–1970).* Viner was born in Montreal in 1892, the son of immigrant parents from Romania. After earning his undergraduate degree from McGill University in 1914, he went to Harvard, where he earned a PhD in 1922. His thesis supervisor was Taussig. Viner joined the faculty at the University of Chicago as an instructor in the fall of 1916. After working for the US Tariff Commission under Taussig during 1917–19, he returned to the University of Chicago, where he became a full professor at age thirty-two. At Chicago, Viner established an international reputation for his work on (1) price theory, in which he anticipated elements of what later became known as the theory of imperfect competition, (2) the theory of international trade—he was the first economist to provide a comprehensive assessment of various terms-of-trade concepts, some of which he originated (Bloomfield 1992, 2080–81), and (3) the history of economic thought, in which he traced the evolution of the theory of international trade.[65] Lionel Robbins described Viner as "the outstanding *all-rounder* of his time in our profession" (emphasis in original, 1970, 2).

Viner mainly taught courses on price and distribution theory and international trade theory and policy. Following the example of his mentor Taussig, Viner ruled by fear in the classroom. His classroom lectures could be both exhilarating and terrorizing for students. Friedman, who took Viner's graduate course in price theory in the fall quarter of 1932–33, described the course as "unquestionably the greatest intellectual experience of my life" (Friedman, quoted from Breit and Hirsch 2009, 70). Samuelson, another Viner student in the early 1930s, described a classroom setting in which Viner fired off questions to students whose names were read off a "diabolical deck of index cards [on which were written the students' names] in his hands through which he shuffled nervelessly." According to Samuelsson:

> Members of the seminar sat tensely around the table, and when the name of the victim was read off the cards, you could almost hear the sighs of relief and the slumping back into chairs of those who had won temporary respite. Indeed, the stakes were high. Three strikes and you were out, with no appeal possible to any higher court. And this was no joke. I remember an able graduate student who, having failed to give an acceptable answer on two previous occasions, was told by Viner: "Mr. ___, I am afraid you are not equal to yourself or this class." ... When one victim alibied, "I am beyond my depth," Viner is supposed to have said, "Sir, you drown in shallow water." (Samuelson 1991, 543)

During most of Viner's tenure at Chicago, along with Knight he was co-editor of the *JPE*.[66] Viner served as special assistant to the US Treasury and as consulting expert to Treasury Secretary Henry Morgenthau Jr. from 1934 to 1939 and occasionally thereafter. He left Chicago for Princeton in 1946, where he taught until his retirement in 1960. He was president of the American Economic Association in 1939–40 and was awarded the Francis A. Walker Medal, in 1962, five years after Knight received the medal.

## 1.3 The Department

It will be useful to mention several features of Chicago's Economics Department before and during the period under consideration.[67] The department was established in 1892, at which time it was called the Department of Political Economy.[68] It was the first separate economics department established in the United States. At its inception, its head was James Laurence Laughlin, who established the *JPE* in that year. Laughlin, who taught at Chicago from 1892 until his retirement in 1916, was a strong supporter of the gold standard, a believer in free markets, and a dogmatic critic of the quantity theory of money.[69] As an administrator, he earned a reputation as someone who emphasized quality in staffing the department and who countenanced diverse political viewpoints.[70] In an essay on Laughlin, Friedman (1987, 140) asserted: "Laughlin's emphasis on quality rather than ideology was combined with an emphasis on research by his faculty, as well as by graduate students as part of their training. A corollary was his belief in personal teaching as opposed to formal lecturing. These have remained key characteristics of the Chicago Department of Economics from that day to this."

In the 1930s, the department was considered to be among the best, if not the best, in the United States. Samuelson (1972, 5) appraised the department as follows: "When I attended the University of Chicago in the early 1930s, it had the best Department of Economics in the country." Throughout the first half of the 1930s, the department had sixteen faculty members.[71] As mentioned, the department chair was Harry Millis (1873–1948), who served in that capacity from 1928 until his retirement in 1938. He joined the Chicago faculty in 1916. Millis was president of the American Economic Association in 1934. His main area of expertise was labor relations. Henry Schultz taught quantitative methods at Chicago from 1926 until 1938 and was a pioneer in the fledging field of econometrics. According to Samuelson (1972, 5), Schultz represented the "wave of the future" while "Knight and Viner represented the giants of the present." On Friedman's return to Chicago during the 1934–35 academic year, he served as Schultz's research assistant and helped write parts of Schultz's 1938 book *The Theory and Measurement of Demand*.[72] Schultz was killed in a car accident shortly after the completion of the book.[73] Other notable members of the department in the early 1930s were the following: (1) Chester Wright was a distinguished economic historian. He taught at Chicago from 1907 to 1944. (2) Harry Gideonse, who was born in the Netherlands, was a specialist in international relations. He taught at Chicago from 1930 to 1937, before going on to become president of Brooklyn College. (3) Simeon Leland, who worked in the area of public finance, taught at Chicago from 1930 to 1946, before becoming dean of the College of Liberal Arts at Northwestern University. (4) John Ulric Neff was an eminent economic historian, who taught at Chicago from 1929 until 1964. In 1941, he cofounded the Committee on Social Thought, which has since been renamed the John U. Neff Committee on Social Thought.[74]

The Economics Department was far from monolithic concerning its thinking on monetary issues. For example, Oskar Lange, an ardent socialist, a critic of the quantity of theory of money, and a major contributor to the neoclassical synthesis, taught macroeconomic theory in the department from 1939 to 1945.[75] Hyman Minsky, an undergraduate student at the University of Chicago from 1937 to 1941, wrote the following about the views of the members of the department: "The department had room for radicals like Lange, liberals like Douglas, middle of the roaders like Viner as well as the beginnings of a conservative group in Knight, Simons, and Mints" (Minsky 1985, 211).[76] Likewise, from 1939 to 1955 the University of Chicago housed the Cowles Commission—later named the Cowles Foundation—the members of which sometimes interacted with, and taught in, the Department of Economics.[77] Members of the Cowles Foundation developed a probabilistic framework for estimating simultaneous equations that eventuated in large-scale Keynesian macroeconometric models developed by Lawrence Klein.[78] The ultimate goal of these models was to gain policy insight. The versions of these models produced in the 1950s and 1960s featured a large role for fiscal policy and a small role for monetary policy in the economy. In addition to the above-mentioned individuals, Friedrich Hayek held an independently funded position at Chicago from 1950 to 1962. Neither Lange, nor Hayek, nor members of the Cowles Commission could be considered part of the Chicago monetary tradition.

A notable aspect of the department was the faculty's diversity. In the early 1930s—a time when there were very few women in the economics profession—the Chicago faculty included two women: Hazel Kyrk (1886–1957), who was listed as associate professor in the 1932–33 University of Chicago *Catalogue*, and Mary Barnett Gilson (1877–1969), who was listed as instructor. Kyrk made pioneering contributions in the areas of consumption theory and income distribution.[79] She was promoted to full professor in 1941. Gilson's area of specialization was industrial relations. She taught at Chicago from 1931 until her retirement in 1942. She was promoted to assistant professor in 1933. The department's diversity was also reflected in the relatively large number of Jewish faculty members.[80] During a period in which American universities practiced discrimination against hiring Jews, four of the sixteen faculty members listed in the

1932–33 University of Chicago *Catalogue* were Jewish: Director, Viner, Schultz, and Gideonse. By way of comparison, Friedman taught at the University of Wisconsin during the 1940–41 academic year but was not retained; Rose Friedman maintained that anti-Semitism played a role in the decision by Wisconsin's Economics Department not to extend her husband's contact.[81]

## 1.4 This Study

The remainder of this book describes the emergence and development of the Chicago monetary tradition, as reflected in the works of members of The Group in the years both before the Keynesian revolution and during the high tide of Keynesian influence, into what became known as monetarism. I broadly identify monetarism as a body of research, grounded on the quantity theory of money, that emphasized that money matters.[82] This characterization of monetarism is similar to that given by Nobay and Johnson (1977, 477), Mayer (1978, 1), K. Hoover (1988, 10), and Meltzer (1998, 8).[83] Friedman's research, as that of Clark Warburton, differed from that of Friedman's Chicago predecessors in that it was empirically based. As was that of his Chicago predecessors, Friedman's work was grounded on the quantity theory of money and stressed the causal dominance of money on nominal income.

It is important to distinguish between the "Chicago monetary tradition," the primary focus of this study, and the "Chicago school." The Chicago monetary tradition represented a group of economists who used the quantity theory of money to emphasize that money matters. As mentioned above, the Chicago monetary tradition was policy centric: by and large, its members advocated monetary-policy rules to reduce uncertainty and maintain economic stability, money-financed fiscal deficits to combat depressions, 100 percent reserve requirements on demand deposits, and flexible exchange rates. Although the members of the Chicago monetary tradition were, for the most part, adherents to the view that free markets work better than other social structures in organizing economic activity, this view was not a defining characteristic of the Chicago monetary tradition.[84]

The term "Chicago school" is taken to refer to a loose grouping of economists noted, first and foremost, for its advocacy of a private-enterprise economy and limited government (Miller 1962, 64–65).[85] Members of the

Chicago school hold that free markets allocate resources, distribute incomes, and organize economic activity more efficiently than other types
of social organizations (Humphrey 2013, 95). The role of the government
is to provide a stable monetary and fiscal framework (Hetzel 2013, 201).

The origin of the Chicago school can be traced to Knight's 1924 article "Some Fallacies in the Interpretation of Social Cost." In that article,
Knight stated that "free enterprise is not a perfectly ideal system" (1924,
605). Nevertheless, Knight established the notion that the free-market
system is the most efficient way to allocate scarce resources. The market
system breaks down, he argued, only when the state fails to "define and
protect property rights, enforce contracts and prevent non-contractual
(compulsory) transactions, maintain a circulating medium, and most especially prevent that collusion and monopoly, the antithesis of competition,
into which competitive relations constantly tend to gravitate" (1924, 606).
As the notion of a Chicago school developed in the 1950s and 1960s, it
also came to be associated with the Chicago monetary tradition's proposals in the area of monetary policy — notably, the advocacy of rules, flexible
exchange rates, and 100 percent reserve requirements.[86] Consequently,
the term "Chicago school" is broader than the "Chicago monetary tradition." As we shall see in chapter 6, in the early 1950s, Chicago economists referred to their positions on free markets and the role of money
in the economy under the appellation "Chicago tradition," which I treat
as identical with "Chicago school." As we shall also see, the characteristics that marked both the Chicago monetary tradition and the Chicago
school were modified in the late 1940s and the 1950s, the former under
the influence of Friedman and Mints, and the latter under the influence of
Friedman and Director.[87]

The following narrative is more or less chronologically based. The period of time covered is 1927 to 1960. The year 1927 saw the first sprouts of
the characteristics that would distinguish the Chicago monetary tradition.
That year marked (1) Paul Douglas's initial published proposals to combat
business depressions with money-financed fiscal deficits and maintain economic stability by following a monetary rule and (2) Frank Knight's first
published criticism of the fractional-reserve banking system. The advocacy
of the government's fiscal position to generate changes in the money supply, monetary rules for long-run stability, and criticisms of fractional-reserve
banking became cornerstones of the Chicago monetary tradition. The year
1927 also saw the arrival of Knight, Simons, and Director at Chicago. The
year 1960 saw the publication of Milton Friedman's book *A Program for*

*Monetary Stability*, which marked the completion of his transformation of the Chicago monetary tradition's framework, from that which he had taken over in the late 1940s, to his particular monetarist structure.[88]

Chapter 2 describes the origins of the Chicago monetary tradition in the late 1920s and the early 1930s. Chapter 3 deals with disagreements among members of The Group—on issues of economic policy in the case of Viner and other members, and ideology in the case of Douglas and other members. The latter disagreement provides light on the emergence of Chicago as a center of free-market thinking in the 1930s. Chapter 4 deals with two issues that have been featured in the recent doctrinal-historical literature—namely, the origins of the 100 percent reserves scheme and monetary-policy rules. I show that precedence for both those ideas in the 1930s belongs to Chicago economists. Chapter 5 describes the development of the Chicago monetary tradition mainly from the mid-1930s to the mid-1940s. During that decade, Chicago economists continued to advance the view that money matters amid a rapidly growing consensus in the economics profession that downplayed the role of monetary factors in the business cycle and the importance of monetary policy as a stabilization tool. Three Chicagoans—Knight, Simons, and Viner—published reviews of the *General Theory*; the review by Viner was, on balance, favorable; the reviews by Knight and Simons were highly critical. Chapter 6 deals with the views of the members of The Group on money in the mid- and late 1940s, a period that saw changes in the composition of The Group—Simons died in 1946; Viner left for Princeton in 1946; Knight stopped writing on the subject of money; and Douglas ran (successfully) for the US Senate in 1948. But the year 1946 also saw the return of Director to Chicago (in the Law School) and the appointment of Friedman to Chicago's economics faculty. Mints, who had not published anything other than book reviews from 1931 to 1944, emerged in the mid- and late 1940s as the preeminent proponent of what became known as "the Mints-Simons program" of money.[89] Meanwhile, from his position as a US senator, in the late 1940s Douglas was joined by Mints and Friedman in helping to forge the famous "accord" between the Fed and the Treasury in the first example of the postwar influence of the Chicago monetary tradition on policy. Chapters 7 and 8 describe the extension of the Chicago framework into what became Friedman's monetarist economics. Chapter 9 presents a summary and conclusions.

A main conclusion that emerges from this study is that the origins of the Chicago monetary tradition are richer, deeper, and more intricate than has heretofore been recognized. Chicago economists Simons, Mints, Director, Douglas, and Knight, who doctrinal historians have, by and large, considered to have been marginal or peripheral influences on Friedman's monetarist framework, appreciably and fundamentally influenced Friedman's monetary thought. In the midst of the Keynesian revolution, which downplayed the role of money in economic activity and advocated a much-expanded role for government engagement in economic affairs, those economists established a stronghold at the University of Chicago Economics Department in which the fidelity to the importance of money and the advantages of free markets were defended and preserved, and from which the monetarist counter-revolution emerged.

## CHAPTER TWO

# The Group

During the early 1930s, University of Chicago economists developed a comprehensive and cohesive set of policy measures for combating the Great Depression. Formulated within the framework of the quantity theory of money, the Chicagoans argued that, during extreme economic crises, the conversion of reserves into loans by the banking system cannot be relied on as the primary vehicle through which monetary policy can generate a recovery. Instead, they believed that the Federal Reserve should print money to finance the federal government's fiscal operations. In modern terminology, this policy constitutes unconventional monetary policies.[1] The Chicagoans also argued that monetary policy should not be constrained by a fixed exchange-rate regime.

In 1931 and 1932 the Chicagoans organized and hosted two major conferences, featuring some of the most distinguished economists of the day, that focused on the causes of, and policy responses to, the Depression. The theme of the 1931 conference was "Unemployment as a World Problem"; the participants included Alvin Hansen and John Maynard Keynes. The theme of the 1932 conference was "Gold and Monetary Stabilization"; the participants included Hansen, Irving Fisher, Gottfried Haberler, and John H. Williams. As mentioned in the previous chapter, the latter conference eventuated in a telegram sent to President Herbert Hoover, advocating, among other measures, expansionary open-market operations and an easing of rediscounting requirements. The telegram was signed by twenty-four conference participants, including twelve Chicagoans—but not by Paul Douglas, who had actively participated in the conference discussions. In addition to that telegram, during 1932 and 1933, the Chicagoans drafted and circulated (to other academics and to Washington policy makers) four other memoranda. Because, with several exceptions, the Chicagoans had not published their individual views on monetary economics before 1934, the contents of these departmental memoranda are essential to the understanding of the development of the Chicago monetary tradition.[2]

In this chapter, I show that an analysis of (1) the records of the 1931 and 1932 conferences hosted by the Chicagoans; (2) the five 1932 and 1933 memoranda (the aforementioned 1932 telegram to President Hoover and the four Chicago memoranda); (3) written correspondence of the Chicagoans; and (4) other documents reveals the following.

- In responding to the Great Depression, the Chicagoans accorded primacy to the view that open-market operations and rediscounting operations would be ineffectual; expansionary monetary policy should, therefore, be implemented through the government's fiscal operations. Douglas played the primary role in developing the view that fiscal deficits, and not open-market operations or rediscounting, should be used to effectuate monetary expansion during depressions. Douglas's proclivity toward activism was likely the driving force underlying Chicago's collective activism.
- To help reduce the severity of the business cycle, to prevent runs on banks, and to enable improved control over the supply of money, the Chicagoans advocated what became known in the 1930s as the "Chicago Plan of Banking Reform." The "Plan" would require that commercial banks maintain reserves of 100 percent, in the form of notes and deposits of the Federal Reserve Banks, against their deposit liabilities.[3]
- In terms of longer-run policy that could help prevent depressions from occurring, or at least lessen the severity of depressions, the Chicagoans favored a monetary-policy rule. By 1933, Henry Simons and Aaron Director had developed the view that a monetary rule (implemented strictly through the federal budget) that entails a continuous expansion of the money supply would not be consistent with a policy of balancing the federal budget over the course of the business cycle and would, under fractional-reserve banking, lead to a continuous transfer of "property rights," or seigniorage, to private banking institutions.
- A key characteristic that distinguished the monetary economics of the early 1930s Chicagoans from that of much of the profession at the time was the view that the gold standard should be abolished in favor of exchange-rate flexibility accompanied by a monetary policy aimed at achieving a domestic objective. In a November 1933 memorandum, Simons and Director developed a penetrating but neglected critique of the gold standard that foreshadowed key criticisms of fixed-exchange-rate systems made by Milton Friedman in his classic paper "The Case for Flexible Exchange Rates" (1953b).

- During 1933 a deep rift emerged between Douglas, on the one side, and Director and Simons, on the other, regarding both the short-term objectives of monetary policy and the specific type of long-term monetary-policy rule that should be followed, with Douglas favoring (over the long term) a monetary-growth rule, under which the price level would be kept stable, and Director and Simons favoring a rule under which the quantity of money would be held constant and the price level would be allowed to decline by about 3 percent a year. Simons and Director used the occasion of the November 1933 memorandum to take sharp issue with Douglas's positions.

This chapter documents the emergence of the Chicago monetary tradition during the period 1927–33. The chapter begins by discussing Douglas's writings on the subject of money in the late 1920s and the early 1930s and the writings on that subject by Lloyd Mints and Director in the early 1930s.[4] The chapter next reviews and assesses the discussions and debates that took place during the Chicago conferences of 1931 and 1932. The chapter then describes the four Chicago policy memoranda of 1932 and 1933; the memoranda were produced in (1) April 1932, (2) early 1933 (the precise date was unspecified), (3) March 1933 (revised in April 1933), and (4) November 1933. I show that the policy proposals that were contained in the four strictly Chicago memoranda were fundamentally different from those contained in the telegram sent to President Hoover that emerged from the 1931 conference held at Chicago, although the policy recommendations of the latter telegram are those that have been identified in the doctrinal literature as representative of the early 1930s Chicago monetary tradition.

## 2.1 Douglas, the Chicago Monetary Tradition, and Activism

*Douglas: Contributions, 1927 and 1932*

Although Douglas is best remembered for his pioneering work on production theory, during the period 1927 to 1935 he was a prolific writer on monetary issues, including two formidable books on depressions — *The Problem of Unemployment* (1931), which he co-authored with Director, and *Controlling Depressions* (1935b) — and numerous articles and monographs. Using as his analytic framework the Fisherine equation of exchange, $P = (MV + M'V')/T$, he was careful to note: "The various terms are not, however, as some of the more naive quantity theorists have believed, independent of each other. On the contrary, they are inter-related in a somewhat organic fashion" (1935b, 26).[5] Douglas combined the quantity theory with a transmission mechanism that drew on underconsumptionist analytics.

Douglas's use of underconsumptionist analytics in the late 1920s and early 1930s was based, in part, on the publications of William Foster and Waddill Catchings. Those two writers co-authored a series of works in the 1920s in which they espoused (1) "the dilemma of thrift," under which they posited that, although savings are necessary to generate an increasing stock of capital, savings generate deficiencies in aggregate demand, and (2) if firms save part of their profits to purchase investment goods (used to produce even more goods), consumers would not be able to purchase the resulting output at the going level of prices—there would be an over-production of goods. Prices would, therefore, fall, profits would decline, and depression would ensue. In other words, consumption was bound to fall short of the amount needed to purchase output at a price sufficient to generate a profit for producers (L. Klein 1947, 139; Laidler 1999, 207). Thus, the economy is marked by underconsumption, which leads to a state of persistent depression. To rectify this unstable situation, they advocated that the government undertake money-financed fiscal deficits to increase the money supply in line with the long-term rise in production in order to keep the price level stable.[6]

Influenced by Foster and Catchings, Douglas argued that depressions are caused by the failure of the monetary purchasing power of consumers to increase as rapidly as the annual trend increase in the production of manufactured goods, which he estimated to be 3 to 4 percent per year. With a constant money supply, increases in production would induce a fall in the general price level in order to clear the market of the excess supply of goods. Because present product prices have embodied within them relatively higher costs that have been paid out previously, profit margins would shrink with the fall in prices, and a decline in output would ensue. To prevent depressions, Douglas argued that primary reliance should be placed on maintaining a price index of manufactured goods at a relatively stable level. Attainment of this goal could be achieved "if the quantity of purchasing power were to be increased at the rate of 3 to 4 percent a year, or the long-time rate of production" (1935b, 185).

In several studies, David Laidler argued that Douglas's underconsumptionist views disqualify Douglas from consideration as a quantity theorist; therefore, Douglas should not be treated as part of the earlier Chicago monetary tradition.[7] Laidler's view is based on the following reasoning.

A fundamental aspect of underconsumptionism is that there is a flaw in the capitalist economy, which, left untreated, renders the economy subject to chronic depression. Laidler contended that, in contrast, the quantity theory should be treated as a component of a broader classical tradition under which Say's Law prevails and full employment is the norm in the long run—though that tradition leaves room for monetary shocks to create serious short-term deviations from equilibrium.[8] Since underconsumptionism, under which the economy is subject to chronic depression if left untreated, is not consistent with the classical tradition, Douglas, according to Laidler, should not be treated as a quantity theorist.

The view followed here, in contrast to that of Laidler, is that Douglas was *both* a quantity theorist *and* an underconsumptionist, provided that a quantity theorist is not treated as someone who believes that the quantity theory is part of a classical tradition under which Say's Law prevails in the long run, a view of Douglas shared by Friedman (letter, Friedman to Laidler, April 3, 1998, Milton Friedman Papers, Hoover Institution Library and Archives, Stanford University).[9] Otherwise, Chicagoans such as Knight and Simons, both of whom viewed the economy as inherently unstable, creating perpetual deviations from the classical long-run norm, should also not be treated as having been quantity theorists. Moreover, by casting Douglas strictly as an underconsumptionist, one excludes critical doctrinal evidence on the development of the Chicago monetary tradition.[10] Effectively, excluding Douglas from the cross section of Chicagoans reduces the size of the sample and, thus, also reduces the available information about the development of the Chicago monetary tradition, as will become evident in what follows.

During the early 1930s Douglas was primarily interested in developing both policy responses to the Great Depression and policies that could prevent depressions from occurring. Consequently, several of his key writings during those years omitted any reference to underconsumptionism. These writings, in which he was equivocal about the cause of depressions, included his 1931 book co-authored with Director, a March 1932 paper, "Money, Credit and the Depression," and a 1933 book, *Know America*, which included two chapters (comprising thirty pages in total) on the causes of, and policy responses to, the Great Depression. In the latter publication, Douglas (1933a, 49) wrote:

> It is still not certain as to just what starts the depression on its downward course. There are probably many such causes instead of only one. But the chief cause would seem to be the actual or expected fall in the prices of goods resulting

from the greater increase in the quantity of goods than in the monetary purchasing power which can buy them.

To document Douglas's contributions to the Chicago monetary tradition, in what follows the focus is on two of his papers, "The Modern Technique of Mass Production and Its Relation to Wages," published in 1927, and his 1932 "Money, Credit and the Depression."

In his 1927 paper, which included underconsumptionist mechanics, Douglas discussed the way to prevent economic depressions.[11] To maintain economic stability, he introduced the notion of a monetary rule into the Chicago literature. His specific policy proposal was an early version of the money-growth rule aimed at maintaining a constant price level: "The primary need is for stability in the price level of those goods manufactured under the present technique of mass production and this can be secured by a general and proportionate increase in the supply of monetary purchasing power" (1927, 40). To effectuate the increase in the money supply, Douglas advocated government spending on public works financed by money creation, provided that "proper safeguards could be provided to prevent inflation" (1927, 42). In this way, needed public works could be constructed, and labor employed, "without any added cost" to society (1927, 42).

Douglas considered his policy rule to be a type of "managed currency" system (1927, 42). He argued: "if a combination of philosophers and economists, endowed with courage as well as with judgement, could be given control over our monetary supply, it would be possible for us largely to prevent business depressions" (1927, 42). Consequently, Douglas allowed a certain amount of discretion to policy makers in the implementation of his money-growth proposal.[12] He noted that "great care and restraint would be needed to prevent such an undue issuance of paper money as would enable the government to bid up unduly the prices of commodities and labor" (1927, 42). In order to prevent an "undue issuance" of money, Douglas argued that the issuance should be so limited as: "(1) to prevent the index of unemployment (the present lack of which is one of the shames of American official statistics) from rising above, let us say five percent; (2) to prevent the general price level from rising by more than two or three per cent; (3) to prevent the foreign exchanges from being dislocated" (1927, 42). If a choice had to be made between internal stability and external stability, Douglas argued that external stability should be sacrificed for internal stability. Foreshadowing the position that he was to take on exchange-rate regimes during the Great Depression, in 1927

Douglas did not consider the gold standard to be a holy grail: "Eastern creditors . . . have come to feel that only gold can constitute money. But there is no intrinsic merit in gold itself save that it imposes a natural limit to the quantity of money which can be issued and thus preserves man from the possible consequences of his own folly" (1927, 42).

In the 1932 paper, "Money, Credit and the Depression," published in March of that year—the particular month is significant because the publication immediately preceded the April 1932 Chicago memorandum to be discussed in section 2.5—Douglas described the notion that a fractional-reserve banking system can amplify the business cycle.[13] In that connection, he discussed the self-reinforcing effects of a fractional-reserve banking system: "If and when a general suspicion of the banking system develops, depositors will try to turn their deposits into cash and hold them in reserve. . . . The effect is to decrease the quantity of money offered for goods and hence to again to cause prices to decrease" (1932a, 79). Douglas also discussed the difficulty, created by fractional-reserve banking, of pursuing expansionary monetary policy through the conversion of reserves into loans:

> if only a few banks start such a policy [of expanding loans] and the others do not follow suit, then the checks drawn on the newly created accounts will mostly find their way into other banks. The expanding banks will then have large adverse balances to meet which will drain their resources and force them to call a sufficient quantity of their loans to preserve their balance. The expansion of credit by a fraction of the banks during such periods of depression is therefore self-defeating. (1932a, 79)

Douglas argued that expansionary open-market operations would not be effective during the Great Depression because, in the existing conditions of high uncertainty and narrow or nonexistent profit margins, banks would be reluctant to lend and firms reluctant to borrow (1932a, 79). Consequently, "a more direct method of attack should be made upon the problem of building up monetary purchasing power" (1932a, 80). To this end, he called for money-financed fiscal deficits, even if the money expansion meant that the gold standard had to be abandoned:

> The sums necessary to pay for . . . governmental deficits can be met by issuing bonds which can then be used as security for Federal Reserve notes, or by issuing money as such. The latter method arouses superstitious fear on the part of many, but if properly managed might be productive of great good in getting

the price level started upward and business restored. . . . The dangers of such a policy would chiefly consist in the alarm which it would create among foreigners and the withdrawal of short-time loans and the sale of securities for foreign transfer which would result. This might possibly carry us off the gold standard. . . . But for us, as for most nations, internal stability is in general more important than stable exchanges. (1932a, 80)

Two points about Douglas's policy framework merit comment. First, Douglas's policy rule aimed to stabilize a narrowly based price index—the index corresponding to manufactured goods. He assumed that price-level stabilization of manufactured goods, his primary policy objective, would correspond to a modest increase—on the order of 2 or 3 percent—in the "general price level." Second, Douglas's monetary rule aimed to control a policy instrument—the growth of the money supply—to achieve a policy objective—a stable price level of manufactured goods.

*Policy Activism, 1930–32*

During the period from January 1930 to January 1932, Douglas signed at least five statements calling for countercyclical policies to combat the Great Depression—mainly large-scale public-works construction, which, he believed, should be financed by money creation. Here, I list these statements and provide brief descriptions of their contents as evidence (1) of Douglas's policy activism and (2) that his activism preceded the University of Chicago's group activism of the early 1930s.

1. *January 1930.* Douglas signed (along with eighty-four other individuals from the academic and business communities) a petition of endorsement of a bill introduced to the US Senate by Senator Robert Wagner.[14] The bill called for increased spending on public works to combat the Depression. One other member of the Chicago economics faculty, department chair Harry A. Millis, signed the petition.
2. *May 1930.* Douglas was one of five "originators and first co-signers"—along with Frank Graham (Princeton), Ernest Patterson (University of Pennsylvania), Frank Taussig (Harvard), and Claire Wilcox (Swarthmore)—of a petition "adamantly opposed" to the sharp tariff increases called for under the Smoot-Hawley Bill (quoted from Barber et al. 1997, 6).
3. *January 1931.* On January 5, 1931, the privately organized Emergency Committee of Federal Public Works released a statement signed by twenty leading economists, including Douglas, John Maurice Clark (Columbia), and John

R. Commons (Wisconsin), calling on the federal government to undertake a $1 billion public-works program (Dorfman 1959, 5:674–75).

4. *January 1932.* On January 11, 1932, Douglas was one of thirty-one economists to submit a report to Congress advocating a $5 billion program (over an eighteen-month period) for public-works spending to deal with "the third winter of depression" (*Congressional Record* 1932a, 1657). The economists argued that the spending should be financed by the issuance of government bonds, which "could be used as the basis for advances to member banks from the Federal reserve banks, . . . [and thus] could easily be absorbed with the aid of our credit system" (*Congressional Record* 1932a, 1656).

5. *January 1932.* On January 16, 1932, Douglas was one of thirty-five economists to issue a statement calling for a "commercial banking policy cooperating with the Reserve Banks in checking credit decreases and encouraging increases, including (a) an increase in sound [government] investments, (b) cooperation in aiding necessary treasury financing, (c) borrowing from the Federal Reserve Banks when necessary to meet these and other sound needs" (*New York Times*, January 16, 1932, 30).

Apart from Douglas and (on one occasion) Millis, I am not aware of any instance prior to the time of the Hoover telegram at the end of January 1932 in which a Chicago economist was involved in an action that could be considered policy activism (e.g., a signed public statement, congressional testimony) aimed at combating the Great Depression.[15] Given that (1) Douglas's policy activism preceded the collective activism of the Chicago economics faculty, (2) in the 1930s Douglas had established a reputation at Chicago as a "man of action,"[16] and (3) collective activism did not characterize the behavior of other university economics departments during the early 1930s, the inference can be drawn that Douglas very likely played a leading role in underpinning Chicago's group activism during the early 1930s.

## Douglas and Director: The Problem of Unemployment *(1931)*

The 1931 book *The Problem of Unemployment*, co-authored by Douglas and Aaron Director, was written mainly in the summer of 1930, during which time both Douglas and Director had stayed at Swarthmore College.[17] In a conversation with Friedman in 1996, Director stated that he regarded it as generous of Douglas to have included his name as co-author.[18] Director's attribution of generosity to Douglas undoubtedly reflected Director's humility. In a 1934 letter from Douglas to Chester C. Maxey, who taught economics at Whitman College, Douglas wrote about Director's contribution to the book as follows: "During the year 1929–1930 he was my research assistant. We worked together at Swarthmore College under the auspices of the Swarthmore Unemployment Study for six months in 1930, and wrote jointly the book *The Problem of Unemployment*. He was an equal author in every respect" (letter, Douglas to Maxey, October 29, 1934, Paul Douglas Papers, Special Collections Research Center, Joseph Regenstein Library, University of Chicago).

The book by Douglas and Director was, in part, a wide-ranging survey of then-existing theories of the business cycle and of policies that had been proposed to ameliorate the cycle. Additionally, the book dealt with such issues as the extent and costs of unemployment, the non-cyclical causes of unemployment (namely, technological and seasonal causes), policy initiatives to reduce the costs of unemployment, such as unemployment insurance, and measures to reduce the amount of frictional unemployment, for example, the establishment of public employment offices providing a centralized location to which both employers and job applicants would be referred, lessening the costs of searching for jobs. Here, I focus on the cyclical analysis and policy measures provided by Douglas and Director. As will become evident later in this chapter, their business-cycle analysis and policy views presaged core Chicago views that emerged in 1932 and 1933.

*The business cycle*. Using the classification scheme presented by A. C. Pigou in his book *Industrial Fluctuations* (1927), Douglas and Director analyzed the initiating factors of the business cycle in terms of "(a) Real Causes, (b) Psychological Causes, and (c) Monetary Causes" (Douglas and Director 1931, 168). The authors expressed the view: "there is no method of isolating these various impulses and arranging them in order of importance. In actual economic life they are inextricably mixed and tend to reinforce each other" (1931, 169). In light of the difficulty of attributing causation to the cycle, Douglas and Director proceeded to analyze the mechanics of the cycle following a disturbance to an economy in equilibrium.[19]

The authors began their analysis with an economy at the bottom of a depression. In such a situation, they argued, the following conditions pertained: (1) stocks of goods and materials have been depleted; (2) the price level has fallen and is low; (3) the elimination of inefficient business units and less efficient workers have reduced costs; (4) industrial strife is relatively small; (5) banks have accumulated large reserves; and

(6) technological improvements have taken place during the depression period (1931, 169). In light of the low price level and the depleted stocks of goods and materials, eventually, consumers buy more goods, and businesses begin to replenish their inventories and to hire more workers. In addition, banks start to increase their lending, prices begin to rise, and confidence improves: "Once prices begin to increase, there is a general expectancy of their continued rise" (1931, 171). The rise in prices leads to a greater demand for credit, an accompanying rise in deposits, and "a further increase in the price level" (1931, 171). The rise in prices takes place before increases in business costs—notably, interest rates and wages—so that profits rise (1931, 172). Moreover, the process is cumulative: "The economic mechanism indeed gathers headway in the same cumulative fashion in which it shows up during the recession and depression phases of the cycle" (1931, 170). Although Douglas and Director noted that the economy had self-correcting properties, they also believed that those properties could be slow to develop, thus necessitating policy interventions.

In their analysis of the depression phase of the cycle, Douglas and Director identified the following factor related to the monetary system that can trigger that phase. Specifically, "technical improvements and savings do at times help to cause and to prolong business depressions and consequently to create unemployment. This is when they can cause the volume of goods in society as a whole to increase faster than the supply of money and credit and therefore cause an inevitable fall in the general price level" (1931, 181). Thus, profits and output would fall. In parallel with the business-cycle analysis presented in Douglas's 1927 paper "The Modern Technique of Mass Production and Its Relation to Wages," Douglas and Director (1931, 181) argued: "production takes time and . . . in a period of falling prices, businesses will be buying raw materials and hiring labor at an earlier and higher price level to be sold as finished commodities at a later and lower price level." Consequently, businesses will reduce production and lay off workers. The authors concluded their discussion of the contractionary phase of the cycle as follows: "It is not pretended that this [i.e., the faster increase in output than the rise in the money supply] is the sole cause of business depressions but it is a factor which can initiate a period of depression and accentuate one initiated by other factors" (1931, 182).

*Countercyclical policy.* Douglas and Director's countercyclical policy focused on measures that would bring about changes in the money supply. The authors assessed both policies that work through the banking system—open-market operations, changes in reserve ratios, and rediscounting policy—and policies that increase the money supply more directly. In their appraisal of monetary-policy measures, Douglas and Director used the quantity theory of money as their analytic framework:

> we need make no decision as to the validity of a rigid form of the Quantity of Theory of Money—which is now much disputed. All we need to assume is that an increase in the quantity of monetary purchasing power—whether in the form of gold, bank credit, or increase in the velocity of circulation—will lead to an increase in the general price level, or a decrease in the value of money, and that on the other hand, a decrease in the quantity of monetary purchasing power will lead to a decrease in the general price level or to an increase in the value of money. As bank credit is today the most important and flexible element of purchasing power, it follows that a contraction in bank credit will check an increase in a rising price level and that an expansion of bank credit will check a decline. (1931, 236–37)

Douglas and Director believed that measures that work through the banking system would be more effective in stemming a rise in the price level than in preventing a fall in the price level "in view of the increasing unprofitableness of business" that accompanies periods of declining prices."[20] During the contractionary phase of the cycle, Douglas and Director opted for "more direct methods for seeing to it that the increased potential credit is actually put into circulation so that it can buoy up prices" (1931, 245). Their preferred method was that of public-works expenditures. They presumed that such expenditures would help raise employment regardless of the financing of the expenditures. They also presumed, however, that tax-financed or bond-financed expenditures would be accompanied by crowding-out effects. The authors thus advocated public-works projects, preferably financed by "the issuance of added money by the government rather than by taxes" to combat depressions (1931, 248).

In addition to the advocacy of money-financed fiscal deficits during depressions, the book by Douglas and Director contained several other arguments that were to become core characteristics of the Chicago monetary tradition. First, the authors explicitly introduced the view that rules are to be preferred to discretion into the Chicago literature. In this regard, after assessing Irving Fisher's compensated-dollar proposal,[21] they criticized the proposal for being "tied up with the consequences of the future gold production of the world" (1931, 235). Nevertheless, they argued that

"Professor Fisher's proposal has the merit of being automatic and not depending on the discretion of government or banking officials" (1931, 235). Second, Douglas and Director proposed the following monetary-growth rule: "If the supply of money and credit were to increase commensurately with the increase in production, the price level would be held constant and the goods produced would be sold at prices which would permit industry to go on with undiminished profits and without curtailment of activity" (1931, 183). Third, the authors expressed the view that a rule aimed at stabilizing the domestic price level would necessitate the abandonment of the gold standard and, thus, should entail a move to flexible exchange rates: "It is thus possible for one nation to stabilize its price level . . . if it is willing to go off the gold standard and allow its exchanges to fluctuate" (1931, 251).

Two final points in connection with the Douglas and Director book are important. First, as noted, Douglas and Director thought that monetary-policy measures that operated through the banking system—notably, open-market operations and rediscounting—would be ineffective in combating depressions. In this connection, in his discussion of the monetary-policy measures contained in that book, Laidler (1999, 224) argued:

> The overall skeptical stance on the powers of discount-rate policy and open-market operations expressed by Douglas and Director was so pronounced . . . that I believe it is a mistake to treat that book . . . as an important building block in the so-called Chicago tradition from which Milton Friedman's ideas are thought to have derived, its advocacy of steady money growth notwithstanding.[22]

As will be shown in the pages that follow, it was precisely *because* of its overall skeptical stance of the powers of discount-rate policy and open-market operations that the book *accurately reflected* the Chicago monetary tradition of the early 1930s. Second, there is, nevertheless, one aspect of the book that would not have been viewed favorably by laissez-faire advocates like Knight, Simons, and—after he became a disciple of Knight—Director himself. Reflecting the socioeconomic environment of the Great Depression, Douglas and Director (1931, 60–63) provided a favorable assessment of the experience of economic planning under the first Five-Year Plan in Russia.[23] The authors stated that "at the very time when, because of the world-wide depression," unemployment had been rising in the rest of the world, in Russia unemployment had been falling and real wages had been rising (1931, 61). Moreover, the Russian Five-Year Plan had led to "an extraordinary increase in the tempo of industrialization." A planned economy, they stated, "may well have a greater capacity to prevent depressions and to keep the laboring force more steadily employed than an uncoordinated system of private establishments necessarily motivated by profit" (1931, 62). They concluded their assessment of planning in Russia as follows:

> The greater industrial stability which Russia has evidenced, as compared with the rest of the industrial world during the past year and a half, is of course not conclusive evidence of the superiority of a planned economy. This favorable record may not be maintained in the future and the fierce energy which now characterizes the program of industrial reconstruction may slacken to a very slow tempo. But the whole contrast should raise in the minds of open-minded men the possibility at least of organizing the production forces of the western world and of extending to the industrial system as a whole some of those methods of setting standards, of planning, and of coordinating which have been so effective within establishments. (1931, 63)

For the reasons discussed in the following chapter, I ascribe this favorable assessment of the Russian Five-Year Plan to Douglas. In all likelihood, this assessment provided an initial shot in what would become open departmental warfare on ideology between Douglas and Knight and the latter's disciples, Simons and, as of 1932 and after, Director.

## 2.2 Director, 1930–33, and Mints, 1930

*Director*

In addition to his 1931 book with Douglas, during the early 1930s Director published three other works that dealt with, at least in part, policies to combat the Great Depression or the analytics of the business cycle or both. The views expressed in those works were consistent with the views contained in the Douglas and Director volume.

In 1930, Director published an article, "Making Use of Public Works," in the periodical *Survey*. In that article, Director advocated the use of public works to combat depressions. He argued that the level of spending on public works should be adjusted to moderate the business cycle. As mentioned in chapter 1, J. R. Davis (1968, 477) cited a 1931 lecture by Viner (to be discussed in chapter 3) as "one of the first important statements of the 'simple truth' of compensatory role for government spending in this country"; under the notion of compensatory finance, a government should spend more and tax less during a depression, and spend less and tax more during the expansionary phase of the cycle. Director expressed a similar view in his 1930 paper: "it seems clear that planned public works can, to an appreciable extent, increase the demand for labor in times of depression and decrease it in times of prosperity" (1930, 428).

In 1932, Director published the monograph *Unemployment*, in which he presented a theory of the business cycle. The theory comprised several key elements. First, Director thought that the role of prices in a capitalist economy is to act as a coordinating mechanism for economic activity: "It is essential to point out that in a capitalistic society, the stimulus to economic activity is the making of profits, and the mechanism of coordinating the economic behavior of a countless number of business men is the pricing process" (1932, 23). Second, Director did not single out an initiating cause of the business cycle—he stated that "there is much dispute about the nature and variety of . . . initiating factors of the business booms [and depressions]" (1932, 24)—but the mechanism driving the cycle, he argued, is the combination of changes in prices and sticky costs (1932, 24). Once prices begin to change, wages and interest costs lag, and, therefore, profits, output, and employment move in the same direction as prices (1932, 25–26). Third, in the downward phase of the cycle, for example, the process is exacerbated by the effects of changes in prices on expectations of further price reductions and on the contraction of credit by banks (1932, 24–25). Moreover, once a downturn in economic activity has started, there is no limit as to how far the downturn will proceed: "there is no certainty of recovery from a widespread and serious depression. In such a period there is always the possibility of a complete breakdown in our economic organization" (1932, 28). Consequently, Director thought it was of "great importance" to take "action to check the violent fluctuations in business activity" (1932, 28).

To reduce the severity of economic fluctuations, Director advocated two types of policies. First, he proposed the use of countercyclical fiscal policy as follows: "the planning of public construction over long periods of time, contracting the expenditures in times of prosperity when there is full employment in private industry and expanding the expenditures in times of depression when there is much unemployment" (1932, 35). Second, Director argued that "the most significant line of action is that to be taken by . . . the Federal Reserve System" (1932, 37). He did not, however,

appear to be confident of the power of monetary policy to produce a recovery once a depression was underway. During a depression, he argued,
businesses are reluctant to borrow because of "a lack of confidence" while
banks "are cautious and reluctant to extend credit" (1932, 38). To smooth
the business cycle so that a situation in which monetary policy is ineffective does not arise, Director argued that the central bank should "so
regulate the volume of bank credit as to check any boom which develops,
and counteract any depression which begins" (1932, 38).

In 1933, Director published the monograph *The Economics of Technocracy*.[24] Technocracy was a social movement that became popular in the
United States for a brief period in the early 1930s. Its proponents contended
that economies based on the price system are incapable of allocating scarce
resources efficiently. Those proponents argued that the 1929 depression was
an inevitable result of the technological improvements of the 1920s, which
had the effect of displacing labor with machinery, culminating in the huge
rise in unemployment of the early 1930s. The proponents promoted a society headed by technical experts, including scientists and engineers.

In his monograph, Director argued that technocracy was incompatible with a system of free enterprise and private property. He criticized
the technocratic thesis that the depression that had started in 1929 was
the result of prior technological improvements. He argued that several
special factors, including the debts imposed on the defeated countries following World War I and tariffs—factors "wholly unrelated to the technical changes of the twenties"—had combined to initiate the depression
(1933, 21). Once the initial decline and economic activity had started, the
process worked along the lines that Director had presented in his 1932
monograph: prices declined and, with a rigid cost structure, "a maladjustment between costs and selling prices" ensued (1933, 23). What made the
depression that began in 1929 deeper than previous downturns? Director
attributed the severity of the depression to the "greater rigidity of the
economic system," which was the result of a rise in organized labor and
"formal combinations among employers." As a result, he argued, "our system is shot through and through with informal understandings to make
competition less and less effective" (1933, 23–24).

## Mints

During the period 1919 to 1930, Mints published four articles. Two of the
articles were published in the *JPE* in 1923 and were titled "Open Market
Borrowing to Finance the Production of Goods Sold for Future Delivery"

(February) and "Expansion of Fixed and Working Capital by Open Market Borrowing" (April). A third article, "Financing a Promotion by Selling Receivables," was published in 1925 in the *University Journal of Business*. Reflecting Mints's specialization at that time in the area of financial organization, none of these articles had anything to do with monetary economics; each was a case study of the financial problems dealt with by specific firms. Mints's 1930 article "The Elasticity of Bank Notes," was also published in the *JPE*; that article brought him into the realm of monetary policy. The article was concerned with what was then known as the commercial loan theory of banking. As discussed in some detail in chapter 6, the proponents of that theory held that if only "real" commercial bills (those bills financing the production of goods) are discounted, the expansion of bank credit will be in proportion to what the proponents called the "needs of trade." Thus, inflation cannot occur, since credit and output expand together. Moreover, the currency will have what the proponents called a desirable "elasticity" in the sense that such a currency would automatically expand and contract based on the "legitimate" needs of borrowers. The theory provided a guiding principle underlying the 1913 Federal Reserve Act (Friedman and Schwartz 1963, 169; Meltzer 2003, 70–71).

In his 1930 article, Mints took issue with the view embedded in the commercial loan theory of banking. He argued that the elasticity of a currency depends on the ability of banks to make loans, which depends on the existence within the banking system of adequate reserves, and is not a matter of the kind of security underlying the notes issued. In turn, the existence of adequate reserves, he argued, was "entirely a question of the presence within the banking system of a non-profit-seeking institution [i.e., a central bank] possessed of sufficient resources [e.g., gold reserves under the gold standard] for the purpose" (1930, 470–71). Mints's criticism of the commercial loan theory of banking would form the core thesis of his next substantive publication—his 1945 book *A History of Banking Theory*. In that book he renamed the commercial loan theory of banking, calling it the "real bills doctrine," the name used to identify the theory since that time.[25]

## 2.3 The 1931 Conference

As mentioned, in 1931 and 1932 the University of Chicago hosted two conferences on the causes of, and policy responses to, the Great Depression.[26] The 1931 conference was held from June 23 to July 2. The economic backdrop was the collapse of the economy. From its peak level, attained in August 1929, industrial production had fallen by 31 percent by June 1931; wholesale prices had fallen by about 30 percent during that period and by an annual rate of 20 percent since the start of 1931. The money supply (M1) had fallen by 10 percent between August 1929 and June 1931.[27] The economic collapse had undertaken a global character and was accompanied by the threat of a breakdown of capitalism in Europe amid a series of coups in Eastern Europe and the rise of the Nazi Party in Germany (Meltzer 2003, 334). In July 1931, *Time* magazine published the contents of a letter that Bank of England governor Montagu Norman had written to his counterpart at the Bank of France, Clément Moret, a few months earlier. The letter included the following warning: "Unless drastic measures are taken to save it, the capitalist system throughout the civilized world will be wrecked within a year. I should like this prediction to be filed for future reference" (quoted from Ahamed 2010, 5).

Each of the Chicago conferences comprised several keynote addresses and a series of roundtable discussions, the latter of which included lead presentations by designated speakers, followed by general discussions among conference participants. The 1931 conference featured a keynote lecture delivered by Keynes entitled "An Economic Analysis of Unemployment."[28] Keynes also led a roundtable discussion on countercyclical policies. By and large, participation by the members of The Group at the 1931 conference was minimal. Douglas did not attend. Viner, who was on leave at the Postgraduate Institute of International Studies at Geneva during the 1930–31 academic year, also did not attend. Knight participated in only one of the fourteen roundtables and contributed only a single, innocuous intervention.[29] Simons attended several roundtables, but he intervened only once with an inconsequential remark. Director and Mints contributed substantive remarks that anticipated what would emerge as core elements of the Chicago monetary tradition over the next few years; I discuss their interventions below.

Two other Chicagoans played active roles in that they helped lead roundtable discussions—Henry Schultz and Harry Gideonse. Schultz co-led, along with Carter Goodrich (Columbia University), a roundtable called "Is Wage Cutting the Way Out?" Schultz and Goodrich argued that the case in favor of cutting wages to restore profit margins during depressions, which they characterized as the "traditional" remedy, is not clear-cut; while cutting wages might raise the supply of output, the effects of lower wages on aggregate demand also needed to be considered. Schultz and Goodrich concluded: "Wages rates are not sacrosanct, but cutting is no panacea. [There is a] necessity for diagnosis of a given situation" (Harris Foundation 1931, 1:191).[30]

Gideonse led a roundtable titled "International Capital Movements and Unemployment."[31] Gideonse's presentation dealt with two main questions. (1) Were capital flows inherently unstable and, thus, a factor behind the high unemployment that marked the Great Depression? His answer to that question was in the negative. To the extent that capital flows had been unstable, he argued, they reflected the effects of unstable economic fundamentals—and not an inherent characteristic of the flows themselves (Harris Foundation 1931, 2:358). (2) In light of the accumulations of large amounts of international reserves (mainly gold) by some countries in the second half of the 1920s and the early 1930s—Gideonse mentioned the specific case of France—what could be done to prevent large movements of official capital? Gideonse called for an organized and coordinated effort among governments "to direct to some extent the forces involved and to mitigate some of the harm that is possibly done by the peculiar psychological movements of our money markets" (Harris Foundation 1931, 2:365).

## Keynes, Mints, and Director

The analytic background to Keynes's keynote lecture was his book *A Treatise on Money* (1930), which was published less than a year before the conference. In that book, Keynes argued that business cycles are caused by alterations in profits; in turn, profits are driven by an excess of investment over saving. He repeated this argument in his keynote lecture:[32]

> The cure of unemployment involves improving business profits. The improvement of business profits can come about only by an improvement in new investment relative to saving. An increase of investment relative to saving must also, as an inevitable byproduct, bring about a rise in prices, thus ameliorating the burdens arising out of monetary indebtedness. The problem resolves itself, therefore, into the question as to what means we can adopt to increase the volume of investment. (Keynes 1931, 34–35)

In the *Treatise*, to raise investment and prices and, thus, to combat depressions, Keynes stressed the role of monetary policy for open economies operating under a fixed-exchange-rate regime characterized by international cooperation; in the absence of such cooperation, he advocated a program of public investment. Thus, in the *Treatise*, Keynes wrote:

> it is the action of the lending countries of the world which mainly determines the market rate of interest and the volume of investment everywhere. Thus, if the chief lending countries would co-operate, they might do much to avoid the major investment disequilibria. (1930, 2:337)

In the absence of such cooperation, Keynes continued:

> there remains in reserve a weapon by which a country can partially rescue itself when its international disequilibrium is involving it in severe unemployment. In such an event open-market operations by the central bank intended to bring down the market rate of interest and stimulate investment may, by misadventure, stimulate foreign lending instead and so provoke an outward flow of gold on a larger scale than it can afford. In such a case ... the Government must itself promote a programme of domestic investment. (1930, 2:337)[33]

In his keynote lecture, Keynes discussed three specific measures that could be used to raise investment relative to saving and, thereby, to increase profits and reduce unemployment. One method would be to raise confidence, with the aim of stimulating private investment. However, Keynes believed that "there is perhaps not a great deal that can be done deliberately to restore confidence" (Keynes 1931, 36). A "second line of approach" would be to undertake a program of public investment; Keynes doubted that such a program could be put into operation at short notice and on a scale large enough to be effective (Keynes 1931, 37–38). The third method, which Keynes preferred, was the use of open-market purchases of short-term government securities to lower the short-term interest rate and, through the term structure, lower the long-term rate on private securities. He stated: "There is a normal relation between the short-term rate of interest and the long-term, and in the long run the banking system can affect the long-term rate by obstinately adhering to the correct policy in regard to the short-term rate" (Keynes 1931, 40).[34]

Ostensibly, there was a contradiction between Keynes's policy position in the *Treatise*, in which he advocated public investment to deal with depressions, and his position in his keynote lecture, in which he expressed doubts about the effectiveness of public investment. Keynes cleared up the apparent contradiction during a roundtable discussion led by Otto

Nathan (German Ministry of Economics), who had presented a paper titled "Public Works Construction and Unemployment."[35] During that roundtable discussion, Keynes pointed out that, in the *Treatise*, he had argued in favor of public-works spending during depressions for Great Britain because it was an open economy and at the center of the gold-standard system. In the case of that country, operating on the interest rate, he believed, would be ineffective because interest-rate cuts would generate gold outflows. Contrarily, Keynes believed that these characteristics of the British economy allowed Britain to borrow at the world interest rate regardless of the return on investment. Hence, for that economy, public-works spending would not crowd out private investment and, thus, had a comparative advantage relative to open-market operations in combating depressions. The case of the United States economy was, he argued, different: "Here you can function as though you were a closed system. . . . For such a system I would use as my first method operating on the long term rate of interest" (Harris Foundation 1931, 2:303). Regarding the use of public-works spending to combat depression in the United States, Keynes stated: "I think in this country deliberate public works should be regarded much more as a tonic to change the state of business conditions, but the means of getting back to the state of equilibrium should be concentrated on the rate of interest" (Harris Foundation 1931, 2:303).

In light of both (1) the earlier roundtable (led by Nathan) during which the use of public-works spending as a countercyclical device was discussed, and (2) several interventions by Keynes during the course of other roundtable discussions in which he expressed his views about antidepression policies, Keynes's remarks for his roundtable presentation "Is It Possible for Governments and Central Banks to Do Anything on Purpose to Remedy Unemployment" focused mainly on technical issues related to the implementation of monetary policy.[36] He believed that the conduct of open-market operations in raising banks' purchases of private-sector securities in Great Britain would be more effective than in the United States because, in the former country, banks are not normally indebted to the Bank of England since the bank keeps its interest rate above the market rate; in the United States, however, the Fed typically keeps its discount rate below the market rate so that banks are "normally indebted to the Federal Reserve System." Consequently, when the Bank of England engages in open-market purchases "there is nothing that the markets has ready to pay off"; the amount of funds available to the banks is increased by the amount of central-bank purchases, which the banks can use to buy long-term securities or to lend or to do both. In contrast, in the case of the United States, open-market purchases can be used by the banks to reduce their indebtedness to the Fed rather than to increase their lending or their purchases of long-term financial instruments (Harris Foundation 1931, 2:447–48). Despite these characteristics of the US financial system, Keynes concluded his comparison of the relative effectiveness of open-market purchases in Great Britain and the United States with the following assessment: "even in this country there is no reason to suppose that buying and selling governments [i.e., bonds] will not expand or contract the basis of credit, but I do have to concede that it works more slowly than it does in Great Britain, and it might have to be on a larger scale" (Harris Foundation 1931, 2:447).

During the discussion that followed Keynes's roundtable presentation, Mints made several comments that indicated his preference for both (1) public-works spending relative to open-market purchases of government securities and (2) open-market purchases of private securities instead of purchases of government bonds to combat the depression. Concerning the former issue, the following exchange between Mints and Keynes took place.

MR. MINTS: I should like to revert for a moment to the question of the relative importance of lowering the interest rate and public works. As I understand your argument, you want to reduce the interest rate in order to bring about an equivalent between saving and investment. As a matter of fact, won't public works bring about precisely the same results, not through decreasing the interest rate, but increasing the rate of return for business firms, thereby increasing the rate of investment, even at current rates of interest?

MR. KEYNES: Certainly; therefore I am in favor of an admixture of public works, but my feeling is that unless you socialize the country to a degree that is unlikely . . . you have shot your bolt, and you are no better off. (Harris Foundation 1931, 2:493–94)

Concerning the second issue, Mints questioned the need to use open-market purchases of government bonds to lower long-term interest rates on private securities. Mints considered this method to be indirect and wondered whether a more direct method might be used.

MR. MINTS: Your means of reducing a long-term rate of interest has been an indirect means. I wonder what you would say to a more direct means, namely purchasing industrial and public utility bonds by the member banks themselves.

MR. KEYNES: I think that is against the law.

MR. MINTS: The law can be changed. (Harris Foundation 1931, 2:479)

Director's intervention was made following Alvin Hansen's roundtable presentation "Business Cycles, Price Levels, and Unemployment."[37] In that presentation, Hansen had expressed the view that the empirical evidence indicated that long-term, or secular, declines in the price level tended to be accompanied by reductions in the growth rates of the production of goods and that this phenomenon was more pronounced than the opposite tendency of long-term rises in the price level to be accompanied by increases in the growth rates of production. Hansen argued: "in the periods of long-run downward trends in prices . . . the rates of increase in the production of goods are slowed down very much compared with the periods of the upswing" (Harris Foundation 1931, 1:54). He continued: "We also find that revolutions tend to develop in the down-swing of the long waves" (Harris Foundation 1931, 1:55). To deal with this problem, Hansen argued that policy should aim "to stabilize not indeed the cyclical movements in prices, but the price trend." One way of achieving this objective would be to devise "a special kind of price index, a price index which omits the commodities peculiarly sensitive to the business cycle" (Harris Foundation 1931, 1:65).

Director took issue with Hansen's concern with the effects of a long-term fall in the price level. The following exchange between Director and Hansen took place.

MR. DIRECTOR: What is the sequence of events in a period of declining prices which leads you to emphasize control of trend rather than control of the cyclical elements?

MR. HANSEN: I should say that the sequence of events is something like this: All your fixed charges, interest on bonds, your salaries, even your wage rates, practically all the cost factors, continue to stay relatively high [during periods of secular declines in prices] except the price of raw materials. . . . Until that has worked itself out, you are in no position to get to recovery. . . . If the fundamental forces on the monetary side tend to produce a fall of fifteen points, your internal price structure is thrown out of line more dramatically, and the lag before you reach the readjustment itself takes a much longer time, hence the longer depression in the periods of long-run price decline.

MR. DIRECTOR: If the secular trend changed at a changing rate. But if the secular changes were at a constant rate, it seems to me that once the adjustment is

made to, say a three per cent fall in the price of finished goods, and the changes
in the prices of the factors of production—wages, and so on—come somewhat
later, once that adjustment was made you could go on indefinitely with the
price falling at that per cent, say three per cent, the adjustment continually being made without any difficulty at all. (Harris Foundation 1931, 1:77)

As will be discussed below, Director's view that an *anticipated* fall in the
price level of 3 percent a year would *not* have harmful effects on economic
activity became an argument underpinning the advocacy of a constant-
money-supply rule in the Chicago memorandum of November 1933.

A final observation about the message that Keynes brought to the Chicago conference merits comment. Keynes's diagnosis of the Great Depression in terms of insufficient investment relative to saving underscored
a deeper concern—namely, the view that the capitalistic system is unstable
and might need to be supplemented with state control over investment.
Thus, following Hansen's roundtable presentation "Business Cycle, Price
Levels, and Unemployment," Keynes commented:

> I should agree that the capitalistic society as we now run it is essentially unsta-
> ble. The question in my mind is whether one could preserve the stability by the
> injection of a moderate degree of management; whether in practice it is beyond
> our power to do this, and that we will have to have some further plan of control.
> I should like to try the central bank method first, uncertain how far in practice
> it would lead us. If that proved to be incapable of keeping things reasonably
> steady, then I should go in for a very great degree of state control of the rate of
> investments. (Harris Foundation 1931, 1:93)

The participants at that particular roundtable included Director, Mints, and
Simons. Keynes's remarks likely did not go over well with the Chicagoans.
In the next few months, they would put forward an alternative diagnosis of
the Great Depression in terms of a rigid price-cost structure and an inherently unstable fractional-reserve banking system. They would also formulate a policy package that aimed to limit state control over investment.

## 2.4 The 1932 Conference

The 1932 conference was held from January 27 to January 31. Three aspects of that conference are pertinent for the debate about a 1930s Chi-

cago monetary tradition and its possible relationship with Friedman's monetary economics: (1) a lecture delivered by Viner titled "International Aspects of the Gold Standard"; (2) the previously mentioned telegram sent to President Hoover, signed by twenty-four conference participants, providing a series of policy recommendations for combating the Great Depression; and (3) an exchange between Douglas and James Harvey Rogers (Yale University) on the most effective means of generating monetary expansion during the depression. As I document below, both the Viner lecture and the telegram to President Hoover were subsequently used to present an inaccurate characterization of the Chicago monetary tradition.

## Viner's Criticism of the Federal Reserve

The focus of Viner's lecture was on what Viner acknowledged was "too sympathetic an account of the way in which the gold standard has functioned" (Viner 1932a, 34–35); that part of Viner's presentation will be discussed in the next chapter. What I want to highlight here are the links in Viner's lecture to Friedman's monetarist framework.

At one point during his presentation, Viner criticized Federal Reserve policy during the Great Depression. Viner argued:

> The Federal Reserve Board has revealed to the outsider no greater capacity [than other central banks] to formulate a consistent policy, unless a program of drift, punctuated at intervals by homeopathic doses of belated inflation or deflation and rationalized by declarations of impotence, can be accepted as the proper constituents of central bank policy. While the New York Federal Reserve Bank has made more effort than any other central banking institution to develop a program and a technique of credit control with a view to stabilization, it has at critical moments found itself at cross-purposes with and inhibited from action by, a Federal Reserve Board with an attitude toward its functions resembling with almost miraculous closeness that of the Bank of England during its worst period. (1932a, 28)

Viner attributed the Fed's inept policy response to the organizational structure of the Federal Reserve System, which he characterized as "overly complex, too decentralized, and too much subject to regional pressure to act quickly and decisively in the international sphere" (1932a, 28). This argument presaged Friedman and Schwartz's (1963, 407–19) thesis that the Federal Reserve's structure in the early 1930s prevented the Fed from acting effectively.[38]

In a February 1933 lecture delivered at the University of Minnesota, Viner again criticized the Fed's policies during the Depression;[39] in that lecture Viner called on the Fed to undertake expansionary open-market operations to combat the Depression. As mentioned in the previous chapter, Friedman (1972) would use both Viner's criticisms of the Federal Reserve's policies during the Great Depression and Viner's advocacy of expansionary open-market operations during that episode as evidence of the character of the earlier Chicago quantity-theory tradition.

*The Hoover Telegram*

On the final day of the conference, a committee of six participants— Hansen, Schultz, Viner, Fisher, Charles Hardy (Brookings Institution), and John H. Williams (Harvard)—drafted a statement of policy recommendations, based on the conference discussions, that was sent to President Hoover; twenty-four conference participants—twelve Chicagoans and twelve non-Chicagoans—signed the telegram;[40] as noted, Douglas did not sign the telegram. The policy recommendations were as follows: (1) the liberalization of the collateral provisions underlying issuance of Federal Reserve notes by permitting the substitution of government securities for commercial paper, and preferential treatment of the discount rates on commercial paper backing the notes "as necessary prerequisites to the following recommendations with respect to open-market operation[s]";[41] (2) "open-market operations with the double aim of facilitating necessary government financing and increasing the liquidity of the banking structure"; (3) encouragement of the Reconstruction Finance Corporation (RFC) to make loans on assets not eligible for rediscounting, as stipulated under the RFC Act;[42] (4) the maintenance of the government's program of public works and public services "at a level not lower than that of 1930–31"; (5) the "reduction or cancellation of intergovernmental debts"; and (6) a "substantial lowering of tariffs and other barriers to world trade" (Harris Foundation 1932, 413–15).

What is noteworthy is what is *missing* from these recommendations. (1) There is no recommendation that the government *expand* public-works spending—only that the level of such spending should be *maintained* at the 1930–31 level. (2) There is no mention that public-works spending should be financed by an expansion of the money supply—the monetary-policy recommendations were strictly limited to open-market operations and rediscounting. (3) There is no mention that the United States should abandon the gold standard if adherence to the gold standard conflicted with domestic stabilization. The absence of these measures from the Hoover telegram is the reason Douglas did not sign the telegram, as discussed below.

## The 1932 Conference and Friedman

Both the address by Viner and the telegram sent to President Hoover have had the effect of injecting diversionary ingredients into the debate about the relevance of early 1930s Chicago monetary thinking to Friedman's monetarist framework. Crucially, in his defense of a relationship between an earlier Chicago monetary tradition and his work, Friedman (1972) used both the part of Viner's lecture critiquing Federal Reserve policy and the emphasis of the Hoover telegram on traditional monetary measures as evidence of such a relationship. Thus, after quoting the part of Viner's lecture dealing with Federal Reserve policies during the Great Depression, Friedman (1972, 940–41) asked:

> What, in the field of interpretation and policy, did Keynes have to offer those of us who learned their economics at a Chicago that was filled with these views? Can anyone who knows my work read Viner's comments and not see the direct links between them and Anna Schwartz's and my *Monetary History* (1963), or between them and the empirical *Studies in the Quantity Theory of Money* (1956b)? Indeed, as I have read Viner's talk for the purposes of this paper, I have myself been amazed to discover how precisely it foreshadows the main thesis of our *Monetary History* for the depression period, and have been embarrassed that we made no reference to it in our account.

Friedman also quoted the recommendation made in the Hoover telegram in support of monetary policies operating through the banking system to combat the Great Depression. After doing so, Friedman (1972, 937) noted that "the manifesto from which I have quoted the recommendation of open-market operations was issued at the Harris Foundation lectures — and was signed by twelve University of Chicago economists."[43] Friedman (1972, 937) also stated that "so far as policy was concerned, Keynes had nothing to offer those of us who had sat at the feet of Simons, Mints, Knight, and Viner."

Friedman's above defense of the Chicago monetary tradition was diversionary for two reasons. First, the defense injected the idea that a characteristic feature of early 1930s Chicago thinking was the notion that the Fed had deepened the Great Depression, thereby anticipating the thesis of Friedman and Schwartz (1963), into the debate concerning a Chicago monetary tradition. Second, the defense created the impression that the earlier Chicagoans favored monetary-policy operations that worked through the banking system to combat the Depression, thereby anticipating Friedman's views of the 1950s and after about the implementation of monetary policy. Both of these arguments used by Friedman to characterize the earlier Chicago monetary tradition became embedded in the subsequent doctrinal literature. Thus, Laidler (1999, 228) stated: "Nowadays we are accustomed to thinking of that institution [the University of Chicago] as the home, in the early 1930s, of an intellectual tradition, based on the quantity theory of money, that advanced a monetary theory of the cycle in general and the Great Depression in particular, [and] took a rather optimistic view of the powers of orthodox monetary policy."[44] The effect of injecting these two characteristics—that is, a monetary interpretation of the Great Depression and belief in the effectiveness of open-market operations into the discussion about the Chicago monetary tradition—was that, apart from Viner's position, it provided a misleading characterization of the 1930s Chicago monetary thinking. As will be documented, the advocacy of monetary-policy measures that work through the banking system and a monetary interpretation of the Great Depression—Viner aside—were *not* part of the early 1930s Chicago monetary tradition. Nevertheless, based on Friedman's 1972 defense of that tradition, Laidler and Sandilands (2002a, 525) stated:

> The recommendations to President Hoover that emerged from the Harris Foundation conference of January 1932 . . . (along with Jacob Viner's contribution to the conference that produced them) are the earliest of the sources cited by Milton Friedman . . . as epitomizing the economics of the Chicago tradition of the 1930s, from which, he claimed, his own work ultimately drew its inspiration.

## Douglas versus Rogers

On January 29, 1932, the conference included a session entitled "Relation of the Federal Reserve System to the Gold Standard," chaired by James Harvey Rogers (Yale). During that session, a heated exchange erupted between Rogers and Douglas over the most effective way to combat the depression. Rogers favored measures that operated through the banking system (e.g., expansion of collateral eligible for rediscounting) within the framework of the gold standard. Douglas had a very different view. The exchange was as follows.

MR. DOUGLAS: May I ask whether it might not be expeditious and better to approach the question from the standpoint of monetary issue, rather than from banking policy? Would you have any objection to meeting the government deficit with an issue of paper money?

MR. ROGERS: I think that would be very dangerous. I think that is simply heretical....

MR. DOUGLAS: In an emergency isn't that the quickest way to get something done? ...

MR. ROGERS: My objection to the greenback proposal [i.e., money-financed fiscal deficits] is that, well, I think of the consternation that would come in various parts of Europe—and not only in France....[45]

MR. DOUGLAS: May I, as a heretic, ask you a question? I take it your objection is that you could not meet the deficit through a paper money issue and retain the gold standard.

MR. ROGERS: I wouldn't go that far, but it would bring a much more severe threat to it.

MR. DOUGLAS: I should like to inquire whether the checking of the business depression, and the rise of the price level to counteract the long-time inequities in the fall of the price level—whether the advantages of that would be a greater danger than a depreciation of the [exchange rate of the] currency. (Harris Foundation 1932, 184–85)

Douglas's proposal that money-financed fiscal deficits be used to combat the depression, even if such a policy meant that the gold standard had to be abandoned, was met with ridicule by some conference participants. This circumstance is evidenced by Douglas's intervention during the conference discussions the following day:

MR. DOUGLAS: I should like to make a statement [that] ... relates to an issue raised at the conclusion of yesterday morning's meeting. . . . When I suggested that it would be better to build up monetary purchasing power directly through the currency system rather than the banking system, and to put this increased purchasing power in the hands of consumers themselves through an issue of paper money to meet part or all of the public requirements, to finance demands for relief, and thus more speedily lead to an increased demand for consumers' goods, that proposal was declared by the leader of the discussion [Rogers] to be heresy, and his declaration was approved by a salvo of "amens" about the table. (Harris Foundation 1932, 295)

The incident in question left a lasting mark on Douglas. Several years later, in his book *Controlling Depressions*, he would recall the incident at the conference as follows (1935b, 117): "Professor James H. Rogers, declared that if the banks only had the funds there were such abundant opportunities for investment that they would be speedily placed out, with the result that employment, production and purchasing power would all greatly increase. Those who, like myself, expressed their disbelief that any real stimulation of business would follow, were either laughed aside or regarded as rather loose-brained heretics."

The above documentation provides clear-cut evidence that Douglas did not sign the Hoover telegram because he was strongly opposed to the absence of any reference to a policy of money expansion operating through the fiscal system, even if that policy meant going off the gold standard. As we will now see, the April 1932 Chicago memorandum was to comprise a very different set of policy recommendations from those of the Hoover telegram.

## 2.5 Pettengill Memorandum

In April 1932 Congressman Samuel Pettengill (Indiana) solicited the opinions of various economists on the advisability of either issuing government bonds or printing money to liquidate "adjusted compensation certificates," which were bonuses paid (in the form of certificates redeemable in cash at a future time) to US military personnel for services rendered in World War I.[46] Pettengill's solicitation was in the form of a series of specific questions about the liquidation of the certificates. In response, twelve Chicagoans, including Director, Douglas, Cox, Knight, Mints, Simons, and Viner, wrote a three-page (single-spaced) memorandum that dealt with the causes of the business cycle, the appropriate policy response to the Depression, and the role of the gold standard.[47] In a cover letter to Congressman Pettengill, department chair Millis wrote that the memorandum "has been developed in a committee of two, in conference, and in Round Table" (Pettengill Memorandum 1932, 524).

*The character of the business cycle*. The memorandum argued that recovery from depression could be generated by two alternative methods:

(1) costs (including nominal wages, rents, and other "sticky" prices) could be reduced in order to raise profit margins; (2) federal expenditures could be increased to raise prices and thus, given "sticky" costs, also raising profit margins.[48] The Chicagoans argued that the economy's structure was such that

> the volume and velocity of credit [i.e., $M'$ and $V'$] is exceedingly flexible and sensitive, while wages and pegged prices are highly resistant to downward pressure. This is at once the explanation of our plight and the ground on which government action may be justified. Recovery can be brought about, either by reduction of costs to a level consistent with existing commodity prices, or by injecting enough new purchasing power so that much larger production will be profitable at existing costs. The first method is conveniently automatic but dreadfully slow; and it admits hardly at all of being facilitated by political measures. The second method, while readily amendable to abuse only requires a courageous *fiscal policy* on the part of the central government. (emphasis added, Pettengill Memorandum 1932, 524)

Note that the above characterization of the business cycle corresponds to Patinkin's "summary propositions, nos. 1 and 2," concerning the Chicago analysis of the business cycle described in chapter 1.

*Policies operating through the banking system.* The Hoover telegram had focused on monetary measures that eased the conditions of the banks. The Pettengill memorandum produced an about-face: "Little is to be gained merely by easing the circumstances of banks, in a situation where, by virtue of cost-price relations, everyone, including the banks, is anxious to get out of debt. Such measures may retard deflation and prepare the way for recovery; but they cannot much mitigate the fundamental maladjustments between prices and costs" (Pettengill Memorandum 1932, 524).

*The preferred policy response.* The Chicagoans contended that policy action should "take the form of generous Federal expenditures, financed without resort to taxes on commodities or transactions" and in such magnitude as to bring about inflation (Pettengill Memorandum 1932, 525). How should such expenditures be financed? The Chicagoans argued in favor of fiscal deficits financed with money creation, either directly or through the banking system:

> On other grounds, the issue of greenbacks seems most expedient; but this method must be ruled out unless one is ready to abandon gold immediately, for it would create the greatest danger of domestic drain. Large sales of Federal

bonds in the open market would be much less alarming; but the probable effect upon the prices of such bonds must give us pause, especially since a marked decline might jeopardize the position of many banks. It would certainly be better for the Government to sell new issues directly to the reserve banks or, in effect, to exchange bonds for bank deposits and Federal reserve notes. Much may be said, indeed, for issuing the bonds with the circulation privilege, thus permitting the reserve banks to issue Federal reserve bank notes in exchange; for this procedure does not much invite suspicion, has supporting precedent, and would greatly reduce the legal requirements with respect to gold. (Pettengill Memorandum 1932, 525)[49]

Note that the emphasis on money creation to counter the depression corresponds to Patinkin's "summary proposition, no. 4." Note, also, that both the adverse assessment of monetary policies that operate via the banking system and the advocacy of changes in $M$ produced via the government's fiscal position to implement monetary policy correspond to my "summary proposition, no. 5a."

*The gold standard.* The Chicagoans referred to the "remote" possibility that expansionary fiscal policy might force an abandonment of the gold standard (Pettengill Memorandum 1932, 525). As I document in chapter 3, the memorandum's relatively weak position on abandoning the gold standard represented a compromise position, forged to secure Viner's signature on the memorandum.

*Compensatory finance.* The Chicagoans favored a policy under which the budget would be balanced every four or five years (Pettengill Memorandum 1932, 526).

*Policy rules.* The Chicagoans made it clear that they favored policy rules although they were not ready to specify a specific rule: "We shall not undertake at this time to indicate any definite rules. . . . For the not too distant future, however, most careful and intelligent management will be imperative" (Pettengill Memorandum 1932, 526). The support of policy rules corresponds to my "summary proposition, no. 6."

Thus, in contrast to the Hoover telegram, the Pettengill memorandum gave essentially no weight to the effectiveness of policies operating through the banking system. Instead, it advocated "generous" fiscal expenditures financed by money creation.[50] Unlike the recommendations of the Hoover telegram, which advocated international policies focused on tariff reductions and cancellations of debts, the Pettengill memorandum did not refer to such policies; instead it considered the possibility of abandoning the gold standard. The fact that the Pettengill memorandum was strictly a product of Chicago strongly suggests that its contents, and not those of the Hoover telegram, reflected the views that were in the air at Chicago during the early 1930s. This conclusion is reinforced by an examination of the 1933 Chicago memoranda, which are discussed below.

## 2.6 The 1933 Documents

### The Setting

Between 1929 and 1933 the US banking system imploded.[51] From 1930 to 1932 more than five thousand banks, accounting for about $3 billion in deposits (7 percent of total deposits), suspended operations. In late 1932 and early 1933 the crisis in the banking system grew progressively worse as depositors sought to convert their deposits to cash, and banks and businesses deleveraged; in 1933, another four thousand banks, accounting for more than $3.5 billion in deposits, closed their doors. By March 4, 1933, the day that Franklin Roosevelt assumed the US presidency, banks in a majority of states had been either closed or subjected to limits on withdrawals imposed by state governments. On his first full day in office, Sunday, March 5, Roosevelt issued a proclamation that closed all banks, first from March 6 to March 9, then later for two additional days. At the time that Roosevelt assumed the presidency, bank deposits were not federally insured.[52]

### Balancing the Budget

On December 5, 1932, President Hoover published his administration's budget program for the fiscal year 1933–34. Hoover (1932, xvii) considered the budget deficit incurred during the previous fiscal year to have been a "disaster." The 1933–34 fiscal year program recommended "drastic reductions in expenditures and increased revenues" (financed, in part, by higher tax rates) in order to balance the federal budget (Hoover 1932, xvii).[53] Hoover (1932, xvii) concluded his budget report as follows: "I can not too strongly urge that every effort be made to limit expenditures and avoid additional obligations . . . in the interest of the very integrity of the finances of the Federal Government."

In early 1933 a group of Chicagoans, including Douglas, Simons, and Viner, published a thirty-page pamphlet, *Balancing the Budget* (Bane et al. 1933), which sharply criticized the fiscal tightening underlying Hoover's budget.[54] The main arguments made in this document included the following. First, the consequence of policies aimed at tightening the federal budget during periods of recession "will be the retardation of business recovery" (Bane et al. 1933, 2). Second, increases in taxes should not be used to raise revenues during recessions (Bane et al. 1933, 28): "The time to *lower* tax rates is during a depression" (Bane et al. 1933, 23). Third, the volume of public-works expenditures should not be curtailed (Bane et al. 1933, 29). Fourth, there are two main methods of financing a fiscal deficit: borrowing and money issuance. In this connection, "the repercussions of the ordinary fiscal operations of the federal government on the nation's currency system must not be ignored" (Bane et al. 1933, 11); and "what is needed today is an increase in the circulation of money and credit" (Bane et al. 1933, 19). Fifth, the budget should be balanced with reference to the business cycle: "The balancing of budgets should be regarded as a series of long-term operations in which deficits will be incurred and debts increased during years of economic adversity while Treasury surpluses and the rapid retirement of the public debt will be planned for during years of prosperity" (Bane et al. 1933, 11).

*The March–April Memorandum*

Against the backdrop of a further deterioration of the economic and financial situation in the first few months of 1933, and in the absence of federal deposit insurance, in March 1933 Chicago economists prepared an untitled, five-page statement that proposed both long-term banking reform and short-term measures to reverse the economic contraction and the collapse of the banking system; as shown in chapter 4, Knight and Simons were the progenitors of the banking-reform measures, which were based on the English Bank Act of 1844. Signatories of the statement included Cox, Director, Douglas, Knight, Mints, and Simons—but not Viner.[55] There were at least three versions of the particular statement—a March 15 version, a March 16 version, and an April version, the last of which contained substantive changes made by Simons in response to a letter from Fisher; the specific date of the April version is uncertain.[56] The two March versions were sent to about forty individuals, including Secretary of Agriculture Henry Wallace. Wallace forwarded the March 16 version to President Roosevelt with a positive appraisal of its contents.[57] Both of the March versions were introduced by an identical letter from Knight. The letter concluded with the following: "P.S. We hope that you are *one* of the forty odd who will get this who will not think we are quite looney. I think Viner really agrees but does not believe it good politics" (letter, Knight to Wallace, March 16, 1933, Frank H. Knight Papers, Special Collections Research Center, Joseph Regenstein Library, University of Chicago).

The Chicagoans proposed an immediate guarantee of deposits by the Federal Reserve Banks to prevent a further decline of the money supply (through conversions of deposits into cash) and the "gradual liquidation" of then-existing banks, the deposits of which "would be paid off in [Federal Reserve] Notes or in drafts upon the Reserve Banks" (Knight et al. 1933a, 3).[58] In turn, ownership of the Federal Reserve Banks would be taken over by the federal government, which would exercise "full supervisory *control* over the management of these institutions," and the notes of the Federal Reserve Banks would be declared full legal tender (emphasis in original, Knight et al. 1933a, 2). Thus, the government would be given the exclusive privilege of creating money. Existing banks would be dissolved and replaced by two new kinds of institutions: (1) an institution "which shall be required to maintain reserves of 100% in lawful money and/or deposits with the Reserve Banks" (Knight et al. 1933a, 2)—basically, a "warehouse" for funds that acted "exclusively as a depository and agency for the transfer of funds . . . deriv[ing] earnings solely from service charges"; and (2) "a distinct class of institutions, in the general form of investment trusts," which would "engage in the business of short-term lending, discounting, and acceptance; [the investment trusts] would be prohibited from accepting demand deposits" (Knight et al. 1933a, 3). The investment trusts would be allowed to invest or to lend only funds invested by their shareholders and, possibly, their bondholders. Although not explicitly stated in the March document, the guarantee of deposits by the Federal Reserve was offered as a short-term solution to the confidence problem associated with a fractional-reserve banking system; the 100 percent reserve scheme and the other banking-reform proposals, were seen as longer-lasting solutions. The advocacy of the 100 percent reserves scheme corresponds to my "summary proposition, no. 7."

The macroeconomic-policy proposals of the document were as follows.[59]

*March versions*. The two March versions were essentially identical, with one significant difference, as explained below. Both versions began with a statement that conveyed the consensus held by the Chicagoans on policy issues:

> It is evident that drastic measures must soon be taken with reference to banking, currency, and federal fiscal policy. In such a situation, it seems desirable that there should be some statement of opinion by academic economists, *especially*

*by groups of whose members hold substantially similar views.* (emphasis added,
Knight et al. 1933a, 1)

The Chicagoans argued that the government's short-term policy objective should be to increase wholesale prices by 15 percent (Knight et al.
1933a, 1). To effectuate such an increase, they called for a "substantial increase of federal emergency measures (for unemployment-relief and for
public works)" financed by money creation:

> The proposal for increasing the price level contemplates additional issue of
> Federal Reserve Notes against federal securities, for the purposes of cover-
> ing the fiscal deficit and of meeting forthcoming maturities. It is not unlikely,
> given the stimulus of the guarantee arrangement, that quite moderate mea-
> sures might suffice to bring about the specified price-level change. Substantial
> increase of federal, emergency expenditures might, however, prove necessary.
> (Knight et al. 1933a, 4)[60]

Corresponding to my "summary proposition, no. 5a," there was *no* mention of the use of monetary policies that operate through the banking system; changes in the money supply needed to be generated entirely through
the government's fiscal position.

The Chicagoans recognized that the implementation of the above policies would *not* be consistent with the requirements of the gold standard.
Consequently, they argued that the gold standard should be abandoned—
corresponding to my "summary proposition, no. 8." Their specific recommendations included the following: (1) suspension of free gold coinage;
(2) embargo on all gold imports; (3) prohibition of the export of gold
by private individuals; (4) mandatory exchange of gold holdings by US
residents for Federal Reserve notes; (5) suspension of all gold contracts;
and (6) "substantial" export of US government and Federal Reserve gold
holdings (Knight et al. 1933a, 5).[61]

The above policy measures left open the issue of a specific long-term
monetary rule. Here the March 15 and March 16 documents, viewed together, hinted of a simmering debate on policy rules among some of the
Chicagoans. The March 15 version contained the following statement:

> The measures outlined above . . . would leave one major problem still to be
> faced, namely, that of long-run currency management. Within our group, there
> are slight differences of opinion as to what constitutes the most desirable policy.

Some of us favor a stabilizing of the total quantity of circulating media; some, a stabilizing of total "circulation" ("MV") per period; some favor more complex formulas (e.g., stabilizing per-capita "circulation.") *On the other hand, none of us favors, as a long-run policy, price-level stabilization.* This policy [raising wholesale prices by 15 percent], however, seems to us quite satisfactory as a short-run expedient. (emphasis added, Knight et al. 1933a, 5)

Recall that Douglas favored a money-supply-growth rule that aimed to stabilize the price level. The above statement, however, does not refer to a monetary-growth rule, and it explicitly *excludes* a long-run policy that aims to stabilize the price level. Therefore, this part of the statement could not have been agreeable to Douglas; in the March 16 version (Knight et al. 1933b), the sentence, "On the other hand, none of us favors, as a long-run policy, price-level stabilization," was deleted. I conjecture that it is likely that Douglas was responsible for the deletion.

*April version.* Irving Fisher, to whom the March 15 version of the March memorandum had been sent, addressed a letter, dated March 19, 1933, to Simons, commenting on the memorandum. Fisher was concerned that the short-term objective of increasing the price level by 15 percent would prove to be inadequate, mainly because it would not fully offset the rise in the real burden of debt resulting from the fall in the price level that had occurred in the years preceding and during the Great Depression; in his letter, Fisher estimated that, since 1926, wholesale prices had fallen by about 40 percent (letter, Fisher to Simons, March 19, 1933, Henry C. Simons Papers, Special Collections Research Center, Joseph Regenstein Library, University of Chicago).

In a letter, dated March 24, 1933, responding to Fisher, Simons took issue with Fisher's view that a larger than 15 percent increase in the price level was warranted to take account of the debtor-creditor relationship (letter, Simons to Fisher, March 24, 1933, Henry C. Simons Papers, Special Collections Research Center, Joseph Regenstein Library, University of Chicago). In any case, Simons wrote that the 15 percent figure was arbitrary. Simons's views about the debtor-creditor relationship and the arbitrary nature of the 15 percent figure were reflected in a revised version, produced by Simons in April 1933, of the memorandum. In a letter from Simons to Beardsley Ruml, dated April 10, 1933, Simons wrote that the revised version consisted of an additional three pages "of stuff which is intended to displace that last page of the recent statement (privately circulated) on banking reform" (Henry C. Simons Papers, Special Collections Research Center, Joseph Regenstein

Library, University of Chicago).[62] The April version took issue with the aim of using monetary policy to address the rise in the real burden of debt resulting from the fall in the price level. In the part of the new version dealing with the objective of an increase in the price level of 15 percent in the short term, the revised text added the following:

> The objective of monetary policy should now be conceived, we insist, in terms of the volume of employment, with only incidental regard for the circumstances of debtors and creditors. In other words, currency measures should aim to correct, and to avoid over-correcting, the general maladjustment between product-prices and operating costs. Our recommendation of a fifteen percent increase in wholesale prices has little or no statistical foundation; the figure represents merely our guess of what would be necessary. (Knight et al. 1933c, 5)

The April version warned that any increase in prices had to be modest so that it would not eventuate in the "unhealthy developments of a furious boom" (Knight et al. 1933c, 5). Concerning long-term currency management, the April version added the following:

> We feel that any body like the Reserve Board should only be entrusted with a largely technical and strictly administrative function of applying some *explicit rule* of currency-management—the *rule* being chosen by Congress and incorporated in legislation under circumstances designed to minimize the possibility of frequent or drastic change. (emphasis added, Knight et al. 1933c, 7)

Why did Simons take issue with Fisher on the matter of the magnitude of the rise in the price level needed to help bring about a recovery? The answer has to do with different perceptions about the big, bad actor in the early 1930s depression. As we have seen, in 1933 the Chicagoans assigned the lead role in the depression to the fractional-reserve banking system. The Chicagoans believed that it had been the buildup of *bank* debt, in the form of demand deposits, prior to the Great Depression, and the multiple contraction of demand deposits in the early 1930s, that accounted for the severity of the depression. The year 1933 also saw Fisher publish the paper "The Debt-Deflation Theory of Great Depressions." In that paper, Fisher (1933b) argued that it was the rise in the *overall* level of real debt—generated by deflation—that led to defaults on consumer loans and mortgages, bank insolvencies, and reductions in lending and spending, which were the source of the severity of the depression.

The contrast between those two ways of looking at the role played by debt was brought out in an exchange of letters between Knight and Fisher in December 1933. In a letter from Knight to Fisher, dated December 12, 1933, Knight wrote that the argument made by Fisher in his article "The Debt-Deflation Theory" "disturbs me profoundly." Knight continued:

> I think I agree with your general position as I always understood it before, namely, that the severity of depressions is primarily due to price deflation. But in the article the concept of debt seems to me ruinously ambiguous, and not only that, but the wording is such that a reader almost inevitably gets the wrong impression. If one went through the paper and simply wrote "commercial bank debt" in place of the bare word "debt" at practically every point, I should agree with the argument almost entirely. . . . *Surely it is the liquidation of bank debt with the resulting contraction in circulation—both quantity and velocity—which is the crux of the matter. Isn't it?* (emphasis in original, letter, Knight to Fisher, December 12, 1933, Frank H. Knight Papers, Special Collections Research Center, Joseph Regenstein Library, University of Chicago)

Why was Knight disturbed by Fisher's debt-deflation theory? Because, as he stated in his letter, Knight thought that the debt-deflation theory had political implications. It was, Knight wrote, "certain to be seized upon politically by farmers and other debtors and used as the basis of political pressure in directions which are more likely to do harm than good." Thus, whereas the Chicagoans' theory of the business cycle led them to propose a reform of the banking system, the Chicagoans believed that Fisher's debt-deflation theory was politically charged and could lead to more widespread changes in the structure of the economy than would a reform of the banking system.

Fisher replied to Knight's letter on December 26, 1933. In his letter, Fisher maintained that it was the *total* volume of debts—and not just bank debt—that was the root cause of the severity of the early 1930s depression. He wrote:

> While "commercial bank debts" hold a special place in the [depression] mechanism because they affect the *volume* of the circulating medium, all debts, in so far as they are hard to meet or create fear that they can not be met, affect, I believe, the *velocity* of circulation. And *in a depression*, velocity changes more than volume and can not be ignored as playing a big role. (emphasis in original, letter, Fisher to Knight, December 26, 1933, Frank H. Knight Papers, Special Collections Research Center, Joseph Regenstein Library, University of Chicago)

In other words, once a depression gets under way, the reductions in
money and near moneys ($M$ and $M'$ in Fisher's equation of exchange) play
supporting roles in the depression; the big, bad actors underlying the severity of the depression are the declines in the velocities of circulation of
money and near moneys ($V$ and $V'$) produced by the self-reinforcing debt
dynamics associated with price declines. In his letter to Knight, Fisher
wrote: "So I would amend your underscored sentence to read: 'It is the
liquidation of *any* debt with the resulting contraction of *velocity* of circulation and in particular of bank debt with the contraction of *quantity* as
well'" (emphasis in original). Since the decline in the real value of all debt
was at the heart of the severity of the depression, it would be necessary to
raise the price level sufficiently in order to restore the real value of debt
to its predepression level. Thus, antidepression policy was not, as had been
argued in the November 1933 memorandum (see below), simply a matter
of restoring profit margins by raising product prices; it was a matter of
raising the entire price structure (including wages and other costs). Fisher
believed that the latter would require a much larger rise in the price level
than the rise needed to restore profit margins. Fisher concluded his letter
as follows: "I even think that reflation of the *general* price level will carry
with it a considerable step toward the restoration of the balance, i.e. will
partly cure maladjustments in the price structure" (emphasis in original).

Several points are important. First, there was an unambiguous continuity between the macroeconomic-policy proposals of the April 1932
Pettengill memorandum and those of the March–April 1933 memorandum. Both memoranda stressed the need of money-financed fiscal deficits,
rules for the conduct of long-term monetary policy, and the need of policy
to pursue domestic economic objectives—even if that policy meant the
abandonment of the gold standard.[63] In addition, both memoranda left
out any role for policies that operate through the banking system. Second, concerning the March–April memorandum, the short time interval
between the March 15 version of the memorandum and the April version permitted the clarification that "long-term currency management"
should be viewed as synonymous with long-term monetary-policy *rules*.
Specifically, in characterizing long-run monetary policy, the March 15
version referred to the "major problem . . . of long-run currency management," without mentioning monetary rules. The April version, in contrast, referred to "some *explicit rule* of currency management (emphasis
added)." Third, the April version included, and the March versions did *not*
include, the need to have whatever monetary rule that might be chosen
"incorporated in legislation." The need of a rule embedded in legislation

became a recurring feature of Simons's subsequent writings.[64] Fourth, Fisher's view that the rise in the price level in the short term should be (1) sufficiently large to fully offset the rise in the real burden in debt that had occurred since 1926, and (2) based on an explicit price index—a view rejected in the April 1933 version of the memorandum—was shared by Douglas as I now document.

## Douglas: 1933

During the period from mid-April 1933 to early June 1933—that is, around the time of the drafting of the March–April memorandum—Douglas completed a monograph titled *Collapse on Cycle*.[65] The monograph contained arguments that Douglas had made in his earlier work, including (1) the need of money-financed deficits to combat the depression (Douglas 1933e, 23), (2) the need to choose domestic economic stability over adherence to the gold standard (Douglas 1933e, 17), and (3) the need of a "managed currency" system under which the money supply would increase between 3 and 4 percent a year to maintain price stability (Douglas 1933e, 19). Douglas also supported the 100 percent reserves scheme to "do away with the creation of purchasing power by private banks" (Douglas 1933e, 19). In addition, Douglas expressed two arguments, both of which had been made by Fisher in his letter to Simons of March 19, 1933, and with which Simons had disagreed. First, Douglas emphasized the point that deflation had increased the debt burden: "The fall in prices has not only largely created the depression but it has increased the real burden of debtors" (Douglas 1933e, 15). Second, in contrast to Simons, Douglas believed that the decision about the necessary policy-induced rise in the price level should be informed by the fall in prices that had, in fact, occurred since 1929 and that the rise could be achieved without leading to "uncontrolled or open-end inflation" (Douglas 1933e, 15–16).[66] He wrote: "If there is any intelligence in the seats of the mighty the rise in prices will be checked after prosperity is restored by balancing the budget and beginning to pay off the accumulated debt and to retire the note issue. If there is no such intelligence then we are probably doomed anyway" (Douglas 1933e, 16).[67] Thus, in contrast to Simons's view, Douglas believed that (1) the price level should be increased by a magnitude that takes account of the increase in the real burden of debt incurred during the Great Depression; (2) the rise in the price level should be based on a price index with the year 1929 serving as the base; (3) prices, therefore, should be raised by 40 percent; and (4) such a price rise could be secured without producing a runaway inflation.

*The November 1933 Memorandum*

The main text of the November 1933 memorandum, titled "Banking and Currency Reform," was fourteen and one-half pages in length; additionally, the memorandum included a five-and-one-half page appendix, "Banking and Business Cycles" and a seven-page supplementary memorandum, "Long-Time Objectives of Monetary Management."[68] Simons drafted the November 1933 memorandum, but in a letter, dated October 2, 1934, to Douglas (cited in the previous note), he wrote: "Actually I did write the thing alone; but it would never have been written except for my conversations with other people, Mr. Director especially; and it never would have been circulated without favourable critical reports from yourself and other members of the group. So what is uniquely my own is merely the phrasing."[69]

The period between the issuance of the March–April 1933 memorandum and the November 1933 memorandum had seen a substantial change in the economic and banking landscape. A robust recovery took place in the second and third quarters of 1933.[70] Although approximately four thousand banks did not reopen following the March bank holiday, the banking crisis had come to an end (Meltzer 2003, 424). An important factor that had helped stabilize the banking system was the Banking Act of 1933, signed into law in June of that year.[71] The Banking Act of 1933 separated investment banking from commercial banking: commercial banks, which accepted deposits and made loans, were no longer permitted to underwrite or deal in securities, while investment banks, which underwrote or dealt in securities, were no longer allowed to have close connections, such as overlapping directorships, with commercial banks. Importantly, the Banking Act of 1933 created the Federal Deposit Insurance Corporation (FDIC), which insured deposits up to $2,500 on a temporary basis, effective in January 1934. Deposit insurance was made permanent in July 1934, and the insured amount was raised to $5,000. Friedman and Schwartz (1963, 434) expressed the following view: "Federal insurance of bank deposits was the most important structural change in the banking system to result from the 1933 panic, and, indeed . . . the structural change most conducive to monetary stability since state bank note issues were taxed out of existence immediately after the Civil War."

In light of the foregoing developments, the November memorandum, in contrast to the March memorandum, did not address the issue of the safety of bank deposits. Nevertheless, the November document, like its

March predecessor, advocated 100 percent reserves on demand deposits and, in doing so, put forward the following additional advantages of the 100 percent reserves scheme: (1) it would reduce the frequency and the severity of the business cycle, and (2) it would make money creation the exclusive privilege of the state, the state alone obtaining the seigniorage from money creation. As in the March memorandum, the November memorandum argued that the 100 percent reserves scheme would allow the monetary authorities to better control the money supply. In making the latter argument, the memorandum directly tied the amplitude of the business cycle to the existence of fractional-reserve banking. Although the objective of preventing the socialization of investment and the political control over investment was not explicitly stated in either the March document or the November document, in his *A Positive Program for Laissez Faire*, Simons (1934a, 332–33n19) stated, "The so-called 100 per cent scheme was suggested, at least by its Chicago proponents, largely, if not primarily, with the notion that reform along such lines would serve to minimize the danger of increasing political control over the direction of investment, i.e., the danger, both of socialization of banking in its present form and of 'financial planning' administration by organizations of private banks."

The November memorandum (including the appendix and supplement) focused on four main *policy* issues: (1) banking and currency reform—essentially a carryover of the March proposals;[72] (2) analysis of alternative long-term monetary rules; (3) analysis of the workings of the gold standard; and (4) the implementation and objectives of macroeconomic policies. The appendix presented the Chicagoans' theory of the business cycle. In what follows, I discuss the memorandum's business-cycle theory and its position on the latter three macroeconomic policy issues. I show that the November memorandum's position in favor of a *specific* long-term monetary rule differed markedly from the neutral position taken in the March–April memorandum, and that this shift in positions could not have been agreeable to Douglas. I then show that the supplement was written after the main text and the appendix were written and that the supplement had not been distributed to Douglas until October 1934. There was a reason for that circumstance. The supplement contained a sharp critique of a rule based on money-supply growth—a critique that appeared to be specifically aimed at Douglas's monetary-growth proposal.

*Business-cycle theory.* The appendix, "Banking and Business Cycles," began by considering the case of an economy *without* a fractional-reserve banking system. In such an economy "there will be some tendency toward cumulative maladjustment over periods of a few years" for two reasons.[73] First, the prices of the factors of production, especially wages, tend to be sticky because of both "inertia" and "the existence of trade unions," the latter of which introduces elements of monopolistic pricing into the setting of wages (Simons et al. 1933, appendix, 1). Consequently, with sticky costs of production, rises in the general price level produce rises in profits, breeding optimism. Second, the rise in profits and the increase in optimism reduce "idle reserves of cash"—that is "the velocity of circulation will increase." This rise in the velocity of circulation, in turn, raises the volume of business and product prices further and, thus, leads to "still larger earnings" (Simons et al. 1933, appendix, 2). The process continues "until the initially sticky prices which govern costs do finally move upward markedly and rapidly—or until some fortuitous disturbance (perhaps a mere speculative scare) happens to establish a sharp reversal of the trend in product prices" (Simons et al. 1933, appendix, 2).

The introduction of a fractional-reserve banking system into the picture greatly exacerbates the business cycle. Underlying this circumstance is the fact that rises in profits generate rises in loans so that "new money (deposits) are created; these changes bring still larger earnings, which in turn induce further expansion of loans" (Simons et al. 1933, appendix, 3). The situation is "even more chaotic" in the contractionary phase of the cycle than in the expansionary phase. Under a fractional-reserve banking system:

> Each bank seeks to contract its loans; but none augments its reserves unless it contracts more rapidly than the rest. Every reduction in bank loans means reduction in the community's effective money [$M$ and $M'$]; and this in turn means lower prices, smaller volumes of business, and still lower earnings. Moreover, in a county where wages and freight rates (to name only the most important items) are as inflexible as they are in the United States, there is no limit, in the absence of drastic federal interference, to the deflation which may ensue. (Simons et al. 1933, appendix, 5)

In concluding their discussion of the business cycle, Simons et al. (1933, appendix, 6) wrote: "We maintain that the cycle problem is a problem of cost-price maladjustments (or the inertia of operating costs), on the one hand, and of the short-run changes in the quantity and velocity of effective money [$M$ plus $M'$] which aggravate these maladjustments." As was the case with the Pettengill memorandum, the above depiction of the business cycle corresponds to Patinkin's "summary propositions, nos. 1 through 3."

*Monetary-policy rules.* As pointed out, Douglas favored a money-supply-growth rule to attain long-run price-level stabilization. Also recall, that (1) the March 15 version of the March–April 1933 memorandum included the statement: "On the other hand, none of us favors, as a long-run policy, price-level stabilization," and (2) in an about-face, the March 16 version deleted that statement. I conjectured that Douglas was responsible for that deletion. The November memorandum, however, included a second about-face. In the discussion of the long-term objective of monetary policy, the following statement, which could not have met with Douglas's approval, appeared: "we do not favor long-run price-level stabilization" (Simons et al. 1933, 6). Additionally, the March–April memorandum had taken a neutral position on the preferences among the Chicagoans on the issue of the choice among monetary rules with the wording, "Within our group, there are slight differences of opinion as to what constitutes the most desirable policy" (Knight et al. 1933a, 5).[74] By the time of the November memorandum, positions had hardened, with the wording: "We have rather *strong convictions* as to the relative merits of different rules for long-run monetary policy" (emphasis added, Simons et al. 1933, 8).

As will be discussed in chapter 4, the November 1933 memorandum's detailed assessment of alternative rules, and its overall advocacy of rules, can be considered the initiation of the long-running debate in the literature about rules versus discretion. The memorandum's starting point for the assessment of alternative rules was a situation in which the economy was in equilibrium in which "cost-price maladjustments have been minimized" (Simons et al. 1933, 1). The objective of any long-term rule was to "build the price structures of the future in such a way that only a minimum of change in the sticky prices will be necessary to full employment" (Simons et al. 1933, 1). To this end, six monetary rules were considered: (1) a fixed quantity of money; (2) a fixed quantity of money per capita; (3) a uniform rate of increase in the quantity of money; (4) the maintenance of a stable price level; (5) the maintenance of a moderately declining price level; and (6) the maintenance of the gold standard (Simons et al. 1933, 5). Rules (3), the money-growth rule, and (4), the stable-price rule, were considered equivalent, as were rules (1), fixed quantity of money, and (5) a moderately declining price level (given expected increases in output and population). Whatever monetary rule was chosen, it would need to be embedded in legislation, with the Federal Reserve's role being confined to "carrying out the rule" but the Federal Reserve "vested with no broad discretionary power" (Simons et al. 1933, 5).

The memorandum's supplement came out strongly in favor of the fixed-money-supply/declining-price-level combination, the advantages of which included the following.[75] First, it would help ensure independence in monetary-policy formulation: "the financing of [government] expenditures merely by increase of the Reserve Banks' circulation" would be eliminated; such monetary financing "is so easy and attractive from the legislator's point of view." Thus, a fixed-money rule would contribute to a balanced budget (Simons et al. 1933, supp., 4–5). Second, echoing Director's intervention at the 1931 Harris Foundation conference, the supplement took a benign view of anticipated declines in the price level under the rule. The supplement stated that the resulting price decline "consequent upon stabilizing the quantity of money [would be] of a different order of magnitude from that experienced in periods of depression. Prices would fall, to be sure, but only at an average rate of, perhaps, three percent per annum." Such a rate of decline would be unimportant "for ordinary business operation" and "relative to the inevitable dispersion of relative price change" (Simons et al. 1933, supp., 6). Third, regarding the effects on equity, "satisfactory relations between debtors and creditors depend primarily upon the establishment and maintenance of certainty with respect to monetary conditions." What is important is that "anticipations of both parties shall be approximately realized. . . . If there is certainty of declining prices, or an unchanging quantity of money, the prevailing rates of interest will be lower than they would be if a stable price level were assured" (Simons et al. 1933, supp., 6). Fourth, while a rule that aims to stabilize the quantity of money would not make allowance for countercyclical monetary policy, cyclical changes in velocity "are unlikely to be of a serious magnitude" in light of the increased certainty provided by the fixed-money-supply rule (Simons et al. 1933, supp., 3). Finally, a fixed-money-supply (declining-price-level) rule had the merit of simplicity, making it easy to understand (Simons et al. 1933, supp., 2).

The supplement's position on the constant-money-growth/stable-price-level rule was highly negative and included sarcastic asides aimed at adherents of such rules. As explained below, there is reason to believe that these comments were aimed at Douglas. The main criticisms of the constant-money-growth/stable-price-level rule were the following. First, it implied "continuous unbalancing of the federal budget" (Simons et al.

1933, supp., 7); recall, the Chicagoans believed that changes in the money supply should be effected through changes in the fiscal balance; a continuous increase in the money supply implied continuous fiscal deficits. Second, and related to the first point, continuous fiscal deficits would encourage political interference in monetary-policy decision-making; therefore, it would leave "too much room for administrative discretion" (Simons et al. 1933, supp., 7): "The spectacle of Congress battling continuously over the question of 'just how much inflation' is neither inspiring nor reassuring" (Simons et al. 1933, supp., 5). Such a rule, the Chicagoans argued, "is sadly lacking in definitiveness." As a result, the rule "leaves too much room for administrative discretion and political manipulation" (Simons et al. 1933, supp., 7). In a barb that seemed aimed at Douglas, the memorandum stated: "This will be clear immediately to anyone [e.g., Douglas] familiar with the technical statistical problems of price-level management" (Simons et al. 1933, supp., 7). Third, continuous injections of money into the economy to maintain a stable general price level could lead to price bubbles in specific markets, leaving the economy vulnerable to the bursting of the bubbles, a prime example having been the 1929 stock-market crash: "We had substantial price-level stability long before the last crisis: Would it be possible again to inject enough 'stimulant' to maintain prices without setting in motion almost uncontrollable forces?" (Simons et al. 1933, supp., 7). Fourth, as argued in the main text of the memorandum, under a fractional-reserve banking system, a continuous increase in the stock of money would mean that the banking sector would share unfairly in the seigniorage; specifically, both the banks' non-interest-bearing obligations and their interest-bearing assets would increase so that a "continuous gratuitous transfer of property rights to these private institutions" would take place (Simons et al. 1933, 12). Then, there was another barb that seemed aimed at Douglas:

> We wish to call attention especially to this point. It seems of decisive importance; but it appears never to have occurred to most students of banking and currency policy. While we do not favor price-level stabilization as a rule of monetary policy, most of the issues here are, we admit, debatable. But any scheme which contemplates continuous dilution of the circulating media by private institutions cannot evade the charge of being preposterous on that score. (Simons et al. 1933, 12–13)

*The gold standard.* The main text of the November memorandum was highly critical of the gold standard as a rule. Among other things, it argued that the gold standard permitted either too much or too little monetary-policy discretion. If a country had large gold reserves, "the monetary authority is left with excessive freedom for arbitrary, discretionary action, since wide changes in the gold stock might be permitted without effort to neutralize the movements" (Simons et al. 1933, 9). Conversely, a country with a small gold stock, or with a narrow range of permittable exchange-rate fluctuation, "would be exposed to disturbance from every change in currency and credit conditions abroad" (Simons et al. 1933, 9). The overall judgment of the gold standard was as follows:

> The gold standard has always been a fair-weather system, functioning smoothly only so long as convertibility really mattered to no one concerned. It can hardly survive a serious war anywhere; and most countries discard it readily under pressure, whether of war or depression. (Simons et al. 1933, 10)[76]

More generally, the Chicagoans' appraisal of the relative merits of fixed and floating exchange-rate systems presaged arguments made by Friedman (1953b) in his classic paper on floating exchange rates. First, regarding the argument that fixed exchange rates reduce the costs of exchange-rate uncertainty and thus facilitate trade relative to floating rates, the Chicagoans argued: "Long-term stability of exchanges is nowise essential to orderly commodity trade; given orderly internal currency management, an adequate futures market for foreign exchange would surely arise, and nothing more is necessary for purposes of commodity trade" (Simons et al. 1933, 9). Second, the Chicagoans argued that what matters for international economic integration "is long-run certainty," and not "short-run stability of the exchanges" (Simons et al. 1933, 10). Long-run certainty would best be achieved by following a domestically oriented monetary rule with flexible exchange rates. Third, the Chicagoans made the case that fixed exchange rates encourage protection while flexible exchange rates would reduce protection: "If the leading nations maintained really independent currency systems, managed internally according to rules which took no account of changes in foreign trade, the grosser fallacies of protection might be transparent to many laymen." By allowing changes in tariff levels to work their effects on exchange rates, instead of on the domestic price level and the quantity of money, "protectionism would lose much of its current plausibility" (Simons et al. 1933, 10).[77]

*Macroeconomic policies.* The November memorandum proposed that, during a transition period of two years, the monetary authorities inject sufficient credit to achieve a price-level objective. In contrast to the March–

April memorandum, which advocated an increase in wholesale prices of 15 percent, the November memorandum did not provide a specific target for the price-level increase: "No drastic increase in the price-level should be attempted, but only such moderate increase as would actually be necessary to reasonably full employment at existing operating costs of industry" (Simons et al. 1933, 6). As was the case in Simons's April 1933 revision to the March 1933 memorandum, the November memorandum argued that the issue of the real burden of debt should not be a consideration in the conduct of short-term stabilization policy:

> In general, we maintain that the cycle problem is a problem of cost-price mal-adjustments (or the inertia of operating costs), on the one hand, and of the short-run changes in the quantity and velocity of effective money which aggravate these maladjustments. It follows as a corollary, incidentally, that the problem of unemployment is not, to an important extent, a problem of debt. (Simons et al. 1933, appendix, 6)

In contrast to both the March–April memorandum and the 1932 Pettengill memorandum, the November 1933 memorandum specified that a monetary rule should be implemented through open-market operations (Simons et al. 1933, 5–6). The latter memorandum's position on the use of open-market operations needs to be viewed in light of the effects of such operations in accommodating the government's fiscal operations. The November 1933 memorandum provided an example under which the quantity of money would need to be increased by $1 billion during a given period. Four options in which such an increase could be effectuated were presented:

> a. by conversion of one billion dollars' worth of interest-bearing federal debt into non-interest-bearing debt, in the form of note and deposit liabilities of the Reserve Banks—i.e., by open-market purchases of federal securities;

> b. by open-market purchase, by the Reserve Banks, of other investment assets— bonds of state and local governments, corporate bonds, or commercial paper;

> c. by increase of federal expenditures, without increase of taxes, the funds being provided merely by expansion of notes and deposits of the Reserve Banks;

> d. by reduction in federal taxes, or even by refunding of taxes already assessed, without reduction of expenditures, the funds again being provided merely by expanding the Reserve Bank circulation. (Simons et al. 1933, 13)

Methods (a) and (b) are equivalent to exchanging fiat currency for debt, whereas methods (c) and (d) are equivalent to the direct issuance of currency to cover fiscal expansion.[78] Which would be the preferred method? The Chicagoans' answer was the method that put the needed increase in the money supply directly into circulation: "at the present time, increase of expenditures or reduction of taxes would be far more immediately effective toward raising prices than conversion of the federal debt into the non-interest-bearing form"—that is, the preferred method was money-financed fiscal expansion (Simons et al. 1933, supp., 13).

### Simons, Douglas, and the November 1933 Memorandum

As documented above, in his letter to Douglas dated October 2, 1934, Simons wrote that he (Simons) had been responsible for drafting the November 1933 memorandum although the memorandum would not have been written in the absence of discussions with Director, and without "favourable critical reports" from Douglas "and other members of the group."[79] Simons's letter to Douglas provided several other pieces of valuable information: the supplementary statement, which included the critical appraisal of the constant-money-growth/stable-price-level rule, had evidently been completed after the main part of the memorandum and its appendix. The letter made clear that the supplement had not been shared with Douglas, probably because Simons recognized that the sarcastic tone of his criticisms of Douglas's policy rule would not go over well with Douglas. Specifically, in his October 2, 1934, correspondence addressed to Douglas, Simons attached the supplement, along with his forthcoming contribution, *A Positive Program for Laissez Faire: Some Proposals for a Liberal Economic Policy* (1934a), to the Public Policy Pamphlet series and "some other letters and papers." Here is what Simons wrote in his letter:

> I'd like for you to see a supplementary statement which was sent to a few people after the original memorandum. . . . I've been on the point of asking you to read the whole thing and am now regretful of my hesitance. I'm afraid that *you will find it irritating at many points*; but I am genuinely interested to know how you would react to the whole thing. (emphasis added)

As discussed in chapter 3, several months later Douglas would successfully lead a move to deny both the awarding of tenure to Simons and the extension of Director's appointment.[80]

## 2.7 Conclusions

The evidence presented in this chapter demonstrated what the Chicago monetary tradition of the early 1930s was—and what it was not.

*What it was.* Using the Fisherine equation of exchange, $MV + M'V' = PT$, the Chicagoans emphasized the inherent instability of $V$, the velocity of circulation of money, in the absence of a rule for long-term money management. Changes in $V$ were considered to be the source of the business cycle and, through the effect of changing price expectations on profits and output, a contributor to the cumulative character of the cycle. Additionally, the cumulative character of the cycle was greatly aggravated, the Chicagoans believed, by the perverse nature of a fractional-reserve banking system, which evokes self-perpetuating changes in the volume and velocity of demand deposits ($M'$ and $V'$). This depiction corresponds to Patinkin's "summary propositions, nos. 1 through 3."

The early 1930s Chicago monetary tradition was policy centric and policy activist. It emphasized the need of changes in the money supply to counteract the business cycle (Patinkin's "summary position, no. 4"). In turn, the Chicagoans advocated changes in the government's fiscal position, rather than open-market operations or discounting operations, to generate the necessary changes in the money supply (my amended "summary proposition, no. 5a"); they also believed that the budget should be balanced over the business cycle. To moderate, if not eliminate, the cycle, the Chicagoans advocated monetary rules and 100 percent reserve requirements on demand deposits. They also argued that the gold standard should be abolished in favor of exchange-rate flexibility so that monetary policy could focus on domestic economic stabilization (my added "summary propositions, nos. 6 through 8."

The idea that changes in the money supply should be generated through the government's fiscal position was first proposed at Chicago by Douglas in his 1927 article. In that article, Douglas advocated a monetary-growth rule, and he argued that the gold standard was not a holy grail. Likewise, Douglas and Director (1931): (1) proposed that changes in the money supply be effected through the government's fiscal position; (2) advocated flexible exchange rates; and (3) argued that rules are preferable to discretion. Douglas's policy activism likely played an important role in underpinning Chicago group activism, which during the 1931 to 1933 period included the hosting of two major conferences on the Great Depression and the production of four policy memoranda.[81]

*What the Chicago tradition was not.* As discussed in chapter 3, except for Viner, the Chicagoans did not implicate the Federal Reserve in initiating or perpetuating the Great Depression; none of their early 1930s memoranda refer to the Fed's possible role in the Great Depression. Moreover, and again except for Viner, the Chicagoans did not favor monetary-policy measures that work through the banking system to combat the Depression.

Thus, the picture that emerges about the nature of the early 1930s Chicago monetary tradition from the evidence presented in this chapter is very different from that which emerged from the Patinkin-Friedman debate, and the aftermath of that debate. Patinkin (1969) failed to identify the emphasis placed by the early Chicagoans on (1) money-financed fiscal deficits, (2) monetary-policy rules, (3) 100 percent reserves against demand deposits, and (4) the abandonment of the gold standard in favor of flexible exchanges. Each of these characteristics rendered the Chicagoans distinguishable from most of the economics profession in the early 1930s; taken together, they rendered the Chicago monetary tradition *unique.* The picture that emerges is also very different from that depicted by Friedman (1972) and Laidler (1993), both of whom singled out (1) a monetary interpretation of the Great Depression and (2) belief in the efficacy of open-market operations and rediscounting operations as characteristics of the early 1930s Chicago monetary tradition. Except for Viner, neither of those characteristics held currency among the members of The Group in the early 1930s. As we will see in the following chapters, the advocacy of money-financed fiscal deficits, monetary-policy rules, 100 percent reserves, and flexible exchange rates continued to mark the Chicago monetary tradition through the late 1940s, including in Friedman's initial work on money.

## CHAPTER THREE

# Controversies

The discussion in chapter 2 raised several issues that were left unaddressed. For one thing, Jacob Viner refused to sign the key March 1933 memorandum, even though it was signed by the other members of The Group.[1] Why did Viner refuse to sign it? Did Viner really agree with the memorandum, but did "not believe it good politics" to sign it, as stated by Frank Knight in his cover letter to the memorandum? Moreover, if Viner did not, in fact, believe that signing the March 1933 memorandum was "good politics," why did he not only sign but also help draft the January 1932 telegram sent to President Hoover? Could the reason that Viner signed one memorandum, but not the other, be that the policy proposals in the two documents were very different, as established in the previous chapter? That circumstance, however, leads to another question. If, as has been shown, the policies presented in the Hoover telegram were not representative of the views that characterized the Chicago monetary tradition, what are the implications of that circumstance for the literature that has attempted to infer a Harvard influence on Chicago by using the Hoover telegram as a central piece of evidence?

Another issue that was raised (but not addressed) in chapter 2 concerned the forceful endorsement of Soviet economic planning in the 1931 book co-authored by Paul Douglas and Aaron Director. I conjectured that Douglas was the source of this endorsement. In this chapter, I provide evidence to support that conjecture. I also demonstrate that Douglas's strong predilection toward activism and his favorable view of economic planning increasingly became a source of friction with Knight. What had earlier been a warm friendship between Douglas and Knight deteriorated into open hostility, with Douglas forcefully and ultimately successfully opposing Knight's drive in late 1934 and early 1935 to award tenure to

Henry Simons and to retain Director on the faculty. Though Douglas won the battle, Knight won the war. In the 1930s, Douglas became increasingly involved in city of Chicago politics and, in the 1940s, went off to engage in combat in World War II, while Knight developed a cohort of disciples who would carry on his free-market principles to future generations of Chicago economists.

This chapter deals with three issues: (1) the relationship between Viner's policy views and those of the core members of The Group in the 1930s; (2) the relevance of Viner's policy views and those emanating from Harvard in the early 1930s in understanding the character of the Chicago monetary tradition; and (3) the dispute between Knight and Douglas over both political beliefs and the retentions of Simons and Director on the Chicago faculty.

## 3.1 The Case of Jacob Viner

We have touched on Viner's views on the origins of the Great Depression.[2] Specifically, we saw that in lectures delivered at the conferences held at the University of Chicago in January 1932 and at the University of Minnesota in February 1933, Viner criticized the Federal Reserve's inept response to the Depression and called on the Fed to undertake expansionary open-market operations. We also saw that Viner was one of six co-drafters of the Hoover telegram that emerged from the Chicago conference; that telegram called for expansionary open-market and discounting operations. Finally, we saw that, in Friedman's defense of a direct linkage between his views and those of the earlier Chicago monetary tradition, Friedman cited Viner's Chicago and Minnesota lectures, as well as the Hoover telegram, as evidence of such a linkage.

Should Viner's views on (1) the Great Depression and (2) the efficacy of monetary policy be taken as evidence of an early 1930s Chicago monetary tradition? Research by Nerozzi (2009) and by Alacevich, Asso, and Nerozzi (2015) has painted a different picture from that put forward by Friedman. Those authors provided evidence showing that Viner, whom we saw had written his PhD dissertation at Harvard under the supervision of Frank Taussig, held policy views in the 1930s that were similar to those held by other Harvard-educated economists;[3] these authors concluded that Viner's monetary views were marked by a distinct Harvard, rather than a Chicago, orientation. Adding to the ambiguity of the relationship

between Viner's views and those of his Chicago colleagues was Viner refusal to add his signature to the critical March 1933 memorandum; as mentioned in chapter 2, that memorandum introduced what became known
as the "Chicago Plan of Banking Reform" into professional discussion
(Hart 1935; R. Phillips 1995). Moreover, as mentioned in chapter 1, in a
1969 letter to Don Patinkin, Viner made it clear that he did not consider
himself to have been a member of a 1930s "Chicago school" that had been
engaged in an organized effort to support the quantity theory of money
and laissez-faire doctrine. As we will see in chapter 7, Viner expressed a
similar view during a 1951 conference sponsored by the University Chicago Law School.

In what follows, I consider Viner's policy views during the period 1931
to 1936. I demonstrate that Viner's views on key policies rendered him
an outlier among the core group of Chicagoans who had a strong interest in monetary issues. Viner was the *only* Chicagoan to hold the Fed ac-
countable for the Great Depression during the early 1930s and the *only*
Chicagoan who was a proponent of expansionary monetary policies that
operate through the banking system. Moreover, Viner's positions on such
policy issues as (1) the monetary financing of fiscal deficits, (2) 100 percent
reserves, and (3) rules versus discretion differed fundamentally from the
positions taken by the other members of the core Chicago group. Thus,
although his views on the Fed's role in the Great Depression and the desirability of conducting monetary policy through open-market operations
presaged Friedman's monetarist economics—as Friedman claimed—
Viner's views on those issues were not representative of the components
of the 1930s Chicago monetary tradition. I also show that a fundamental
factor underlying the differences in policy positions between Viner and
the other Chicagoans was their respective views on the role played by the
fractional-reserve banking system in the business cycle. Each of the other
members of the Chicago core group thought that such a system contained
an "inherent" tendency toward self-perpetuating instability, subjecting the
economy to periodic crises. Viner, as we shall see, held a different view of
the matter.

Moreover, Viner was a strong advocate of the gold standard. Yet, he
signed the April 1932 Pettengill memorandum, which raised the "remote"
possibility that the gold standard might have to be abandoned. Why did
he sign that document?

To set the stage, let us recall the main conclusions that emerged from our
earlier discussion of the 1932 and 1933 documents. First, the Chicagoans

favored money-financed fiscal deficits to combat the Great Depression; as I show below, however, Viner took exception to that view. Second, although twelve Chicagoans, including Viner, signed the January 1932 Hoover telegram calling for monetary measures that operated through the banking system, that telegram reflected the sometimes conflicting views of a wide spectrum of economists, including the views of Viner, a co-drafter of the telegram.[4] Third, there was a critical difference between the external policies proposed in the Hoover telegram and the corresponding policies proposed in the three strictly Chicago memoranda that dealt with external policies.[5] The Hoover telegram called for debt relief and tariff reductions but said *nothing* about the gold standard. The three strictly Chicago documents either suggested (April 1932 memorandum) or advocated (March–April and November 1933 memoranda) an abandonment of the gold standard. Fourth, to attain longer-term economic stability, the three Chicago documents proposed, in addition to the abandonment of the gold standard, 100 percent reserves on demand deposits, and monetary-policy rules. Fifth, there was *no* mention in *any* of the 1932 and 1933 memoranda of the role that the Federal Reserve may have played in precipitating or exacerbating the Great Depression. In the three strictly Chicago memoranda, the severity of that episode was attributed *only* to the inherent tendency of a fractional-reserve banking system to generate self-perpetuating business cycles.

## Viner's Policy Views, 1931–36

I describe Viner's views on policy issues during the early 1930s and compare those views with the positions set out in the above-mentioned strictly Chicago documents. The issues addressed are the following: (1) the gold standard; (2) the use of cost reductions to combat the Great Depression; (3) the relative efficacy of generating changes in money through the banking system compared with doing so through the government's fiscal position; (4) the origins of the Great Depression; (5) the 100 percent reserves scheme; and (6) rules versus discretion. I identify issues on which Viner's views changed during 1931–33. I substantiate the important differences that existed on each of the foregoing issues between Viner and the other Chicagoans, thus explaining Viner's refusal to sign the March 1933 memorandum. In addition, I provide previously undiscovered evidence indicating that Viner signed the April 1932 Pettengill memorandum—despite the memorandum's oblique suggestion that the United States might have to leave the gold standard at some point—because that suggestion was an about-face from an earlier draft of that memorandum that called for the immediate abandonment of the gold standard.

My data sample includes, but is not confined to, the following works by Viner: (1) a lecture, "Problems of International Commercial and Financial Policy" delivered in 1931 at the Institute of Politics in Williamstown, Massachusetts (1931b);[6] (2) the lecture "International Aspects of the Gold Standard," delivered at the conference held at Chicago in January 1932 (1932a); (3) the lecture "Balanced Deflation, Inflation, or More Depression," delivered at the University of Minnesota in February 1933—that is, before the United States left the gold standard on April 20, 1933 (1933a);[7] (4) a lecture, "Inflation as a Possible Remedy for the Depression," delivered at the University of Georgia in May 1933, that is, after the United States left the gold standard; and (5) the paper "Recent Legislation and the Banking Situation," published in the *American Economic Review* (*AER*) in March 1936 (1936a). Although I had occasion to briefly refer to both the Chicago and the Minnesota lectures earlier, the following discussion presents a fuller account of those lectures.

## The Gold Standard

Viner's belief in the efficacy of policies to facilitate balance-of-payments adjustment under the gold standard played an important role in shaping his views about the policies needed to combat the Great Depression. These policies consisted of both cost reductions and macroeconomic measures that were formulated so as not to jeopardize the US commitment to remain on the gold standard. Viner's interest in the workings of the gold standard stemmed from his PhD dissertation, in which he examined external adjustment in Canada between 1900 and 1913 (Viner 1924).[8] During those years, Canada's economy presented several interesting aspects. The country had no central bank, precluding the possibility of sterilization operations; it imported large amounts of capital from the United Kingdom; and Canadian banks held large quantities of their short-term assets in New York banks. Viner found that both relative price changes and capital flows played an equilibrating role in bringing about balance-of-payments adjustment, confirming the automatic character of the adjustment mechanism under the gold standard.[9] In his dissertation, Viner found that short-term capital movements, in the form of changes in Canadian deposits with New York banks, contributed to the equilibrating process, helping to stabilize exchange rates within the gold points, thereby minimizing the need of specie movements.

Viner's lecture at the 1932 Chicago conference provided an assessment of the operation of the gold standard. The basic case for the gold standard, he argued, was the automatic character of adjustment. The process, Viner (1932a, 19–20) argued, worked as follows. A country with, say, a balance-of-payments surplus would experience an accumulation of gold, resulting in an expansion of domestic credit (assuming that the gold inflows were not sterilized). The expansion of domestic credit would push down interest rates and raise prices in the country. Both the rise in domestic prices and the decline in domestic interest rates would help restore balance-of-payments equilibrium—the rise of domestic prices by reducing net exports of goods and services, and the fall in interest rates by bringing about an outflow of gold and short-term capital to other countries as investors searched for higher yields.

That process, however, operated very differently in the pre–World War I period compared with the postwar period. In the former period, adjustment tended to take place automatically, with the Bank of England exercising responsibility at the center of the system. Viner argued that the foregoing adjustment mechanism had "encountered countervailing forces" in the reconstructed postwar gold exchange standard (Viner 1932a, 20).[10] He singled out the following factors that prevented the effective functioning of the postwar regime. First, in the 1920s the Federal Reserve sterilized large amounts of gold inflows, thwarting the operation of the adjustment mechanism in the United States. To the extent that the gold inflows were not sterilized, some of the inflows were used for stock-market and real estate speculation, rather than for purchases of goods and services (1932a, 20). Second, the Banque de France and the French Treasury had adopted a "deliberate" policy of accumulating large amounts of gold in the late 1920s, again thwarting the operation of external adjustment (1932a, 20–22). Third, "international co-operation" among central banks and national treasuries, which marked the prewar gold standard, was abandoned in the postwar years. This circumstance reflected, in part, the decline of England as the "good administrator of the gold standard" and the failure of the United States and France to assume that role (1932a, 26–27).[11] Fourth, compared with the pre-1914 period, the responsiveness of trade flows to changes in relative prices had declined in the postwar years in light of increased wage rigidities and the imposition of higher tariffs during the latter period. Fifth, the unwise peace settlement following World War I had contributed to the growing instability of the international political environment (1932a, 24–25). Consequently, Viner argued, "the gold standard, strained beyond the breaking point, crashed." That crash, however, was not attributable to the gold standard itself; the gold standard, he stated, "was . . . not responsible for all these difficulties" (1932a, 25). Instead, Viner believed that the collapse of the gold standard was a result of "the anarchic way the gold standard has been operating" (1932a, 25).

Viner, therefore, did not want the United States to leave the gold standard. "The gold standard," he stated, "is a wretched standard, but it may conceivably be the best available to us" (1932a, 37). He concluded his presentation as follows: "it seems wise for countries still on the gold standard [including the United States at the time] to exploit more fully its possibilities of exercise before abandoning it as utterly incorrigible" (1932a, 39).[12]

The following puzzle emerges from the above discussion. Since Viner was a strong advocate of the gold standard, why did he agree to sign, along with eleven other Chicagoans, the April 1932 Pettengill memorandum? In that memorandum the Chicagoans argued: "It is well to face the possibility, though it seems *remote*, that adequate fiscal inflation might force us to abandon gold for a time" (emphasis added, Pettengill Memorandum 1932, 525). They continued:

> If the time comes, as it probably will not, when we must choose between recovery and convertibility, we must then abandon gold, pending the not distant time when world recovery will permit our returning to the old standard on the old terms. The remote possibility of our being forced to this step, however, should not influence our decision now. (Pettengill Memorandum 1932, 526)

I conjecture that the preceding statement represented a compromise position between those of the Chicagoans, including Director, Douglas, Knight, Mints, and Simons, who believed that the United States should immediately abandon the gold standard, and Viner, who wanted the United States to remain on the gold standard. My conjecture is based on the following previously undiscovered evidence. The final version of the Pettengill memorandum was dated April 26, 1932. An earlier draft of the memorandum was dated "April 1932," without a specific date. It was almost an exact duplicate of the final version, with the part on the gold standard being an exception.[13] The draft included—but the final version omitted—the following statement:

> It should be recognized, however, that any program of fiscal inflation which does not begin by cutting loose from gold is doubly precarious: we might lose

gold to foreigners and domestic hoarders, and thus be forced gradually to the necessity of suspending our currency laws; or, protecting gold, we might abandon inflation, and revert to fiscal deflation, at a stage such that the whole enterprise would prove disastrous. Great damage can be done by a policy which involves abandoning gold "by inches," with desperate and persistent effort to maintain convertibility. It is not unlikely that we would be forced to choose between gold and recovery. This being the case, we should abandon gold in advance, suddenly and, if possible, un-expectedly. The shock would cause little serious disturbance; while protracted uncertainty and strain would do much harm. (Pettengill Memorandum: Draft 1932, 5)

The idea of abandoning the gold standard "in advance" of other policy measures would have been firmly opposed by Viner. His signature on the final memorandum came when the policy recommendation with regard to gold was reversed.

### The Deflation Alternative

Previous studies of Viner's policy views have suggested that Viner was *not* an advocate of cost cutting during the Great Depression. J. R. Davis (1971, 42) argued that "Viner considered the argument for 'induced balanced deflation' little more than a mistaken supposition." Rotwein (1983, 273n35) stated that Viner had considered the idea of cutting wages and other costs during the early 1930s, "but [Viner] argued that it would cause widespread distress, encounter strong social resistance, and probably meet with little success." Nerozzi (2009, 589) correctly noted that Viner thought that balanced deflation should be part of a countercyclical policy package, but that "monetary policy should be the engine with which to actively boost recovery." In fact, consistent with the operation of the gold standard's adjustment mechanism, Viner believed that cost reductions were an essential response to the Great Depression although he became less confident about the effectiveness of cost reductions during the course of the early 1930s.

In his 1931 Williamstown lecture, Viner advocated nominal wage cuts as part of a package response to the Great Depression; the package also comprised countercyclical fiscal policy and expansionary open-market operations. The components of what he called (1931b, 183) his "wage [reduction] policy" were as follows: (1) a "substantial horizontal reduction of wage rates in all industries in which they have not yet occurred"; (2) a "pledge" by employers to maintain their total payrolls; (3) a "pledge" by employers to raise future wage rates in line with future increases in prices; and (4) similar reductions in rents, interest rates on loans, and other costs as necessary (1931b, 183). Viner then stated that recovery would not come about until the "prevailing cost and price levels ... are such as to assure a satisfactory profit on new operations." He concluded: "Either, therefore, prices must be raised, or wage rates must be cut, and if there is no price recovery, *wage reductions are a necessary preliminary to business recovery*" (emphasis added, 1931b, 184). For the policy to be effective, the cost reductions, and the pledges to maintain total payrolls and raise wages in the future, would have to be coordinated through government intervention. Evidently, Viner's proposal was not received favorably by participants at the Williamstown roundtable. According to the roundtable report, objection to Viner's proposal was raised on the ground that "only a dictator could put [the proposal] into effect." Viner replied: "we underestimate the power of [governmental] leadership" (Viner 1931b, 185).

Why did Viner advocate nominal wage cuts to combat the Great Depression? He provided the answer in a 1932 review of the book *The Problem of Maintaining Purchasing Power*, by P. W. Martin. In his review, Viner noted that, in the face of sticky wages, profit margins could be increased either by injecting purchasing power into the economy or by cutting costs. He argued, however, that adherence to the gold standard placed a limit on the use of the former policy. He thought that "perhaps undue emphasis" had been placed on the "manipulation of purchasing power" in light of the need to conform to the gold standard's rules of the game: "for a single country under the gold standard and suffering from severe unemployment, deflation of monopoly prices and of money costs may be the only way out" (1932b, 419).

Viner returned to the issue of cost cutting during his February 1933 lecture at the University of Minnesota. He distinguished between two kinds of cost-cutting policies.

1. The "Do Nothing" policy, under which the "self-corrective process" drives costs down. This process "*does* tend to bring depressions to an end, and ... has always hitherto succeeded in doing so" (emphasis in original, 1933a, 7). Viner argued, however, that "the price structure is shot through with rigidities" (1933a, 9). Consequently, while the self-corrective mechanism would "eventually" restore profit margins, Viner stated that he was "becoming more and more convinced" that the mechanism "won't do so quickly enough to forestall wholesale economic collapse" (1933a, 10).

2. The "Induced Balanced Deflation" policy, under which "the government has a
   deflating role to play" in coordinating wage reductions (1933a, 15). The government could also play a role, he argued, in facilitating debt write-downs and in
   reducing utility charges (1933a, 16–17).

Viner acknowledged that the latter policy would "inevitably involve hard-
ships and inequities in individual cases." Nevertheless, "to have its maximum beneficial effect, it would be necessary that a program of induced
balanced deflation should be pursued rigorously and simultaneously along
the whole front of undeflated costs" (1933a, 19).

By the time of Viner's May 1933 lecture at the University of Georgia,
circumstances had changed. The banking crisis had peaked; upon assuming the presidency in March, Franklin D. Roosevelt shut down the banks,
and, in April, the United States (temporarily) left the gold standard. In
his May lecture, Viner acknowledged that his earlier policy of "balanced
deflation" had been strongly tied to the gold standard's rules of the game:

> Until we went off the gold standard, it seemed to me that [along with mildly ex-
> pansionary monetary and fiscal policies] the only safe path for our government
> to follow in endeavors to bring about artificial recovery from the depression was
> the method of balanced deflation, that is to exercise pressure on business costs
> so as to restore equilibrium between costs and prices, and so offer to business
> men an inducement to give employment to the productive factors. (1933b, 121)

Viner added that, in 1931, he had not believed that the depression would
"last forever." He had anticipated that, in the absence of expansionary
monetary and fiscal policies, a policy of "induced balanced deflation" would
be accompanied by "social costs and strain" and "wholesale bankruptcies, major redistributions of national wealth, protracted continuation of
unemployment in pronounced degree" (1933b, 121). Viner continued: "I,
nevertheless, advocated [induced balanced deflation] because I saw no
other available alternative. I blundered seriously on one point. I did not
see that this country could go off the gold standard with as little trouble,
as little controversy, as proved to be the case" (1933b, 122).

## Macroeconomic Policies

Viner and the other Chicagoans agreed about the need to increase the
money supply in order to generate inflation and, thus, combat the Depression. They disagreed, however, over the most effective means of bringing

currency expansion into effect. As documented, the other Chicagoans favored money-financed fiscal deficits in order to put newly created money directly into circulation. Viner held a different view.

In his 1931 lecture in Williamstown, Viner advocated expansionary policies, both fiscal and monetary, provided that the expansionary policies did not jeopardize the gold standard. With regard to fiscal policy, Viner criticized the US Treasury for its "traditional policy, based on sound principles of public finance, of taxing heavily, spending lightly, and redeeming debts" during the Depression. Such a policy, he argued, "is sound in periods of prosperity and business expansion, but is unwise and inappropriate for a period of depression" (1931b, 182). During periods of depression, "a precisely opposite policy should be followed, of taxing lightly, spending heavily, and borrowing" (1931b, 183). Viner thought that the fiscal deficits should be financed by borrowing, either from private investors or from the banking system or from both: "in so far as the funds spent by government are primarily financed . . . by borrowing from existent funds which otherwise would have remained uninvested, or by expansion of bank credit which would otherwise would been unexploited, the public works . . . so financed during a period of economic depression are from the national point of view almost costless" (1931b, 183).[14] With regard to monetary policy, Viner called on the Federal Reserve to "begin market operations on a considerable scale, buying up securities" (1931b, 184). He believed that expansionary open-market operations would, by increasing the reserves of the banks, force the banks to make new loans (1931b, 183).

In light of Viner's advocacy of expansionary fiscal and monetary policies, what was his view about the possibility of financing fiscal expansion through money creation? That policy was espoused in the April 1932 Pettengill memorandum, which Viner signed; the untitled March 1933 memorandum, which he refused to sign; and the November 1933 memorandum. Viner thought that the need to remain on the gold standard precluded such a policy. In a letter to John Commons (University of Wisconsin), dated September 21, 1931, Viner wrote:

> The scheme, therefore, should be either one of credit expansion through governmental assistance and stimulations plus maintenance of the Gold Standard, or greenback and departure from the Gold Standard. I believe it would be much more possible to get action on the former plan than on the latter, and in any case I believe the former plan is more desirable. . . . I believe that, from the point of view of tactics, there is great deal to be said for choosing mild ways of formulating strong programs. (quoted from Nerozzi 2009, 589)

Viner expressed a similar view is his February 1933 Minnesota lecture. There, he cautioned about the use of budget deficits, financed either by "the issue of legal tender greenbacks [i.e., money financed] or by borrowing from the banks" because those deficits could "cause general fear of an early departure from the gold standard" (1933a, 25).

By the time of his May 1933 lecture in Georgia, Viner was less sanguine about the effectiveness of open-market operations.

> What this [method] does is to increase the cash reserves of the banking, and therefore, it is hoped, to give the banks the desire to put their idle funds to work. But the bankers have learned in recent years, not how to make money without lending, but that under certain circumstances the rate at which they lose money is less if they stop lending, so it is conceivable that the banking system would welcome the additional liquidity and would not increase its loans or investments. (1933b, 131)

He continued to favor fiscal deficits "financed by borrowing from the banking system, with the hope that what the banks lend is newly created credit or credit which otherwise would have remained idle and not funds that would otherwise have been used by private business" (1933b, 133).[15]

## The Great Depression

What caused the Great Depression? As discussed, criticism of the role of the Federal Reserve was a theme of Viner's work in the early 1930s. In his 1931 lecture in Williamstown, he cited figures to show that (1) Federal Reserve credit had decreased since 1929, (2) total deposits of all member banks in the system had also decreased, and (3) the indebtedness of member banks to the Federal Reserve System had reached "a low figure" (1931b, 188–89).[16] Anticipating a key argument made by Friedman and Schwartz (1963, chap. 7), Viner attributed the Fed's policy stance, under which the Board had refrained from undertaking "market operations on a considerable scale," to the void left by the death of Benjamin Strong, who had been the governor of the Federal Reserve Bank of New York: "It would be equally true to say that, except under Governor Strong, the Federal Reserve Board has avoided having a definite policy; it has acted in a purely opportunistic manner" (1931b, 189).[17] Viner presented a similar critique of Fed policy in his February 1933 lecture in Minnesota:

> At no time . . . since the beginning of the depression has there been for as long as four months a net increase in the total volume of bank credit outstanding.

On the contrary, the government and Federal Reserve bank operations have not nearly sufficed to countervail the contraction of credit on the part of the member and non-member banks. There has been no net inflation of bank credit since the end of 1929. There has been instead a fairly continuous and unprecedentedly great contraction of credit during this entire period. (1933a, 21–22)

There were two important differences in the early 1930s between Viner's views and those of the members of The Group on the business cycle in general, and the Great Depression in particular. First, in contrast to Viner, in their individual writings during the 1930s none of the other Chicagoans expressed the view that the Fed played a detrimental role in the Depression. Likewise, none of the Chicago memoranda, discussed above, criticized the Fed's policy during the Depression. Yet, at least several of the Chicagoans were aware that the Fed's policy in the early 1930s had come under attack. During the first half of the 1930s, Lauchlin Currie published the book *The Supply and Control of Money in the United States* (1934b) and several articles in which he presented data on the decline of the money supply to criticize the role of the Federal Reserve in bringing on the Great Depression.[18] Two of the articles, "Treatment of Credit in Contemporary Monetary Theory" (1933) and "The Failure of Monetary Policy to Prevent the Depression of 1929–32" (1934a), were published in the *JPE*, then coedited by Knight and Viner. As discussed below, Currie's book was reviewed favorably in the *JPE* by Simons. Clearly, at least several of the Chicagoans were aware of Currie's work.

Why, then, did the Chicagoans, other than Viner, fail to criticize the Fed's policy? This brings us to the second crucial difference between Viner's views on business-cycle theory and the views of the other members of The Group. In his analysis of the business cycle, Viner *never* mentioned the role played by a fractional-reserve banking system in the cycle—not even in his discussions of the cumulative nature of the cycle (1931b, 189; 1933b, 7). In contrast, the other Chicagoans thought that the fractional-reserve banking system was the major reason for economic instability. Thus, as noted in chapter 2, the April 1932 Pettengill memorandum attributed the severity of the Depression to the "exceedingly flexible and sensitive" volume and velocity of credit; along with the rigid cost structure, the Chicagoans argued, "this is at once the explanation of our plight" (Pettengill memorandum 1932, 524). The *purpose* of the March 1933 memorandum was to propose a method—the 100 percent reserves scheme—to eliminate fractional-reserve banking in order to lessen the severity of the business cycle. The November 1933 memorandum contained an appendix on business cycles that was titled "*Banking* and Business Cycles" (emphasis added). In that appendix, Simons et al. (1933, appendix, 3) wrote: "if some malevolent genius had sought to aggravate the affliction of business and employment cycles, he could hardly have done better than establish a system of private deposit banks in the present form." Earlier, in 1927, Knight provided the following assessment of the fractional-reserve system: "important evils result, notably the frightful instability of the whole economic system and its periodical collapse in crises, which are in large measure bound up with the variability and uncertainty of the credit structure if not directly the effect of it" (Knight 1927b, 732).[19]

Apart from Viner, therefore, the Chicagoans attributed the collapse of the money supply to the nature of the fractional-reserve banking system. That system, they believed, was the primary cause of the severity of the Great Depression; the inherent feature of the system was a self-perpetuating decline in the money supply during depressions. Thus, in 1934 Simons wrote the following about the cause of the Great Depression: "It is no exaggeration to say that the major proximate factor in the present crisis is commercial banking" (1934a, 54). In his favorable review of Currie's 1934 book, in which Currie provided statistical data documenting the decline in the money supply that occurred during the early 1930s, Simons expressed the view that the data presented by Currie were not needed to convince him (Simons) about what the fractional-reserve banking system had produced—namely, a sharp decline in the money supply and the collapse of economic activity. Simons (1935a, 556) stated: "For critical students, however, Dr. Currie's inductive verifications will be largely gratuitous—although everyone will be grateful for the excellent statistical compilation and analysis. In general, the author's fundamental insights are so sound that failure of statistical confirmation would only indicate error or inadequacy in the statistics."

*100 Percent Reserves*

The early 1930s Chicago memoranda attributed the severity of the Great Depression to the massive contraction of demand deposits that occurred during that episode. Viner held a similar view. In his 1936 paper "Recent Legislation and the Banking Situation," he noted that the Depression was more severe in the United States than in most other countries. He attributed responsibility for this circumstance to "the mass withdrawals of cash by the banks, the forced liquidation of their assets . . . in their desperate attempts to remain open[,] the repeated waves of banking failures . . . [and] the final closing of the system as a whole." The weakness of the banks, he argued, "must be held largely responsible" for the severity of the Depression in the United States (1936a, 106).

Where Viner differed fundamentally from the other Chicagoans was in (1) the *diagnosis* of the factors underlying the banking system's weakness, and the (2) needed policy response to rectify that weakness. For the other Chicagoans, the problem was seen in the "inherent instability" of fractional-reserve banking; the policy response was the 100 percent reserves scheme. Viner disagreed.

In his 1936 *AER* paper, Viner argued that the problem with the US banking system was that it comprised small and isolated units: "I am convinced [that the weakness of the banking system] lies in the fact that of all the modern banking systems it alone has adhered predominantly to the eighteenth-century model of individual small-scale units, as distinguished from large-scale banking institutions with many branches" (1936a, 107). Several factors contributed to this situation, including "jealousy of encroachment on state autonomy," "small-town jealousy of the metropolitan areas," and "fear of undue concentration of financial power in the great metropolitan centers" (1936a, 107). The unit-based architecture, Viner argued, exposed the US banking system to the kinds of periodic crises experienced by English banks in the nineteenth century: "American bank-closings of 1931 to 1933 were but a typical reproduction of the normal events of an English business depression before the development of branch banking on a large scale" (1936a, 107).

The solution to the banking problem, Viner thought, was twofold. The first part lay in the development of branch banking. Such a system would have several advantages: (1) it would provide risk diversification for each "independent unit in the banking structure"; (2) the larger units inherent in branch banking could afford to attract personnel with "a higher grade of talent"; (3) by reducing the number of executive positions it would facilitate "the achievement of co-operative action in emergency situations"; and (4) the large size of the institutions would "give to them a prestige and an appearance of strength, which . . . is extremely valuable in a crisis" (1936a, 108). Viner believed that many industries were dominated by large firms that had been responsible "for many of our economic woes." Although the size of these firms needed to be reduced, Viner thought that "an exception should be made for banking" (1936a, 107). The second part of the solution, Viner argued, was the federal deposit-insurance program:

"deposit insurance should be expected substantially to lessen the danger of [bank] runs, and thus increase the ability of the banking system as a whole to meet a depression without engaging in drastic liquidation to ensure liquidity" (1936a, 111).

In espousing a twofold solution, comprising branch banking and deposit insurance, to stabilize the banking system, Viner went against the views of his Chicago colleagues.[20] In the November 1933 memorandum his colleagues expressed the following view about branch banking and deposit insurance:

> Branch banking, another proposed remedy [for banking crises], contemplates a system composed of, say, twenty-five private institutions and their enormous network of branches. This implies, as we see it, an intolerable concentration of power in private hands. It threatens dangerous domination of industry, and even of the Treasury, by the banks. It promises substantial safety for depositors, to be sure, but only because the government could never afford to let private institutions of this kind fail. Under such a system, as under deposit guarantee, the government could not escape direct responsibility to depositors in any severe emergency. (Simons et al. 1933, 2)

Two other points about Viner's view of the 100 percent reserves scheme in particular, and the 1930s Chicago memoranda in general, merit comment. First, in Hart's (1935, 105) review of the 100 percent reserves scheme, that author noted that proponents of the scheme believed that, as the Fed bought government bonds from the commercial banks in exchange for newly issued Federal Reserve notes to implement the scheme, the Fed's purchases of debt would amount to the cancellation of a large part of the national debt. Hart, however, called that purported advantage "fallacious" (1935, 115). He stated that while it would be possible to achieve cancellation of the national debt, the interest charge on the debt, which is "the economic substance of the debt, would be replaced by [a] subsidy on checking accounts" to compensate the banks for the "forced sale" of a substantial part of "their earning assets" (1935, 115n1). After presenting that argument, Hart wrote: "This is the consideration which . . . Professor Viner has suggested to the writer" (1935, 115n1).[21] Second, in a letter, dated August 19, 1935, from Simons to James Angell, Simons wrote the following about the November 1933 memorandum: "Viner has communicated your request for a copy of our 1933 memorandum on banking and currency. . . . Viner is a bit sensitive about the memorandum. He should be absolved of all responsibility. He had no part in the preparation of the memorandum, and he has never evidenced sympathy with the proposals" (Henry C. Simons Papers, Special Collections Research Center, Joseph Regenstein Library, University of Chicago).

## Rules versus Discretion

Reflecting his strong attachment to the gold standard, Viner was a proponent neither of domestic monetary rules nor of policy discretion. Instead, he favored the adjustment of the money supply under the gold standard's rules of the game with limited room for discretionary sterilization operations. Thus, in his 1932 lecture at the Chicago conference, Viner considered two alternatives to the gold standard: (1) a "rigid formula," such as that embedded in the English Bank Act of 1844, which aimed to minimize the ability of the central bank to engage in discretionary monetary policy at the domestic level by establishing a ratio between the gold reserves of the Bank of England and the notes that the bank could issue; and (2) discretionary management by the monetary authorities. Regarding the former alternative, Viner stated:

> Some economists seek an avenue of escape ... in a rigid formula of the Act of 1844 type, which would leave little or no opportunity to the central banker to exercise his discretion. If I may express an individual view, we know too little as yet of the possibilities of stabilization to take any major steps in that direction. (1932a, 37)

As will be discussed in chapter 4, the English Bank Act of 1844 provided the intellectual underpinning of the Chicago proposal for the 100 percent reserves scheme. Viner's negative view of the 1844 Bank Act was one reason for his refusal to support the 1933 Chicago memoranda that advocated such a scheme. He maintained that view in his 1936 *AER* paper: "we still have a long way to go before we can frame with assurance the desirable objectives and limits of credit control and a mechanical procedure to be followed in executing it. . . . [The] concrete issues which [the Federal Reserve] faced were always complex and involving a conflict of legitimate objectives, instead of being reducible to the statistically definable objective and the arithmetically definable procedure for attaining it which figure so prominently in much of the recent academic literature on credit control policy" (1936a, 115–16). Regarding the choice between discretionary management of monetary policy and the gold exchange standard, Viner expressed his preference for the latter. Discretionary policy, he argued, would involve "the necessity of reconciling ourselves to the persistence of management which falls far short of perfection, and of knowledge still far from complete as to the proper objectives and technique of even perfect management" (1932a, 39).

## Conclusions

Responding to Patinkin's critique of Friedman's claim of a direct connection between his (Friedman's) monetary economics and the ideas that characterized the early 1930s Chicago monetary tradition, Friedman (1972) made use of Viner's views to substantiate that claim. While Viner's views on the monetary origins of the Great Depression, the void left by the death of Benjamin Strong in that episode, and the Fed's failure to employ expansionary open-market operations to combat the Depression clearly anticipated the theses of Friedman and Schwartz (1963), those views were not representative of the Chicago monetary tradition.

Furthermore, those were not the only areas in which Viner's views differed from those of the other Chicagoans. In contrast to Viner, the other Chicagoans believed that (1) the gold standard should be abandoned in favor of flexible exchange rates; (2) a fractional-reserve banking system is "inherently" unstable and, thus, 100 percent reserves should be imposed on demand deposits;[22] (3) cost cutting would be ineffective in combating the Depression; (4) expansionary monetary policy should be conducted through the government's fiscal position; and (5) monetary rules are preferable to discretionary policies. It is noteworthy that Friedman's views on each of the above five areas in the late 1940s and early 1950s were similar or identical to the views of the other Chicagoans. The differences between Viner's positions on fundamental policy issues and the positions of the other Chicagoans on those issues explain Viner's refusal to add his signature to the March 1933 memorandum that constituted the "Chicago Plan of Banking Reform." Contrary to Knight's explanation, Viner's refusal to add his signature was not simply because he did not believe it was "good politics." Nevertheless, Knight's explanation has had an enduring effect on the literature dealing with Viner and the Chicago monetary tradition. Thus, Van Overtveldt (2007, 160) argued that "although he was in agreement with the economics of the [Chicago] plan for the most part, Jacob Viner did not sign because he thought it was politically impossible to realize."[23]

In light of the above discussion, why was Friedman not aware that the other Chicagoans' views differed from those of Viner? And why did Friedman single out Viner's views in his aim to establish a linkage between his monetarist framework and the work of his Chicago predecessors? Viner was one of the four Chicagoans who had been identified by Friedman in his 1956 "Restatement" of the quantity theory as having influenced his (Friedman's) thinking on monetary issues—the others being Simons, Mints, and Knight. In contrast to those other Chicagoans, however, in the first half of the 1930s, Viner had established a track record of publications on monetary-policy issues. Viner published four lectures on monetary issues in the early 1930s; Friedman discussed the contents of two of the lectures—the 1932 lecture delivered at the Chicago conference and the 1933 lecture delivered at Minneapolis—to support his claim of a Chicago quantity theory tradition. In both lectures, Viner criticized the Federal Reserve's policies during the Depression and argued in favor of expansionary open-market operations.

The following question arises. How did Friedman come upon those lectures? There are two main possibilities. First, Viner may have presented his views on monetary and fiscal policies, and referred to his published 1931 (at Williamstown) and 1932 (at Chicago) lectures in his price theory course, which Friedman took in the fall of 1932, with the effect that Friedman had been exposed to, and influenced by, Viner's policy views.[24] That explanation, however, is implausible. In a letter to Patinkin, dated November 24, 1969, Viner wrote the following about what he taught in his courses: "As far as my teaching at Chicago was concerned . . . I chose to exclude from my courses considerations of monetary-fiscal doctrine [and] of business cycles" (quoted from Patinkin 1981b, 265).

The second possibility is more plausible. As mentioned in chapter 1, Friedman was not a doctrinal historian. In debating Patinkin, who was an eminent scholar in the field of the history of monetary doctrine, it would have been natural for Friedman to turn to the secondary literature on 1930s macroeconomics that interpreted and analyzed evidence derived from primary sources.[25] As it turned out, in 1968, J. Ronnie Davis published the paper "Chicago Economists, Budget Deficits, and the Early 1930s" in the *AER*. In his paper, Davis discussed Viner's 1933 lecture at Minneapolis and the 1932 telegram sent to President Hoover; that telegram, advocating expansionary open-market operations, emerged from the Chicago conference at which Viner delivered his lecture on the gold standard. In his exposition of the early 1930s Chicago quantity-theory tradition, Friedman (1972) provided evidence from three sources: Viner's 1932 and 1933 lectures, and the Hoover telegram; Friedman also cited, and quoted from, Davis's paper. I conjecture that having read Davis's paper, Friedman turned to and read those three works, which he then used to draw an incomplete and misconstrued depiction of the policy content of the early 1930s Chicago quantity-theory tradition.

## 3.2 Dangerous Curves Ahead: The Road from Cambridge, Massachusetts, to Chicago

Friedman's reliance on (1) Viner's views both on the monetary origins of the Great Depression and on the efficacy of policies that work through the banking system, and (2) the Hoover telegram calling for easing collateral requirements and expansionary open-market operations, to depict the character of the Chicago monetary tradition had a substantial—but diversionary—effect on the understanding of that tradition in the subsequent doctrinal literature. The diversionary effect stemmed from the following circumstance: since Friedman had produced evidence tying his views with those set forth in early 1930s Chicago archives, it was therefore reasonable for other researchers to accept that evidence as valid. Thus, Laidler (1993, 1068) followed Friedman, claiming that the 1930s Chicago tradition "offered a monetary interpretation of cyclical fluctuations in general and the Great Depression in particular, [and] an optimistic view of the power of monetary policy."[26] Studies by Laidler (1993; 1999, chap. 9) and Laidler and Sandilands (2002a) furnished evidence showing that those characteristics marked the views of Harvard economists in the late 1920s and early 1930s. As mentioned in chapter 1, those authors argued that the Harvard views preceded and influenced the views of the Chicago monetary tradition, the effect of which was to deflate the latter's originality. A similar judgment was made by Alacevich, Asso, and Nerozzi (2015, 402n31), who after discussing the views of Harvard-trained economists, including Viner, concluded that those views reinforced the claim that "there was a strong Harvard link . . . to the Chicago School."

Was there, as claimed, a "strong Harvard link" to the ideas that characterized the early 1930s Chicago monetary tradition? In this section, I assess the validity of that claim. Effectively, two rounds of evidence were presented in support of the claim. The first round consisted of evidence provided in Laidler (1993; 1998a; 1999, chap. 9). The second round comprised evidence furnished in Laidler and Sandilands (2002a). I describe, in turn, the evidence presented in each of the two rounds. I then appraise the relevance of the evidence concerning the character of the Chicago monetary tradition.

*Round One*

Ralph Hawtrey, an economist of the UK Treasury, played an important role in Laidler's (1993; 1998a; 1999, chap. 9) narrative.[27] In a pair of early studies, Hawtrey (1913; 1919) provided several original insights into the operation of the monetary system. The insights included the following: (1) an emphasis on the instability of the behavior of demand deposits (i.e., credit) in the business cycle; (2) a focus on the variability of the currency-deposit ratio as a crucial attribute of the cycle; (3) a deemphasis on the role of stock-market speculation and its collapse in foreshadowing cyclical downturns; and (4) the identification of the dangers of treating the "needs of trade" (Laidler 1993, 1077) — that is, the real bills doctrine — as independent of the monetary system. Hawtrey believed that a deflationary spiral could always be broken, no matter how low the bank rate, through expansionary open-market operations; there was a limit, he believed, to the amount of funds the sellers of securities would wish to hold idle (Laidler 1998a, 8). Anticipating Friedman and Schwartz (1963), Hawtrey blamed the Federal Reserve for causing the Great Depression. In doing so, he attributed the Fed's inept policies to the void in leadership left by the death of Benjamin Strong (Laidler 1993, 1080), again anticipating Friedman and Schwartz (1963).

Laidler (1993) brought to light the previously undiscovered influence of Hawtrey's views on Harvard economists. Hawtrey was a visiting professor at Harvard during the 1928–29 academic year.[28] He was brought to Harvard by Allyn Young, who was "a great admirer" of Hawtrey's work, was influenced by that work, and did much to disseminate Hawtrey's views (Laidler 1993, 1074–80).[29] Young was a pioneer in the development of banking statistics. He wrote a monograph, *An Analysis of Bank Statistics for the United States* (1928a), in which he documented the pronounced seasonal movements of currency out of, and into, the New York financial market. The data revealed New York's central place in what had become an integrated national banking system (Laidler 1993, 1080–81; 1999, 198–99). In his work, Young foresaw the consequences of what he viewed as the fragmented nature of the Federal Reserve System, thus anticipating

an argument made by Friedman and Schwartz about the causes of the
Great Depression. Young died unexpectedly in 1929. Before his death, he
had been working on a treatise on monetary economics.

Two other Harvard economists were central to Laidler's narrative—
Currie and John H. Williams. Currie was a graduate student at Harvard in
the late 1920s and early 1930s. He had been slated to serve as Young's assistant in 1928–29 but instead acted in a similar capacity for Hawtrey during
the latter's visit to Harvard. In an analysis of the US monetary system, Currie's PhD thesis combined Hawtrey's monetary theory of the cycle with
Young's careful empirical orientation.[30] In the early 1930s, Currie (1933;
1934a; 1934b) argued that the Federal Reserve System had mismanaged
monetary policy in the late 1920s and early 1930s. In this way, Currie held
the Federal Reserve responsible for precipitating the Depression.

Williams, like Viner, wrote his PhD thesis at Harvard.[31] He taught at
Harvard from 1921 to 1957. Williams supervised Currie's PhD thesis. Along
with Viner, Williams participated in the January 1932 conference at Chicago
and, as mentioned in chapter 2, with Viner, was one of the six conference
participants who drafted the Hoover telegram that emerged from the conference. On behalf of the other five draftees, he also prepared a paper that
sought to explain the motivation underlying the policy proposals in the telegram (Laidler 1993, 1091; 1999, 238). In Williams's paper, that author struck
a positive tone—more so than Viner's paper presented at the conference—
about the effectiveness of open-market operations and discounting operations in combating the Depression (Laidler 1993, 1092–94; 1999, 238).[32]

Laidler drew two links between the views of the Harvard-connected
economists—including Hawtrey—and Chicago views. First, he pointed to
a link between Harvard views and those of Friedman. Laidler wrote that
an objective of his work was

> to draw attention . . . to the essential similarity between Friedman's interpreta-
> tion of the causes of the Great Depression and his views on what appropriate
> monetary policy could have accomplished between 1929 and 1933, and the posi-
> tions taken by Hawtrey, Williams, and Currie on the same questions. (1993, 1100)

Laidler (1993, 1088) also wrote:

> Now it is clear that in the writings of Hawtrey, Young, and Currie are to be
> found many elements of what Friedman [1972] has termed the "Chicago Tra-
> dition": a monetary approach to cycle theory that derived from but went far

beyond the quantity theory of money as it was then understood as a proposition about the relationship between money and the price level; opposition to the "real-bills" doctrine; a belief that the Great Depression was largely the result of inept policies pursued by the Federal Reserve System under the influence of that doctrine; confidence in the effectiveness of properly conceived monetary policies to alleviate the Depression; and a version of the 100 percent money scheme; all are there.

Second, Laidler postulated a link between the views of Williams and the early 1930s Chicago tradition. The basis of that link was Williams's positive assessment of the power of monetary policy in his paper at the Chicago conference and the connection between the views contained in that paper and the views in the Hoover telegram. Laidler wrote: "if we follow Friedman in looking to the 1932 Harris Foundation conference for evidence of that 'hopefulness' that he tells us marked the Chicago tradition, we shall find more of it in the contribution of Williams than anywhere else; and if we look further afield, we shall also find it in the work of Hawtrey—by then published—and Lauchlin Currie—then in progress" (1993, 1094).

## Round Two

In January 1932, the year and month in which the Hoover telegram emerged, three young members of the Harvard economics department— Currie, Paul J. Ellsworth, and Harry D. White—co-drafted an untitled seventeen-page memorandum in which they recommended a set of policy measures to combat the Depression. The measures were the following: (1) rigorous open-market purchases by the Federal Reserve; (2) an easing of collateral requirements on banks by allowing government bonds to be used as collateral against the issuance of Federal Reserve notes; (3) a program of public-works construction financed by issuance of bonds, which would be made eligible both for rediscounting at the Fed and as collateral for Federal Reserve notes (as under [2] above); (4) the cancellation of intergovernmental debts; and (5) a reduction in tariff duties.

The untitled Harvard memorandum was rediscovered by Laidler and Sandilands, who issued it, along with an introductory note by those two economists, as a working paper in 2000.[33] It was then published, along with a revised introduction, in *History of Political Economy* in 2002.[34] Concerning the intended audience of the Harvard memorandum, Laidler and

Sandilands (2002a, 516) expressed the following view: "It is not known how widely this memorandum circulated, but the fact that it is a piece of policy advocacy, combined with its relatively polished style, makes it inconceivable that it was meant for the eyes and files of its authors alone." As to the substance of the memorandum, the very close similarity between its policy recommendations and those contained in the Hoover telegram (discussed in chapter 2) is striking. In fact, all five policy proposals of the Harvard memorandum are essentially the same as those in the Hoover telegram. The latter document included a sixth policy recommendation— the encouragement of the Reconstruction Finance Corporation to make loans on assets not eligible for collateral.

Thus, in their introductory note to the memorandum, Laidler and Sandilands (2002a, 525) pointed to

> the extremely strong similarities between the Harvard memorandum and the recommendations to President Hoover that emerged from the Harris Foundation conference of January 1932. These recommendations (along with Jacob Viner's contribution that produced them) are the earliest of the sources cited by Milton Friedman . . . as epitomizing the economics of the Chicago tradition of the 1930s, from which, he claimed, his own work ultimately drew its inspiration.

In light of those "strong similarities" between the policy recommendations of the Harvard memorandum and the Hoover telegram, Laidler and Sandilands (2002a, 529) drew the following conclusion:

> the similarities between this [Harvard] memorandum's contents and those of the famous Harris Foundation [i.e., Hoover telegram] recommendations of 31 January 1932 provide conclusive evidence that many of the ideas that characterise the pre–*General Theory* "Chicago Tradition" in monetary economics . . . were also current at Harvard at the time when that tradition was developing.

In a letter to Laidler, dated January 22, 2001, Friedman expressed the following observation on the memorandum:

> [It] is a truly remarkable and impressive document, and it certainly supports your position that Chicago had no monopoly on the quantity theory approach to the Great Depression and to measures required to recover from it. I have no doubt, as you suggest in your introductory comments, that more than

coincidence explains the similarity of the views expressed by the Harvard trio and the recommendations coming out of the Harris conference. (quoted from Laidler and Sandilands 2002a, 518n4)[35]

Alacevich, Asso, and Nerozzi (2015) reached a similar assessment. Those authors reviewed the writings, including the Harvard memorandum of January 1932, of Currie, Viner, and Williams during the early 1930s and drew the following conclusion:

> Currie, Viner, and Williams believed that heavy deflationary forces were at work all over the world as a consequence of the war and the postwar settlements, and blamed the onset of the crisis on the policies pursued by the Fed, which, in an awkward attempt to curb speculation and preserve adherence to the Commercial Loans [i.e., real bills] criteria, provoked a sudden monetary contraction at home and abroad. This monetary interpretation anticipated the main lines of Friedman's and Schwartz's analysis of the Depression and, together with the recommendations [in the Hoover telegram] stemming from the 1932 Chicago Harris Foundation Conference, played an important role in the establishment of the monetary tradition, whose main apostles have been known to reside in the economics department at the University of Chicago. (2015, 404)

How did the strong similarities between the Harvard memorandum and the Hoover telegram find their way from Cambridge, Massachusetts, to Chicago? Laidler and Sandilands provide the following explanation:

> one of the non-Chicago economists involved in drafting the recommendations [of the Hoover telegram] was John H. Williams of Harvard. . . . The record of his oral contributions to the Harris Foundation conference suggests that he was probably familiar with the Harvard memorandum. . . . These considerations constitute strong circumstantial evidence of a Harvard influence on one of the Chicago tradition's earliest documents. (2002a, 517)

## Discussion

At this stage of our discussion, the following conclusions emerge. First, concerning the link between Currie's work on the monetary origins of the Great Depression and Friedman's view on that subject, Laidler (1993) contributed to the literature by demonstrating the way that Hawtrey and Young's work shaped Currie's views. However, Friedman and Anna

Schwarz's *A Monetary History* (1963), which established the monetary hypothesis of the Great Depression as a convincing interpretation of the origins of that event, contained no references to either Currie or Young. Friedman and Schwartz did cite both Hawtrey and Williams, the former on a single occasion and the latter on two occasions, none of which had anything to do with the Depression.[36] Thus, there is no evidence of a direct link between the views at Harvard during the early 1930s and the monetary hypothesis of the Great Depression developed by Friedman and Schwartz.

There appears, however, to have been an indirect link between Currie's view, and, thus, the views at Harvard, in the early 1930s, and Friedman and Schwartz's monetary hypothesis of the Great Depression. Currie attributed the Federal Reserve System's mismanagement of monetary policy during the Depression to the prevalence of ideas related to the commercial loan theory of money, or real bills doctrine, within the system, particularly at the Federal Reserve Board in Washington. In later chapters we will see that (1) in the early 1930s Viner held a similar view; (2) in the mid-1940s Mints formulated a real bills interpretation of the Federal Reserve's policies during the Great Depression; and (3) one of the criticisms leveled at the Federal Reserve System's policies during the Great Depression by Friedman and Schwartz was the system's adherence to the real bills doctrine. Consequently, a plausible argument can be made of an indirect link running from Currie's real bills interpretation of the Great Depression through the similar interpretations of Viner and Mints, and, ultimately to Friedman and Schwartz.[37]

Second, there were informal links between Harvard of the late 1920s and early 1930s and Chicago of those years. (1) As Laidler (1993, 1020) pointed out, Young had been Knight's PhD thesis supervisor at Cornell.[38] Laidler (1993, 1020) also pointed out that, in 1928, Young had been offered, but turned down, the position of chair of the Economics Department at Chicago. (2) As mentioned, the coeditors of the *JPE*, Knight, and Viner, thought sufficiently well of Currie's work to publish two of Currie's articles in that journal. As also mentioned, Currie's 1934 book *The Supply and Control of Money in the United States* was favorably reviewed by Simons (1935a) in the *JPE*. (3) Hart, who taught at Chicago in the 1930s, had been Currie's undergraduate student at Harvard and kept in touch with his former teacher after he (Hart) moved to Chicago.[39] Hart, who published a comprehensive assessment of the 100 percent reserve proposal in the *Review of Economic Studies* (Hart 1935), drew Currie's attention to work on the 100 percent reserve scheme at Chicago (Laidler 1999, 240).

Third, the teaching material at Chicago provides some evidence of a Currie-Chicago connection. In the early 1950s the reading list for the second semester sequence of Mints's graduate course on money, titled "Banking Theory and Monetary Policy," included the section "The Organization and Operation of the Federal Reserve System." That particular section comprised six reading assignments, one of which was Currie's 1934 book.[40] This information suggests that Currie's work may have been viewed with some significance by Mints and was known to Friedman. However, in 1951, Mints coedited (with Friedrich Lutz) the American Economic Association's *Readings in Monetary Theory*, an important volume in its day that reprinted twenty classic articles on money from the period 1917 to 1949. None of those articles was by Currie. Significantly, a forty-five-page "Classified Bibliography of Articles on Monetary Theory," with which the volume ends (with about twenty articles per page), did not include any of Currie's works. The bibliography was compiled by Harlan M. Smith, who expressed his "indebtedness . . . above all to Professor Mints, not only for his direct contribution to the bibliography but for his constant advice" (Lutz and Mints 1951, 459).

Fourth, Laidler and Sandilands provided convincing evidence of a direct link between the Harvard memorandum of January 1932 and the Hoover telegram of that same month. The similarities in the policy proposals in the respective documents *were* too similar to have been coincidental. Williams, as argued by Laidler and Sandilands, acted as a transmitter of ideas from Harvard to the Hoover telegram.

Fifth, the evidence of a direct link between the Harvard memorandum and the Hoover telegram does *not* establish Williams as a transmitter of ideas from Harvard to Chicago. As shown in the previous section, except for Viner, the Hoover telegram was not representative of the views of the Chicago monetary tradition. Hawtrey, Young, and Williams, like Viner, were supporters of the gold standard. Hawtrey, Young, and Currie were supporters of discretionary policies; along with Viner, they opposed monetary policy rules. Except for Currie, who developed a 100 percent reserves scheme in 1934—a decade after the scheme had been considered by both Knight and Simons (as discussed in chapter 4)—none of those economists supported the idea that demand deposits should be backed with 100 percent reserves. Therefore, it can be concluded that Laidler (1993; 1999) and Laidler and Sandilands (2002a; 2002b) uncovered important evidence showing that Harvard economists, influenced by Hawtrey, *anticipated* Friedman's ideas on (1) the monetary origins of the Great

Depression and (2) the effectiveness of open-market operations. The Harvard economists did not, however, directly *influence* Friedman's views.

## 3.3 Turbulence on the Midway: The Protagonists

In chapter 2, we saw that disagreements on monetary policy had emerged in 1933 — between Douglas, on the one side, and Simons and Director, on the other. These disagreements concerned both short-term and long-term policy objectives. The disagreements on short-term policy objectives related to: (1) the required increase in the price level needed to combat the Great Depression; (2) whether that increase should be based on a statistical price index; (3) whether a policy of reflation could lead to runaway inflation; and (4) whether policy should take into account the increase in the real burden of debt incurred during the Great Depression. The disagreements on long-term policy objectives related to the preferred monetary rule, with Simons and Director favoring a rule that fixed the quantity of money, and Douglas preferring a money-supply-growth rule. The disagreements manifested themselves in both the April (revised) version of the March memorandum and the November memorandum — especially in the supplement to the latter document, which had not been made available to Douglas until October 1934. The criticisms in the November memorandum of the views of a senior member of the faculty (Douglas) by two junior, untenured members (Simons and Director) may have been a factor contributing to Douglas's opposition to the retentions of Simons and Director on the Chicago faculty.

Two additional factors contributed to Douglas's position against the retentions. First, neither Director nor Simons had established a reputable track record of publications that could be used to support the continuation of their respective positions on the faculty. Specifically, neither economist had published an article in an established economics journal during the first half of the 1930s, a noteworthy shortcoming for two scholars who must have enjoyed preferred access to Chicago's in-house publication outlet, the *Journal of Political Economy* (*JPE*). In the case of Director, while he did co-author *The Problem of Unemployment* (1931) with Douglas, his contribution to that publication may have been viewed by other faculty members — however unfairly — in the context of his official position (at the time of the writing of the book) as a research assistant to Douglas. Director's other publications during the first half of the 1930s — his

1930 *Survey* paper "Making Use of Public Works," and his two pamphlets *Unemployment* (1932) and *The Economics of Technocracy* (1933)—were intended for general audiences and did not contain original research. A similar circumstance applied to Simons. As mentioned in chapter 2, his first substantive work was his 1934 pamphlet *A Positive Program for Laissez Faire*. Although (as we shall see) that publication would, over time, achieve the status of a near classic, at the time of its publication it was not considered—at least by Douglas—to be a contribution worthy of retaining Simons on the faculty.

Why did both Director and Simons fail to publish (on their own) anything substantive in the first half of the 1930s despite the fact that (1) they both presumably enjoyed preferred access to the *JPE* and (2) the retention of their positions on the Chicago faculty was dependent on a good publication record? A reason, provided by Milton Friedman, runs as follows. Simons and Director were disciples of Frank Knight. As mentioned, Simons was Knight's student at Iowa, and Simons moved to the University of Chicago from Iowa with Knight in 1927. Meanwhile, Director, who had been brought to Chicago by Douglas, increasingly fell under Knight's influence and, by 1932, had also become a disciple of Knight.[41] Friedman provided the following explanation—specifically with regard to Director, and inferentially, with regard to Simons (during the first half of the 1930s)—about their weak publishing records:

> Aaron Director was, just as men like Homer Jones and George Stigler; a true disciple of Knight's. Although much influenced by Knight, I do not consider myself to be such a disciple. I was much more interested in the scientific aspects of economics than in the philosophical ones. Those close to Knight like Aaron, Homer and to a somewhat lesser extent George, tended to become inhibited in their writings because Knight always sought for absolute perfection. Although Frank Knight himself was prolific, people like Aaron Director were always afraid of being debunked. Knight's specialty was debunking. (Friedman interview with Van Overtveldt, November 1, 1986, quoted from Van Overtveldt 2007, 71–72)[42]

In a letter dated July 6, 1942, addressed to Frank A. Fetter, Simons provided a similar characterization of Knight's influence on his (Simons's) career.[43] In the letter, Simons noted that Knight initially had a stimulating effect on Simons's career but that, subsequently, Knight's influence became inhibiting. Simons wrote:

Knight was nearly perfect as an influence at the next stage; but his usefulness was ultimately limited, partly because of a kind of a political diffidence, defeatism, and irresponsibleness, and partly because his attainments of distinction only served to make him on balance a heavier importer of approbation. (Henry C. Simons Papers, Special Collections Research Center, Joseph Regenstein Library, University of Chicago)

With his 1934 publication *A Positive Program for Laissez Faire*, Simons was able to break away from the inhibiting influence exerted by Knight on his disciples. That publication marked the first of what would become a long list of publications by Simons on policy issues. Knight, who, as mentioned, believed that economists should not engage in debates about policy issues in the public arena—a belief that did not prevent Knight, himself, from engaging in such debates—could not have been pleased with Simons's 1934 publication. Nevertheless, as we shall see, he strongly supported Simons's retention on the economics faculty.[44]

Another factor that likely influenced Douglas's position on the retentions of Simons and Director related to the deteriorating personal relationship between Douglas and Knight. Following Knight's appointment to the Chicago economics faculty in 1927, the two economists had developed a close friendship.[45] In the early 1930s, however, an acrimonious disagreement arose between Douglas and Knight on political beliefs, especially on the issue of economic planning. As I document below, the disagreement became apparent in their respective publications in the early 1930s and spilled over to their personal relationship. By the early 1930s, the two Chicagoans communicated only through written correspondence, even though they occupied offices next to each other. As we shall see, Simons's positions on political issues were in sharp contrast to those of Douglas.

### Economic Planning: Douglas versus Knight

*Douglas.* In chapter 2, we saw that in their book *The Problem of Unemployment* (1931), Douglas and Director provided a favorable assessment of the experience with planning in Soviet Russia. I conjectured that Douglas was the likely source of that assessment. The following account of Douglas's political views in the late 1920s and early 1930s provides the basis of my conjecture.

In the 1920s, Douglas became intrigued with the communist experiment underway in the Soviet Union, and in the summer of 1927, he served as an economic adviser on a trade-union delegation to the Russian Republic.[46] The goal of the delegation was to assess economic conditions under the communist government.[47] The delegation produced a 1928 report, *Soviet Russia in the Second Decade*, coedited by Stuart Chase, a prominent economics writer; Robert Dunn, a member of the American Civil Liberties Union; and Rexford Guy Tugwell, professor of economics at Columbia University. The report consisted of fifteen chapters dealing with various aspects of the Russian economic and political system (e.g., education, justice administration). Douglas authored three of the chapters and co-authored a fourth chapter with Dunn.[48] Douglas's assessment of communism was generally favorable. For example, in the chapter, "Labor Legislation and Social Insurance," he described—approvingly—"the relatively short [working day] in Russia" (Douglas 1928, 220), and stated that the social-insurance system provided "very full protection to the workers against the risks of accident, illness, unemployment, old age and death" (Douglas 1928, 221) while the health-care system provided "free medicine" for all citizens (Douglas 1928, 225).

A striking aspect of the chapters contributed by Douglas is the author's evident self-restraint in his criticisms. For example, Douglas wrote the section of chapter 8, "The Trade Union Movement," dealing with wage determination. That section described an astonishingly complex wage-negotiation process that involved a multitude of bureaucratic layers. At no point did Douglas question the efficiency or the practicality of the process. In his autobiography *In the Fullness of Time*, Douglas wrote the following about the report: "For our report, I wrote a section strongly condemning the Soviet violation of civil liberties, but when the report appeared these charges were greatly watered down, presumably by Coyle, who had read and corrected the proofs" (Douglas 1971, 54). Albert E. Coyle was the editor of a periodical published by the Brotherhood of Locomotive Engineers. Coyle was one of four union representatives who signed a separate, ninety-six-page report, *Russia after Ten Years*. Coyle's name appeared neither as an editor nor as an author of the report *Soviet Russia in the Second Decade* (374 pages).

Although Douglas was active on public issues in the late 1920s and early 1930s, supporting, among other causes, stronger unions, the breakup of monopolistic firms, unemployment insurance, and social security, he was not allied with any particular political party. In the midst of the Great Depression, in 1932 he published the book *The Coming of a New Party*, in which he advocated the creation of a political party similar to the Labour

Party in England. In that book, Douglas compared the performance of the US economy since the onset of the Great Depression to that of the Russian economy, with Soviet Russia coming out on top. Echoing the very positive appraisal of the Russian experience with planning provided in *The Problem of Unemployment*, Douglas made the following arguments in his 1932 book. (1) Under Soviet Russia's planning system resources were allocated according to social needs. In the United States, in contrast, there was a widespread misallocation of productive resources, with "lurid" overdevelopment of some industries, such as coal mining and textiles (1932b, 92–93). (2) The Russian government's monopoly of foreign trade and its internally managed currency had avoided the global decline in prices and the sharp rise in unemployment that had occurred in the United States since the beginning of the Great Depression. (3) In Soviet Russia, the laying down of productive standards in the five-year plan provided a sense of "common purpose" to Russian workers, a quality that was absent among the US workers: "a very large proportion, and perhaps a majority of the Russian industrial workers, have come to feel that the five-year plan is intended to benefit them as a class, whereas the American workers have no such faith that such is either the design or the effect of the economic policies of their employers" (1932b, 92–93). In concluding his comparison of the US and Russian economies, Douglas struck an almost revolutionary tone:

> If the beginnings toward a genuine planned economy are, consequently, to be made, they must be carried through over the opposition of the capitalists themselves. Even if their political power were broken, as long as they were in control of industry they would resist having production quotas assigned or the elements of price control imposed by society. It seems, therefore, that a truly planned economy is almost impossible under capitalism and only practical under socialism. (1932b, 96)

Douglas provided a similar tone in an article, "Karl Marx the Prophet," published in the *World Tomorrow* in March 1933. In that article, Douglas reviewed the following theories developed by Marx: (1) the economic interpretation of history; (2) the labor theory of value and the theory of surplus value; and (3) the inevitable cataclysm of capitalism. The labor theory of value, Douglas stated, entailed six factors that "according to Marx, would lead capitalistic society to break down": (1) the concentration of production; (2) the disappearance of the middle class; (3) the increasing reserve army of the unemployed; (4) the increasing misery of workers; (5) the increasing severity of crises; and (6) the emergence of a strong militant working class (1933b, 257). In his article, Douglas did not endorse Marxism, but he nevertheless provided a sympathetic treatment of Marx's views. Marx, Douglas stated, "pointed out the fundamental absurdity of depending on the wealthy to introduce socialism and instead demonstrated that it was the working class which was the driving force of the socialist movement because it as a class had the most to gain from it" (1933b, 256). Douglas (1933b, 257) called the *Communist Manifesto* "that keen and marvellously written pamphlet." He concluded his appraisal of Marx's work as follows:

> Such then is the sweep of history which Marx envisaged. That he is mistaken on many points goes without saying, and perhaps his greatest achievement was not in the intrinsic logic of his theories as in the way [he] removed the inferiority complex of large masses of workers and made them feel that they are the class which is destined to take power. Just as the apparent fatalism of Calvinism removed the doubts of its followers and gave them the consciousness that they were the elect of God, so has Marxism given not only hope but apparent certainty to the dispossessed. Marx thus ranks as one of the creators of the present, and his influence on the predictable future bids fair to increase rather than to diminish. (1933b, 257)

*Knight.* In 1932, Rexford Guy Tugwell, who had coedited the 1928 study on Russian communism to which Douglas had contributed, published the paper "The Principle of Planning and the Institution of Laissez Faire" in the *American Economic Review*; Tugwell had delivered the paper at the meeting of the American Economic Association (AEA) in December 1931.[49] In his 1932 *AER* paper, Tugwell called for "the abandonment, finally, of laissez-faire" (1932, 76) and its replacement with national planning. He argued that government and the political system had been corrupted by business; eliminate business, and the political system would be purified.[50]

Knight responded to Tugwell's arguments in a 1932 *JPE* article, "The Newer Economics and the Control of Economic Activity."[51] The ostensible purpose of Knight's article was to review the book *Modern Economic Society*, by Sumner Slichter.[52] As were many of Knight's writings, the review was filled with discursive asides.[53] Knight ridiculed Tugwell's presentation at the AEA meeting as follows: "A little high-grade utopian-reformist

soap-boxing should provide excellent—let us say—'messianic relief' from
the nerve-strain of the solemn stodginess of a meeting of a learned society. But—but perhaps it is out of place to remark as to how out of place
it would be to think of such a performance in the light of a contribution
of any social problem" (1932a, 475). Knight also took on Tugwell's notion
that the political process had been corrupted by business. Knight argued
that differences among members and shady dealings characterized all
kinds of social groups. Thus, one could not argue (as Tugwell had) that
politics had been corrupted by business and that elimination of the latter
would purify the political system. Political groups, like other social groups,
were subject to internally generated corruption. In his criticism of Tugwell's view, Knight may have been hinting that all was not well among the
members of the Chicago economics faculty. Knight stated:

> The intrinsic purity of politics may be questioned on more substantial grounds,
> in addition to the obvious query as to why it is so easily corrupted. Interesting
> to note, its connotation does not vary noticeably when used regarding other as-
> sociations other than government, engaged in activities where the contact with
> "the dead hand of business" is not evident to view. The general observation
> of mankind has noted the presence of much the same phenomena wherever
> groups large in size and heterogeneous in interest attempt to gather for any
> purpose. . . . Has Professor Tugwell found . . . college faculty politics categori-
> cally different from "political" politics? (1932a, 475–76)

Knight followed his 1932 critique of planning in the *JPE* with an article, "Can We Vote Ourselves Out of the Fix We Are In?," published in
the periodical the *Christian Century* in April 1933. In that article, Knight
(1933a, 153) expressed the view that planning was incompatible with the
democratic form of government. He wrote, "Democracy's cure for its own
shortcomings is to make itself still more democratic." In contrast:

> Effective planning and control seem most likely to come through a seizure of
> power by force and appeal to the mob mind on the part of the fanatics for the
> bare, abstract idea, with little or no thought as to what, concretely, they will
> do with the power when they get it; and the next stage would be the ruthless
> treatment of the population as the guinea pigs for an indefinitely prolonged,
> trial-and-error experiment in utopia building. (1933a, 153)

Knight characterized those authors—presumably including Douglas—who
wrote in favor of planning as "authors [who] are obviously wandering in

an intellectual wilderness, or more accurately, a wilderness" (1933a, 153). The writings of "socialists and communists [who] speak of action," he stated, comprise "weasel words, in brief, essentially lies" (1933a, 153).

## Simons versus Douglas

Simons joined Knight in the latter's assault on planning. The main objective of *A Positive Program for Laissez Faire* was to lay down the kind of legal and institutional framework within which free competition could function effectively. *A Positive Program for Laissez Faire* was published near the bottom of the Great Depression, and, as evidenced in Douglas's works, the perception that free enterprise and laissez-faire had failed greatly strengthened support within the academic community for government intervention in economic activity. Simons's objective was to provide a set of principles to guide government intervention in economic affairs with the aim of allowing the market system to be the primary mechanism of organizing the production and distribution of goods and services (H. Stein 1987, 334). He proposed a division of labor between the government and the market under which the former would be responsible for (1) maintaining overall economic stability by setting the conditions for a stable currency, (2) keeping the market competitive through the rigorous enforcement of antitrust policy, and (3) preventing extremes in the distribution of income.[54]

Simons viewed planning as an especially dangerous form of interference in economic affairs. Like Knight, he believed that planning could be implemented only through a seizure of power: "it seems unlikely that any planners or controllers, with the peculiar talents requisite for obtaining dictatorial power, would be able to make decisions wise enough to keep an elaborate economic organization from falling apart" (1934a, 52). Thus, Simons thought planning incongruous with a democratic form of government: "The real enemies of liberty in this country are the naïve advocates of managed economy or national planning" (1934a, 41).

In addition to their differences on planning, Douglas and Simons differed in their assessments of the New Deal. In an article, "The New Deal after Ten Weeks," published in the periodical the *World Tomorrow*, in June 1933, Douglas provided a glowing appraisal of the Roosevelt administration's policies, including its policies to control prices (1933c, 419). He also praised Roosevelt's choice of advisers, including Tugwell, "all of whom are at once extremely competent and humane." In light of the Roosevelt administration's actions, Douglas argued: "there is a healthier atmosphere in Washington now than there has been in the last fifteen years. The new Administration is not frightened by any problem and is apparently ready to be in general as bold in action as conditions necessitate and the state of public opinion permits" (1933c, 418). Douglas maintained that the Roosevelt administration should engage in price and wage fixing: the new administration, he stated, should establish "governmentally supervised cartels . . . as a means of preventing cut-throat competition [and], in partnership with the industries . . . fix minimum wages and maximum hours" (1933c, 419). Douglas continued: "This scheme will necessitate the organization of labor" (1933c, 419). Noting that, in early June 1933, Roosevelt had submitted legislation for the purpose of fixing prices and wages, Douglas argued that Roosevelt "is making an effort at once to save and to liberate capitalism" (1933c, 419).

The legislation to which Douglas referred was signed into law on June 16, 1933, creating the National Recovery Administration (NRA). Under the direction of General Hugh Johnson, the objective of the NRA was to eliminate "cut-throat competition" by bringing industry, labor, and government together to create codes of "fair practices" and to set prices.[55] In the fall of 1933, Douglas was appointed to the NRA's Consumer Advisory Board.

In contrast to Douglas, Simons was concerned that the New Deal's actions to increase government intervention in economic affairs would pave the way toward authoritarianism.[56] He provided an assessment of the New Deal in general, and the NRA in particular, in two 1934 publications—his pamphlet *A Positive Program for Laissez Faire* and a March 12 article published in the *Chicago Tribune* newspaper, under the headline "Finds New Deal Queer Jumble; Aims Conflict." In the former publication, he wrote about the New Deal and its supporters in the following terms: "It is easy to devise phrases for denouncing the Roosevelt program and the so-called New Deal. On the other hand, one hesitates to condemn, knowing that condemnation will invoke applause from persons whose political philosophy has nothing in common with one's own" (1934a, 75). With regard to the NRA, Simons (1934a, 75) wrote: "No diabolical ingenuity could have devised a more effective agency for retarding or preventing recovery (or for leading us away from democracy) than the National Recovery Act and its codes."

Simons provided a similar assessment in his *Chicago Tribune* article.[57] He characterized the actions of the Roosevelt Administration as an "orgy of legislative witch-hunting, ill-conceived slogans, and misleading slogans."

He expressed the view that those actions constituted a substitution of "planning for competition" involving a "transition to economic and political arrangements which few people can envisage even vaguely." The NRA was singled out for special attention: "directed by Gen. Johnson, [the NRA] served ... to increase critical rigidities in the price structure, to aggravate cost-price maladjustments" (1934b).

It is relevant to point out both an important similarity and an important difference regarding Douglas and Simons's respective views on price and wage rigidities. Both Chicagoans believed that monopolistic firms had thwarted competition, causing prices to be rigid. Both advocated the rigorous enforcement of antitrust policy to help restore price competition in industry. They differed, however, on the issue of wages. As demonstrated in Douglas's June 1933 article (discussed above) published in the *World Tomorrow*, Douglas thought that labor needed to become better organized so that it could negotiate on an equal footing with monopolistic firms. In his book *Controlling Depressions*, he argued:

> Unless the strong organization of the employers ... is balanced by an equally strong organization of labor and the consumers, we are likely to have our society dominated even more completely than in the past by the concentrated power of capital. This is, indeed, the economic essence of fascism. (1935b, 245)

Simons had an entirely different view of the matter. He believed that labor unions had already organized into monopolistic organizations. Thus, both industrial corporations and labor unions needed to be broken up. He expressed the view that one response to the problem of monopolistic firms and unions was that of planning. He believed, however, that planning would entail the "political control of relative prices, relative wages, and investment" (1934a, 319n1); it would thus entail "an end of political freedom" (1934a, 45). Simons's association of planning with political control over investment and the resulting end of political freedom helps explain his hostile reaction to Keynes's *General Theory*, as discussed in chapter 5.

The difference on political issues between Douglas and Simons during the course of 1934 came into the open in an exchange of letters between the two Chicagoans in January of that year. Douglas was actively involved at the time in Chicago's city politics. On January 23, 1934, he sent a letter to Simons informing him (Simons) of a "movement" that had "developed in various parts of the City, which wants a new deal for Chicago" (Paul

Douglas Papers, Special Collections Research Center, Joseph Regenstein Library, University of Chicago). The movement, Douglas wrote, was called the "People's Political Alliance," of which Douglas was a member. Attached to the letter was a platform that put forward the Alliance's positions—or "planks"—on various issues. One such plank, for example, was concerned with taxes; it called for the "imposition of taxes upon profits of corporations and upon large incomes" (plank 2). Plank 12 was as follows: "Support of the Roosevelt policies affecting wages and hours of labor." The plank called for higher minimum wages and reduced working hours. In his letter, Douglas wrote: "If after the final platform is drafted and submitted to you, you would be willing to endorse both it and the movement, it would of course be of great aid to all of us." It should be noted that, as of January 1934, Simons had not yet published either his *Chicago Tribune* article or his pamphlet *A Positive Program for Laissez Faire*.

Simons replied to Douglas in a letter dated January 25. The letter began: "Replying to your inquiry of the 23rd, I must say that I disapprove [of] almost every feature of the second plank [i.e., on taxes] in the proposed platform." Regarding plank 12 on minimum wages, Simons wrote: "You already know that I would disapprove Plank 12 or any proposal for enforcement of a grand hierarchy of wage minima" (Henry Simons C. Papers, Special Collections Research Center, Joseph Regenstein Library, University of Chicago). Simons's reactions to other planks were equally dismissive. Douglas could not have been pleased either with Simons's reply to his (Douglas's) letter, or with Simons's two 1934 publications. The following year, in a letter, dated January 5, 1935, addressed to Knight, Douglas appraised Simons's 1934 *A Positive Program for Laissez Faire* in the following, sarcastic terms: "the one point where I think Simons has made a contribution is on the pamphleteering and propagandistic elements of his work" (Paul Douglas Papers, Special Collections Research Center, Joseph Regenstein Library, University of Chicago).

*The Knight-Douglas Correspondence*

As mentioned, what had started in the late 1920s as a warm friendship between Douglas and Knight turned into an acrimonious exchange of views in the early 1930s via those economists' publications. It culminated, beginning in late 1933, in confrontational exchanges of letters. The letters—at least the ones that have survived—consist of two sets of exchanges: (1) an exchange of three letters—two written by Knight and the third written by Douglas in December 1933; and (2) an exchange of five letters—three written by Knight and two written by Douglas—in January 1935. The underlying difference of opinion marking the first set concerned the role of the economist in the public arena. The main area of contention in the second set concerned Douglas's opposition to providing tenure to Simons and retaining Director on the Chicago faculty. Both sets were characterized by a toxic demeanor. Here I describe the contents of the exchanges.

*December 1933.* The letter that initiated the exchange was written by Knight and was dated December 21. It brought into the open the hostility that existed between the former friends. Knight wrote: "I have felt for some time that you and I seem to be developing a tendency for each to feel a little 'off' at the other, chiefly, it seems because each feels the other feels that way." Knight then wrote concerning what he believed to be the root cause of the hostility: "We disagree pretty widely, I guess, about the role of scientific economics and economists in the current political situation. Frankly, I think that those who go into politics, particularly under present conditions, are committing suicide on behalf of the profession as a whole."[58] Knight stated that he and Douglas should meet to help clear up their differences (Frank H. Knight Papers, Special Collections Research Center, Joseph Regenstein Library, University of Chicago).

Douglas replied in a letter dated December 22. He expressed the view that Knight had disparaged Douglas both in public and in private because of the latter's participation in political movements: "it has been quite evident from your personal conversations and your public speeches and what you have said to many others that you regard me as something of a charlatan and a demagogue. I am not wholly stupid, although probably partially so, and therefore what you actually think of me has not failed to sink in." As to the possibility of a one-on-one meeting with Knight to help clear up their differences, Douglas was not receptive, saying that he thought that it might "exacerbate the situation" (Paul Douglas Papers, Special Collections Research Center, Joseph Regenstein Library, University of Chicago).

Knight concluded the 1933 exchange with a letter dated December 27. He expressed "shock" at the tone of Douglas's letter and denied having disparaged Douglas in public: "To my knowledge I have not said anything discreditable of you, as to intelligence or sincerity, in public or private." He also disclaimed having called Douglas a "charlatan" and a "demagogue": "As far as I know there is absolutely no ground for bringing words like charlatan and demagogue into the discussion and I wonder, what could have put them into your mind. I am deeply, even bitterly disappointed and desgusted [*sic*] with the status of economics and intellectual leadership and even more with conditions within the political 'science' professions — but have never blamed any individual" (Frank H. Knight Papers, Special Collections Research Center, Joseph Regenstein Library, University of Chicago).

*January 1935.* The trigger for the exchange of letters between Douglas and Knight was a departmental meeting held on December 23, 1934, in which Douglas led a move to terminate the appointments of Director and Simons.[59] Both Douglas's role in the public arena and Knight's purported classroom derision of Douglas's public activities continued to be a main area of disagreement.

The exchange began with two letters from Knight, *both* written on January 5. In the first letter, Knight referred to the leading role played by Douglas in the December 23, 1934, meeting to terminate the appointments of Director and Simons: "This comes home to me personally because your animus is undoubtedly due in part to the men you are trying to 'get' being friends of mine." Knight continued with a lightly veiled threat: "I merely write to say that they *are* friends of mine, in a somewhat special sense, and that if you succeed in getting their throats cut without the interests of our group and its work being rather clearly in evidence, as they are not now, I am not going to make any pretence of liking it." Knight concluded by referring to his differences with Douglas on political and economic issues: "I think you have been displaying an attitude of resentment toward me, for which there is no reason, except insofar as differences of political and scientific opinion are to you a personal affront" (Frank H. Knight Papers, Special Collections Research Center, Joseph Regenstein Library, University of Chicago).

Douglas took the liberty of circulating Knight's letter to each member of the department.[60] Knight was not happy with that circumstance, prompting the second letter from Knight to Douglas on January 5: "I am disappointed that you saw fit to put it in circulation, presumably as an exhibit or something, rather than try to settle things between ourselves." He explained — in personal terms — the reason Director and Simons needed to be retained: "I 'feel' as if eliminating these men is eliminating me, and that when it is done I would simply be 'through' with the group, morally and sentimentally. . . . If these men do not belong in the group, I do not belong." Knight then drew a distinction between himself, strictly a thinker, and Douglas, a man of action: "I know that the world was made for your type of being, and not my type, and in a way I understand the contempt of the man of action and the fighter for indecision, for the disposition to think rather than to do something, and to feel baffled even in thinking" (Frank H. Knight Papers, Special Collections Research Center, Joseph Regenstein Library, University of Chicago).

That same day—January 5—Douglas replied to Knight with a ten-page letter. He made the following points. First, neither Director nor Simons had demonstrated the capacity to publish high-quality research. Moreover, Simons had been "a student and instructor since 1923 I believe ... and ... Director has been here as a student and instructor since 1927," but neither had "submitted a [PhD] thesis."[61] Second, both Simons and Director had exhibited acerbic personalities (as evidenced in the sarcastic asides in the November 1933 memorandum). Concerning Simons, Douglas wrote:

> Along with others in our department I have found Simons to be openly scorn-ful not only of those who, dealing with the same problems as those in which he was interested, reached different conclusions, but equally so of those who dealt with a different set of problems. Only those who thought precisely as he did could escape his sharp and scornful disapproval.

Concerning Director, Douglas expressed the view that "like Simons, he was becoming personally unpleasant in his classes." Third, Douglas again raised the issue regarding Knight's persistent and sharp criticisms of Douglas: "for at least two years and probably more you have been at-tacking my motives before groups of students, classes, fellow members of the faculty and upon occasion the general public." Douglas charged that Knight had referred to Douglas, among other things, as a "publicity seeker" and as "loose-witted" (Paul Douglas Papers, Special Collections Research Center, Joseph Regenstein Library, University of Chicago).

Knight responded with a letter dated January 9. He again criticized economists, such as Douglas, who sought to play a role in the public arena. He argued that such individuals were motivated by "a competitive exhi-bitionism and thirst for power." Implicitly referring to Douglas, Knight stated: "the 'reform' interest is especially subject to this mixture of mo-tives ... [and] the intellectual life of the great universities is a place where it is peculiarly inappropriate, and saddening, and discouraging in its significance ... and that in fact it seems to me one of the places where it is the worst" (Frank H. Knight Papers, Special Collections Research Center, Joseph Regenstein Library, University of Chicago).

The final letter in the 1935 series of correspondence was written by Douglas on January 10. The main point raised concerned Knight's argument that those individuals engaged in social reform were, in fact, participating in a form of "exhibitionism." Douglas responded: "I have literally spent far more time licking stamps and stuffing literature in boxes and in going to dull committee meetings than in making speeches." He stated that "the powerful enemies" that he had made in his public dealings far outweighed the friends he had made, and that his public efforts to reduce utility rates had led to moves among the university trustees to have him dismissed. If Knight, however, had made up his mind that Douglas was indeed a "hopeless exhibitionist, these considerations will . . . have no effect upon you." Douglas concluded: "There may be certain points in my letter to which you will desire to reply. If not, so far as I am concerned, I shall regard the correspondence as closed and not write any further letters upon this general range of issues" (Paul Douglas Papers, Special Collections Research Center, Joseph Regenstein Library, University of Chicago). Knight did not reply, and the correspondence ended.

*Discussion*

The following points merit comment. First, regarding Douglas's argument that the published output of Simons and Director was not sufficient to support their retention on the faculty, Douglas was probably correct. Both Simons and Director had failed to establish successful publishing records as of 1935.[62] Moreover, neither had been able to complete his respective PhD dissertation, even though both began their graduate work at Chicago in 1927.[63] Second, it appears that Knight had, in fact, criticized Douglas in public gatherings. George Stigler, a newly arrived student at Chicago in 1933 and eventual disciple of Knight, expressed the following view: "I would find it hard to believe Knight's disclaimer of criticism of Douglas, because Knight had no capacity for silence" (G. Stigler 1988, 186). Third, Knight's criticism of economists who took stands on political matters in the public arena evidently did not extend to himself; he was certainly willing to criticize the political views of others in the public arena. Fourth, the dispute was settled as follows. Simons was retained on the faculty but was denied tenure. In 1939, he obtained a second, part-time, appointment in Chicago's Law School. He was promoted to associate professor, with the backing of the Law School in 1942.[64] Director was released (in 1935) and went on to work for the US government during World War II. Fifth, after

Douglas published the book *Controlling Depressions* in 1935, he became increasingly engaged in politics, and, as we shall see, his work at Chicago in monetary economics in the second half of the 1930s essentially stopped, with two exceptions.[65] With his increased involvement in politics, Douglas, in contrast to Knight, did not establish a cohort of disciples to carry on his research in labor economics or his political philosophy.[66] Increasingly, Douglas distanced himself from the Economics Department until he went off to combat in World War II.

From the mid-1930s through the mid-1940s, work on monetary economics at Chicago was spearheaded by a small group of free-market economists: Knight, Simons, and Mints. Beginning in 1946, a group of former Knight students and protégés returned to Chicago in teaching positions. The group included Friedman (Economics Department), Director (Law School), and W. Allen Wallis (Graduate School of Business), all of whom returned in 1946.[67] They were joined by George Stigler, who accepted a position in the Graduate School of Business in 1958. The critical mass, in quality and numbers, necessary for the intergenerational transmission of ideological attitudes formed around what was known as "Knight's affinity group" (Reder 1982, 7).[68] On his return from military service to Chicago in 1946, Douglas was struck by the change that had taken place in the Economics Department. In his autobiography *In the Fullness of Time*, he wrote about that change:

> I found myself increasingly out of tune with many of my faculty colleagues and was keenly aware of their impatience and disgust with me. The University I had loved so much seemed to be a different place. Schultz was dead, Viner was gone, Knight was openly hostile, and his disciples seemed to be everywhere. . . . My emotions turned outward. (1972, 128)

His emotions having turned outward, Douglas successfully ran for US Senate in 1948 and served for three terms in that institution.

## 3.4 Conclusions

This chapter began by considering Jacob Viner's policy views of the early 1930s. I showed that, while Viner's views on the monetary origins of the Great Depression and the desirability of expansionary open-market operations clearly foreshadowed the theses of Friedman and Schwartz (1963),

those views were not representative of the 1930s Chicago monetary tradition. I also showed that those were not the only areas in which Viner's
views differed from those of the other Chicagoans. In contrast to Viner's
views, the other Chicagoans believed that (1) the gold standard should
be abandoned in favor of flexible exchange rates, thereby facilitating a
focus on domestic-policy objectives; (2) 100 percent reserve requirements
should be imposed on demand deposits to deal with the inherent instability that characterizes a fractional-reserve banking system; (3) deposit
insurance and branch banking were undesirable because they exposed the
banking system to increased government intrusion in decision-making;
(4) cost cutting was not an appropriate response to the depression; (5) expansionary monetary policy should be conducted through the government's fiscal position; and (6) domestic monetary rules are preferable to
either discretionary policies or the gold standard's rules of the game. The
differences between Viner's views and the views of the other Chicagoans
on the foregoing policy issues explain Viner's refusal to sign the March
1933 Chicago memorandum.

As I will show in subsequent chapters, in the late 1940s and early 1950s,
Friedman's views on the above set of six policy issues were similar, or
identical, to those of the early 1930s Chicagoans (apart from Viner). Nevertheless, in his articulation of a link between his views and those of the
earlier Chicagoans, Friedman (1972) chose to focus on Viner's views on
the monetary origins of the Depression and the need of expansionary
monetary policies that operate through the banking system. I attributed
that circumstance to Friedman's reliance on the secondary literature on
monetary doctrine. Other researchers followed Friedman in characterizing the early 1930s Chicago monetary tradition in terms of a belief in
the monetary origins of the Depression and the effectiveness of monetary
policies that work through the banking system. The result has been a mis-
representation of the nature of that tradition and a belief that the Chicago
tradition relied on ideas from sources outside of Chicago—which, in turn,
effectively undercuts the originality of early 1930s Chicago ideas.

Although Viner's views on the monetary origins of the Great Depression and macroeconomic policies were not representative of the 1930s
Chicago monetary tradition, as we will see in chapter 6, Viner's view on
the monetary interpretation of the Great Depression found its way into
Mints's work in the mid-1940s. Mints's work, in turn, was known to Friedman and reflected in Friedman and Schwartz (1963). In this way, an indirect link will be established between the views of Viner and those of

Friedman and Schwartz on the role played by the Federal Reserve System's adherence to the real bills doctrine in explaining the system's performance in the late 1920s and early 1930s.

Finally, I showed the way Chicago monetary economics in the 1930s became associated with free-market views. Knight, the self-described "thinker," took on "man of action" Douglas, in a battle over political beliefs. At stake were the positions of Knight's disciples, Simons and Director, on the University of Chicago economics faculty. The short-run settlement of the battle was Solomonic: Simons, who had been up for tenure, was retained on the faculty, without tenure, and Director was let go. Over time, the reticent scholar's (i.e., Knight's) focus on the economics department overshadowed the "man of action's" (i.e., Douglas's) focus on extradepartmental matters. Director returned to the University of Chicago and— along with a cohort of Knight's disciples, including Friedman, Stigler, and Wallis, the personalities of whom did not fit the Knight template— disseminated Knight's free-market beliefs to future generations of Chicago economists.

## CHAPTER FOUR

# The "Chicago Plan"

## *Doctrinal Aspects*

Two essential components of the 1933 "Chicago Plan" were the following: (1) a reform of the banking system, including the requirement that demand deposits be backed by 100 percent reserves; and (2) the imposition of a policy rule on the monetary authorities. The two components were *not* inexorably linked. The 100 percent reserves scheme aimed, among other things, to allow the monetary authorities to control the supply of money better. Once that control was attained, the monetary authorities could, in principle, practice discretionary policy or apply a rule; the 100 percent reserves scheme would facilitate either the implementation of a rule or the conduct of discretionary policy.[1] The Chicagoans, of course, favored a rule.

What contributions—if any—did the Chicagoans make to the contemporaneous literature on banking reform and policy rules? As mentioned in chapter 2, the banking-reform measures in the 1933 Chicago memoranda were based on the English Bank Act of 1844, the components of which will be discussed in this chapter. Moreover, as will also be discussed below, the idea that bank deposits should be backed with 100 percent reserves was proposed in the 1920s in a book by Frederick Soddy, a 1921 British Nobel laureate in chemistry. Frank Knight reviewed Soddy's book in 1927. This circumstance has given rise to the present-day consensus that Knight and the other Chicagoans adopted Soddy's idea, resulting in the prevailing view that the Chicago 100 percent reserves scheme lacked originality. Did the Chicago scheme derive from Soddy's proposal, as asserted in the recent literature?

Similarly, the notion that monetary policy should be based on a rule was inherent in the operation of the gold standard, which was first adopted (de facto) by England in 1717 (Bordo 1992, 267). In chapter 2, we saw that, in their November 1933 memorandum, the Chicagoans considered the gold standard to have been a type of monetary-policy rule although they were critical of its properties. Beginning in 1911, and over the next thirty-five years, Irving Fisher persistently argued that monetary policy should be based on a rule that aims to stabilize the domestic price level. In light of the longevity of the gold standard and Fisher's work on rules, what contribution, if any, did the Chicagoans bring to the literature on monetary-policy rules?

To ascertain the contributions made by the Chicagoans in the areas of banking reform and monetary rules, we will need to probe the nature of an earlier literature that gave rise to the Chicago proposals for (1) 100 percent reserve requirements, and (2) monetary-policy rules. As discussed in this chapter, the British debates on money in the first half of the nineteenth century—comprising the Bullionist Controversy in the first quarter of that century, and the banking school–currency school debate in the second quarter—provided the foundations for both proposals. The next section describes those debates and their relation to the Chicago proposals on banking and monetary-policy reform. The chapter then describes Soddy's work in the 1920s on 100 percent reserves and appraises whether the Chicago 100 percent reserves proposal derived from Soddy's formulation. Finally, the chapter discusses Fisher's work on policy rules and compares his price-level-stabilization proposal to the contributions emanating from Chicago, notably in the works of Henry Simons and Lloyd Mints in the 1930s and 1940s.

## 4.1 The Nineteenth-Century British Debates

To explain the nineteenth-century debates that gave rise to the ideas of 100 percent reserves and monetary policy rules, we must consider the institutional and historical settings that gave rise to the debates. I begin with a description of the British financial system and the key role played by the Bank of England in that system.

The Bank of England was established in 1694 to create a market for, and an institution to manage, the government debt arising from England's participation in wars against France (Laidler 1992, 256). The cost of fighting the war put England on the edge of bankruptcy. In 1694, a group of merchants offered to lend the government £1.2 million in perpetuity at an interest rate of 8 percent in return for the authority to set up a bank with the right to issue £1.2 million in banknotes—the first officially sanctioned paper currency in England—and be appointed the sole banker to the government (Ahamed 2010, 77). The offer by the merchants was accepted, and the new bank opened its doors for business (under joint-stock ownership) with the name the Governor and Company of the Bank of England. The bank's principal lines of business were to help finance the government's borrowing requirements and to discount commercial bills of exchange in the London discount market.

At the end of the eighteenth century, the Bank of England held a legal monopoly of joint-stock banking in England. At that time, the English banking system was structured into three parts. At the center was the Bank of England itself, which catered to the needs of the government and large-scale commerce, and issued banknotes.[2] The second component of the system was a group of about fifty small, private banks in London, which received deposits, discounted bills, accepted drafts, but did not issue notes. Rounding out the system was a large group of "country banks" outside of London that issued notes in small denominations for local businesses (Cameron 1992, 124).[3] The "circulating medium" in the 1790s consisted of gold coins and—to a lesser extent—silver coins, and Bank of England and country-bank notes. Bills of exchange and bank deposits were widely used as means of payments in wholesale transactions (Laidler 1992, 256). The monetary system was underpinned by the expectation that (1) country-bank notes would easily be convertible into Bank of England notes and gold coins (country banks tended to hold Bank of England notes in their reserves), and (2) Bank of England notes would be easily convertible into gold.

The banking system's development into this tripartite structure, which included a circulating medium comprising gold and silver coins and banknotes, had outpaced developments in monetary theory.[4] International monetary theory at the end of the eighteenth century was based on the Humean quantity-theoretic, price-specie flow doctrine analyzed by both Cantillon (1755) and Hume (1752).[5] That doctrine dealt with purely metallic currency systems. As mentioned in chapter 3, the basic idea of Humean theory was that—assuming an initial position of balance-of-payments equilibrium—an increase in the domestic money supply would raise prices (including the prices of domestically produced exports) in the domestic economy. This circumstance would lead to a reduction in competitiveness and, thus, a rise in imports, a decrease in exports, and a trade deficit as the country in question lost competitiveness. The resulting trade deficit would be accompanied by an outflow of gold, a contraction of the domestic money supply, and a fall in the domestic price level, restoring competitiveness and balance-of-payments equilibrium. In this way, the price-specie-flow mechanism provided the means by which arbitrage in gold among nations and regions served to keep national and regional price levels in line and to maintain balance-of-payments equilibrium (Bordo 1992, 268–69).[6] The price-specie-flow mechanism did not, however, address the operation of the mixed gold and paper money system that was in place in Britain at the end of the eighteenth century. Thus, it lacked the capacity to adequately explain movements in the price level. The description of the operation of a mixed-currency system would have to await the currency debates of the early nineteenth century, as discussed below.

Amid this institutional and theoretical setting, in 1793 the British government declared war on revolutionary France, precipitating a drain of gold from the British banking system. During the next few years, the Bank of England came under strain, mainly because of the large demands for advances by the government to finance participation in the war (Viner 1937, 122). Early in 1797, a general panic, initiated by rumors of a French landing on English soil and exacerbated by failures among country banks, precipitated a flight to safety into gold. In February 1797, the Bank of England reported to the government that its gold reserves had fallen to such a low level that it would not be able to remain open.[7] On February 26, 1797, the bank requested—and the government approved—a prohibition of the bank's exchanging its notes for specie. A parliamentary act in May 1797 validated the restriction on the conversion of the bank's notes into specie and "temporarily" extended the restriction. The "temporary" restriction remained in place until 1821.

With the suspension of convertibility, Britain moved to a flexible-exchange-rate regime. From the start of suspension in 1797 to the end of the Napoleonic Wars in 1815, there was a widespread perception that British prices had risen sharply.[8] This perception was based on the premium of bullion over the face value of paper currency and the discount of sterling against other currencies relative to the metallic parities of the pound and those currencies. The suspension of specie payments set the stage for "the two great monetary debates" of the nineteenth century (Humphrey 1974, 6): (1) the Bullionist Controversy that took place in the first two decades of that century; and (2) the banking school–currency school debate that took place during the middle of the century.

*The Bullionist Controversy*

The participants in the Bullionist Controversy[9] included bankers, lawyers, and statesmen.[10] The key issue addressed was the following: what caused the premium of bullion and the depreciation of the pound sterling following the suspension of convertibility? Bullionist writers attributed gold's premium and the pound's depreciation to an overissue of banknotes by the Bank of England (Humphrey 1974, 6; Laidler 1992, 257).[11] Bullionist writers included John Wheatley, Henry Thornton, Thomas Malthus, and David Ricardo. The bullionists traced the overissue of banknotes to the suspension of convertibility. If convertibility had been in place, an overissue of notes would have been prevented since banks would have ensured that they had sufficient reserves to cover their convertible liabilities (Flanders 1989, 31–32).[12] Not having been subject to convertibility requirements, banks overissued notes. Therefore, if the requirement of convertibility were enforced, there would be no need of further regulations (apart from mandatory convertibility) to ensure against excess issue of paper money (Viner 1937, 223).

The antibullionists defended the Bank of England against the charge that it had overissued banknotes and, thus, caused the depreciation of the exchange rate and the rise in the price of gold. Antibullionists, including Robert Torrens and James Mill, attributed the rise in prices to deficient English harvests, which raised the price of commodities, like wheat.[13] In their view, the premium on bullion reflected a deterioration in the balance of payments in light of extraordinary importations of grain and heavy military remittances by Britain to its allies (Viner 1937, 138). Using the real bills doctrine, they also argued that—if banknotes had been issued against the discount of short-term commercial bills drawn to finance real goods in the process of production and distribution—it was not possible for the quantity of money to be excessive, and to thus cause inflation.[14] Under that condition, the nominal quantity of banknotes would be determined by the real volume of goods under production.[15] The Bank of England, the antibullionists argued, had restricted its issues of notes to real bills of exchange. In doing so, it responded to the real needs of trade.[16] For these reasons, the bank could not have been responsible for the rise in prices during the Napoleonic Wars (Humphrey 1988b, 4–5; Laidler 1992, 258–59).

The bullionists countered as follows.[17] First, they criticized the real bills doctrine. They argued that the process of tying one nominal value, that of the money supply, to the nominal value of commercial bills renders the price level indeterminate in the absence of specie convertibility. Once disturbed, prices and money could chase each other upward or downward indefinitely. With specie convertibility, however, excessive monetary expansion would lead to a drain of reserves, forcing the Bank of England to raise its lending rate to protect its reserves (Laidler 1992, 259). Second, the bullionists extended the Humean metals-based model to take account of a mixed-currency system. In so doing, they provided another reason that the real bills doctrine could, in the absence of convertibility, lead to an indeterminate price level. Noting that new banknotes enter the economy through an expansion of bank loans, bullionists argued that the demand for banknotes depends on the relationship between the rate of interest charged on the loans and the expected rate of return on new capital projects.[18] Should the loan rate be set below the expected profit rate, the supply of bills offered for discount (and thus the money supply) could expand without limit (Humphrey 1974, 5; Laidler 1992, 258–59).[19]

*David Ricardo*

One crucial—but largely overlooked—contribution to the literature on money during the period under consideration merits acknowledgment because it is relevant to the origination of Chicago ideas on 100 percent reserves. The year 1824 saw the publication of Ricardo's pamphlet *Plan for the Establishment of a National Bank.*[20] In that pamphlet, Ricardo identified several issues that presaged key features of the English Bank Charter Act of 1844 and the 1933 Chicago 100 percent reserves proposal.

First, Ricardo distinguished between the two key functions of a central bank—the money-issuing function and the money-lending function:

> The Bank of England performs two operations of banking, which are quite distinct, and have no necessary connection with each other: it issues a paper currency as a substitute for a metallic one; and it advances money in the way of loan, to merchants and others. . . . That these two operations of banking have no necessary connection, will appear obvious from this,—that they might be carried on by two separate bodies, without the slightest loss of advantage, either to the country, or to the merchants who receive accommodation from such loans. (1824, 1)

Based on that reasoning, Ricardo argued that the "privilege of issuing money" could be taken from the Bank of England and given to a new, government-owned National Bank, without any "impairment" to the economy: "We should then, as now, carry on all the traffic and commerce of the country, with the cheap medium, paper money, instead of the dear medium, metallic money" (1824, 2). Ricardo assumed that the government-issued paper money would be backed by gold.[21] Under his proposal, the Bank of England, though deprived of its money-issuing function, would remain in a position to profit from its lending activities (1824, 5).

Second, Ricardo argued that, with the creation of a government-owned National Bank, the state, rather than the privately owned Bank of England, would derive seigniorage. He reasoned that, under the prevailing setup, the Bank of England held large amounts of government debt on its balance sheet: "the Government not only owes the Bank fifteen millions, its original capital, which is lent at three percent interest, but many more millions, which are advanced on Exchanger bills . . . and other securities" (1824, 2–3). Under Ricardo's plan, the new National Bank would purchase the Bank of England's government securities with new paper notes. Ricardo argued: "the sole effect of depriving the Bank of this [money-issuance] privilege, would be to transfer the profit which accrues from the interest of the money so issued from the Bank to Government" (1824, 10).

Ricardo had considered the issue of seigniorage several years before writing his pamphlet. In an 1815 letter to Thomas Malthus, Ricardo wrote:

I think the Bank an unnecessary establishment getting rich by those profits which fairly belong to the public. I cannot help considering the issuing of paper money as a privilege which belongs exclusively to the state.—I regard it as a sort of seigniorage, and I am convinced, if the principles of currency were rightly understood, that Commissioners might be appointed independent of all ministerial control who should be the sole issuers of paper money,—by which I think a profit of from two to three millions might be secured to the public. (letter, Ricardo to Malthus, September 10, 1815, quoted from Ricardo 1951, 268)[22]

Third, anticipating the modern literature on central bank independence, in his 1824 pamphlet Ricardo called for the National Bank to be independent. He was concerned that the directors of the Bank of England had typically been appointed to their positions based on their political affiliations and not based on their professional qualifications. The National Bank would be governed by five commissioners "not removable from their official situation but by a vote of one or both Houses of Parliament. . . . The Commissioners should never, on any pretence, lend money to

Government, nor be in the slightest degree under its control or influence" (1824, 11). The government would cover its funding needs through taxation or by borrowing from the private sector, "but in no case should it be allowed to borrow from those who have the power of creating money" (1824, 13).

Earlier, Ricardo had expressed concern about the consequences of incompetent management of the Bank of England. In a letter, dated July 9, 1821, addressed to Malthus, Ricardo wrote:

> I very much regret that in the great change we have made from an unregulated currency to one regulated by a fixed standard [that is, following the return to convertibility in 1821] we had not more able men to manage it than the present Bank directors. If their objective had been to make the revulsion as oppressive as possible, they could not have pursued measures more calculated to make it so than those which they have actually pursued. . . . They are indeed a very ignorant set. (quoted from Viner 1937, 178n14)

## The English Bank Charter Act of 1844

With the end of the Napoleonic Wars in 1815, the British economy entered a deflationary phase that persisted through the 1820s.[23] Following parliamentary debates on the issue, convertibility was reinstituted in 1821. Three severe financial crises—in 1825, 1836, and 1839—marked the following twenty years. The crises took the form of bank runs as holders of banknotes and banks' depositors sought refuge in the safety of gold. The crisis of 1825 gave rise to the view among some commentators that—contrary to the belief of the bullionists—convertibility would not be sufficient for maintaining confidence in the mixed-currency system. The discussions about the causes of the crisis marked the beginning of the debate between members of the currency school and the members of the banking school. Members of the currency school included Samuel Jones Loyd (later Lord Overstone), Robert Torrens, and George W. Norman. Members of banking school included John Fullarton, John Stuart Mill, Thomas Tooke, and James Wilson.[24] The debate, which lasted into the middle of the nineteenth century, focused on the way to ensure against the overissue of notes so that convertibility could be maintained.

The members of the currency school were the intellectual heirs of the bullionists (Humphrey 1988b, 6).[25] But, whereas the bullionists thought that convertibility on its own would ensure Humean adjustment under a mixed paper and metal system, currency school proponents believed that, under convertibility, banks frequently issued notes in amounts greater than would have occurred under a pure metallic standard. Those "overissues" of notes raised prices and fostered gold outflows, culminating in severe commercial crises. Consequently, there was a need, they believed, to arrest gold drains in their early stages so that the severity of commercial crises could be reduced (Daugherty 1942). What was required was convertibility *plus* special restrictions on the issuance of banknotes so that a mixed currency of notes and gold fluctuated in amount exactly as a wholly metallic system would have done under identical circumstances—a view called the "currency principle" (Humphrey 1974, 7; O'Brien 1992, 564).[26]

Banking school advocates, appealing to real bills reasoning, expressed the views that (1) convertibility of notes was automatically regulated by the needs of trade, ensuring monetary stability, and (2) even if that were not the case, there would be no point in regulating only notes since deposits would raise the same problem posed by notes (Schumpeter 1954, 727). They argued that the quantity of notes in circulation was adequately controlled by competitive processes. Under convertibility, the quantity of notes would not exceed the needs of business for any appreciable length of time—the "banking principle" (Viner 1937, 223). Members of the banking school also maintained that the Bank of England could not force an excess issue of notes on the market since no one would borrow at interest unnecessarily. Any excess would be extinguished as borrowers paid back costly interest-bearing loans to the bank; the idea that excess note issue would be returned to the bank was called the "law of reflux" (Humphrey 1988b, 5).[27] In light of these factors, members of the banking school argued that statutory control on the issuance of banknotes was unnecessary.[28]

The Palmer rule, adopted in 1827, but first publicly explained in 1832 by J. Horsley Palmer, then governor of the Bank of England, was an initial attempt to implement the currency school view that a mixed-currency system should behave exactly as a fully metallic currency. The rule specified that, when the foreign exchanges were at par, the Bank of England should hold securities amounting to two-thirds of its total liabilities of notes and deposits, and specie reserves of one-third of its total liabilities of notes and deposits. Thereafter, the quantity of securities would be held fixed. All fluctuations in the bank's combined notes and deposits would, except under special circumstances, be equal to the fluctuations in the bank's holding of specie. Palmer (1832, 72) stated that in this way "the circulation of the country [would be] regulated by the action of the foreign exchanges."[29] This rule amounted to the imposition of a 100 percent marginal reserve requirement on the bank's liabilities of notes and deposits (O'Brien 1992, 564; Demeulemeester 2019, 79–80). The rule, however, apparently was not implemented in practice.[30]

The debate between the currency school and the banking school culminated with the English Bank Charter Act of 1844—sometimes called the Peel Act after the then prime minister Sir Robert Peel. The Bank Act of 1844 marked a triumph for currency school ideas. The main elements of the Bank Act of 1844 were as follows.[31] (1) Following Ricardo's proposal in his 1824 *Plan for the Establishment of a National Bank*, the Bank of England was split into two departments: an Issue Department and a Banking Department. In contrast to Ricardo's proposal, the bank remained under private ownership.[32] (2) The Issue Department was limited to an issuance unbacked by bullion—the fiduciary issue—of fourteen million pounds (Viner 1937, 220).[33] Above that amount, the Issue Department could issue notes only in exchange for gold (or within certain limits, silver). Whereas the Palmer rule aimed to impose a 100 percent reserve requirement on the bank's total liabilities, the 1844 Bank Act established a 100 percent reserve requirement on the bank's note liabilities. (3) The Banking Department *functioned* as a private bank. Nonetheless, it occupied a special place in the banking system because the reserves of the London bankers consisted, in part, of deposit balances held on the books of the Banking Department.[34] The Banking Department's reserves mainly comprised notes issued by the Issue Department. These reserves would increase if a Bank of England customer deposited funds or if loans were repaid. The Banking Department could also create deposits; there was no reserve requirement on that department's deposits. (4) No new banks of issue could be established. Those in existence received compensation if they relinquished the right of issue. Those banks that continued to issue notes were limited to an amount equal to the average circulation in the three months immediately preceding the passage of the Bank Act of 1844 (Daugherty 1942).[35]

*Rules versus Discretion?*

Before proceeding to discuss the relevance of the currency school–banking school debate for the contemporary rules-versus-discretion literature, it is necessary to define terms.[36] I use Mishkin's (2018) definitions of "rules" and "discretion":

> A *rule* requires that monetary policy is essentially automatic: it involves a precise prescription for how monetary policy should react to a set of economic

circumstances. One example of a monetary policy rule is the constant-money-growth rule advocated by Milton Friedman, in which the money supply is set by the central bank to grow at a constant rate. A more recent alternative is the classic Taylor (1993) rule in which the policy interest rate, the federal funds rate, is set to be a weighted average of an output gap (actual output minus potential output) and an inflation gap (actual inflation minus the target inflation rate). The polar opposite of a monetary policy rule, according to the traditional classification of policy regimes, is based on *discretion*. Discretion, in its purist form, involves monetary policy makers setting their policy instruments on a day-to-day basis as economic events unfold, with no public commitments about its objectives or actions. (emphasis in original, Mishkin 2018, 225)

The following points provide context to my discussion below about the relevance of the nineteenth-century British monetary debates to the rules-versus-discretion literature of the 1920s and 1930s. First, both the currency school and the banking school "were staunch supporters of the gold standard" and in the efficacy of the Humean adjustment process (Schumpeter 1954, 727). That is, both groups were in favor of a rule — the gold-standard rule. Where they differed was in how to best operate the gold standard so that it could secure economic stability. Neither group believed that policy instruments should be set on "a day-to-day basis as economic events unfold[ed], with no public commitments about [the policy makers'] objectives or actions" (Mishkin 2018, 225). Second, both groups believed that the restriction of 1797 to 1821 had induced commercial "revulsions," and recurring booms and banking crises (Viner 1937, 221; Mints 1945a, 74). The objective of both groups was to prevent or at least ameliorate such episodes. Third, the currency school believed that, in the absence of regulation on the issue of notes, a system with a convertible paper currency could lead to excess note issuance for sufficiently long periods to endanger the maintenance of convertibility and generate financial crises (Viner 1937, 223). Thus, the currency school advocated regulation of paper notes — a circumstance that, as we have seen, led to the Bank Act of 1844, the aim of which "was to create conditions in which changes in the currency would occur exclusively as an *automatic* response to international gold movements and *not at all upon the initiative of the Bank*" (emphasis added, Viner 1937, 178).

The banking school opposed the mechanism embedded in the Bank Act of 1844. The members of the banking school believed that (1) the capacity of banks to discount real bills and (2) the law of reflux, in the presence of convertibility, would normally be sufficient to guard against gold drains and financial crises. If a gold drain should nevertheless occur, the banking school advocated two lines of defense. These defensive measures were spelled out by Tooke in his *An Inquiry into the Currency Principle* (1844). First, Tooke advised that the Bank of England should hold a sufficiently large quantity of gold reserves—on the order of fifteen million pounds—to allow the bank to withstand a gold outflow without endangering convertibility. Second, should the level of reserves fall to ten million pounds, he advised that the bank should raise its discount rate (Tooke 1844, 115–17). Fullarton (1845, 229–39) held similar views, although he was less confident than Tooke about the effectiveness of hikes in the discount rate in stemming gold outflows.[37]

Some currency school advocates framed their debate with the banking school in the context of rules versus discretion. They believed that the implementation of the currency principle would constitute a rule but that alternative ways of conducting policy—including hikes in the discount rate to stem gold outflows—were equivalent to discretion. Loyd argued:

> Without this *rule* [i.e., the currency principle], all must be left to the irregularity and uncertainty of individual *discretion*. The manager of the circulation must undertake to foresee and to anticipate events, instead of merely making his measures conform to a self-acting test. . . . In the exercise of such a *discretion*, the manager of the circulation . . . will, in nine cases out of ten, fall into error; whilst the interests of the whole community, and the fate of all mercantile calculations, will be dependent upon the sound or unsound *discretion* of some individual or body; instead of depending upon their own prudence and judgment, exercised under the operation of a fixed and invariable law, the nature and provisions of which are equally known to every body. (emphasis added, 1844, 21; quoted from Demeulemeester 2019, 80)

Loyd's view about what constituted discretion is problematic. In particular, Loyd did not recognize that methods of conducting policy other than based on the currency principle—such as the real bills doctrine—could also constitute a rule under which the gold standard could operate. In an 1837 publication, he characterized the currency principle as follows: "By this means, and *by this means only*, can we obtain in paper circulation varying in amount exactly as the circulation would have varied had it been metallic" (1837, 15). Contrary to Loyd's perception of the matter, a policy can be viewed as having been based on a rule if the policy is systematic and predictable. For example, an increase in the discount rate to stem gold outflows, as under the banking school framework, does not constitute a discretionary regime any more than does a hike in the interest rate in response to a rise in inflation under the Taylor rule.

Correspondingly, some members of the banking school thought that their policy framework entailed a discretionary element. As mentioned, Tooke had argued that the Bank of England should hold a sufficiently large quantity of reserves so that it could withstand a gold outflow without endangering convertibility. In that way, the bank would be able to distinguish between a gold outflow that was self-correcting and an outflow that would be long lasting, requiring an interest-rate increase.[38] Although in 1844 Tooke had set a lower limit for reserves of ten million pounds before the bank would need to raise interest rates, he was not always specific about the amount at which the lower limit should be set. In parliamentary testimony in 1848, he was asked about the limit at which the bank needed to act. He replied: "I am quite sure that you must leave it to the discretion of some men or body of men; no doubt they are fallible in their judgement, and Bank directors have sometimes signally failed in their judgement" (quoted from Arnon 1991, 138).

The use of the terms "rules" and "discretion" were commonplace in the currency school–banking school debates. To illustrate, consider one parliamentary committee's *Report from the Select Committee on Banks of Issue*, published in 1840. The committee heard evidence from ten experts, including Palmer, Norman, Loyd, and Tooke. During the hearings—amounting to some four hundred pages—the terms "rule" or "rules" were used 123 times; the term "discretion" was used eighteen times.

The widespread use of these terms, together with the misinterpretation of activist rules (such as the Taylor rule) as discretionary policies, apparently motivated some doctrinal historians to conclude that the rules-versus-discretion literature originated in the currency school–banking school debates. Thus, O'Brien expressed the following view:

> Another way of looking at the distinction between the Currency and Banking principles is to view it as a distinction between rules and discretion. This is because at some point the reality of long-run equilibrium values will force even the adherents of the Banking principle into discretionary action. This was indeed recognised by the leading member of the Banking School, Thomas Tooke, who proposed that the Bank of England should hold a gold reserve of between £10 million and £15 million and that it should avoid taking contractionary

action on a discretionary basis, only pursuing monetary contraction if the reserve, starting at £15 million, fell below £10 million. . . . The Currency School sought to link the money supply automatically to the balance of payments while the Banking School relied on discretion to avert the catastrophe of a sustained departure from long-run equilibrium values, resulting in the suspension of convertibility. (2007, 98–99)[39]

Likewise, in a paper on the development of monetary rules, Laidler (2002, 17–18) stated:

> Severe crises involving internal drains and bank failures occurred under convertibility in 1825, 1836 and 1839, and these eventually prompted a renewal of debate about the proper conduct of the Bank of England, the so-called Currency School–Banking School controversy. Here the issue of rules versus discretion in the specific matter of coping with crises, which had lain just below the surface of earlier exchanges, was squarely joined. The Banking School were content with the then existing institutional status quo, but urged the Bank of England to adopt what amounted to the principles of discretionary policy.[40]

Similar views have been expressed by, among others, Humphrey (1988b, 4), Flanders (1989, 34), Arnon (1991, chap. 9; 2010), Schwartz (1992, 151), and Goodhart and Jensen (2015, 21).

Did the currency school–banking school debate presage the 1930s literature—and, in particular, the literature emanating from Chicago—on rules versus discretion in monetary policy? The following points are relevant. First, contrary to what *recent* doctrinal historians have argued, the nineteenth-century debates were *only* about rules. Specifically, they were about the way to regulate changes in the money supply to ensure economic stability via the gold-standard mechanism. The currency school believed that a restriction—the currency principle—needed to be added to convertibility to attain economic stability. The banking school believed that convertibility would be sufficient to ensure Humean adjustment and economic stability. Thus, the difference between the two schools centered on which *particular rule* would achieve greater economic stability.

It is important to point out that the pre-1970s secondary literature on the currency school–banking school debate did *not* interpret that debate within the context of rules versus discretion. In particular, that literature took the position that *both* schools opposed discretion. Here is what Viner had to say:

Both schools were hostile to discretionary management. The currency school thought that the currency could be made nearly automatic again merely by limiting the issue of bank notes uncovered by specie. The banking school held that there was no acceptable way of escape from the discretionary power of the Bank of England over the volume of deposits, although the "banking principle," according to which the issue of means of payment could not be carried appreciably beyond the needs of business under convertibility, set narrow limits to this discretionary power. (1937, 389)

Similarly, Schumpeter (1954, 727) expressed the view that the currency school and the banking school "were equally averse to monetary management." Mints (1945a, 100) stated: "it was precisely this [discretionary management] that the currency school desired to avoid, while the banking school took no definite position on this question." Robbins (emphasis in original, 1958, 122) expressed the following view: "The grand point of difference [between the two schools] concerned the means of securing . . . convertibility. Whereas . . . it was the contention of the Currency School that a strict regulation of the volume of note issue was necessary, it was the leading contention of the Banking School that, *provided the obligation of convertibility was maintained*, no further regulation was required." Blaug (1962, 185) argued: "It is clear that at bottom neither school recognized the necessity of discretionary management of the currency. The Currency School wanted to regulate the note issue . . . while the Banking School balked at the idea of any monetary management whatever."[41]

What happened to produce an about-face among more recent doctrinal historians compared to the position their predecessors adopted concerning the applicability of rules versus discretion in the currency school–banking school debate? Dellas and Tavlas (2022) conjecture that, with the ascendance of the rules-versus-discretion debate since the 1970s, doctrinal historians developed the idea that the banking school's opposition to the Bank Act of 1844, and its belief that the Bank of England should maintain large reserves and use its discount rate after a certain lower reserves limit had been reached to maintain economic stability, could be interpreted as a discretionary policy. In that way, the debate could be interpreted as having contemporary relevance. Note, however, that that banking school's policy involved "a prescription for how monetary policy should react to a set of economic circumstances" (Mishkin 2018, 225). Thus, it was a rules-based policy.[42]

The main difference between the two schools concerned the amount of *activism*—as opposed to discretion—that could be used in response to internal and external drains of gold. The members of the currency school believed that the currency principle would normally suffice; thus, the need of further policy action was not expected. The members of the banking school believed in policy activism, but the activism should *not* be arbitrary. In the event of a gold drain, they believed that the Bank of England should use its discount rate to regulate gold outflows. Fullarton (1845, 214–15) put the banking school view as follows:

> The principles on which it might be deemed desirable that the affairs of the Bank should be administered, under certain given contingencies, might perhaps be embodied in resolutions, or by some other means might be made the subject of a general understanding between the State and the Bank, but not in a shape that would be of any legal effect in fettering the discretion of the administrative body. The most important part of this understanding would necessarily be, that the Bank should, under all circumstances, steadily aim at the possession of as large a reserve in bullion as the vicissitudes of trade might permit, without considering how the interests of its proprietors might be affected by the accumulation.

Fullarton and the other proponents of the banking school did *not* argue that the Bank of England should be allowed to change its policy in an arbitrary and unsystematic way—a policy that would have constituted a discretionary regime.

What about the currency school's position in the event of a gold drain following the passage of the Bank Act of 1844? As it turned out, a financial crisis occurred in 1847. During the first three months of that year, the Bank of England's gold reserves fell from fifteen million pounds to ten million pounds. The bank responded to the crisis by raising its discount rate (Daugherty 1943, 241). Thus, the bank's response was consistent with the views of banking school advocates, including Tooke and Fullarton. What about the views of currency school advocates? Here is how Robbins (1958, 119) characterized the views of Torrens and Loyd (i.e., Overstone).

> Now neither Torrens nor Overstone, the chief [currency school] writers concerned in this connection, were disposed to deny the possibility of such emergencies. Nor, when there had actually occurred a crisis of this degree of severity, which happened in the autumn of 1847, were they disposed to criticize the action of the government of the day in promising an indemnity to infringements of the Bank Act. Each of them expressed the view that what had happened was both necessary and sensible.

Consequently, even on the issue of using the discount rate to respond to exceptional gold drains, the views of the currency school and the banking school were essentially the same.

As discussed later in this chapter, beginning with the work of Simons (1936a), and continuing through the work of Friedman (1960) and Taylor (2017), the proponents of rules have aimed to make policy actions more predictable, reducing *policy uncertainty* and, thus, supporting private-sector spending. Policy uncertainty, however, was not an element of the nineteenth-century debates.

There was a specific reason that the rules-versus-discretion literature—with its emphasis on the need for monetary-policy certainty—originated in the 1930s. With the end of World War I in 1918, the Fed began to manipulate its discount rate and to engage in open-market operations to achieve its objectives. During the 1920s, the Fed pursued several objectives. These objectives were, at times, pursued simultaneously. The priority assigned by the Fed to its objectives changed from year to year. Thus, the Fed's reaction function changed in an unsystematic way during that decade and culminated in the Great Depression (Friedman and Schwartz 1963, chap. 7). The Fed's objectives included the restoration of the international gold standard, the prevention of inflation, the mitigation of business fluctuations, and, in 1928–29, the dampening of stock-market speculation (Meltzer 2003, 261–67). It pursued these objectives amid a fragmented Federal Reserve System and a power struggle between the New York Fed and the Federal Reserve Board in Washington. Friedman and Schwartz (1963, 297) characterized monetary policy during the 1920s as follows: "Inevitably, in the absence of any single well-defined statutory objective, conflicts developed between discretionary objectives of monetary policy. The two most important arose out of the re-establishment of the gold standard abroad and the emergence of the bull market in stocks." Mints, who followed Simons in developing the rules-versus-discretion issue, characterized the Fed's discretionary policies in the 1920s as follows:

> During the 1920's this belief [in the power of central-bank policy] was greatly strengthened, and what were held to be the goals of central-bank action were more explicitly formulated. The most unfortunate aspect of this development was the general belief that the central bank should be given wide discretionary powers to take whatever action seemed to it wise in given circumstances. The Federal Reserve System was created and was operated (and still is) in accordance with this point of view. (1950, 8)

In light of the above account of the currency school–banking school debates, why have contemporary doctrinal historians identified those debates with the genesis of the rules-versus-discretion literature? As mentioned, with the rise of the rules-versus-discretion debate, especially in the 1970s and 1980s, doctrinal historians, it seems, appropriated the use of the word "discretion" in the contemporary usage of that term to describe the banking school's position in the nineteenth-century debates. As documented, members of both schools used the word "discretion" to describe the banking school's policy. However, by equating the terms "rules" and "discretion" with today's meanings to the terms with the meanings they had in the nineteenth-century debates, contemporary writers have gone beyond what the earlier writers meant by those concepts.

To conclude, the nineteenth-century debates between the currency school and the banking school were essentially about the type of automatic mechanism that worked more efficiently in bringing about balance-of-payments adjustment under the gold standard. To the extent that the word "discretion" entered into the debates, the discretion concerned whether the monetary authorities should use their policy instruments to react to exceptional circumstances—that is, to excessive gold outflows. In such circumstances, the currency school believed that restrictions on the issuance of Bank of England notes would produce automatic adjustment. The banking school believed that the bank should raise its discount rate—that is, policy should be activist, but predictable. Those debates had little—if anything—to do with the rules-versus-discretion literature of the 1930s and after.

*100 Percent Reserves*

We have seen that the Bank Act of 1844 imposed a 100 percent reserve requirement on the Bank of England's note liabilities above a fiduciary issue. What were the similarities and differences between the Bank Act of 1844 and the Chicago proposal for 100 percent reserves? In other words, what value added did the Chicagoans bring to the table? The similarities were as follows.

- Both the Bank Act of 1844 and the Chicago proposal aimed to moderate the amplitude of economic fluctuations and prevent banking crises resulting from the conjunction of banks' lending and the money creation embedded in lending.
- Both the Bank Act of 1844 and the Chicago proposal assumed that discretion exacerbated the cycle and contributed to banking crises.

- Both featured a reform of the banking system through the separation of the money-creation function from the money-lending function of banks.

- The Bank Act provided that some of the notes issued by the Bank of England would be fiduciary in character because a fixed maximum amount of government debt was to be held on the balance sheet of the Issue Department (the Bank Act did not place a limit on the amount of government debt that could be held by the Banking Department). The Chicago proposal also envisaged that the issuing of money be made against the acquisition of bonds by the monetary authority, thereby providing a way to significantly reduce (if not eliminate) government debt. The November 1933 memorandum stated: "At the end of the transition period, the Reserve Banks should find themselves in possession of additional investment assets (perhaps exclusively bonds) about equal in value to the amount of the present federal debt" (Simons et al. 1933, 4). Thus, in both cases, there would be government debt as an asset on the balance sheet of the monetary authority used as a backing for the currency (in addition to gold under the Bank Act of 1844).

The above similarities were significant, and, as I document in what follows, both Knight and Simons acknowledged the indebtedness of the Chicago 100 percent reserves scheme to the 1844 Bank Act.

There were, however, important differences between the Bank Act of 1844 and the Chicago proposal.

- The Bank Act separated the Bank of England into two departments. The Banking Department provided money-lending services, competing with other private banks. Under the Chicago proposal, private banks would be limited to deposit-transferring activities. Investment trusts would engage in lending activities.

- The Bank Act applied a marginal 100 percent reserve requirement to Bank of England notes, both to secure their convertibility into gold and to ensure that paper money would vary in correspondence with the flows of bullion (the currency principle). Bank deposits were left out of the reform. The Chicago scheme stipulated that commercial bank deposits be fully covered by reserves in the form of Federal Reserve notes or deposits with the Federal Reserve; gold-reserve requirements against Federal Reserve liabilities would be completely abolished.

- The above-mentioned currency principle, embedded in the Bank Act, represented a policy rule that constrained the Bank of England's issuing of notes, in order to make the total of metallic and paper currency behave exactly as would a purely metallic currency. Under the Chicago proposal, institutional reform was aimed at increasing control of the money supply; the monetary authority could, in principle, follow a rule or engage in discretion—in the particular case of the Chicago proposal, monetary control would be accompanied by a rule.

The rule would be domestically focused; the gold standard would be replaced with flexible exchange rates.

- Under the Bank Act of 1844, seigniorage remained with the private owners of the Bank of England. Under the Chicago proposal, the government would own the central bank and, thus, earn the seigniorage (consistent with Ricardo's proposal).
- The Bank Act was not concerned with the socialization of the banking sector — socialization of banking was not an issue in Britain in the middle of the nineteenth century. An objective of the Chicago proposal was to prevent the socialization of the banking sector — that *was* an issue in the United States in the 1930s.

## Conclusions

The substance of the nineteenth-century debates between the currency school and the banking school was very different from that of the discussions on rules versus discretion in the 1930s. The participants in the nineteenth-century debates aimed to preserve the gold standard. They endeavored to apply a principle on note issuance so that a mixed-currency system would work automatically — as though it were a fully metallic system. The use of discretion — manipulating a policy instrument in an unsystematic way to achieve a policy objective — was not part of the debates.

To reduce the possibility and severity of financial crises, the Bank Act of 1844 placed a 100 percent marginal gold-backing requirement on the notes issued by the Bank of England. The 1930s Chicagoans aimed to replace the gold standard with a fiat-money regime. They endeavored to reduce the frequency and severity of business cycles by (1) requiring 100 percent reserve backing — in the form of central-bank fiat money — on demand deposits of commercial banks and (2) eliminating monetary-policy discretion in domestic economic affairs. The currency school–banking school discussions culminated in the Bank Act of 1844, a forerunner, but by no means an exact preconception of, the Chicago proposal for 100 percent reserves. In the next section, I assess the Chicagoans' contributions to both banking reform and policy rules in terms of the contemporaneous literature of the 1920s and 1930s.

## 4.2 Soddy versus Knight and Simons

Following the circulation of the March and November 1933 Chicago memoranda calling for 100 percent reserves, the idea took off.[43] During the next few years numerous articles about the proposal, authored by leading econo-mists of the day, appeared in the literature.[44] Irving Fisher embraced the idea in 1934 and became a leading advocate, making the adoption of the 100 percent reserves proposal his chief policy objective during the remain-der of his lifetime. His unflinching support continued almost to the day of his death on April 29, 1947; on March 27, 1947, he wrote a letter to President Harry S. Truman urging the enactment of "a law which will sever the tie that now binds bank loans to the volume of checkbook money" (quoted from Allen 1993, 715).[45] The idea was debated in Congress, and several pieces of congressional legislation that included the 100 percent reserve requirement were introduced.[46]

On the other side of the Atlantic, however, the attribution of the idea was greeted by one individual with great consternation. Frederick Soddy, who, as mentioned, had been awarded the Nobel Prize in Chemistry in 1921, had published a book, *Wealth, Virtual Wealth and Debt*, in 1926, in which he proposed 100 percent reserve requirements on demand deposits.[47] In his review of the book the following year, Knight (1927b) saw merit in the idea. However, the two 1933 Chicago memoranda and much of the subsequent academic literature, including articles by Simons (1934a; 1936a), on the sub-ject failed to mention Soddy's origination of the idea. Soddy was furious. He "repeatedly upbraided" Fisher in a mistaken belief that Fisher had failed to give him credit (Dimand 1993b, 70).[48] Likewise, Soddy reprimanded Knight and Simons for not having cited Soddy in the two 1933 Chicago memo-randa. As I discuss below, Alvin Hansen also chimed in. In his book *Full Recovery or Stagnation?* (1938), Hansen chided Simons and other propo-nents of the 100 percent reserves scheme for failing to give credit to Soddy as the originator of the proposal.[49] In a review of Hansen's book, Simons (1939) relented, citing Soddy, but the citation was embellished with sarcasm (see below). Simons wrote numerous subsequent articles containing the 100 percent reserves idea, but he never again cited Soddy. After his 1927 re-view of Soddy's book, Knight also never again referred to that author.

Soddy's claim of origination produced an effect. There is currently a widely held view—though not unanimous agreement—that Soddy was the progenitor of the Chicago 100 percent reserves scheme and that the Chicago economists—especially Knight—took the idea over from Soddy. Ronnie Phillips (1995, 46–47) wrote: "The ideas of the Chicago economists on banking reform were influenced by Soddy. . . . Frank Knight, . . . one of the greatest economic minds of the twentieth century, embraced the he-retical proposal of a noneconomist to transform the banking system radically." Barber (1996, 90) stated: "Soddy . . . had sparked the contemporary [i.e., 1930s] discussion with a pamphlet calling for 100 percent reserves in 1926." Laidler (1999, 240) expressed the view that the 100 percent reserves scheme was "labelled 'the Chicago Plan,' and with considerable justice, if we set aside the claims of Frederick Soddy (1926), whose work was known to Frank Knight." Similarly, Benes and Kumhof (2012, 17) wrote: "[The Chicago Plan] was first formulated in the United Kingdom by . . . Frederick Soddy. . . . Frank Knight . . . picked up the idea almost immediately." Daly, who published an article on Soddy's economics (see Daly 1980), expressed the view that "Soddy's advocacy of full reserve banking was later picked up by . . . Frank Knight and others of the Chicago School" (Daly 2016, 2).[50]

Did Soddy's 1926 proposal for 100 percent reserves influence Chicago thinking on that issue? If so, why did the Chicagoans, especially Knight and Simons, the main propagators of the 100 percent reserves scheme at Chicago, fail to acknowledge the influence of Soddy? The following discussion addresses these issues.

### Soddy on Money, the Trade Cycle, and 100 Percent Reserves

In his book *Wealth, Virtual Wealth and Debt* (1926), Soddy distinguished between what he called "real wealth" and "virtual wealth." Real wealth comprised physical objects such as buildings and machines, while virtual wealth consisted of money and represented claims on real wealth.[51] Real wealth, Soddy argued, is subject to inescapable entropy laws of thermodynamics (i.e., depreciation), while virtual wealth is subject to laws of mathematics, compounding at the rate of interest instead of depreciating. He believed that a major problem with the economic system is that the banks, through their lending activities, had taken over the power to create money from the government. He also believed that when a single bank makes a loan, the bank can multiply deposits up to the limit set by reserve requirements. Under a gold standard,

> the banker can safely lend part of his depositors' money; but what is not so clear is that he can lend many times as much as the [gold reserves] as the whole nation possesses—in fact, create it to lend it at will. . . . Now the whole secret of the system is contained in the fact that when a bank creates a loan and lends £100 to a borrower, to do so it need only have £15 of its depositors' money, or whatever the "safe" ratio may be. (Soddy 1926, 153–54)

Soddy went on to argue that, with an initial deposit of £100, and with a reserve ratio of 15 percent, an individual bank can create an additional £566 of money. He also argued that, in practice, the amount of additional money that a bank can create is even larger because the reserve ratio is closer to 7 percent than 15 percent: "At least since, if not before, the War the figures suggest rather a 7 per cent 'safe' limit than 15 per cent. On this basis a client depositing £100 of cash in current account enables the bank to loan £1,330" (Soddy 1926, 154).

Soddy believed that three main consequences follow from the power of banks to create money. First, the banks gain seigniorage; the interest paid by the borrower on the loan is a "cost to the community" that the banks are paid because they possess the power to create money (1926, 155). Second, "the community is robbed"; since demand deposits can be created much more rapidly than new physical wealth can be created, the creation of deposits leads to an excess of money relative to physical wealth, resulting in inflation. Third, the trade cycle is greatly amplified (1926, 157).

Soddy's trade-cycle theory was based on a transmission process emanating from changes in the supply of gold. Essentially, the author argued that injections and withdrawals of gold into, and from, the economy underpinned the cycle and that fractional-reserve banking system amplified the cycle. In a country *without* a highly developed banking system, the process operated as follows:

> Not only during the War, but also after the gold discoveries of last century, trade greatly flourished, and general prosperity resulted. Now this prosperity directly stimulates the luxury demand for gold for jewellery and ornament, and in countries—still the majority—without a highly developed banking system, for saving. Thus the money tends to disappear again, the stimulus due to abundance of money receives a check, and a period of depression ensues. Then these hoards and stores, before taken out of the circulation, tend to reappear and again help to inaugurate a boom. The trade cycle, in some part at least, must be due to the use of a metal as the basis of currency, which is gradually withdrawn as industry expands and comes back as it contracts, exactly the opposite to what is required of a currency. Even the ease with which the precious metals can be melted up without loss, and converted from coin to merchandise and back again an innumerable number of times at trifling cost, which has been held to make them especially suitable for coinage, is a fatal defect. Just as the industrial system has been laboriously tuned up to a higher level of production, the medium of exchange turns into an article of luxury, and with it goes the wave of prosperity. (Soddy 1926, 180)

In a country with a well-developed banking system, the ability of banks to create and destroy money greatly exacerbates the trade cycle:

> By the use of credit money, based upon a small proportion of gold, the quantity of money becomes subject to much greater and more violent variation than before, and the exchange value of gold in terms of goods oscillates. The causes which are inherent in the use of gold as a luxury article, as well as a medium of exchange, are greatly exaggerated, producing the trade cycle. (Soddy 1926, 181)

Soddy derived the following policy proposals from his economic analysis: (1) a constant price index to help prevent fluctuations in the purchasing power of money; (2) flexible exchange rates to facilitate equilibrium in the balance of payments; and (3) 100 percent reserve requirements on demand deposits to moderate fluctuations in both the quantity of money and the price level, and to eliminate the seigniorage prerogative of the banks. Concerning the 100 percent reserves proposal, he stated:

> Banks create and destroy money arbitrarily and with no understanding of the laws that correlate its quantity with the national income. They have been allowed to regard themselves as the owners of the virtual wealth which the community does not possess, and to lend it and charge interest upon the loan as though it really existed and they possessed it.... The banks should by law be required to keep national money, £ for £ of their liabilities for customers' "deposits" in current account [i.e., demand deposits] and only be permitted to lend money genuinely deposited into their keeping by its owners, who give up the use of it for the stipulated period of the loan and receive receipts in legal form. (Soddy 1926, 296, 298)

Under Soddy's proposal, "[the] State [would] recover its sole prerogative in the issue of money, and make it impossible for the banks to issue money" (Soddy 1926, 196). The money would be issued to finance national expenditure instead of reliance on taxation or debt financing or both; it would also be issued to redeem interest-bearing government debt. The withdrawal (and destruction) of money would occur through taxation or the sale of a "National loan" (1926, 297). To initiate the proposed system, "some £2,000,000,000 of National interest-bearing Debt should be cancelled and the same sum of national money (non-interest-bearing National Debt) issued to replace the credit created by the banks" (1926, 298). The banks would derive income from service charges for maintaining demand deposits and from lending funds deposited in savings accounts.

Two points about Soddy's treatment of the business cycle warrant comment. First, Soddy did not spell out a specific transmission mechanism through which fluctuations in gold flows are related to the business cycle. He simply argued that "the trade cycle . . . *must* be due to the use of a metal as the basis of currency" (emphasis added) and that a fractional-reserve banking system amplified the cycle. Soddy may have had a Hume-type price-specie-flow mechanism in mind, but, if he did, he did not spell it out. In contrast, the Chicagoan theory of the business cycle, which emphasized the role played by autonomous changes in the velocity of circulation of money, flexible product prices combined with sticky costs, and self-justifying expectations, exacerbated through the behavior of a fractional-reserve banking system, was a coherent and relevant explanation of the occurrence and depth of the Great Depression.

Second, Soddy believed that an *individual bank* was the entity likely to create money equivalent to a multiple of an initial deposit. The Chicagoans, however, recognized that the banking system taken as a whole—but not an individual bank—possessed the capacity to multiply deposits on a given reserve base. Recall, in this connection, the discussion in chapter 2 of the expansionary phase of the business cycle contained in the November 1933 Chicago memorandum. During the expansionary phase of the cycle, the Chicagoans argued, banks increase their lending, thereby creating new money (demand deposits). In turn, these developments lead to increases in earnings, which induce a further expansion of loans. What distinguished the Chicagoans' analysis of the role played by banks in the cycle from Soddy's analysis was that the Chicagoans focused on the banking *system*, whereas Soddy dealt with an individual bank. In contrast to Soddy, the Chicagoans recognized that an individual bank would *lose* reserves if it attempted to expand its loans faster than other banks. Thus, in their description of the role of the banking system in the expansionary phase of the cycle, they stated that, as banks increase their lending, "new money (deposits) are created; these changes bring still larger earnings, which in turn induce further expansion of loans. During such expansion, no *single bank* losses reserves, unless it expands more rapidly *than the rest*" (emphasis added, Simons et al. 1933, appendix, 3). I return to this issue below.

### Knight and Simons on Soddy

*Knight.* In his review of Soddy's book, published in the *Saturday Review of Literature*, Knight (1927b) criticized Soddy's effort to contribute to the theory of wealth,[52] but praised that author's assessment of fractional-reserve banking. Knight began his review as follows: "Somewhat to the reviewer's surprise, this book has proven well worth the time and effort of a careful reading. Surprisingly, because in general, when the specialist in natural science takes time off to come over and straighten out the theory of economics he shows himself even dumber than the academic economist" (Knight 1927b, 732). Concerning Soddy's criticism of fractional-reserve banking, Knight stated:

> The practical thesis of the book is distinctly unorthodox, but is in our opinion both highly significant and theoretically correct. In the abstract, it is absurd and monstrous for society to pay the commercial banking system "interest" for multiplying several fold the quantity of medium of exchange when (a) a public agency could do it at negligible cost, (b) there is no sense in having it done at all, since the effect is simply to raise the price level, and (c) important evils result, notably the frightful instability of the whole economic system and its periodical collapse in crises, which are in large measure bound up with the variability and uncertainty of the credit structure if not directly the effect of it. Nor is the cost a bagatelle; if the amount of created bank currency in the United States be placed roughly at thirty-five billions and the average rate of bank interest at six per cent, it will be seen to amount to well over twice the interest on the national debt, and to several per cent of the total national income. Yet we must emphasize the qualification, "in the abstract." (Knight 1927b, 732)

Knight pointed out that there would be practical problems associated with a scheme that aimed to proscribe banks from lending, and thus creating, money. In this connection, he noted that the participants in the currency school–banking school debates had grappled with such problems:

> Many serious problems are raised by the proposal to prohibit banks from following the "'treasonable practice of uttering false money." The author has apparently never heard of the controversy over the banking versus the currency principles—as he has not heard of the mathematical economists and several generations of predecessors in the endeavour to create an exact science of economics—and he shows no recognition of the real and important relations between commercial banking and the creation of new capital and its guidance into use. (Knight 1927b, 732)

Knight concluded his review of the book with the following appraisal: "in general it is a brilliantly written and brilliantly suggestive and stimulating book" (Knight 1927b, 732). However, Knight never again cited Soddy in his (Knight's) writings.[53]

*Simons.* Simons referred to Soddy on two occasions. The first was in an overlooked article published in the November 1935 issue of the periodical the *Christian Century.* The article was titled "Depression Economics"; it was a review of three books, one of which was Soddy's *The Role of Money*, published in 1934.[54] In his 1934 book, Soddy again put forward the idea of 100 percent reserves on demand deposits. Much in line with Knight's (1927b) review of Soddy's 1926 book, Simons praised Soddy's advocacy of 100 percent reserves but was highly critical of Soddy's views on other economic issues. Regarding the former, Simons (1935b, 1421) stated that "Soddy's conclusions and proposals . . . merit intelligent consideration; and the supporting argument, when relevant, is often stimulating. So long as he sticks to the subject of banking, Soddy writes with considerable penetration." Regarding Soddy's views on economic issues more broadly, Simons (1935b, 1421) stated: "Soddy's other [views] will be insufferable to critical readers. His critical comments on traditional economics indicate that he has read little and understood even less" (Simons 1935b, 1421). On the issue of 100 percent reserves, Simons provided a cautionary remark that indicated how his view had changed since the circulation of the 1933 memoranda: "Even here, however, his [Soddy's] insight is limited — witness his categorical distinction between demand deposits and savings accounts, and his innocence of what would really be involved in preventing effectively the private use of money substitutes" (Simons 1935b, 1421). What did Simons mean by his use of the language "what would really be involved"? I return to this issue below.

The second occasion on which Simons referred to Soddy was in a generally critical review in 1939 of Hansen's 1938 book *Full Recovery or Stagnation?*[55] As previously mentioned, in that book Hansen prodded the Chicago group, along with other proponents of the 100 percent reserves proposal, for not giving credit to Soddy.[56] Hansen (1938, 111) stated: "Credit for originating this plan is usually given to a group of Chicago economists who circulated a mimeographed memorandum in 1933. It is strange that most of the leading writers on this proposal should quite overlook the fact that the 100 percent reserves plan had been publicized several years earlier by Sir Frederick Soddy." Hansen (1938, 112) then quoted Soddy's formulation of the 100 percent reserves proposal as stated in Soddy's *Wealth, Virtual Wealth and Debt.* An accompanying footnote listed four writers who had discussed the proposal but who did not give credit to Soddy; among the names were those of Albert Hart (a signatory of the March 1933 memorandum) and Simons.[57]

In his review of Hansen's book, Simons addressed Hansen's prodding of Simons and other proponents of the Chicago proposal for not acknowledging Soddy as follows: "since Hansen has chided us [i.e., the Chicago group] for not mentioning Soddy as an earlier proponent of 100 percent reserves, I must say that, while it is sometimes permissible to expound ideas without tracing out their historical antecedents, it is hardly appropriate, after one has brought up the matter in this instance, to stop with mention of Soddy!" (1939, 293). The sarcastic demeanor of Simons's "acknowledgment," with the clear suggestion that there had been antecedents other than Soddy, indicates that Simons did not regard Soddy as someone who influenced the Chicago proposal for 100 percent reserves. If that was indeed the case, then why not?

### Why Knight, and Most Probably Simons, Originated the 100 Percent Reserves Scheme: The Evidence

The preceding discussion has laid out the following facts: (1) Soddy proposed the 100 percent reserves scheme in his 1926 book *Wealth, Virtual Wealth and Debt*; (2) Knight reviewed that book in 1927 and praised the notion of 100 percent reserves; (3) Simons reviewed Soddy's 1934 book *The Role of Money* and, like Knight, praised the idea of 100 percent reserves; (4) the 1933 Chicago memoranda, which did not give credit to Soddy, advocated the 100 percent reserves scheme, and the scheme became identified with the Chicago group; and (5) despite the vocal consternation of Soddy, supported by Hansen, the Chicagoans failed to give Soddy credit after 1933 for the origination of the 100 percent reserves scheme. Why not? In what follows, I provide evidence leading to the conclusion that Knight—and most probably Simons—originated the 100 percent reserves scheme before 1926.

*1. Simons's letter to Fisher, January 19, 1934.* In a letter to Fisher explaining the origins of the Chicago proposal, Simons wrote:

> I got started toward this scheme of ours about ten years ago, by trying to figure out the possibilities of applying the principle of the English [Bank Charter] Act of 1844 to the deposits as well as to the notes of private banks. The Act would have been an almost perfect solution of the banking problem, if bank issue could have been confined to notes. (letter, Simons to Fisher, January 19, 1934, quoted from R. Phillips 1995, 67)

Two essential points about this letter are the following. First, Simons stated that his thinking about the 100 percent reserves idea originated "about ten years" ago, which would have placed the origination date to the early part of 1924 (or late 1923, since the letter was written in January 1934), that is, before the publication year of Soddy's book. Simons's qualification with the adjunct "about," however, leaves the precise origination year subject to uncertainty. Second, Simons credited the inspiration for the idea to "the English Act of 1844," and not to Soddy. As mentioned, in his 1927 review of Soddy's *Wealth, Virtual Wealth and Debt*, Knight had noted that Soddy seemed to have been unaware of the currency school–banking school debate that led to the Bank Act of 1844. An implication of both Simons's letter to Fisher and Knight's 1927 review of Soddy's book is that the catalyst underlying the Chicago 100 percent reserves proposal was the English Bank Charter Act of 1844.

   *2. Knight on Soddy's claim of precedence.* In a 1937 letter to Fisher, Soddy complained that the "Chicago group" had failed to give him (Soddy) credit for originating the 100 percent reserves proposal. Fisher communicated Soddy's complaint to Knight as follows:[58]

> Professor Soddy seems to be hinting that the Chicago group derived the 100% money idea from him, inasmuch as you had reviewed his "Wealth, Virtual Wealth and Debt" in 1927, and there are a few sentences in this book on a "L [pound sterling] for L" reserve. As I have been explaining to him that my idea of 100% money was largely due to the Chicago group's, I would be glad if you would tell me whether there is anything in his notion that it all traces back to him. (letter, Fisher to Knight, August 27, 1937, Frank H. Knight Papers, Special Collections Research Center, Joseph Regenstein Library, University of Chicago)

Knight replied as follows:

> I completely disclaim getting the one hundred per cent money idea from Soddy or anybody else, as far as I am personally concerned. I was always skeptical about the theory of pyramiding, and think I have taught practically the one hundred per cent doctrine from the beginning of work as teacher, in 1917. Of course I always explain to classes that it was distinctly heterodoxy doctrine. I don't presume to speak for Simons, or any one else. (Simons was one of my "gang" in the elements course at Iowa City from about 1920 on, but may perfectly well have been infected with that idea before that, for all I know.) It is true that I reviewed Soddy's first edition, and expressed agreement with this

phase of his doctrine; and, of course, I had not, and have not, published anything on the subject. (letter, Knight to Fisher, September 2, 1937, Frank H. Knight Papers, Special Collections Research Center, Joseph Regenstein Library, University of Chicago)

3. *The Iowa connection.* Knight taught at Cornell during the 1916–17 academic year and at Chicago during the 1917–19 academic years, before joining the faculty at the University of Iowa. He taught at Iowa from 1919 to 1927, before departing again for Chicago. At Iowa, Knight was initially an associate professor; he was promoted to professor in 1923. Simons joined the University of Iowa faculty in 1920 as an instructor, while also taking courses in economics; he was promoted to associate professor in 1924. While at Iowa, he became a disciple of Knight, becoming a member of Knight's "gang," and he followed Knight to Chicago in 1927. Another member of the Iowa faculty during the stints of Knight and Simons at that institution was Chester Arthur Phillips, who joined the faculty as a professor in 1920; Phillips taught at Iowa until 1952. Knight taught a principles course for undergraduates, a history-of-thought course for both undergraduates and graduates, and a theory (methodology) course for graduates. Simons taught public finance for both graduates and undergraduates. Phillips mainly taught money-and-banking courses for both undergraduates and graduates.[59]

In 1920, Phillips published the book *Bank Credit*, in which he made a major contribution to the banking literature. Phillips (1920, 32) stated that his objective was to "draw a sharp line of distinction between credit extension by an individual bank, and that of banks taken in the aggregate." He succeeded in attaining that objective.[60] Specifically, Phillips "brought home to the economics profession the crucial distinction between the reserve loss of a [single] competitive bank that expands its loans versus multiple expansions by the banking system as a whole" (Humphrey 1987, 8). Before the publication of Phillips's book, the "commonly held [view] by prominent banking economists . . . [was] that the typical *bank* can use a given input of reserves to multiply deposits. . . . Phillips's contribution was to show that those successive actions and reactions [of an initial increase in lending by a single bank] result in a system-wide expansion of deposits, even though any individual bank could expand its deposits only slightly" (emphasis added, Timberlake 1988, 300).

Phillips's contribution would have certainly been known to, and discussed by, his Iowa colleagues Knight and Simons; according to Rockoff

(2015, 47), Phillips's book was on Simons's reading list at Chicago.[61] As mentioned, the distinction between the reserve loss of a single bank that expands its loans and the multiple system-wide expansion of deposits marked the analysis contained in the Chicago memorandum of November 1933 and helped differentiate that analysis from that of Soddy. The likely exposure of Knight and Simons to Phillips's work on that distinction, and its incorporation in the November 1933 memorandum, suggest that the assessment in that memorandum underlying the analysis about the role played by the banking system in exacerbating the business cycle was provided by Knight or Simons or both, and originated before the publication of Soddy's 1926 book.

4. *Business cycles.* There is, to my knowledge, a single surviving document from Knight's teaching material while he was at Iowa. That document is an undated exam (or quiz), titled "Business Cycles," and it likely derives from Knight's principles course. Several of the questions in that document refer to "the recent [economic] crisis." The US economy experienced a sharp contraction in 1920–21. The contraction began in January 1920 and ended in July 1921; real output fell by 33 percent. Friedman and Schwartz (1963, 232) referred to that contraction as follows: "this contraction [although] relatively brief . . . ranks as one of the severest on record." Since the document "Business Cycles" refers to "the recent crisis," I conjecture that it was completed shortly after that episode—that is, during the 1921–22 or the 1922–23 academic year.

The document consisted of thirty-six questions, most of which had multiple-choice answers. One focus of the exam questions was the role played by credit expansion and contraction in the business cycle. Seven of the questions pertained to that issue; another three questions concerned the behavior of the "bank rate of interest" during the business cycle. The seven questions on credit behavior are reproduced in table 4.1 (with the numbering of the questions corresponding to that in the original document). The questions on the reserve ratio—that is, reserves to deposits—during the cycle (questions 15 and 23) indicate that Knight placed an emphasis on the creation and the destruction of credit during the business cycle since a mechanism through which credit contracts, for example, during the contractionary phase of the cycle is through deleveraging, or liquidation (question 8), as banks convert their loans into cash. In this connection, Friedman and Schwartz (1963, 244) referred to "businessmen's . . . experience of loan liquidation in 1920–21."[62] Question 10 suggests that Knight thought that credit contraction played a critical role in the 1921–

TABLE 4.1.  **Frank Knight's Exam on the Business Cycle: Questions Related to Credit (University of Iowa, Early 1920s)**

| Number (as listed in the original) | Question |
| --- | --- |
| 4 | Rank the following in the order of their sensitiveness or amount of change they undergo during the business cycle<br>• Retail prices<br>• Wholesale prices<br>• Interest rates<br>• Bank loans and deposits<br>• (E) Physical production |
| 6 | The main direct cause of the business cycle is<br>• Overexpansion and collapse of bank credit<br>• Overproduction of certain basic commodities<br>• Waves of business optimism and pessimism<br>• Variation in farm crops<br>• Speculation |
| 8 | By "liquidation" is meant<br>• Making of loans by business men to tide over a crisis<br>• Payment of debts out of income<br>• Payment of debts by sale of property<br>• Reduction of debts by mutual cancellation<br>• Reduction of debts to banks by long-term financing |
| 10 | Reduction in total volume of bank loans [in the recent crisis] was … |
| 15 | *During the period of liquidation,* the reserve ratio in banks is<br>• Increasing<br>• Decreasing<br>• Constant [italics in original] |
| 23 | During the *boom* period of the cycle, the reserve ratio in banks is<br>• Increasing<br>• Decreasing<br>• Constant [italics in original] |
| 36 | The most hopeful method of controlling the business cycle is<br>• To undertake public works during depression<br>• To regulate the issue of bank credit<br>• To provide unemployment insurance for wage earners<br>• To disseminate information regarding business conditions |

22 episode since students were expected to know the precise amount of credit contraction. One of the questions (number 36) hints that Knight may have discussed the possibility of regulating bank credit to control the business cycle. Clearly, the exam questions suggest that, in the first half of the 1920s, Knight had been analyzing the role played by the banking system in the business cycle.

*Discussion*

The foregoing discussion on the origin of the Chicago 100 percent reserves proposal has laid out the following evidence.

- First, in his 1927 review of Soddy's book, Knight noted that Soddy had not recognized that the idea underlying 100 percent reserve requirements featured in the nineteenth-century debate between the banking school and the currency school. As we have seen, the currency school's victory in that debate culminated in the English Bank Charter Act of 1844. We have also seen that there were important differences between the modalities of the Bank Act of 1844 and those of the Chicago proposal.
- Second, Simons used the occasion of a 1934 letter to Fisher to attribute the inspiration for the Chicago 100 percent reserves proposal to the Bank Act of 1844. Simons did not mention Soddy in that letter. Simons's comment about when he began thinking about the proposal indicated that his thinking pre-dated the year of publication of Soddy's 1926 book.
- Third, in his 1937 letter to Fisher, Knight categorically "disclaimed" the suggestion that he got the 100 percent reserves proposal from Soddy. By explicitly stating in his letter that Simons was "one of my gang" in the "elements" [i.e., principles] course at Iowa in the 1920s, Knight placed Simons in a position to confirm the veracity of Knight's statement that he (Knight) "taught practically the one hundred percent doctrine" at Iowa.
- Fourth, even discounting the claims of origination in the above-cited letters of Simons and Knight, the indirect evidence from the early 1920s on what would emerge as the Chicago framework about the role of the banking system in exacerbating the business cycle, and the distinction placed in that framework between the effects of the banking system versus those of individual banks on the cycle suggest that Knight, and most probably Simons, had analyzed the destabilizing effects of fractional-reserve banking prior to the publication of Soddy's book. As mentioned, a feature that distinguishes the business-cycle theory underlying Soddy's proposal from that underlying the Chicago proposal is the difference between the effect of credit expansion by a *single bank* and the effect of credit expansion by the *banking system*. The Chicagoans differentiated—but Soddy did not—between (1) the capacity of the banking system as a whole to multiply deposits on a given change in the reserve base and (2) the behavior of an individual bank, which tended to be constrained in its lending by the amount of new funds received (apart from an amount retained as reserves). That crucial distinction was emphasized in Chester Phillips's 1920 book. The distinction would have been known to that author's Iowa colleagues Knight and Simons.[63]

- Fifth, Knight emphasized, probably in 1921–22 (if not earlier), the role of credit expansion and contraction, working through changes in the reserve ratio, in exacerbating the business cycle in his principles course at Iowa. In the early 1920s, Knight also appears to have considered regulating bank credit—that is, bank deposits—to control the business cycle.

## Why Wasn't Soddy's Work Cited?

Even though Soddy's work did not influence the development of the Chicago Plan, why was it not cited in the 1930s Chicago literature as a matter of standard professional courtesy? After all, Soddy's 1926 book had been reviewed—receiving mixed assessments—in several professional journals shortly after its publication. Consider the following examples. In a generally critical review in the *Economic Journal*, Roy Harrod (1927, 272) wrote: "In his destructive passages Mr. Soddy does not appear to have a sufficiently firm grasp of the economic doctrines commonly held by present or earlier writers to make his criticisms pointed or telling." A similar assessment was made by A. G. Silverman (1927, 277) in a review in the *American Economic Review*: "[Soddy's] proposed solutions [i.e., 100 percent reserves and elimination of private issuance of money] . . . seem to involve evils greater than those connected with our present system." James Angell, who in the mid-1930s would become an advocate of 100 percent reserves, reviewed the book—generally favorably—in the *Political Science Quarterly*. Paradoxically, given his subsequent views, Angell was critical of Soddy's *specific* proposal of 100 percent reserves because, according to Angell "it rests on a familiar misunderstanding of the nature of banking and of the actual limits on the volume of lending" (1927, 623). The *Times Literary Supplement* (*London Times* 1926, 565) also reviewed Soddy's book. Daly (1980, 471) reported that the content of that review included the following: "[It is] sad to see a respected chemist ruin his reputation by writing on a subject about which he was quite ignorant."

There are several possible reasons for the absence of references to Soddy's work in the 1930s Chicago literature on 100 percent reserve requirements. First, the Chicago documents that launched the 100 percent reserves scheme in 1933 were memoranda—not articles published in scholarly journals in which citations to the previous literature could have been expected. Second, an absence of citations to previous works was just Simons's way of doing things; most of his well-known papers are more like policy memos than conventional journal articles and contain few references. Thus, Bordo and Rockoff (2013a, 171) pointed out that "Simons generally did not waste a lot of ink citing his predecessors." In contrast, in his scholarly 1945 book *A History of Banking Theory*, Simons's Chicago colleague Lloyd Mints, did cite Soddy as a proponent of the 100 percent reserves scheme (Mints 1945a, 270). Third, Soddy was viewed as an outsider by the economics profession and, with justification, a crank. He considered economics to be "a pseudoscience in need of a totally new beginning" (Daly 1980, 471). He argued that an international conspiracy of bankers sought to establish global dominance (Soddy 1926, chap. 14).

*Simons's Misgivings*

By early 1934, Simons began to express misgivings about the practicality of the 100 percent reserves scheme in the presence of financial-market innovation. The application of 100 percent reserve requirements to demand deposits, he recognized, could be accompanied by the development of financial (debt) instruments that were close substitutes for demand deposits but were not subject to 100 percent reserves. In these circumstances, the new instruments could instigate the same instability previously posed by demand deposits. In a January 1934 letter to Douglas, he wrote that he had been

> a little upset lately about the banking scheme—trying to figure out how to keep deposit banking from growing up extensively outside the special banks with the 100% reserves. Just what should be done, for example, to prevent savings banks (a) from acquiring funds which the depositors would regard as liquid cash reserves or (b) from providing through drafts a fair substitute for checking facilities? (letter, Simons to Douglas, January 24, 1934, Henry C. Simons Papers, Special Collections Research Center, Joseph Regenstein Library, University of Chicago)

In a July 1934 letter to Fisher, Simons expressed his concern that the imposition of 100 percent reserve requirements would cause risks to migrate to other parts of the financial system:

> In fact, I am more and more convinced of the importance of the point on which we seemed somewhat [to] disagree. Much is gained by our coming to regard demand deposits as virtual equivalents of cash; but the main point is likely to be lost if we fail to recognize that savings-deposits, treasury certificates, and even commercial paper are almost as close to demand deposits as are demand

deposits to legal-tender currency. The whole problem which we now associate with commercial banking might easily reappear in other forms of financial arrangements. There can be no adequate stability under any system which permits lenders to force financial institutions into effort at wholesale liquidation, and thus to compel industry to disinvest rapidly—for orderly disinvestment on a large scale is simply impossible under modern conditions. (letter, Simons to Fisher, July 4, 1934, Henry C. Simons Papers, Special Collections Research Center, Joseph Regenstein Library, University of Chicago)

Simons's concerns about the effects of alternative financial instruments led him to have doubts about the practicality of the 100 percent reserves idea applied only to demand deposits. In his July 1934 letter to Fisher, Simons expressed those concerns as follows: "little would be gained by putting demand-deposit banking on a 100% basis, if that change were accompanied by increasing disposition to hold, and increasing facilities for holding, liquid 'cash' reserves in the form of time deposits" (letter, Simons to Fisher, July 4, 1934). Simons called time deposits "an effective substitute medium for purposes of cash balances"; he argued that they would subject the economy, even in the presence of 100 percent reserves on demand deposits, to the same kind of inflationary and deflationary episodes, and banking crises, as those experienced in the absence of 100 percent reserves on demand deposits (letter, Simons to Fisher, July 4, 1934).[64]

Simons expressed similar misgivings about the effectiveness of the 100 percent reserves scheme in an exchange of letters with Friedrich Hayek in December 1934. Hayek initiated the exchange with a letter to Simons dated December 1, 1934, that commented on Simons's *A Positive Program for Laissez Faire*. Hayek expressed great sympathy for the general spirit of the pamphlet but cautioned about the practicality of the 100 percent reserves scheme:

> If it is not possible—and it clearly is not—to regulate the quantity of all media of exchange including even the very liquid resources which will occasionally be used in lieu of cash balances, then it is also impossible to regulate any arbitrarily selected part of the total quantity of money according to any "simple rule or principle of monetary policy." (Henry C. Simons Papers, Special Collections Research Center, Joseph Regenstein Library, University of Chicago)

In a letter dated December 18, 1934, Simons expressed agreement with Hayek's argument:

I agree enthusiastically with your comments on the 100% plan, and am happy
to say (pardonably, I trust) that they are no longer applicable to my position. I
have completely repudiated the position taken in the Addendum to the mimeographed [November 1933] memorandum (taken only tentatively there) as to the
merits of fixing the supply of *circulating media.* (emphasis in original; Henry C.
Simons Papers, Special Collections Research Center, Joseph Regenstein Library, University of Chicago)

Simons added that he had been unable to explain the problem of near
monies to Fisher: "Incidentally, I'd give a lot to be able to make clear your
point (and mine) to several over-hasty and overly enthusiastic converts—
above all, to Irving Fisher, with whom I've spent hours and hours without
making him see what you have expressed so clearly."

The misgivings about the 100 percent reserves scheme that Simons
expressed in his 1934 letters to Douglas, Fisher, and Hayek, respectively,
would carry over to Simons's publications (e.g., Simons 1936a, 331n17; Simons 1942a, 191). As explained in the next chapter, from the mid-1930s,
he regarded the scheme "as merely one phase or one step in the total
reordering of our financial structure which aims at virtual elimination
of private fixed-money contracts, especially those of short maturity" (Simons 1942a, 191). The "reordering" of the financial system would include
(1) the conversion of public debt into currency and consols, simplifying the conduct of debt management, and (2) the replacement of debt
financing by corporations with equity-only financing. With such a reform
of the financial structure, banks would be required to hold reserves in currency and Federal Reserve deposits against 100 percent of their deposits.
In his 1944 paper "On Debt Policy," Simons expressed qualified support
for the 100 percent reserves proposal as follows: "Thus, we only repeat
proposals for the 100 percent reserves scheme—for which I still have no
great enthusiasm save as part of a gradualist program whose objective is
recognized (and consistently pursued) as gradual reduction and ultimate
denial of borrowing and lending powers to all corporations, especially as
regards obligations of short term" (1944a, 229).

## Conclusions

Simons's solution to the problem posed by the existence of financial assets that, like demand deposits, were seen as unstable was to propose a
reform of the financial system in a way that would reduce the quantity of

near monies and the instability of the debt structure. He continued to advocate the 100 percent reserves scheme throughout the remainder of his lifetime, but only within the context of a long-term, fundamental reform of the financial system. Knight never again referred to the scheme in his published works after his 1927 review of Soddy's book.

Simons's concerns about the potentially destabilizing role of non-banks presaged a major characteristic of the 2007–8 financial crisis. Financial innovation led to the development of financial institutions that can offer commercial-banking-type services without being subjected to the regulations applying to commercial banks. The runs on financial institutions during that crisis were not on commercial banks, but on institutions like mutual funds and investment banks. This episode suggests, as Simons fully recognized, that 100 percent reserve requirements on commercial banks' deposits would not be sufficient to prevent financial crises. Simons's solution to the problem of runs on non-banks was to ban short-term-debt issuance by non-banks.[65]

There is currently a widely held view that Chicago economists took over the idea from Soddy in 1933. Based on the evidence presented in this chapter, I conclude that, for Knight, and very probably for Simons, the principle underlying the English Bank Charter Act of 1844 was the wellspring of their advocacy of 100 percent reserves against demand deposits — an idea that aptly came to be known as the Chicago Plan of Banking Reform. Further, I contend that their advocacy of this policy prescription, based on the potentially destabilizing effects of the multiple-deposit expansion and contraction that can occur under a fractional-reserve banking system, predated the publication of Soddy's *Wealth, Virtual Wealth and Debt* in 1926.

## 4.3 Monetary-Policy Rules: Fisher versus Chicago

I have argued that the context of the nineteenth-century British debates on money was different from that of the debates on rules versus discretion in the 1930s.[66] The nineteenth-century literature focused on the automaticity properties of a mixed-currency standard. There was no discussion about discretionary monetary policy—indeed the idea of a domestically oriented monetary policy had yet to be formulated. If, then, the nineteenth-century British debates were not about rules versus discretion, where did the literature about rules versus discretion in monetary policy originate?

To address that question, we will have to probe into the nature of the policy framework developed by Irving Fisher and compare that framework with the views of Henry Simons and Lloyd Mints on policy rules.[67] As we will see, in the 1920s Fisher began advocating that monetary policy should aim to stabilize the price level. Simons, who had proposed a policy rule under which the quantity of money would be held constant in the November 1933 Chicago memorandum, began advocating a stable-price-level rule of the Fisher type in the mid-1930s. In the mid-1940s, he would be joined by Mints in advocating a price-level-stabilization policy.[68]

With both Simons and, later, Mints supporting a rule that would stabilize the price level, there has long been a presumption in the literature on the development of monetary rules that the rules proposed by Fisher and by Simons and Mints were essentially the same (Patinkin 1973a, 332–33; Weber 1980, 673; Fischer 1990, 7; Humphrey 1990, 7; Laidler 1999, 242; 2010, 72; Bordo and Rockoff 2013a, 170–71). The standard narrative runs as follows. Fisher and the two Chicagoans advocated policy rules intending to moderate the amplitude of the business cycle. While, as we shall see, the business-cycle theories underlying the rules put forward by Fisher and the Chicagoans were fundamentally different—Fisher, for the most part, attributed the cycle to an unstable money supply whereas Simons and Mints, by and large, thought that an unstable velocity of circulation of money was a primary cause of the cycle—the monetary-policy conclusions derived from the respective theories of Fisher and the Chicagoans were essentially the same—namely, monetary policy should follow a rule that aims to stabilize the price level and, thus, moderate the business cycle. Laidler (2010, 72) expressed the policy equivalence of the standard narrative as follows: "Simons . . . combined the quantity theory [of money] with a rule-based approach to monetary policy similar in many essentials to Fisher's, and with a broader commitment to *laissez faire*, while mention should also be made of . . . Lloyd Mints, who came to share his views."[69] Similarly, Bordo and Rockoff (2013a, 170) stated: "In advocating a mandate of price stability, Fisher was on the same page as Henry Simons and Lloyd Mints at the University of Chicago."[70] It follows from the standard narrative that, since the objectives of more recent rule-based policy frameworks, including those of Friedman (1960) and Taylor (1993), have also been to stabilize the price level and output growth, a direct continuity runs from the earlier rules of Fisher, Simons, and Mints to modern rules.[71]

The standard narrative presented the following puzzle. As mentioned earlier in this chapter, in the mid-1930s Fisher became an enthusiastic supporter of the 100 percent reserves proposal. In his 1935 book *100% Money*, devoted to the proposal, Fisher gave credit to Simons and his Chicago colleagues for having earlier advanced the idea (Fisher 1935a). In the Chicagoans' work on the price-level-stabilization rule, however, Simons did not give credit to Fisher for having earlier advanced that particular rule, while Mints, who did acknowledge Fisher, misstated—according to Patinkin (1973a)—the aim of Fisher's proposal. Patinkin (1973a, 332–33) expressed the puzzle in the following terms:

> In the writings [on policy rules] of Simons, I have not found any reference to these views of Fisher. And though Mints (1950, 10) did recognize that Fisher was "in more recent years . . . the strongest supporter of stabilizing the price level," he wrongly implied that this was only because of considerations of distributive justice to creditors and debtors, and not because price stability was "a necessary condition for the effective operation of a competitive system." As has just been emphasized, however—and as Mints himself had earlier recognized (1945a, 272)—this was precisely Fisher's view of the matter. In contrast, Fisher (1935a, ix) did refer to the Chicago School, and particularly Henry C. Simons, as being among the primary advocates of "100 percent money"—a proposal to which Fisher gave his unequivocal support. In order to avoid any possible misunderstanding, I wish to emphasize that what I find puzzling here is the relation of the Chicago School to Fisher's policy views, as distinct from his theoretical contributions.

Several explanations were subsequently offered to explain the puzzle. Patinkin (1993, 33) and Dimand (1998, 193) noted that, by the mid-1930s, Fisher had developed a reputation in the profession as something of a crank; he was viewed as being, among other things, a vegetarian and a prohibitionist who had made widely inaccurate predictions about the stock market;[72] consequently, the Chicagoans may have wanted to distance themselves from Fisher. Moreover, as noted earlier, Simons generally did not waste a lot of ink citing his predecessors. In what follows, I provide another possible explanation for the treatment of Fisher by the Chicagoans.

Specifically, I argue that there were subtle, but important, differences in the rationales underlying the policies put forward by the Chicagoans and by Fisher; therefore, the Chicago economists may not have considered Fisher's policy orientation to be a close progenitor of their monetary-policy framework. Beginning in the early 1920s, Fisher's aim was *not* to limit the discretionary powers of the monetary authorities but to ensure that the authorities were provided with sufficient powers over the selection and the use of policy instruments to pursue a particular outcome—price-level stability. I provide evidence that shows that Fisher's price-level-stabilization framework involved considerable discretion in the use of policy instruments and some ambiguity in the choice of policy objective.

The basis of monetary rules proposed by Simons and Mints was very different from that of Fisher. In contrast to Fisher, the words "rules versus authorities" were a central part of their lexicon; and, also in contrast to Fisher, they provided comprehensive assessments of alternative policy rules. Simons and Mints emphasized the role of discretionary policies in generating *monetary-policy* uncertainty—as opposed to price-level uncertainty—as the prime mover of the amplitude of the business cycle; a policy rule, they believed, would tie the hands of the monetary authorities and thereby stabilize private-sector expectations, helping to also stabilize the velocity of circulation of money. To Simons, a price-level rule was a second-best rule. His preferred rule under ideal conditions, including a reformulation of the financial sector and 100 percent reserve requirements, was one that fixed the quantity of money—a policy instrument—and produced a falling price level and stable output growth. The argument that the main rationale for a policy rule is to reduce monetary-policy uncertainty (by tying the hands of the monetary authorities) provides a direct link to the rules-based frameworks proposed by Friedman and Taylor.

There exist several precedents for the views expressed in what follows. First, the idea that Simons's rationale for rules grew from the conviction that discretionary monetary policy could be a major source of instability was previously noted by Director (1947a, vii), Friedman (1967), Cagan (1978), and Bordo (2019). Second, as noted in chapter 1, in the debate about the relationship between the 1930s Chicago monetary tradition and Friedman's monetary framework, Parkin (1986, 112) emphasized the continuity stemming from the Chicago emphasis on rules "running from the 1930s to Friedman and coming all the way up to . . . the rational expectations framework developed by Robert E. Lucas." None of these researchers, however, dealt with the distinction addressed in what follows—namely, the different underpinnings of the Fisher and the Chicago rules.

*Fisher on the Business Cycle and Stabilization Policy*

Fisher's views about the mechanisms generating the business cycle and the policy responses needed to moderate the cycle changed during the course of his career.[73] A common theme underlying his business-cycle theory was the role played by price-level changes in driving the cycle; a common element underlying his policy prescription was the need to maintain price-level stability. I focus on Fisher's views on these subjects from the time of the publication of his *The Purchasing Power of Money* (assisted by Harry Gunnison Brown) in 1911 until the mid-1930s.[74] My aim is to demonstrate that Fisher's formulation of a policy rule is only a distant relative of subsequent instrument rules, including those of Friedman and Taylor, the latter two of which aim to ensure that the conduct of monetary policy itself does not impose uncertainty on the economy.[75]

## Business-Cycle Theory

In his *Purchasing Power of Money*, Fisher attributed economic fluctuations to monetary shocks that, he thought, could be generated through gold discoveries, and were transmitted to the real economy through the incomplete pass-through of expected inflation to nominal interest rates. Fisher used the linear approximation connecting the nominal interest rate, $i$, the real interest rate $r$, and expected inflation, $\pi$, $i = r + \pi$, to show that the behavior of the rate of interest is largely responsible for the cycle.[76] A positive monetary shock, for example, would raise inflation, but nominal interest rates would adjust to inflation with a lag so that the real interest rate, $r = i - \pi$, would decline:[77]

> Not only will lenders require, but borrowers can afford to pay higher interest in terms of money; and to some extent competition will gradually force them to do so. Yet, we are so accustomed in our business dealings to consider money as one thing stable,—to think of a "dollar as a dollar" regardless of the passage of time, that will reluctantly yield to this process of readjustment, thus rendering it very slow and imperfect. When prices rise at the rate of 3 per cent a year, and the normal rate of interest—*i.e.* the rate which would exist were prices stationary—is 5 per cent, the actual rate, though it ought (in order to make up for the rising prices) to be 8.15 per cent, will not ordinarily reach that figure; but it may reach, say, 6 per cent, and later, 7 per cent. This inadequacy and tardiness of adjustment are fostered, moreover, by law and custom, which arbitrarily tend to keep down the rate of interest. (Fisher 1913a, 57–58)

As a result, profits would rise—and here is the source of the business cycle: because "the rate of interest [the businessman] has to pay will not adjust itself immediately" (Fisher 1911b, 59), the rise in profits leads to an increase in borrowing from the banks and a rise in deposits. And this, in turn, raises prices further and also raises the velocity of circulation of both money and deposits.

Fisher's formal presentation of the business cycle was based on the equation $MV+M'V'=PQ$, where, as before, $M$ is the stock of money in circulation, $V$ is the velocity of circulation of money, $M'$ is the level of deposits subject to check, $V'$ is the velocity of circulation of deposits, $P$ is the average price of the considerations traded for money, and $Q$ is the physical volume per year of those considerations. In the event of a positive monetary shock, the business-cycle sequence was the following:

1. Prices rise.
2. Velocities of circulation ($V$ and $V'$) increase; the [nominal] rate of interest rises but not sufficiently.
3. Profits increase, loans expand, and the Qs (i.e., the real volume of trade) increase.
4. Deposit currency ($M'$) expands relatively to money ($M$).
5. Prices continue to rise; that is, phenomenon no. 1 is repeated. Then no. 2 is re-peated, and so on. (Fisher 1913a, 63)

During the twenty or so years following the publication of *The Purchasing Power of Money*, Fisher made several refinements to the business-cycle theory developed in that book. First, in a 1919 article, "Stabilizing the Dollar," he argued that monetary shocks engender changes in the price level, which, in turn, affect profits not only through the effect of lagged adjustments of interest rates on profits but also through the effect of lagged adjustment of nominal wages on profits. To Fisher, the labor unrest experienced in the United States following World War I was, in part, the result of the lagged adjustment of nominal wages to prices, which meant that, as prices rose, real wages declined. That lagged adjustment, he argued, "relates itself to the whole question of the distribution of wealth and to labor unrest. The disproportion between the level of wages and the soaring price level has . . . been responsible for much of the recent labor agitation" (1919, 158). Fisher made a similar argument in his 1920 book *Stabilizing the Dollar*:

> The process is like this: when prices rise, great profits are made because . . . the "profiteer" or stockholder wins without effort from the bondholder and from

the employees on salary or wages. His easy profits lead him to "extend himself" until, when interest charges, rents, salaries, and wages do catch up, his prosperity ceases, he gets caught in debt, becomes bankrupt, and involves others in a chain of bankruptcies. (1920, 66)

The resulting fall in prices, Fisher argued, causes "social discontent," penalizing the debtor class, especially the farmer (1920, 68).[78] Second, Fisher argued that it is not price-level changes per se that underlie the cycle, but price-level *uncertainty*—that is, the failure to perceive the extent of price-level changes and to fully adjust interest rates, wages, and other costs in light of changes in prices. In his 1920 book, he wrote: "The chief indictment, then, of our present dollar is that it is uncertain. . . . Business is always injured by uncertainty. . . . One of the results of such uncertainty is that price fluctuations cause alternate fluctuations in business; that is, booms and crises, followed by contractions and depressions" (1920, 65).

During the Great Depression, Fisher came to a theory of the business cycle very different from the monetary theory of the cycle described above. As mentioned in chapter 2, this new theory was his debt-deflation theory of depression. A key feature of the theory was that "*new opportunities to invest at big prospective profit* . . . such as through new inventions, new industries, development of new resources, opening of new lands or new markets" fuel a boom followed by a recession (emphasis in original, 1933b, 348).[79] The new opportunities to invest lead to overconfidence, and overconfidence leads to over-indebtedness. The ensuing downturn, however, need not lead to a major depression. For the latter to take place, two factors—or "diseases"— have to be in place—"namely, *over-indebtedness* to start with and *deflation* following soon after" (emphasis in original, 1933b, 341). The process underlying severe depression, Fisher argued, worked as follows:

> The two diseases act and react on each other[;] . . . deflation caused by the debt reacts on the debt. Each dollar of debt still unpaid becomes a bigger dollar, and if the over-indebtedness with which we started was great enough, the liquidation of debts cannot keep up with the fall of prices which it causes. . . . Then, *the very effort of individuals to lessen their burden of debts increases it, because of the mass effect of the stampede to liquidate in swelling each dollar owed*. . . . The more debtors pay, the more they owe. (emphasis in original, 1933b, 344)

In common with Fisher's monetary theory of the business cycle, changes in the price level were the major force driving the dynamics of the cycle.

In contrast with that theory, the effect of the lagged nominal-interest-rate adjustment on the real interest rate played a subsidiary role in the debt-deflation theory.[80] Both of Fisher's theories led to the conclusion that to smooth the business cycle, policy should aim to stabilize the price level. As Fisher stated in his exposition of the debt-deflation theory, "If the debt-deflation theory of great depressions is essentially correct, the question of controlling the price level assumes a new importance; and those in the drivers' seats—the Federal Reserve Board and the Secretary of the Treasury . . . will in the future be held to a new accountability" (1933b, 347).

*Price-Level Stabilization*

But what about Fisher's position on rules versus discretion? How did Fisher's altered view on the business cycle affect his policy views? Under both business-cycle theories, stabilization of the price level was essential. To stabilize the price level, in his *Purchasing Power of Money* (Fisher 1911b, chap. 13) Fisher introduced the idea of a "compensated dollar," an idea that would remain part of his stabilization proposals, though with diminishing emphasis, for the next twenty-five years.[81] Importantly, Fisher thought that the proposal would be compatible with the gold standard. Although the modalities of the scheme changed over time, the basic plan was as follows. Fisher proposed that the monetary base should consist entirely of "gold bullion certificates." These certificates would entitle the holder, on any date, to convert dollars into gold bullion "of such a weight as may be officially declared to constitute a dollar for that date" (1920, 104). Specifically, the certificates would be convertible into a varying amount of gold linked to a general index of prices. Whenever the price level, for example, exceeded that of an "established" index comprising commodities in a certain period, the price of gold would be lowered by the same percentage in the next period (1920, 105).[82] In his 1920 book *Stabilizing the Dollar*, Fisher termed this procedure for adjusting the weight of gold bullion an "*adjustment rule*" (emphasis in original, 1920, 105).[83]

To explain, assume (as did Fisher) that the amount of gold in a dollar would be adjusted every two months. If the price level were, say, 1 percent above the "ideal composite" index in a certain two-month period, Fisher supposed that the monetary authority would increase the amount of gold in a dollar by 1 percent in that period, which is the same thing as saying that the dollar had appreciated by 1 percent relative to gold. If the price level failed to decline sufficiently, the monetary authority would increase the amount of gold in a dollar in the following two-month period.[84] Fisher noted that the attainment of price-level stability—or, as he called that objective, a stable dollar—would not "banish all complaint in the financial, business, and industrial world, much less serve as a substitute for progressive economies" (1920, 110). He added, however,

> It is no exaggeration to say that stabilizing the dollar would directly and indirectly accomplish more social justice and go farther in the solution of our industrial, commercial, and financial problems than almost any other reform proposed in the world to-day; and this it would do without the exertion of any repressive police force, but as simply and silently as setting our watches. (1920, 111–12)[85]

Three points about Fisher's compensated-dollar plan, in particular, and his overall price-level stabilization scheme, more generally, merit comment. First, as mentioned, Fisher continued to favor the plan, though not as a stand-alone policy, at least until the mid-1930s (Fisher 1934, 396). I return to this issue below. Second, while from 1911 to the publication of *Stabilizing the Dollar* in 1920, Fisher viewed his compensated dollar as an automatic mechanism—recall, he had referred to it as an "adjustment rule"—in the early 1920s he began to associate the compensated dollar with discretion in the use of instruments. In congressional testimony on December 18, 1922, in support of the first Goldsborough Bill—which aimed to mandate the Federal Reserve to stabilize the price level under the compensated-dollar plan—he indicated that the plan would leave room for considerable discretion on the part of the authorities:

> So it is just like steering a bicycle or an automobile. If it deviates a little you turn the wheel slightly and if that is not enough you turn it some more, or if you turn too much you turn it back, and keep the automobile in pretty nearly a straight line. Nobody can steer a machine with absolute straightness; but it is amazing how straight you can steer it if you only touch the wheel a little here and there; and that is exactly what we mean by . . . trial and error every two months. (Fisher 1922a, 25)

Following the Federal Reserve's success in using open-market operations in stabilizing the price level in the first half of the 1920s, those operations—along with the changes in the gold content of the dollar under the compensated-dollar plan, rediscounting operations, and (in the 1930s) changes in reserve requirements—constituted important, though not exclusive, parts of Fisher's policy arsenal for pursuing price-level stability.[86] He made numerous appearances throughout the 1920s and 1930s before congressional committees during which he argued that the Federal Reserve should be mandated to pursue price-level stability. In his testimony before the Committee on Banking and Currency of the House of Representatives in 1926, Fisher stated: "You have got to have your gold control [through the compensated dollar] as well as your credit control [through open-market operations and rediscounting], if you are going to prevent the terrible evils of inflation and deflation in the future" (quoted from Barber 1998, 33).

But—and here is a key difference from the 1930s and 1940s Chicago position and the second point worth mentioning—for both "gold control" and "credit control," Fisher believed that the authorities should be given discretionary powers. The use of discretion in Fisher's "gold control" policy was evident in his 1926 testimony before the House Committee on Banking and Currency. According to Barber (emphasis added, 1998, 33), in that testimony "[Fisher] held that the Federal Reserve's stabilizing role might be compromised unless *discretionary authority* to alter the gold content of the dollar were available." The notion that the Federal Reserve should be given the power to alter the gold content of the dollar remained an essential part of Fisher's policy platform into the 1930s (1932, 216; 1934, 396). On at least one occasion, he added an additional discretionary element to the power that should be entrusted to the authorities: "I would . . . remove the present restrictive limits on the gold content of the dollar . . . so as to avoid some day finding no further adjustments permissible under the law. Also I would keep redemption in gold *discretionary* on the part of the government" (emphasis added, 1934, 396). Regarding "credit control," in his 1928 book *The Money Illusion*, Fisher stated:

> When my *Stabilizing the Dollar* [1920] was written, I relegated credit control to the Appendix. . . . My aim was to make the whole plan of stabilization—both gold control and credit control—as "automatic," that is as free from discretion as possible. . . . Since that time, however, as has been shown in this book, *discretionary* credit control has actually come into existence. This, when duly perfected and duly safeguarded, will greatly simplify and improve the technique of stabilization and will make gold control secondary to credit control. (emphasis added, 1928, 192–93)

Similarly, in his 1935 book *100% Money*, Fisher wrote the following about what he called "entrusting" the authorities with conducting open-market operations:

We have long ceased to have any "automatic" system. Our system is already full of discretion. . . . The question now is not at all whether we shall have an automatic (unmanaged) or a discretionary (managed) currency. The question is whether we prefer the present irresponsible management or a responsible management with the definite objective of stabilization. (1935a, 195–96)

The third point meriting comment about Fisher's price-level framework is that on several occasions during the early 1930s Fisher argued that price-level stabilization need not be the only objective assigned to the monetary authorities. In this connection, he expressed the view: "The Federal Reserve System might well exercise such diverse functions as the care of the commodity price level and the care of the stock market price level" (1932, 133; see also 1933c, 105). In the case that two such objectives were assigned to the monetary authorities, Fisher did not elaborate on the weights to be given to the two objectives or to whether the weights would be preassigned by an institutional body such as the US Congress or would be set by the individuals in charge of monetary policy.

Fisher's emphasis on a wide range of discretionary policy instruments and the possibility of using those instruments to achieve up to two objectives deprived the framework of the simplicity and the clarity that marked the rules-based framework developed by Simons and Mints (as discussed below).[87] Joseph Reeve (1943, 165) reported: "In his voluminous testimony before the House hearings on this [the Goldsborough Bill of 1932], he [Fisher] suggested more than twenty other methods [apart from open-market operations] of increasing the volume or velocity of the circulating medium, all of which he believed had some merit." These methods would be assigned to a monetary authority with the power to use them at the authority's discretion. In both his 1932 book *Booms and Depressions* and his 1934 book *Stable Money*, Fisher again presented more than twenty measures for increasing the price level—what Fisher called "reflation"—and then stabilizing the price level.[88] In addition to the measures mentioned above, other measures included such proposals as a stamped-money scheme;[89] President Roosevelt's 1933 policy of raising the price of gold in an ad hoc—sometimes daily—manner (while keeping the United States on the gold standard);[90] the use of the profits from the higher price of gold to issue a supplemental currency designated as "yellowbacks" (to distinguish them from greenbacks); the rationing of credit; the assumption of overdue private debts permanently by government agencies in order "to forestall credit deflation" (Fisher 1933c, 106), and the provision by the

Reconstruction Finance Corporation of interest-free loans to private enterprises that agreed to enlarge their payrolls.[91]

In proposing that the above-mentioned powers be assigned to the monetary authorities, Fisher was effectively entrusting the authorities to use those powers to stabilize the commodity price level and, possibly, the stock-market price level. He was not aiming to tie the hands of the authorities in setting the policy instruments. Concerning the mandate that he proposed be assigned to the authorities to change the price of gold at their discretion, Fisher stated: "But if and when the retention of a constant price of gold and the maintenance of a fairly constant level of prices are found to be incompatible, a change can and should be made. The authorities *can be trusted* not to make it any sooner than need be" (emphasis added, 1932, 216).

### Discussion

Fisher's policy framework comprised diverse, time-varying tools, which typically provided further (in addition to open-market operations, rediscounting operations, and changes in reserve requirements) discretionary powers to the monetary authorities—for example, the determination of the gold content of the currency under the compensated-dollar scheme and the responsibility to decide whether, for domestic economic agents, the currency would be redeemable into gold. Some of Fisher's proposals were decidedly oddball, such as the stamped-money proposal. The proposal that the Fed target stock prices in addition to commodity prices introduced additional ambiguity into his framework. All the policy tools, Fisher believed, would operate alongside the international regime of the gold standard. Recent writers on the doctrinal foundations of monetary rules have singled out the price-stabilization component of Fisher's framework while overlooking the fact that Fisher had not formulated a simple, easy-to-understand, and coherent framework for monetary policy. Moreover, in contrast to the frameworks of subsequent advocates of rules, including Friedman and Taylor, Fisher's framework did not explicitly aim to reduce monetary-policy uncertainty.

### Simons on Policy Rules

Let us recall the ideas put forward on policy rules at Chicago from 1927 to 1933.

- We saw that, beginning in 1927, Paul Douglas advocated a rule under which the money supply would grow at the rate of 3 to 4 percent a year—a rate that Douglas equated with the rate of increase of production over the long term. Douglas's rule aimed to maintain a stable price level and prevent depressions. Douglas did not assess the performance of alternative rules in any of his writings in the late 1920s and early 1930s.
- In their 1931 *The Problem of Unemployment*, Douglas and Director supported a money-growth-rate rule. Those authors critiqued Fisher's compensated-dollar proposal but argued that the proposal had the merit of being automatic and not dependent on "the discretion of government or banking officials" (1931, 233).
- The April 1932 Pettengill memorandum, signed by twelve Chicagoans, made it clear that a monetary-policy rule would be desirable over the medium term. The memorandum did not refer to any specific rule.
- The March 1933 memorandum, signed by eight Chicagoans, listed three possible rules: (1) a rule that stabilizes the quantity of money; (2) a rule that stabilizes the total turnover $(MV)$; (3) a rule that stabilizes the money stock per capita. The memorandum did not provide an assessment of these rules; nor did it indicate a preference for a particular rule.
- The November memorandum, which was unsigned, but drafted by Simons with support from Director, was the outcome of discussions among the members of The Group. It provided a detailed comparison of the attributes of six rules; the preferred rule fixed the quantity of money. The memorandum argued that what is important is not the choice among alternative rules, but the selection of some precise rule because, compared with a discretionary regime, a rules-based regime would reduce uncertainty, although Simons et al. (1933) did not specifically refer to monetary-policy uncertainty.

The November 1933 memorandum carries significant historical importance. Nothing approaching its analysis of alternative rules had appeared previously in the economics literature. What the memorandum had done was to frame the central issue facing monetary policy in terms of rules versus discretion. True, in the 1920s Fisher and others had proposed that policy should follow a rule that stabilizes the price level. And during the nineteenth century members of the currency school and the banking school favored rules under which the gold standard could operate. But neither Fisher nor the participants in the nineteenth-century English debates criticized discretionary policies as such. The November 1933 Chicago memorandum was of a different character. Discretionary policies were singled out as the big, bad actor on the economic stage. Thus, the memorandum can be considered to have marked the genesis of the subsequent debate on the merits of rules versus discretion in monetary policy.

In the several years following the publication of that memorandum, Simons pushed forward the idea that rules are preferable to discretion. His next substantive endeavor into the rules-versus-discretion issue was his 1934 *A Positive Program for Laissez Faire*. Four potential rules were identified in that pamphlet: (1) a rule that fixes the quantity of money; (2) a rule that fixes the total turnover $(MV)$; (3) a rule that stabilizes an index of commodity prices; and (4) the gold standard. Simons (1934a, 63) dismissed the latter option as "totally inadequate and undesirable as a rule of national currency policy." However, in contrast to the November 1933 memorandum's preference of a rule that fixed the quantity of money, in his 1934 pamphlet, Simons did not take a position concerning which particular rule might be preferable. He stated: "There will be wide differences of opinion as to what the specific rule of monetary policy . . . should be, but this is not the place to discuss the relative merits of different possible rules" (1934a, 63). His view on the preferred rule was in a state of transition, as evidenced by his next publication on rules.

That publication was "Rules versus Authorities in Monetary Policy," which was published in the *JPE* in 1936. Whereas the November 1933 memorandum came out in favor of rules because they would reduce uncertainty, without specifying the particular kind of uncertainty, in his 1936 article Simons specified the kind of uncertainty that he viewed as the source of economic instability. He argued that a main rationale for a rule should be to reduce *monetary-policy* uncertainty:

> An enterprise system cannot function effectively in the face of extreme uncertainty as to the action of the monetary authorities or, for that matter, as to monetary legislation. We must avoid a situation where every business venture becomes largely a speculation on the future of monetary policy. (1936a, 161)

Then, in what appears to have been an anticipation of the Lucas critique, Simons expressed the view that it would not be possible to assess the merits of monetary rules in an economy that has not previously operated with rules. The adoption of rules in such an economy would effectively amount to a regime change:

> Generally speaking, it is very difficult to judge the merits of any precise rule of monetary policy on the basis of experience in an economy where no such rule

has obtained and where economic behavior has been profoundly influenced by extreme monetary uncertainty. The primary objective of reform should be that of minimizing this kind of uncertainty for the future. From the point of ultimate operation, it seems likely that many different rules would serve about equally well. (Simons 1936a, 330n12)

Simons made it clear that a rule should ideally tie the hands of the authorities—not only by setting an objective for monetary policy—but also by applying the rule to an instrument of policy; otherwise, the authorities would be given too much discretion in policy implementation. Thus, in his assessment of price-level stabilization rules, Simons argued that such rules "define programs in terms of ends, with little discussion of appropriate means; they call for an authority with a considerable range of discretionary action and would require much intelligence and judgement in their administration" (1936a, 169). A rule that fixes the quantity of money would both bind the authorities to a policy instrument—the money supply—and deliver an objective—economic stability. Such a rule, Simons argued, had several other advantages: (1) it "defines policy in terms of means [i.e., the policy instrument] not merely in terms of ends"; (2) it "is ideally simple and definite"; (3) "it is clear enough and reasonable" to be easily understood; and (4) because the money stock would be tied to the government's fiscal position, "it is compatible with the rule of balancing government revenues and expenditures" (1936a, 163–64).

Despite those advantages of a rule that fixed the quantity of money, by 1936 Simons had begun to favor a rule that stabilized the price level. What was the reason underlying the change in his thinking? Let us recall that in 1934 Simons had begun to have doubts about the effectiveness of the 100 percent reserves scheme if it applied only to demand deposits. Underlying those doubts were Simons's concerns about the influence of near-money substitutes on the stability of the demand for a narrow measure of money. A similar reasoning motivated his shift to a price level rule. As he explained, because of the inherent instability of velocity under a financial system dominated by short-term debt instruments, the "limitations [of the fixed-quantity rule] have to do mainly with the unfortunate character of our financial structure—with the abundance of what we may call 'near moneys'—*with the difficulty of defining money* in such a manner as to give practical significance to the conception of quantity" (emphasis added, 1936a, 171). Thus, "the obvious weakness of a fixed quantity lies in the danger of sharp changes on the velocity side" (1936a, 164). In line with his view that, in the absence of financial-system reform, financial innovation would undermine the working of the 100 percent reserves scheme, Simons thought that the "fixing of the quantity of circulating media might merely serve to increase the perverse variability in the amounts of 'near moneys' and in the degree of their general acceptability, just as the restrictions on the issuance of bank notes presumably served to hasten the development of deposit (checking account) banking" (1936a, 164). Once the necessary reforms to the financial system were in place to make the system more resilient against changes in velocity,[92] Simons believed that a "a rule calling for outright fixing of the total quantity of money . . . definitely merits consideration as a preferable solution in the more distant future" (1936a, 183).

### Simons, Mints, and Fisher

With the passing away of Simons in 1946, the mantle for assessing alternative rules and upholding the superiority of rules over discretion in stabilizing monetary expectations was picked up by his Chicago colleague Lloyd Mints. As we shall see in chapters 6 and 7, in his work from the mid-1940s to the early 1950s, Mints would, like Simons, provide comprehensive assessments of alternative rules. In what follows, I will briefly refer to Mints's writings on rules to show that he differentiated between the justifications for rules provided by Simons and Fisher.

As mentioned, in his writings Simons did not cite Fisher's work on price-level stabilization, a circumstance that has long been a puzzle to doctrinal historians. To help explain that puzzle, I have argued that Fisher was not a supporter of monetary rules in the sense of Simons: Fisher did not provide assessments of alternative rules; he did not compare rules with discretion — indeed, his framework entailed considerable discretion in the use of policy instruments; and he did not discuss the role of rules in reducing monetary-policy uncertainty.

Although Simons did not refer to Fisher's work on price-level stabilization, Mints *did* refer to Fisher's policy framework. And, in doing so, Mints expressed the view that Fisher's framework was not on a par with that of Simons. Consider the following.

- In his 1945 book *A History of Banking Theory*, Mints referred to Fisher, along with John Commons and Gustav Cassel, as "chief advocates of price-level stabilization" (1945a, 272). In an implicit reference to Fisher's willingness to use a multitude of policy instruments (that is, in addition to monetary-policy instruments),

Mints noted that, in contrast to Commons and Cassel, Fisher "has not been so ready ... to believe that the central bank alone could achieve this end [i.e., price-level stabilization]" (1945a, 272). Immediately following that comment, Mints made clear that he considered Simons's rules-based framework to be of a different character from the frameworks of other writers: "At any rate the problem of a legislatively prescribed and definite rule, as opposed to discretionary action by the central bank, has been explicitly presented, and very definitely defended, *only* by H. C. Simons" (emphasis added, Mints 1945a, 162).

- In his 1950 book *Monetary Policy for a Competitive Society*, Mints drew a distinction between the advocacy of *price* stability by Fisher and the espousal of *monetary* stability by Simons: "Irving Fisher has been the stoutest advocate of price-level stabilization. Henry Simons has been the more convincing, although he was more interested in the fundamental problem of monetary stability than in this particular criterion of [i.e., price-level] stability" (Mints 1950, 126).
- Mints made a similar argument in the introductory chapter of *Monetary Policy for a Competitive Society*: "Irving Fisher has been the strongest supporter of a policy of stabilizing the price level" (1950, 10). Then, after implying that Fisher was primarily concerned about considerations of distributive justice between debtors and creditors, Mints wrote:

Monetary stability, as evidenced by a stable price level, has seldom been looked upon as a necessary condition for the effective operation of a competitive system. Nevertheless, some few writers have seen the essential need for monetary stability and have proposed deliberate efforts to maintain price-level stability for this reason, rather than merely on grounds of justice. (1950, 10)

In assessing the state of play of previous work on price-level stabilization, Mints again distinguished between Simons's contributions and the work on stabilization by other economists, including Fisher:

Henry C. Simons saw most clearly the essential character of the need for monetary stability. While he believed that stabilization of the price level is (for the present, at least) the most feasible policy for this purpose, he was much more interested in pointing out the urgent need for *some* definite and announced criterion than in this, or any other, specific indicator of stability. His work was consistently directed toward the statement of the proper rules and conditions for the effective functioning of a competitive society, and he looked upon a rule for monetary stability as one of the most important of such conditions. (emphasis in original, Mints 1950, 11)

A final point about the differences in the policy perspectives between Fisher and Simons is important to mention. As discussed earlier, Fisher had been highly supportive of Roosevelt's discretionary policy concerning the price of gold in 1933. Moreover, the ascendancy of Roosevelt to the presidency in March 1933 had been followed by numerous measures that increased the government's role in the economy and restricted competition. Fisher was supportive of these measures. In his book *Mastering the Crisis*, published at the end of 1933,[93] Fisher wrote:

> In economic affairs . . . the comparatively recent idea of regulation has super-seded the dogma and brutal rule of *laissez faire*, and has been abundantly vin-dicated in doing so. . . . Today it [i.e., business] plans ahead on an unprecedented scale; and perhaps planners should take government into partnership. . . . Mr. Roosevelt is doing things which a generation ago—nay, a decade ago—would have been denounced as "socialism." (1933c, 107–8)

Simons had a decidedly different view of Roosevelt's gold policy and of the latter's policy interventions into economic affairs. In his March 1934 article on the New Deal, published in the *Chicago Tribune*, he char-acterized Roosevelt's gold policy "as a resort to cutthroat competition in the international field" that aimed "to shift unemployment to other nations."[94] As for Roosevelt's measures that sought to increase the role of the government in the economy, Simons (1934b) wrote:

> Of crucial importance now is the question of whether it will be possible af-ter the orgy of legislative witch-hunting, ill-conceived measures, and mislead-ing slogans, to retain or re-establish the essential foundations of political and economic freedom. Will it be possible to secure a stable system of rules under which a free enterprise system can function effectively?

For Simons, the rules of the game concerning money aimed to reduce monetary uncertainty to support the market-based economy.[95] For Fisher, any relationship between the policy of price-level stabilization and the preservation of the market economy was of a second order of importance.

### Fisher in the Mid-1930s

By the mid-1930s, Fisher's policy framework had undergone several nota-ble changes. First, the experience of the Great Depression provided Fisher with additional reasons for advocating that the monetary authorities be assigned a price-level objective. He expressed the view that the Fed could have prevented the Great Depression had it acted to ease monetary policy after the October 1929 stock-market crash. In this connection, Fisher (1935a, 115) pointed out that the Federal Reserve, under the leadership of Benjamin Strong, governor of the Federal Reserve Bank of New York, had pursued a policy of price-level stabilization before Strong's death in 1928; had Strong lived, Fisher suggested that the Great Depression could have been avoided, an argument that anticipated Friedman and Schwartz's (1963) indictment of the Fed.

Second, Fisher began to qualify the amount of "trust" that could be delegated to the monetary authorities. In particular, he began to argue that the authorities should not simply be directed to achieve a price-level objective, but should be disciplined for failure to achieve that objective. In a 1934 appearance before Congress for a bill calling for the creation of a Monetary Authority that would be directed to stabilize the price level, he stated:

> There should be a provision that if at any time for 3 successive months there is a deviation from that norm by as much as 10 per cent, then the board is automatically removed by that fact. It need not be impeachment proceedings and not by the President, but simply by the fact, and it would be the duty of the President to proclaim the facts—here are the facts, and according to law those men are out. (Fisher, Hearings before the Subcommittee of the Committee on Banking and Currency, House of Representatives, February 1, 1934, 28; quoted from Barber et al. 1997, 1)

Third, likely reflecting the influence of the Chicagoans, in the second edition of his book *100% Money*, published in 1936, Fisher recognized the possibility of monetary rules other than the price-level objective. As pointed out by Loef and Monissen (1999, 103n8), Fisher listed the following alternatives: a fixed total money supply; a fixed per capita money supply; and a per capita money supply at a fixed fraction of per capita income (1936, 22–27). Other than listing the alternatives and stating that his preferred rule was to stabilize the price level, Fisher did not provide a discussion of the merits of the rules or a comparison of the rules.

In the mid-1930s, Fisher publicly stated that his policy framework entailed more discretion than the Chicago fixed-quantity-of-money rule. In congressional testimony on March 22, 1935, he explained the difference between his price-level framework and the Chicago framework as follows:

Yes; you could do away with the whole management of currency. . . . All you would need to do would be to decree that we should increase our per capita circulation until it reached $250, or whatever you decided on, and then keep it there. That is really what was proposed by these — or substantially what was proposed by these economists at Chicago. Personally, I would prefer to have some discretion enter in order to get a higher degree of stabilization. This is like running your automobile with a robot instead of with a chauffeur. I would rather have a chauffeur and give him a little discretion, although he would be told where he is to go. (Fisher 1935b, 541–42)

As we shall see in the next chapter, in the late 1930s Fisher joined Paul Douglas and four non-Chicago economists in proposing a rules-based framework remarkably similar to that provided in the Chicago November 1933 memorandum and in Simons's writings of the mid-1930s.

### Garfield Cox

How widespread was the preference for rules at Chicago in the 1930s? I conjecture that the environment at Chicago in the 1930s featured discussions among members of The Group about the merits of alternative rules. The conjecture is based on both the unpublished 1932 and 1933 Chicago memoranda, which highlighted the stabilizing properties of rules, and the published works of Douglas, Director, and Simons in the first half of the 1930s, which advocated rules. To further support that conjecture, I now introduce a 1936 unpublished two-page document by Garfield Cox. The document was titled "Forums Conducted by Dr. Garfield V. Cox: General Theme; Business Cycles, Booms and Depressions; Can We Manage Money and Credit?" The forums were sponsored by the Colorado Springs Board of Education.

We were introduced to Cox in chapter 1, where it was mentioned that, in a 1980 interview, Mints stated that he considered Cox to have been a member of the 1930s Chicago school. In chapter 2, it was noted that Cox, who taught in the Business School in the 1930s, was one of twelve signatories of the 1932 Pettengill memorandum and one of the eight signatories of the March 1933 memorandum calling for the adoption of 100 percent reserves and the adoption of a policy rule.[96] In chapter 3 (n. 57), we saw that Cox had been critical of New Deal economic measures.

Cox's area of specialization was business forecasting. He published several books in the late 1920s that assessed alternative forecasting techniques.[97] During the 1930s, his journals output almost entirely consisted of (1) the evaluation of alternative forecasts produced by forecasting services, such as Babson's Statistical Organization, Harvard Economic Society, and Moody's Investor Service, and (2) book reviews, mainly of books on forecasting. In his published output, he seldom ventured away from a strict comparison of alternate forecasts. He rarely expressed views on economic policy.[98]

A notable exception to the absence of policy statements in Cox's published work occurred in a 1936 review (in the *Journal of Business of the University of Chicago*) of Lauchlin Currie's 1934 book *The Supply and Control of Money in the United States*, in which Currie advocated 100 percent reserve requirements on demand deposits. Cox called the book "an important book" (1936b, 93). He stated that the book "reflects competence in the analysis of banking statistics and genuine theoretical insight" (1936b, 94). However, he criticized the book on two fronts. First, concerning the 100 percent reserves proposal, Cox stated that the proposal overlooks the problem posed by the existence of near moneys: "[the proposal] oversimplifies the problem of distinguishing for control purposes between what is money and what is not money" (1936b, 94). As discussed above, Simons had reached an identical view in the mid-1930s. Second, Cox criticized the book because of the absence of a rule to control the quantity of money: "[the book] neglects the difficult, controversial, and crucial question of the proper objectives of a policy of control of the money supply" (1936b, 94).

Cox's unpublished 1936 document served as the basis of his presentation in Colorado Springs. The document aimed to motivate discussion in the forums, conducted by Cox, but not to advocate a specific policy. The dates of the forums listed on the document were September 21–25, 1936. It is clear from the wording at the beginning of the document that Cox was an adherent of the Chicagoan view that the business cycle is amplified by the behavior of the banking system and that policy should aim to stabilize the price level. Thus, the document began as follows:

In earlier sessions we have pointed out that our present credit system intensifies the instability of business because we inflate the currency when we borrow from banks and deflate it when we repay them. This expansion and contraction of the currency makes for short-time fluctuations in the general price level which affect the prospect for business profits and increase or decrease the volume of spending. Experts do not agree as to whether stabilization of the price level should be the *sole* objective of monetary policy, but there *is* general agreement among them that *preventing wide swings* of the price level is *one* desirable objective. (emphasis in original, Cox 1936c, 1)

What could be done to (1) prevent wide swings in bank lending and (2) stabilize the price level? Concerning the former question, one possibility, according to the document, was to put "the *creation* of circulating medium entirely in the hands of a government-appointed monetary authority, a step which would involve the abolition of the right of commercial banks to combine lending with the handling of checking deposits. This would mean, in effect, the abolition of commercial banking" (emphasis in original, Cox 1936c, 1).

Concerning the issue of stabilizing the price level, the document put forward the following rules:

The various proposed *objectives* of control by a monetary authority.

a) A fixed total quantity of circulating medium.

b) A fixed amount of circulating medium per capita.

c) A steady increase in the circulating medium at the same rate as the average annual increase in the physical volume of production and trade.

d) Stabilization of the international purchasing power of the dollar (should we have an international monetary standard?)

e) Stabilization of the internal purchasing power of the dollar (what domestic price index should be stabilized?)

f) Stabilization of the general prospect for profits. (emphasis in original, Cox 1936c, 1–2)

The document did not assess the merits of the respective rules. It concluded that, although it might not be possible to achieve "perfect control of credit, it should be possible (barring another world war) to achieve a considerably greater degree of success in the future than has been accomplished in the past" (Cox 1936c, 2).

Thus, Cox appears to have held the following views: (1) the fractional-reserve banking system amplifies the business cycle, creating credit (demand deposits) during cyclical upswings and destroying credit during cyclical downturns; (2) one way of dealing with that situation would be to deny the ability of commercial banks to lend funds from checking deposits (that is, impose 100 percent reserves on demand deposits); and (3) monetary policy should be based on a rule.

## 4.4 Conclusions

This chapter has dealt with the originality of Chicago views on the issues of rules versus discretion in monetary policy and 100 percent reserve requirements. Contrary to the widely held view among contemporary doctrinal historians, I have argued that the rules-versus-discretion debate did not originate in the currency school–banking school engagement of the eighteenth century in Britain. Both sides of that engagement were hostile to discretionary management. Both sides were in favor of an automatic mechanism to regulate the quantity of money and, thus, to stabilize the economy. Neither group believed that policy instruments should be adjusted continuously as economic events unfolded, with no public commitments about the policy makers' objectives or actions, which is the contemporary view of discretionary policies. The main difference between the two schools concerned the amount of policy *activism*—as opposed to discretion—that could be used in response to internal and external drains of gold. I conjectured that, with the ascendance of the rule-versus-discretion issue to center stage beginning in the 1970s, historians sought to use the terms employed in past policy debates and inappropriately attributed properties that do not correspond to their modern meaning to the terms found in the nineteenth-century debates. My interpretation of the role played by the rules versus discretion issue in the currency school–banking school debate corresponds to that shared by doctrinal historians before the 1970s.

There also exists a widely held view among doctrinal historians that the rules proposed by Irving Fisher in the 1920s and 1930s and Chicagoans Henry Simons and Lloyd Mints in the 1930s and 1940s were essentially the same. Each of those economists advocated a policy rule that stabilized the price level, intending to moderate the business cycle. I have argued that there were important differences between the policies put forward by the Chicagoans and by Fisher. Fisher's aim was *not* to limit the discretionary powers of the monetary authorities but to ensure that those authorities were provided with sufficient powers over the selection and the use of policy instruments to pursue a particular outcome—price-level stability. In contrast to Fisher, Simons and Mints advocated a policy rule because they believed that it would tie the hands of the monetary authorities and thereby stabilize private-sector expectations. In contrast to Fisher, Simons and Mints emphasized the role of discretionary policies in generating *monetary-policy* uncertainty. Simons's preferred rule under a reformed financial system fixed the quantity of money—a policy instrument. There was a specific reason that the rules-versus-discretion literature—with its emphasis on monetary-policy certainty—originated in the 1930s. During the 1920s the Federal Reserve practiced discretionary policies. Its reaction function changed in an unsystematic way during that decade, culminating in the Great Depression. In reaction to the Fed's unsystematic policies, Chicago economists sought to avert the damage produced by discretion. My argument that there was a fundamental difference between the policy frameworks of Fisher and the Chicagoans helps resolve the long-standing puzzle concerning why the Chicagoans did not give Fisher adequate credit for having motivated their policy framework. Specifically, the Chicagoans did not consider Fisher to have been a close progenitor of their policy orientation.

On the issue of 100 percent reserve requirements on demand deposits, the catalyst of that proposal was the English Bank Act of 1844. Like the motivation underpinning the Bank Act of 1844, the Chicago proposal for 100 percent reserves aimed to moderate the amplitude of economic fluctuations and to prevent banking crises. Both the Bank Act of 1844 and the Chicago proposal assumed that policy discretion exacerbated the business cycle. Both aimed to reform the banking system through a separation of the money-creation function from the money-lending function of banks. In contrast to the Bank Act of 1844, which applied 100 percent marginal-reserve requirements to Bank of England notes, the Chicago proposal aimed to ensure the security of demand deposits by fully backing such deposits with central-bank notes and banks' reserves with the central bank. The Chicago proposal aimed to provide better control of the money supply. Under the Bank Act of 1844, seigniorage remained with the private owners of the Bank of England. Under the Chicago proposal, the government would own the central bank, thereby earning the seigniorage. The Bank Act of 1844—and, therefore, the Chicago proposal—was inspired by David Ricardo's idea of a state-owned central bank comprising an Issue Department and a Banking Department.

In 1926, Frederick Soddy, a Nobel laureate in chemistry, published a book in which he proposed the 100 percent reserves scheme. Knight reviewed the book a year later. Following the strong interest generated by the Chicago proposal in 1933, Soddy claimed that the Chicagoans did not give him credit for having originated the idea of 100 percent reserves on demand deposits. Soddy's claim of origination gained traction. There is currently a widely held view that Soddy was the progenitor of the Chicago 100 percent reserves scheme. Correspondingly, there is also a widely held view that the 1933 Chicago proposal for 100 percent reserves was developed almost concurrently with similar proposals that emerged around that time, especially that of Lauchlin Currie, who came up with a 100 percent reserves scheme in 1934. I have provided evidence that both Knight and Simons developed the idea in the early 1920s, based on a modification of the modalities of the 1844 English Bank Charter Act of 1844. Thus, I conclude that, on the issues of both monetary-policy rules and 100 percent reserves, the Chicagoans deserve considerable credit for originality.

## CHAPTER FIVE

# Into the Academic Wilderness

We have seen that Chicago economists developed a policy-centric approach to the quantity theory of money during the late 1920s and early 1930s. That approach included the use of money-financed fiscal deficits to combat the Great Depression, flexible exchange rates to allow policy makers to pursue domestic economic objectives, monetary-policy rules to reduce the uncertainty inherent in discretionary policies, and 100 percent reserve requirements on demand deposits to help control the money supply and to stabilize credit creation and the business cycle.[1] A singular characteristic of the Chicago monetary tradition was its use of group memoranda, based on discussions in departmental meetings and social gatherings, to forge and promote common policy positions. We have also seen that Jacob Viner often disagreed with the other core Chicagoans on policy issues. He refused to sign the key March 1933 memorandum that introduced the idea of 100 percent reserves into professional discourse and that espoused flexible exchange rates, policy rules, and fiscal deficits financed by money creation. Moreover, in 1933 and 1934 a schism based primarily on political differences formed between Paul Douglas, on one side, and Frank Knight, Aaron Director, and Henry Simons, on the other. The schism resulted in Director's release from the faculty and the denial of tenure to Simons. Amid what had become a fractious environment among the core members of The Group, after 1933 the practice of producing joint policy memoranda at Chicago ceased. That practice would resume in the late 1940s with the arrival of Milton Friedman on the scene.[2] For about fifteen years after 1933, the views of the members of The Group on monetary issues were expressed solely in their individual works.

In this chapter, I discuss the writings of the core group of Chicago-ans mainly from the mid-1930s to the mid-1940s. Those years marked a revolution in thinking about macroeconomic issues. The revolution was provoked by the publication of John Maynard Keynes's *The General Theory of Employment, Interest and Money* (1936a), the policy message of which quickly swept through the economics profession. In his book, Keynes advocated fiscal deficits to combat depressions and provided a theoretical basis for the deficits. The tenor of those years was well captured in the 1948 publication by the American Economic Association (AEA) of the volume *A Survey of Contemporary Economics*, edited by Howard Ellis.[3] The volume was the product of the Committee on the Development of Economic Thinking and Information, established by the AEA in April 1945. Ellis stated that the primary purpose of the volume was to provide an account of the "main ideas—both analytical devices and their practical application to public policy—which have evolved during the last ten or fifteen years" (Ellis 1948, v). The most cited entry—by far—in the index of names at the end of the volume was that of Keynes, who received seventy citations. The second-most-cited author was John Hicks, who received thirty-four citations. The volume comprised thirteen chapters, each of which surveyed an important field of economics; each chapter was authored by a prominent contributor to the field being surveyed. The volume included a survey paper titled "Monetary Theory" authored by Henry Villard.[4] In the introduction to his paper, Villard wrote the following about the status of the subject of money in the academic community at that time:

> In the same way recent monetary theory directly reflects the unprecedented depression which rocked the industrialized world during the nineteen-thirties; in the United States, perhaps worse hit than any other country, the increase in productive capital, which had averaged 6 per cent a year for the first three decades of the century, over the 'thirties as a whole was negligible in amount. As a result the center of interest has in general shifted from the factors determining the quantity of money and its effect on the general level of prices to those determining the level of output and employment. In addition, the purely monetary devices for control, on which great store had been laid, were found to be broadly ineffective, taken by themselves, in bringing about recovery from the Great Depression. And finally, as a result of the way in which the war was financed, it seems quite likely that it will prove impossible to use such devices for the effective control of a future boom. The general change in emphasis is well indicated by the altered character of university courses: in 1930 an outstanding elementary text devoted 144 of its 1250 pages to Money and Banking

and 16 to the Business Cycle; in 1947 a new elementary text devoted 205 of its 700 pages to National Income and Employment and 55 to Money and the Interest Rate! (Villard 1948, 314)[5]

What reception did the Chicagoans give to the *General Theory*? Did they, like most other members of the economics profession, succumb to the Keynesian revolution? As mentioned in chapter 1, Harry Johnson (1971, 10–11) accused Friedman of having "invented" the notion that a "small band of the initiated" at Chicago resisted the Keynesian revolution while preserving the fundamental truth of the quantity theory "through the dark years of the Keynesian despotism." In this and the following chapters, I assess the validity of Johnson's accusation.

This chapter focuses on the works of Simons, Douglas, Knight, Viner, and Director on the subject of money. Simons's work on money formed part of a broader program aimed at supporting a free-market system; this chapter describes that program. Like Simons, Knight supported monetary rules to eliminate discretion and prevent the government from destabilizing a well-functioning free-market system. In this context, I discuss the reasons that led Knight to advocate laissez-faire. During the decade examined in this chapter, Lloyd Mints appears to have been absorbed in writing his scholarly book *A History of Banking Theory*, published in 1945. As mentioned previously, Mints did not publish anything, apart from book reviews, from 1931 until 1945. I deal with Mints's writings from 1945 onward in the next two chapters. Although Director was away from Chicago during most of the period under consideration, that economist published an overlooked article on monetary policy in 1940, an article that was very much in the spirit of the Chicago monetary tradition. I discuss the contents of that article in this chapter. In the following chapters, I describe Director's contributions to the 1952 conference volume *Defense, Controls, and Inflation*, a volume that Director edited, and previously undiscovered *unpublished* writings on money by Director in the decade following his return to Chicago in 1946. A priori, Douglas would seem to have been susceptible to Keynesian views—Keynes (1936a, chapter 22, section 4, and chapter 23, section 7) acknowledged that the *General Theory* had roots in underconsumptionism, to which Douglas had subscribed in the late 1920s and the early 1930s. As I will show, however, during the mid- and late 1930s Douglas became increasingly concerned with keeping investment decisions in *private* hands. During those years, Douglas moved closer to the policy views held by Simons, Knight, and Director. Three

Chicagoans—Viner, Knight, and Simons—published reviews of the *General Theory*. The review by Viner was, on balance, favorable; the reviews by Simons and Knight were highly critical. I discuss those reviews and other writings by those three economists in the late 1930s and early 1940s in this chapter.


## 5.1 Simons


With the publication of *A Positive Program for Laissez Faire* in 1934, Henry Simons inaugurated an agenda supporting a libertarian society. During the next twelve years—that is, until his death in 1946—Simons produced a series of essays that restated and refined that agenda. Simons's support of a free-market system was a response to the rise of totalitarian regimes in Europe and what he perceived as the cartelization of business under the aegis of the Roosevelt administration.[6] His writings were polished, loquacious, acerbic, embellished with grand pronouncements, and free of technical jargon, mathematics, and statistics (Lewis 1946, 668; H. Stein 1987, 335). Those writings influenced both his colleagues and his students. Herbert Stein (1987, 335) characterized Simons's literary style in the following terms:[7] "It was not very difficult but difficult enough to leave the reader with a sense of accomplishment at having recognized its merits. He gave his readers and students a feeling of being initiated into a select club that had great insights that politicians, businessmen, and most economists were intellectually, morally, and ethically incapable of appreciating." As an example of Simons's literary style, consider his comparison of a competitive economic system with a system based on the welfare state presented in his 1945 paper "The Beveridge Program: An Unsympathetic Interpretation."[8]

> [The] strength [of the competitive system] is in its implied political philosophy. Its wisdom is that of seeking solutions which are within the rule of law, compatible with great dispersion or deconcentration of power, and conductive to extensive supranational organization on a basis that facilitates indefinite peaceful extension. Certainly another kind of system, ruled by authorities, *might be* more efficient and more progressive—if one excludes liberty as an aspect of efficiency and capacity for freedom and responsibility, among individuals and among nations, as a measure of progress. Discretionary authorities, omniscient and benevolent, surely could in some sense do better than any scheme involving democratic, legislative rules and competitive dispersion of power. After any

disturbing change they could promptly effect the same arrangements which competition would achieve slowly or with "unnecessary" oscillations. Indeed, they could probably avoid all real disturbances by anticipating them! But some of us dislike government by authorities, partly because we think they would not be wise and good and partly because we would still dislike it if they were. (emphasis in original, 1945a, 308–9)

Among those whom Simons strongly influenced were Aaron Director, Lloyd Mints, Allen Wallis, and Milton Friedman—none of whom took a course with Simons.[9]

In chapter 3 we saw that the main objective of *A Positive Program for Laissez Faire* was to lay down the components of a program aimed at preserving the values of a simple, unregulated market system for allocating resources to competing uses. Simons set down the specific components of that program as follows.

The main elements in a sound liberal program may be defined in terms of five proposals or objectives (in a descending scale of relative importance):

I.    Elimination of private monopoly in all its forms. . . .

II.   Establishment of more definite and adequate "rules of the game" with respect to money. . . .

III.  Drastic change in our whole tax system, with regard primarily for the effects of taxation upon the distribution of wealth and income. . . .

IV.   Gradual withdrawal of the enormous differential subsidies implicit in our present tariff system. . . .

V.    Limitation upon the squandering of our resources in advertising and selling activities. (Simons 1934a, 57)

The placement of the "elimination of private monopoly" at the top of the list reflected Simons's belief that monopoly is "*the great enemy of democracy, in all its forms*" (emphasis in original, 1934a, 43).[10] He believed that monopolies were responsible for price and wage rigidities, converting what would have been (in the absence of the rigidities) a price cycle into an output cycle with no downward limit. Moreover, monopolies interfered with efficient (equal productivity) allocation of resources (Lewis 1946, 699). His views concerning monopolies, however, changed over the years. In 1934, he thought that the "abolition of private monopoly . . . is the *sine qua non*" of a free-market policy (1934a, 57); he viewed industrial monopolies and labor unions on an equal footing (1934a, 48–49). By the 1940s, Simons no longer considered industrial monopolies a force to be reckoned with. In his 1944 paper "Some Reflections on Syndicalism," he asserted that "enterprise monopoly . . . is a skin disease, easy to correct . . . and usually moderate in its abuses, since its powers are necessarily small, and since the danger of political reckoning is never very remote" (1944b, 130). Similarly, in a 1945 paper (published posthumously in 1948), "A Political Credo," he wrote: "Industrial monopolies are not yet a serious evil" (1945b, 35).[11] In that latter paper he argued that "the hard monopoly problem is labor organization" (1945b, 35).[12] The growth of labor unions, he thought, had been encouraged by the policies of Franklin Delano Roosevelt's administrations. In his 1942 paper "Hansen on Fiscal Policy," Simons wrote: "In labor policy, however, we have sown the wind. Government, long hostile to other monopolies, suddenly sponsored and promoted widespread organization of labor monopolies, which democracy cannot endure, cannot control without destroying, and perhaps cannot destroy without destroying itself" (1942a, 193).[13]

Why did Simons consider labor unions to be an overriding problem? For one thing, he considered the effects of the labor union movement on the capitalist system to be essentially the same as those of the communist movement. Simons (1944b, 150) asserted: "Unionists are much like our Communist friends. . . . Communists are out to destroy capitalism; unionists are out to destroy competition in labor markets." More precisely, Simons's enmity toward labor unions reflected the following factors. In a free-market economy, he believed, wages are set at levels that bring forth an adequate supply of labor in competition with other employment opportunities; trade unions block this process. They restrict entrance into specific trades. They impose cost-increasing working rules in the trades in which they operate. They impede cost-reducing innovations and practice "racial and sex discriminations." They lead to barriers to the mobility of labor among related trades. Their impacts on wage rates "preclude the expansion of production and employment in their field" (1944b, 130–31). Because "they have little to fear" from presidential administrations, Congress, or the courts, "they enjoy an access to violence which is unparalleled in other monopolies" (1944b, 130). The unorganized workers lose as a result of the unions because they are denied access to higher-wage areas and are forced to compete with workers who would otherwise have been employed in the (restricted) higher-wage occupations had those occupations been open to competition. These factors, Simons thought, were a major reason for the low levels of private investment in the 1930s and the early 1940s.

Simons believed that natural monopolies—"areas where competition is notoriously inadequate" (1942a, 195)—should be socialized. In 1934, he singled out two such industries: "the railroads [and] the utilities" (1934a, 51). In the early 1940s, the railroads had been dropped from the list, while oil extraction and life insurance had been added (1942a, 195).

Concerning the establishment of "more definite and adequate 'rules of the game' with respect to money," Simons believed that the role of government is to make the rules and to ensure that they are followed. The government's role, in other words, is constitutional, as opposed to administrative (Hardy 1948, 307). To Simons, active management of the currency by the government would mean that the government was a player in the game, thus violating the liberal creed (Carlson 1988, 3). Simons put it as follows:

> The liberal creed demands the organization of our economic life largely through individual participation in a game *with definite rules*. It calls upon the state to provide a stable framework of rules within which enterprise and competition may effectively control and direct the production and distribution of goods. The essential conception is that of a genuine division of labor between competitive (market) and political controls—a division of labor within which competition has a major, or at least proximately primary, place. (emphasis added, 1936a, 160)

As discussed in chapter 4, in *A Positive Program for Laissez Faire* Simons did not single out a preference for a particular monetary-policy rule—in contrast to the view expressed in the November 1933 memorandum in which the preferred rule fixed the quantity of money. We saw in that chapter, however, that in his 1936 paper "Rules versus Authorities in Monetary Policy," Simons came out in favor of a rule that stabilizes the price level. He recognized that such a rule would necessarily provide the authorities with discretion to determine the quantity of money—but he was concerned that the high degree of substitutability between money and "near moneys" would render a fixed-money-supply rule inoperable.[14] Thus, by 1936 he favored a price-level-stabilization rule pending a reform of the financial system such that a fixed-money-supply rule could be implemented. By the 1940s, his preference for a rule that stabilizes the price level had firmed. In his 1944 paper "On Debt Policy," he wrote:

> I persist in the notions that stabilization of the value of money, however unrealized, is the only rule or principle of monetary-fiscal policy we have ever had, that it is the only rule really available to a democratic society, and that only

by recognizing and by accepting this rule explicitly can legislatures be made responsible financially or business be spared intolerable monetary uncertainty. (1944a, 224)

As also discussed in chapter 4, from the mid-1930s Simons argued that the financial system should be reformed in such a way that short-term, private fixed-money contracts (e.g., commercial paper, call loans, corporate bonds) would be eliminated; under the proposed reform, public debt would be converted into currency and consols, and debt financing by corporations would be replaced by equity-only financing. Over time, the consols would be converted into money (Simons 1945b, 38; 1946, 239). The proposal aimed to minimize variations in the velocity of circulation of money.[15] Effectively, implementation of the proposal would lead to a prohibition of all (private-sector and government) short-term fixed-money contracts, which Simons regarded as de facto money. Combined with Simons's call for 100 percent reserves, the changes in the financial system would put the monetary authorities in a position to better implement a monetary rule. The changes in the financial system that Simons proposed, however, would markedly restrict the scope for private-sector activity in the credit market. Effectively, Simons believed that a monetary rule could best be made viable in a highly regulated financial system.[16] Such a system would have prevented a wide range of financial transactions between borrowers and lenders and acted as a brake on the accumulation and allocation of capital (Rockoff 2015, 16).

In the implementation of the policy rule, Simons considered that the US Treasury should be the responsible institution; changes in the quantity of money, he thought, should be effected through variations in the government's fiscal position.[17] He believed that measures that operated through the banking system would be ineffective. Thus, in "Rules versus Authorities in Monetary Policy," he explained:

The task [i.e., control over the quantity of money] is certainly not one to be intrusted to banking authorities, with their limited powers and restricted techniques, as should be abundantly evident from recent experience. Ultimate control over the value of money lies in fiscal practices—in the spending, taxing, and borrowing operations of the central government. Thus, in an adequate scheme for price-level stabilization, the Treasury would be the primary administrative agency; and all the fiscal powers of Congress would be placed behind (and their exercise religiously limited by) the monetary rule. (Simons 1936a, 175)[18]

Similarly, in his paper "Hansen on Fiscal Policy," Simons criticized the view that changes in the money supply could be attained only through central-bank action. In assessing Alvin Hansen's conversion to Keynesian economics, Simons wrote:

> But another distinction conceals the conversion, namely, distinction between monetary and fiscal measures. Hansen, advocating the latter, thus dissociates himself nominally from monetary theorists by representing such people as advocates of mere central-bank action. This provides a lonely category for Mr. [Ralph] Hawtrey, while denying classification to those for whom central-bank action is a feeble, inadequate, and anomalous implementation of monetary policy. If the name at issue be granted to those advocating schemes of monetary compensation or stabilization which would employ all the borrowing, spending, taxing, and issue powers of the central government, then Hansen not only belongs among them but stands as an extremist in that company. (1942a, 190)[19]

Why did Simons consider central-bank action to be a feeble and inadequate way to implement monetary policy? He believed that monetary policy had to operate on the quantity of money to be effective. Central-bank actions, however, entail the substitution of high-powered money for short-term government debt, which Simons considered de facto money. Consequently, those actions, he believed, would not change the quantity of money (reserves plus currency) plus near monies and, thus, would be ineffective. The notion that monetary-policy measures that operate through the banking system are ineffective was a common feature of the Chicago monetary tradition of the 1930s and 1940s.[20]

In his works published toward the end of his life, Simons allowed some scope for open-market operations to complement fiscally generated changes in the money supply. Thus, in his 1944 paper "On Debt Policy," he argued the federal government "may perhaps, on some occasions properly borrow money; that is, open-market operations are a convenient, traditional, and perhaps desirable temporizing means of currency regulation" (1944a, 220). Similarly, in his paper "The US Holds the Cards," also published in 1944, Simons stated that the "main implementation of monetary stabilization should be found in changes of the relative flows of federal revenues and expenditures," but with "traditional open-market policy . . . [used] as secondary or temporizing measures" (1944d, 158).[21] As we will see in the next chapter, Lloyd Mints would also advocate the combined use of changes in the government's fiscal position and open-market operations to attain changes in the money supply.

The tax system played two essential roles in Simons's framework. First, Simons viewed the progressive-income-tax system as the major instrument for mitigating inequalities that arise in a capitalist society. Since progressive income taxation did not interfere substantially with the operation of the market, it provided the most appropriate means for achieving greater equality.[22] Simons wrote: "Our proposal with reference to taxation is based on the view (1) that reduction in inequality is immensely important; (2) progressive taxation is both an effective means and, within the existing framework of institutions, the only effective means to that end" (1934a, 65).[23] Consequently, he called for "drastic alteration in the rate structure of the personal income tax, with more rapid progression" (1934a, 67). Under the proposal presented in *A Positive Program for Laissez Faire*, Simons envisaged that "something like 10 percent of the whole national income would pass, via personal income taxation into the hands of government" (1934a, 68).

Second, he thought that a progressive income tax should be the mainstay of federal revenue; in times of depression, the money supply should be increased by lowering the income tax—preferably by changing personal exemptions (and, if necessary, "across-the-board" decreases in rates); once a "suitable scale of marginal or bracket [tax] rates had been established, these rates should not be manipulated" (1945c, 281). He generally opposed the use of government expenditures to generate changes in the fiscal deficit since higher deficits would imply a larger government role in economic activity.[24] He believed that the relevant measure of income for taxable purposes should be the taxpayers' consumption of goods and services (but excluding capital expenditures) plus the addition to the taxpayers' net assets during the accounting period.[25] Under his measure, capital gains, gifts, inheritances, and bequests would be treated as income—anything that increased the consumer's relative command over real resources (G. Stigler 1974, 4). Viewing the personal income tax as the only equitable tax, Simons advocated the abolition of sales taxation and the taxation of corporate earnings.[26]

Simons thought that competition should extend beyond national borders. Consequently, he strongly supported free trade. "Free foreign trade," he declared, "would largely frustrate all major enterprises in economic centralization or in direct federal control of relative prices, wages or production" (1945b, 24). He viewed "the enormous differential subsidies inherent in our present tariff system as one of the worst deviations from a free economy" (1934a, 57). Among other things, he opposed tariffs because he considered them a form of subsidies borne by the consumers in proportion to their consumption and because tariffs supported particular industries whose products would otherwise be imported (1934a, 69). In the 1940s, he was hopeful that the negotiations between the United States and Britain for a new world economic order would help achieve a significant reduction in tariffs.

Simons's proposal to eliminate tariffs was also tied to his belief in the efficacy of flexible exchange rates. In a 1934 paper, "Currency Systems and Commercial Policy," he affirmed that a fixed-exchange-rate regime, such as the gold standard, is "conducive to protectionism because it renders obscure the adverse effects of higher tariff duties. The immediately beneficial effect on newly protected industries is evident; but the burden on other industries is not evident at all" (1934c, 346). Anticipating an argument made by Friedman in his 1953 paper "The Case for Flexible Exchange Rates," Simons expressed the view that adjustments to shocks under fixed exchange rates "work themselves out through a slow and elaborate change in the whole structure of domestic prices and wages" (1934c, 346). In contrast, under flexible exchange rates, "disturbances to trade would involve an initial change in the [nominal] exchange rates" (1934c, 347). Thus, a flexible-exchange-rate regime would avoid the costly changes to wages and output associated with adjustments to shocks under fixed-exchange-rate systems. Regarding the frequently made argument that flexible exchange rates would be excessively volatile and, thus, hamper international trade, Simons—again anticipating an argument made by Friedman (1953b)—stated: "Given orderly internal management of independent currencies according to specified rules, adequate future markets for foreign exchange would surely develop. Thus the risks of exchange rate fluctuations would be assumed by specialists—and probably at no real cost to the community except for what the specialists might have produced in other employments" (Simons 1934c, 347).[27]

Simons also opposed tariffs because he thought they encouraged a larger government role in economic affairs. In his 1944 article "The US Holds the Cards," he argued: "We cannot have the traditional federal interference with private importation without being driven into other governmental economic policies that are anathema to conservatives and simply incompatible with liberty, individualism, or free enterprise" (1944d, 159). He continued: "The real issue concerns a more extreme and epochal

choice, namely, a choice between free external trade and national, collectivist monopolies of foreign trade" (1944d, 159). In the 1940s, his free-
trade program extended beyond the elimination of tariff barriers. It also
included the "elimination of quota restrictions, import preferences or
discrimination, export subsidies, and bilateral or barter trading" (Simons
1943, 244).

More generally, Simons's 1944 paper "The US Holds the Cards" dealt
with the post–World War II international monetary order. In this connection, Simons advocated a system under which national authorities would
follow rules that aimed to stabilize the domestic price level. Price-level
stabilization, he believed, would secure "reasonable stability" of exchange
rates (1944d, 200). Correspondingly, he thought that the Keynes-White
plan would be compatible with a system under which national authorities
practiced price-level stabilization. Thus, the plan, if adhered to, would produce exchange-rate stability. For that reason, he supported that plan. As
we shall see, in 1943 he wrote a letter to Keynes in which he complimented
Keynes for his work on devising a blueprint for the international monetary system. One final point about Simons's views in "The US Holds the
Cards" deserves mention. Simons accurately predicted the ascendance of
the US dollar as the leading international currency in the postwar world:
"the dollar surely will be," he stated, "the predominant world currency"
(1944d, 157).[28]

The fifth and final element of Simons's 1934 program was the limitation of resources used for advertising. In his *A Positive Program for Laissez Faire*, Simons expressed the view that "the enormous sum [spent] on
advertising led to unlimited 'economic waste'" (1934a, 71). Nevertheless,
he acknowledged that "unlike the other [four] proposals, it is not immediately indispensable for survival of our economic and political system"
(1934a, 72). In his subsequent writings, this proposal was withdrawn from
his program.

Among the classical writers who helped shape Simons's views were
Adam Smith and Jeremy Bentham. In a 1941 paper, "For a Free-Market
Liberalism," Simons (1941, 105) called Smith and Bentham "the great po-
litical philosophers of modern democracy." Simons credited Smith and
Bentham for providing the following "special insight":

> that political and economic power must be widely disbursed and decentral-
> ized in a world that would be free; that economic control must, to that end, be
> largely divorced from the state and effected through a competitive process in

which participants are relatively small and anonymous; and that the state must jealously guard its prerogatives of controlling relative prices (and wages), not for the purpose of exercising them directly itself but to prevent organized minorities from usurping and using them against the common interest. (1941, 105)

Simons's agenda for a free-market economy encompassed a considerable variety of governmental services. In *A Positive Program for Laissez Faire* (1934a, 68), he described those services: "There are remarkable opportunities for extending the range of socialized consumption (medical services, recreation, education, music, drama, etc.) and, especially, for extending the range of social welfare activities." In the same publication, he wrote: "There are endless possibilities for increasing and improving the community's 'free income' in the form of governmental services, especially through extension of social welfare activities" (1934a, 76).

In retrospect, some of Simons's views appear to have been highly interventionist. This appraisal especially applies to Simons's views in the early part of his career on such issues as the use of antitrust legislation to restructure industry and the nationalization of natural monopolies, and to his proposals throughout his career to restrict the scope for private-sector activity in financial markets. However, Simons's writings need to be viewed in light of the political environment at the time in which he wrote, an environment in which, as mentioned, many American intellectuals favored an expanded role for government in economic affairs. In this connection, Friedman, in referring to the political environment during which *A Positive Program for Laissez Faire* was published, stated: "Remember, probably in 1934 when it appeared, I would say that close to a majority of the social scientists at the University of Chicago were either members of the Communist party or very close to it" (quoted in Kitch 1983, 178).

## Simons and Hansen

We already encountered Alvin Hansen's name in this and previous chapters. In the present chapter, we saw that Simons, in his 1942 article "Hansen on Fiscal Policy," expressed the view that Hansen's definition of monetary-policy actions—a definition that confined such actions to central-bank measures—was overly restrictive; specifically, Hansen's definition excluded money-supply changes produced through the government's fiscal position. As mentioned, the 1942 article on Hansen was a review of Hansen's 1941 book *Fiscal Policy and Business Cycles*. The review was published in the

*JPE* and, at thirty-six pages, was one of the longest articles that Simons ever published.[29] Why did Hansen's book merit such a lengthy review in Simons's estimation? To address that question, we must briefly consider Hansen's policy views both in his 1941 book and in the years preceding the publication of that book. Doing so will shed light on the impact of the Keynesian revolution on the economics profession of the early 1940s and the nature of the resistance to Keynesian ideas that emerged among members of The Group.

Hansen taught at the University of Minnesota from 1919 to 1937. In the fall of 1937, he became the first Littauer Professor of Political Economy at Harvard, where he remained until his retirement in 1956.[30] At Harvard, Hansen and John H. Williams established the Fiscal Policy Seminar; Barber (1987, 200) credited Hansen's involvement in the seminar for bringing Hansen close to the center of the contemporaneous debate on policy issues.

During the 1920s and through the mid-1930s, Hansen was a critic of policies that he viewed as major deviations from laissez-faire. He had been markedly unsympathetic to policies, shaped in the 1920s, that aimed to contain cyclical downswings through accelerated spending on public works (Barber 1985, 163–64). Hansen attributed business cycles to exogenous factors, such as technological developments, territorial and population changes, and alterations in the accessibility of natural resources; these factors induced changes in profit expectations relative to interest costs and generated changes in investment (Brown 1989, 1). In the early 1930s, Hansen maintained that public-works spending, though well intentioned, served to prolong the cost reductions needed to bring about recovery from depressions (Hansen 1932, 366); he attributed the severity of the Great Depression, in part, to longer-term structural factors, including the decline in capital spending opportunities produced by the completion of Europe's postwar reconstruction, reduced rates of growth in two major capital-absorbing sectors in the United States—the automobile and the residential construction industries—and declining population-growth rates (Barber 1987, 195).

Against this personal intellectual backdrop, Hansen wrote two reviews of Keynes's *General Theory*. One review, aimed at a wide academic audience, was published in the *Yale Review* in June 1936. The second review, aimed at professional economists, was published in the *JPE* in October 1936. Both reviews were very critical of Keynes's book.

In the *Yale Review*, Hansen wrote that Keynes had abandoned the analytical edifice of the *Treatise on Money* under a barrage of damaging attacks by critics of the book who considered each theoretical structure to be "untenable" (Hansen 1936a, 828). Hansen predicted that the *General Theory*'s analytical edifice, under which equilibrium could be reached at less than full employment, was "not tenable except upon the assumption of an approach to a rigid economy in which costs are highly inflexible and supplies are monopolistically controlled" (1936a, 829). Hansen asserted that "it is reasonably safe to predict that Keynes's new book will, so far as his theoretical apparatus is concerned, fare little better that did the *Treatise*" (1936a, 829). Nevertheless, the review betrayed an indication of his future views concerning secular stagnation. In particular, Hansen pointed out that Keynes's theory of unemployment equilibrium depended on the assumption that the marginal efficiency of new investment is low, which Hansen called a "state of technological stagnation"; in such a state the marginal efficiency of capital would fall below the lowest attainable rate of interest, thereby preventing investment from equaling saving at full employment.

Hansen's review in the *JPE* was similarly critical of the *General Theory*. He again observed that criticisms leveled at the *Treatise* left "the theoretical structure [of that book] without a foundation and compelled either abandonment or a radical reconstruction" (1936b, 669). In Hansen's estimation, several flaws marred Keynes's new theoretical structure. First, one factor that underpinned Keynes's thesis that equilibrium could be reached at a point below full employment was Keynes's assumption that the marginal propensity to consume is stable and its value is less than one. Hansen argued that Keynes's presentation of the marginal propensity to consume was muddled because Keynes had failed to provide precise definitions—for example, whether the relevant definition of income is "anticipated income" or "realized income." Hansen maintained that "these difficulties and obscurities arise from Keynes's failure to give exact definitions and to employ them consistently" (1936b, 675–76). Second, Hansen asserted that the condition of underemployment equilibrium "is not possible" without "one necessary condition"; that condition, he argued, was "cost rigidity (including wage rates) and monopolistic control of supplies," a condition that would be "made much worse should it turn out that we are approaching a society in which the outlets for investment are likely to prove more limited than in the past century" (1936b, 680). That condition, Hansen alleged, had been foreseen in classical economic analysis; and it would form the core of Hansen's subsequent articulation of the secular-stagnation thesis. The fate of the *General Theory*, Hansen concluded, would be similar to the fate of the *Treatise*. In the final paragraph, Hansen expressed the following view: "The book under review is not a landmark in the sense that it lays a foundation for a 'new economics.' ...The book is more a symptom of economic trends than a foundation stone upon which a science can be built" (Hansen 1936b, 686).[31]

By the late 1930s, Hansen had undergone an intellectual epiphany; he had become a convert to, and propagator of, Keynesian economics. The conversion is illustrated in two books—*Full Recovery and Stagnation* (1938) and *Fiscal Policy and Business Cycles* (1941). The former volume is a compilation of Hansen's essays, some of which had been previously published, including the 1936 review of the *General Theory* published in the *JPE*. The 1938 reprint of the *JPE* review of the *General Theory*, however, included additions to, and deletions from, the original article—these changes were *not* acknowledged in the 1938 book. For one thing, the passage, in the original article (1936b, 675–76) discussed above, in which Hansen criticized Keynes's obscure presentation of the consumption function, was deleted in the reprinted version. In later work, Hansen would emphasize Keynes's "clear" presentation of the consumption function. Thus, in a 1947 article on the *General Theory*, Hansen wrote: "It has been my conviction for many years that the great contribution of the *General Theory* was the clear and specific formulation of the consumption function" (Hansen 1947, 135).[32] Second, the passage about cost rigidity, also discussed above, was revised in a way that linked Hansen's concern about the possibility that investment outlets might have become more limited than in the past to the secular-stagnation thesis. In this connection, the 1938 version of Hansen's review of the *General Theory* added the following text:

> But the marginal efficiency of capital is determined in part by the cost of production of investment goods. From this it follows that flexibility in the cost-price structure is extremely important, though Keynes takes little, if any, cognizance of this problem. And, in particular, in an economy not expanding into new territory or experiencing a rapid population growth, the outlets for investment are made much worse under the condition of cost rigidities and monopolistic price and wage policies. (1938, 27)

Finally, the concluding, critical passages of the original *JPE* article—quoted at the end of the preceding paragraph—were deleted.

The basic thesis of *Fiscal Policy and Business Cycles*—which was the subject of Simons's 1942 review in the *JPE*—is that the primary force driving business cycles is net investment. During the nineteenth and early part of the twentieth centuries, investment in the United States was underpinned by new inventions, population growth, and the opening-up of new territories, factors that Hansen had identified in his earlier writings. These factors had, at one time, been powerful enough to support rising levels of income and relatively full utilization of resources. However, population growth and the expansion into new territories seemed to have come to an end by the early part of the twentieth century. Hansen believed that technological innovations would not be able, on their own, to provide sufficient investment opportunities to absorb saving and ensure full utilization of resources. Consequently, to ensure full employment the government needed to step into the breach with more vigorous public investment. Hansen (1941, 117) argued: "This policy involves greatly enlarged government expenditures." Otherwise, cyclical depression would likely be transformed into secular stagnation. To prevent that possibility, Hansen proposed a "dual production system, which is clearly a hybrid between a private capitalistic economy and a socialized economy" (1941, 401). Under the system, part of the economy (railways, public utilities) would be run as a state enterprise; part (manufacturing) would be run under private ownership.

Hansen maintained that public investment should be financed by debt issuance. He argued: "The assumption that a large public debt is inherently and necessarily under all circumstances an evil is not warranted" (1941, 156). An internally held debt, he maintained, "represents a transfer of funds *within* the community" (emphasis in original, 1941, 172). Moreover, the services provided by the debt, "which are offered without charge to the community, may . . . increase the taxable capacity in the sense of increasing the taxable monetary income" (1941, 170).

In his earlier works, Hansen wrote that countercyclical monetary policy could be used to dampen the business cycle.[33] In *Fiscal Policy and Business Cycles*, Hansen expressed a very different view about the effectiveness of monetary policy. In making the argument that changes in investment drive changes in output, Hansen maintained that both "the money supply ($M$) and its utilization ($V$) adjust themselves to the demands of the underlying real factors" (1941, 38).[34] In a chapter titled "Monetary Policy in the Depression," he assessed the Federal Reserve's policies during the Great Depression. Hansen argued that expansionary open-market operations in 1930 (1) helped cushion the stock-market crash, (2) "supplied the [cash to satisfy the] increasing demand for currency and gold," and

(3) provided the means by which the banks reduced "their indebtedness to the Reserve Banks without effecting too drastic a decline in member bank reserves" (1941, 77). Yet, these and other easing measures by the Fed, Hansen maintained, were not effective during the Great Depression for two reasons. First, investment demand depends on long-term interest rates, whereas "the interest-rate structure that can be reached by the Central Bank [is that pertaining to] short-term rates" (Hansen 1941, 80). Second, in any case, there "is increasingly . . . considerable doubt among economists as to how effective . . . the low rate of interest would be, at least within reasonable limits, as a means of increasing investment" (1941, 330). That is, Hansen perceived that the interest elasticity of investment was extremely low. Hansen's verdict on what was learned about the effectiveness of monetary policy during the Great Depression was the following: "the decade of the thirties offers abundant evidence that cheap money alone is not adequate" (1941, 82).

Simons was agitated by Hansen's book. Two characteristics can be said to have marked Simons's review. First, reflecting his agitation, the review was highly negative. After conceding that the book had some "attributes of excellence," Simons wrote: "But I have come to bury Hansen—albeit respectfully and despairingly" (1942a, 185). Second, despite the thirty-six-page length of the review, Simons made essentially no effort to convey to the reader what was in Hansen's book. Hence, the review was not so much a critical appraisal of Hansen's book as it was a series of counterpunches to key arguments made by Hansen.

At the outset of his article, Simons noted that the economics profession, especially its younger members, was being swept away by Keynesian thinking, which called for "perpetual deficits and uninterrupted increase in the federal debt." Specifically, the *General Theory* provided a theoretical rationale for the policies of the New Deal. In the persona of Alvin Hansen, the Keynesian revolution had claimed a very important convert: "Now, from the ranks of older, distinguished economists, comes Professor Hansen to argue their [i.e., the Keynesians'] case and to espouse their cause" (Simons 1942a, 184). Simons then explained the motivation underlying his review of Hansen's book.

His book is the academic apology par excellence for the inner New Deal and all its works. It may well become the economic bible for that substantial company of intellectuals, following Keynes and recklessly collectivist, whose influence grows no less rapidly in academic circles than in Washington. So, as an unreconstructed, old-fashioned liberal, I must counteract as best I can, hoping to diminish slightly the impetus which the book must give to trends of thought and action which to me seem wholly dangerous. (1942a, 185)

Hansen, as we saw, believed that, barring technological innovations, the capitalist system had reached its growth limits, necessitating government intervention to maintain economic growth. Simons's view of the matter was very different. He asserted that "the productivity curve for new capital is extremely flat" and that "investment opportunities are and have been nearly limitless" (1942a, 192). Why, then, had investment been weak in the 1930s? Simons attributed that weakness to the political climate fostered by the New Deal: "The period . . . witnessed almost revolutionary change, profoundly adverse to investors and enterprise, in the political situation and outlook." That political climate "practically defied people to invest privately or to behave enterprisingly" (1942a, 193).

Simons then contrasted his interpretation on the events of the 1930s with Hansen's interpretation. Hansen believed that expansionary monetary policy had been tried but had been found wanting: "Hansen looks at the thirties and infers that 'monetary policy' is not enough" (Simons 1942a, 194). Therefore, the government needed to step in, "borrowing and spending . . . the redundant savings which private business fails to absorb" (1942a, 194). Simons, however, argued that once "fiscal measures"—by which he meant changes in the quantity of money—had stabilized the price level, they "have done their bit and cannot wisely be relied upon further" (1942a, 195). He maintained that private investment should be allowed to steer economic growth, "avoiding that dangerously easy solution of displacing private by governmental investment and avoiding debt increase like the plague" (1942a, 195).

As mentioned, Hansen believed fiscal deficits should be financed by debt—instead of by newly created money. Simons, in contrast, maintained that fiscal deficits, if they were necessary, should be financed by money creation, instead of through debt issuance. Both ways of financing fiscal deficits had their drawbacks, but the drawbacks of money-financed deficits were more easily recognizable and, therefore, correctible:

Currency issue, merely because its effects are more immediate and its dangers well recognized, is likely to be used cautiously and in moderation. Its excesses set off danger signals for everyone to see; and popular distaste for inflation sets proximate limits on legislative extravagance and reluctance to tax. . . . Borrowing,

on the other hand, permits legislatures to indulge freely their spending proclivi-
ties, piling up difficulties for legislatures in the future. Inflationary extravagance
is countered by deflationary borrowing; and the trick can be made to work for
quite a time. (Simons 1942a, 197)

In his book, Hansen argued that the buildup of internally held debt
is not an unmitigated evil because it is merely a transfer of income flow
from one group of the population to another. Simons agreed: "The debt,
of course, we shall owe to ourselves" (1942a, 197). Moreover, Simons acknowledged that increases in debt could increase the value of public assets and provide a larger tax base. But he saw the potential for political
upheaval in rising debt. He wrote: "the magnitude and rate of increase of
internal debt is a measure of political instability and exposure to revolution." At some point, "taxpayers or claimants of governmental dispensa-
tions will revolt against deprivations in the name of bond holders" thereby
"jeopardizing the political order" (1942a, 197). Consequently, Simons believed that Hansen's blueprint for economic policy would lead to a "moun-
tain of governmental money substitutes (debt) which threaten indefinite
inflation if the confidence of creditors is ever impaired." Specifically, Simons asserted that "Hansen proposes with borrowing to avoid long-term,
secular inflation by continuously courting inflation catastrophe" (1942a,
199). In addition, should the government follow a path of continuously
borrowing to absorb savings, it would neglect measures needed to revital-
ize private investment and enterprise; instead, it would "extend collectivism indiscriminately" (1942a, 201).

Hansen's forceful support and propagation of Keynesian economics
would earn him the moniker "The American Keynes."[35] As we shall see
in chapters 6 and 7, in the mid-1940s and early 1950s Hansen would defend Keynesian economics against the quantity-theory views of Mints and
Friedman.

## Simons and Keynes

Simons published a scathing review of the *General Theory* in the July 2,
1936, issue of the magazine *Christian Century*.[36] In his review, Simons focused on the policy aspects of Keynes's book. He began by opining that
Keynes "is popularly accepted as one of the authentic geniuses of his generation." The *General Theory*, itself, "is full of brilliant insights and occasionally devastating criticism of other writers" (Simons 1936b, 1016).

Then, however, came the appraisal of the book's policy message: "Nowhere, moreover, can one discover, even from insinuation, the nature of the monetary system which the argument presupposes. Thus the author gives us a theory of unemployment, interest and money which attains generality by being about nothing at all" (1936b, 1016). In particular, Simons asserted that the policies advocated by Keynes would result in "a highly diffuse kind of political interference" in economic affairs. Keynes had advocated, according to Simons, a system under which

> the state should use taxation to curtail private saving; it should supplement private consumption and investment with its own spending; and it should force down and keep down the rate of interest to promote new enterprise. At times the author seems to suggest outright fixing of the volume of investment and of the rate of interest by the government. (1936b, 1017)

Simons contrasted the Keynesian system with the kind of system that he (Simons) advocated:

> Mr. Keynes nowhere suggests this need for economy in the kinds of governmental interferences; and he seems to disregard, or grossly to underestimate, the possibilities of controlling all the variables which his analysis emphasizes merely by controlling the quantity of money—*i.e.*, by ordering fiscal practice (spending, taxing, borrowing and currency issue) in terms of deliberate monetary policy. He overlooks the need (clearly suggested by his own analysis) for the minimizing of monetary uncertainties and the achievement of a monetary system based on definite and stable rules. Thus, while expressing decided preference for an economic system of free enterprise, he does not seriously consider what monetary arrangements or what implementations of monetary policy are most and least compatible with that system. (1936b, 1017)

In 1943, Simons and Keynes exchanged letters. The occasion for the exchange was Keynes's 1943 paper "Proposals for an International Clearing Union" published by the British government.[37] In a letter dated June 10, 1943, Simons wrote to Keynes to express his "enthusiastic praise and endorsement" of the plan. Simons then baited Keynes to express his opinion about his (Keynes's) American disciples, such as Hansen:

> These are the considered opinions of an American economist who, by slight reputation, has been bitterly anti-Hansen and, if not wholly anti-Keynesian,

utterly opposed to your extreme American disciples. (I sometimes suspect that
you may not be much more tolerant than I am toward that weird amalgam
of your doctrines and Schumpeter's preposterous Entwicklungstheorie [evo-
lutionary theory of economic development] which constitutes the extreme
"American Keynesism"[*sic*].) (Henry C. Simons Papers, Special Collections
Research Center, Joseph Regenstein Library, University of Chicago)

Keynes did not take the bait. He replied with a letter dated July 16, 1943,
expressing his gratitude to Simons for finding the Clearing Union paper
"so satisfactory." He added that discussions about the Clearing Union
were "going on with the United States Treasury" and that he was "hopeful
that some agreed version may eventually emerge." Keynes did not refer
to his "American disciples" (Henry C. Simons Papers, Special Collections
Research Center, Joseph Regenstein Library, University of Chicago).

## 5.2 Douglas

In 1935 Douglas published two studies on the subject of money and the
business cycle: a book, *Controlling Depressions*, that he wrote during
1934;[38] and an article, "Purchasing Power of the Masses and Business Depressions," which appeared in the volume *Economic Essays in Honor of
Wesley Clair Mitchell*.[39] The latter article, which was written before Douglas's book had been completed, summarized many of the main arguments
provided in the book. Nevertheless, the time interval between the completion of the article and that of the book revealed several salient changes in
Douglas's thinking about the causes of, and required policy responses to,
the business cycle.

Both publications started by taking issue with the idea that the economic system, in its monetary aspect, is naturally in equilibrium and is
unbalanced only by exceptional factors. On the contrary, Douglas argued
that the economic system would not normally be in equilibrium unless deliberately kept there. In both works, he argued that two principal theories
(discussed below) could be used to explain the causes of depressions. The
two theories were as follows.

*Underconsumptionism.* As he had in many of his earlier writings, Douglas ascribed depressions to the failure of wages, salaries, and farm incomes
to increase in line with the rise in output of the mass-production industries.
The result of this circumstance was that, at some point, the prices of the

products of these industries had to be "slashed" to clear the market of the excess supply of goods. Consequently, "profit margins would begin to be swept away" (Douglas 1935a, 113), output would be cut, and depression would ensue.

*Monopolistic pricing.* Douglas also attributed depressions to a second cause—namely, "the failure of industry, because of 'friction,' monopoly and quasi-monopoly, to reduce prices commensurately with the reduction in [unit labor] costs." During the 1920s, he argued, "undue profits were piled up and undue investments made" (Douglas 1935b, 77). Three consequences followed from the excessive rise in profits. First, the profits stimulated investment in capital producing industries, drawing "large quantities of labor into these lines." Corporate yields rose, stimulating "the great stock market boom of 1925–1929" (1935b, 58). Second, excessive profits gave rise to "wild speculation" in real estate investment, especially with regard to "urban skyscrapers and hotels, and in the suburban real estate" (1935b, 58–59). Third, to maintain prices and profits, production and employment in consumer-goods industries had to be restricted, reducing purchasing power (1935b, 59). With the increases in both wages and employment having been less than the rise in output, the economy arrived at the point at which prices had to be slashed. Thus, profits fell, and the Great Depression ensued.

In Douglas's 1935 article "Purchasing Power of the Masses and Business Depression," which, as noted, was completed before *Controlling Depressions*, the underconsumptionist theory was discussed before the monopolistic-pricing theory. In *Controlling Depressions*, the monopolistic-pricing theory was presented before the underconsumption theory. Moreover, in assigning priority to the causes of the Great Depression in that volume, Douglas made it clear that monopolistic pricing was primarily to blame for that episode: "*by far the major responsibility* for [the Depression] must be laid at the doors of those American industrial combinations which by keeping prices up and dampening down production created an inflation of profits which both helped on wild speculation and threw considerable numbers out of work" (emphasis added, 1935b, 59).

In both of his 1935 publications on depressions, Douglas provided detailed discussions of the "cumulative causes" of the business cycle.[40] These causes included the effects of declining prices on both profits and price expectations, which, in turn, led to falls in the velocity of circulation of both money and credit.[41] Using the Fisherine equation of exchange, $MV + M'V' = PT$, Douglas argued that, as prices declined, "another pair of forces are set into motion. These are the decline in the rapidity of circulation of money and the similar decline in the circulation of credit" (1935b, 25).[42] Moreover, once $V$ and $V'$ start to decline, a depression feeds on itself:

> The decrease in the quantity of credit and the decline in the velocity of circulation of both money and credit naturally cause the general level of prices to fall.... Since the combined shrinkage in the turnover rate of money and credit and in the volume of credit is greater than the decrease in production, the inevitable result is, therefore, that prices must fall still further. (1935b, 26)

Similarly, Douglas used the quantity theory to explain the determination of the price level: "the level of prices depends, if other things are equal, not merely on the quantity of money but also on its velocity and even more upon the quantity and velocity of bank credit" (1935b, 163).

As is evident from the above discussion, Douglas believed that the demand for, and supply of, money and credit (demand deposits) played a key role in amplifying the business cycle. In his 1935 article "Purchasing Power of the Masses and Business Depressions," he stated: "I am, indeed, one of those who believe that the banks as such should not 'create' any purchasing power, and that this should be a function of society, which should obtain the basic rate of interest on such credit. But this, though an important issue, I shall not develop further here because of lack of space" (1935a, 129). To that statement, he added the following footnote: "I hope to treat this topic more fully in a forthcoming book, *Controlling Depressions*" (1935a, 129n25).

That is precisely what he did. *Controlling Depressions* contained an entire chapter—chapter 9 (twenty-three pages)—on reform of the banking system. In that chapter, Douglas argued along lines similar to Simons. The latter economist, as we saw, had assigned a major responsibility for the Great Depression to the fractional-reserve banking system. Douglas stated: "the creation of credit by the private banking system leads to confusion and instability. The banking system is, indeed, in large part responsible for the severity of existing depressions and its weaknesses go right to the very heart of its own structure" (1935b, 177).[43] What could be done to stabilize the banking system? In the November 1933 memorandum, Simons and Director had argued against the use of branch banking: "It promises substantial safety for depositors, to be sure, but only because the government could never afford to let private institutions of this kind fail" (Simons et al. 1933, 2). Douglas (1935b, 177) wrote: "It is sometimes proposed that all those dangers [produced by private-sector credit creation] could be averted . . . through the medium of extensive branch banking. Even here, however, safety to depositors would not primarily be given by any soundness in the credit system as such but simply because the government could not afford to let any bank of such magnitude fail." What about the option of nationalizing the banking industry? As mentioned, an objective of the November 1933 memorandum was to prevent the socialization of bank lending. Here is what Douglas wrote about the socialization of the banking system:

> I see in it one large source of danger. That lies in making a governmental agency the sole body to make commercial loans to private industry. Were the government to become the only banker, we can easily imagine some of the pressures to which it would be subjected in determining who should be given credit and how much credit should be loaned to the different applicants. Even with the greatest precautions, political influence rather than the efficiency of the applicants would be likely to be the controlling force in many of these decisions. (1935b, 183–84)

What, then, could be done to stabilize the creation of credit? Douglas thought that it would be necessary to separate the creation of credit from the retailing of credit. "The ablest proposal in this direction," he wrote, "is . . . that which a group of my colleagues at the University of Chicago under the leadership of Mr. H. C. Simons have set forth" (1935b, 184). After describing the proposal made in the November 1933 memorandum, Douglas discussed the benefits of the 100 percent reserves scheme. These included: (1) revenue provision for the government; (2) the safety of deposits; (3) control over the quantity of money; (4) the moderation of the business cycle; and (5) the retention of the allocation of resources in private hands (1935b, 185–88).

Douglas made another notable concession to the views of Simons, Director, and Knight in *Controlling Depressions*. Recall from chapter 3 that in 1933 Douglas had been appointed to the Consumer Advisory Board of the National Recovery Administration (NRA). Also recall that in 1933 Douglas had expressed support for the NRA's mandate to engage in price and wage fixing (1933c, 419). In *Controlling Depressions*, Douglas continued to support the NRA's efforts to raise wages—a view that set him apart from Simons, Director, and Knight—but he was critical of the NRA's efforts to engage in price fixing. The original purposes of the NRA, he argued, "were worthy." However, "far from restoring competition in the monopolistic industries, they [the NRA codes] have extended these monopolistic practices into many industries which were formerly competitive" (1935b, 234). He continued:

> The real abuses of the NRA lie ... in the price and production policies which have been fostered, rather than in the wage policies. These abuses have operated greatly *to restrict* the area of price competition and to enlarge that of monopoly and quasi-monopoly. ... The NRA has virtually made it mandatory upon the employers to combine. They had to get together to submit a code and they have to stay organized to administer it. (emphasis added, 1935b, 235)

Douglas (1935b, chap. 12) argued in favor of increased flexibility in the structure of prices by the restoration (as far as possible) of competitive conditions. Where such flexibility could not be implemented, like Simons, he supported the socialization of monopolies.

As in his earlier publications, in his 1935 studies, Douglas argued that to combat depressions it was necessary to increase the money supply. He continued to believe that monetary policies that work through the banking system were not likely to be effective during depressions. He argued that the Federal Reserve had conducted expansionary open-market operations at various stages of the Great Depression but that "the hoped-for expansion of loans and of business did not occur. ... The banks used their new reserves to get out of debt to the Federal Reserve System and avoid paying interest to the latter" (1935b, 117). To combat depressions, Douglas argued that the government should incur fiscal deficits, with the government budget normally balanced "over the period of a major cycle as a whole" (1935b, 135). Of the three ways of financing the deficit—taxes, bond issuance, and money creation—the former method, he believed, "is inferior during a depression to the other two methods" since it crowds out private expenditure (1935b, 137). Concerning taxation, he considered highly progressive income taxes to be the least objectionable form of taxation (1935b, 137). Regarding the choice between bond-financed and money-financed deficits, Douglas favored the latter method since "the issuance of paper money would ... be a completely fresh creation" of purchasing power and would not involve payment of interest (1935b, 138). He acknowledged that a major objection to money-financed deficits was that the deficits "would soon lead to almost limitless inflation" (1935b, 139). He countered that objection with the argument that, historically, money-financed fiscal deficits had led to inflation only in special circumstances—namely, in countries with "an inadequate system of taxation combined with large continuing sources of public expenditure, such as war" (1935b, 139).

To help prevent depressions, Douglas believed that a rule should govern the money supply (1935b, chap. 10). He considered three types of rules: (1) one under which the money supply increases at a rate of 3 to 4 percent per year to stabilize the price level; (2) one under which the money supply rises at a rate that slightly exceeds the rate of increase in production so that the price level rises slowly; and (3) a rule, as under a fixed quantity of money per capita, that aims to achieve a slightly falling price level. It will be recalled that the latter rule was advocated in the November 1933 memorandum.

Douglas asserted that a major theoretical argument in favor of a policy that aimed to attain a "slight continuous rise in the price level" was that, with "money costs lagging behind the advances in production," profit margins would steadily increase, raising production "to the fullest degree" (1935b, 198). He argued, however, that there was "little evidence to indicate that slowly rising prices would appreciably increase production above what it would be under a stable general price level with flexible individual prices" (1935b, 201).

Douglas was very critical of the policy under which the price level would decrease slowly. He stated: "If we examine [the proposal for] . . . a constant total supply of money, with a consequent tendency for the price level to decrease at the rate of from 3 to 4 percent, we shall bring out in sharp outline the difficulties which are inherent in any such program" (1935b, 203). He pointed out that if prices fell by 4 percent a year, by the end of the twentieth century they would be one-seventieth of what they were at their initial level. He continued: "Even an annual decrease of only 2 per cent a year would mean a halving of the price level every 33 years" (1935b, 203). Douglas's judgment of the proposal to maintain a constant money supply (per capita) was the following: "This [i.e., the enormous decline in prices after a period of years] is almost enough in itself to reveal the economic absurdity of any such program" (1935b, 203).

Concerning a rule that aimed to stabilize the price level under a money-growth rule, Douglas argued that such a rule would help eliminate "abnormal profits which come when costs lag behind upward movements in prices, with an attendant over-stimulation of investment, and with a frequent failure of the monetary purchasing power . . . of consumers to keep pace with the output of mass production goods" (1935b, 195). In contrast to the criterion of a slowly falling price level (which favored rentiers over borrowers) and a slowly rising price level (which favored businesses over labor), a constant price level would be neutral in its distributive effects. He concluded his evaluation of the alternative rules as follows: "It would seem . . . that a stable general price level is superior to either falling or rising prices, and that in all probability it is the criterion which should be adopted" (1935b, 208). As in his previous writings, the criterion would be pursued under a regime of flexible exchange rates (1935b, 151–52).

Thus, by 1935 Douglas's views had undergone several changes that brought them closer to the views of his Chicago colleagues Simons, Director, Knight, and (as we shall see) Mints.[44] Douglas had come to assign a major responsibility for the depth of the Great Depression to the fractional-reserve banking system. Like his Chicago colleagues, he advocated the 100 percent reserves scheme for the same reasons as those provided in the November 1933 memorandum. His view on the causes of depressions had shifted toward an increased weight on the role played by monopolistic pricing in conjunction with a fractional-reserve banking system. Whereas he had earlier been a supporter of the NRA's codes of conduct, in 1935 he had come to believe that the NRA's price-fixing elements had contributed to the severity of the Depression. Moreover, as was done in the November 1933 memorandum and Simons's 1934 *A Positive Program for Laissez Faire*, Douglas analyzed the advantages and disadvantages of alternative monetary rules. Apart from Douglas and the other Chicagoans, I know of no other American economist who had performed such an assessment by the mid-1930s.

In the second half of the 1930s and the early 1940s, Douglas's research focused mainly on estimations of the Cobb-Douglas production function and on studying historical developments in wages.[45] He did, however, return to the issue of money in the late 1930s.[46]

In the fall of 1938, Douglas, joined by Irving Fisher, Frank D. Graham (Princeton), Earl J. Hamilton (Duke), Willford I. King (New York University), and Charles R. Whittlesey (Princeton), drafted a five-page memorandum, *A Program for Monetary Reform*. During the winter, the memorandum was widely circulated, and, in March 1939, it was sent to President Roosevelt. By July 1939, the memorandum had been expanded to forty pages. The foreword to the memorandum stated that "235 economists from 157 universities and colleges have expressed their general approval of this 'Program'; 40 more approved it with reservations; 43 have expressed disapproval" (Douglas et al. 1939, 3).[47]

The basic problem addressed by *A Program for Monetary Reform* was what the authors perceived to be the "wholly inadequate" monetary system, which was "unable to fulfill its function" of employing "productive resources to the fullest practicable extent" (Douglas et al. 1939, 2). The authors stated that their proposed program was not intended to be a panacea for what they called "the depression problem." Rather, the program aimed "to eliminate one recognizable cause of great depressions, the lawless variability in our supply of circulating medium" (Douglas et al. 1939, 4).

What was that one "recognizable cause" of depressions? The authors adopted the argument made in the November 1933 memorandum and subsequently by Simons (1934a; 1936a). Specifically, they maintained that the absence of a monetary rule embedded in legislation under a single monetary authority had led to a situation in which discretionary policies fostered monetary uncertainty:

> So long as we have no law determining what our monetary policy shall be *there will always be uncertainty as to the external and internal values of the dollar.* Consequently, there is an ever-present danger of abuse of discretionary powers. . . . The Secretary of the Treasury, for instance, has discretionary power to issue silver certificates. . . . The Board of Governors of the Federal Reserve System may change the reserve requirements of banks, may buy or sell Government bonds in the open market, may change discount rates, and in other ways effect the volume of credit and so the purchasing power of the dollar. . . . Our monetary system is thus permeated with discretionary powers. (emphasis added, Douglas et al. 1939, 10–11)

The program proposed by Douglas et al. comprised three elements. First, the authors pressed for the creation of an independent Monetary Authority in which the power to create money would be centralized. Second, to simplify the Monetary Authority's task of controlling the money supply, and to ensure the safety of demand deposits, they called for 100 percent reserve requirements on demand deposits. In doing so, Douglas et al. proposed that banks should be allowed to invest the funds contained in their time deposits. In this way, the 100 percent scheme would lead to a separation—within each bank—of its demand-deposit department from its time-deposit department. Thus, the scheme would result in a separation of "the two functions of lending and the creation of money supply . . . much like that of 1844 in the Bank of England which separated the Issue Department from the Banking Department" (Douglas et al. 1939, 35). Third, they proposed that the US Congress mandate the Monetary Authority to follow a rule: either a constant per capita volume of money—à la the proposal in the November 1933 memorandum—or a stable-price-level rule. Under the constant (per capita) money-supply rule, the authors noted that, with technological improvements and increases in real income, "the price level would fall" (Douglas et al. 1939, 15). That criterion was vehemently rejected by Douglas in his *Controlling Depressions*. True to form, following the presentation of that criterion in the 1939 memorandum, there was a footnote stating that Douglas, and another co-author, Willford King, "do not approve of this criterion" (Douglas et al. 1939, 15).

In 1941, the six co-authors of the *Program*, joined by John R. Commons (University of Wisconsin), submitted an almost identical document to President Roosevelt. They were supported by some four hundred economists (or 85 percent of those expressing an opinion). The president responded that the statement "will receive careful study" (quoted from Allen 1993, 714). Those economists who expressed approval of the *Program* did *not* include Simons, Knight, Director, or Mints, who had co-authored the March 1933 Chicago memorandum with Douglas. One possible reason for this circumstance may have been that the other Chicagoans thought that what had been proposed in the March 1933 memorandum was sufficient— thus, there was no need to be repetitive. Another plausible explanation is that the other Chicagoans, especially Simons, had moved on in their thinking. In particular, they may not have viewed the policies, especially the 100 percent reserves scheme, contained in *A Program for Monetary Reform* as practical under the existing financial system. In a letter dated, February 3, 1937, addressed to Fisher, Simons wrote that his thinking about the practicality of the 100 percent reserves scheme had changed since the inception of that scheme in 1933:

> I'm afraid you'll find me either useless or a liability in connection with any drive for definite legislation for carrying out the 100% scheme. As you may infer from my *JPE* article, I have little faith in any simple legislative prescription. To me, the scheme (whatever its potentialities during the banking crisis) is significant only for its definition of an ideal objective of gradual reform; and in such a gradual unfolding, changes outside formal banking seem even more

important and indispensable than the things which we stressed in the beginning.[48] (Henry C. Simons Papers, Special Collections Research Center, Joseph
Regenstein Library, University of Chicago)

## Discussion

During the course of the 1930s, Douglas's views on the 100 percent reserves scheme, the role of monopolistic pricing in fostering the business
cycle, the negative impact of the NRA's price controls in the Great Depression, the need of policy rules to reduce the uncertainty fostered by
discretionary policies, and the desirability to keep investment decisions in
private hands emerged in such a way that they brought Douglas's views
close to those of Simons, Knight, Director, and Mints. Nevertheless, Douglas's opinions differed from those of his Chicago colleagues in his belief
that wage earners needed to be better organized and that the government should play a larger role in the economy (including in the setting
of wages). Although Douglas's view of the chief generating cause of depressions changed during the 1930s, he continued to employ the Fisherine
equation of exchange as a tool to analyze the business cycle. Despite his
belief in underconsumptionism, Douglas, in common with his Chicago
colleagues, did not succumb to the Keynesian revolution. His post-1936
works contained few references to Keynes's *General Theory*. As will be
discussed in chapter 6, in the early 1950s, while a US senator, he used the
quantity theory to help forge the "accord" between the US Treasury and
the Federal Reserve. In his autobiography *In the Fullness of Time*, Douglas referred to the influences on his thinking during the 1930s as follows:
"I was strongly influenced by Joan Robinson's 1933 study, *The Economics
of Imperfect Competition*. She was one of Keynes's favorite pupils, but I
think she was on sounder ground than Keynes in his *The General Theory
of Employment, Interest and Money*" (1972, 351n9). Douglas had the following to say about both the Keynesian revolution and the experience of
communism in Russia:

> The Keynesians ... did not convince me. ... They favored a continuous injection
> of publicly created purchasing power to build up production and employment.
> This meant continuing government deficits. . . . I wanted the private sector to
> carry out the major economic activities. I opposed the all-encompassing state
> employer. The experience of Russia showed how an inner group of experts and
> politicians could tyrannize over the mass of mankind. (1972, 455)

## 5.3 Knight

In chapter 3, we saw that, in the early 1930s, Frank Knight was highly critical of social organizations based on planning; he viewed planning as incompatible with democratic government. He emphasized the idea that markets perform an essential function as a social mechanism for achieving voluntary cooperation among diverse economic units (Minsky 1985, 214). Yet, as we shall see, Knight was also critical of laissez-faire.[49] He argued that the free-market system tends to produce monopoly, which dilutes competition. Consumer sovereignty, he believed, is distorted by advertising. He also argued that income goes to the owners of the means of production, and not to the factors of production themselves. These characteristics of the free-market system, along with the prevailing patterns of inheritance, undermined arguments that aimed to justify the market's distribution of wealth.[50] Despite these defects of the free-market system, Knight defended that system against proposals to increase the role of the government in economic activity. As we shall now see, Knight was highly critical of Keynes's *General Theory*, basing his criticism, in large part, on Keynes's theory of money and the implications of Keynes's book for the role of government in the economy.

During the second half of the 1930s and the early 1940s, Knight produced two substantive articles on the subject of money and the business cycle: (1) "Unemployment: And Mr. Keynes's Revolution in Economic Theory," in the *Canadian Journal of Economics and Political Science* in 1937; and (2) "The Business Cycle, Interest, and Money: A Methodological Approach," published in the *Review of Economics and Statistics* in 1941.[51] The 1937 article was—as its title indicates—an assessment of Keynes's *General Theory*; the 1941 article provided an account of Knight's business-cycle theory. In addition to those articles, Knight taught a graduate course, Business Cycles, at the University of California, Berkeley, during the fall semester of 1936.[52] A transcript of Knight's lectures—delivered several months after the publication of the *General Theory*—was compiled by Perham C. Nahl, who was a PhD student at Berkeley. The lectures suggest a teaching style that was, at times, discursive and disjointed.[53] Nevertheless, the lectures shed light on Knight's thinking on both the business cycle and Keynes's contributions to the economics literature. Nahl attached the lecture notes to a letter addressed to Knight dated May 11, 1937 The letter began as follows: "At the conclusion of your course last semester I asked if you would like to have a copy of the class notes, to which you replied in the affirmative. So—here they are—finally" (Frank H. Knight Papers, Special Collections Research Center, Joseph Regenstein Library, University of Chicago). There is no record of a reply by Knight. In what follows, I describe the main elements of Knight's 1936 lectures. Then, I discuss his 1937 and 1941 articles, respectively.

### Lectures on Business Cycles (1936)

The twelve lectures were delivered from August 26, 1936, to November 18, 1936. There were three required readings for the course: Keynes's *General Theory*, John M. Clark's *Strategic Factors in Business Cycles* (1934), and the introduction to Wesley C. Mitchell's *Business Cycles: The Problem and Its Setting* (1927).[54] The fact that Knight retained Nahl's compilation of the lectures suggests that the lecture notes accurately, if incompletely, reflected what Knight taught in the course. They were published in 2016 in the *Review of Keynesian Economics*, along with an introductory article, "Two Minds That Never Met: Frank H. Knight on John M. Keynes Once Again—a Documentary Note," co-authored by Carlo Cristiano and Luca Fiorito. In my discussion of the lectures, the page numbers correspond to those in the published version.[55]

In his introductory remarks to the class, Knight noted that he had "been called a reactionary and a 'die hard.'" He then stated: "I have always had the reformer interest as well as the practical interest in economics." The "basic problems" that needed to be addressed in economics, he argued, "are philosophical—we must solve them before any progress can be made" (Knight 1936c, 80).[56]

The main part of the course was a commentary on the theory of the business cycle. The classical economists, Knight stated, had "nothing to say about . . . cyclical analysis. [They] contemplated a relatively frictionless economy" (1936c, 85).[57] This circumstance reflected the emphasis that those economists placed on the long run—after the economy had settled into an equilibrium position. Knight noted, however, that equilibrium was "simply a direction in which economic forces are pulling." He stated that "other forces may block" the economy from settling into an equilibrium position (1936c, 85). In this connection, classical economists did not appreciate the role played by money and credit in generating deviations from equilibrium: "Classical economists *failed* to treat cycles or monetary phenomena partly through ignorance (a failure to realize their importance) and partly because of a perfectly legitimate tendency toward abstraction" (emphasis in original, Knight 1936c, 83).[58] He characterized the business cycle as follows:

> Economic theory is a mechanical analysis. Any mechanical "governor" will oscillate—it will not act until some change takes place. . . . Thus there is a time lag. The baffling thing about business cycles is their irregularity—lack of periodicity. Cycles should have period, amplitude, regularity, phases. A business cycle represents an inherently unstable situation . . . which means that irregularities are self-aggravating—that there is a natural tendency toward oscillation. (Knight 1936c, 84)[59]

Knight repeatedly stressed the role played by money and credit in the business cycle. Here are some examples.

- "What throws economic life as a whole into *the* cycle? . . . The answer is to be found in the banking and credit mechanism" (emphasis in original, 1936c, 84).
- "Expansion and contraction of credit are tied up with commercial banking. The banks build up deposits by lending to business—business borrows when it thinks times will be good, and this money is put into circulation. More money in circulation makes other businesses prosper (the essential phenomenon of the upswing in business)—this is the synchronizing force" (1936c, 84).
- "The cycle is due mainly to credit expansion and contraction—control of credit would cut down the catastrophic nature of the cycle, but there would still be cyclical movements—even if . . . cash were . . . the [only] velocity factor" (1936c, 85).
- "The essential role of money is speculative—to meet contingencies. The greater the contingencies the more money needed (liquidity preference). All money dealings constitute a speculation in money. Speculation has a cumulative effect—self-aggravating, necessarily oscillatory. Speculation causes things to happen that people think are going to happen—the only thing they do not know is the limits" (1936c, 85).

The "pyramiding" of credit—reflecting the role played by the fractional-reserve banking system in enabling the system to expand credit by a multiple of deposits—explained four-fifths of the amplitude of the cycle (1936c, 85).

In addition to stressing the role of money and credit, Knight emphasized the role of lags—or frictions—in the business cycle: "In my business cycle theory I would begin with [lags]. . . . Whenever you have lags, inertia, or self-aggravating (stimulating) tendencies you will get oscillations"

(1936c, 92). When prices are expected to rise, businesses build up their stocks of goods, leading to further price rises. During the upswing of the cycle, for example, the "lag of costs (wages, rent, interest) behind prices" plays an important role in perpetuating the cycle (1936c, 92).

The basic elements of the cycle were, according to Knight, the following. (1) During the expansionary phase of the cycle, the quantity of money rises. Using the quantity-theory equation $MV = PT$, Knight stated that some economists believed that "$P$ is not necessarily affected by an increase in $M-T$ may compensate for it. But this is true only if the assumption is made that you have unemployed resources" (1936c, 92). Thus, prices rise. (2) Costs lag behind, and, therefore, profits rise. (3) Speculation of additional price rises takes place. Businesses build up their stocks. The "anticipated price rise . . . [is] self-aggravating" (i.e., self-perpetuating) (1936c, 92) (4) Banks expand credit: "bank expansion works cumulatively when business is good but there is a limit to lending" (1936c, 91). (5) Firms use newly created credit to finance investment: "The major characteristic of the business cycle is the fluctuation in investment. . . . Money and credit [are] the center of fluctuations in investment" (1936c, 85). (6) "Costs [eventually] catch up with prices and go beyond—reverse sets in" (1936c, 92). (7) In contrast to the expansionary phase of the business cycle, the contractionary phase appears to be subject to no downward limit. Knight posed the following questions, without providing an answer: "The most mysterious thing about this [contractionary phase] is: What stops the downswing? Why is it that once a contraction of credit sets in, it does not continue contracting until there is none left?" (1936c, 84).

To ameliorate the business cycle, Knight asserted that the government needed to control *both* money and credit—but the lecture notes do not refer to specific proposals. Knight stated: "The monetary theory of the business cycle is important because [money and credit are] something which you can really influence or control. Why should the government not regulate *credit* as well as money?" (emphasis in original, 1936c, 85).[60]

Beginning with the seventh lecture, held on October 14, 1936, Knight focused on the *General Theory*. In his notes for that seventh lecture, Nahl wrote: "From this point to the end of the course, most of the discussion centered about Keynes's *General Theory of Employment, Interest, and Money*. Notes here are not very complete or organized . . . controversial points [were] not conducive to extensive notes" (Knight 1936c, 93).

The central arguments made by Knight about the *General Theory* were the following. (1) The context in which Keynes wrote the *General Theory* was an important factor that influenced Keynes's thinking. In particular, "Keynes was evidently very much influenced by business conditions in Great Britain in the late 20s—a 'stabilized stagnation'—an 'equilibrium' with a great amount of unemployment" (1936c, 85).[61] (2) The book represented "a lost opportunity." Instead of analyzing the weaknesses of classical economic theory, Keynes tried "to stand [that theory] on its head" (1936c, 81). (3) Keynes attempted to develop "a theory of equilibrium with unemployment" (1936c, 94). According to Knight, "Keynes ignores boom and recessions" (1936c, 95). Related to that, "Keynes's system overlooks or neglects lags which . . . are the crux of the cycle problem" (1936c, 97). "Consequently, there is no cycle theory in Keynes because the norm is unemployment" (1936c, 85). (4) The theory of liquidity preference "seems to be the best part of [Keynes's] book" (1936c, 85). "The heart of the cycle problem," Knight argued, is "what happens when people hoard money. . . . A contraction in the flow of money hurts the system" (1936c, 96). In contrast to Keynes, classical economists thought that the main function of money was to act as a medium of exchange. Knight stated: "Money is used to get around the 'non-coincidence of barter'" (1936c, 95); Keynes correctly perceived that "more emphasis should be placed on 'money as a store of value,' liquidity preference" (1936c, 95).

Several comments are in order. First, the business-cycle theory that Knight presented in the course was essentially the same as that presented in the 1932 and 1933 Chicago memoranda; the main elements of the cycle were the lagged effects of variations in the quantity and velocity of money and credit, combined with sticky costs. Second, whereas the Chicagoans focused on the velocity of circulation of money, Keynes focused on the demand for money in his *General Theory*. The Chicagoans thought that the economic system had a natural tendency to be out of equilibrium. They also believed that there was no downward limit to the velocity of circulation of money. Once the price level starts to fall, expectations of further price declines become self-justifying, leading to further hoarding of money. The result is that a cumulative process is set into motion with no natural limit. The analytic tool used to describe the cycle was Fisher's equation of exchange. Third, Keynes believed that, in a liquidity trap, the demand for money—the reciprocal of velocity—could approach infinity. Once the interest rate has fallen to a certain level, liquidity preference may become virtually absolute in the sense that almost everyone prefers to hoard cash rather than debt, which yields so low a rate of interest (Keynes 1936a, 207).[62] Thus, the Chicagoans and Keynes held similar views about money's behavior during the downward phase of the cycle, although they used different analytical tools to reach their respective views. Fourth, Knight maintained that the high unemployment of the 1930s could be explained by incorporating frictions in the adjustment of costs relative to prices and the procyclical behavior of a fractional-reserve banking system into the classical analysis. In contrast, Keynes thought that a new analytical structure was needed to explain the Great Depression.

## Knight and Keynes

Knight's 1937 review of the *General Theory* was combative and sarcastic.[63] Knight began the review as follows: "What Mr. Keynes ostensibly does in his already widely discussed volume published over a year ago is to effect a revolution in general economic theory" (1937, 100).[64] Keynes, alleged Knight, believed that he had set forth a theory of stable equilibrium. Like the classical theory, it was free from cycles; unlike that theory, Keynes's theory was characterized by a large amount of involuntary unemployment—not due to frictions such as sticky wages—in equilibrium. In the introduction to his review, Knight stated: "I may as well state at the outset that the direct contention of the work seems to me quite unsubstantiated" (1937, 100). Instead of contributing a theory of equilibrium with involuntary unemployment, Keynes's book made an "indirect contribution to the theory of business fluctuations" (Knight 1937, 100). Effectively, Keynes had developed a "special case" of classical theory.

Knight asserted that Keynes's description of classical doctrine amounted to the setting up of "straw men for purposes of attack" (1937, 101). Knight (1937, 101) stated that "the doctrines so labelled [as classical] seem to be quite at variance with, and often contradictory to, anything I was ever taught as classical doctrine in any modern sense—and I went through the academic 'mill'; and they are certainly alien to anything I have ever taught as such, and I have been rated, and have supposed myself, an adherent of the general type of position referred to by the term." Instead of starting with a "drastically simplified" theoretical structure that proceeded "by stages toward the complexity of real life," Keynes's procedure was one that replaced "conventional assumptions which do not tell the whole story, and were never represented as doing so, with some antithetical proposition, or familiar qualification, which is then treated as quite general, though the context of the book itself makes clear enough that the argument cannot be taken as meaning what it says" (1937, 101). Keynes, according to Knight, *assumed* that involuntary unemployment is a normal state of affairs without showing "how unemployment comes to pass" (1937, 106n8).

The review was punctuated with sarcastic remarks. For example, after quoting a passage from the *General Theory* in which Keynes maintained that the inducement to invest depends on the relation between the schedule of the marginal efficiency of capital and the complex of interest rates, Knight wrote: "The first difficulty in following up and interpreting this statement is the confusion between what is dependent upon the actual magnitude of a variable and what is dependent on changes in that variable. It is no exaggeration to say that the book is 'packed' with examples of this confusion" (1937, 104n5). At another point, Knight referred to the revolutionary ideas that Keynes *thought* he had produced:

> Since it has become quite the fashion to account for differences in intellectual position by psycho-analysing, or somehow "explaining," one's opponent (and the example of following the fashion having in this case been set by Mr. Keynes), it may be permissible to note that our civilization of to-day, being essentially romantic, loves and extols heretics quite as much as its direct antecedent a few centuries back hated and feared them. The demand for heresy is always in excess of the supply and its production always a prosperous business. (1937, 122n22)

In his concluding section, Knight expressed the view that Keynes believed that he had presented a theory of unemployment equilibrium; in fact, Keynes's book often dealt with a short-period situation:

> The next general comment which must be made on Mr. Keynes's book as a whole is that it is inordinately difficult to tell what the author means. This is true in particular because on general issues it appears certain that he does not mean what he says. The theory is ostensibly one of equilibrium with extensive involuntary unemployment . . . and in the bulk of the exposition there is no explicit reference to cycles or oscillations and little hint that such phenomena exist. Now I for one simply cannot take this new and revolutionary equilibrium theory seriously, and doubt whether Mr. Keynes himself really does so. Scattered through the work are innumerable references to the short period, several which indicate that reactions are more or less reversible. (Knight 1937, 121)

To shed light on Knight's—and, more generally, the Chicago group's—adverse reception of the *General Theory*, my discussion of Knight's review focuses on three issues: (1) Keynes's critique of the classical view that "saving always involves investment" (Keynes 1936a, 83); (2) Keynes's theory of liquidity preference; and (3) the policy implications of the *General Theory*.

*Saving and investment.* Knight quoted what he called "the two most important sentences in [Keynes's] book": "The error [in the classical view that saving always involves investment] lies in proceeding to the plausible inference that, when an individual saves, he will increase aggregate investment by an equal amount. [This] conclusion ... fails to allow for the possibility that an act of individual saving may react somewhat on someone else's savings and hence on someone else's wealth" (Knight 1937, 108; quoting from Keynes 1936a, 83–84). In the *General Theory*, Keynes went on to argue: "Every such attempt to save more by reducing consumption will so affect incomes that the attempt necessarily defeats itself" (Keynes 1936a, 84). Consequently, an increase in saving can be destabilizing.

Knight claimed that the idea that an increase in saving can be destabilizing could also be analyzed via the Fisherine equation of exchange: "In familiar language this, of course, means simply that the saving may be hoarded and by reducing monetary circulation lead to sales reductions or price declines with all the consequences of these in train; but familiar terms and modes of expression seem to be shunned on principle in this book" (Knight 1937, 108). Thus, Knight did not think that there was anything novel about Keynes's analysis of saving—apart from Keynes's incorporation of new terms to explain established concepts.

Correspondingly, in discussing the mechanics of the multiplier, Knight expressed the view that it was preferable to assess the effects of changes in expenditure through the $MV = PT$ framework rather than through income-expenditure analysis:

It is undoubtedly true that [as Keynes wrote] "the logical theory of the multiplier ... holds good continuously, without time lag, at all moments of time. ..." This is rigorously correct because all money which exists at all must exist in some "hoard" at any moment of time. But it would surely be more realistic to assume that an addition to the monetary circulation simply continues to circulate at the prevalent velocity. (1937, 110)

*Theory of liquidity preference.* Keynes criticized classical economists for regarding the rate of interest "as the factor which brings the demand for investment and the willingness to save into equilibrium" (1936a, 173).

In chapter 14, "The Classical Theory of the Rate of Interest," Keynes provided examples from several authors who extolled that theory. One of those authors was Knight. In this connection, Keynes cited Knight's article "Capital, Time and the Interest Rate," published in *Economica* in 1934. After affirming that Knight's article contained "many interesting and profound observations on the nature of capital," Keynes stated: "the theory of interest is given precisely in the traditional classical mould" (1936a, 176n3).[65] Specifically, Keynes quoted a passage from Knight's 1934 *Economica* article in which Knight defined equilibrium in the area of capital production as taking place at "such a rate of interest that savings flow into the market at precisely the same time-rate or speed as they flow into investment producing the same net rate of return as that which is paid savers for their use" (Knight 1934a, 282).[66]

In the *General Theory*, Keynes maintained that "the rate of interest cannot be a return to saving or waiting as such. For if a man hoards his savings in cash, he earns no interest, though he saves as much as before" (1936a, 166–67). Instead, Keynes introduced the idea that the rate of interest is the price that "equilibrates the desire to hold wealth in the form of cash with the available quantity of cash" (1936a, 167). Consequently, a reduction in the rate of interest would increase the amount of cash that people wish to hold; the demand for money would exceed the supply of money. If the rate of interest were raised, "there would be a surplus of cash which no one would be willing to hold" (Keynes 1936a, 167). According to Keynes's liquidity-preference theory, the quantity of money, in "conjunction with liquidity-preference, determines the actual rate of interest in given circumstances" (Keynes 1936a, 168).

Knight considered the liquidity-preference theory of interest-rate determination to be restrictive. He criticized Keynes for "repeatedly" arguing that the rate of interest is *not* the price that equates the demand for resources to invest with the readiness to abstain from consumption: "According to Mr. Keynes, interest is purely a monetary phenomenon": it is the price that equates the desire to hold wealth in the form of cash with the available quantity of cash (Knight 1937, 112). Knight, however, asserted that the interest rate is determined by a broader set of factors than those posited by Keynes:

> It is self-evident that at any time (and at the margin) the rate of interest equates *both* the desirability of holding cash with the desirability of holding nonmonetary wealth *and* the desirability of consuming with that of lending and so

with both the other two desirabilities. For, to any person who has either money or wealth in any form, or to anyone who holds salable service-capacity, all three of these alternatives are continuously open. (emphasis in original, Knight 1937, 112–13)

Thus, Knight described the desire of holding money as an alternative to holding other forms of wealth—an analytical construct that did not appear in any of his earlier writings. Knight's use of this construct can be regarded as having been influenced by Keynes's theory of liquidity preference.[67] As we shall see, the use of liquidity-preference theory formed an important part of Knight's theory of money in his 1941 article "The Business Cycle, Interest, and Money: A Methodological Approach," and in Mints's work beginning in 1945.

*Policy implications.* The final chapter of the *General Theory* was titled "Concluding Notes on the Social Philosophy towards Which the General Theory Might Lead." In that chapter, Keynes discussed the policy implications of his book. These included an increased role of the state in "guiding" consumption through taxation and "partly by fixing the rate of interest" (1936a, 378). Additionally, Keynes downplayed the effectiveness of monetary policy. He argued: "it seems unlikely that the influence of banking policy on the rate of interest will be sufficient by itself to determine an optimal rate of investment. I conceive, therefore, that a somewhat comprehensive socialization of investment will prove the only means of securing an approximation to full employment" (1936a, 378). Keynes envisaged an economic system entailing increased socialization, but in which "the necessary measures of socialization can be introduced gradually" (1936a, 378).

As Simons (1936b) had done in his review of the *General Theory*, Knight criticized both the social-philosophical and the monetary-policy implications of Keynes's book. Concerning the social-philosophical implications, Knight commented: "Any government in effective control of the economic life of a nation can certainly set aside any fraction of the social product it may decide upon, and can also invest it in any way it pleases" (1937, 118–19). Keynes's solution to the problem of involuntary unemployment, Knight affirmed, was a "'somewhat comprehensive socialization of investment'" combined with a low-interest-rate policy (1937, 119). Knight continued:

> I can only comment that phrases like socialization of investment, with no indication of what procedure is in mind, sound (to me) more like the language of the soap-box reformer than that of an economist writing a theoretical tome for

economists. Even the "influence of banking policy" cannot, in fact, be carried far without the banking authority passing upon the soundness of, and taking responsibility for, real investment for long periods, which would necessitate a large measure of actual management. That is, this in itself involves socialization of investment, which again certainly cannot be carried far without largely "socializing" economic life in general, and this means taking it out of business and putting it into politics. (1937, 119)

Concerning the monetary-policy implications of the *General Theory*, Knight's assessment was revealing. He stated that the "value of the book" was its emphasis on "the need of a sound monetary theory," but the book itself had not contributed to the construction of such a theory (1937, 123). Knight *agreed* with "Mr. Keynes's conception of [monetary] inflation as the cure for depression and unemployment." He wrote: "With this general position, I happen to be in sympathy" (1937, 123). Knight argued, that "the case of money . . . is the most important factor in the general tendency to oscillation in an economic system" (1937, 123n24). Where Knight parted ways with Keynes was in the latter's belief that the central bank should keep its foot on the monetary gas pedal at all times—not only during cyclical downturns. Specifically, he asserted that "it is hard for me to believe that Mr. Keynes had tried very hard to picture in his mind the effects on the competitive economy of having a political banking authority dedicated to the permanent policy of maintaining an artificially low rate of interest" (1937, 119). Knight questioned whether Keynes had thought through the implications "of having a central bank unremittingly pumping money into the system by an arbitrarily low interest rate" (1937, 119). In other words, by keeping the interest rate artificially low, Knight believed that the central bank would ultimately lose control over the money supply and inflation.

*Postscript.* The editor of the *Canadian Journal of Economics and Political Science* wrote to Keynes asking if he wanted "to write a counter-blast" to Knight's review (Patinkin 1979, 300). Keynes replied as follows:

I read his passionate expiring cries, but controversial-minded though I am, I could not discover any concrete criticism to reply to. In fact, I really felt that there was nothing at all to be said. Indeed with Professor Knight's two main conclusions, namely, that my book caused him intense irritation, and that he had great difficulty in understanding it, I am in agreement. . . . The truth is, I feel sure, that our minds have not met, and that there is scarcely a single particular in which he has seen what I was driving at. (quoted from Cristiano and Fiorito 2016, 69)

*Discussion*

An overriding feature of Knight's review of the *General Theory* was its critical and combative tone. That tone notwithstanding, the review revealed several important reasons that the Chicagoans resisted both the analytical structure and the policy message of the *General Theory*. As previously emphasized, the Chicago version of the quantity theory had been formulated in such a way that it assumed that a basic feature of economic life is the danger of sharp changes in the velocity, or the hoarding, of money, a feature that was greatly exacerbated by the perverse behavior of a fractional-reserve banking system. In this connection, Knight singled out the central role played by increases in the demand for money, or declining velocity, in his review of the *General Theory*: "it is the speculative motive for holding money which varies widely in connection with the cycle and immediately causes the trouble. (What *causes* this variation is the *central problem* of cycle theory)" (emphasis added, 1937, 114). The Fisherine equation, employed by Chicagoans, focused on the use of money to purchase goods. Hence, expectations of the price level underpinned changes in velocity. The theory of liquidity preference focused on money's role as an asset. Therefore, expectations of interest rates on bonds underpinned changes in the demand for money. Formulated during a period (1932 and 1933) when the US banking system was on the verge of collapse and had to be shut down, the Chicago quantity-theory framework explained both the banking crisis and the very high unemployment rates of that period.

As was the case for Simons, Douglas, Director, and Mints, Knight believed that the Depression could be combated, and the socialization of investment averted, through the use of money-financed fiscal deficits, 100 percent reserve requirements, and monetary-policy rules. Keynes envisaged that fiscal deficits would form a permanent feature of economic life and that the share of government spending would rise secularly. Knight, along with Simons, Douglas, Director, and Mints, wanted to balance the budget over the cycle and limit the amount of government involvement in economic activity.

*Theory of the Business Cycle, 1941*

Amid the Keynesian revolution's ascendancy, Knight published the paper "The Business Cycle, Interest, and Money: A Methodological Approach," in the May 1941 issue of the *Review of Economics and Statistics*. The article was the most complete description of the Chicago version of the business cycle published to that time. The article also extended the Chicago tradition's business-cycle theory in ways that anticipated elements of the monetary analysis contained in Friedman's 1956 "Restatement" of the quantity theory. Additionally, the article included a critique of the socialist state and a defense of the capitalist system.

Knight began with the observation that one of the most important criticisms made against the capitalist system by its "attackers" centered on the tendency of that system to give rise to business cycles. Correspondingly, a criticism frequently made against classical economic theory was that "it has overlooked or ignored the existence of cycles and depression which the critics assert is inherent in such a system" (1941a, 202). As in his 1936 lectures on the business cycle and his 1937 review of the *General Theory*, Knight considered that criticism to be valid: "Economic theory, as expounded in the orthodox tradition, down until very recent times has ... failed to recognize the business cycle as a reality, and to inquire into the causality of the cycle" (1941a, 202).[68] The purpose of Knight's article was "to show that purely abstract theorizing about the free-market system ... should long ago have led students [of economic theory] to expect cyclical changes as a matter of course" (1941a, 202). Knight then proceeded to present a business-cycle theory.

As he had done in his 1936 lectures at Berkeley, Knight began with an analogy of a "machine self-regulated by a governor." The workings of such a machine always control the regulated phenomenon—such as a thermostat set to regulate the temperature of a room—"within some limits, between which it oscillates in a more or less regular or rhythmic cycle. This follows from the inevitable presence of 'lag' in the working of the mechanism" (1941a, 203). The same logic applied to the economic system:

> In the presence of a lag between cause and effect, the function-and-variable conception of cause and effect itself is valid only for long-run tendencies; it applies to the equilibrium situation only, giving no information as to the quantitative relation between the cause and the effect (the independent and the dependent variable) at any moment of time. Variations in an economic cause can never be expected to produce strictly simultaneous variations in its effect. (1941a, 203)[69]

Thus, if a disturbance hits the system, the response may be subject to a lag with "an indeterminate interval." Knight maintained that the "phenomenon of 'disturbance' is especially important in monetary theory" (1941a, 204).

Knight claimed that the two basic phenomena of the business cycle are (1) speculation in money and (2) the fact that changes in costs lag behind changes in the prices of products. Regarding speculation in money, he stated:

> Cyclical analysis properly begins with the fact that the general price level, the reciprocal of the purchasing power of money, is subject to . . . psychological tendency. . . . An incipient tendency of prices (of products in general) to rise creates the impression of an upward trend (a downward trend in the value of money). . . . The motive for holding money idle . . . is speculation for a rise in its future value [i.e., an expected change in the price level]. . . . Since cash holdings yield no return in any other form, any cash held longer than necessary to bridge over the regular non-coincidence of receipts and disbursements must be expected to increase in value (relative to other wealth) at a rate equal to the yield of any property to be had in exchange for the money at existing prices—with allowance for the uncertainty in both alternatives. (1941a, 210)

Concerning the role of sticky costs in the business cycle, Knight asserted that lags in the response of costs, especially wages, relative to prices, convert oscillations in prices into oscillations in profits and production (1941a, 212–13).[70]

But what about the role of money in the business cycle? A key characteristic of the cycle, Knight claimed, is that "the tendency for increase or decrease in speculation holding of money (i.e., disposition to hold which reflects itself in general prices, the quantity of money being held constant) to feed upon itself cumulatively is subject to no such effective check as results from the accumulation of a consumable commodity with a fairly definite demand curve" (1941a, 211). Furthermore, once the cumulative process has started, "in the case of money, just what does set a boundary to a movement of general prices in either direction, and especially the downward movement, becomes something of a mystery." Importantly, "the general condition of instability is further accentuated by the role played in economic society by the banks" (1941a, 211). Banks, Knight noted, create money through lending, and they withdraw money from circulation by cutting back their overall level of assets: "For reasons which are familiar, the consequences of short-period lending are peculiarly serious" (1941a, 212).

What was the analytic framework underlying Knight's account of the business cycle? Knight noted that his account—what he called "a simplified picture, or 'theory' of the behavior of money" (1941a, 213)—was grounded

on a particular theory. That theory was the Fisherine equation of exchange.
He wrote:

> For present purposes, the following assumptions seem justifiable: (*a*) The total
> quantity of money (*M* in the Fisher equation) is constant, including both "cash"
> and the lending (deposit-creating) power in the hands of the banking system.
> (*b*) The transactions-velocity of circulation of money in effective use (we may
> call it "active *V*") is also constant. This means that changes in "total *V*" reflect
> transfers from idle reserves or hoards (where *V* = 0) to active use, or in the
> opposite direction (hoards, including idle lending power of the banks). In con-
> sequence, finally (*c*) changes in general prices (*P*) reflect changes in "active *M*."
> That the division between active and idle funds is not definite or determinate
> goes without saying, and the other assumptions are more or less unrealistic,
> but the whole group of assumptions seems to be a close enough approximation
> to the facts to function as a hypothesis for a general explanation of the cycle.
> (1941a, 213)

Beginning with an economy at the bottom of a depression, Knight described the cycle in terms of the following sequence. (1) An "incipient
upward tendency in business conditions" acts "cumulatively," resulting "in
increased disbursements, especially to labor" (1941a, 213–14); prices rise.
(2) Costs lag behind the rise in prices; thus, profits rise. (3) Bank lending rises; thus, deposits (*M'*) and the velocity of circulation of deposits
(*V'*) increase. (4) The demand for consumption goods increases, which,
in turn, increases the demand in the production-of-goods industries.
(5) Investment rises. (6) Prices and profits continue to rise; "idle funds"
(including lending power) are exhausted (that is, velocity rises). (7) The
process comes to an end because the "absorption of unemployed labor,
and perhaps . . . a drawing-in of 'inferior' workers . . . [leads to] a rise in
wages, probably gaining upon the rises in prices of consumption goods. . . .
This situation will certainly lead to a 'crisis' and the reversal of the whole
process." Knight continued:

> But reversal may come about from other causes, such as the overtaking of
> prices by costs, a crop failure or any calamity in the business world, or mere
> "psychology." Too much attention has been given to this problem of the cause
> of the collapse. The essential fact is merely the unstable equilibrium. As already
> noted, we do not try to find out what particular cause upsets an object balanced
> upon a sharp point. (1941a, 214)

In what follows, I focus on three aspects of Knight's article: (1) its anticipations of Friedman's monetary economics; (2) its policy recommendations; and (3) its defense of capitalism.

*Anticipations.* Knight presaged specific aspects of Friedman's monetary framework. First, he argued that human capital should be included in the determination of wealth:

> In all essentials, the training or retraining of a laborer—of a [Robinson] Crusoe or a worker for wages in contemporary society—is a matter of investment or the transfer of investment; and the economically rational management of such activity involves the same kind of investment-yield calculation as the production of any material instrument or the replacement of one such instrument by another—presumably in response to a change in the form of consumption demand. (1941a, 217)

Friedman's incorporation of human capital in his concept of permanent income constituted an important part of his work on the demand for money (Friedman 1956a) and the consumption function (Friedman 1957b).

Second, Knight incorporated the Fisherine distinction between nominal and real interest rates into his discussion.[71] He stated:

> In a capital-using economy, with effective freedom to invest (and specifically with new investment going forward in substantial volume), it is (to repeat) self-evident that if loans of money are made, the effective rate must tend to be approximately equal to the rate of return on investment, regardless of the value unit in terms of which computations are made. In long-term contracts involving any stipulated exchange ratio, this contractual price will of course be influenced, in a mathematically simple way, by the general market anticipation of future price changes and the prevalent attitude toward any recognized risk of such changes. And if any contract calls for payments of "money" at future dates, the amounts will be affected in the same way by any expected change in the value of the money unit. The loan of money at interest is such a contract. (1941a, 218)

Recognition of the effect of anticipated price changes on the loan rate of interest enabled Knight to make a distinction, emphasized in Friedman's (1956a) work, between nominal and real interest rates. Thus, Knight asserted: "The stipulated rate in loan contracts becomes a monetary phenomenon precisely to the extent that prospective changes in the value of the unit in which such contracts are drawn is the predominant (eventually the only) factor in the calculations of borrowers and lenders" (1941a, 221).

Knight used the distinction between nominal and real interest rates to criticize Keynes's theory of liquidity preference. Keynes, in his *General Theory*, was correct, argued Knight, that the rate of interest is, at any time, a measure of the unwillingness of those who possess money to part with it in exchange for bonds (1941a, 221). However, Keynes based "his whole argument for the monetary theory of interest on the familiar fact that open-market operations can be effective" in reducing interest rates. In doing so, Keynes fell into a "simple methodological fallacy"—he denied "that other things need to be considered" (1941a, 221–22). Knight argued that Keynes's failure to take other factors into account rendered Keynes's liquidity-preference theory "analytically absurd" (1941a, 222). The crucial factor that Keynes failed to consider is the expected change in the price level. Thus, Knight explained:

> The rate of interest in its normal aspect as the rate of return on investment is the ratio between two value [nominal] magnitudes, income and wealth. A change in the unit of value can affect this ratio only as it affects one of its terms *more* than it affects the other. There may (or may not) be such a differential effect for a time, after a monetary change. Of course, if created currency is used exclusively to buy bonds, or even to construct new equipment, it can temporarily raise the relative price which the principal, or source, will yield. Such an occurrence is a temporary disturbance only. As a monetary change diffuses through the economy, it comes to affect all classes of prices in the same way, and at equilibrium any relative price will be the same as before the monetary change occurred—except in so far as in the meantime changes may have occurred in the factors which really control the price relation in question. (emphasis in original, 1941a, 222–23)

Knight's distinction between the nominal interest rate and the real rate, and his account of the monetary-transmission mechanism in the above quotation, presaged Friedman's description, in his 1967 presidential address before the American Economic Association, of the effects of an increase in the rate of growth of the money supply on economic activity. Friedman's account ran as follows. (1) "The *initial* impact of increasing the quantity of money at a faster rate than it had been increasing is to make interest rates lower for a time," stimulating spending. (2) "Rising income will raise the liquidity preference schedule and the demand for loans." (3) "[It] may also raise prices, which would reduce the real quantity of money." Together, the three effects will "tend [after a year or two] to return interest rates to the level they would otherwise have had" (1968a, 6). Friedman continued:

> A fourth effect, when and if it becomes operative, will go even farther, and definitely mean that a higher rate of monetary expansion will correspond to a higher, not lower, level of interest rates than would otherwise have prevailed. Let the higher rate of monetary growth produce rising prices, and let the public come to expect that prices will continue to rise. Borrowers will then be willing to pay and lenders will then demand higher interest rates—as Irving Fisher pointed out decades ago. (1968a, 6)

Thus, Friedman and Knight both believed that an attempt by the monetary authorities to lower interest rates by expanding the supply of money would, over time, raise interest rates. The view that expansionary monetary policy would ultimately raise interest rates was not a prevalent view among economists in the early 1940s, when Knight published his article.

*The question of policy.*[72] As we have seen, Knight's 1941 paper provided a theory of the business cycle in which the behavior of money is the big, bad actor in the cycle. What measures could be taken to dampen the cycle? Knight expressed the following view: "Some means must be found for preventing individuals, business units, and banks, acting separately or in conjunction, from behaving in such a way as to change drastically and rapidly the amount of effective money [i.e., $M$ and $M'$ in the Fisherine equation of exchange] in active use—or the velocity of circulation of the total stock of medium, actual and potential" (1941a, 223).

What should be the objective of monetary policy? Knight favored a price-level-stabilization rule but recognized that such a rule would involve substantial discretion in the use of policy instruments. He argued that "general prices ... must be maintained at a relatively stable level, and the public must be given confidence that this action will be taken" (1941a, 223). To attain an "approximate constancy in general prices" would necessitate "deliberate action based on constant attention, correcting or offsetting incipient tendencies to expansion or contraction" (1941a, 224–25). What agency should be entrusted with the goals of price-level stabilization? Knight did not say. It was clear, however, that he was concerned with the matter of discretion: "Serious problems are involved in finding a reliable indicator of the actual monetary position and its changes, in devising a prompt and effective mode of action on the monetary situation, and especially in the political and administrative field, in safely delegating the necessary authority to any human political agency for exercise on behalf of society" (1941a, 225).

Through what means should changes in the money supply be implemented? Knight, again, had little to say—with one exception. He did not consider changes in interest rates—operating through open-market operations or discount-rate changes—to be an effective way of conducting policy: "To be sure, interest is an element in cost of production. . . . But, clearly, in view of the way in which enterprises are commonly organized and financed, the borrowing rate on money, including the rate of yield at which bonds can be sold and the bank rate, is relatively quite unimportant in comparison either with the effects of wage changes or with the role of speculative [i.e., expectations of changes in the price level] considerations" (1941a, 215).

*Capitalism versus collectivism.* Knight concluded his article with a brief comparison of the capitalist and the collectivist systems. He maintained that "if a collectivist, or socialist, state is to preserve any of the traditional economic liberties of individuals, it also must operate on the basis of money and market transactions; with prices of products and of productive services controlled by competition, in essentially the same manner as in the enterprise system. The fact that the government would be the chief owner of productive wealth, and the 'entrepreneur' in the great bulk of economic activity, would not change things in that regard" (1941a, 225). In that connection, Knight observed: "The totalitarian-communistic regime in Russia, if it ever seriously tried to get away from the pecuniary market structure as the general framework of economic organization, certainly did not succeed, but ran into disastrous consequences and soon gave up the attempt" (1941a, 225–26). Since prices would have to be determined by competitive forces in a socialist system, Knight asserted that the monetary situation in a collectivist economy would have the same character that it has in a free-enterprise system and, in particular, "the same tendency to cyclical oscillation" (1941a, 226). While a collectivist state would be able to carry out certain "remedial action"—for example, to prevent unemployment— more easily than could a free-market society, Knight explained that

on examination these conditions [necessary for the remedial action to take place] will be found to root in arbitrary power over the activities and lives of individuals. As has been remarked before, there is no problem of unemployment in a penitentiary. In any other sense, the argument for collectivism from the standpoint of the problem of the business cycle does not seem to have much force. The general presumption is that ... the control of all the features of a national economy by a central authority would present much greater difficulty than the control of one feature. (1941a, 226)

## Knight, Simons, and Laissez-Faire

Like his former student Henry Simons, Knight had been deeply alarmed by the emergence of communism in the Soviet Union and National Socialism in Germany. Like Simons, he viewed the policies of the New Deal as part of a movement toward political radicalism in the United States. In a letter dated May 9, 1934, addressed to Friedrich Hayek, Knight wrote: "This to me is the meaning of the 'New Deal'; it is just a detail in the general movement of west European civilization away from liberalism to authoritarianism" (quoted from Burgin 2009, 522). Some months later, in a letter dated October 3, 1934, addressed to William H. Kiekhofer, Knight wrote that he believed that the policies of the New Deal were further manifestations of "a fundamental historical drift of western civilization toward bureaucratic tyranny" (quoted from Burgin 2009, 518).[73]

Additionally, like Simons, Knight was critical of the then-existing liberal order. Market economies, he believed, had demonstrated several adverse characteristics. First, as noted earlier, Knight believed that market economies bred inequality, with income often determined by luck and inheritance. In a 1923 paper, "The Ethics of Competition," he wrote: "The income does not go to 'factors'; but to their owners, and can in no case have more ethical justification than has the fact of ownership. The ownership of personal or material productive capacity is based on a complex mixture of inheritance, luck and effort, probably in that order of importance" (1923, 56). He continued: "of the three considerations named certainly none but the effort can have ethical validity" (1923, 56). Concern with the inequality fostered by the free-market economy was a persistent theme in Knight's writings throughout his career. In his 1950 presidential address "The Role of Principles in Economics and Politics," before the American Economic Association, he stated:

> The most serious limitations of the free-market economy and major problems set by it, arise from the fact that it takes the "units," individuals, families, etc. as "given," which is entirely unrealistic. ... But in the distribution of economic

resources atomistic motivation tends powerfully toward cumulatively increasing inequality. For all productive capacity—whether owned "property" or personal qualities—is essentially "capital," a joint creation of pre-existing capacity (or the result of "accident"). And those who already have more capacity are always in a better position to acquire still more, with the same effort and sacrifice. This applies about as much to personal capacity as to property, though the latter is a more convenient way of passing on "unearned" advantage to heirs or successors. It is a gross injustice—by one of several conflicting norms of justice generally accepted in liberal society. (1951, 271)

Second, in the early part of his career, Knight, like Simons, believed that market economies naturally tend to generate monopolies. In his 1923 paper "The Ethics of Competition," he expressed the view: "No error is more egregious than that of confounding freedom with free competition as is not infrequently done. As elementary theory itself shows, the members of any economic group can always make more by combining than they can by competing. . . . The workings of competition educate men progressively for monopoly" (1923, 52). And like Simons, Knight's views concerning monopolies changed over the years. Early in his career, he put industrial monopolies, labor monopolies, and monopolies in many parts of agriculture on an equal footing as impairments to the functioning of the free markets.[74] By the early 1940s he had come to believe that government policies foster monopolies. In a 1941 paper, "The Meaning of Freedom," Knight argued:

> But it is needful to state that the role of "monopoly" in actual economic life is enormously exaggerated in the popular mind and also that a large part of the monopoly which is real, and especially the worst part, is due to the activities of government. In general (and especially in the United States under the New Deal), these have been very largely such as to promote, if not directly to create, monopoly rather than to create or enforce the conditions of market competition. (1941b, 103)[75]

By the time of his 1950 AEA presidential address, Knight no longer considered industrial monopolies to be a major evil. "The public," he stated, "misconceives its nature and grossly exaggerates the extent and power of business monopolies" (1951, 220); Knight had come to believe that industrial monopolies are "temporary and functional"; "but where monopoly really bites is in the legal brigandage of organized wage-earners and farmers" (1951, 270).

Finally, and again like Simons, in his early writings Knight was critical of the role played by advertising in manipulating wants. In a 1934 paper, "Social Science and the Political Trend," he wrote: "one of the most fundamental weaknesses of the market system is the use of persuasive influence by sellers upon buyers, and a general excessive tendency to produce wants for goods rather than goods for the satisfaction of wants" (1934b, 422).[76] Like Simons, Knight's concern with the effects of advertising diminished during his career.

In terms of attitudes toward the free-market system, Knight, however, differed from Simons. While both economists pinpointed flaws in the operation of the market system, Simons, as we have seen, provided a program for reforming the system to improve its *functioning*. Knight, in contrast, mainly took on the role of a critic. He was more comfortable in exposing the weaknesses of economic systems, including the free-market and socialist systems, than in proposing reforms.[77] Thus, after pointing out in his AEA presidential address that a free-market economy fosters inequality, Knight wrote: "The question is, what can be done about it?" (1951, 272). He did not attempt to provide an answer.

Why, then, did Knight support the free-market system despite its faults? The reason had to do with his belief that only such a system could provide the freedom of choice required to allow individuals to set and pursue their own objectives—and not necessarily because such an order would produce superior economic results.[78] He made this reason clear in a 1932 reply to a comment made by Sumner Slichter, in which Slichter had defended economic planning:[79]

There has been, and must be, a question how far it is *comparatively* better social policy (I am aware of the redundancy but wish to be clear) to have individuals make their own choices in economic life and how far better to have them dictated—by anybody else who can be thought of in the position of dictating them. Even if it were proved (a) that some specified individual would make these choices more wisely than the one affected, (b) that that particular individual would be the one to make them under some hypothetical political arrangement, and (c) that the said arrangement could be had by wishing for it—still the question would not at all be settled in favor of dictation. What I want from the preachers of control, and do not get in *Modern Economic Society*, in this "Comment," or anywhere else, is something I can understand on the subject of *who* is to make the economic choices for the individual *who* admittedly makes them quite "imperfectly," or *how* this choosing functionary is to be selected, and *how* the individual affected is to be brought to accept them; and, in general, what kind of (a) individuals and (b) social order the preachers are either assuming or working toward. (emphasis in original, 1932b, 823–24)

By the time of his 1950 AEA presidential address, Knight's view was that the freedom provided under the market system had, if anything, strengthened. He stated:

> The ethic of liberal civilization holds (I repeat) both that men want to be free and have a right to be and that they ought to be free, even if they themselves feel that their affairs might possibly be technically better managed for them as slaves by some possible master. Of course even these assumptions in an extreme version are made only for the purposes of theory; everyone admits that in practice governments have to set some limits to individual freedom and freedom of association and to perform many functions on behalf of the community as a whole. If only economics could really teach people the simple and obvious fact, which most of them already know but refuse to accept, that anyone producing for exchange is producing for himself, as much as Crusoe, but merely a thousand times more effectively because he does it indirectly by producing for the needs of others. If this were realized, it would surely put an end to all the insane or diabolical revolutionary propaganda and most of the stupid criticisms of the "capitalist system" that menace our free institutions. (1951, 264)

One more point about Knight's AEA presidential address should be mentioned. The address contained a single reference to Keynes—a reference that summed up Knight's assessment of the Keynesian revolution. Here is what Knight had to say: "The latest 'new economics,' and in my opinion rather the worst for fallacious doctrine and pernicious consequences, is that launched by the late John Maynard (Lord) Keynes, who for a decade succeeded in carrying economic thinking well back to the dark ages" (1951, 252).[80]

## 5.4 Viner

We have seen that Jacob Viner was a dissenter from the core policy positions advocated by the other members of The Group in the first half of the 1930s. To assess the consistency of Viner's policy views over time, I discuss the following writings by Viner on macroeconomic issues in the

second half of the 1930s and early 1940s: (1) the article "Mr. Keynes on
the Causes of Unemployment," published (as part of a symposium on the
*General Theory*) in the *Quarterly Journal of Economics* (*QJE*) in 1936;[81]
(2) the 1937 book *Studies in the Theory of International Trade*, which, although concerned with the doctrinal development of trade theory, sheds
light on Viner's thinking about the quantity theory and monetary-policy
rules; and (3) an overlooked article, "Inflation: Menace or Bogey?," published in the *Yale Review* in 1942. I then discuss Viner's 1939 presidential
address to the American Economic Association, titled "The Short View
and the Long View in Economic Policy," published in the *AER* in 1940.
In his presidential address, Viner presented his views on the sustainability
of a free-market system after ten years of mostly economic depression;
he also offered a reason for the weakness of private investment spending
throughout those years.

*Review of the* General Theory

Viner's review of the *General Theory* was, on balance, critical but constructive. His bottom line was that Keynes had not established a "general
theory" as intended; that is, Keynes had not achieved a breakthrough that
truly went beyond what existing work had to offer in explaining depressions. Like Knight in his appraisal of the *General Theory*, Viner asserted
that the book was a difficult read. In addition, like Knight, Viner complained about Keynes's contrivance of new terms: "no old term for an old
concept is used when a new one can be coined" (1936b, 147).

Viner's main criticism of the *General Theory*—what Viner called "the
most vulnerable part of his [Keynes's] analysis"—was Keynes's contention that the rate of interest is determined "by the schedule of liquidity-
preferences and the available quantity of money, the prevailing rate of
interest being simply that price for the sacrifice of liquidity at which the
desire to hold cash is equated with the available quantity of cash" (1936b,
157). Like Knight, Viner rejected Keynes's purely monetary theory of interest. Viner argued that the transactions demand for money—and the
forces of consumption and investment that underpin that demand—also
determine the interest rate:

> The transactions-desire for cash is for cash to be used and not for cash to be
> held unused. It must therefore vary positively with the volume of investment,
> of income, and of expenditures for consumption. In so far as it consists of

demand for cash from entrepreneurs for business uses, it is but a reflection of their investment demand for capital. In so far as it is a demand for cash from consumers who are living beyond their current income, it is the demand for consumption loans of older theory. Whatever its origin, demand for cash for transaction purposes is, dollar for dollar, of equal influence on the rate of interest as demand for cash for hoarding purposes. The demand for capital and the propensity to save (which is the reciprocal of the propensity to consume) are thus restored—tho, I admit, in somewhat modified and improved fashion—to their traditional rôles as determinants of the rate of interest. (1936b, 158–59)[82]

Viner noted that full employment "rarely occurs" under Keynes's theoretical framework (1936b, 151). A key factor contributing to "the persistence of 'involuntary' unemployment lies with the persistence of interest rates at levels too high to induce employers to bid for all the labor available at the prevailing money rates of wages" (1936b, 151). The high interest rates, coupled with Keynes's assumption that "the marginal productivity function of capital and therefore the investment demand for capital have little elasticity," contribute to the persistence of unemployment (1936b, 153).

Viner contended that a major difference between Keynes's analysis and the classical framework was Keynes's belief that a reduction in nominal wages would not reduce unemployment: "[Keynes's] view is that a lowering of money wage-rates . . . would chiefly alter the relative rates of wages of different labor groups. It would not be likely to increase the aggregate volume of employment" (1936b, 160). Viner, who had supported wage reductions in the early 1930s as a way to combat the Great Depression, argued that Keynes had failed to take into account the classical doctrine's view that declines in prices during depressions lag behind declines in wages, thus raising profits, investment, and output:

What I understand to be the current doctrine is different. It looks to wage-reductions during a depression to restore profit-margins, thus to restore the investment-morale of entrepreneurs and to give them again a credit status which will enable them to finance any investment they may wish to make. It relies upon the occurrence of a lag between the reduction in wage-rates and a response in reduced volume of sales at the previous prices, during which interval entrepreneurs find prices to be higher than marginal costs and extensions of output therefore profitable, provided buyers can be found for the increased output. (1936b, 162)

With the rise in output, payrolls would increase "to provide the incomes with which the increased output can be bought" (1936b, 162).

Apart from the generally favorable tone of Viner's review, two aspects of that review distinguish it from the reviews of the *General Theory* by Simons and Knight. Both aspects concern issues *not* covered in Viner's review. First, Viner wrote *nothing* about the social-philosophical implications of the *General Theory*. Second, Viner said *nothing* about the monetary-policy implications of Keynes's book; indeed, the words "monetary policy" or "interest-rate policy" do not appear in Viner's review. As we saw, Keynes's contention that—to preserve capitalism—comprehensive socialization of investment, combined with a policy of low interest rates, would be needed was at the heart of the critiques of the *General Theory* in the reviews by Simons and Knight.[83]

### Studies in the Theory of International Trade

In early 1932, Viner began writing the book *Studies in the Theory of International Trade*. He thought that he would be able to complete the book within the year. In a letter dated January 27, 1932, to Bertil Ohlin, Viner wrote: "The depression here has involved me in all sorts of committee work and memoranda writing, as well as in lecturing than I care to do. I am beginning now to write a book on international trade theory and I hope to have it finished before next Christmas" (quoted from Nerozzi 2009, 587). In the event, Viner was far too optimistic. The book was published in 1937. It quickly became a classic in economic doctrine.

For the present study, four points about Viner's doctrinal-historical study are important to mention.[84] First, using the quantity theory Viner specified a causal relationship between the quantity of money and the price level (1937, 40–45), with the strength of the relationship depending on the factors that determine the velocity of circulation of money. Viner noted that both long-term structural factors and short-term cyclical factors affect velocity. Concerning the structural factors, he singled out "improvements in the means of communication, and . . . the development of clearinghouse and other arrangements for 'economizing currency'" (1937, 130–31). The predominant short-term factor affecting velocity, Viner indicated, was "changing degrees of confidence in the future value of the currency" (1937, 131). He added: "On both *a priori* and empirical grounds, however, velocity should be expected to rise as the volume of means of payment and the price level was rising" (1937, 131).[85]

Second, Viner suggested that monetary-policy rules are not practical; hence, rules were not likely to be followed by central banks. Thus, in discussing an exchange-rate system under which the price of the domestic currency is pegged to a commodity, such as gold, but where "the ratio of the amount of the currency to the amount of specie is subject to the discretion of a central authority," Viner wrote:

> If the controlling agency were operating on the basis of a clearly formulated and simple policy or rule of action, which was made known to the public, it would be possible to describe the international mechanism as it would operate under such policy. But central banks do not ordinarily disclose their policy to the public, and the evidence seems to point strongly to a disinclination on the part of central bankers as a class to accept as their guide the simple formulae which are urged upon them by economists and others, or to follow simple rules of their own invention. All central banks find themselves at times facing situations which appear to demand a choice between conflicting objectives, long-run versus short-run, internal stability versus exchange stability, the indicated needs of the market versus their own financial or reserve position, and so forth, and they seem universally to prefer meeting such situations *ad hoc* rather than in accordance with the dictates of some simple formula. (1937, 391)

Third, in reviewing the bullionist and antibullionist positions in the debates over monetary policy, Viner believed that the advocates of a national paper, or fiat, currency had made a better case for such a currency than had the advocates of an international metallic standard for their position.[86] Viner thought, however, that the underlying issue was not between a metallic standard and a paper standard, but between stable (or fixed) exchange rates and unstable (or fluctuating) exchange rates. Viewed in that context, Viner judged that the advocates of fiat money had "theoretically a moderately inferior and under ordinary practical conditions a seriously inferior" case than did the proponents of fixed exchange rates (1937, 216–17). He thought that fluctuating exchange rates give rise to risks and uncertainties that hamper international trade and investment. Although the development of forward exchange markets and other facilities for hedging might help to reduce exchange-rate risk, Viner believed that those facilities would "provide only a strictly limited palliative" (1937, 217).

Finally, Viner's discussion of the Bank of England's policies during the first half of the nineteenth century clarified an ambiguity that was contained in his lecture at the 1932 Chicago conference. As documented in chapter 2, in that lecture Viner criticized the Federal Reserve's policies during the Great Depression with the argument that the Fed's "attitude towards its functions" had resembled "with almost miraculous closeness that of the Bank of England during its worst period" (1932a, 28). But Viner failed to explain what he meant by his reference to the Bank of England's policies. He also failed to specify what period of time he had in mind in referring to the Bank of England's "worst period." Five years later, *Studies in the Theory of International Trade* provided clarification.

Chapter 5 of *Studies* included a section in which Viner assessed the Bank of England's policies during the nineteenth-century currency debates.[87] Here is the way that Viner judged the bank's performance: "It nevertheless appears to me that the evidence available warrants that during the period from about 1800 to about 1860 the Bank of England almost continuously displayed an inexcusable degree of incompetence or unwillingness to fulfill the requirements which could reasonably be demanded of a central bank" (1937, 254). What were the policies that led to the bank's incompetent performance during the period in question? Viner maintained that the bank failed to (1) make systematic use of discount policy, (2) make adequate use of open-market operations, (3) hold adequate gold reserves and interest-earning securities, (4) adequately distinguish between internal and external gold drains, and (5) formalize a policy of cooperation with other central banks (1937, 256–76). Viner did not single out a specific policy framework under which the Bank of England operated during this period. This circumstance reflects the fact that Viner believed that the bank's management never formulated a consistent policy framework, with the result that policy changed frequently and inconsistently. He stated: "During this entire period, the management of the Bank showed an almost complete inability to profit not only from its own recent experience, and from the advice so freely offered to it by outsiders, much of it excellent, but even from 'the practice of the forefathers' in the eighteenth century" (1937, 255). Thus, the picture that emerges from his account of the Bank of England's policies is one in which the root cause of the bank's "worst period" was incompetent management.

In our discussion of the Bullionist Controversy in chapter 4, we saw that bullionist writers laid the blame for the inflation in England at the beginning of the nineteenth century squarely at the door of the Bank of England. The bullionists argued that the bank's directors operated under the assumption that if banknotes were issued against the discount of short-term commercial bills drawn to finance real goods in the process of production, it would not be possible for the quantity of money to be excessive and thus to cause inflation—that is, the directors operated under the real bills perspective pushed forward by the antibullionists.[88] In chapter 3 of his book, Viner provided extensive coverage of the debates surrounding the inflationary phase of the Bullionist Controversy. In that connection, he wrote that the antibullionists "claimed that as long as currency was issued only by banks, and was issued by them only in the discount of genuine and sound short-term commercial paper, it could not be issued in excess of the needs of business, since no one would borrow at interest funds which he did not need" (1937, 148). This assertion is an obvious reference to the real bills doctrine. Thus, it can be reasonably conjectured that, in his critique of the Bank of England's policy in his 1932 Chicago lecture, Viner was likely referring, at least in part, to the bank's reliance on the real bills doctrine at the beginning of the nineteenth century.[89] As we shall see, criticism of monetary policy on the basis that the central bank followed the real bills doctrine was a feature of the work of Mints (1945a) and Friedman and Schwartz (1963).[90]

*Controlling Wartime Inflation: Viner's Position*

As mentioned, Viner's article "Inflation: Menace or Bogey?" was published in June 1942. The military buildup in the United States to World War II, followed by the country's entry into the war (in December 1941), had precipitated a surge in inflation. In his article, Viner reported that "the wholesale price level rose at a rate of approximately 10 per cent per annum from September, 1939, to May, 1942" (1942a, 690). In the article, Viner dealt mainly with two issues: (1) an enumeration of the costs of inflation; and (2) an analysis of the ways to control inflation. Regarding the costs of inflation, Viner affirmed that "the effect of the rise in prices is almost unalloyedly evil" (1942a, 686). In particular, inflation leads to income and wealth redistribution: organized labor and those with liabilities fixed in nominal terms gain; the "salaried class," "unorganized labor," those with claims in nominal terms, and the "*rentier* class" (e.g., pensioners, those livings on fixed incomes), lose.[91] "In this fact [the unequal distribution of the effects of inflation]," Viner argued, "lies the great menace of inflation" (1942a, 687).

In light of the government's large wartime spending requirements, how could "the necessary additional transfer of spending power from the public to the government" be achieved without triggering even higher inflation? Viner ruled out financing government spending through taxation. He argued:

"In the present war, tax structures are already so steeply progressive that great increases in tax revenues are now physically unattainable except by increased taxation of low incomes, thus making the tax system less instead of more progressive" (1942a, 696). Instead of taxation, he advocated two methods. The first—and less important—method was to have the government borrow to finance its spending. Viner thought that the government should, as far as possible, not borrow from "funds which otherwise would remain idle" (1942a, 697). He wrote: "It is government expenditure and not government borrowing which is inflationary; and given the expenditures, the borrowing is anti-inflationary unless it is borrowed from funds which if not lent to the government would remain idle, or is borrowing from the banks of funds created to be lent to the government, when it is neutral" (1942a, 696).

The second—and more important—method to contain inflation, Viner claimed, was to impose price controls: "The development of direct controls as preventatives of inflation has greatly lessened the importance of the traditional fiscal device of taxation" (1942a, 695–96). Viner expressed the belief that direct price controls would prevent the buildup of inflation: "My failure fully to share the feeling that others are expressing of urgent need for more to be done immediately to check inflation is probably due to the greater confidence I have in the efficacy of the direct controls already in operation or in prospect as anti-inflation measures" (1942, 700). As in his review of the *General Theory*, in the case of his 1942 article Viner did not consider the possible use of monetary policies. As in his 1936 review, the words "monetary policy" or "interest-rate policy" do not appear in his 1942 article.

## The Free-Market System

Viner having worked for the US Treasury for about seven years, his 1939 presidential address to the American Economic Association mainly dealt with his views about the ability of academic economists to adapt to the policy arena. However, another issue that occupied his attention was the future of the free-market system following ten years of economic depression and in light of the rise of the fascist and communist regimes in the 1930s. Viner noted that "the liberal tradition in Anglo-American thought" operated according to the following "economic dogma"—mainly that "under a system of free individual enterprise a higher level of economic well-being was attainable than under any other form of economic organization" (1940, 11). Viner expressed the view that the acceptability of that dogma "has been destroyed or seriously impaired even for many economists by ten years of sustained and severe depression" (1940, 11). He believed that the emergence of monopolistic industries had undermined the case in favor of the efficiency of the free-market system. He stated:

> Whether now, after several generations of unrestrained grant of corporate charters and of great development of mass-production requiring large economic units for its operation, it is still possible, through proper regulation and restriction by government of the activities of large corporations, to restore an essentially competitive price system, is a question to which I freely confess I do not see a clear answer. (1940, 12)

To deal with the rise of monopolistic industries, Viner advocated the stricter enforcement of antitrust laws. Like Douglas, but unlike Director, Knight, and Simons, Viner did not think that labor unions posed a problem for the functioning of the economic system. Like Douglas, he called for "encouragement to and protection of labor monopolies" (1940, 13). With the enforcement of the antitrust laws, and a strengthening of labor unions, the capitalist system, he thought, had a chance to survive: "All that I suggest, therefore, with respect to the dogma that free competition can substantially survive if government gives it due protection and encouragement, is not that its validity under modern conditions is obvious, but that we have not the right definitely to reject it before it has been given an honest and thorough test" (1940, 13).

Another issue that concerned Viner was the weakness of private investment during the Great Depression. Why had investment been so weak during much of the 1930s? Because Viner had been advising the US Treasury since 1933, his answer to that question was surprising: Viner indirectly cited the antibusiness rhetoric of the Roosevelt administrations as a contributing factor to the weakness of private investment. He noted that the "spokesmen for capital have ... been claiming for some six years that a political shadow *has* been cast over the security of their investments, and that this has been responsible for the low rate of new investment, and consequently for the persistence of depression" (emphasis in original, 1940, 13). Viner was not willing to dispute that view. He stated: "to my perhaps naïve mind, the dogma still carries some shreds of credibility" (1940, 14).

After he stopped advising the Treasury, Viner's view of the role played by antibusiness rhetoric in the weak US economic performance in the

1930s had sharpened. Thus, in a 1953 interview, Viner, no longer working for the US Treasury, reported on his response to President Franklin Roosevelt during a meeting when the latter suggested that he would renew his "warfare against business." The meeting took place in 1936; it comprised a group of administration officials and was part of regular sessions that Roosevelt held with those officials. Here is Viner's account of his intervention at the meeting.

> In one instance, he [Roosevelt] tried out on the group an idea he had of renewing his warfare against business, prodding business. They all agreed that what he [was] suggesting was clever, would be effective politically, and so on. I spoke up and said that I didn't think that was exactly what the country needed, that while he felt things were quiet, it still was true that there had been no reconciliation between the New Deal and business. Business still was suspicious and hostile. There still were anywhere from six to nine million unemployed after three or four years of the New Deal. He [Roosevelt] had failed to produce real recovery. . . . My own guess as an economist was that the major reason was that business men just were living in an atmosphere of [a] lack of long-run confidence, and therefore were not investing and were not optimistic. Therefore, what he was thinking of doing was a mistake. (Viner 1953, 17)

Viner (1953, 17) then gave Roosevelt's response:

> He [Roosevelt] said "Viner, you don't understand my problem. If I'm going to succeed and if my administration is going to succeed, I have to maintain a strong hold on my public. In order to maintain a firm hold on [the] public I have to do something startling every once in a while. I mustn't let them ever take me for granted."

Viner (1953) went on to say that, after he spoke up, Roosevelt gave instructions to Treasury Secretary Robert Morgenthau to make sure that Viner would no longer attend these meetings.

*Postscript 1.* Patinkin (1979) reported that, in 1940, Viner evidently proposed that Keynes be awarded an honorary doctorate in connection with the fiftieth anniversary of the University of Chicago. In a letter dated August 6, 1940, from Knight to Viner, Knight expressed "shock" at having heard that Viner had made such a proposal. Knight continued: "I regard Mr. Keynes's neo-mercantilist positions in economics in general, and with respect to money and monetary theory in particular, as essentially taking the side of the man-in-the-street, against the effort of the economic thinker and analyst to get beyond and to dispel the short-sighted views and prejudices of the former. . . . His work and influence seem to me supremely 'anti-intellectual' " (quoted from Patinkin 1979, 301). Viner's proposal was turned down.

*Postscript 2*. In 1963, Viner published an article, "Comment on My 1936 Review of Keynes's *General Theory*," in which he provided an updated assessment of Keynes's book. Viner's years at Princeton had led to an increased admiration for the *General Theory*. He wrote:

> I found the *General Theory* dazzling in its brilliance, and, if interpreted as primarily and admittedly a contribution to short-run theorizing, a veritable landmark, in both its positive and negative or critical aspects, in the history of our discipline. If I failed to make this clear, it was the consequence of inadequacy of exposition, not of intent. My appreciation of the quality and originality of its analysis as *short-run* analysis has grown since rather than shrunk, as I have struggled with its difficulties and as my understanding of it has improved thanks to the efforts of its many dedicated exegetes and perhaps also to my own later efforts, with the assistance of my students, to master its intricacies of thought and peculiarities of vocabulary. Within the boundaries of short-run analysis, and especially of short-run depression analysis, I regard the claim made for its having achieved a "Keynesian revolution" in economics as a permissible manifestation of an enthusiasm for which there is substantial justification. (emphasis in original, 1963, 419)

## 5.5 Director

After leaving the University of Chicago in 1935, Aaron Director worked for the US Treasury for two years. He then began writing a PhD thesis under Viner on the quantitative history of the Bank of England. Director traveled to England in 1937 to research the dissertation but was denied access to the bank's records. He spent the fall semester of 1938 at the University of Chicago, where he worked on his thesis and actively engaged in discussions with the members of The Group, particularly Knight, Simons, and Mints. He then returned to Washington, where he worked at the Brookings Institution before World War II and for several government agencies during the war.[92]

In 1939, Simons, with the support of Knight and Mints, made a strong — albeit unsuccessful — attempt to bring Director back to the Chicago faculty.

The attempt was prompted by news in early 1939 that Albert Hart would
be leaving Chicago for the University of Iowa at the end of the academic
year, thus creating a vacancy on the economics faculty. In a three-page
(single-spaced) letter, dated February 20, 1939, addressed to department chair Chester Wright, Simons (also writing on behalf of Knight and
Mints) asserted: "There can be only one happy solution [to the problem
created by the impending departure of Hart] for us, namely the reappointment of Aaron Director." Simons then made the following case for the
reappointment:

> I would submit that Aaron was an excellent teacher and is likely to be much
> better now than he ever was. This may be impugned as the testimony of one
> biased by close friendship; but it is also testimony based on more evidence and
> better evidence than was or is available to anyone else, save possibly Mints—
> i.e., on evidence available only to a departmental counselor. For the above-
> average students, there has been no better teacher around here in my time;
> and, in view of the low quality of our students during Aaron's last years here,
> it was sheer folly to conduct courses with much regard for the lower half of the
> students. The records will show, I believe, that, among those who elected the old
> 299 (Honors) courses, more of them elected to work with Aaron than with all
> other members of the staff combined. (Henry C. Simons Papers, Special Col-
> lections Research Center, Joseph Regenstein Library, University of Chicago)

In his letter, Simons noted that Douglas would likely object to the
reappointment. If Douglas were to object, Simons wrote that "it would
appear to be a matter of Douglas's interests against the far more immediate and substantial interests of (at least) Knight, Mints, and myself." In a
follow-up letter, dated March 3, 1939, addressed to Wright, Simons wrote
about the influence that Director exerted on his (Simons's) work and the
work of others:

> Aaron has been more useful to me than all other people in the university com-
> bined. He greatly influenced everything I have written and all my teaching here.
> Frankly, I find it hard to do writing which meets my own standards, or to make
> innovations in my courses, except in connection with a lot of discussion and
> exchange of ideas with persons of similar interests. I'm one of those extreme
> individualists who become relatively ineffectual when left to themselves; and,
> in spite of the efforts and good intentions of other people, I have been, qua
> economist, alone since Aaron left. Certainly I am worth more to the University

with Aaron around than without him. We have a rare capacity for helping and stimulating each other; and I'm by no means the only person with whom he does and can do this sort of thing. When he was back in the Fall [of 1938], I acquired again the delightful feeling of belonging to a real (and rather numerous) community of economists hereabouts. The people in question seem congenial enough all the time, and willing to help one another; but the intentions become fruitful only with Aaron around to help us in the business of helping one another. (Henry C. Simons Papers, Special Collections Research Center, Joseph Regenstein Library, University of Chicago)

In the event, Director was not rehired at that time. His return to the faculty of the University of Chicago would have to wait until 1946.

In 1939, Director worked on the paper "Does Inflation Change the Economic Effects of War?," which he presented at the annual AEA meetings in December 1939; the paper was published in the *American Economic Review* in March 1940.[93] The paper is notable because it is the only academic article that Director ever published on monetary policy; it also appears to be the only article that Director published on *any* subject during his absence from Chicago from 1935 to 1946.[94] The fact that the article was completed soon after discussions among Director and his former colleagues—including Simons, Knight, and Mints—suggests that its contents reflect, in part, the thinking of other members of The Group. Therefore, it is relevant to describe the contents of the article even though Director was not formally a member of the Chicago faculty at the time it was written.

*Controlling Wartime Inflation: Director's Position*

Like Viner's 1942 article "Inflation: Menace or Bogey?," Director's 1940 article "Does Inflation Change the Economic Effects of War?" dealt with the problem of transferring resources from the private sector to the government in a wartime economy (i.e., with full employment) without generating inflation. Unlike Viner, however, Director placed monetary policy front and center of his discussion.

Director began with the assumption that a wartime economy would lead to full employment, with a buildup of inflationary pressures.[95] Under such conditions, what "monetary framework" should the authorities follow? Director answered: "A given criterion, such as a stable price level or fixed quantity of money, may therefore be adopted" (1940, 351).[96] In the interim, to ensure that "approximately full employment is established," Director argued that "monetary policy must be oriented around the task of increasing the aggregate output of the community, as well as making a portion of it available for the war effort" (1940, 351). In advocating that monetary policy be assigned the role of attaining full employment while preventing inflation, Director acknowledged that the emphasis he placed on the use of monetary policy was out of fashion: "but we have generally assumed that both inflation and deflation are monetary phenomena in the sense that they could be prevented by monetary policy. The *recent discrediting of monetary policy* as a means of combating deflation need not concern us" (emphasis added, 1940, 352).

Director then turned to the issue of the transfer of resources from the private sector to the government under the assumptions of a fully employed, wartime economy and a given monetary policy. How should the funds needed for military expenditures be obtained—from borrowing or taxation? In contrast to Viner, who, as noted, favored government borrowing supported by price controls, Director preferred the taxation method and opposed price controls. He presented the following arguments in favor of increased taxation. First, he expressed the view that "we are more likely to adhere to a policy of monetary stability if a much larger fraction of war expenditures is obtained through taxation" (1940, 353). Second, and in contrast to the taxation method, Director argued that "large-scale borrowing is itself likely to promote monetary expansion. Even if the central bank had both the power and inclination to maintain monetary stability, war will subordinate its own policy to that of the treasury. . . . But treasuries are reluctant to pay high rates of interest, both because of the increased monetary cost of waging war and because of the adverse effect of high interest rates on institutions with large holdings of fixed interest-bearing assets" (1940, 358). Third, borrowing to finance war expenditures can lead to "the existence of a large public debt" (1940, 359). Director asserted:

> The theory of deficit financing in the present decade [has] led to a too widespread belief that the size of the public debt is not a matter of great importance. It is no doubt true, though not very significant, that the larger the debt and the larger the interest payments required, the larger will be the income out of which taxes can be paid. The real problem associated with a public debt is that of transferring income from income recipients as a whole to those in possession of public debt. (1940, 359)

Director next discussed deficit financing during periods of unemployment, such as the situation that existed in late 1939. How should fiscal deficits be financed in such periods? His answer was in the spirit of the Chicago monetary tradition; he advocated money-financed fiscal deficits to combat unemployment: "We should . . . give further consideration to the substitution of central bank credit for public borrowing" (1940, 360). Director noted that "[the] opposition to the creation of money by the state rests on the fear that the state will not exercise the necessary restraint, and that private banks will compete with the state in the creation of money, using the money created by the state as a reserve" (1940, 360). How could the problem of the creation of credit by the private sector be dealt with? Director's answer was again very much in accord with the Chicago monetary tradition; he recommended the imposition of 100 percent reserve requirements on the banks: "The latter difficulty [i.e., the problem posed by the creation of credit by the banks] can, however, be overcome by applying the principle of Peel's Act [of 1844] to the deposits created by the central bank for government war expenditures" (1940, 360).[97]

In concluding his paper, Director stressed what he perceived to be the connection among monetary policy, wartime inflation, and authoritarian control. He argued that the use of controls, instead of monetary policy, to stem inflation would give rise to increased governmental intrusion into economic affairs. His final sentence read: "If we can prevent inflation by monetary means, we may forgo, some at least, of the authoritarian control that might otherwise be imposed" (1940, 361).

## Discussion

The views expressed by Director in his 1940 *AER* article were direct extensions, applied to a wartime economy, of the views of The Group in the early 1930s. Correspondingly, Director's views were very different from those of the majority of American economists in the late 1930s and early 1940s. Unlike much of the profession, the views of which had been influenced by Keynes's *General Theory*, Director believed in the efficacy of monetary policy in steering the economy toward full employment and, once full employment had been achieved, in preventing inflation. Specifically, to combat unemployment, he advocated the use of money-financed fiscal deficits. Moreover, unlike much of the profession (including Viner), Director opposed the use of controls during wartime; he believed that controls would increase the role of government in the economy and, once imposed, would be difficult to reverse. He favored implementing a monetary rule during wartime—either a rule that stabilizes the price level or a rule that fixes the quantity of money. To deal with the potential inflationary effects of credit creation by the banks, Director advocated 100 percent reserve requirements on demand deposits.

## 5.6 Chicago and the Keynesian Revolution: Observations

In the previous chapter, I argued that in the early 1930s the Chicagoans originated the twentieth-century debates about rules versus discretion in monetary policy and the idea of 100 percent reserves on demand deposits. Using the Fisherine analytic framework, those economists stressed the important role played by money in the economy. The emphasis that the Chicagoans placed on the instability of a fractional-reserve banking system in the absence of deposit insurance enabled those economists to explain both the severity of the Great Depression and the banking crises of the early 1930s. At a time when most of the economics profession favored fixed exchange rates, the Chicagoans called for the adoption of flexible exchange rates.

This chapter has described the views of Simons, Douglas, Knight, Director, and Viner on money and the business cycle from the mid-1930s to the mid-1940s. Except for Viner, the Chicagoans continued to espouse views presented in their 1932 and 1933 memoranda—namely, they continued to assign the quantity of money a paramount role in the business cycle and to advocate monetary measures to ameliorate the cycle. In terms of their theoretical framework, the Chicagoans used the Fisherine equation of exchange, emphasizing the instability of the velocity of circulation of money and the roles of changes in price expectations and the fractional-reserve banking system in exacerbating the cycle. In terms of policies, the Chicagoans continued to proffer money-financed fiscal deficits to combat depressions, flexible exchange rates so that policies could focus on the domestic economy, monetary-policy rules, and 100 percent reserve requirements. Simons advocated these policies within the context of a modified laissez-faire market system.

The advocacy of deficit spending to combat unemployment was also the policy message of Keynes's *General Theory*. We have seen, however, that Simons and Knight were highly critical of the *General Theory*. Correspondingly, Director and Douglas remained immune to the Keynesian virus throughout their careers; as we shall see in chapter 7, Mints was also very critical of Keynesian economics. Among The Group, only Viner appears to have had a generally favorable opinion of Keynes's book and to have been susceptible to the Keynesian revolution. What explains this circumstance—namely, that, while the *General Theory* ushered in a revolution in macroeconomics, Keynes's book failed to gain a foothold among the majority of the Chicago quantity theorists? There are two fundamental explanations—one relating to the short-term policy implications of Keynes's book and the other relating to its longer-term policy implications.

*The short term.* Patinkin argued that "the advocacy *per se* of public-works expenditure was not the purpose of the *General Theory*; rather it was to *provide a theory* which would, among other things, rationalize such a policy" (emphasis added, Patinkin 1987, 24).[98] For Keynes, the purpose of a fiscal deficit was to increase aggregate demand to offset declines in private spending. That is, the deficit aimed to increase government spending, $G$, in the income-expenditure relation (closed-economy version), $Y = C + I + G$. For the Chicagoans, the purpose of a fiscal deficit was to increase $M$, the money supply, in the equation of exchange, $MV = PT$. While other American economists advocated public-works expenditure before the publication of the *General Theory*, a characteristic that distinguished the Chicago framework from much of the profession in the 1930s was the application of the quantity theory in a way that provided a theoretical rationale for (money-financed) public-works expenditure. Thus, both the Chicagoans and Keynes advocated fiscal deficits to combat depressions, but they used different theoretical frameworks to reach their policy conclusions.

Having developed a theoretical rationale for deficit spending during depressions, the Chicagoans were less attracted to the use of Keynesian income-expenditure theory to justify such spending than were economists at other institutions.[99] Hyman Minsky, who, as mentioned in chapter 1, was an undergraduate student at Chicago in the late 1930s and early 1940s, wrote the following: "Before the implications of the *General Theory* for policy had been worked out—and without first revolutionizing theory—Simons and others had put forth a policy 'regime' that was consistent with the *General Theory*" (Minsky 1985, 220). Concerning the reception of the *General Theory* at Chicago, Minsky (1985, 221) asserted: "Only Lange (and perhaps Douglas) of the senior faculty was sympathetic to Keynes, but perhaps this was due to the prior acceptance by the other members of the faculty of the need for a strong expansionary fiscal policy during the depression. Having reached this 'Keynesian' policy conclusion by

observing the economy, orthodox economists at Chicago felt no strong
need to revolutionize economic theory" (1985, 221).[100]

Both the Chicago economists and Keynes (of the *General Theory*)
believed in the inefficacy of monetary measures that operated through
the banking system in combating depressions. The Chicagoans—Viner
excepted—maintained that during periods of low confidence businesses
would not want to borrow and banks would be reluctant to lend. Keynes—
and especially his disciples—believed that, at low rates of interest, monetary policy would not be effective in light of the high interest elasticity
of the demand for money or the low interest elasticity of investment or
both.[101] Nevertheless, the Chicagoans and Keynes reached very different
conclusions about the role of money in the economy. As indicated in the
quotation from Villard's survey article "Monetary Theory," cited at the beginning of this chapter, by the mid-1940s a degradation in the role assigned to the quantity of money and "purely monetary devices for control" had taken place in the economics profession. In contrast, Simons,
Knight, Douglas, and Director continued to assign money the central role
in business-cycle theory and in stabilization policy. Although those economists did not believe that policy measures that operated via the banking system would effectively secure changes in the quantity of money in
times of depression, they thought that the necessary changes in the money
supply could be achieved through adjustments in the government's fiscal
position. As we shall see, these views characterized those of Mints and
Friedman in the late 1940s and early 1950s.

*The long term.* Both the Chicagoans and Keynes in the *General Theory* sought to preserve the capitalist system. They differed, however, in
their respective conceptions of capitalism. For the Chicagoans—especially
Simons, Director, and Mints—the ideal economic system was characterized by a division of labor between the government and the market.
Simons, Director, and Mints sought to establish a modified system of
laissez-faire, entailing a small government sector, suitable for the twentieth century. The government would be responsible for maintaining a
competitive market, avoiding extremes in the distribution of income, and
setting rules to minimize monetary uncertainty. This system would preserve liberty and equality by preventing concentrations of power. Knight
emphasized the capacity of laissez-faire to provide citizens with freedom
of choice; because of that freedom, it was the best among economic systems. The Chicagoans advocated fiscal deficits as a temporary palliative.
Recall, the Chicagoans—including Douglas and Viner—believed that the

government's fiscal position should be in balance over the course of the business cycle.

Keynes saw in capitalism an inherent fragility; he believed that this fragility could be surmounted by conscious management via state intervention. In a 1939 article, "Democracy and Efficiency," published in the *New Statesman and the Nation*, Keynes depicted his framework as one that sought "the particular amalgam of private capitalism and State Socialism which is the only practical recipe for present conditions." He also stated: "In contemporary conditions we need, if we are to enjoy prosperity and profits, so much more central planning than we have at present that the reform of the economic system needs as much urgent attention if we have war as if we avoid it" (Keynes 1939, 121). As Moggridge (emphasis in original, 1992, 455), in his biography of Keynes, noted, Keynes envisaged "a solution to the economic problem [that] lay in a *managed* capitalism. This involved a rejection of *laissez faire*." Specifically, Keynes envisaged a system characterized by secular fiscal deficits and government-directed investment. In contrast, Simons, Knight, and Director strongly opposed government-directed investment. By the mid-1930s, Douglas came to share that view although he favored more government involvement in economic affairs than did Simons, Knight, and Director. Viner attributed the weak performance of private investment in the 1930s to the antibusiness policies of the Roosevelt administrations.

Thus, while the Chicagoans wanted to preserve capitalism in a way that minimized the role of government in economic affairs, Keynes wanted to reform capitalism by substantially increasing the role of government in the economic system. This circumstance, along with the degradation assigned to the role of money, helps explain the negative appraisals of the *General Theory* by Simons and Knight. In this connection, Simons, in his 1936 review of Keynes's book, viewed the book as an attack on traditional free-market economics. Simons wrote: "Not content to point out the shortcomings of traditional views, Mr. Keynes proceeds to espouse the cause of an army of cranks and heretics simply on the grounds that their schemes or ideas would incidentally have involved or suggested mitigation of the deflationary tendencies of the economy" (Simons 1936b, 1017). In criticizing Keynes's attack on traditional economics, Simons worried about the use to which that attack could be put. He wrote: "The reviewer is not inclined to be more generous toward monetary orthodoxy than is Mr. Keynes. But the sophistical academic leg-pulling which he perpetrates in this volume, however delightful and entertaining in its proper place, should not be done publicly in times like these, least of all by persons of Mr. Keynes' repute" (Simons 1936b, 1017). So dim a view did Simons take of the *General Theory*'s policy stance that he regarded Keynes's attack on economic orthodoxy as running the risk that Keynes "may only succeed in becoming the academic idol of our worst cranks and charlatans—not to mention the possibilities of the book as the economic bible of a fascist movement."[102] Hence, Simons concluded that "only a kind fate can spare [Keynes] the approbation which he has invited from fools" (Simons 1936b, 1017).[103]

## CHAPTER SIX

# The Resistance

A conclusion that emerged from the evidence presented in the previous chapter is that a "small band of the initiated" at Chicago—to use Harry Johnson's jargon—resisted the emerging Keynesian revolution in the decade following the publication of Keynes's *General Theory* in 1936. During that decade, Chicago economists continued to advance the view that money matters amid a developing Keynesian consensus that downplayed the role of monetary factors in the business cycle and the importance of monetary policy as a stabilization tool. This chapter and the next two move the discussion forward in time. The present chapter deals with the views of the members of The Group on money mainly during mid- and late 1940s—a period that saw the emergence of elements that would constitute part of the monetarist counter-revolution against the then-Keynesian consensus. To be sure, changes in the constitution of The Group had occurred. Henry Simons died in 1946. Jacob Viner—who, as we saw, was, at best, a borderline member of The Group in terms of economic policies—left Chicago for Princeton in 1946. After the early 1940s, Frank Knight's writings focused almost exclusively on issues of methodology and philosophy.[1] Paul Douglas, whose interests had veered to the politics of the city of Chicago in the late 1930s and early 1940s, enlisted in the US Marines as a private in 1942; at the age of fifty, he was one of the oldest individuals ever to have joined the Marines.

Amid this change, however, there was also continuity. A somewhat reconstituted "membership" of The Group continued to push forward "the fundamental truth of the quantity theory"—again using Johnson's jargon. As we will see, Lloyd Mints, who had not published anything apart from book reviews from 1931 to 1944, stepped up to the plate. Between 1945 and his retirement in 1953, Mints, building on the early 1930s Chicago monetary framework, especially Simons's program for preserving the values of a market system, published two major books and several articles on money that made important, original contributions later pushed forward by Milton Friedman. This chapter discusses Mints's work in the mid-1940s; the next chapter discusses his contributions in the early 1950s. The year 1946 saw the return of Aaron Director to Chicago. Director, who was appointed to the Law School faculty, closely interacted with members of the Economics Department. Although he published nothing on the subject of money after his return to Chicago, in this chapter and the next, I provide evidence showing that he carried forward the main ideas developed earlier by Simons and Knight on the role of money in a laissez-faire economy to the Chicago of the 1940s and 1950s. The year 1946 also saw the appointment of Friedman to Chicago's economics faculty, filling the void created by the departure of Viner. Reconstructing the 1930s and 1940s Chicago monetary framework, especially that of Simons and its development by Mints, Friedman, among other things, applied statistical tools to extend and advance that framework. In the present chapter, I discuss Friedman's initial monetary framework, which was straight out of the Simons-Mints narrative. Finally, the year 1946 saw the return of Douglas to Chicago's Economics Department. Douglas's pre–World War II focus on politics continued, and in 1948 he was elected to the US Senate. However, his role in advancing Chicago monetary thinking did not end with his new responsibilities. In his first few years in the Senate, Douglas emerged as the central figure in forging the famous "accord" between the Federal Reserve and the US Treasury in 1951. In doing so, he was joined by Friedman, Mints, and other members of Chicago's Economics Department in the first example of the postwar influence of the Chicago tradition on monetary policy.

During the period covered in this chapter, the Keynesian revolution in economics was completed.[2] A key feature of Keynesian thinking on money during the period was that monetary policy had, at best, modest effects on economic activity (Meltzer 2003, 612). Fiscal policy—that is, changes in government expenditures and tax receipts—was considered the primary way to affect economic activity. To keep the Treasury's financing costs on debt low during the war, in 1942 the Federal Reserve, at the Treasury's request, formally committed to maintaining interest rates on government debt at the low levels that prevailed at that time. The Fed's commitment, which continued throughout the 1940s, subordinated monetary policy to the government's financing requirements. The policy was consistent with the economics profession's thinking about the role of monetary policy after the war. Friedman and Schwartz (1963, 626) characterized the profession's thinking as follows:

> At the end of the war, dominant intellectual opinion in the United States and abroad assigned a minor role to monetary policy. As a result of the Great Contraction, of the widespread success of the Keynesian revolution in academic economic thought, and of the experience with wartime controls which succeeded in suppressing some of the manifestations of the accumulation of money balances, the view was accepted that "money does not matter," that the stock of money adapted itself passively to economic changes and played a negligible independent role. Further, the major postwar problem was widely assumed to be prevention of deflation and depression, not inflation. The wartime accumulation of liquidity was regarded as providing a highly desirable source of postwar purchasing power. The sole role assigned to monetary policy was to keep interest rates low and thereby to facilitate or perhaps, rather, not to hinder investment. This was the view not only within the Federal Reserve System in this country but also in most western countries.

The discussion of the views of the Chicago economists on money that follows should be viewed in the context presented by Friedman and Schwartz; in arguing that money plays an important role in the economy, the Chicagoans were going against the tide of professional thinking.[3]

## 6.1 Out of the Wilderness: Mints

I touched on Mints's views on monetary economics in earlier chapters.[4] In chapter 2, I discussed Mints's 1930 article "The Elasticity of Bank Notes," in which he criticized the view embedded in the so-called commercial loan theory of banking. In that article, Mints argued that, from the standpoint of obtaining elasticity of currencies, there seemed to be no advantage in the requirement that commercial paper serve as security for banknotes. He maintained that the elasticity of a currency depends on adequate reserves within the banking system—and not on the kind of security underlying the notes issued. In chapter 2, we saw that Mints signed several of the 1932 and 1933 Chicago memoranda. In chapter 4, I alluded to Mints's support of a monetary rule. Specifically, I showed that Mints distinguished between the rationales underlying the respective rules of Simons and

Irving Fisher. Mints argued that, in contrast to Fisher, Simons advocated a rule because he (Simons) thought that it would minimize monetary uncertainty—a necessary condition for the effective operation of a competitive economic system in Simons's view.

Following a fifteen-year absence from substantive academic publishing, Mints returned to the publishing fold in 1945.[5] That year saw the publication of his book *A History of Banking Theory in Great Britain and the United States*. The book, which became a classic in the area of doctrinal monetary history, was a critical review of theories put forward in the English-language literature to explain the operation of commercial banks from the second half of the seventeenth century in Great Britain and the late eighteenth century in the United States to the first half of the twentieth century. The year 1945 also saw the publication of Mints's piercing review of Ragnar Nurkse's 1944 book *International Currency Experience: Lessons of the Inter-war Period* in the *AER*. Mints's views on exchange-rate regimes in that review closely foreshadowed in several respects the appraisal subsequently made by Friedman (1953b), which played an influential role in converting the economics profession to favor flexible exchange rates during the 1960s.[6] As we shall see in this chapter, the year 1946 saw Mints engage four leading Keynesians, including Alvin Hansen, in debate over the effectiveness of monetary policy.

After the mid-1940s, Mints published several additional works in the field of money. These works, which are discussed in the next chapter, included articles and comments in journals, and a 1950 book, *Monetary Policy for a Competitive Society*. The book helped solidify Mints's scholarly reputation. Perhaps reflecting his high standing within the profession in the early 1950s, Mints coedited, along with Friedrich Lutz, the volume *Readings in Monetary Theory* for the American Economic Association in 1951.[7]

Mints taught at Chicago from 1919 until his retirement in 1953, the longest consecutive stretch of any of the earlier Chicagoans.[8] Moreover, Mints specialized in monetary economics and taught the graduate course in money and banking at Chicago taken by, among others, Friedman.[9] Mints, however, has long been considered a peripheral figure in the development of monetary economics at the University of Chicago.[10] Discussions of his monetary views, and of their possible influence on the development of monetarism, have been relatively sparse.[11] By and large, those discussions focused on Mints's criticisms of the Federal Reserve's policies during the Great Depression and the similarities of those criticisms with those of Friedman and Schwartz (1963).[12] None of those studies provided a systematic analysis of Mints's original contributions as contained in his publications from the mid-1940s to the early 1950s; nor have those studies assessed the interplay between Mints's contributions and the development of Friedman's monetary thinking during that period.[13]

Why has Mints's work been glossed over in studies on the Chicago monetary tradition? One plausible reason is that previous studies on that subject have focused on the pre–*General Theory* period, 1927–35. As we have seen, during that period Mints published only a single article, "The Elasticity of Bank Notes," in 1930; that article bore little relationship to the characteristics that would mark the Chicago monetary tradition.[14] A second possible reason for the neglect of Mints's work is discussed in chapter 7.

## Mints, 1945

*A History of Banking Theory in Great Britain and the United States* established Mints's scholarly reputation in the economics community.[15] The primary aim of *A History of Banking Theory* was to expose the deficiency of the commercial loan theory of banking, which Mints renamed the "real bills doctrine," within the context a doctrinal survey of the development of the literature on banking and monetary theory from the mid-eighteenth century to the early 1940s.[16] As Mints wrote in the preface, "If there is a central theme in what I have written, it is that this doctrine is unsound in all its aspects" (1945a, 5). The book also presented Mints's views on business-cycle theory and stabilization policy. In the preface, Mints wrote that Aaron Director, Henry Simons, Jacob Viner, and C. R. Whittlesey had "read the manuscript in its entirely" and had made "many useful suggestions for improvement" (1945a, 5).[17]

We briefly encountered the real bills doctrine in chapter 4 within the context of the British Bullionist Controversy that took place at the beginning of the nineteenth century. We saw that the antibullionists used the doctrine to argue that, if banknotes were issued against the discount of short-term commercial bills, the currency would have two desirable properties—(1) it would not be possible for the quantity of money to be excessive or deficient, and, thus, to cause inflation or deflation, respectively, and (2) the currency would have a desirable elasticity so that banks would be in a liquid position at all times. Let us now take a closer look at the arguments underlying these two properties.

The real bills doctrine specified that bank loans should have three qualities: they should be (1) short-term, (2) self-liquidating, and (3) issued against productive projects. The requirement that the loans should be short-term aimed to ensure that banks had adequate liquidity to meet their liabilities (mostly demand deposits), which are subject to immediate call.[18] By the requirement that the loans should be self-liquidating, what was meant was that the loans were expected to be repaid rapidly by the borrower through funds raised by the very transaction being financed. By the requirement that the loans should be productive, what was meant was that the loans were provided to a business firm to finance the production of goods and services (Ritter and Silber 1974, 276n4). When banks make loans with those three qualities, they are said to accept a "real bill" as an asset in their portfolios and to create a corresponding liability—a bank deposit or issuance of a banknote—on their balance sheets. In turn, the doctrine specified that the central bank should lend to commercial banks on collateral consisting of loans that satisfy these three qualities. By regulating the purpose for which credit is extended—that is, the quality of bank assets—the appropriate amount of credit would be ensured (Ritter and Silber 1974, 279; Humphrey and Timberlake 2019, 1–8).

If banks make loans with the foregoing three qualities, then the increase in the money supply (i.e., demand deposits, banknotes) that results from bank lending corresponds (according to the real bills doctrine) to the increase in the value of physical output that the lending financed. Correspondingly, when the output was sold and removed from the market, the loans would be repaid, canceling the borrowers' real bill obligations, and the money supply would be reduced. In this way, by confining lending to only short-term, self-liquidating, and productive loans, the supply of money would vary with the "needs of trade"—it would correspond to changes in output and, thus, would cause neither inflation nor deflation (Ritter and Silber 1974, 276–77; Humphrey and Timberlake 2019, 1–8). Moreover, by confining their lending to only short-term, self-liquidating loans, the banks would be in a liquid position at all times. Thus, banks would be able to satisfy unexpected calls for cash at short notice—the currency would "have a desirable elasticity" (Mints 1945a, 9).

Mints traced the origins of the real bills doctrine to eighteenth-century writers, including John Law and Adam Smith (1945a, chap. 3). The doctrine, he noted, served as a founding principle of the Federal Reserve Act in 1913 and since that time had often underpinned the Fed's policies.[19] Mints asserted that the doctrine "is utterly subversive of any rational attack on the problem of monetary policy" (1945a, 5). That the doctrine continued to thrive in the twentieth century was, in Mints's view, a scandal: "This [persistence of the doctrine] is a scandal, and, so long as it continues, economists are in no position to complain when their ideas in regard to banking legislation are ignored. . . . There has been no improvement to this day on Smith's statement [of the doctrine] and little advance in the criticism of it" (1945a, 10–11). Mints aimed to expose the basic flaw in the doctrine.

Mints noted that, by tying one nominal variable, the money stock, to the nominal value of commercial bills, the potential for procyclical behavior is created. The fundamental error made by proponents of the doctrine, Mints argued, "lay in the fact that they failed to see that, whereas convertibility into a given *physical amount* of specie (or any other economic good) will limit the quantity of notes that can be issued, . . . the basing of notes on a given *money's worth* of any form of wealth—be it land or merchants' stocks—presents the possibility of unlimited expansion of loans" (emphasis in original, 1945a, 30). By specifying "the needs of trade" in nominal terms, the doctrine led to the result that an upward movement in the price level would generate an increase in the money supply, which would enable the upward movement in the price level to continue indefinitely. Thus, the doctrine renders both the money supply and the nominal value of bills indeterminate variables.[20]

Moreover, the doctrine, Mints argued, embodies the potential for self-aggravating feedback loops and, hence, for explosive behavior. Specifically, he asserted that the volume of bills coming due for discount depends on both the quantity of goods and the velocity of turnover of those goods:

> A rigorous adherence to the real-bills doctrine might accentuate fluctuations in bank loans. Inasmuch as velocity tends to rise during prosperity, the ratio of bills to money will then rise also, and consequently banking on these conditions might possibly mean an *aggravated* tendency to expand loans in prosperity and contract them in depression. (emphasis added, 1945a, 38)[21]

Mints concluded: "It is evident that stability in either the quantity or the value of bank money, in consequence of a restriction of discounts to real bills, is fantastically improbable" (1945a, 38).

Concerning Mints's perspectives on business-cycle theory and stabilization policies, the views set forth in *A History of Banking Theory* were in key ways reflective of earlier Chicago thinking. Thus, Mints argued that the business cycle is initiated by autonomous "changes in velocity or in liquidity preferences."[22] Once these changes occur, they trigger adverse expectations that "constitute a serious additional impediment to a return to full employment" (1945a, 220n87). To combat depressions, Mints believed that open-market operations and discounting operations would not be effective tools because, during those episodes, "the impairment of confidence may be so great that an impossibly low, or even negative, [interest] rate would be necessary to induce an increase in the amount borrowed" (1945a, 280). In light of "the unavoidable influence of fiscal policy on monetary affairs," changes in the money supply should be effected mainly through the government's fiscal position, with open-market operations playing a supporting role (1945a, 281).[23]

Evidence of the influence of Simons's views on *A History of Banking Theory* is pervasive. As did Simons, Mints thought that, to minimize uncertainty, monetary-policy implementation should be based on a rule. A rule, he thought, would stabilize expectations and, thus, economic activity (1945a, 263). Like Simons, the particular rule that Mints favored was one that stabilizes the price level (1945a, 275). Like Simons, Mints believed that the Treasury should be the agency responsible for implementing the rule (1945a, 286).

Mints was one of the co-authors of the March 1933 Chicago memorandum that introduced the idea of 100 percent reserves into the American economics literature. In *A History*, he reiterated his support for 100 percent reserves: "The attractions of 100 per cent reserves are evident. Such a system would eliminate the autonomous and perverse changes in the quantity of circulating medium which result from variations in the earning assets of the banks, and it would therefore make possible a much more effective control of the quantity of money" (1945a, 270). In supporting the 100 percent reserves scheme, Mints cited several earlier studies that advocated the scheme.[24] In doing so, he referred to the March 1933 Chicago memorandum: "There was also privately circulated in 1933 a mimeographed statement by a small group of economists at the University of Chicago in which this change in the American banking structure was sponsored" (1945a, 270n29).

Mints's support for the 100 percent scheme was not, however, unequivocal. His remarks on the scheme left some doubt about his degree of commitment to the scheme. He stated that "fractional reserve banking should . . . be suppressed" (1945a, 222), but he did not indicate if the *suppression* of fractional reserves meant the *elimination* of the fractional-reserve system. His remarks quoted in the preceding paragraph indicated that he supported the elimination of fractional reserves. However, at another point in his book, he remarked that—in light of the large holdings of government bonds by banks in the 1940s, which provided the banks with a liquid asset—"it may become practicable to raise the reserve requirement to a much higher level than that which now prevails, even though perhaps not to 100 per cent. . . . If the ratio of cash and bonds to liabilities could be raised, say, to 75 per cent, we would secure much of the gain from 100 per cent reserve banking" (1945a, 270–71). As we shall see, the idea that banks' large holdings of government bonds in the 1940s provided them with liquidity and, therefore, eliminated the essentiality of the 100 percent reserves scheme played a role in the qualified adherence to the scheme by Mints and Friedman in the early 1950s.

Finally, and again in line with Simons's views, Mints believed that, for the 100 percent reserves scheme to be effective, "it would be necessary for the legislature to be on the alert to prohibit any alternative and equally harmful devices that might appear" (1945a, 270). By the term "harmful devices," Mints meant financial instruments that were close substitutes for money. In this connection, Mints, like Simons, thought that all short-term-debt instruments should be eliminated (1945a, 218, 262). Mints argued that "the attempt [by banks] to enforce payment of maturing [short-term] obligations [during depressions] will operate greatly to strengthen the deflationary influence on business generally, and consequently short-term [debt] will have a more unfortunate effect on business conditions than long-term debts" (1945a, 219). He also thought that when the government borrows it should issue only consols: "short term obligations as Treasury bills and certificates, and only to a slightly less extent longer-term fixed-maturity bonds, are so acceptable in lieu of cash in 'cash' balances that the use of these instruments in borrowing tends to *monetary confusion*" (1945a, emphasis added, 222).

Mints's book also extended the Chicago monetary perspective in several ways, each of which would become elements of the emerging monetarist framework of the mid-1950s and after.

*Policy lags.* As we saw in chapter 5, in Knight's 1941 article "The Business Cycle, Interest, and Money: A Methodological Approach," that economist had called attention to the fact that monetary-policy actions were subject to lags although Knight had not discussed potential problems created by the existence of lags. Mints provided a more detailed presentation of lags in monetary policy than Knight had done:

> It takes time for men to become aware of new opportunities that are opened up by a reduction in the rate of interest; it takes time to make plans, both business and engineering; and in the case of investments in fixed capital it takes time to obtain bids, let contracts, and actually to get construction under way. Moreover,

under some circumstances it may take some time for the central bank to make its rate policy effective in the sense merely of obtaining the desired influence on the customer rate charged by the member-banks, and it will take still more time to influence the long-term rate. (1945a, 279)

Related to his argument about lags in monetary policy, Mints believed that the effectiveness of discretionary central-bank actions "would require that the [central bank] . . . be able to forecast economic conditions with at least a fair degree of accuracy and for a considerable period of time in advance," an ability Mints thought that central banks did not possess (1945a, 279).[25] For these reasons, Mints thought that central-bank policies that relied on changes in the interest rate to affect economic activity were not as effective as changes in the money supply produced through the government's fiscal position.

*Portfolio theory.* Whereas the 1930s Chicago tradition focused on the effects of changes in velocity on the economy, Mints (1945a, 219–22) assessed the effects of changes in money demand on the economy within a framework that featured a simple portfolio theory of the demand for money. Similar to Keynes in *The General Theory* (1936a), Mints considered wealth to be the variable that constituted the total budget constraint on the holding of assets, including money. For given levels of wealth and money, Mints assessed the effects of relative demand shifts between money and other assets, including commodities, short-term debt, long-term debt, and stock certificates.

*The historical-monetary narrative.* Although *A History of Banking Theory* was primarily a study of monetary doctrine, in the final part of the book—amounting to more than twenty pages—Mints provided a critique of the Federal Reserve's discretionary policies since that institution's inception in 1913. The conceptual framework underlying Mints's historical-monetary narrative was the real bills doctrine—that doctrine provided the cohesive thread tying Mints's critiques of the Fed's policies together. Thus, in commencing his historical-monetary narrative, Mints (1945a, 265) wrote: "The theoretical position of the Federal Reserve Board is of more than incidental interest. The Board has at all times shown a considerable amount of faith in the real-bills doctrine." As we shall see in the following two chapters, the historical-monetary narrative as a basis with which to critique discretionary policies was used with considerable effectiveness by Friedman in the 1950s and after.

*The Great Depression.* As part of his historical-monetary narrative, Mints used the real bills doctrine to critique the Federal Reserve's role in exacerbating the Great Depression. He noted that in 1928 and 1929 the Fed had become "much concerned over the supposed danger that the growth of speculative loans" posed—that is, the Fed, in line with the precepts of the real bills principle, had focused on the quality of bank credit instead of the quantity of money (1945a, 267). Specifically, reflecting its concern with stock-market speculation, the Fed raised interest rates and dissuaded banks from engaging in lending related to stock purchases. Moreover, in the early 1930s "the Board twice referred to the need for liquid assets on the part of the Reserve banks, and it clearly was earning assets, not cash to which reference was made. This point of view is strictly a real-bills position" (1945a, 268).[26] Although Mints did not blame the Fed for bringing on the Great Depression, he asserted that "vigorous monetary action ... could [have been] successful in preventing the [1929] collapse from resulting in a serious depression. ... The chief trouble was not with the years preceding 1929 but with the monetary policy of the government, or absence thereof, during the years following 1929" (1945a, 275).

The following points regarding Mints's view of the role played by monetary policy in the Great Depression merit comment. First, Mints had been critical of the Fed's policies in the Great Depression before his published criticisms. McIvor (1983, 889) reported that Mints's classroom criticisms of the Fed's policies during the Great Depression provided "the basis for lively discussions in [Mints's] graduate monetary policy course" in the late 1930s.[27] Mints implicitly expressed a similar view in a 1940 review of a book authored by Edwin Kemmerer on the structure and functions of the Federal Reserve System. In his book, Kemmerer (1938) praised the Fed's action to raise the discount rate during the autumn of 1931 (after Great Britain left the gold standard). Mints (1940, 602) made it clear that he disagreed with Kemmerer's positive appraisal of the Fed's actions in the early 1930s. Second, Mints's view that the Fed *deepened* the Great Depression may have reflected Viner's influence. As discussed in chapters 2 and 3, during the early 1930s Viner criticized the Fed's policies for their role in deepening the Depression.[28]

*Cost-push inflation.* At a time when the economics profession overwhelmingly believed that cost-push factors, working through the wage-setting behavior of unions, were the primary determinant of inflation,[29] Mints (1945a, 274–75) argued:

> No proponent of price-level stabilization would deny that other factors than the quantity of money do, indeed, have their influence on the price level. It is precisely because of this fact that it is contended that variations in the quantity

of money will, or may, be necessary to stabilize the level of prices. . . . From this point of view the case for attempting to stabilize the price level by monetary means lies in the fact that the quantity of money is the one easily and deliberately controllable factor and in the belief that variations in the stock of money can be so managed as largely to offset disturbing fluctuations in other factors, particularly the velocity of circulation. (1945a, 274–75)

*Review of Nurkse.* Mints did not express views on exchange-rate arrangements in his 1945 book. He did, however, express such views in his review of Nurkse's book *International Currency Experience.*[30] Nurkse (1944) argued against floating exchange rates on the basis of the experience of the 1920s and the 1930s.[31] Based on the experience of the French franc in the 1920s, Nurkse (1944, 118) argued that freely floating rates inevitably lead to destabilizing speculation and unstable exchange rates. He also argued that the experience of the 1930s, following the devaluation of sterling in 1931, led to a series of competitive devaluations and overshooting of exchange rates because of the destabilizing nature of speculative capital flows (Nurkse 1944, 123). Nurkse advocated an adjustable-peg system, very much like Bretton Woods, supported by capital controls and discriminatory exchange controls. He also expressed the view that "regulation of the quantity of money has proved relatively ineffective even in steadying the level of prices" (1944, 106). The reviews of the book by economists were overwhelmingly favorable.[32] Mints's review was an exception.

Mints provided three major criticisms of Nurkse's theses. First, he argued (1945b, 194) that exchange controls typically involve the "undervaluation of the domestic currency," leading to "discriminatory" commercial policies (1945b, 194). Second, he challenged Nurkse's view that regulation of the quantity of money had proved ineffective at maintaining price stability:

> There is little evidence to support this statement. There was no serious attempt to prevent the decline in the volume of money in the United States for nearly three years following the beginning of the depression in 1929. Before we can say that regulation of the quantity "has proved" ineffective we must make an attempt at such regulation. (1945b, 194)

Third, Mints challenged Nurkse's interpretation of exchange-rate movements during the interwar period:

Nurkse is opposed to freely fluctuating exchange rates. However, this opposition seems to be founded in very large part upon a belief that the difficulties of the 1930's are inherent in any system of free exchanges. It is one thing to condemn, as one must, exchange fluctuations which are the consequence of widespread internal instability, and of consequent speculation in, and flights from, particular currencies; and it is quite a different thing to condemn, as one need not, such exchange fluctuations as would occur under conditions of internal stability. It is more than a little anomalous to condemn fluctuating exchange rates under conditions which a system of fixed exchanges could not survive. It is doubtful that fluctuating exchanges, under conditions of internal monetary stability, would create an undue discouragement to trade; or that they would be disequilibrating under the same conditions. (1945b, 193)

As mentioned, Mints's criticism of Nurkse's interpretation of the interwar system foreshadowed Friedman's influential criticism of Nurkse. Friedman (1953b, 176) wrote:

Nurkse concludes from the interwar period that speculation can be expected in general to be destabilizing. However, the evidence he cites is by itself inadequate to justify any conclusion. . . . In general, Nurkse's discussion of the effects of speculation is thoroughly unsatisfactory. At times, he seems to regard any transactions which threaten the existing value of a currency as destabilizing even if the underlying forces would produce a changed value in the absence of speculation. . . . It is a sorry reflection on the scientific basis for generally held economic beliefs that Nurkse's analysis is so often cited as the "basis" or "proof" of the belief of destabilizing speculation.

### Mints, 1946

In 1946, Mints published the paper "Monetary Policy." The paper was the centerpiece of a symposium published in the *Review of Economics and Statistics (REStat)*. Four other economists, Howard Ellis, Alvin Hansen, Michal Kalecki, and Abba Lerner—all prominent members of the profession—provided comments on Mints's paper; their comments were published alongside Mints's paper.[33]

The objective of Mints's 1946 paper was to lay down the components of a package that would ensure equilibrium at a high level of employment. To that end, Mints maintained that "we shall have to give more heed than hithertofore to the need for protecting the freedom of the market from

encroachment by both businessmen and laborers" (1946, 60). Like Knight
and Simons, Mints defended the free-market system against the encroachments that he perceived were inherent in Keynesian policies. Like Knight
and Simons, Mints asserted that only the free-market system provided the
freedom of choice required to allow individuals to set and pursue their
own objectives. Mints wrote:

> An expansion of the volume of public expenditures . . . would increase the
> area within which the public authorities would determine the allocation of
> resources, in other words, the ends of economic activity. We defend political
> democracy in part because it permits the will of the majority to prevail, but in
> this one respect a competitive economic system has more to commend it. In a
> system of free markets the desires of even very small minority groups are duly
> registered, and the appropriate amount of resources is devoted to their satisfac-
> tion. I do not mean to imply that the technique of the market can be applied
> to political affairs, or that this criterion alone can serve as the final basis for
> an appraisal of democracy or of private enterprise; but it does suggest that we
> should not resort to political control in areas where the mechanism of the mar-
> ket will function, unless there are overwhelmingly strong reasons for so doing.
> (1946, 64)

Let us recall Simons's agenda for a libertarian society. We saw in chapter 5 that in his 1934 *A Positive Program for Laissez Faire* Simons set
forth a program consisting of five elements: (1) the elimination of private
monopoly in all its forms; (2) the establishment of a monetary rule; (3) a
restructuring of the tax system; (4) the elimination of tariffs; and (5) limitations on advertising activities. I pointed out that the last component (i.e.,
limitation on advertising activities) was dropped from the list in Simons's
later writings. As explained in chapter 5, the rationale for eliminating private monopolies was to increase price and wage flexibility. A monetary
rule aimed to reduce monetary uncertainty. We saw that the tax system
played two essential roles in Simons's framework. First, the progressive
income tax, supported by changes in personal exemptions, would be the
mainstay of federal revenue and would be used (through its effect on the
government budget) to underpin countercyclical changes in the quantity
of money. Simons, we saw, opposed the use of government expenditures
to generate changes in the fiscal deficit because he thought that increased
government spending during cyclical contractions would become permanent and, therefore, would increase the role of the government in the

economy. Second, the progressive tax system would be the main instrument for achieving greater income equality.

Mints's views on economic reform were similar to, but less comprehensive than, those of Simons.[34] Like Simons and Knight, Mints did not support a system of unfettered laissez-faire. In particular, Mints believed that the government had two essential roles to play in the economy. The first role was to counter monopolistic practices. Mints maintained:

> A simple governmental policy of laissez-faire is indefensible in an enterprise economy, since if the government is purely passive private groups will then not fail to take advantage of the opportunity to impose monopolistic restrictions of various kinds on the community. Such restraints will mean not only outright reduction of output, but also a rigid price structure. Unless we have a fairly flexible price system a dynamic economy will be subject to an inordinately high level of frictional unemployment. (1946, 60)

Therefore, Mints argued that the government should "vigorously oppose the development of monopolistic restrictions" (1946, 62).

The second essential role of government in Mints's framework was in the area of money. Like Simons, Mints asserted: "If we had a definite, announced monetary policy, based upon legislation and firmly accepted . . . there would be no reason why aggregate demand should continue to decline after an initial disturbance" (1946, 60).[35] A monetary rule, Mints believed, would stabilize expectations and reduce uncertainty. Following Simons, Mints preferred a rule that stabilizes the price level because of its "simplicity," its "definiteness," and its characteristic of offsetting changes in velocity (1946, 60). Also following Simons, Mints asserted: "Any one of a number of possible guides to monetary action" would be about "equally acceptable" (1946, 60). In this connection, he mentioned two rules other than price-level stabilization: (1) an increase in the quantity of money at a constant rate equivalent to the rate of increase in output, and (2) the stabilization of per capita money incomes (1946, 60).

To effectuate changes in the quantity of money, Mints, as Simons before him, pointed out that "the fiscal operations of the national government unavoidably have monetary consequences" (1946, 63). In this connection, he noted that "the federal finances may, and at times do in practice, become the major factor in determining the quantity of money in circulation" (1946, 63). Consequently, he thought that the government's fiscal position should be used to change the money supply during depressions, with open-market operations playing a secondary role. In depression conditions, open-market operations and changes in the discount rate were, Mints maintained, weak stabilization instruments (1946, 63). Open-market operations, he thought, operated on too narrow a base to be effective during depressions—they affect "only a small proportion of individuals and corporations"—while changes in the discount rate are subject to the problems posed by long lags and an interest-inelastic demand for funds (1946, 63).

Apart from the effects of the progressive-income-tax structure on revenue, how would fiscal deficits be achieved during depressions? Like Simons, Mints favored changing tax-exemption levels, supported, if needed, by a general retail sales subsidy, while keeping the volume of government expenditures constant (1946, 64). Mints was concerned that an expansion of the volume of government expenditures "for the purposes of monetary policy would mean that the aggregate of such expenditures would be larger than otherwise" (1946, 64). If changes in tax-exemption levels and the retail tax subsidy were not sufficient to produce the desired budget deficit, Mints thought that "the tax rates themselves" would have to be changed (1946, 63). To implement monetary policy, Mints favored the establishment of a Monetary Agency, under which the money-creation powers of both the Federal Reserve and the Treasury would be consolidated (1946, 64). However, he thought it would be "impossible" to provide a politically independent agency "since the final monetary authority is and must be the legislature" (1946, 63). Mints recognized that a price-level rule would involve discretion in the use of policy instruments: "some discretionary authority would have to be granted to the agency [the Monetary Authority]" to achieve price-level stabilization (1946, 65). Should the government need to issue debt to finance the deficit, it should be only in the form of consols.

As noted, an underlying objective of the 1946 paper was to warn against the hazards inherent in proposals that relied on an enhanced role of government expenditures to support economic activity. Mints believed that those proposals reflected two influences: (1) the idea that government spending should be raised to counter recessions, and (2) the notion that government spending would have to increase to counter secular stagnation. Regarding countercyclical policy, Mints, as mentioned, favored raising tax exemptions and the provision of a retail tax subsidy during recessions to support an increase of the money supply. To reduce income inequality, he argued that exemptions should only be raised for lower-income groups: "It may be doubted ... that any reduction in the tax collections from the higher income brackets should be made" (1946, 65–66). Concerning the secular-stagnation thesis, Mints wrote: "even though secular stagnation is neither present nor imminent, a program of price level stabilization would actually avoid more than frictional unemployment if such conditions should develop" (1946, 62).

Building on the earlier Chicago framework, Mints's 1946 paper extended that framework in several ways.

*The Great Depression.* In his 1945 *A History of Banking Theory*, Mints had criticized the Federal Reserve for not having taken "vigorous monetary action" following the initial decline in economic activity in 1929 (1945a, 275). In his paper "Monetary Policy," Mints supported his criticism of the Fed's policy in the early 1930s with empirical evidence. In that connection, he showed that, whereas the wholesale price index had fallen from 96 in 1929 (1926 = 100) to 73 in May 1931, and to a low of 63 in May 1933, "the volume of money dropped to a low level in the summer of 1933 which was 25 per cent below that of 1929" (1946, 62–63). Mints argued that "open market operations were not employed on a scale sufficient to increase the reserves of the member banks, despite the fact that the volume of circulating medium (deposits and hand-to-hand currency) was actually declining" (1946, 62). Mints concluded his assessment of the Fed's policies as follows: "one cannot say that the Federal Reserve System made any serious attempt to maintain the quantity of money in the early thirties. We therefore are not justified in asserting that the course of events during those years has proved the inadequacy of conventional central-bank measures" (1946, 63).

Mints's position on the efficacy of open-market operations, however, lacked clarity. On the one hand, he argued that, because open-market operations "immediately affect the cash balances of only a small proportion of individuals and corporations," those operations "are unlikely to be sufficiently effective in the presence of severe disturbances" (1946, 63). For that reason, he favored the use of fiscal deficits to generate changes in the money supply during depressions. On the other hand, Mints criticized the Fed for not having made a serious attempt to employ open-market operations on "scale sufficient to increase the reserves of the member banks" in the early 1930s (1946, 62). Thus, although he argued that open-market operations are not effective during depressions, he criticized the Fed's failure to undertake open-market purchases in the early 1930s.

How can this apparent contradiction be resolved? The resolution is the following. Mints believed that the most effective tool to combat depressions was the use of money-financed fiscal deficits. Nevertheless, he thought that expansionary open-market operations should also be employed to complement money-financed fiscal deficits during depressions. During normal economic conditions, however, the roles of money-financed deficits and open-market purchases would be reversed. In this connection, it is relevant to note that, in his enumeration of the way his proposal that a Monetary Agency should aim to stabilize the price level would operate, Mints thought that open-market operations should be the agency's primary tool. For example, he argued that if the price level fell below its numerical objective, "the Monetary Agency would immediately enter the open market and purchase government bonds" (1946, 65). Should the price level remain below the objective, Mints stated: "if the decline [in the price level] were not halted in a very short time, exemption levels under the income tax would be raised. The deficit thus created would afford an opportunity to inject additional money into circulation" (1946, 65). In situations of economic recession, the priority assigned to money-financed fiscal deficits and open-market operations in expanding the money supply would be reversed, with the fiscal deficits assigned the lead role, but supported by open-market purchases.[36]

*Causes of the business cycle.* As mentioned, a core characteristic of the Chicago monetary approach from the early 1930s to the mid-1940s was the hypothesis that the business cycle is caused by autonomous shifts of velocity (or shifts in the demand for money). In his 1946 article, Mints considered the idea that the business cycle could also be caused by changes in the supply of money: "A depression is initiated by a decline in aggregate demand. Whether this decline is caused by a reduction in the quantity of money, or by an increase in liquidity preferences, is a matter of secondary importance" (1946, 60).

*Cash-balance effect.* Hitherto, the Chicagoans viewed the transmission mechanism as operating both through the interest-rate channel and through direct spending (flow) effects under which increases in the money supply raise spending on consumption and investment, leading to changes in prices, and via sticky wages, to changes in profits and production.[37] Mints introduced the possibility of a wealth (or stock) effect into the monetary-transmission mechanism. Specifically, he argued that an expansionary monetary policy could counter the effects of a negative shock to aggregate demand in the following way: "by means of an addition to the cash balances of the public . . . the maintenance of aggregate demand could be assured" (1946, 67).

*What monetary policy can do.* Mints believed that monetary policy should aim to maintain unemployment at a rate consistent with a minimum level of frictional unemployment:

> In a changing economy readjustments are constantly necessary, and frictional unemployment of some minimum amount is therefore unavoidable. This is a problem, however, which cannot be solved by monetary means. It requires . . . information available to the public, particularly to workers, concerning the regions and industries in which additional workers are in demand, and geographic and occupational mobility. (1946, 67)

Mints's argument that monetary policy cannot reduce unemployment below its frictional level was a forerunner of Friedman's (1968a) hypothesis of a natural rate of unemployment.

In the above discussion, I noted similarities between the views of Simons and Mints. In chapter 1, I numerated eight summary propositions that marked the early 1930s Chicago monetary tradition. The presentation of the views of The Group in chapter 2 provided evidence that the Chicagoans adhered to those propositions, with Viner being an outlier. It will be useful at this point to take stock of where Simons and Mints stood concerning those propositions in the mid-1940s. This exercise will allow us to see where the views of those two Chicagoans may have differed from the early 1930s Chicago framework and from each other's views. It will also allow us subsequently to identify the elements of the Simons-Mints framework that Friedman adopted when the focus of his research turned to the subject of money in the late 1940s. The eight summary propositions are the following.

*Summary proposition, no. 1. $MV + M'V' = PT$.* Both Simons and Mints used this framework, Fisher's equation, to analyze the business cycle. Mints, as Knight had done earlier, alternatively used a portfolio-balance model of the demand for money.

*Summary proposition, no. 2.* The economic system is inherently unstable because of autonomous changes in $V$; changes in $V$ are cumulative in nature. Simons and Mints subscribed to that view. Mints also argued that changes in $V$ could be greatly moderated by a monetary rule, which would help stabilize expectations and put a brake on the downward phase of the cycle. Mints discussed the possibility that changes in $M$ could also *initiate* the business cycle.

*Summary proposition, no. 3.* The fractional-reserve banking system exacerbates the cycle. Both Simons and Mints subscribed to that view.

*Summary proposition, no. 4.* The aim of stabilization policy is to effectuate countercyclical changes in *M*. Both Simons and Mints subscribed to that view.

*Summary proposition, no. 5.* During depressions, changes in *M* should be generated by the government's fiscal position; open-market operations and rediscounting operations are ineffective policy instruments. Both Simons and Mints subscribed to that view. Nevertheless, Mints thought that open-market purchases should complement money-financed fiscal deficits during depressions. He also maintained that open-market operations should play the lead role in stabilizing the price level in normal situations. In Simons's writings toward the end of his career, he saw a suppoting role for open-market operations in stabilization policy.

*Summary proposition, no. 6.* Long-run stabilization requires the use of monetary-policy rule to reduce uncertainty. Both Simons and Mints subscribed to that view. The view underpinned their respective proposals for a monetary rule.

*Summary proposition, no. 7.* The 100 percent scheme would help moderate the cycle. Simons subscribed to that view, but, by the mid-1930s, it had become but one element in his proposal to reform the financial sector. Mints also subscribed to that view, but his attachment to the 100 percent reserves scheme was not unequivocal. He thought that the large amounts of government bonds that banks held on their balance sheets secured the banks against unexpected liquidity requirements, reducing the urgency of the scheme.

*Summary proposition, no. 8.* To be able to pursue domestic economic objectives, there is a need of flexible exchange rates. Both Simons and Mints were strong exponents of flexible exchange rates. Each made contributions to the literature on exchange-rate regimes that foreshadowed arguments later made by Friedman.

It will also be useful to identify some other areas in which the views of Simons and Mints were in agreement. Again, the exercise will allow us to take stock of the Chicago monetary tradition as of the mid-1940s.

1. *Free-market system.* Both Simons and Mints believed that the free-market system provided individuals the freedom of choice to set and pursue their own objectives. Simons and Mints aimed to protect that system from the encroachments that they thought were inherent in Keynesian policies. Knight shared that view.

2. *Economic reform.* Both Simons and Mints favored the elimination of monopolies to foster wage and price flexibility.
3. *Financial system.* Both Simons and Mints believed that the financial system should be reformed. Both believed that short-term debt instruments should be eliminated. Both thought that, when the government borrows, it should issue only consols.
4. *Tax system.* Both Simons and Mints thought that the progressive tax system should be the mainstay of federal revenue. Both also favored the use of personal exemptions to manipulate tax revenues. Simons believed that the progressive income tax should be the major instrument for achieving greater equality. In addition to the progressive income tax, Mints favored the use of differential treatment of exemptions among income groups to achieve greater equality.

## The Discussants

Now I turn to views set down by the four discussants of Mints's 1946 article. I present their comments in the order presented in *REStat.*

*Alvin Hansen.*[38] Although agreeing with Mints that "anti-monopoly and monetary policy are important," Hansen did not subscribe to Mints's monetary interpretation of the Great Depression. That episode reflected, according to Hansen, the "structural financial defects of the twenties," by which he meant the absence of necessary institutions such as the Federal Housing Administration, the Federal Deposit Insurance Corporation, and the Securities and Exchange Commission (1946, 69). Hansen thought that the absence of those institutions contributed to the speculative excesses of the late 1920s. He stated: "Had these institutions been in existence throughout the twenties, many unsound elements in the boom would have been absent or present in less degree" (1946, 69). Hansen believed that antidepression policy required both reductions in taxes (in the form of higher exemptions and lower tax rates) and increases in government spending. Higher levels of government spending were also required to deal with the problem posed by secular stagnation (1946, 70). The potential for such spending, Hansen thought, was boundless: "I am convinced that a study of the serious deficiencies in this country will indicate that large public outlays are necessary.... [A] rational use of our resources ... requires large public outlays (much larger than we have had in the past)" (1946, 70–71). In some industries [such as private construction], government spending would need to play the role of a "balance wheel" to keep those industries from falling into recession (1946, 70).

Hansen thought that fiscal deficits should be bond financed; the idea that "the issue of bonds is deflationary while the issue of currency is inflationary is surely a vast oversimplification" (1946, 71). The money supply, Hansen asserted, determines the "rate of interest—not the price level" (1946, 72). He maintained that a stable-price-level rule "by itself alone is no adequate criterion on the basis of which it can be decided how much of a deficit shall be financed from borrowing from the public and how much by multiplication of the money supply" (1946, 72).

A noteworthy aspect of Hansen's paper was its argument that Mints's and Simons's views should be treated as a single framework. Thus, after discussing the Mints and Simons ideas that (1) there is a "sharp dichotomy between 'currency' and 'consols'" (1946, 72) and (2) "there is some virtue in limiting the property claims of society wholly to equities and money," Hansen referred to these ideas under the designation "the Mints-Simons program" (1946, 73). Hence, the perception that the monetary ideas emanating from Chicago needed to be treated separately from those of the rest of the economics profession was gaining traction.

*Howard Ellis.* Ellis took issue with Mints's view that a rule that stabilizes the price level would be consistent with full employment. Ellis asserted: "Price level stability, while it constitutes one of several legitimate aims of monetary and fiscal policy, does not constitute the only or even the most important aim and it is certainly not synonymous with full employment" (1946a, 76). "Fiscal and monetary measures," Ellis argued, needed to be complemented with "some defensible national wage policy." He noted that such a national wage policy would have to confront the question of the way it could be implemented "without authoritarian determination of wage rates" (1946a, 76). Ellis discussed the possibility of imposing price controls and quantity rationing, noting that those policies had been recommended by a group of economists at the Oxford Institute of Statistics in a 1944 study, titled *The Economics of Full Employment*[39] (I will have occasion to return to the Oxford study below). A policy that aimed to reach full employment without triggering "sporadic outbursts of inflationary spending in a society assured of jobs for all" raised the possibility that "price control and rationing would have to be available for immediate use" (1946a, 75). Increasing the supply of money, he argued, would not be sufficient to bring about full employment. Instead, Ellis argued that "the maintenance of a liberal capitalist regime requires an attack upon unemployment along a very broad front" (1946a, 75). Finally, Ellis agreed with Hansen's view that spending on public works should not be "bound by an absolute rule" (1946a, 76).

*Abba Lerner*. Lerner's comments on Mints's paper were critical and derisive. The focus of Lerner's remarks was Mints's ill-fitted use of the quantity theory of money in what Lerner perceived was a Keynesian world; in that world, the quantity theory had been rendered obsolete. In this connection, Lerner expressed the view that "there is an astonishing overemphasis [in Mints's paper] on the amount of money in existence as key to the volume of spending" (1946, 77). He asserted such concepts as government debt, government borrowing, and fiscal deficits "seem very strange in the company of a quantity theory of money approach which seeks to stabilize P (a *wholesale* price level!) by variations in M, the amount of money. It is as if Professor Mints had hibernated right through the Keynesian revolution, and had recently awakened bright and fresh, to show great skill in innocently playing the old games with the new instruments he had found lying around" (emphasis in original, 77–78). Mints, Lerner argued, assumed that an increase in the quantity of money would be successful in raising "effective demand" because of "the optimistic assumption of a very elastic marginal efficiency of investment and a very inelastic marginal liquidity preference; so that a small fall in the rate of interest from a small increase in the amount of money will always put things right" (1946, 81). Lerner strongly disagreed with this view: "What is missing almost completely from Professor Mints's analysis is the Keynesian clarification of how liquidity is not enough" (1946, 79). While Mints correctly saw that more direct measures, "such as government spending or the encouragement of consumer spending," were needed during depressions, Mints's paper, Lerner argued, had the effect of "slurring . . . some of the complications because of the use of the quantity equation approach" (1946, 79).

*Michal Kalecki*. Kalecki, who was one of the co-authors of the 1944 Oxford study *The Economics of Full Employment*, to which Ellis had referred, was critical of Mints's policy proposals. Kalecki pointed out that, while "Mints himself is not very confident of the effectiveness of the open market policy," Mints nevertheless proposed open-market operations as one of two methods for "increasing effective demand," the other method being money-financed fiscal deficits (1946, 82). In particular, Kalecki thought that open-market operations on a very large scale would be required to reduce the interest rate sufficiently to stimulate demand. Thus, Kalecki did not think that open-market purchases were "the best way of stimulating consumption, either from a social or an economic point of view" (1946, 82). To stimulate consumption, he favored increasing tax exemptions, but "only up to a certain level"; reduction or abolition of contributions to social insurance by the poor; and a "subsidation of prices of mass consumption goods only" (82–83). As Hansen had argued, Kalecki favored permanent increases in government expenditure to deal with "the long-run 'deflationary gap.'" In this connection, Kalecki argued: "there are so many urgent tasks to be tackled by public authorities, as Professor Hansen points out in his paper, that they would raise the public expenditure to a level which exceeds the probable tax revenue" (1946, 83).

Additionally, Kalecki advocated the use of government expenditure to counterbalance cyclical fluctuations in private investment. By maintaining full employment, countercyclical government expenditure would result in a situation in which "the fluctuations in private investments would be much smaller than under *laissez faire* and the regular investment cycle would probably disappear altogether" (1946, 83). Kalecki believed that the fiscal deficits generated by his proposals should be financed by issuing "short-term securities while the short-term rate of interest is maintained by the central bank at a low but stable level" (1946, 83). As we shall see later in this chapter, Chicago economists, including Mints, strongly opposed the Fed's then policy of interest-rate pegging. Finally, on the issue of trade unions, Kalecki thought that it "is indeed fortunate that trade unions exist" to protect workers' wages in an economic environment of imperfect competition (1946, 84).

*Discussion*

The 1946 symposium on monetary policy in the *Review of Economics and Statistics* has provided the occasion to consider The Group's monetary economics within the context of the views of four prominent members of the economics profession. How did the Chicagoans' views that (1) money plays an important role in the economy and (2) the quantity theory of money should be used to assess economic conditions square with the views of those four members of the profession? It is noteworthy that none of the non-Chicagoans thought that monetary policy on its own would be sufficient to maintain full employment. None of those economists supported a monetary-policy rule. Lerner and Kalecki asserted that the effectiveness of monetary policy was constrained by a low interest elasticity of investment and high interest elasticity of money demand. Hansen stated that monetary policy could not bring about full employment.[40] Ellis asserted that fiscal and monetary measures should be complemented with a national wage policy. The non-Chicago economists who expressed a view on deficit financing—Hansen and Kalecki—stated that deficits should be financed by issuing bonds—but not by money creation. Hansen argued that money influenced interest rates—money did not influence prices. He expressed the view that the Great Depression was caused by structural defects in the US economy of the 1920s. Lerner took Mints to task for having "hibernated right through the Keynesian revolution." That statement pretty much summed up the overall appraisal of Mints's paper.

Two additional comments are warranted. First, as mentioned, Hansen blamed the Great Depression on structural "defects" in the US economy of the 1920s; among those "defects," he singled out the absence of certain institutions, one of which was the Federal Deposit Insurance Corporation (FDIC). Concerning the specific case of the FDIC, Hansen, without elaborating, stated that its absence was an important example of a "seriously deficient" banking structure (1946, 69). It should be noted that Friedman and Anna Schwartz argued that, had the FDIC been in existence in the late 1920s and early 1930s, it would have prevented the large shifts from deposits to currency that took place and the resulting banking crises. Specifically, in their *Monetary History*, Friedman and Schwartz attributed the severity of the Great Depression, in part, to the absence of the FDIC. They argued that the greater part of the 1929–33 decline in the money stock was a consequence of the large number of bank failures that took place, the effects of these failures on the deposit-currency ratio, and "the failure of the Federal Reserve to offset the fall in the ratio by a sufficient increase in high-powered money" (1963, 441). Friedman and Schwartz (1963, 441) wrote: "Had federal deposit insurance been in existence in 1930, it would very likely have prevented the initial fall in the deposit-currency ratio in late 1930 and hence the tragic sequence of events that fall set in train, including the drastic decline in the money stock." In contrast to Friedman and Schwartz, Hansen did not assign a pivotal role to the absence of the FDIC in the Great Depression; the FDIC was only one of several institutions that he singled out. Nor did Hansen discuss the fall in the deposit-currency ratio and the resulting fall in the stock of money as crucial elements in the Great Depression.

The second comment concerns the advocacy of wage and price controls. We saw that Ellis raised the possibility of imposing (1) controls on prices and (2) rationing so that inflation could be kept in check at full employment. We also saw that price and wage controls and rationing were recommended by a group of economists—a group that included Kalecki—in the Oxford study *The Economics of Full Employment* (1944). Although

Hansen and Lerner did not discuss the possibility of using price and wage controls and rationing to control inflation in their discussions of Mints's paper, in other publications of the 1940s they did so. Thus, the discussants of Mints's paper shared the view that inflation could not be controlled by monetary measures alone. For example, in his 1944 book *The Economics of Control*, Lerner advocated a policy called "general rationing"—a policy that, according to Lerner, had originally been proposed by Kalecki.[41] To contain aggregate demand under that policy, the amount of money that could be spent on goods and services—the particular goods which the government had determined to be scarce—would be limited; the amount permitted to be spent would be equal to "what would be left by the simpler but too heavy load of taxation that would (otherwise) prevent inflation" (A. Lerner 1944, 53). Consequently, an individual's income "is not taxed away but left with the individual though it is not available for current expenditure on the scarce goods. It may be spent on goods that are not scarce or it may be saved and released for expenditure only when the emergency is over" (1944, 53). Correspondingly, in Hansen's 1949 book *Monetary Theory and Fiscal Policy*, that economist wrote the following about inflation control: "Any attempt to control inflation by monetary means alone is likely to turn the economy into a nose dive. . . . Monetary restraint can, in conjunction with other measures, play a useful role." What were those other measures? Hansen wrote: "a firm use of fiscal policy, minimum direct controls, including allocation of scarce materials for essential uses, construction permits, and rationing (for example of food imports)" (1949, 166).

The advocacy of direct controls to check inflation by Ellis, Hansen, Kalecki, and Lerner provides evidence that the Keynesian revolution brought with it not only an emphasis on demand management but the idea that monetary policy was not sufficient to control inflation. As Nelson (2020, 1:128) pointed out, that idea emanated from a cost-push view of inflation under which autonomous forces could trigger a wage-price spiral. Keynesians argued that wage and price controls, and other forms of incomes policy, would be needed to keep the wage-price spiral in check.

The picture that emerges from the symposium is one in which Chicago economists—in particular, Simons and Mints—had come to be recognized as outliers within the economics profession in the mid-1940s. With Simons's death in 1946, Douglas's engagement in World War II and his postwar immersion in politics, and Knight's retreat from work in monetary economics, Mints would have been left on his own to push forward the Chicago monetary tradition's views but for the appointments of Director and Friedman to the Chicago faculty in 1946.

## 6.2 Director, 1947

Director returned to the University of Chicago in 1946 to head the newly formed Free Market Study (FMS) Project, which was housed in the Law School. The objective of the project was to promote free-market ideas to counter the then-rising tide of collectivist doctrine (Van Horn 2020).[42] Specifically, the FMS aimed to investigate the kinds of legal and institutional *changes* that would be necessary to create and preserve an effective competitive environment (Caldwell 2011).[43] In addition to Director, the other members of the FMS were Friedman, Knight, and Theodore Schultz, all members of the Economics Department; Garfield Cox, dean of the Business School; Wilber Katz, dean of the Law School; and Edward Levi, a professor in the Law School.[44] Van Horn (2020) reported that the FMS "undertook some empirical studies geared toward countervailing collectivism and reinvigorating liberalism."[45] The idea that Director should head the FMS had been pushed forward by Hayek and Simons.[46] After Simons's death, and following the offer made to Director to join the Law School, Hayek wrote to Director encouraging him to accept the offer with the following argument: "It seems to me ... the only chance that the tradition which Henry Simons created will be kept alive and continued at Chicago" (letter, Hayek to Director, July 10, 1946, quoted from Van Horn 2010a, 267).[47]

Director taught at the Law School from 1946 until his retirement in 1965.[48] During his time at the Law School, he established a reputation as a revered, but enigmatic, figure. His legacy as a revered figure stems from the key role he played in establishing the field of law and economics as a separate discipline and, in 1958, founding the *Journal of Law and Economics*.[49] His reputation as an enigmatic figure reflects the fact that he left very little behind in terms of a written track record through which to assess his contributions. During his career in the Law School, his views became known through his teaching. His influence on the profession was revealed in the writings of his students, many of whom became distinguished legal scholars, and through his influence on Law School colleagues.[50] As George Stigler put it, "most of Aaron's articles have been published under the names of his colleagues" (quoted from University of Chicago News Office 2004, 2).

Director's published output in monetary economics was, if anything, even sparser than his published writings on law and economics. In fact, following the publications of his book *The Problem of Unemployment*, co-authored with Douglas, his two early 1930s monographs (Director 1932; 1933), and his 1940 article "Does Inflation Change the Economic Effects of War?," each of which was discussed in previous chapters, Director published nothing original on the subject of money.[51]

The scarcity of Director's published writings in monetary economics is regrettable because his two appointments at the University of Chicago co-incided with crucial stages in the development of that subject at Chicago and because of Director's intimacy with the two leading figures underpinning those stages. As we saw, Director's initial teaching stint at Chicago from 1930 to 1934 coincided with the emergence of the Chicago monetary tradition in the early 1930s, with Simons increasingly taking on the leadership role. Until the time of Simons's death in 1946, Director and Simons had been the best of friends (Coase 1998, 602). Director's second stint at the University of Chicago, beginning in 1946, coincided with Friedman's appointment to Chicago's economics faculty and with the emergence of Friedman's monetarist framework from the late 1940s to the mid-1950s. As was the case with Director and Simons, Director and Friedman were intimate friends. Director was Friedman's brother-in-law, Friedman having married Director's sister, Rose; the two brothers-in-law had a close personal relationship (Friedman and Friedman 1998, chap. 14).[52]

In addition to his close relationships with Simons and Friedman, Director also interacted closely with other members of the Economics Department during his stints at Chicago. As discussed in chapter 1, during the early 1930s members of the University of Chicago's economics faculty, including Director, met regularly in departmental meetings and Sunday social gatherings at Knight's home to discuss the causes of the Great Depression and to formulate policy responses to the Depression. Following his appointment to the Law School, Director "was responsible for generating a great deal of interaction among members of the Law School Faculty, the Economics Department, and the Business School"; he also participated in, and occasionally hosted, "bull sessions" among members of the economics faculty (Milton Friedman, quoted from Friedman and Friedman 1998, 194–95).

Having been at the University of Chicago during two crucial stages of the development of monetary economics at that institution, having had close personal relations with the two leading figures of each of those stages, and having participated in regular discussions among members of the Economics Department during those stages, Director was in a unique position to shed light on the relationship between the monetary frameworks of those stages. In this and the following chapters, I provide evidence that makes Director's role in carrying forward the Chicago monetary tradition's message on money from the Chicago of the early 1930s to the Chicago of the late 1940s and 1950s less enigmatic. In particular, I show that Director brought the earlier Chicago views on the important role of money in the economy and the need of policy rules with him to his second stint at Chicago. I also show that, like Knight, Simons, and Mints, Director pushed forward the need of a modified laissez-faire system. In presenting Director's views, I rely on unpublished works by that economist. I begin with a 1947 presentation made by Director at the first meeting of the Mont Pèlerin Society. In chapter 8, I discuss unpublished works of Director from the mid-1950s.

## Mont Pèlerin

The Mont Pèlerin Society was Hayek's creation.[53] Following invitations from Hayek, in 1947, thirty-nine scholars, mostly economists, with some historians and philosophers, met to discuss the state of classical liberalism, including ways to strengthen liberalism in a world increasingly characterized by bigger governments. Three Chicagoans were among the participants—Director, Friedman, and Knight.[54] The first meeting of the Mont Pèlerin Society took place from April 1 to April 10, 1947.

Director addressed the Mont Pèlerin Society gathering on April 1, 1947.[55] His remarks had two objectives: first, to provide an overview of the reasons underlying the state's encroachment in economic life and, second, to identify those areas in which state intervention was needed to make the competitive order work more efficiently.

Director began his presentation with the observation that a steady shift from individualism to authority as the basis of the organization of economic affairs had taken place over several generations. This shift, he argued, had become "part of a definite design to adopt an entirely different type of economic organization than the one to which we are accustomed" (1947b, 1). In some countries, he maintained, the shift had been completed. Elsewhere, it was proceeding at a rapid pace. Director mentioned three factors that contributed to this shift. First, in light of the economy's poor performance in the 1930s, he stated that the free-market system was justifiably under attack because it had not performed well. Second, he argued that advances in technology had increased the efficiency of large-scale enterprises, which, in turn, favored monopolistic firms. The rise of those firms led to a reduction in competition and an "intolerable loss of product." Preventing firms from becoming monopolistic required "an intolerable amount of governmental intervention" (1947b, 2). Additionally, Director maintained that the acceptance of the secular-stagnation thesis by many economists contributed to the idea that private investment opportunities were being exhausted, requiring a large and secularly increasing governmental participation in economic life. Third, Director argued that the "incomplete character of the theory of liberalism developed in the nineteenth century" had changed little in the ensuing century; as a result, liberalism had not risen to the occasion of addressing the economic challenges of the mid-twentieth century. Liberalism, he stated, provided "no role for the state in economic life beyond the enforcement of contracts and performing certain economic functions which cannot be undertaken by individual enterprises" (1947b, 3).[56] In light of these factors, liberalism had not been up to the task of competing with ideologies that promoted state interventionism in economic affairs.

Specifically, liberalism was not able to deliver in three essential areas: (1) it had not been able to deal with an economic system that featured a "substantial amount of monopoly"; (2) it had not adequately provided stable rules of the game with respect to money; and (3) it had fallen short in meeting the democratic standards of equality (1947b, 4). What, then, were the kind of measures that liberalism needed to take so that it would be able to overcome these weaknesses? Director proposed the following.

*Monopolistic power.* Similarly to Simons, Director stated that "trade unions . . . constitute the most serious type of monopoly organization" (1947b, 7). Director maintained that the "law against monopoly and combinations in restraint of trade" should be applied to labor unions. With regard to monopolistic firms, he asserted that their size could be limited through the application of specific legislative measures such as the prohibition of "corporate ownership of other corporations" (1947b, 7). He also favored the application of antitrust laws although he considered those laws to be stopgap measures.

*Monetary stabilization.* Director argued that there was almost universal recognition that "the competitive market is not a suitable means of regulating the supply of money" (1947b, 8). Yet, "the liberal tradition" had offered little in the area of money "apart from the Bank Act of 1844" (1947b, 8).[57] Thus, the liberal economic tradition had not addressed the issue of a suitable monetary regime.

The essential prerequisite for monetary stability for a competitive society, Director asserted, was "definite control over the quantity of money"
(1947b, 8). That control, in turn, could be achieved by either a gold-backed
currency or "the direct assumption by the state of the responsibility for
issuing the currency" (1947b, 8–9). A gold-backed currency had "two advantages": (1) the supply of money would not be determined by the state;
and (2) it would require fixed exchange rates. However, it would be costly
in terms of resources and stability, and it would depend on the supplies
produced by the gold industry (1947b, 9).

Director's preferred method to control the quantity of money was to
have the state regulate the supply to maintain price stability. He stated:
"The prospect of providing *monetary certainty* for enterprise so that it
need no longer gamble on the behavior of discretionary authorities may
accomplish a great deal in solving the problem of variations in aggregate
output and employment" (emphasis added, 1947b, 9). In addition, a monetary rule, Director argued, would provide "an escape ... out of the confusion of fiscal behavior" since it would set a limit on the amount of money
that could accompany fiscal expansion (1947b, 9).

*Equality*. Director expressed the view that one of the original tenets of
liberalism was "the greatest good for the greatest number." However, liberalism, he said, had fallen short of satisfying the strong humanitarian impulses of its founding fathers. Instead, a "misguided humanitarianism" had
led to a series of ad hoc interventions in economic affairs, including pro-
tective tariffs, minimum-wage laws, and agricultural protection schemes,
each of which had created new inequalities to replace those that had been
redressed. Director asserted that the adoption of measures that provide
monetary certainty and the elimination of monopolistic power would help
reduce inequalities, but those measures would not be sufficient.[58] He favored increased reliance on the progressive income tax to reduce inequalities, "extended to include subsidy payments to those with low incomes
but leaving a margin for incentive to work"; he recognized, however, that
such reliance would negatively affect aggregate output. He stated: "We
should be prepared to pay this price" (1947b, 4).

## 6.3 Cox, 1947

In chapter 4, I provided evidence showing that Cox supported monetary
rules in the mid-1930s. I noted, however, that Cox's published work rarely
included discussions about policy issues. His work was narrowly focused

on the assessment of various forecasting techniques and a comparison of alternative forecasting exercises.

Against this backdrop, in 1947 Cox published the paper "Free Enterprise *vs.* Authoritarian Planning" in the *Journal of Business*. Cox's views in the paper were very similar to those made by Knight, Simons, and Mints in their published work, and by Director in his April 1, 1947 presentation to the Mont Pèlerin Society. Cox argued that a global trend toward socialism had been taking place: "From the gradual socialism of Great Britain to the planned economy of Soviet Russia the area of free markets has shrunk or vanished" (1947, 59). He stated that he felt a "deep concern" about the issue. For that reason, he wanted to present an analysis of the factors that had led to the rise of collectivism (1947, 59).

To do so, Cox provided a brief historical account of the emergence of the free-market economy. From Adam Smith's day onward, he argued, in English-speaking countries, the development of freer and wider markets went hand in hand with the diffusion of economic initiative and responsibility, the spread of education and cultural participation among people, and the growth of political democracy and international interdependence (1947, 60). This development had proceeded for about a century, from the fourth quarter of the eighteenth century to the final quarter of the nineteenth century. Two factors, however, reversed this process toward freer markets. First, "swiftly changing technology," under a system in which the market determined "where and how labor and capital should be invested," dealt "harshly with many persons" (1947, 60). In those circumstances, it was a natural human instinct, Cox asserted, to believe that "a select group of capable managers with a desire to serve the general welfare could direct the economy better than the market" (1947, 60). Second, the view had emerged among some advocates of free markets that the state should not interfere at all in economic affairs. Like Simons, Mints, and Director, Cox believed that this circumstance gave rise to three major problems—the first two of which were the rise of private monopolies and money-induced business cycles:

> Even the wisest and best-informed liberals failed to sense the amount of intelligent positive action necessary to maintain the satisfactory functioning of free enterprise. In part they underestimated and in part misunderstood the problems of private monopoly and pressure groups. They neglected the problems of booms and depressions and the large part of the monetary system plays in them, though all concerned have long agreed that monetary policy must be primarily the responsibility of the state. (1947, 61)

The third major problem confronting the free market, according to Cox, was income inequality. He maintained that liberals had not adequately addressed this issue, leaving it up to others to do so. As a result, "reformers have attacked the problem of great economic inequality by price- and wage-fixing rather than by such methods of taxation and government spending as are consistent with the maintenance of a free-market economy" (1947, 61). In various sectors of the market, Cox maintained, "strong interests" contrived to control the market on their own behalf, resulting in anticompetitive associations, such as labor unions, and anticompetitive practices, such as the imposition of tariffs and subsidies.

Cox expressed the concern that some Americans had been impressed with "the production records of the Soviet and Nazi dictatorships" and, as a result, would vote to give US politicians "a mandate to undertake a planned economy" (1947, 62). The collectivist trend in the United States, he argued, had started with the policies of the New Deal. He warned that planning would lead to the concentration of power in the hands of a few. Cox expressed particular concern with the rise of organized labor, which, he asserted, "has been behaving as irresponsibly as the more ruthless of the industrial captains of a generation ago—and more dangerously to the general welfare" (1947, 64). He called for government intervention to reduce the size of monopolistic firms and labor unions.

What was needed most to restore the viability of the free-market system, Cox argued, was "a theory of appropriate state action to improve the rules of the game" (1947, 65). In other words, as did Simons and Mints, Cox thought that the state's role in economic affairs should be constitutional, rather than administrative. There was, a need, he stated, "for better and clearer rules in matters which are already the acknowledged responsibility of the state" (1947, 65). As an example, he referred to "the field of monetary-fiscal policy." For generations, governments had pursued discretionary policies, resulting in a "bewildering hodgepodge" in "our monetary structure and federal tax, spending, and debt arrangements." In concluding, he stated:

> If, in the monetary-fiscal field which is peculiarly its own, our government can formulate and administer a few definite, understandable rules favorable to satisfactory levels of business activity, it will thereby lessen the occasion for its intervention in details. Only an intelligently selective and economical use of bureaucratic power can save enough areas of free market to protect basic civil, political, and cultural liberties that we cherish. (1947, 65)

*Discussion*

As did Simons, Mints, and Director, Cox called for action to deal with monopolistic organizations although Cox did not provide specific proposals. Like those other Chicagoans, Cox did not believe that the free-market system had addressed the issue of inequality. Like those other Chicagoans, Cox stressed the need of rules in the field of money. During the mid-1940s, the above-mentioned Chicagoans were in a very small minority in advocating monetary rules. In the late 1940s, they would be joined by another advocate of rules—Milton Friedman.

## 6.4 The Return of Friedman

*Pre-Chicago*

After spending the 1940–41 academic year in a teaching position at the University of Wisconsin, Friedman moved to the US Treasury in December 1941; he remained at the Treasury until early 1943.[59] At the Treasury he worked on the subjects of inflation, taxation, and fiscal policy. Nelson (2020, 1:91–92) reported that not only had Friedman arrived at the Treasury with a Keynesian perspective, but his employment at the Treasury reinforced that perspective.[60]

In May 1942, Friedman submitted a memorandum to the House Ways and Means Committee in which he dealt with ways to control inflation.[61] To achieve that objective, Friedman argued that consumer spending would have to be restricted. The best way to do that, he argued, was via income taxation. The other ways of avoiding inflation that he mentioned in his memorandum were through price controls and rationing, controls on consumer credit, reduction in government spending, and selling war bonds to the public. He made no mention of money or monetary policy (Friedman 1942b). Looking back on that episode over half a century later Friedman wrote: "The most striking feature of this statement is how thoroughly Keynesian it is" (Friedman and Friedman 1998, 112).[62] Given Friedman's criticisms of controls in the 1970s and, indeed, in his and George Stigler's *Roofs or Ceilings? The Current Housing Problem* (Friedman and Stigler 1946) not long after his 1942 congressional memorandum, was he really in favor of price controls in 1942? As Nelson (2020, 1:84) pointed out, Friedman was an employee of the federal government at that time and, hence, hardly free to criticize government policy, and price controls were a part of government policy at the time.

The Keynesian perspective on spending and inflation in Friedman's congressional memorandum—including the omission of monetary factors from that testimony—was mirrored in a comment he wrote on an article by Walter Salant on inflation (Friedman 1942a). When Friedman reprinted that article in his *Essays in Positive Economics* in 1953, he made several additions to correct for the omission of monetary effects from his original discussion.[63] In this connection, Friedman (1953e, 253n2) explained: "the omission from that [i.e., original] version of monetary effects is a serious error which is not excused but may perhaps be explained by the prevailing Keynesian temper of the times."

By the mid-1940s, however, Friedman had begun to alter his views on the cause of inflation substantially. Nelson (2020, 1:121–22) noted that in a 1944 review of the book *Saving, Investment, and National Income*, by Oscar Altman, Friedman put distance between himself and Keynesian income-expenditure theory.[64] In an April 1946 University of Chicago Round Table radio discussion, *What Can Be Done about Inflation?*, Friedman singled out what he termed the "two pillars to the [inflation] problem" (NBC 1946). The first was "the large volume of money and money substitutes in the hands of the public," and the second, "the great volume of unused lending power in the hands of the banks." In further contrast to his 1942 congressional testimony, Friedman argued against price controls, including rent controls, and also against the Federal Reserve's then policy of pegging the interest rates on government securities.

Similarly, in a statement published in the *Congressional Record* on April 16, 1946, Friedman called for the elimination of price controls, imposed by the Office of Price Administration (OPA), to reduce inflation. He also wrote:

> We can and must take measures now to control the basic causes of inflation by limiting the supply of cash and bank deposits. This will require that Government collect as much and spend as little as possible; that we put the Federal Reserve System once again in control of the volume of cash and deposits by drastically raising reserve requirements and that we pin down the liquid assets in the hands of the public by a realistic debt policy, even if that means higher interest rates on the Federal debt. (Friedman 1946, A2336)

As we shall see, Friedman's above suggestions that the government's fiscal position should be used to determine the quantity of cash and that 100 percent reserve requirements be used to control the supply of deposits became key features of his first major work in monetary economics—his

1948 paper "A Monetary and Fiscal Framework for Economic Stability."
As we shall also see, his call for "a realistic debt policy" foreshadowed
his efforts in the late 1940s and early 1950s to put an end to the Federal
Reserve's policy of pegging interest rates.

## Chicago

Friedman joined the Chicago economics faculty as an associate professor
in the 1946–47 academic year.[65] Although he expressed views on monetary issues in various forums during his first few years on the Chicago
faculty, Friedman's primary research interest during those years was price
theory.[66]

In 1951, Friedman was awarded John Bates Clark Medal, the award
given by the American Economic Association to economists under the
age of forty for an outstanding contribution to economic research. Friedman received the Clark Medal largely based on his theoretical work—
notably his joint work with Leonard Savage in which those researchers
developed a theoretical approach to the utility analysis of risk and measurement of utility (Nelson 2020, 1:176).[67]

The year 1948 saw Friedman embrace monetary economics as a primary field of interest. In doing so, Friedman brought a skill set to the table
that Simons and Mints did not have—namely, a very strong knowledge
of theoretical and applied statistics. During the 1933–34 academic year,
Friedman held a fellowship at Columbia University, where he studied
statistics under Harold Hotelling, a mathematical statistician and economist.[68] Back in Chicago for the 1934–35 academic year, Friedman worked
as a research assistant for Henry Schultz, who was writing a book on statistical demand analysis.[69] By the mid-1940s, Friedman had demonstrated
the potential to be a statistician of considerable stature.[70] In contrast to
Friedman, Simons never employed statistical analysis in his work; indeed,
Simons's work was marked by a complete absence of the use of data. While
Mints used data to highlight the importance of money in various historical
episodes, Mints's use of data did not include statistical techniques, such as
correlation analysis.

Two points about Friedman's statistical approach are important to highlight.[71] First, the statistical approach that Friedman brought to his work
on money was the application of correlation analysis to a wide array of
data to develop quantitative and qualitative evidence. In Friedman's view,
scientific investigation was necessarily a sequential process, proceeding in

successive approximations.[72] Theory provided the initial starting point for empirical investigation, with its results then feeding back on theory and leading to its refinement. As Heckman (2012) put it, Friedman's approach was one that "*distilled* wisdom from the data and learned from the data" (emphasis in original). Throughout, Friedman eschewed formal statistical testing and avoided the use of statistical analysis to draw conclusions about cause and effect.[73] The second point is that Friedman was in important respects a Bayesian. He did not use formal Bayesian tools, but he viewed probability from a personal perspective to assess various states of the world: the purpose of empirical analysis, in Friedman's view, was to assess the support that empirical work provided for a theory and parameter values (Dwyer 2016, 582).[74]

Two occurrences marked Friedman's 1948 move into monetary economics. First, Friedman began his collaboration with Schwartz on *A Monetary History* in that year. In preparation for the project, in September 1948, Friedman completed a fifteen-page unpublished document, "Preliminary Plan for Completion of Data for Study of Monetary Factors in Business Cycles." Second, in 1948, Friedman published the article "A Monetary and Fiscal Framework for Economic Stability," in the *AER*, in which Friedman, for the first time, proposed a monetary rule.[75] Both the unpublished paper and the *AER* paper provide evidence of the considerable influence of the Chicago monetary tradition on Friedman's thinking on monetary issues by the late 1940s. In what follows, I consider each of those papers in turn.

The unpublished document framed the objective of the Friedman and Schwartz project as follows: "It is clear that the first stage of this study is to compile and put into systematic form some quantitative data that will provide the chief basis for whatever inferences we can make about the behaviour of monetary and banking phenomena during business cycles and about their role in generating, or determining the character of business cycles" (Friedman 1948b, 1). While most of the document dealt with data requirements for the project, it also touched on the project's expected analytic framework. That framework was the Fisherine equation of exchange, and its particular form was that of the Chicago monetary tradition. Specifically, Friedman maintained that shifts in velocity, exacerbated by a fractional-reserve banking system, were the primary drivers of the business cycle. Friedman wrote:

> For cyclical analysis, interest attaches not only and perhaps not mainly to the total
> quantity of circulating medium but also to its form and to the interchangeability

of different forms. The most dramatic monetary episodes of business cycle history all relate to attempts on the part of the general public to change the form in which they held the circulating medium, in particular, attempts to convert bank deposits into hand-to-hand currency, and to a somewhat lesser extent, to convert hand-to-hand currency into gold. (1948b, 2)

Once a movement from bank deposits to currency starts during a business contraction, Friedman claimed that there is "hardly any limit to the 'velocity of circulation'" of money (1948b, 3). Why are changes in the form in which the circulating medium is held a source of instability? Friedman stated:"[because] there is no sharp dividing line between 'money' and 'near-moneys' or between 'near-moneys' and 'securities proper'" (1948b, 5). In light of the "interdependence" of the various financial instruments that constitute the circulating medium, "monetary and banking phenomena play a crucial role in the generation of business cycles and in determining their character" (1948b, 9).

There is a clear-cut relationship between the analytic structure of Friedman's unpublished 1948 document and that of the 1930s and 1940s Chicago monetary tradition. (1) At a time during which the economics profession overwhelmingly used the Keynesian income-expenditure approach to assess the business cycle, Friedman used the Fisherine equation of exchange to analyze the cycle. Monetary forces, in his view, underpinned the business cycle. (2) Friedman diagnosed that the fundamental problem driving the business cycle was the inherent instability of the velocity of circulation, occasioned by the close substitutability between the circulating medium and other financial instruments. (3) Once a downward movement in velocity had started, there was "hardly any limit to the velocity of circulation of money."

The core of Friedman's policy position in the late 1940s was presented in his 1948 *AER* paper.[76] In that paper, he proposed a rule under which fiscal policy would be used to generate changes in the money supply automatically. His proposal comprised four key elements. First, to deal with what Friedman regarded as the "inherent instability" of a fractional-reserve banking system, he called for 100 percent reserve requirements. Under the proposal, open-market operations would be abolished.[77] Second, to eliminate the Fed's discretionary power, Friedman called for the adoption of a monetary rule under which changes in the stock of money would be linked to the federal budget.[78] The stock of money would be increased when there was an increase in the budget deficit—by the amount of the deficit.

It would be decreased when there was a surplus in the budget—by the amount of the surplus. The budget would be balanced over the course of the business cycle or, alternatively, it would lead to a deficit sufficient to provide some specified secular increase in the quantity of money (1948a, 137). All existing Treasury securities would be converted into consols so that, as an interim measure, only two kinds of government liabilities would exist—money and consols. Eventually, the issuance of consols would be discontinued and the existing public debt retired so that money would be the only government-issued debt. Third, the volume of government expenditure on goods and services, excluding transfers, would be predetermined by the community based on the value attached by the community to public services; the volume would "presumably change only slowly" (1948a, 136). A program of transfer payments would also be predetermined and not changed in response to cyclical fluctuations although the absolute level of outlays would, of course, vary automatically over the cycle. Fourth, the tax system would place primary emphasis on the progressive income tax with rates and exemptions "set in light of the expected yield at a [hypothetical] level of income corresponding to reasonably full employment at a predetermined price level" (1948a, 137). The progressive-income-tax *structure* would *not* be changed in response to cyclical fluctuations in economic activity. Changes in the level of public services or transfer payments would require changes in the tax structure. The international-exchange-rate arrangement under which the proposal would operate was flexible exchange rates (1948a, 142). The proposal aimed to stabilize aggregate demand and balance the budget at full employment (1948a, 145).

Friedman's two 1948 papers—his unpublished memorandum for the project with Schwartz and the *AER* paper—provide important evidence of the influence of earlier Chicago views on his monetary economics at the beginning of his engagement in that field of study. I noted above the Chicago monetary tradition's markings on Friedman's analytic framework as evidenced in his background memorandum for his work with Schwartz. Now I consider the linkages between the policy views of the Chicago monetary tradition and those in Friedman's 1948 *AER* paper.

As was the case for the 1930s Chicago monetary tradition, in his *AER* paper, Friedman: (1) preferred a monetary rule; (2) emphasized the importance of money and identified the federal budget's position as the means to generate changes in the money supply; (3) believed that the federal budget should be balanced over the course of the business cycle to maintain a constant quantity of money, or should be in deficit to secularly increase the quantity of money; (4) advocated the 100 percent reserves scheme; and (5) backed flexible exchange rates. Additionally, similar to Simons and Mints in their works in the 1940s, Friedman would (1) fix the volume of government expenditure (excluding transfer payments);[79] (2) limit government debt instruments to only consols and money; (3) ultimately, eliminate consols so that money would be the only government-issued debt instrument; and (4) allow the progressive tax system to produce countercyclical changes in the budget with a tax structure that would not be varied in response to cyclical fluctuations.[80]

There were additional similarities. The 1930s Chicagoans stressed the role of price and wage rigidities in their business-cycle analysis. Friedman wrote the following about his proposal in the *AER*: "Rigidities in prices are likely to make this proposal, and indeed most if not all other proposals for attaining cyclical stability, inconsistent with full employment" (1948a, 142). The 1930s Chicagoans had argued that increases in the money stock would have a large impact on nominal spending if the increases entered circulation through the government's fiscal position but not if they entered circulation through other means. That identical view underlined Friedman's proposal.[81] Knight and Simons had emphasized that monetary-policy operations are subject to long lags. Friedman's 1948 *AER* article introduced the notion of "long and variable lags" into the literature (1948a, 144).

There were also a few differences between earlier Chicago views and Friedman's views in 1948. First, whereas Simons and Mints favored a price-level-stabilization rule, Friedman favored a rule under which the budget would be either balanced or in deficit at a hypothetical level of income corresponding to reasonably full employment—depending on whether the government's goal was to keep the quantity of money constant or to increase the quantity of money. Second, unlike Friedman, Simons wanted to eliminate both short-term government and *private* debt instruments, whereas Friedman proposed that only short-term government debt instruments be eliminated.[82] Third, Friedman's 1948 *AER* paper retained an element of his early 1940s Keynesian views. Specifically, Friedman argued that increases in fiscal deficits raise aggregate demand irrespective of the way the deficits are financed—Friedman nevertheless argued that money-financed deficits had larger effects on economic activity than deficits financed by the issuance of longer-term securities.[83] He also argued that issuing debt to finance deficits was more expansionary than levying taxes (1948a, 140). Fourth, Friedman argued that policy-induced changes in the money supply affect economic activity primarily through a fiscal multiplier effect of deficit spending.[84] Like Mints had argued in his 1946 paper, Friedman maintained that for a *given* price level, the increase in the stock of money resulting from a fiscal deficit "must further raise the real value of the community's stock of assets and hence the average propensity to consume" (1948a, 152). Unlike Mints, however, Friedman also argued that, should aggregate demand fall and the price level decline, the community's "real value of . . . money and government bonds" would rise, increasing "the fraction of any given level of real income that the community will wish to consume" (1948a, 150).[85] Thus, Friedman thought that real wealth effects would arise either from an increase in the nominal supply of money for a given price level or from a decrease in the price level for a given nominal quantity of money.

In his 1948 *AER* article, Friedman criticized discretionary policies because they are subject to lags that, in turn, are difficult "to forecast accurately" (1948a, 145).[86] However, as pointed out by Nelson (2020, 1:141), Friedman's concept of a hypothetical level of income corresponding to reasonably full employment is subjective since it is based on the judgment as to what constituted "reasonably full employment." Friedman recognized this problem, but he thought that if the determination of the full-employment level of income were made periodically at relatively long intervals, it would help reduce the forecasting problem: "The determination of the income goal admittedly cannot be made entirely objective or mechanical. At the same time, this determination would need to be made only at rather long intervals—perhaps every five or ten years—and involves a minimum of forecasting" (1948a, 139).[87]

The above discussion of Friedman's views at the time that he began his specialization in monetary economics paints a picture of an economist who was thoroughly familiar with, and subscribed to, the monetary economics of the 1930s and 1940s Chicago monetary tradition. While Keynesian income-expenditure mechanics were part of Friedman's thinking in 1948, his analytic and policy framework was overwhelmingly—and down to the smallest detail—straight out of the Simons et al. monetary playbook.[88] The evidence presented earlier in this study documented the existence of a distinctive Chicago monetary tradition in the 1930s and 1940s, during which time Chicago economists resisted the advance of the Keynesian revolution. The present section has documented that, as of 1948, Friedman's thinking on money *was part* of the Chicago monetary tradition.

How did Friedman come to adopt the views of the Chicago monetary tradition? Consider the following. (1) During his 1932–33 academic year as a graduate student at Chicago, Friedman took courses with Knight, Mints, and Viner—but not with Simons. The course with Mints provided exposure to Mints's policy views. Friedman returned to Chicago as a research assistant for the 1934–35 academic year, during which period he may have had additional exposure to Chicago thinking on money. Friedman's exposure to Chicago monetary views of the early 1930s may have included the 1932 and 1933 Chicago unpublished memoranda; in his 1967 paper "The Monetary Theory and Policy of Henry Simons," Friedman drew heavily on the November 1933 memorandum in presenting Simons's views. This fact, however, does not prove that Friedman had read the memorandum in the 1930s or the 1940s. (2) As noted, during the early 1940s, while employed at the Treasury, Friedman had largely accepted Keynesian analysis, with its emphasis on fiscal policy and its deemphasis of monetary policy.[89] Thus, while Friedman had been exposed to Chicago monetary views in the early 1930s, he had not, as of the early 1940s, become an advocate of those views. (3) While living in the Washington, DC, area during the early 1940s, Friedman spent considerable time interacting with his brother-in-law, Aaron Director, who was also living in the Washington, DC, area at the time (Friedman and Friedman 1998, chap. 7). As we have seen, in 1940 Director published a paper in the *AER* in which he emphasized the importance of money and advocated a monetary rule and 100 percent reserves. Thus, Friedman may have been influenced by Director on monetary issues. (4) After his return to Chicago in 1946, Friedman interacted with Director, Knight, and Mints.[90] Director and Mints were among seven individuals whom Friedman thanked for "helpful criticisms and constructive suggestions" on his 1948 *AER* paper (1948a, 153).[91] (5) Despite not having taken a course with Simons, by 1948 Friedman had read, absorbed and been deeply influenced by Simons's work.[92] Friedman's 1948 *AER* paper acknowledged his indebtedness to three of Simons's works: Simons's 1934 *A Positive Program for Laissez Faire* and his 1936 "Rules versus Authorities in Monetary Policy," concerning monetary rules and 100 percent reserves; and Simons's 1944 paper "On Debt Policy," concerning the idea of a financial system in which there would only be two kinds of government debt instruments—consols and money.[93]

Thus, while it appears that Friedman had come under the influence of Keynesian ideas after he left Chicago in the mid-1930s, something that would have been natural for a young scholar beginning his career at the start of the Keynesian revolution, his return to Chicago in 1946 provided the occasion for interactions with Chicago colleagues Director, Knight, and

Mints, and an orientation with the ideas of Simons. With those ideas serving as a foundation, in the late 1940s Friedman set off on a research agenda on money that would culminate in the monetarist counter-revolution against the Keynesian orthodoxy.

## The Return of Chicago Activism

The year 1948 saw the return of group activism at Chicago in support of the importance of money. The catalyst for the activism was the US post-war inflation, which reached (consumer prices, year on year) 8.3 percent and 14.4 percent in 1946 and 1947, respectively. In January 1948, eight Chicagoans, including Director, Friedman, Knight, and Mints, published a letter in the *New York Times* titled "Control of Prices: Regulation of Money Supply to Halt Inflation Advocated."[94] The letter was in response to the government's attempt to control inflation by imposing controls on individual prices. The Chicagoans were extremely critical of that policy. They made the following points. (1) Variations in the general price level are "in the main determined by variations in the quantity of money." (2) The quantity of money is dependent on the volume of reserves. (3) The Fed and the Treasury "are amply equipped with technical power to control the volume of money and, hence, the general level of prices." (4) The "greatest contribution" that monetary policy can make is "stabilization of the price level." (5) What is needed to control the general price level "is a legislative rule directing the monetary authorities to maintain stability" (Director et al. 1948).

Why had the Fed failed to use its powers to control the quantity of money and, thus, inflation? The Chicagoans argued that the Fed's ability to control the quantity of money had been constrained because of its wartime agreement with the Treasury to support the prices of Treasury securities, an issue the resolution of which I now discuss.

## 6.5 Douglas, Chicago, and the "Accord"

In 1942 the Federal Reserve formally committed to maintaining interest rates on government debt at the low levels prevailing at that time. To implement this policy, beginning in April 1942, the Fed fixed ceiling rates on government securities at 0.375 percent for Treasury bills and 2.5 percent for long-term bonds, with intermediate rates on intermediate maturities

(Meltzer 2003, 580). Under this policy, the Federal Reserve was a residual buyer of Treasury securities. The policy goals were to stabilize the government securities market, allow the federal government to engage in low-cost debt financing during World War II, and avoid potential losses to bondholders (commercial banks and the non-bank private sector) from higher interest rates, thereby contributing to economic stabilization.[95] To maintain the pegs on interest rates, the Fed lost control over both the size of its portfolio of Treasury securities and the money supply. Effectively, the Federal Reserve "put itself at the service of the wartime Treasury" (Meltzer 2003, 579). The Fed's policy was consistent with the dominant view among economists at the time, under which the task of monetary policy was to support budgetary finance (Meltzer 2003, 580–81).

After the war, the Fed had difficulty extracting itself from its agreement with the Treasury. In 1946 and 1947, it attempted to deviate from the agreement. Following the surge in inflation in 1946,[96] the Fed made it known that it intended to raise rates but was forced by the Treasury to back down (Friedman and Schwartz 1963, 610–22). Meltzer (2003, 582) expressed the view that two events altered the Fed's subservient relationship with the Treasury. The first event was the start of the Korean War in June 1950, which led to concerns about a renewed rise in inflation. In the event, wholesale prices increased at an annual rate of nearly 8 percent in the first half of 1950; they rose at a rate of 22 percent in the second half of the year.[97] The rise in inflation called for a tightening of interest rates. In August 1950, the Fed once again tried to extract itself from its agreement with the Treasury; once again the Fed was forced to back down (Friedman and Schwartz 1963, 610–11). The second event that altered the Fed's relationship with the Treasury was the arrival of Paul Douglas to the Senate, and, in particular, his engagement in the Treasury-Fed dispute. According to Meltzer (2003, 582), Douglas's engagement "altered the political balance" in favor of the Fed.

*The Road to the Accord*

Douglas began his term in the Senate in January 1949.[98] During his first year in the Senate, he was appointed a member of the Joint Committee on the Economic Report (hereafter, Joint Committee). In July 1949, the Joint Committee announced the formation of the Subcommittee on Monetary, Credit, and Fiscal Policies (hereafter, Subcommittee). The Subcommittee's mandate was to conduct "a thorough study and report on our monetary policy, on the machinery for monetary policy formation and execution, and in general on the problem of coordinating monetary, credit, and fiscal policies with general economic policies" (Subcommittee Statements 1949, 1). Douglas was appointed chairman of the Subcommittee.[99] Reflecting his standing within the economics profession, he dominated the Subcommittee's hearings.[100]

In preparation for the hearings on its mandate, the Subcommittee sent separate questionnaires to (1) "officials occupying responsible positions in governmental and quasi-governmental agencies" and (2) "a large number of bankers, economists and others" (Subcommittee Statements 1949, 1). Correspondingly, in November and December 1949, the Subcommittee held hearings on "Monetary, Credit, and Fiscal Policies." Based on its investigations, the Subcommittee published three documents.

1. A Collection of Statements Submitted to the Subcommittee on Monetary, Credit, and Fiscal Policies by Government Officials, Bankers, Economists and Others (hereafter, Subcommittee Statements), published in November 1949. The 443-page document included replies to the questionnaires by government officials, bankers, and economists.
2. Hearings before the Subcommittee on Monetary, Credit, and Fiscal Policies (hereafter, Subcommittee Hearings), published in January 1950. This document included the prepared statements read before the Subcommittee by high-level government and Federal Reserve officials.
3. Report of the Subcommittee on Monetary, Credit, and Fiscal Policies (hereafter, Subcommittee Report), published in January 1950. This document was the Subcommittee's—mainly Douglas's—assessment of the roles of monetary and fiscal policies.

Although the Subcommittee had a broad mandate, Douglas made the Treasury-Fed dispute on pegging interest rates the key focus of the hearings. Among those who testified before the subcommittee were Thomas McCabe, chairman of the Federal Reserve; Marriner Eccles, a member of the Fed's Board of Governors and a former Fed chairman;[101] Secretary of the Treasury John Snyder; and Leon Keyserling, acting chairman of the Council of Economic Advisers. It is accurate to state that Douglas's interventions had one specific purpose—namely, to expose the Fed's inability to conduct an independent monetary policy and, thus, to control money and inflation, in the face of its subordination to the Treasury.

To convey the tenor of both (1) Douglas's position on the Treasury–Federal Reserve agreement on interest-rate pegging and (2) the economics profession's view on the respective roles of fiscal and monetary policies at the time of the hearings, in what follows I report on (1) exchanges between Douglas and Fed officials Eccles and McCabe; (2) a joint statement on fiscal and monetary policies submitted to the Subcommittee by a group of sixteen leading economists; and (3) an overview of the answers provided by some forty economists to the Joint Committee's questionnaire. As a preview, only one of those forty-odd economists emphasized the role of the money supply in the economy. That economist was Lloyd Mints.

*Douglas and Eccles*

Eccles appeared before the Subcommittee on November 22, 1949. He began by reading a long statement in which he described the Federal Reserve System's functions and structure. He explained that, in light of its commitment to support the government securities market, the Fed needed an additional tool to restrain credit during periods of inflationary pressures. That tool, he stated, was the extension of the Fed's ability to set reserve requirements to include the reserves of non-member banks (in addition to member banks, which were already subject to reserve requirements): "if the Congress intends to have the Reserve System perform its functions, then you should by all means arm it with alternative means of applying restraints. The *only* way to do that is through revision and modernization of the mechanism of reserve requirement" (emphasis added, Subcommittee Hearings 1950, 216). There was *no* reference in the statement to the constraint placed on the Fed by its agreement to peg the prices of Treasury securities. Reflecting the thinking of the economics profession at the time, there was *no* reference to the supply of money.

Douglas, however, stressed the importance of the money supply. Following Eccles's presentation, Douglas initiated an exchange of views by noting that the Fed had "three main methods . . . to control the general supply of money and credit"—rediscounting, open-market operations, and changes in reserve requirements (Subcommittee Hearings 1950, 225). Douglas then led a reluctant Eccles through a series of questions concerning the Fed's policy of pegging rates. Douglas aimed to draw an acknowledgment from Eccles that the Fed was unable to take the necessary open-market operations to stem inflation in light of its commitment to peg the prices of Treasury securities:

SENATOR DOUGLAS. Well, I take it that you believe that during the period of expanding prices, and a period in which there is a tendency toward inflation, one

way of checking this would be, if it could be made effective, for the System to
sell Governments in the open market and thus draw down the. . . .

MR. ECCLES. It cannot be made effective.

SENATOR DOUGLAS. That is the next point I was coming to. But if it could be made
effective, that is what you would like to have done?

MR. ECCLES. Oh, yes; if the banks or the public would buy securities out of the
portfolio of the System, that would be fine.

. . .

SENATOR DOUGLAS. Well, now, that was the next point. Are you saying that the
weapon of the open-market operations has been virtually made inoperative to
check inflation because of the readiness of the System to buy unlimited quantities of Governments at relatively pegged prices?

MR. ECCLES. That is correct. (Subcommittee Hearings 1950, 226–27)

Douglas then asked Eccles to describe the first occasion (that is, in
1946) during which a confrontation between the Fed and the Treasury had
occurred over monetary policy. As will be apparent, Douglas supported
the Fed's need to be independent of the Treasury more than did Eccles:

SENATOR DOUGLAS. May I ask: When did the Federal Reserve first suggest raising
the short-term rate on Treasury bills?

MR. ECCLES. In 1946.

SENATOR DOUGLAS. But it was not carried into effect until the middle of 1947?

MR. ECCLES. Yes. I think that is true. We had a buying rate of bills of three-eighths.

SENATOR DOUGLAS. Was there a disagreement in Government circles?

MR. ECCLES. There was.

SENATOR DOUGLAS. You felt the short-time rate should go up?

MR. ECCLES. The Open Market Committee felt it should go up.

SENATOR DOUGLAS. The Treasury did not think it should go up?

MR. ECCLES. That is correct.

SENATOR DOUGLAS. Why did you think it should go up?

MR. ECCLES. Well, I felt that you had no flexibility in the market at all. You could,
as many of the banks were doing, sell the shorter securities to us and buy the
longer-term securities. This practice, which we call playing the pattern of rates,
tends to force the long-term rate down as long as short-term rates are not
permitted to rise. In other words, we had a spread between short-term rates
and long-term rates that didn't make sense, in view of the support policy. Why
should anyone want to handle any short-term securities at seven-eighths if you
could get 2½ percent for a demand liability in long-term securities?

SENATOR DOUGLAS. You were in favor of the pegging of the long-term rate?

MR. ECCLES. I couldn't figure out any alternative. I didn't like it. (Subcommittee
Hearings 1950, 229)

Douglas pressed forward with his line of inquiry.

SENATOR DOUGLAS. Well, this is something that puzzles me a bit: As I remember
it, the Federal Reserve System was supposed to be an independent agency; the
Treasury, another independent agency. Yet, it is inevitable that the views of one
be taken into consideration by the other, and highly desirable. What is the machinery for coordinating the policies of the Reserve System with the policies of
the Treasury?

. . .

SENATOR DOUGLAS. Mr. Eccles, I can quite understand that during the period of
the war, when the amounts collected in taxes and subscribed for bond purchase
out of current income were not sufficient to meet the total cost of the war, we
had to create credit by banks. But in the period of 1946 and the first part of
1947, of which you speak, the Government did not have a deficit; it had a surplus, so that the policy of low rates on short-time securities was not necessary
for current financing. You can say that it was desirable for refunding, but not
for current financing.

MR. ECCLES. There was no current financing. It was all a problem of refunding.

SENATOR DOUGLAS. Then the question comes, For how long will the refunding
needs of the Treasury dictate Reserve policy? Is this going to continue forever?

MR. ECCLES. I think so. If Congress would, as a result of hearings of this sort, make
it apparent that this support policy on the part of the Open Market Committee
was not desirable, I think you would find, maybe, a greater independence on the
part of the Open Market Committee. (Subcommittee Hearings 1950, 230–32)

In pursuing his line of inquiry into the Fed's subordination to the Treasury a short time later, Douglas initiated the following exchange:

SENATOR DOUGLAS. I would like to ask: Would it serve a useful purpose if Congress were to instruct the Treasury further as to the policies to be followed in
debt management and the procedures of cooperating with the Federal Reserve
System?

MR. ECCLES. I think it would be of great assistance. (Subcommittee Hearings 1950,
235)

Eccles did not go so far as to maintain that the Fed should be made independent of the Treasury. He stated: "I don't know that it would be practical . . . to create an independent Reserve Board" (Subcommittee Hearings 1950, 236). Douglas, however, persisted that the Fed's commitment to peg interest rates was an obstruction to its ability to implement monetary policy:

SENATOR DOUGLAS. Mr. Eccles, in connection with the responsibilities of the Treasury for debt management, which you now say you do not propose to change, does not that necessarily carry with it, in the final analysis, control over credit policy and therefore over money policy?

MR. ECCLES. Well, you could make a good argument for that.

SENATOR DOUGLAS. Isn't that just a statement of fact under the present situation?

MR. ECCLES. I would question that. Certainly the desirability of it.

SENATOR DOUGLAS. I am not speaking about the desirability of it. I am just saying, isn't that a statement of the situation?

MR. ECCLES. Well, I must admit that that is where the logic of the situation leads you; I must admit that.

. . .

SENATOR DOUGLAS. I want to make it clear that I am not advocating that. I am merely raising the question as to whether, in the present situation, the power of the Treasury to manage the debt, which you do not question, does not, as a matter of fact, also carry with it the virtual control over credit and monetary policy. That is all. (Subcommittee Hearings 1950, 237–38)

### Douglas and McCabe

Fed chairman McCabe appeared before the Subcommittee on December 3, 1949. Like Eccles before him, McCabe read a lengthy statement in which he described the Federal Reserve System's structure and functions. He expressed the view that the Fed's primary function was to support the Treasury's financing requirements. What role did that leave for monetary policy in stabilization? McCabe stated: "[There] are still powerful instruments in the promotion of high-level economic stability. They must operate, however, in close conjunction with appropriate fiscal, debt management, and other governmental policies" (Subcommittee Hearings 1950, 463). Like Eccles, McCabe did not make a single reference to the quantity of money. Moreover, McCabe was even more conciliatory toward the Treasury's dominance of the Fed than Eccles had been. Referring to the reported confrontation between the Treasury and the Fed in 1946 and 1947, he stated that it was "not true" that there had been a disagreement between the two agencies (Subcommittee Hearings 1950, 465).

At that point, Douglas interrupted McCabe's presentation. Douglas read a passage from an official Fed document reporting that the Fed wanted to raise rates in 1946 but was prevented from doing so until the Treasury concurred in 1947.[102] Douglas then initiated a line of questioning the aim of which was to establish the Fed's lack of independence. In doing so he became increasingly irritated with McCabe's evasiveness.

SENATOR DOUGLAS. Did you concur in the general opinion of the Federal Reserve authorities that the rate on short-time securities should have been raised at that time [i.e., in 1946]?

MR. MCCABE. Yes.

SENATOR DOUGLAS. For what reasons?

MR. MCCABE. We were just coming into the postwar period, and the evidences then were that we were entering an inflationary period. This was an instrument of Federal Reserve control that we felt should be applied to check the inflationary influence we felt was developing.

SENATOR DOUGLAS. Was it your feeling, if the interest rate on short-time governments were allowed to rise, that the interest rate on loans to private borrowers would also rise?

MR. MCCABE. You see, the whole credit structure is closely related to the Government-bond market and very sensitive to the Government-bond market. So, if there is a rise in Government bonds, there is a stiffening of rates throughout the whole credit structure.

SENATOR DOUGLAS. Stiffening, you mean, is the euphonious term for an increase?

MR. MCCABE. Increase; yes.

SENATOR DOUGLAS. The way in which reality can be muffled in Washington with soft words is really quite amazing. You thought, therefore, that this would check undue private borrowing?

MR. MCCABE. It would help.

SENATOR DOUGLAS. But you did not put the policy into effect?

MR. MCCABE. The Federal Reserve was attempting to persuade the Treasury that that was the proper course to pursue.

SENATOR DOUGLAS. Did you have the legal powers to put it into effect even though the Treasury did not concur!

MR. MCCABE. The Federal Reserve, through its open-market operations, could upset the proposed policy of the Treasury.

SENATOR DOUGLAS. But you did not exercise your legal power because you wished to "cooperate" with the Treasury?

MR. MCCABE. At that time, we were emerging from a war period into a postwar period, and we had this colossal public debt. And at that time I was not Chairman of the Board. I would assume that its position was that it did not want to do anything that would upset [it]. (Subcommittee Hearings 1950, 466–67)

Despite McCabe's evasiveness, Douglas pressed ahead with his argument that the Fed's agreement with the Treasury prevented the former institution's effectively carrying out its policies. Not wanting to antagonize the Treasury, McCabe continued to be evasive. At one point, he stated: "a splendid degree of cooperation exists between the Treasury and the Federal Reserve" (Subcommittee Hearings 1950, 422). Exasperated by McCabe's unwillingness to address the Fed's lack of independence from the Treasury, Douglas again interrupted:

SENATOR DOUGLAS. Here is the difficulty that we legislators labor under: We work to untangle a jigsaw puzzle and we generally find that the question directly addressed to the Government official is for a period in which he did not serve, or over an area for which he does not feel responsible, so that the Government official with perfectly good grace can say, "Well, it is impossible for me to answer." And the poor frustrated legislator goes around in a merry-go-round hunting for the pea underneath the walnut and never finds it, and merely finds one administrative official after another telling him to look somewhere else. (Subcommittee Hearings 1950, 468)

The following points emerge from the appearances of Eccles and McCabe before Douglas's Subcommittee. First, Douglas emphasized the need of monetary policy to control the supply of money and credit. Neither of the Fed officials mentioned the supply of money in their remarks, nor did they state that monetary policy played an important role in the economy. Second, neither Eccles nor McCabe was willing to criticize the Fed's subservient relationship with the Treasury—even though their respective appearances before the Subcommittee gave them ample opportunity to do so; indeed, Douglas encouraged them to do so.[103] Douglas, who commanded the respect of his congressional colleagues on economic issues, took the lead in 1949 in paving the way for an end to the Fed's submissiveness to the Treasury's wishes on matters of monetary policy.

*Joint Statement by Academic Economists*

As part of its mandate on monetary, credit, and fiscal policies, in August 1949 the Subcommittee sent a questionnaire to economists, bankers, and executives of other financial institutions. The questionnaire was signed by Senators Douglas and Flanders, both of whom were members of the Subcommittee. The questionnaire consisted of twenty questions. Most of the questions contained subquestions. The majority of the questions related to monetary policy, which was unusual in light of the minor role assigned to monetary policy in academic and official circles at the time. Of the twenty questions, the first twelve were concerned with monetary policy, four others dealt with institutional issues related to the banking sector (for example, the division of authority in supervising banks), two related to the Treasury's debt-management policies (including the relationship of those policies to monetary, credit, and fiscal policies). Another two questions addressed the role of fiscal policies in the economy. Here, I single out the following three questions. Question 1 sought opinions on the "guideposts and objectives" of monetary policy. It also asked for "major criticisms" of "our monetary and credit policies in the past." Question 2 sought opinions on the Fed's policy of pegging interest rates on government securities. Question 17 was the main question on fiscal policy. It sought opinions on "the guiding principles of the Government's overall taxing and spending policies." It also asked whether the budget should be balanced annually, over the course of the business cycle, or should be either in deficit or in surplus at all times.

In addition to publishing answers to the questions from some forty economists—more about that shortly—the Subcommittee published a document titled "Economists' Statements on Federal Expenditure and Revenue Policies." The document was a joint response to the questionnaire by a group of economists. It consisted of two parts—part A, "Federal Expenditure and Revenue Policy for Economic Stability," and part B, "Fiscal Policy in the Near Future." The document was signed by sixteen economists, including Howard Ellis (University of California),[104] John Kenneth Galbraith (Harvard University), Albert Hart (Columbia University), Paul Samuelson (Massachusetts Institute of Technology), Sumner Slichter (Harvard University), Arthur Smithies (Harvard University), and Jacob Viner (Princeton University).[105] The document was eight (single-spaced) pages in length. A remarkable feature of the document was its exclusive focus on fiscal issues even though it was a response to a questionnaire focused on monetary policy.

The sixteen economists expressed the view that annual budget balancing is both difficult in practice and unsound in principle; the budget should be adjusted to the particular economic circumstances at the time of formulation. They argued that the government has a significant role to play in economic stabilization: "We must not rely on the private economy, unaided by Government action, to perform that task. The Government must not shirk the responsibility placed upon it by the Employment Act, and fiscal policy is one of the most promising instruments it possesses" (Subcommittee Statements 1949, 438).[106] What policies should be used to combat inflation? The economists stated: "The survival of a relatively free and stable price system depends heavily on our willingness to fight inflation by *fiscal* methods" (emphasis added, Subcommittee Statements 1949, 438).

A striking feature of the statement is that only a single sentence in the document referred to monetary policy; in so doing, the sentence made it clear that monetary policy should include the Fed's role in managing the government's debt. That sentence appeared in the concluding paragraph of part A. It read:

> In this statement, we have confined ourselves to fiscal policy of the Federal Government. But, while essential, that is only one element in a stabilization policy. The policies of State and local governments can make useful contributions within their more limited spheres. *Monetary and credit policies including debt management must play an active role in their own right and must be properly coordinated with fiscal policy.* All necessary measures must be taken to preserve and stimulate competition. Supported by such measures, Federal fiscal policy offers the best prospect of achieving sustained prosperity within the framework of our existing economic system. (emphasis added, Subcommittee Statements 1949, 440)

*Replies by Economists*

Forty-odd economists who were sent the questionnaire provided individual responses. Not all those economists responded to each of the twenty questions. As mentioned, Mints was among the respondents. Others included Howard Ellis[107] (University of California), Harry Gunnison Brown (Yale University), Seymour Harris (Harvard University), George Halm (Tufts University), and Frank Graham (Princeton University).

Mints's responses to the questions on monetary and fiscal policies were of a different character from those of all other respondents. Unlike the other respondents, he placed the quantity of money front and center of his assessment of monetary policy. Unlike all other respondents, he argued that monetary stability was a necessary and sufficient condition for economic stability. Mints was the only economist to argue that monetary policy should follow a rule—he advocated a monetary-growth rule. In response to the first question dealing with (1) the objectives and guideposts of monetary policy and (2) criticism of past monetary policy, Mints was the only economist to argue that the money supply should be the objective of monetary policy. He was the only economist to criticize the Fed's policy in the Great Depression. His response to the first question included the following:

*Guideposts and objectives.* "The primary aim should be a stable index of wholesale prices. As a means to this end the stock of money should increase at a rate about equal to the rate of growth in the economy. If we definitely announced that it would be the sole aim of the monetary agents of the Government to stabilize an index of the price level (wholesale) I am convinced that the system itself would without further action maintain a high level of employment and output. There might be some minor variations in employment, but I am doubtful that they would be of much consequence" (Subcommittee Statements 1949, 290).

*Criticism of past policies.* Mints stated: "In my opinion credit policies since the institution of the Federal Reserve System could hardly have been worse. It failed to adopt any announced and definite criterion, it allowed the volume of money to decline in the depressions following 1920 and 1929, during the recent postwar period it did nothing to prevent inflation, and in the first half of 1949 it actually reduced its holdings of governments and absorbed bank reserves" (Subcommittee Statements 1949, 290).[108]

The majority of economists responded that the primary objective of monetary policy should be the stabilization of employment or the price level or both. Only one other respondent—Seymour Harris—mentioned the money supply. Unlike Mints, Harris treated the money supply as one of several indicators of monetary conditions—and not as an objective of monetary policy. Harris wrote: "Those responsible should watch gold flows, monetary supplies, exchange rates, prices and the rate of interest as factors influencing economic conditions; and output, employment, and unemployment are the ultimate objectives of monetary policies. In general, the monetary authorities should try to keep interest rates low as a stimulus to business activity" (Subcommittee Statements 1949, 292).

Concerning the (second) question on the Fed's policy on interest-rate pegging, most of the forty-odd respondents supported the policy—

although many respondents thought that the Fed should be given some "flexibility." Seven economists, including Mints, thought that the policy should be terminated. Mints's response was unequivocal: "I think the Federal Reserve System should completely ignore the prices of Government bonds. The Government itself should have no policy in regard to this matter other than selling at whatever yield may be necessary for the purpose of obtaining the funds that are to be acquired by borrowing" (Subcommittee Statements 1949, 300).[109]

Concerning question 17, having to do with the "guiding principles" of fiscal policy, almost all respondents thought that the budget should be balanced over the course of the business cycle. Harris put that view as follows: "The guiding principle should be to contribute to a healthy economy. An annual balancing of the budget is undesirable. Debt should be accumulated in periods of [economic] decline and retired in periods of overexpansion" (Subcommittee Statements 1949, 401).

Once again, Mints was an outlier. He wrote: "I do not subscribe to the view that the expenditures of the Federal Government should be varied cyclically." The level of expenditures, he maintained, should be determined based on the merits of the projects for which funds would be spent "without regard to the question of monetary policy." He recommended that tax credits be adjusted to produce countercyclical changes in the money supply. To provide sufficient money creation, Mints thought that the budget would always have to be in deficit: "I see no way of avoiding an annual Federal deficit, to be met with new money, of a sufficient amount to prevent the price level from falling." With the level of expenditures determined independently of the state of the economy, the annual additions to the money supply needed to maintain a stable price level would be estimated. Tax credits would then be adjusted "to equal the difference between those two items" (Subcommittee Statements 1949, 398–99).

*Subcommittee Report, 1950*

On January 13, 1950, Douglas submitted the Subcommittee's (fifty-page) *Report* to Senator Joseph O'Mahoney (Wyoming), the chairman of the Joint Committee on the Economic Report. The Subcommittee's *Report* emphasized the important role played by the quantity of money in the economy. It recommended that the Fed should be freed from its agreement with the Treasury to peg interest rates. At a time during which the role of fiscal policy dominated professional thinking about stabilization policies, the *Report* enumerated the limits of fiscal policy. Finally, the *Report* noted the Fed's failure to ease monetary policy after the onset of the Great Depression.

*Role of monetary policy.* The *Report* stated that the Federal Reserve possessed "three principal weapons"—open-market operations, alterations in the discount rate, and changes in reserve requirements—"which it can use to control the over-all supply and cost of money and credit" (Subcommittee Report 1950, 19). Those "weapons," however, had not been used effectively in the past to help maintain economic stability. Why not? An important reason, maintained the *Report*, was the view that monetary policy is a weak policy instrument. The *Report* stated:

> We reject the idea, held by a few economists and others, that for stabilization purposes little or no reliance should be placed on monetary policy and that we should rely exclusively on other measures, such as fiscal policies. (1) It is highly doubtful that fiscal policy would be powerful enough to maintain stability in the face of strong destabilizing forces even if monetary policy were neutral, and a conflicting monetary policy could lessen still further the effectiveness of fiscal policy. (2) Monetary policy is strong precisely where fiscal policy is weakest; it is capable of being highly flexible. (Subcommittee Report 1950, 18)

*Role of fiscal policy.* The *Report* stated that the federal budget should be balanced over the course of the business cycle. Reflecting Douglas's view during the 1930s that deficits financed by money creation are effective in combating depressions, the *Report* argued: "In a depression period, when production, prices and employment are declining and when there is a considerable amount of unutilized capital and labor, a Government deficit financed by bank-created credit will therefore help to offset the decline in the total volume of private purchasing power" (Subcommittee Report 1950, 6). Two factors, however, limited the effectiveness of a "flexible" fiscal policy: "(1) The unreliability of economic forecasting" and the associated difficulty of predicting cyclical turning points meant that cyclical actions could be procyclical rather than countercyclical (Subcommittee Report 1950, 14–15). "(2) The long period required to enact revenue laws and the inflexibility of expenditure programs" meant that discretionary fiscal measures could not be relied on to ameliorate the business cycle (Subcommittee Report 1950, 15). The *Report* went on to argue: "one of the greatest limitations on the effectiveness of fiscal policy as a stabilization device is to be found in its inflexibility—the long period typically required to formulate, enact, and put into operation tax changes and the time required to start, stop, slow down, and speed up expenditure programs" (Subcommittee Report 1950, 17).

*Interest-rate pegging.* The *Report* recommended that the Fed be freed from its commitment to peg rates on Treasury securities. It stated: "The vigorous use of a restrictive monetary policy as an anti-inflation measure has been inhibited since the war by considerations relating to holding down the yields supporting the prices of United States Government securities" (Subcommittee Report 1950, 2). The *Report* also maintained that "the advantages of avoiding inflation are so great, and that a restrictive monetary policy can contribute so much to this end, that the freedom of the Federal Reserve to restrict credit and raise interest rates for general stabilization purposes should be restored" (Subcommittee Report 1950, 2).

*The Great Depression.* In its August 1949 questionnaire, the Subcommittee had invited economists and bankers to criticize the Fed's past policies. As we saw, Mints used the occasion to criticize the Fed for its failure to prevent the decline in the money supply in the first few years of the Great Depression. The Subcommittee's *Report* took a similar track. It stated: "Our monetary history gives little indication as to how effectively we can expect appropriate and vigorous monetary policies to promote stability, for we have never really tried them" (Subcommittee Report 1950, 18). The *Report* then referred to the role of monetary policy in specific episodes:

> For example, the effectiveness of these policies during the late 1920's was seriously reduced by the Federal Reserve's lack of powers for the selective control of security loans. After 1929, a vigorous easy-money policy was not adopted until bank reserves had been allowed to shrink for more than 2 years, thousands of banks had failed, and general business confidence had dwindled; and after World War II its use as a restrictive measure with which to combat inflation was very seriously hampered by considerations relating to the management of the Federal debt. With our improved banking structure and the benefit of our past experience, we should be able to look forward to more effective monetary management characterized by timely, vigorous, and flexible actions. (Subcommittee Report 1950, 18–19)

## The 1951 Chicago Memorandum and Douglas

The resurgence of inflation during 1950 put upward pressure on market interest rates. To help stem that pressure, the Fed purchased Treasury securities at an accelerating pace throughout the year. The Federal Reserve's commitment to peg interest rates on government securities occasioned widespread concern within and outside the Federal Reserve System that the policy would lead to large increases in the money supply and inflation (Friedman and Schwartz 1963, 610–11; Hetzel and Leach 2001a). In the fall of 1950, the Fed publicly reaffirmed its commitment to maintain orderly conditions in the government securities market but also affirmed its priority to curb inflation. In private, Fed officials pressed the Treasury for higher interest rates, but the Treasury resisted (Hetzel and Leach 2001a).[110] The Fed again was forced to back down. From June 1950 to the end of the year, the Federal Reserve credit outstanding rose by $3.5 billion (Friedman and Schwartz 1963, 611).

In January 1951, a group of Chicago economists circulated a memorandum to Washington officials in which the Chicagoans warned that the Federal Reserve's "ill-conceived policy" of pegging interest rates, "presumably under the influence of the Treasury," was "highly inflationary." Seven Chicagoans, including Friedman and Mints, signed the memorandum.[111] The Chicagoans presented a table with data showing that, from the end of May to the end of December 1950, demand deposits — "the most active component of the money supply" — had increased by "over 8 percent." With currency having increased slightly, "the total circulating medium rose by 7 percent." The Chicagoans argued that "this increase in the money supply was made possible primarily by Federal Reserve purchases of government securities [which] . . . rose by . . . $3,500,000,000, or 20 percent." The rise in demand deposits had fueled the surge in inflation: "This is about as clear a case of purely monetary inflation as one can find." The "surge in inflation," the Chicagoans continued, could not be attributed to fiscal policy: "During the second 6 months of 1950, the Federal Government took in substantially more than it paid out. The Federal budget was, therefore, if anything, deflationary rather than an inflationary force during the period." What was needed, the Chicagoans maintained, was "a vigorous monetary policy designed to make credit tight, to prevent an increase in the quantity of money or, if necessary, to decrease the quantity of money in order to offset a rise in the rate of use of money." Instead of following such a policy, the Fed had "provided additional reserves to the banking system," which had fueled the rise in the money supply. What the Chicagoans called "rear guard actions" to control inflation, including selective credit controls, moral suasion, and rises in reserve requirements, were "all doomed to failure so long as the Federal Reserve System stands ready to buy unlimited amounts of Government bonds at essentially fixed prices." The Chicagoans called for an end to the Fed's policy of pegging interest rates on Treasury securities: "Monetary policy cannot serve two masters at once. It cannot at once buttress a strong fiscal policy in preventing inflation and be dominated by the present misconceived cheap money policy of the Treasury" (Friedman et al. 1951).

One of the officials who received the memorandum was John D. Clark, the vice chairman of the Council of Economic Advisers. On February 2, 1951, during his appearance before the Joint Committee on the Economic Report, Clark brought the memorandum to the Joint Committee's attention as an example of a *misguided* explanation of the surge in inflation. Clark referred to "the view expressed by the Chicago economists" as asserting that inflation is a monetary phenomenon, but he argued that the existing situation "is the very reverse of [this] situation"—prices had risen "in July, August, and the first part of September ... when there was almost no change in the volume of money" (*Congressional Record* 1951, 1469 [February 22]).

Senator Joseph O'Mahoney (Wyoming), the chairman of the Joint Committee on the Economic Report, supported the policy of pegging interest rates. During a meeting of the full Senate on February 22, 1951, O'Mahoney asked that Clark's February 2 statement be printed in the record of the February 22 meeting as an attachment to his (O'Mahoney's) remarks. There was no objection. However, Douglas, whose speeches on the Senate floor had made him a national celebrity, took the floor.[112] He stated: "in view of the great importance of the subject, I am constrained to do what perhaps I should not do; namely discuss the alleged points of difference between the Federal Reserve Board on the one hand, and the United States Treasury, upon the other" (*Congressional Record* 1951, 1470). Douglas then proceeded to give the Senate a long lecture based on the quantity theory of money.[113] In doing so, he defended the position taken by his former Chicago colleagues in their January memorandum. The points covered by Douglas included the following.

*Money matters.* Douglas began by acknowledging that a rise in interest rates on government securities would increase the government's cost of financing its debt. He contended, however, that "this misstates the real issue, which is whether we shall have any control over the total volume of credit. The interest rate is merely a consequence of the relative supply of credit in relation to demand" (*Congressional Record* 1951, 1470). The Fed's policy, Douglas asserted, had led to a rise in the quantity of money, which underpinned the surge in inflation since the start of the Korean War: "the increase in the general supply of money spreads through the entire economy" (*Congressional Record* 1951, 1470). Thus, "the primary reason for the large increase in prices since June has been the expansionist credit policies which have been carried through by the Federal Reserve System under the stimulus of the Treasury" (*Congressional Record* 1951, 1471). Could the rise in inflation have been abetted by expansionary fiscal policy? Like the Chicagoans in their memorandum, Douglas did not subscribe to that view: "the inflation has not been caused by an excess of Government expenditures over receipts" (*Congressional Record* 1951, 1471). He continued: "No; the inflation has come through an expansion in private credit . . . made possible by the Federal Reserve at the dictates of the Treasury" (*Congressional Record* 1951, 1471). Douglas then warned about the consequences of inflation.

> Every historian knows that inflation has been a great destroyer of the vast middle classes and of governments. It has paved the way for dictatorships and overthrow of democratic institutions. By wiping out the middle classes and separating society into the two classes of the propertyless on the one hand and the rich speculators on the other, it paved the way for fascism and communism on the continent of Europe. It is a destroyer almost as evil as war itself. In the eyes of those who want to destroy democracy and capitalistic institutions it is a cheap way of achieving their collapse. It costs the enemy nothing in lives or treasure. It is really a supreme folly for a nation which is arming against the threat of invasion from without to let this invader, inflation, bring ruin from within. (*Congressional Record* 1951, 1471)

*The evidence.* Like the Chicagoans in their memorandum, Douglas provided evidence to show that the Fed's purchases of Treasury securities had caused the jump in inflation between June 1950 and the end of that year. The Chicagoans had cited the $3.5 billion increase in the Fed's holdings of Treasury securities during that period. Douglas stated that the Fed's "net purchases . . . have totaled over $3,500,000,000 since June." These purchases had contributed to a 10 percent increase in demand deposits, which underpinned the rise in inflation.[114] Using the Fisherine equation of exchange, Douglas argued: "The combined effect of an increased supply of dollars and an increased velocity of dollars has permitted prices to increase despite a significant increase in total production since June" (*Congressional Record* 1951, 1472). Douglas noted that the Truman administration had imposed price controls to stem inflation. Those controls, he argued, would fail: "No system of Government price controls can permanently or greatly reduce the pressure toward high prices if there is an ever-increasing amount of bank credit" (*Congressional Record* 1951, 1475).

*The quantity theory.* Douglas provided the Senate with several descriptions of the equation of exchange. As a general description of the quantity theory, he stated:

> If we have $100 to offer for 100 units of goods, it follows that the average price of each unit will be $1. Then, if we increase the quantity of money offered to $200, but the quantity of goods remains the same as before, the average price per unit will now rise to $2. This is inflation. If the supply of money is reduced to $50 but the quantity of goods is not changed, then the average price falls to 50 cents. That is deflation.... What we face today, however, is too much money in relation to available goods. (*Congressional Record* 1951, 1472)

Referring to the six months ending in December 1950, Douglas asserted:

> Dealing with the question of complexity, let me point out this fact: The increase in the total supply of bank credit has been about 10 percent. The increase in the total quantity of physical production has been apparently about 10 percent. The increase in the velocity of circulation of money and credit has been about 10 percent. The increase in prices has been about 10 percent.... It is interesting to note that if we divide the relative increase in the total amount of money plus the increase in velocity of circulation by the increase in the quantity of goods produced, we get an increase of about 10 percent in price. (*Congressional Record* 1951, 1477)

*The Fed's policy.* Douglas emphasized that the rise in interest rates that would follow cessation of the Fed's policy of pegging interest rates would *not* be effective in lowering inflation: "I certainly do not argue that a rise in the interest rate ... would appreciably reduce the demand for loans. I think that economists and bank authorities have in the past erred in overstressing this point" (*Congressional Record* 1951, 1478). To lower inflation, it would be necessary to reduce the growth of the money supply. Douglas then explained: "What I am saying is that we should try to control credit not by raising the price [of credit] but by helping to shut off the supply" (*Congressional Record* 1951, 1478).

In concluding his intervention, Douglas called for an end to the Federal Reserve policy of pegging interest rates on Treasury securities. He asked that several statistical tables that showed the rises in the money supply, prices, and inflation since the onset of the Korean War, and other documents that supported his position, be included as appendixes to his intervention. One of those documents was the 1951 Chicago memorandum. It was attached to Douglas's intervention under the title "Statement of Milton Friedman, Fredrick H. Harrison, Lloyd A. Meltzer, Lloyd W. Mints, D. Gale Johnson, Theodore W. Schultz, and H. G. Lewis of the Department of Economics, University of Chicago: The Failure of the Present Monetary Policy" (*Congressional Record* 1951, 1481–82).

Douglas's February 22, 1951, speech before the Senate was widely reported in the press and made a large impact in swaying public opinion in favor of granting independence to the Fed.[115] Among those who reacted favorably to the speech was Milton Friedman. In a letter, dated March 6, 1951, addressed to Douglas, Friedman wrote:[116]

Dear Paul,

I have just seen your speech on monetary policy in the Congressional Record for February 22, 1951, and I cannot refrain from writing to congratulate you on it. It was a magnificent speech. I particularly liked your repeated emphasis that the real issue is the control of the money supply, not of the rate of interest.

It looks as if your good fight is paying big dividends. From here, however, it is hard to judge what is going on—whether the Reserve Board has become virtuous for good or only for the moment.

The behavior of the bond market in recent days certainly confirms the belief you expressed that removal of the peg should not mean a "panic" or anything like it.

More power to you.

Sincerely yours,
Milton Friedman

Following a meeting between Federal Reserve and Treasury officials, on March 4, 1951, the Treasury and the Fed put out a joint statement in which they announced that they had "reached full accord with respect to debt management and monetary policies to be pursued in furthering their common purpose to assure the successful financing of the Government's requirements and, at the same time, to minimize monetization of the public debt" (quoted from Eichengreen and Garber 1991, 184). The precise provisions of the accord were never published (Hetzel and Leach 1951b, 57).[117]

In his autobiography *In the Fullness of Time*, Douglas reflected on his February 1951 speech before the Senate. He expressed the view that the Fed's policy of purchasing a "large quantity of government bonds at par on the open market at low interest rates" in 1950 had led to inflation (1972, 332). That policy, he maintained, "seemed like a vindication of the quantity theory of money, supposedly known to every student of elementary economics" (1972, 332). At that point in his autobiography, Douglas presented (in a footnote) an algebraic form of the Fisherine equation. Douglas then pointed out that shortly after his February 1951 speech, "the Treasury and the Reserve agreed to an 'accord,' removing from the Reserve the need to buy such an unlimited quantity of government bonds as would maintain a low and constant interest rate" (1972, 333). Douglas then disclosed that one of the members of his Subcommittee, Congressman Wright Patman (Texas), was not pleased with the role that Douglas played in bringing about the accord: "My friend Wright Patman has never forgiven me for the accord and has consistently denounced it as an infamous agreement. I have told him that while his knowledge of the mechanics of the Federal Reserve System is unequaled, he is being stubborn in refusing to admit the truth of the quantity theory" (1972, 333).

*Postscript.* In his 1982 *Journal of Money, Credit and Banking* lecture "Monetary Policy: Theory and Practice," Friedman identified four specific episodes to show how little progress had been made over many years in the practice of monetary policy; he argued that what progress had been made had come from pressures outside the Federal Reserve System. One of the episodes concerned the Fed's policy of pegging interest rates from 1942 to 1951. Friedman then asked: "Why was the program ended? Did the initiative to end it come from within the [Federal Reserve] system?" (Friedman 1982, 104). Friedman answered the question in the negative. He argued that the initiative to end the program came from outside the system. Friedman cited three "sources of outside pressure," the first two of which were the following:

> One was the Korean War, which produced a change in anticipations that in turn led to a sharp jump in monetary velocity and to the emergence of inflation. The second, and, in my opinion, *unquestionably the more important* in terms of the immediate effect, was pressure from Senator Paul Douglas, the famous

University of Chicago economist—*the first recent example of the influence of the Chicago school on monetary policy.* Senator Douglas conducted a series of hearings on monetary policy. Throughout those hearings, he kept hammering away on the undesirability of pegging bond prices. I have very little doubt that his pressure played a critical role in finally producing the Federal Reserve–Treasury accord. (emphasis added, Friedman 1982, 104–5)[118]

To sum up, Douglas distinguished between the supply of money—which he thought played a crucial in the economy—and the price of credit—the role of which he thought was much less important. His views on money—both in the early 1930s and in the early 1950s—were based on the quantity theory of money. In earlier chapters, we saw that Douglas was an important member of the Chicago monetary tradition in terms of his views on monetary and fiscal policies. In this chapter, we have seen how Douglas put the Chicago tradition's views to work, helping to bring about the Treasury–Federal Reserve accord.

## 6.6 Conclusions

This chapter has dealt with the views on money of the members of The Group mainly during the mid- and late 1940s. As we saw, changes in the composition of The Group had occurred. Mints emerged as a major player in monetary economics in the academic community, helping to fill the void left by the death of Simons in 1946. Mints engaged leading Keynesians of the day in academic combat, forging what became known in the profession as the "Mints-Simons program." The key monetary elements of that program had been set out in the early 1930s Chicago memoranda. Moreover, by the early 1950s, the Chicago singular advocacy of flexible exchange rates was called the "Friedman-Mints scheme" (Kindleberger 1953, 302). Director returned to Chicago—to the Law School—in 1946. He pushed forward the idea that the quantity of money is an important variable and its behavior needs to be regulated by the government under a regime of monetary rules and 100 percent reserves. Together with Mints and Cox, Director articulated a vision under which the competitive, free-market order could be made to work more efficiently. Characteristically, both in the late 1940s and, as we shall see, in the 1950s, Director's views on money were communicated by oral means; he published nothing on the subject of money after his return to Chicago. Friedman joined the Chicago economics faculty in 1946. Two years later he made a permanent move into monetary economics. His initial monetary framework, from which he would launch the monetarist counter-revolution, was essentially that of the "Mints-Simons program." In the late 1940s and early 1950s, Friedman, Mints, and other Chicagoans combined forces with their former colleague Douglas to strike the first major victory for the Chicago monetary tradition, helping to reinstate the independence of monetary policy and reinstitute the importance of money in policy debates. What remained to be done was to translate that initial victory into a successful counter-revolutionary movement. The process of doing so would involve a reformulation of the Chicago monetary tradition's framework.

## CHAPTER SEVEN

# The Counterattack

The 1950s saw a transformation of the Chicago tradition's monetary framework. The view that changes in the money supply, and not autonomous changes in the velocity of circulation of money, precipitated turning points in major business cycles became an essential part of a revised framework. The idea that inflation is a monetary phenomenon, caused by attempts to reduce the unemployment rate below its frictional level, became accepted. Velocity, or its reciprocal, the demand for money, was no longer viewed as subject to autonomous shifts; instead, the demand for money came to be seen as functionally stable. The Federal Reserve's pernicious role in the Great Depression, an idea that had been anticipated by Jacob Viner in the early 1930s and Lloyd Mints in the mid-1940s, emerged as a keystone of the Chicago monetary narrative. The perception that the fractional-reserve banking system meant that the economy is inherently unstable was discarded. The idea that money-supply changes should be generated through the government's fiscal position came to be seen, initially, within a longer-run perspective of using that position to increase the money supply secularly, before being discarded in favor of open-market operations as the instrument of choice. The 100 percent reserve proposal remained part of the monetary framework although its status was downgraded—from essential to desirable. Left untouched in the transformation were the emphasis placed on the role of money in the economy, the critical need of policy rules to diminish monetary-policy uncertainty, and the strong advocacy of flexible exchange rates.

The central players in the transformation were Mints, before his retirement in 1953; Aaron Director, often behind the scenes; and, increasingly, Milton Friedman, leading the charge against the Keynesian orthodoxy. Each of those economists paid homage to the intellectual legacy he inherited from Henry Simons. Mints used uncomplicated data analysis to advance Chicago views. Friedman employed cutting-edge statistical analysis, placing the Chicago monetary approach on a firm empirical foundation.[1] Friedman's work with Anna Schwartz throughout the 1950s played a decisive role in the transformation of his thinking. As we will see, non-Chicagoan Clark Warburton performed an important function in that transformation.

This chapter and the next describe the transformation of the Chicago monetary tradition's framework from what Alvin Hansen called the "Mints-Simons program" in the 1940s to Friedman's monetarist framework of the late 1950s. The present chapter focuses on the years 1950 to 1953. In 1950, the notion of a distinctive Chicago school of economics appeared in the economics literature.[2] In an article, "Contemporary American Economic Thought," published in the *Doshisha University Economic Review* in February 1950, Martin Bronfenbrenner (1950, 6) stated:

> The so-called Chicago school of economic policy, whose intellectual parent is Frank H. Knight but whose best-known publicist is Henry C. Simons . . . believes those optimum conditions [production at minimum cost for maximum satisfaction, with each resource paid according to its contribution measured by marginal productivity] would in fact be realized quickly and painlessly in a free economy . . . if these three conditions were satisfied: (1) Elimination of all seriously monopolistic restrictions on the supply of goods and labor; (2) Monetary policy devoted to maintaining a stable price level, or alternatively a stable level of Government expenditure . . . ; and (3) Mitigation of inequality by taxation (particularly the progressive income tax) rather than by interference with the pricing of goods and services.[3]

In this chapter, I cover published and unpublished works (several for the first time in the literature) by Mints, Director, and Friedman. In describing the transformation of the Chicago monetary tradition's framework, I report on the proceedings of an April 1951 Chicago Law School conference, organized by Director, on the respective efficacies of monetary and fiscal policies, and price and quantity controls, in counteracting the incipient inflationary pressures emanating from the Korean War. As will be shown, the notion of a "Chicago tradition" that emphasized the roles of money and free markets surfaced at the conference. One of the conference participants was former Chicagoan Viner, who was publicly encouraged (by Director) to declare his allegiance to that tradition. The following account reports how Viner responded.

How did the economics profession receive the emerging monetarism emanating from Chicago? Robert Lucas (1984, 53) remarked: "The Keynesian [consensus] of the 60s was artificial and unhealthy. Look at the way Friedman's work was criticized during that period. I think it is just a disgrace to the profession that he was treated as though he were some kind of nut." Similarly, Robert Barro (1998, 5) expressed the view that, at Harvard in the late 1960s, "Friedman was treated as a right-wing Midwestern crank. Most of the derision applied to his views on money."[4] To shed light on the profession's treatment of Friedman in the 1950s, this chapter also describes exchanges between Friedman and prominent Keynesian economists, including Alvin Hansen, Abba Lerner, Paul Samuelson, and James Tobin. As we shall see, Friedman's challenge to the Keynesian consensus, which downplayed the role of money in the economy, was met with dismissal and reprobation. More generally, in the early 1950s, Chicago views on money and free markets were characterized as "evangelical" (by Tobin), "radical" (by Harry Johnson), and "tinged with fanaticism" (by Dennis Robertson). I begin the narrative with a discussion of Mints's evolving views on money in the early 1950s.

## 7.1 Mints in the Early 1950s

*Mints 1950*

Mints's 1950 book *Monetary Policy for a Competitive Society* was the culmination of a career-long engagement with monetary economics. In the preface, Mints singled out the influences of three people on his views — Friedman, Simons, and Clarence Philbrook.[5] Regarding Friedman, Mints wrote: "I am greatly indebted to Professor Milton Friedman, who has read the penultimate draft of the manuscript. In consequence of his many suggestions several chapters have been rewritten and others have been revised to a greater or lesser extent" (1950, vii). Regarding Simons, Mints stated: "To my late colleague, Professor Henry C. Simons, I owe much. I have been influenced by him to an immeasurable extent" (1950, vii).

Mints and Friedman had an intellectually reinforcing relationship. They frequently commented on one another's work in the late 1940s and early 1950s. During those years, both of them taught the course Introduction to Money and Banking (Econ 230);[6] Mints also taught the more advanced courses Money (Econ 330) and Banking Theory and Monetary Policy (Econ 331). As mentioned, Friedman began teaching at Chicago as an associate professor in 1946 and was promoted to professor in 1948. Mints, who was promoted to associate professor in 1941, remained at that rank until his retirement in 1953; Mints's inability to be promoted to professor likely reflected his lack of publishing output until 1945 and that he never earned a PhD. Besides commenting on each other's work, collaborating on departmental memoranda on monetary policy—specifically, the 1948 commentary on monetary policy (Director et al. 1948) published in the *New York Times* and the January 1951 "Statement" on monetary policy (Friedman et al. 1951) published in the *Congressional Record*—Mints and Friedman, as we shall see, worked closely in formulating a common Chicago position on monetary policy at the April 1951 Chicago-sponsored conference on the effects of price controls.[7]

As had been the case with Simons's work, Mints's objective in his 1950 book was to propose a monetary program that would support a free-market system amid what Mints called "a strong feeling of doubt [within the economics profession] about the merits of free markets" and widespread support for "proposals for public employment for those unemployed by private industry" (1950, 3). As Simons, Mints believed that unfettered laissez-faire was flawed. It engendered (1) "monopolistic restrictions of many kinds," and (2) "the development of fractional reserve banking," and, thus, a monetary system in which private banking institutions had "taken over the control of the stock of money" (1950, 4–5). Consequently, the government had an important role to play in the economy: it needed to (1) ensure that markets are competitive so that prices and wages are flexible, and (2) pursue rules of the game concerning money to maintain monetary stability. "It is my thesis," Mints asserted, that "if provision is made for such over-all requirements as flexible prices and stability of monetary conditions," then "no direct remedies for unemployment will be required" (1950, 4). Mints's book focused exclusively on the monetary requirement of a well-functioning market system. The author had little to say about the antimonopolistic requirement.

*The role of money.* In a departure from earlier Chicago thinking about the passive role of fluctuations in the money supply in initiating the business cycle, Mints assigned a causal role to money. He argued that while "the inherent instability of an uncontrolled fractional-reserve banking system" had often accentuated declines in employment during cyclical contractions, "it is quite possible that in some instances a decline in the stock of money has been the *initiating* factor in bringing on depression, as well as an aggravating factor after the decline has been started" (emphasis in original, 1950, 37). In making the argument that the money supply could be the initiating factor in the business cycle, Mints was influenced by Clark Warburton's work. Mints wrote:

> Clark Warburton contends that the initiating factor in depressions has been a failure of the stock of money to increase equivalently with the "need" for money, "need" being measured by the growth in transactions and the increase in the demand for liquid resources. This failure of the stock of money to increase sufficiently has brought on a decline in prices, so he contends, and this in turn has ushered in the depression. To me Warburton's evidence seems inconclusive, which is equivalent to saying that he may be right. (1950, 37n2)[8]

*Inflation and unemployment.* Mints believed that, if the central bank attempted to bring unemployment below its frictional level, serious inflation would result and unemployment would increase beyond the frictional level.

> The level of production and of employment are not amenable to control by monetary measures, except in the sense that monetary stability will provide the conditions in which a high average level of output and employment will be maintained. If price rigidities are responsible for a high level of frictional unemployment, conditions could be improved by monetary means, if at all, only at the cost of serious inflation; and before the inflation had gone far it is quite likely that this itself would create so great a degree of uncertainty as to make the remedy worse than the disease. (1950, 117–18)

This statement seems closely connected to Friedman's argument in his Nobel lecture that, at the natural rate of unemployment, highly expansionary monetary policy that results in high inflation is likely to lead to high inflation *variability*, raising unemployment (Friedman 1977, 465–68).[9]

*The Great Depression.* Mints (1950, 37–39) presented data on the money supply (deposits plus currency), the wholesale price index, and industrial production during five cyclical downtowns: 1920–21, 1923–24, 1926–27, 1929–33, and 1937–38. Pointing to the "significant decline in the quantity of money and [the] drastic decline in industrial production" in four of those episodes—excluding the 1923–24 episode—he concluded: "To permit the volume of money to vary in this manner reflects a tragic failure in the management of our monetary affairs" (1950, 39).[10] To evaluate the Fed's performance during the Great Depression further, Mints

(1950, 44–49, 179–80) assessed (1) the sequence of changes in discount rates and buying rates on bills and (2) the variations in the Fed's holdings of earning assets (i.e., Federal Reserve credit outstanding) in relation to changes in both the wholesale price index and the index of industrial production. Regarding the Fed's interest-rate policy, Mints (1950, 179–80) noted that both the discount rate and the buying rate on bills were increased sharply in October 1931 after Great Britain left the gold standard and again in March 1932. Mints pointed out that, during periods of sharp downward movements in prices, the Fed should have been increasing its holdings of earning assets. What he found, however, was that, between December 1929 and July 1931, wholesale prices and industrial production dropped by 22 percent and 17 percent, respectively, while the earning assets of the Federal Reserve Banks *declined* by 42 percent (1950, 45).

Mints (1950, 45) noted that the "defenders of the system" argued that the Fed's reluctance to expand the volume of credit during the Great Depression stemmed from the requirement of maintaining convertibility of the dollar under the gold standard. He argued that the convertibility issue would *not* have emerged had the Fed maintained domestic stability: "had there been in effect, in the autumn of 1929, an adequately implemented policy of monetary stabilization, the occasions for the restrictive measures of the Reserve officials to maintain convertibility would never have arisen" (1950, 46). In a criticism of discretionary policy, Mints stated: "I intend that my criticisms of the Reserve System shall be unambiguous and largely adverse; but I do not mean to imply that another group of men, under the same conditions and operating with the same grant of discretionary power, would have done better. It is to discretionary monetary authorities that I object" (1950, 46n5). Mints concluded his assessment of the Fed's role in the Great Depression with: "Neither the Reserve System nor the Federal government made any significant effort to prevent a drastic decline in quantity of money, to say nothing of a much-needed increase, from 1929 to 1932. This is where we blundered" (1950, 129).[11]

As I have documented, Mints's objective was to demonstrate that discretionary monetary policies had rendered the economy "unavoidably and inherently unstable" (1950, 116). He maintained that the "proponents of discretionary authority have not presented a careful defense of their position" (1950, 116). Who were these "proponents of discretionary authority"? Mints singled out one individual. That individual was his former Chicago colleague Jacob Viner.[12]

In 1947, Viner published the article "Can We Check Inflation?" in the *Yale Review*. In that article, he advocated discretionary monetary policy to deal with inflation. Mints (1950, 116–17) reproduced two paragraphs—both advocating discretion—from the article. In those paragraphs, Viner noted that central bankers had often reacted "too little and too late" to incipient inflationary pressures in the past. Mints chastised Viner: "Viner is right in asserting that central bankers cannot be relied upon. Why, then, would he give them great power unaccompanied with a rule for its use?" Mints criticized Viner as one of the "defenders of discretion" who "do not tell us just how it is that a fixed rule will cause trouble" (1950, 117). As we shall see, the 1951 Chicago Law School conference would provide the occasion for a confrontation on the subject of money between Mints and his Chicago colleagues, on the one side, and Viner, on the other side.

As in his earlier works, Mints continued to argue that monetary policy should be conducted both through the government's fiscal position and through open-market operations, with the former method taking precedence. Where monetary expansion was needed, he recommended running a federal deficit financed by new money and monetizing the public debt. The deficit would arise from a reduction in tax revenues, partly the automatic result of a progressive rate structure and partly from variations in tax rates and exemptions.[13]

*Fractional-reserve banking.* In another departure from earlier Chicago thinking, Mints was equivocal in his criticism of fractional-reserve banking. Indeed, his view on the role of a fractional-reserve system in the business cycle appeared to be in a state of transition. On the one hand, he continued to extol the Chicago tradition's view of the "perverse elasticity which is the inevitable concomitant of uncontrolled fractional-reserve banking—fluctuations in employment will occur with a frequency and a severity that will be intolerable" (1950, 9). He argued that:

> If a malignant despot desired to create the utmost confusion among his subjects on questions of public policy, he would surely require that any question of importance invariably be considered jointly with at least one other, unrelated, problem; and if, he had a real genius as his adviser, the latter would immediately suggest that joint discussion of private lending operations and monetary policy would serve the purposes of his master very nicely. Commercial banking presents precisely this incongruous mixture in practice, and therefore the confusion in discussions of monetary and banking policy should occasion no surprise. (1950, 4–5)

The close relationship between Mints's argumentation—and articulation—of the consequences of fractional-reserve banking on economic activity, and early 1930s Chicago views, is unambiguous. For example, as I previously noted (in chapter 3), the November 1933 memorandum "Banking and Currency Reform" contained the wording: "if some malevolent genius had sought to aggravate the affliction of business and employment cycles, he could hardly have done better than to establish a system of private deposit banks in the present form" (Simons et al. 1933, appendix, 3). Similarly, in a 1933 review of Alvin Hansen's book *Economic Stabilization in an Unbalanced World*, Knight wrote: "the devil in person could not have invented a device more obviously 'intended' than is commercial banking to increase the amplitude of any incipient swing by an indefinite magnitude" (Knight 1933b, 244).

On the other hand, Mints downplayed the role of fractional-reserve banking in the business cycle—in contradiction to his above-quoted remarks. Thus, he wrote: "For the most part the banks have probably been accentuating factors in business fluctuations rather than initiators of disturbances" (1950, 7). What caused this about-face? The answer is that he recognized that the creation of deposit insurance in 1934 had sharply curtailed the possibility of bank panics:

> Prior to 1934 it was inevitable that the banks should vary their lending perversely, and that they should aggravate, and possibly even initiate, periods of disturbance. It is unlikely that deposit insurance has eliminated all of this unfortunate characteristic, since it cannot have eliminated other reasons for this perversity than the withdrawals of cash which the public is likely to make when doubts about the conditions of the banks prevail.... However, we should not exaggerate the shortcomings of the banks. (1950, 6–7)

Consequently, Mints provided the following assessment of the 100 percent reserve scheme: "The elimination of fractional-reserve banking would be a very desirable element in the reduction of short-term debt, although ... this is not indispensable" (1950, 186).

*Portfolio theory of money demand.* As in his 1945 study *A History of Banking Theory in Great Britain and the United States*, in his 1950 book Mints argued that the monetary-transmission mechanism needed to be considered within a portfolio-balance framework. In chapter 3, "The Propensity to Hoard and Unemployment," he expressed the view that unemployment could increase because of a rise in the propensity to hoard, the "proximate cause [of which] is a change in the velocity of circulation of money" (1950, 29). What are the alternatives to holding money balances? Mints argued that "an increase, for example, in the demand for cash on the part of a given individual may be at the expense of any one or more of several ways in which he might have disposed of his income" (1950, 30). Mints listed the following possibilities:

1. Purchase of consumers' goods.
2. Purchase of producers' goods.
3. Lend on short term.
4. Purchase of long-term bonds.
5. Purchase of corporation shares. (1950, 30)

Mints was critical of Keynes's liquidity preference theory of interest-rate determination.[14] Mints argued that liquidity preference theory was not a general theory of interest rate determination: "At best, it merely explains *temporary changes* in rates. It may explain why the rate rises temporarily from 4 to 5 per cent, but it does not explain why the initial rate was 4 per cent" (emphasis in original, 1950, 59). Specifically, Mints argued that an increase in the supply of money (or a decrease in the demand for money) will *initially* lower the interest rate at full employment. However, the price level will also rise, bringing the real money supply back to its initial level. Since the theory of liquidity preference does not explain the initial level of the interest rate, it cannot be a general theory of interest rate determination (1950, 59–60).

As Knight had argued that in his critique of the theory of liquidity preference in his review (Knight 1937, 112–13) of the *General Theory*, Mints wrote:

It may be that for some individuals the quantity of money held (in real terms) is a function of the rate of interest, but it does not follow that the rate is determined by the demand for money for hoarding purposes, nor, therefore, that an increase in this demand will raise the rate. We have three factors to be kept in equilibrium: the quantity of money, the rate of interest, and the general price level. (1950, 34)

Changes in expectations about the third factor, the general price level, could lead to a substitution from money into consumer or producer goods, or both, consistent with Mints's presentation of the transmission process described above. Consequently, changes in the quantity of money need not lead to changes in the interest rate.

As I discussed in chapter 5, Knight had presented a portfolio theory of money demand in both his 1937 review of the *General Theory* and his 1941 article "The Business Cycle, Interest, and Money." In that chapter, I noted that Knight had not presented a portfolio theory of the demand for money in any of his writings before his review of the *General Theory*. Thus, I argued that Keynes's theory of liquidity preference likely influenced Knight's use of the portfolio-analytic construct. A similar argument applies to Mints: his use of a portfolio theory of the demand for money can be regarded as having been influenced by Keynes's liquidity-preference theory.

We saw that Friedman had not taken a course with Simons in the early 1930s. We also saw that, when Friedman returned to Chicago in 1946, he had not yet specialized in monetary economics. Nevertheless, by the time that Friedman moved into monetary economics in 1948, he had become very familiar with Simons's work. As discussed in chapter 6, it appears to be the case that, as Friedman started to specialize in monetary economics, he studied and absorbed the works of his Chicago predecessors Simons, Mints, and (probably) Knight. That circumstance accounted for the close correspondence between Friedman's views and the views of Simons and Mints both in his (Friedman's) 1948 *AER* article and in his 1948 unpublished document prepared for his work with Anna Schwartz. I conjecture that, based on his study of the works of his Chicago predecessors, Friedman concluded that the portfolio theory of money demand had been an intrinsic part of Chicago's work on money. What Knight and Mints had *not* done in their writings was to formalize the portfolio theory of money demand in a mathematical setup. Friedman made that formalization in his 1956 "Restatement" of the quantity theory while arguing that his formalization represented a systematic rendering of the monetary thinking of his Chicago mentors.

*Real balance effect.* Mints incorporated the price-level-induced real balance effect, used by Friedman in his 1948 *AER* paper, into his (Mints's) analysis of the dynamics of depressions. Specifically, he argued that declines in prices during depressions will increase real money balances. This increase, he argued, would act as a brake on the downward spiral of velocity during economic contractions. Consequently, as he had argued in his 1946 paper "Monetary Policy," Mints stated that there is a limit to the fall in economic activity in depressions: "there is some indefinite

minimum below which even modern perversely elastic moneys cannot
be reduced, and when this level has been reached any further decline in
the level of prices will raise the volume of cash balances in real terms"
(1950, 34).

*Monetary rules.* Mints (1950, 115–73) provided a careful assessment of
alternative monetary rules, including Friedman's 1948 rule.[15] Apart from
the latter rule, the other rules considered were (1) a rule under which the
*level* of the money supply would be held constant, (2) a rule under which
the money supply would increase "at a rate roughly equivalent to the rate
of increase in the volume of transactions" (1950, 123), and (3) a stable-
price-level rule.

A central argument in the book was Mints's view that economic stability requires monetary stability:

> One of the prime requisites for the automatic and effective functioning of a
> competitive system is monetary stability. A deliberately provided, definite, and
> known monetary policy is a unique and indispensable means of reducing to a
> minimum variations in the expectations of the public. It is as much an essential
> part of the framework of an enterprise economy as is competition or the law of
> contracts. (1950, 9)

Mints argued that a rules-based monetary framework could have prevented the Great Depression.[16] He expressed this argument as follows:

> Today we have utter confusion and uncertainty in our monetary system. We do
> not know when or to what extent the banks may extend or contract the stock
> of money; we do not know what policy the Federal Reserve System will pursue.
> Who would have predicted before 1929 that the Reserve System would take an
> almost completely passive attitude during conditions such as those that devel-
> oped from 1929 to 1932? (1950, 8)

As in his earlier writings, Mints expressed a preference for a rule that
stabilizes an index of wholesale prices because of its simplicity and capacity to offset changes in velocity. In contrast to those earlier writings, however, in 1950 Mints discussed a potential problem with such a rule: "There
must necessarily be some lag between the date upon which monetary action would be indicated by the change in prices and the time at which the
action would become effective in the market" (1950, 138–39). Mints made
it clear that it was not only the *length* of the lag that created a problem, a

problem that he had identified in his previous writings, but the *variability* of the lag that created a problem, a problem that he had not mentioned in his earlier works: "In this way it may seem that an attempt to stabilize an index [of prices] would or might actually accentuate variations in the levels of prices" (1950, 139). The possibility of variable lags that magnify movements in the ultimate target variable was what Friedman (1948a) had noted. In his discussion on this issue, Mints gave Friedman credit: "This possibility was suggested by my colleague, Professor Milton Friedman" (1950, 138n8).

Concerning Friedman's fiscal-based monetary rule, Mints thought that the rule's main advantage was the "nondiscretionary character of its anti-cyclical action" (1950, 223). Mints maintained, however, that the rule suffered from several shortcomings. First, as was the case for the price-level rule, Friedman's rule would be subject to the lagged effects of monetary actions (1950, 172). Second, for the rule to be effective, the reserve ratio would have to be raised to 100 percent so that banks would not be able to offset monetary-policy actions through the creation and destruction of demand deposits. Third, there would be no assurance that the automatic changes in reserves produced under the proposal would generate the "right" amount of money needed to stabilize the economy. Fourth, since the proposal relied on a hypothetical level of income corresponding to a stable budget, it was susceptible to the judgment, and, thus the discretion, of policy makers, who would have to determine that hypothetical level of income. Fifth, the connection between the proposal and key economic variables, especially the price level, "would not be entirely understandable" to the public (1950, 172). In his overall assessment, Mints was not sternly critical: "it would be a reasonably satisfactory alternative to increasing the stock of money at some constant rate or stabilizing the price level, although, to my mind, it is nevertheless somewhat inferior to either of these procedures" (1950, 167).

*Flexible exchange rates.* Mints devoted two chapters—chapter 4, titled "Internal Adjustments to International Disturbances," and chapter 5, titled "Fixed Versus Flexible Exchange Rates"—to the exchange-rate-regime issue. As Friedman had done in his 1948 paper, Mints came out in favor of flexible exchange rates. Mints put forward the following arguments:

1. High exchange-rate volatility reflected volatility in the underlying macroeconomic fundamentals: "Historical periods of exchange instability have been the product of monetary disorder . . . and there is no way of disentangling the

influence of internal affairs from that of movements in the exchange rates"
(1950, 93). As mentioned, Mints (1945b, 193) had argued similarly in his critique
of Nurkse's (1944) study, foreshadowing the analogous critique of Nurkse made
by Friedman in his paper "The Case for Flexible Exchange Rates" (Friedman
1953b, 176n9).

2. Flexible exchange rates would lead to a forward market in foreign exchange in
   which exchange-rate risk for the major currencies could be hedged: "If there is
   a well-organized market for forward exchange . . . the traders themselves can
   avoid the exchange risk at a cost which will raise the price of the product only
   slightly. A national monetary standard would undoubtedly lead to the development of such speculative markets for the more important currencies" (1950,
   93). As noted in chapter 2, a similar argument had been made in the November 1933 Chicago memorandum (Simons et al. 1933, 9). Moreover, as noted in
   chapter 5, Simons had presented the same argument in a 1934 paper, "Currency
   Systems and Commercial Policy" (1934c, 346). Friedman would make the same
   argument in his 1953 paper on exchange-rate regimes (1953b, 174).[17]

3. Speculation in foreign-exchange markets would be stabilizing "in the sense that
   it would reduce the extent of short-run fluctuations . . . [because] speculation
   serves a highly useful purpose, and the profit of the speculator is the reward of
   the bona fide service rendered. If a speculator has a disequilibrating influence,
   he will lose money and be eliminated from the market" (1950, 94). Friedman
   (1953b, 175) argued: "People who argue that speculation is generally destabilizing seldom realize that this is largely equivalent to saying that speculators lose
   money, since speculation can be destabilizing in general only if speculators on
   the average sell when the currency is low in price and buy when it is high."

4. Mints also claimed that the theoretical and empirical cases that flexible exchange rates hamper international trade are ambiguous: "there is little of a
   theoretical nature that can be said, and even that little is inconclusive. Furthermore, there is no reason to suppose that statistical evidence would be of much
   value" (1950, 92–93). Friedman (1953b, 173–74) argued that flexible exchange
   rates do not increase uncertainty and, therefore, do not hamper trade.[18]

Did Mints's arguments on exchange rates precede those of Friedman?
Several points are relevant. First, Mints wrote the preface of his book in
July 1950, an indication that the book manuscript had been finalized by that
time. Friedman's 1953 paper on exchange rates was based on a memorandum that he wrote in the fall of 1950, and the paper went through several
subsequent drafts.[19] Thus, chronologically, Mints's book takes precedence
over Friedman's article. Second, as mentioned, Friedman made extensive

comments on Mints's draft manuscript, resulting in the rewriting of several chapters of that manuscript. Likewise, in the introductory footnote to his 1953 paper, Friedman (1953b, 157) acknowledged that the ideas in the paper owed "much . . . to extensive discussion of the general problem with a number of friends," one of whom Friedman singled out being Mints.[20] Additionally, after Mints retired and Friedman took over teaching responsibility for one of Mints's graduate courses on money (Econ 331), the two chapters on the exchange-rate-regime issue in Mints's 1950 book became staple items on Friedman's reading list. As late as 1965, a question on the final exam (Friedman 1965) required students to provide the central idea in one of four reading assignments, one of which comprised the exchange-rate-regime chapters in Mints's 1950 book. Clearly, there was considerable cross-fertilization between the ideas of Mints and those of Friedman. However, Friedman's (1953b) assessment was more comprehensive and broader in terms of the subject matter covered—as discussed later in this chapter it introduced such ideas as exchange-rate overshooting, optimum currency areas, and the daylight-saving-time argument for flexible exchange rates into the literature (Dellas and Tavlas 2009). This circumstance helps explain the subsequent influence that Friedman's article exerted on the economics profession.[21] Correspondingly, however, Mints's ideas on flexible exchange rates, including his prescient critique of Nurkse's views, do *not* deserve the complete neglect that they have experienced.

### The Chicago Tradition: The Profession's Reactions

The reviews of Mints's book were generally positive. A common feature of the reviews was that the reviewers connected Mints's views to those of a Chicago cohort that was distinctive, idiosyncratic, and eccentric. Consider the following. (1) In a review in the *Accounting Review*, Donald Fergusson (1951, 439) characterized Mints's views as those of "the Chicago banking school." (2) Dennis Robertson reviewed the book in the *AER*. Robertson (1951, 466) wrote: "Banks, as they have actually developed, are in [Mints's] eyes a great nuisance, and Central Banks no better; and it is only out of a laudable desire to be realistic and not to cry (like some of his Chicago colleagues!) for the moon that he is led to assign them a role, though a minor one, is his scheme of operations." Regarding Mints's criticism of government intervention in economic affairs, Robertson (1951, 467) stated that "Mints's uncompromising rejection of all such expedients ... [are] tinged with fanaticism."[22] (3) In his review in the *Journal of Business*, James Tobin (1951a, 233) stated: "Professor Mints, like the late Henry Simons, is an able and devoted architect of the economic structure of a modern liberal society." (4) Harry Johnson reviewed the book—negatively—for the *Economic Journal*. Johnson (1951, 382) began his review as follows: "Professor Mints is a leading member of the Chicago radical school of the late Professor Henry C. Simons." As we shall see, as of 1951, the Chicagoans identified their views on money and free markets as part of a "Chicago tradition."

*Mints, 1951*

In December 1950, Mints presented the paper "Monetary Policy and Stabilization" at the meeting of the American Economic Association. The paper was published in the *AER* in May 1951. In the paper, he turned the earlier Chicago view that the economy is *inherently unstable* because of autonomous fluctuations in velocity on its head. Instead, he argued that the economy is inherently stable, but discretionary policies robbed the "competitive economy ... [of] the proper conditions for the functioning of such a system" (1951b, 189). In particular, Mints expressed the view that discretionary policies destabilized expectations: "[discretion] robs policy of the very thing which is most needed in monetary matters; namely, certainty with respect to monetary conditions" (1951b, 191). In contrast to discretion, under "a definite and announced policy," he argued, "expectations would become a major stabilizing rather than a destabilizing influence" (1951b, 191). Mints also extended the argument made in his 1950 book that deposit insurance had reduced "the danger of runs on the banks" (1951b, 190). He stated that the "relatively larger amounts of government securities" that banks held on their balance sheets than in the past had "undoubtedly reduce[d] the perverse influence of the banks" (1951b, 190).[23] Mints maintained that the "disturbing actions of the bankers and the public" in the past were due to the uncertainty caused by discretionary actions and, "while ideal conditions may require the elimination of fractional reserves, there is no doubt that we could get along very well in the presence of the banks if only we would adopt an announced policy aimed at the maintenance of monetary stability" (1951b, 190).

Mints provided further evidence—in the form of movements of Federal Reserve credit and changes in the wholesale price index—on the destabilizing role that the Fed's discretionary policies had played during six "periods of outstanding need for action" (1951b, 192). The periods that he singled out were the following: 1920–21, 1929–31, 1937–38, 1940–46, 1946–48, and 1948–49. The particular periods were chosen because they involved especially large movements in the price level. Mints found that in four of the periods—1920–21, 1929–31, 1940–46, and 1948–49—credit outstanding and the price level moved in the same direction, indicating that the Fed's open-market operations had been procyclical. Moreover, even though the Fed's earning assets and the price level moved in opposite directions in the remaining two periods (i.e., 1937–38 and 1946–48), the price level moved to a much greater degree than Fed credit outstanding moved so that the monetary authorities deserved little, if any, credit (1951b, 192–93). He concluded: "In the light of this examination we must conclude that when conditions have most urgently demanded monetary action the Reserve System has predominantly followed a policy precisely contrary to that which was desirable" (1951b, 192–93).

## Discussion

By the early 1950s Mints had modified the Chicago tradition's framework in several ways. The fractional-reserve banking system, he had come to believe, was not inherently unstable in the presence of deposit insurance and the large holdings of government securities by banks. Hence, the 100 percent reserve scheme, while desirable, was not indispensable. The economy, he argued, was not subject to velocity shocks, constantly being thrown off course. The economy was inherently stable but was thrown off course by destabilizing changes in the quantity of money, a consequence of discretionary policies. Central-bank action aimed at lowering the unemployment rate below the "frictional" level would lead to "serious inflation" and uncertainty. Once an economic downturn had started, the downturn would *not* proceed without limit. The real balance effect provided an automatic brake on the downward momentum. The effects of changes in the money supply on economic activity could be viewed within the context of a simple portfolio-balance framework. Economic policies, Mints argued, are subject to long and variable lags, so that discretionary policies could amplify the business cycle. In common with the 1930s and 1940s Chicago tradition, Mints believed that changes in the money supply should mainly be achieved through changes in the government's fiscal position; open-market operations should play a secondary role. Also in common with that tradition, Mints enumerated the benefits of flexible exchange rates made by Simons in the 1930s; at the same time, Mints furnished additional arguments in favor of flexible exchange rates.

The changes in Mints's views reflected, in part, the influence of Friedman, whom Mints singled out for credit. In turn, Friedman's views, especially at the time that he became actively engaged in monetary economics in 1948, had been heavily influenced by Mints and Simons. Moreover, Simons, Mints, and Friedman were influenced by, and, in turn, influenced, Director, although the precise trail of influence (in both directions) is blurred because Director left very few markings in terms of published output in monetary economics. Nevertheless, as we shall see in chapter 8, in his unpublished documents and lectures Director continued to carry the torch lit by Simons in the 1930s to the Chicago of the mid-1950s.

## 7.2 Conference on the Economics of Mobilization

In April 1951, the University of Chicago Law School sponsored a conference titled "The Economics of Mobilization."[24] The backdrop to the conference was the Korean War, which began in June 1950. An immediate consequence of the conflict was a surge in domestic demand and prices as spending to fight the war brought government expenditure close to its peak level of World War II (Meltzer 2003, 583). Consumer-price inflation, which ran in negative territory (year on year) in each of the first six months of 1950, accelerated sharply in the months after the start of the war. In April 1951, the month of the Chicago conference, inflation was running at over 9 percent. There was a widespread expectation that the war would produce a large fiscal deficit financed by money growth (Meltzer 2003, 684).[25] In response to the acceleration in inflation that had occurred since the start of the war, in late January 1951 the Truman administration imposed price and wage controls.[26] As discussed in chapter 6, in March 1951, the US Treasury and the Federal Reserve reached an agreement to separate the Treasury's debt management from monetary policy. At the time of the Chicago conference, the monetary-policy implications of the accord were not clear.[27]

The main focus of the Chicago conference was whether direct price controls (including wage controls) were necessary to contain the inflationary pressures stemming from the Korean War. Could monetary policy or fiscal policy or a combination of the two be sufficient to contain inflation? What would be the economic consequences of the controls? The conference was held at White Sulphur Springs, West Virginia, from April 5 to

April 8.[28] There were seventy participants, including academics, government officials, and business and union leaders. The academics included Chicagoans Theodore Schultz (the chair of the Economics Department and, as discussed in chapter 6, a signatory of the Chicago memorandum published in the *Congressional Record* as an appendix to Paul Douglas's February 22, 1951, speech before the US Congress), Director, Cox, Friedman, Knight, Mints, Wallis, and Hayek—the latter economist held an independent position at the University of Chicago funded by the Committee on Social Thought.[29] Non-Chicago academics included Gardner Ackley (Office of Price Stabilization; on leave from the University of Michigan), Alvin Hansen (Harvard), Roy Harrod (Oxford), Ludwig von Mises (New York University), George Stigler (then with Columbia University), and Jacob Viner (Princeton). There were seven sessions: one session on monetary policy, two sessions on fiscal policy, two sessions on direct controls, one session on the rearmament of the British economy, and one session on the long-run consequences of rearmament on free-market institutions. The conference proceedings were published as a book under the title *Defense, Controls, and Inflation*, edited by Director (1952).[30] Although the Chicago contingent was overrepresented (relative to its share of the economics profession), the conference provided the occasion for a contrast between what had emerged as the Chicago tradition's position on the role of monetary policy in the economy and the position of other members of the profession. In what follows, I provide an overview of the discussions on monetary policy, fiscal policy, and direct controls.

*Role of monetary policy.* The first session was "The Role of Monetary Policy." The session opened with statements by Mints and Harrod; it continued with a general discussion and concluded with a summing-up by Friedman. In his statement, Mints argued that the best way to control inflation was through a tightening of monetary policy, supported with an increase in taxes to balance the federal budget. He expressed the view that the Fed should embrace price-level stabilization as a "guide to action." The Fed, he argued, had "the power" to achieve that objective if it were "willing to forsake the bond-support program that it has been following since 1942" (Director 1952, 28–29). Thus, to stem the inflationary pressures emanating from the Korean War, the Fed needed to conduct sales of its earning assets, allowing interest rates to rise. Mints stated, however, that he was "skeptical that we can depend on the Board to follow any such policy." He remarked that he had studied the performance of the monetary authorities since the creation of the Fed, and had isolated what he considered were episodes that called for a "particular need for action." These episodes had been marked by either large rises or large declines in the price level. In those circumstances, to maintain price stability the level of the Fed's earning assets should have moved in the opposite direction from the movements in the price level. There were, he stated, seven such episodes.[31] What he found was that in five of those episodes the Fed's earning assets moved in the same direction as movements in the price level. When the price level rose, for example, the Fed typically engaged in open-market purchases—the opposite of that needed to stabilize the price level. Over the long run, Mints continued, price-level stabilization would require a resort to budget deficits "of a restricted amount for the purpose of supplying the additional money that would be needed to prevent the price level from falling [in light of the long-run rise in output growth]" (Director 1952, 28).

A notable aspect of Mints's presentation was the fact that Mints had come around to the view that the procyclical effects of velocity movements and changes in bank lending under a fractional-reserve banking system could be offset through countercyclical open-market operations. In that regard, he noted that, even in the event of a balanced budget, there "may be a tendency for inflation to develop because of a rise in the rate of use of money or because of a rise in the volume of private loans of the banks." Should those situations arise, the Federal Reserve "has the power to offset those developments if it so chooses. I mean it has the power now. It does not need additional power" (Director 1952, 28).

In his statement, Harrod provided a very different perspective on inflation control. He expressed the view that monetary policy on its own would not be effective in preventing inflation: "I do not believe that in history we can find an example of pure monetary control [i.e., monetary policy] preventing an inflation of the sort with which we are threatened, because the forces are too strong" (Director 1952, 31). He argued that monetary tightening would need to be accompanied by (1) price controls and controls on the physical allocation of materials needed to support the war effort; (2) an increase in tax rates to balance the budget; and (3) a decrease in depreciation allowances on investment to reduce private investment—beyond the decrease produced by the monetary tightening—to offset the increase in government spending associated with the war. Harrod maintained that "history does not show that a tight credit policy can prevent the development of inflation in the kind of situation . . . we have at the present time" (Director 1952, 64).

During the ensuing discussion, those speakers who expressed an opinion on the issue agreed with Harrod's position—namely, that monetary policy, supported with fiscal tightening, would not be sufficient to contain inflation; controls on prices would also be needed.[32] There was widespread agreement among the non-Chicagoans that a monetary-policy tightening that produced contraction of the quantity of money would be offset, at least in part, by an increase in velocity. That view was expressed, for example, by W. Randolph Burgess, who was, at that time, chairman of the National City Bank of New York.[33] Burgess used the occasion to rebuke Friedman, Mints, and the five other Chicago co-authors of the memorandum published as an appendix to Paul Douglas's February 22, 1951, speech in the *Congressional Record*. It will be recalled that the memorandum pressed for the termination of the Fed's policy of pegging interest rates on government securities. Burgess stated that he wanted to "enter a dissent from the complete belief in the document put out by five or seven Chicago professors, which I think vastly overstates the case for monetary policy." Burgess added that he was "distressed" by the document (Director 1952, 35).

In his summary of the discussion, Friedman noted that two positions on inflation control had been put forward. One position was that to which Harrod had subscribed—namely, that in addition to monetary and fiscal restraint, direct controls on prices and rationing would be required to contain the inflation then being experienced. The other position was Mints's. Friedman summarized that position as follows: the monetary tightening, "by its effect on the quantity of money," and "combined with reasonably adequate fiscal policy," could prevent inflation (Director 1952, 65–66). Friedman stated: "I may say, I share [the position] . . . that monetary measures, given a reasonable fiscal policy, could be effective in stabilizing the level of prices" (Director 1952, 48). In subsequent sessions, Director and Knight would support the position of Friedman and Mints. Cox indicated his agreement in a comment on Director's summary of the conference discussions (Director 1952, 17n16).

*Role of fiscal policy.* The next two sessions focused on the role of fiscal measures. There was widespread agreement that fiscal tightening would be needed to contain inflation. The main area of disagreement was the extent of such tightening that would be required. Harrod reiterated his view that "monetary policy cannot be expected to carry the whole burden under present circumstances of defeating the inflationary effect [of excess demand]" (Director 1952, 88).[34] He asserted that either a balanced budget or, possibly, a budget surplus would be needed. Friedman agreed that fiscal policy would have to be tightened, but he argued that the degree of fiscal tightening would not need to be such as to produce a balanced budget. Specifically, he expressed the view that "the range of feasible maneuver in the area of monetary policy is even greater than it is in the area of fiscal policy so far as its effects on incentives and so far as the equity distribution of the burden is concerned" (Director 1952, 95–96). He concluded that, with an appropriately tight monetary policy, a "minor fiscal deficit" would be appropriate (Director 1952, 96).

One additional point about the discussion on monetary and fiscal policies deserves mention. Throughout the previous session on the effectiveness of monetary policy during wartime, both Friedman and Mints framed a monetary tightening in terms of open-market sales of government securities, contrary to the Chicago tradition's approach that money-supply changes should be generated through the government's budget position. During the discussion on fiscal policy, former Chicagoan Viner raised the following question: "Would not a budgetary surplus be one of the means of contacting the supply of money?" Director responded to Viner's question with an intervention that suggested that the Chicago tradition's approach of using the government's fiscal position to change the money supply was giving way to using open-market operations for that purpose: "It [a budget surplus] may be used as a means of contracting the supply of money. Even so, what are the advantages of using tax collections rather than open market operations?" (Director 1952, 89). Friedman's position that a "minor fiscal deficit" could be incurred so long as monetary policy was tight suggested that he had come to the view that open-market operations should be used to implement a monetary tightening—especially given that a fiscal deficit, if financed by money creation, would increase the money supply.[35]

*Price controls and the Chicago tradition.* The discussion on price controls opened with statements by Michael DiSalle, who was the director of the Office of Price Administration, the US government's agency responsible for administering price controls, and Director. DiSalle was a strong proponent of the price-wage freeze. In January 1951, the month in which the freeze was imposed, he supported the freeze by saying it was like "bobbing a cat's tail: better to do it all at once close to the body, otherwise the result would be a mad cat and a sore tail" (quoted from Layman 1994, 110). The basic case made by proponents of price controls was that the market may not be an efficient mechanism for dealing with very large and rapid changes in demand. Moreover, even if fiscal and monetary policies were sufficiently tightened to maintain a stable price level, prices of the most critical and scarce goods would nevertheless rise sharply.[36] As evidence of the effectiveness of such controls, DiSalle pointed to what he considered had been the positive experience with price controls during World War II (Director 1952, 155–58).

Director's statement on the role of price controls was notable for two reasons. First, he succinctly summed up the Chicago tradition's position on controls. Second, Director's statement may have marked the first occasion during which the words "Chicago tradition" were used in a conference forum. Director stated:

> All I plan to do is to state the position that price control should not be used. I apologize for the dogmatic character of the statements I shall make. My excuse is that I find it very difficult to argue the position. This in turn may be due to the fact that the position is so much a part of the Chicago tradition that we have forgotten how to argue the issue. At Chicago the advantages of the market as a method of organizing economic affairs are valued too highly to be laid aside during so-called emergency periods. (Director 1952, 158)

Subsequently, Knight intervened in order "to express my loyalty to the Chicago tradition about which you have heard something. And I think there actually is a tradition in the economics group at Chicago to lean in the direction of free enterprise and of freedom rather than the opposite direction" (Director 1952, 295).[37] He went on to argue that capitalism faced an external threat from the "communist totalitarian system" and an internal threat "from saviors, that is, from reformers" (Director 1952, 296). He criticized monopolies, singling out "labor unions and organized farmers," and protectionism (Director 1952, 296).

Regarding monetary policy, Knight was critical of the use of money creation to finance an enlarged government sector, and the use of price controls to contain the ensuing inflation. He stated:

> Monetary policy is about as bad [as protectionism]—the clamor to make capital cheap or free and to finance governmental largesse without anyone having to pay taxes, by eliminating the "money power" and creating money by fiat. And of late we confront arbitrary price-fixing; for example, the freezing of residential rents. Of course landlords as a class are rich and grasping and tenants poor and virtuous. This surpasses even protectionism and sets a new high for economic stupidity and indefensible justice. (Director 1952, 297)

Having referred to a "Chicago tradition" under which price controls should not be used to control inflation, Director made a not-very-subtle attempt to lure Viner to express his allegiance to that tradition. Viner, after all, was a preeminent figure in the profession, and his inclusion within what Director called the Chicago tradition would have added prestige to such a tradition. Here is what Director stated: "I understand that recently this [Chicago] tradition has been spreading eastward. If that is so, it can perhaps be partly explained by the fact that one of the Chicago economists responsible for establishing this tradition has recently moved in that direction [to Princeton]" (Director 1952, 158).

Director went on to argue that a market-induced rise in prices leads to the discovery and use of substitute goods and services, a function that could not be performed by "any particular group of experts" (Director 1952, 159). The main effect of price controls, he argued, was to repress inflation during the period in which the controls were in effect. With the lifting of the controls, prices would ultimately rise to the level that would have been obtained in the absence of the controls. This observation led Director to provide two additional arguments against controls. First, if the ultimate increase in the price level "is generally the same regardless of price control, then it seems to me there is no advantage in postponing it." That is, it would be best to have prices rise sooner rather than later. Second, Director contended that "open inflation is better than repressed inflation, and it is better precisely because it permits changes in relative prices, which price control, used to stop inflation, must prevent" (Director 1952, 159). Thus, "open inflation" allows the market to perform its function of allocating goods and services. Director's remarks set the stage for clashes between Friedman and both Hansen and Viner. The remarks also set the stage for a reaction from Viner on the Chicago tradition.

Hansen joined the group that advocated price controls. He maintained that as long as "private investment and governmental outlays exceed savings and taxes, prices will rise" regardless of what happens to the money supply (Director 1952, 167). Consequently, he argued that private investment needed to be reduced to counterbalance the rise in government expenditure. One way of doing so would be to "cut out civilian motorcar production altogether" (Director 1952, 167). Criticizing the view put forward by Friedman and Mints that inflation could be contained by curbing money-supply growth, Hansen argued that the cessation of post–World War II inflation in 1948 had nothing to do with monetary factors: "Why did prices stop rising? Well, I submit that it was fundamentally nonmonetary factors." Those nonmonetary factors included increased supplies of agricultural products, of which there had been shortages at end of the war (Director 1952, 166).

Reacting to Hansen, Friedman argued that the inflation experienced during and after World War II was attributable to high monetary growth. Using the evidence that he had marshaled in his then-forthcoming 1952 *AER* paper "Price, Income and Monetary Changes in Three Wartime Periods," he cited the experiences in the United States with inflation during the Civil War, World War I, and World War II.[38] Friedman argued that wage and price controls during those wartime periods served only to "postpone but not to reduce the ultimate price rise." Inflation in each of the wartime periods, he maintained, was strictly determined by the quantity of money (Director 1952, 176).

Viner put distance between his view and what had emerged as the Chicago view. He maintained that controls on prices, along with fiscal and monetary policies, were needed to restrain inflation. Responding to the contention by Mints and Friedman that monetary policy on its own would be effective in restraining inflation, Viner asserted: "I do think there is a tendency toward too simple explanations, and doctrine which explains the course of events in terms of the quantity of money alone, as if nothing else matters, is a grossly simplified explanation. I hope nobody believes in that kind of explanation, even though I occasionally hear talk that sounds that way" (Director 1952, 178). Friedman countered:

> Those of us who have been concentrating on the monetary sources of inflation have . . . been accused, by some of the few and rare individuals here who are our critics [meaning, in particular, Viner], of adopting an oversimplified view of the monetary mechanism. It has been implied that we believe if the quantity of money doubles, prices inevitably double. . . . I want to deny that accusation explicitly. We are not so naïve as all that. (Director 1952, 230)

Friedman went on to explain that the relationship between the money supply and prices is a complex one, with factors other than money affecting prices. Nevertheless, the money supply, he argued, is the most important factor affecting prices and it could be manipulated to offset the effects of other factors (Director 1952, 230–31).

At the concluding session of the conference, Viner took up the gauntlet that Director had thrown down to him about his (Viner's) being part of the "Chicago tradition." The chair of that session asked Viner to provide a summary statement of the conference proceedings. Viner began as follows: "What I will say may disturb some old friends [meaning his former Chicago colleagues] and new enemies here [again meaning his former Chicago colleagues]." He went on to say that some speakers had treated the free market as if it were a virtue, and controls as if they were a vice. He then stated: "But I, unfortunately, do not believe in an excess of virtue. . . . I also believe that there can also be an excess of vice" (Director 1952, 336). He argued that price controls were needed to keep inflation in check. Those controls, Viner noted, would entail an enlarged role for government intervention in the economy, but that enlarged role was necessary. Viner stated: "Despite my free-market convictions, I have never been able to get seriously afraid of American bureaucrats" (Director 1952, 337).

*Discussion*

The occasion of the 1951 Chicago conference sheds light on the origination of the notion of a Chicago monetary tradition. In the previous chapter it was shown that, in the 1940s, the views of Simons and Mints on money and free markets came to be identified under the designation "the Mints-Simons program." In this chapter, we saw that reviewers of Mints's 1951 book identified Mints's views as representative of a distinctive and eccentric "Chicago school." By the time of the 1951 conference, the Chicagoans had come to publicly identify their monetary-cum-free-market framework as "the Chicago tradition." Moreover, the identification of the Chicago tradition as synonymous with the importance of money and free markets had gained acceptance in the economics profession. For example, in an *AER* review of the Chicago conference volume, Richard Heflebower wrote of "two sharply divergent policy programs" discussed at the conference.[39] He continued:

> One which was labelled that of the "Chicago School," consisted solely of vigorous monetary control carried out by Federal Reserve open market operations. No direct controls over wages, prices, or uses of materials, or over total amount or direction of use of investment funds should be imposed. Even a balanced budget, while helpful, would not be fundamental, for a deficit could be offset by still tighter money and the restricting effect of higher interest rates. (Heflebower 1953, 457)

Thus, contrary to Harry Johnson's (1971) assertion, Friedman did not originate—or "invent"—the idea of a Chicago monetary tradition in his

1956 "Restatement" of the quantity theory. The University of Chicago had established a reputation in the economics profession for cultivating the distinctive view that money plays a crucial role in the economy years before the publication of the "Restatement." Indeed, Johnson, himself, had used the words "Chicago radical school" to describe the views emanating from Chicago in his 1951 review of Mints's book. The 1951 conference also makes clear that Viner did not consider himself to have been part of the Chicago tradition after he left Chicago for Princeton. Viner assigned less importance to the role of money in the economy and was less concerned about an expanded role of government in the economy than were the adherents to that tradition.

*Postscript.* Mints's presentation at the conference was based on a fourteen-page background paper, "The Role of Monetary Policy in Mobilization." The paper was not published and has never been cited in the literature.[40] The paper provided additional details on Mints's views. For one thing, Mints viewed a price-level stabilization rule to be compatible with a money-supply growth-rate rule: "Since we shall undoubtedly continue to have a slow expansion in the volume of transactions, this policy [of price-level stabilization] would require a corresponding growth in the stock of money" (1951a, 6). In addition, Mints was more critical of the Fed in his paper than he had been in his presentation at the conference. In the paper, he stated: "The history of the System's actions, its present policy, and its pronouncements on the subject of policy, all combine to make clear beyond a reasonable doubt that it is a totally unreliable monetary authority. . . . One of the first things that is needed in shoring up our monetary arrangements is to deprive both of them [the Fed and the Treasury Secretary] of the privilege of making themselves ridiculous in public" (1951a, 6–7). In this regard, the actions of the monetary authorities had been "disastrously opportunistic" and had failed "to provide the business world with the stability of monetary expectations which is essential to an even-handed carrying on of economic activities" (1951a, 11). Finally, Mints updated the six episodes of significant movements in the price level identified in his December 1950 American Economic Association presentation to include a seventh episode—June 1950 to January 1951. For the latter episode, Mints found that the Federal Reserve's earning assets moved in the same direction as the price level, contrary to the requirements of price-level stabilization. The fact that the paper was located in the Frank H. Knight Papers at the University of Chicago library suggests that the paper was circulated at the April 1951 conference.

*Mints's Final Bow*

In 1953, Mints made his final publishing bow with a comment on monetary policy in the May 1953 issue of the *American Economic Review*.[41] In his comment, Mints attributed the dollar shortage of the early 1950s to the overvaluation of foreign currencies against the US dollar under the Bretton Woods system (1953, 54). Mints criticized the idea that an exchange rate could be pegged at an equilibrium level, noting that equilibrium exchange rates were constantly changing. The Bretton Woods system of pegged exchange rates prevented rates from moving to their equilibrium levels. Hence, "even though . . . the pegged rate were at the equilibrium level originally, it would shortly fail to be" (1953, 54). He argued that "I can think of no other means of bringing about rapid adjustments in an economy" than "a free exchange rate" (1953, 55). Mints criticized the effects of the Bretton Woods system on global trade. In helping to construct that system, he argued that American delegates to the Bretton Woods conference aimed to promote multilateral trade. In so doing, "they believed stability of exchange rates would operate powerfully in this direction." However, the system of pegged rates "has compelled various nations to resort to direct controls of imports and bilateral agreements of precisely the kinds that the government of the United States was hopeful of avoiding" (1953, 55).

The final paragraph of Mints's comment dealt with monetary policy. Mints maintained that he saw "no possibility of avoidance of final governmental responsibility for monetary policy." Consequently, he considered it pointless to suggest that a central bank should be "independent" of the government. What was needed for domestic economic stability, he concluded, was a rule, "indicating by legislation the precise policy to be followed by the monetary agency," thereby eliminating "the delegation of discretionary monetary power to both treasuries and central banks" (1953, 56).

With his retirement in 1953, Mints terminated his engagement with academic research and writing. Before we take leave of Mints, however, we must address a question that was raised but only partially answered in chapter 6: Why have Mints's contributions to the Chicago monetary tradition been underappreciated for so long?"[42] As mentioned in chapter 6, one plausible reason for the neglect of Mints's contributions is that previous studies on the Chicago monetary tradition have focused on the pre–*General Theory* period, 1927–35, whereas Mints's publications were concentrated in the 1945–53 period. Here I want to put forward another factor that helps explain the neglect of Mints's contributions. As the volume, depth, and originality of Friedman's research output during the 1950s and 1960s converted a sizable part of the profession to the view that money matters, Mints's monetary contributions—like those of Clark Warburton (discussed below)—were swept aside. Yet the picture that emerges from the discussion of Mints's works in this study is that Friedman's monetarist economics owed more to the contributions of Mints than has previously been recognized.

### 7.3 The 1951 REStat Symposium

As had been the case with the 1951 Chicago conference, the rise of inflation associated with the Korean War provided the backdrop for another clash of views over the role of monetary policy during that episode—this time in the form of a symposium published in the August 1951 issue of the *Review of Economics and Statistics* (*REStat*).[43] The Chicago conference had been slanted in favor of Chicagoan views—sixteen of the seventy participants held positions with the University of Chicago at the time of the conference. Eighteen years after the conference, Viner reflected back at the conference as follows: "The invited participants were a varied lot of academics, bureaucrats, businessmen, etc., but the program for discussion, the selection of chairmen, and everything about the conference except for the unscheduled statements and protests from individual participants were so patently rigidly structured, so loaded, that I got more amusement from the conference than from any other I ever attended" (Viner, quoted from Patinkin 1981b, 266). In light of this circumstance, the discussions at the conference on the effectiveness of monetary policy and the problems created by price and wage controls, and quantity rationing, cannot be considered to have been representative of the economics profession at large.

The contributors to the 1951 *REStat* symposium were more representative of the profession's views. The symposium's centerpiece was a paper, "The Controversy over Monetary Policy: Introductory Remarks," authored by Seymour Harris, then editor of *REStat*.[44] The commentators on Harris's paper were Friedman, Lester Chandler, James Tobin, and two of the commentators on Mints's 1946 paper "Monetary Policy"—Hansen and Lerner.[45] To provide a flavor of professional thinking on monetary policy at the time of the Korean War, I briefly describe the views on monetary and fiscal policies, and on controls, of the contributors to the symposium. I present the comments in the order presented in *REStat*.

*Harris, 1.* Harris provided the "Introductory Remarks" for the symposium. He began his paper by observing that a debate had erupted about the role of monetary policy in combating inflation: "In the year 1951, the debate is hot" (Harris 1951a, 179). His initial position was that "monetary policy [i.e., a change in the interest rate] has a place in the anti-inflationary fight," but he subsequently abandoned that position (Harris 1951a, 183). His policies for containing inflation evinced support for wide-ranging government intervention in economic affairs. He favored "heavier taxes and compulsory loans (*i.e.*, tax loans) . . . together with income control and, where necessary, adequate price and supply controls" (Harris 1951a, 1984). For good measure, he advocated the "segmentation of markets, with the government security market protected by provision of special supports; the banks are to hold special reserves in government securities" (Harris 1951a, 183). Harris was very critical of Douglas's successful efforts to deliver independence to the Fed. Harris foresaw that Douglas's efforts would have an "unstabilizing effect on the government security market, and . . . adverse effects on the economy" (Harris 1951a, 182). What, then, was Harris's position on the role of monetary policy as an anti-inflation tool? In contradiction to his beginning remarks, near the end of his paper, Harris stated: "I insist that it is not likely to play an important part." On what basis did he reach that conclusion? Harris wrote: "Its relegation to a secondary role rests not only on history but also on the development of Keynesian economics [which attacks] . . . the problem [of inflation] through fiscal policy" (Harris 1951a, 183).

*Chandler.* Chandler was invited to participate in the symposium because he was expected to be "sympathetic . . . to greater use of monetary weapons" (Harris 1951b, 198). Indeed, Chandler turned out to be sympathetic to monetary-policy tools, but not to the kind of tools that operated on the quantity of money. Chandler criticized Harris's paper because it presented "too narrow a concept of monetary policy and its modus operandi," which "as a result [Harris] underestimates the effectiveness of monetary policy" (Chandler 1951, 185). Chandler argued that, in addition to affecting economic activity by changing interest rates, "monetary policy includes a wide variety of actions by a central bank, ranging all the way from warnings and statements of intention to overt acts affecting reserve requirements, the availability of bank reserves, and so on" (Chandler 1951, 185). Chandler did *not* mention the effect of monetary policy on the quantity of money; nor did he express a view on price and wage controls. He supported credit-rationing policies (Chandler 1951, 185).

*Friedman.* Friedman was critical of Harris's paper, pointing out that Harris began the paper with the argument that monetary policy had a role to play in combating inflation, but inexplicably concluding at the end of the paper that monetary policy did *not* have a role to play. Friedman viewed monetary and fiscal measures as "substitutes within a wide range." He maintained that "monetary and fiscal measures are the only appropriate means of controlling inflation. Direct controls—price and wage ceilings, the rationing or allocation of goods, qualitative credit controls—are not appropriate means of controlling inflation" (Friedman 1951c, 187). He expressed the view that, besides being weak instruments for controlling inflation, "direct controls hinder production and distribution, and threaten the foundations of a free society" (Friedman 1951c, 187).

Friedman maintained that a combination of monetary and fiscal policies was needed to prevent inflation. As he had argued at the Chicago conference, he stated that a "good" combination would consist of "a roughly balanced budget" and a monetary policy directed exclusively toward the prevention of inflation. Pending long-run reform of the monetary and banking structures, monetary-policy implementation should take the form of open-market sales of government securities. Friedman stated: "control of the quantity of money through open market operations can and should be a major instrument for controlling inflation" (Friedman 1951c, 188). No consideration should be given, he argued, to the effect of monetary policy on the rate of interest on government securities (Friedman 1951c, 187). Nevertheless, he stated that he did not endorse the use of discretionary open-market operations as a permanent instrument. As a matter of long-run reform, Friedman (1951c, 188) stated: "I would like to see the Federal Reserve System in its present form abolished and replaced by a 100 per cent reserve deposit banking system in which there was no monetary authority possessing discretionary powers over the quantity of money." Underlying that argument was the view that Friedman had expressed in his 1948 *AER* paper: in the absence of a central bank that engages in open-market operations, changes in the money supply would be produced via the government's fiscal position.

Two points regarding Friedman's positions are important to mention. First, in his presentation of the channels through which monetary policy operated, Friedman stated that the "process can be described in either of two alternative languages—that of the quantity theory or of Keynesian analysis" (Friedman 1951c, 189). The juxtaposition of the quantity theory with the Keynesian framework would become a recurrent feature of Friedman's work in the 1950s and after. Friedman proceeded to describe the effects of a tightening of monetary policy using Keynesian language. A rise in interest would reduce investment—which, Friedman argued, included consumer expenditure on durable goods and housing—with the extent of the reduction dependent on the interest elasticity of investment. The interest-rate rise would also reduce consumption in two ways. (1) It would reduce the propensity to consume. (2) It would reduce the capitalized value of future income streams, or wealth. The extent of the rise in the interest rate would depend on the magnitude of inflationary pressure—the volume of attempted expenditure that needed to be reduced—and the interest elasticities of the investment and consumption schedules. The liquidity preference function determined how much the quantity of money had to be reduced to produce the necessary rise in the interest rate (Friedman 1951c, 190).

The second point is that Friedman provided distance between his view on the effectiveness of open-market operations and Simons's view. As we have seen, Simons did not believe that those operations would be effective because they involved the exchange of one financial instrument, money, for another instrument, Treasury securities, the latter of which Simons considered to be an essentially perfect substitute for base money. If Treasury securities were perfect substitutes for base money, they could be exchanged with certainty for money at their face value, and the exchange would not alter interest rates. Friedman, it will be recalled, held a similar view in his 1948 *AER* paper. In his 1951 symposium paper, Friedman held a different view:

> The mere substitution of bonds for money is of no importance *per se*: it makes no difference which asset people hold except as their (spending) behavior, or the behavior of someone else, is influenced by their asset holdings; if they were willing to exchange the one asset for the other at no change in the price of securities, this would be a clear indication that they were indifferent which they held; the fact that the price of securities must be reduced to make them willing to hold more means that they are not indifferent. Hence an open market sale can be said to prevent inflation only insofar as it affects "the" rate of interest. (Friedman 1951c, 189)

If Treasury securities and money were *not* perfect substitutes, to bring about portfolio equilibrium an open-market sale of Treasury securities would lower their price and increase their yield. In those circumstances, open-market operations would be effective.

*Alvin Hansen.* Hansen argued that monetary policy could be useful in helping to prevent inflation; he also argued that "no monetary policy, short of a destructively deflationary one, could have prevented *some* increase in the general price level once the Korean episode suddenly broke loose" (emphasis in original, Hansen 1951, 193). To control inflation, "primary emphasis must be placed on fiscal policy, inclusive of increased taxation, and control of non-defense expenditures; on an increase in saving; and on curtailing investment by qualitative (selective) methods" (Hansen 1951, 194). The qualitative methods included (1) real estate credit control, (2) controls on construction permits, (3) direct control of plant and equipment allocations, (4) inventory control, (5) control of capital issues, and (6) tax schemes to curtail investment (Hansen 1951, 191). Hansen also favored the use of quantitative monetary controls to limit the availability of credit. These latter controls included loan quotas applied to individual banks, thereby freezing the maximum limit of loans to the volume outstanding at a certain date, and a special tax on bank loans.

*Abba Lerner.* Lerner believed that *both* tighter fiscal policy and tighter monetary policy produced undesirable results because they restrained inflation by curtailing output. He held a purely cost-push view of inflation. "The root of the inflationary process," he asserted, "is the very high level of employment" (Lerner 1951, 195). The high level of employment raises the bargaining power of labor "to a point where wage increases are easily obtained and passed on in higher prices of the product.... And so we have inflation" (Lerner 1951, 196). What is needed, he argued, is a "plan" that "will permit individual wage rates to be adjusted in response to change in the relationship between the demand and the supply in the particular labor market, while keeping the average level of wages from rising very much in relation to the increase in productivity." The criterion to be used in determining wages would be "the relationship between the number of men ready and able to take jobs in the particular labor market and the number of men actually employed in it." This ratio, which Lerner called "the index of relative attractiveness," in conjunction with the national average of such ratios, would determine whether the wage (adjusted for productivity) in the labor market in question should be increased — and, if so, by how much (Lerner 1951, 196).

*James Tobin.* Tobin began his paper with a comment aimed at Friedman: "The evangelical advocacy of monetary restriction which has characterized much recent discussion of anti-inflationary policy has been coupled with an equally fervent opposition to direct controls." Tobin's view was very different. He maintained that "in the present circumstances, direct controls are a more useful adjunct to anti-inflationary fiscal policy than monetary restriction" (Tobin 1951b, 196). Underpinning his policy view was his belief that the economy was facing two distinct "species" of inflation: demand-pull pressures, or "gap" inflation, and cost-push pressures, or "income" inflation. Fiscal policy, he argued, was the most effective way to address "gap" inflation. "Only direct controls of wages and prices," Tobin argued, "can be relied upon" to prevent cost-push inflation (Tobin 1951b, 197). What about the role of monetary policy? Tobin argued that "effective monetary policy would require such a large and rapid increase in interest rates that the accompanying capital losses would be almost as unpalatable to holders of liquid assets as inflation itself" (Tobin 1951b, 198).

*Seymour Harris, 2.* Harris had the last word in the debate. He concluded the symposium with "Summary and Comments." The symposium, he observed, had been motivated by the following: "In the last few years a hot controversy has raged concerning the contribution of monetary policy toward the fight against inflation" (Harris 1951b, 198). He noted that Hansen, Lerner, and Tobin had taken his side in the debate given that they tried "to deflate the current campaign in favor of monetary policy" (Harris 1951b, 199). Harris pointed out that Friedman's position was extreme, noting that on the issue of rationing policies, "Professors Friedman and Chandler part company"—Friedman was against rationing while Chandler was in favor of rationing. Harris summarized his own view of the matter as follows: "Monetary policy has been a failure over the last 35 years" (Harris 1951b, 199).

*Discussion*

Friedman was the only one of the six participants in the *REStat* symposium to argue that monetary policy, in combination with a balanced budget, would be sufficient to contain wartime inflation. He was the only participant to define monetary policy in terms of its effects on the quantity of money and to oppose all forms of controls, including rationing policies. The other participants, with the partial exception of Chandler, viewed monetary policy as a weak instrument. Essentially, the 1951 *REStat* symposium was a repeat performance of the 1946 *REStat* symposium in which

Mints represented the Chicago tradition's views; both symposia pitted the Chicago position on money against views that were representative of the rest of the profession. There was, however, an underlying difference between the intellectual backdrops of the two symposia. In contrast to 1946, in 1951 the debate about the role of monetary policy had turned, as Harris stated, "hot." In contrast to 1946, in 1951 the advocacy of tight monetary policy to control inflation was viewed, as Tobin stated, "evangelical." Thus, in the early 1950s, the profession had begun to pay increased attention, and responded with increased agitation, to the views of the Chicago monetary tradition. We shall soon encounter more evidence of this agitation in the persona of Paul Samuelson.

## 7.4 Friedman: The Road to Monetarism 1

Ed Nelson (2020, 1:152) wrote that "in the years spanning 1948 to 1951, Friedman's views on monetary economics underwent a dramatic shakeup, from which emerged his familiar monetarist position." As I documented in chapter 6, Friedman's 1948 papers on money—"A Monetary and Fiscal Framework for Economic Stability," published in the *AER*, and the unpublished "Preliminary Plan for Completion of Data for Study of Monetary Factors in Business Cycles"—were very much within the Simons-Mints (of the 1940s) quantity-theory playbook. Those papers featured the idea that exogenous shifts in velocity, exacerbated by the destabilizing character of the fractional-reserve banking system, accounted for the "inherent instability" of the economic system. In 1948, Friedman called for 100 percent reserves, a policy rule under which money-supply changes would automatically be generated through the government's fiscal position, and flexible exchange rates. Under Friedman's 1948 proposal, open-market operations would be abolished. From the late 1940s to the late 1950s, Friedman's views on money would change in the following ways.

- He came to believe that the demand for money exhibited functional stability. Velocity, the reciprocal of money demand, he found, followed a secular downward trend. Thus, exogenous changes in velocity were not the source of the business cycle.
- Changes in the money supply, in the absence of changes in fiscal policy, precipitated turning points in the business cycle and were the primary determinant of inflation in the long run.

- Open-market operations, and not the government's fiscal position, were the preferred way of changing the supply of money.
- The Federal Reserve possessed the ability to determine the money supply through its control over the monetary base, offsetting changes in the ratios underlying the money multiplier. In any case, the multiplier could be viewed as stable or having a smooth trend.
- The 100 percent reserve scheme was a desirable, but not an essential, requirement for economic stability.
- The Federal Reserve both initiated and greatly exacerbated the Great Depression. The Fed's role in that episode was key to understanding the damaging consequences of discretionary policies.
- Monetary policy should be based on a rule—but not the 1948 fiscal-based rule. The preferred rule was one under which the money supply would grow at an annual rate of 3 to 5 percent to achieve an approximately stable price level.

What caused Friedman's monetary economics to undergo "a dramatic shakeup" in the several years after 1948? His ongoing work with Anna Schwartz played a significant role, but that work was not the entire story. The several years after the initiation of the Friedman and Schwartz research project in 1948 were devoted mainly to data collection and data construction. That work led to a publication, "Price, Income, and Monetary Changes in Three Wartime Periods," published in the *AER* in May 1952. Friedman presented the paper at the December 1951 meetings of the American Economic Association; he referred to the findings of that study at the April 1951 Chicago conference. Although the results presented in that publication contributed to Friedman's emerging monetarism, it accounted for only part of Friedman's changing views. For example, the results did not explain Friedman's switch to open-market operations conducted by the Fed as the preferred monetary instrument since the Fed did not exist in the Civil War and, once it was established, did not start experimenting with open-market operations until after World War I.

To shed light on the way Friedman's views on money changed in the early 1950s, and the reasons for the change, I discuss evidence from the following sources: (1) an unpublished 1949 document, "Outline of Work in the First Phase of the Banking Study: Cyclical Behavior of the Quantity and Rate of Use of Circulating Media," prepared as a status report on his work with Schwartz; (2) the 1951 article "Commodity-Reserve Currency," published in the *Journal of Political Economy*; (3) an unpublished

1951 document, "The Role of the Monetary and Banking System in the Business Cycle," also prepared as a status update of Friedman's collaboration with Schwartz; (4) Friedman's May 1952 *AER* article, mentioned above; and (5) Friedman's testimonies in January 1952 and March 1952, respectively, before the US Congress's Joint Committee on the Economic Report. I discuss these materials in the order presented above.[46] The materials reveal the influence of Friedman's cross-fertilization with Mints; in some key ways, changes in Friedman's views corresponded with changes in Mints's views. The materials also reveal the substantial influence of the ideas set forth by Clark Warburton. Warburton, we saw, influenced Mints. As we shall see, he influenced Friedman even more.

*1949, unpublished document* (Friedman 1949c). The eleven-page 1949 unpublished document "Outline of Work in the First Phase of the Banking Study: Cyclical Behavior of the Quantity and Rate of Use of Circulating Media" presented an analytic framework similar to that in Friedman's two 1948 papers on money, but in the 1949 document Friedman left open the possibility that changes in the quantity of money could be the primary mover of the business cycle, with changes in velocity playing a secondary role. In raising that possibility, Friedman cited Warburton.

As he had in the earlier (Friedman 1948b) unpublished document prepared for his work with Schwartz, in the 1949 document, Friedman underscored the passive role played by changes in the money supply in the business cycle: "Casual study of the data and other studies suggest that . . . the quantity of circulating media *responds* sluggishly to cyclical movements, skipping many minor movements and *reacting* to major movements only after a considerable lag" (emphasis added, 1949c, 1). Friedman added, however, that deviations in the money supply from its trend could lead turning points in economic activity: "Such studies as have claimed a more sensitive relation [of the quantity of money] to cyclical fluctuations (*e.g., those by Warburton*) find it in deviations from trends and in particularly sensitive components of the money supply" (emphasis added, Friedman 1949c, 1).[47]

In Warburton's work on secular trends, that researcher had found that money-supply changes were the primary mover of the business cycle. Warburton also found that a decline in velocity was a secondary, intensifying force in the cycle, but not the initiating force, contrary to Friedman's views in 1949. Thus, after citing Warburton's findings, Friedman noted that they implied that the quantity of money played a key role in generating the business cycle: "If valid they have important implications for *the possible role of monetary factors in generating cyclical fluctuations* and for the possible effectiveness of policies directed at promoting stability by controlling the volume of circulating media" (emphasis added, Friedman 1949c, 1).

*1951, JPE.* The paper "Commodity-Reserve Currency" was published in the June 1951 issue of the *JPE*; given that publication date, the paper was likely completed in 1950. The paper was mainly a critique of monetary regimes based on commodities, such as the gold standard. Friedman argued that commodity standards were costly because of such factors as the use of resources devoted to the production of money and the absence of the flexibility needed to respond to domestic shocks (1951d, 209). Consequently, Friedman favored a fiat-currency regime. That, however, raised the question: "Who is to create the fiat currency and control its issuance?" Friedman answered that "the production of fiat currency is, at it were, a natural monopoly," which explains why governments typically exercise a measure of control over the issuance of the currency. He continued: "Henry Simons ... held the view—which I share—that the creation of fiat currency should be a government monopoly" (1951d, 216–17).

The policy proposals in the 1951 *JPE* paper were a carryover from 1948. Friedman advocated the 100 percent reserves scheme, partly because it would permit banks' lending and investing activities to be free of government control. Moreover, "though [the scheme] is not the only way to eliminate the *inherent instability* of the monetary system, it is a satisfactory way" (emphasis added, 1951d, 220). Friedman continued to espouse his 1948 proposal to use the government's fiscal position to change the money supply. To promote domestic stability, foreign exchanges would be freely determined (1951d, 242). Open-market operations would be abolished.

The article contained one new element although Friedman did not assess its significance. Specifically, Friedman noted that velocity appeared to have been following a long-term downward trend: "In fact, the velocity of circulation has apparently been declining at the rate of something over 1 per cent per year, which would mean that something over a 4 per cent per year addition to the circulating medium would have been required for stable prices" (1951d, 210).

The source that Friedman cited for the velocity estimate was Warburton's 1949 article "The Secular Trend in Monetary Velocity," published in the *Quarterly Journal of Economics* (*QJE*). In his article, Warburton noted that the income velocity of circulation of money declined by about

1½ percent per year from 1919 to 1947 (Warburton 1949, 199).[48] Warburton raised the issue: "Is the apparent downward trend since World War I in the circuit velocity of money a true secular trend?" (Warburton 1949, 197). Alternatively, was that decline in velocity, as Albert Hart (1945) had argued, "a fiction"? To shed light on the issue, Warburton extended the data sample back to 1799 and found that the trend held over the entire period: "These data indicate that the downward trend in monetary velocity is not of recent origin, since it apparently extends back a century and a half" (1949, 199). Hence, Warburton concluded that the decline would continue.[49] Moreover, he argued that velocity had not been an initiating factor in the business cycle but that it accompanied or followed deviations of money growth from its trend. As Warburton (1949, 213) put it: "There is no evidence that disturbances to economic equilibrium originate in an erratic rate of use of money [i.e., from velocity], but there is much evidence that such disturbances [in the quantity of money] result in, and are in turn intensified by, variations from trend in the rate of use of money."

A related point is important. In both Friedman's 1951 *JPE* article and his 1948 *AER* article, his two substantive published works on money during the period 1948 to 1951, Friedman highlighted the "inherent instability" of the monetary system, but he said *nothing* about the role played by the Federal Reserve as an instigator or facilitator of that instability. To be sure, both at Mont Pèlerin in 1947 and in a 1949 "Rejoinder" to comments on his 1948 *AER* paper, Friedman referred to the role played by Fed's interest-rate hikes in the autumn of 1931 (after September, when Britain abandoned the gold standard) in the Great Depression. Friedman's critiques of the Fed on those occasions, however, were succinct and temperate. During the conference of the Mont Pèlerin Society, Friedman referred to the Fed's policy tightening in the fall of 1931 as follows: "The big error was that of 1931" (quoted from Cherrier 2011, 353). In his 1949 *AER* "Rejoinder," the extent of Friedman's criticism of the Fed was a single sentence: "The Federal Reserve System has operated under highly advantageous circumstances, yet I think it likely that on balance its discretionary action has been destabilizing, the most striking example being the sharp deflationary action it took in the fall of 1931" (1949a, 950).[50] Those remarks were much more restrained than the criticisms made by Mints in the late 1940s and early 1950s and, as we shall see, by Warburton.

*1951, unpublished document* (Friedman 1951e). The five-page document "The Role of the Monetary and Banking System in the Business Cycle" provided another status report on Friedman's work with Schwartz.[51]

There was no mention of the role played by the fractional-reserve system in the business cycle and no mention of the "inherent instability" of the monetary system. For the first time, Friedman assigned a *causal* role to changes in the quantity of money in major cycles and a passive role to monetary changes in minor cycles. He wrote:

> On the analytical side, the tentative hypothesis suggested to me by the evidence is that the monetary system has played a very different role in the minor cycles and the severe cycles. The reactions in the minor cycles appear to be essentially passive responses to changes occurring elsewhere. I do not mean that the monetary reactions have had no influence but simply that they have not been the major initiating factors. On the other hand, in the major cycles, there is evidence that monetary reactions have played an active and important role. Put differently, monetary changes may well have been the primary factor responsible for converting mild movements into extreme movements. (1951e, 2)

In the unpublished 1948 document, prepared for his work with Schwartz, Friedman (1948b, 9) had singled out the role played by "monetary and banking phenomena" in the business cycle, by which he meant autonomous shifts in velocity and the destabilizing effects of movements from demand deposits to hand-to-hand currency under fractional-reserve banking. The role attached to "monetary reactions" in the above quotation was of a different character. After stating that "monetary changes" had been the "primary factor" in converting "mild" business cycles into "extreme" business cycles, Friedman stressed the Fed's role in the Great Depression. He wrote: "I think there is very good reason to believe that the great depression might have ended in late 1931 or early 1932 if it had not been for the monetary action taken by the Federal Reserve System in the fall of 1931. This hypothesis is as yet, of course, exceedingly tentative, and requires expansion and testing" (1951e, 2–3). Thus, in contrast to his 1948 position, Friedman placed the Fed's policy at the forefront of major cycles. On the policy side, Friedman was brief: "I have made some suggestions about an appropriate monetary and fiscal framework"; he then referred to his 1948 *AER* paper.

Consequently, beginning in 1951, Friedman stopped emphasizing the idea of an "inherently unstable" monetary system—excluding the 1951 *JPE* paper, which was likely written in 1950. He had begun to consider the hypothesis that changes in the money supply, produced by Federal Reserve policies—and not autonomous changes in velocity—were the big, bad actor in major business cycles; those policies explained the severity of the Great Depression. That hypothesis, and the related hypothesis that the Fed initiated the Great Depression, needed to be empirically confirmed.[52] As I will show, it took Friedman several years to do so. In the meantime, in the absence of empirical evidence inconsistent with his initial hypothesis that the economy was "inherently unstable," in the early 1950s Friedman continued to advocate the main elements of his 1948 policy package.

*1952, AER.* In the 1952 paper, Friedman presented evidence on the determinants of inflation during the Civil War, World War I, and World War II based on data he had constructed with Schwartz. Friedman (1952, 158) pointed out that "in all three cases the rise in prices was almost of precisely the same magnitude, so this critical variable is under control."[53] The determinants of the three inflations that he assessed were the following: (1) federal expenditures in each year as a fraction of national income; (2) the fraction of government expenditures financed through taxes; (3) the increase in output in each war; (4) wage and price controls; and (5) the quantity of money per until of output (Friedman 1952, 158–59). Friedman found that price behavior was proximately explained by the stock of money per unit of output; it could not be satisfactorily explained by an analysis that excluded the stock of money.[54] He also found that none of the other variables helped to explain any of the three inflations.

As in his contribution to the August 1951 *REStat* symposium, Friedman juxtaposed the quantity theory with the Keynesian income-expenditure framework. In his 1952 *AER* paper, however, Friedman went further. He interpreted the quantity theory in a way that was considerably removed from the unstable-velocity version that he had inherited from his Chicago predecessors. In this connection, Friedman argued that the respective theories could each be translated into the language of the other. Consequently, they could be viewed as different frameworks of analysis. He then stated:

> But I take it that the major issue has been about the theories, not as alternative languages, but about empirical hypotheses. In this sense they are different and competitive: the quantity theory asserts in essence that *the velocity of circulation of money is the empirical variable that behaves in a stable or consistent fashion*; the income-expenditure theory, that the propensity to consume, or the consumption function, is the empirical variable that behaves in a stable or consistent fashion. (emphasis added, 1952, 166)

Friedman interpreted the findings in his paper to be consistent with the quantity-theory view of price-level determination.

As noted, Friedman presented the paper at the December 1951 meetings of the American Economic Association. Therefore, by the end of 1951 Friedman had come to the view that a core characteristic of quantity theory was that the velocity of circulation of money behaved in a stable way. However, while the findings presented in the 1952 *AER* paper were consistent with the predictions of the quantity theory, they did not *directly* tackle the issue of the stability of velocity.

*Congressional testimony, January 1952.* On January 31, 1952, Friedman appeared before the US Congress.[55] As he had argued both at the April 1951 Chicago conference and in his paper for the 1951 *REStat* symposium, Friedman maintained that a combination of fiscal policy and monetary policy was needed to contain inflation: "A surplus and an easy money policy, or a deficit and a tight money policy, may have the same combined effect in preventing inflation" (Joint Committee 1952, 334). He maintained that monetary policy, implemented by open-market operations supported "by appropriate rediscount policies," to control member bank reserves, should bear the brunt of any sudden emergence of inflationary pressure (Joint Committee 1952, 334). Friedman also expressed the view that, given the size of a particular fiscal deficit, the way that the deficit is financed affects economic activity. In particular, if the deficit were financed by borrowing from the private sector at whatever interest rate were required, the bond-financed deficits would raise interest rates and, thus, stimulate saving (thereby, reducing consumption); in contrast, money-financed deficits would likely reduce the incentive to save. Thus, money-financed deficits, he advised, would be inflationary whereas bond-financed deficits would be more consistent with a stable price level (Joint Committee 1952, 335).

*Congressional testimony, March 1952.* On March 25, 1952, Friedman again appeared before the US Congress.[56] His arguments during that testimony are key to understanding his conversion from a quantity theorist of the Simons-Mints (of the 1940s) character to a monetarist. Also appearing before Congress on that date was Paul Samuelson.[57] The two economists provided contrasting views about the role of money in economic activity. Friedman's testimony showed that his views on money had changed since 1950–51.

In a prepared statement, Friedman referred to the findings in his 1952 *AER* article. Citing those findings, he maintained that there was a strong relationship between changes in money and prices:

> There is scarcely a case on record in which a substantial rise in the stock of money over a short period has not been accompanied by a substantial rise in

prices, or in which a substantial rise in prices has occurred without a substantial rise in the stock of money. And a similar proposition is valid for declines in prices. There is scarcely a case on record in which a substantial decline in the stock of money over a short period has not been accompanied by a substantial decline in prices, or in which a substantial decline in prices has occurred without a substantial decline in the stock of money. (Subcommittee 1952, 688)

Friedman pointed out that he was not claiming that the relationship between money and prices is a precise one since the relationship depended on the demand for money (or velocity). However, he argued that "there is ample evidence . . . that such changes in attitudes toward holding money [i.e., velocity] are seldom large, at least over short periods of time, if they are not reinforced by changes in the stock of money in the wrong direction. Equally important, they can be offset by compensating changes in the stock of money and so prevented from influencing prices" (Subcommittee 1952, 689). This observation, he argued, held both in times of war and in normal periods.

Friedman maintained that the Federal Reserve possessed ample powers to have prevented inflation both in the post–World War II period and during the Korean War. Specifically, the Fed could have conducted open-market sales with the aim of reducing the money supply to achieve price stability. What prevented its doing so? The Fed, he argued, lacked "the will" because its policies aimed at "avoiding incidental effects on the prices of government bonds rather than [pursuing] . . . the major objective of preventing inflation." Friedman added that there was some evidence that the Fed "has been following [an anti-inflation] policy since the accord with the Treasury of a year ago" (Subcommittee 1952, 689).

Friedman noted that, although he had advocated "discretionary open market operations" to bring about price stability, this circumstance did not mean that he endorsed such operations as a permanent instrument of stabilization. He then launched into a critique of the Fed's historical performance.

Despite the prevailing belief to the contrary, I am convinced that the Federal Reserve System has failed to promote the objectives for which it was established, and that this conclusion is abundantly supported by the historical evidence. The System facilitated inflation in two world wars, permitted or promoted unnecessary inflation immediately after both wars, had much to do with making the great depression of the 1930's as deep as it was, and even failed in the one function that its founders were most convinced it would perform: namely, the prevention of a banking panic. I do not believe that the failure of the System reflects ignorance or incompetence, or malice on the part of the group of men who have guided its destinies. On the contrary, they seem to me an unusually well-informed, able, and public-spirited group. I therefore believe that the solution, if there be one, lies in a fundamental reform of our monetary institutions. (Subcommittee 1952, 691)[58]

Friedman concluded with a call to abolish the Fed and to have it replaced with a 100 percent reserve banking system in which there was no monetary authority possessing discretionary powers over the quantity of money.

Several points are important. First, Friedman stated that (1) there is a strong relationship between money and prices, and (2) the Fed had the power to control the money supply and, thus, inflation. It follows that causation ran primarily from the quantity of money to inflation, and not the other way around. Second, Friedman claimed that velocity, or the demand for money, was essentially stable. If velocity changed in the short run, that change could be countered by open-market operations. As discussed, in the early 1950s Mints had come around to the view that changes in velocity could be offset through open-market operations. Third, Friedman commenced what would be a career-long public criticism of the Fed's performance in the Great Depression. Finally, although Friedman recognized that open-market operations were an effective policy instrument, his proposal that the Fed should be abolished implied that such operations would have to be discontinued.

*Friedman versus Samuelson.* In his prepared statement before the Subcommittee, Samuelson asserted that the idea that monetary policy could operate on the quantity of money was a "sophomoric fallacy." He alleged that it was not possible to identify the quantity of money because "the quantity of money is a fabricated concept." Instead, he maintained that "the real problem of monetary policy open to the central-bank authorities is the problem of its effects upon the cost and availability of credit to spenders" (Subcommittee 1952, 692–93).

Following the prepared statements by the economists appearing before the Subcommittee, a general discussion ensued. One of the issues raised was the validity of the quantity-theory equation, $MV = PT$. Samuelson wrote off the equation as a collection of unobservable terms: "the current edition of the Encyclopaedia Britannica mentions this formula $MV$ equals $PT$, and it says of the four [terms], three are completely unobservable, and must be constructed, and on the basis of my provocative testimony this morning, the fourth [i.e., $M$] has been brought into suspicion" (Subcommittee 1952, 720).

Friedman's view was orthogonal to Samuelson's. Friedman maintained that the quantity equation should be restated with real income, $Y$, replacing transactions, $T$. In that form, "the quantity equation can be defended . . . as one of the few empirically correct generalizations that we have uncovered in economics from the evidence of centuries" (Subcommittee 1952, 720). He noted that, while velocity varied over short periods, "these variations . . . are in general relatively small" (Subcommittee 1952, 720).

As mentioned earlier, during the 1940s Friedman had joined Simons and Mints in assuming that money and Treasury securities were essentially perfect substitutes. That assumption underpinned their view that open-market operations were not an effective instrument since those operations involved the exchange of financial instruments that were essentially identical. Consequently, to motivate holders of Treasury securities to accept more money in exchange for Treasury securities in their portfolios, there was no need of a change in the interest rate on Treasury securities. This assumption was realistic during the period from the early 1940s to the early 1950s, when the Fed pegged the price of Treasury securities, but it no longer applied after the accord commenced. Friedman thought that the change was critical. During the discussion at the congressional hearings, he stated: "When the Federal Reserve dropped the peg on Government bonds, Government bonds ceased to be as close a substitute for money proper as they had been before. They were no longer immediately convertible into money at a known price" (Subcommittee 1952, 721). The fact that money and Treasury securities ceased to be close substitutes opened the door for Friedman to come to believe that changes in the money supply generated via open-market operations could be as effective as money-supply changes produced through the government's fiscal position.

The March 25, 1952, congressional hearings brought out other differences between Friedman and Samuelson, in terms of both substance and personal style. On substance, Samuelson held both a demand-pull theory and a cost-push theory of inflation; wage hikes caused prices to rise, and vice versa, resulting in inflation (Subcommittee 1952, 723). As noted, Friedman argued that inflation is a monetary phenomenon. He stated: "I think the so-called wage-price spiral has been enormously exaggerated, that what we have had has been inflationary pressures pulling both wages and prices up. If we had had a reasonable level of price stability, I think we would not have had much trouble from the so-called wage-price spiral" (Subcommittee 1952, 727). He added that if organized groups were able to push wages or prices up, the way to tackle the problem was by eliminating "the monopolistic conditions" that underpinned the wage-cost pressures. Samuelson believed that there were "certain dilemmas of policy." Specifically, it was not possible to attain both "stable average prices . . . and at the same time . . . maximum employment and production" (Subcommittee 1952, 722). Friedman argued that it *would be* possible to attain both "price stability" and "a high level of output for the economy as a whole" (Subcommittee 1952, 726). Price stability, he argued, would promote a high level of output by providing stable expectations.

On the matter of differences in personal style, Friedman's interventions were matter-of-fact, whereas Samuelson's were marked with sarcastic remarks, typically aimed at Friedman's positions. Friedman did not react to those remarks. Here are some examples of Samuelson's style.

- *Monetary policy*. "The first view [i.e., Friedman's view] . . . and I will overstate this in order to be provocative, is the almost completely fallacious view that the purpose of credit policy is not to affect the cost or availability of credit so much as rather to affect the quantity of money in existence" (Subcommittee 1952, 693).
- *The quantity theory*. "I myself would not make too much of the point that the definition of money is a shifting one, because I have not had the good success that Mr. Friedman has had in the predictive power of this truism" (Subcommittee 1952, 721).
- *The quantity theory*. "Just as I did not believe in the case for tight money because of the previous flimsy argument [made by Friedman] so the backfiring of this argument does not shake my faith. It is strange however that Mother Nature should have played so cruel a trick on the quantity theory. It is not usually so wrong a formula" (Subcommittee 1952, 722).
- *Friedman's use of data*. "Now, it is true that retrospectively I can go over the data, as Mr. Friedman has just done, and find that a slight change in the definition of money . . . will make my retrospective predictions better" (Subcommittee 1952, 721).
- *The empirical validity of the quantity theory*. "In economics empirical correlations are a dime a dozen, and one of the disadvantages of a flimsy argument is that it weakens the good cause that you are favoring" (Subcommittee 1952, 721).

After the session, Friedman submitted a supplemental statement that was included in the *Congressional Record*. In that statement, he expressed the view that income velocity was "a reasonably stable magnitude" and that it had declined over time—from "around 4½ to 5 in the Civil War" to "currently around 1½." He proposed that in the short run the Fed be given a mandate to promote "reasonable stability in the general level of prices," using open-market operations to achieve that objective (Subcommittee 1952, 743). For the long run, Friedman presented a summary of all the elements contained in his 1948 *AER* paper, referring the reader to that paper.

## 7.5 Friedman and Warburton

As documented, the several years after 1948 saw a substantial modification in Friedman's perception of the role of money in the economy. In his June 1951 *JPE* paper "Commodity-Reserve Currency," likely written in 1950, Friedman carried forward his late 1940s view that the monetary system is "inherently unstable" under the fractional-reserve banking system. Friedman's unpublished 1951 memorandum "The Role of the Monetary and Banking System" provided a different perspective. That memorandum did not mention the role of fractional-reserve banking. Instead, Friedman put forward the "tentative hypothesis" that assigned a causal role to changes in the money supply in major cycles and a passive role to monetary changes in minor cycles; one tentative hypothesis that required "expansion and testing" was that the Federal Reserve deepened the Great Depression with its monetary tightening in the fall of 1931. In his 1952 *AER* paper, Friedman presented evidence, based on data from his National Bureau of Economic Research (NBER) project with Schwartz, showing that inflation in three wartime periods could be explained by the money supply per unit of output; fiscal policy, the evidence showed, played no role. He asserted that the quantity theory held that velocity is stable although he did not provide evidence directly related to that assertion. In his January 1952 congressional appearance, Friedman stated that bond-financed deficits involve crowding-out effects. In his March 1952 appearance before the Joint Committee on the Economic Report, Friedman presented the quantity theory as a causal relation running from money to prices. In the absence of the Fed's interest-rate-pegging policy, he argued that open-market operations could be an effective policy instrument. In his published work in the early 1950s, and in his supplemental statement submitted to the Joint Committee in March 1952, Friedman reverted to the policy framework provided in his 1948 *AER* paper "A Monetary and Fiscal Framework for Economic Stability."

Thus, it appears to have been the case that between the completion of (1) "Commodity-Reserve Currency" in 1950 and (2) Friedman's 1951 unpublished memorandum and his March 1952 appearance at the Joint Committee something occurred to reshape Friedman's views about the relative roles of changes in the money supply and velocity in the business cycle, the inherent-instability characteristic of fractional-reserve banking, the role of the Federal Reserve in the Great Depression, and the effectiveness of open-market operations. We saw that Mints's views on these subjects also changed in the early 1950s. In Mints's case, that economist gave credit to Warburton for persuading him that changes in the money supply, and not autonomous variations in velocity, could be the primary mover of business cycles. We also saw that Friedman referred to Warburton in his (Friedman's) unpublished 1949 memorandum and his 1951 *JPE* article. Specifically, Friedman cited evidence provided by Warburton showing that disturbances in the quantity of money precipitated movements away from economic equilibrium, which, in turn, were intensified by variations away from the trend in velocity. It is time to take a closer look at Warburton, his work, and the role he appears to have played in helping shape Friedman's evolving monetary views.

Warburton (1896–1979) earned his PhD from Columbia University in 1932. In 1934, he joined the Federal Deposit Insurance Corporation (FDIC), where he continued to work until his retirement in 1965. Between 1943 and 1953, he published more than thirty articles on monetary economics, most of them empirically oriented and many in leading journals. Cargill (1981, 92) reported that "in 1953 he received pressure from the [US] Treasury to cease publishing and making presentations, marking a sudden stop to his research productivity." Warburton did not resume his research activities until 1962, when he was temporarily employed by the House Banking Committee. After retiring from the FDIC, he taught for one year at the University of California, Davis. In a tribute to Warburton, Cargill—who was one of three students who attended a seminar offered by Warburton at Davis—recounted that "he [Warburton] did not have a dynamic personality and was not comfortable in a classroom environment" (Cargill 1981, 90). Cargill also recounted a revealing classroom incident: "To my suggestion that he must be pleased that the Friedman and Schwartz evidence was being seriously debated in the profession, he [Warburton] responded with utter frustration because he had argued many of the same points during the 1940s and early 1950s and had been ignored" (Cargill 1981, 90).

Using the Fisherine equation of exchange, Warburton stressed the importance of empirical verification of competing theories.[59] He employed both quarterly and annual data in his empirical studies and compared series of deviations of money and velocity from their trend values using standard NBER reference dates of business cycle peaks and troughs. His studies provided evidence showing that deviations from trend movements of the quantity of money generally preceded, and velocity lagged, turning points in economic activity. While accepting the validity of the quantity theory of the price level in the long run, he believed that what he called "erratic" money growth was largely responsible for economic instability. Specifically, wage and price stickiness caused monetary disturbances to be transmitted initially to output, and then to prices. As mentioned, during the late 1940s and early 1950s Warburton concluded that a 3 to 5 percent annual rate of increase in the money supply would provide stable prices at full-employment levels over the long run, mitigating extreme fluctuations in economic activity.[60]

Warburton emphasized the role of monetary policy in both precipitating and deepening the Great Depression. Since its inception, the Fed, he believed, had displayed excessive concern over the character of bank assets. As a result, it failed to guarantee convertibility between deposits and currency during the Great Depression—that is, it failed to act as a lender of last resort (1946b, 302). In addition, because of its emphasis on qualitative rather than quantitative guides to its actions, the Fed paid insufficient attention to the control of the quantity of money (1946b, 301–8). Warburton presented evidence showing that declines in the growth of bank reserves and of the money supply during the late 1920s and early 1930s to rates below their long-term trends occurred following the Fed's adoption of a tight monetary policy in the late 1920s, which, he argued, preceded the 1929 decline in economic activity by several quarters (Warburton 1950, 190).[61] Warburton believed that, throughout the Great Depression, the Fed possessed the capacity to undertake expansionary open-market operations and to discount eligible paper. These operations would have increased the money supply. He argued that, had the Fed maintained a steady money-growth rate of 3 percent per annum (the rate experienced during the period 1923–28) in the late 1920s and the early 1930s, the United States would have experienced "a moderate business depression . . . in 1930"—but not a Great Depression (Bordo and Schwartz 1979, 50).

Although Warburton's views on monetary issues predated many of the tenets of the monetarist counter-revolution, including those on the role of monetary forces during the Great Depression and monetary rules, Warburton has been treated as someone who, writing in the heyday of Keynesian economics, "was a one-man show ... [and] out of step with the [Keynesian] times" (Cargill 1981, 92). Other than providing commentary on drafts of Friedman and Schwartz's *A Monetary History* (1963) during the mid- and late 1950s, Warburton has been considered as a researcher who anticipated subsequent developments in monetary economics, but not as someone whose views directly shaped the future course of monetary economics. Thus, Bordo and Schwartz characterized Warburton as a "*forerunner* of ideas that became current long after he had first enunciated them" (emphasis added, 1979, 44) while Cargill called Warburton a "*precursor* [of] many of their ideas" as expressed in Friedman and Schwartz's *A Monetary History* (emphasis in original, 1981, 90).[62] This strictly precursor characterization of Warburton is especially surprising because in *A Monetary History* Friedman and Schwartz acknowledged Warburton as follows:

> We owe an especially heavy debt to Clark Warburton. His detailed and valuable comments on several drafts have importantly affected the final version. In addition, time and again, as we came to some conclusion that seemed to us novel and original we found that he had been there before. (1963, xiii)

In their study, Friedman and Schwartz referred to eleven of Warburton's publications. That figure is greater than the number of works they cited by any other author, including Friedman himself.

In fact, Warburton likely exerted a direct—and, possibly, a profound—impact on Friedman's monetary views at the time during which those views were undergoing a marked change. Between June 22, 1951, and November 21, 1951, Warburton and Friedman carried on a correspondence in which Warburton sharply criticized Friedman's monetary framework. The correspondence comprised thirteen letters, seven from Warburton and six from Friedman.[63] Several of the letters exceeded four single-spaced pages in length. The trigger for the correspondence was Friedman's article "Commodity Reserve Currency," which, as discussed, was published in the June 1951 issue of the *JPE*. In a letter, dated June 22, 1951, that initiated the correspondence, Warburton wrote to Friedman about the latter's policy views:

I disagree with you decidedly with respect to the desirability of attempting to control the money supply through government deficits and surpluses. Also, I think you vastly exaggerate government interference with lending and investing activities resulting from the fractional reserve system, when such a system is guided by a central bank which uses its power to promote stability of the monetary unit.

Warburton added that Friedman's framework needed to be subjected to professional assessment. He concluded the letter with: "Perhaps I may attempt this in the near future."

In a reply, dated July 6, 1951, Friedman wrote:

Re fractional reserves . . . their existence greatly complicates the task of a central bank. . . . For they mean that the central bank must continuously intervene in order to offset changes in the form in which people desire to hold their money—what I have described as the inherent instability of a fractional reserve system like our present one. You will surely grant that the task of a central bank trying to provide stability is not so easy that strictly unnecessary difficulties should be added; surely, one should try to provide as stable a framework as possible to maximize the chance that such a central bank could be successful.

As to Warburton's suggestion that he might attempt a critical assessment of Friedman's proposal, Friedman wrote: "I quite agree that someone should give my proposal a thorough going over. I hope very much that you will attempt to do so. Perhaps one of us can convert the other in the process."

By October 1951, Warburton had written a sixty-two-page draft in which he critiqued Friedman's monetary framework. Both Friedman and Mints had commented on the draft. Given the length of the opus, it was split into two separate papers, "Monetary Difficulties and the Structure of the Monetary System" and "Rules and Implements for Monetary Policy," published in the December 1952 and March 1953 issues, respectively, of the *Journal of Finance* (*JF*).[64] In what follows, I first describe the main issues covered in the correspondence between Warburton and Friedman. I then discuss Warburton's critiques of Friedman's views in his two *JF* papers.[65]

## The Correspondence

During the course of the correspondence, Warburton made the following arguments. First, the Fed failed to carry out its responsibilities as a lender of last resort in the early 1930s, thereby exacerbating the Great Depression. Second, Warburton *suggested* that the Fed, which he believed had become obsessed with the problem of speculation in the stock market, had initiated the Great Depression with its policy tightening in 1928 and 1929.[66] Third, Warburton attributed the Fed's inept policies during the Great Depression to the incompetence of Fed officials. Under the legal requirements of the early 1930s, the Fed was mandated to hold as collateral a reserve of 40 percent in gold and additional collateral of 60 percent comprising either gold or eligible paper against the issuance of Federal Reserve notes. Consequently, the conversion of bank deposits into cash—which amounted to an increase in the circulation of Federal Reserve notes—during the early 1930s meant that the Fed needed to back these notes with additional collateral—gold or eligible paper. To engage in open-market purchases—effectively, increasing the quantity of Federal Reserve notes—the Fed would have to pledge part of its holdings of gold above minimum-reserve requirements—that is, its "free gold"—or hold sufficient eligible paper on its balance sheet.[67] During the early 1930s, Federal Reserve officials pleaded that they held insufficient amounts of collateral to offset, through open-market operations and discounting operations, the effects on the quantity of money arising from shifts from deposits to currency (Friedman and Schwartz 1963, 691–93).

In his correspondence with Friedman, Warburton presented data that had been published in Federal Reserve documents of the early 1930s. The data showed that the Fed possessed sufficient collateral to reverse (through large-scale open-market operations or discounting, or a combination of the two) the increases in the currency-to-deposit ratio, and, thus, could have prevented the contraction of the money supply that took place in the early 1930s. Such actions would have increased confidence, he argued, stemming the flight from deposits to currency. Consequently, the monetary system was not, as Friedman had argued, "inherently unstable." It was *rendered* unstable during the Depression by the passive behavior of Fed officials.

### The JF Articles

Warburton's 1952 *JF* paper focused on three issues: (1) the stability characteristics of a fractional-reserve banking system; (2) Fed policy during the Great Depression; and (3) a rule for monetary policy based on money-supply growth. The paper began by noting the pronounced similarity between Friedman's proposal for monetary reform and those of Simons and Mints:

> it is similar to proposals for monetary reform developed during the past two decades by Professors Lloyd W. Mints and the late Henry C. Simons. In fact, Friedman's proposal is a combination of the "Chicago plan" for replacement of fractional bank reserves by 100 per cent reserves and a device for carrying out an assumption of Simons that "monetary policy must ultimately be implemented through fiscal arrangements." (1952, 328)

*Fractional-reserve banking and monetary stability.* A key assumption underlying Friedman's 100 percent reserves proposal, Warburton pointed out, was that the monetary system is inherently unstable because "the monetary system holds the wrong kind of assets" (1952, 329). Friedman's proposal, argued Warburton, was based on the view that the system's inherent instability could be addressed by effectuating "a drastic change . . . in the character of the assets which could be monetarized"; under the proposal, banks would hold only non-interest-bearing obligations issued by the federal government, and those obligations would comprise 100 percent of banks' deposits (1952, 329). Consequently, banks would not be able to create (or destroy) money through their lending (or deleveraging) operations with the private sector. Warburton thought that Friedman's diagnosis of the problem of monetary instability, and proposed remedy, were mistaken:

> Any monetary system has a dual character, for in issuing obligations which serve as circulating medium in the community, some person or organization of the community must be the first recipient and user, and the creation or issue of money therefore serves to finance those economic activities for which the recipient (in the case of customary banking operations, the borrower from the bank) uses the money. The proposal to eliminate obligations of business concerns and of individuals from bank assets, and to confine bank assets to government obligations, is therefore an assumption that a monetary system having the dual-purpose character of financing business enterprises and of providing circulating medium is inferior to a dual-purpose system which finances government and provides circulating medium. This argument seems to me specious. (1952, 329–30)

The key weakness in Friedman's analysis, Warburton believed, was Friedman's assumption that there would necessarily be "inherent instability in the total quantity of circulating medium whenever there are shifts

from one type of medium [e.g., demand deposits] to another [e.g., Federal
Reserve notes]" (1952, 335). Warburton continued:

> This argument rests on the assumption, which Friedman fails to make clear,
> that the amount of "reserves" is inflexible and may not be varied in accordance
> with changing amounts required when one type of deposit or currency is con-
> verted into another type. This assumption is not in accord with reality under the
> present monetary system, when "reserves" consist of deposit balances in (i.e.,
> liabilities of) a central bank with broad powers to change the amount of those
> balances by acquiring or relinquishing assets. That is to say, in discussing the
> "inherent" instability of a fractional reserve monetary system, Friedman does
> not distinguish between a banking system operating with fractional reserves
> consisting of "standard" money [e.g., gold coin] and one with reserves consist-
> ing of balances at a central bank. In fact the two systems differ profoundly from
> each other. (1952, 335)

The central difference, according to Warburton, was the following. Under
a "standard" commodity-money regime—such as the classical gold standard of the late nineteenth century—the conversion of demand deposits
into currency would lead to a contraction of reserves (since the currency—
the gold coins—had served as reserves) and, therefore, a contraction in
the quantity of money. The "problem" of "convertibility" under the gold
standard consisted of "two phases": (1) the "convertibility of deposits into
hand-to-hand currency [e.g., gold-backed notes]"; and (2) the "convertibility of currency [notes] and hence deposits also, into gold" (1952, 335).
The latter phase had been eliminated in 1933 when the United States left
the gold standard; the former phase had been addressed in 1913 with the
creation of the Federal Reserve (1952, 335).

Specifically, Warburton pointed out the Federal Reserve Act of 1913,
which established the Fed, gave that institution the ability to offset the
contractionary effects of shifts from deposits to currency on the quantity
of money (1952, 335–37). The act allowed the Fed to issue paper notes
collateralized by both gold (or gold certificates) and eligible commercial
paper. Thus, the act provided potential for an "elastic" currency. If the Fed
wanted to increase banks' reserves, it could issue Federal Reserve notes
collateralized, in part, with eligible paper. Amendments to the act in 1916
and 1917 expanded the type of collateral that could be used to issue Federal Reserve notes to include "United States government obligations, bills
of exchange purchased from member banks, [and] bankers acceptances

purchased from any source" (1952, 337). As a result, Warburton argued that "since 1917 there has been ample provision in the structure of the monetary system for convertibility of deposits into currency without producing instability through an adverse effect on bank reserves and hence on the amount of deposits or the total circulating medium" (1952, 340). Warburton continued:

> Further changes in the conditions of acquisition of assets by Federal Reserve Banks, for use either as collateral against Federal Reserve notes or as a means of increasing the reserve accounts of member banks, were made by the Glass-Steagall Act of 1932, the Banking Acts of 1933 and 1935, and by other amendments.[68] These changes have removed the vestiges of the circumstances which were thought to be obstacles to the conversion of deposits into currency, in any amount demanded by the public, without disturbance of the reserve balances of member banks. (1952, 341)

Warburton further argued that Friedman, like Simons before him, had failed to distinguish between the way the monetary system had been managed and its inherent characteristics; Friedman and Simons confused poor management with structural deficiencies:

> The arguments of Friedman and Simons regarding "inherent instability" of the present monetary system reveal a lack of discrimination between the actual characteristics of the present monetary system ... and the way the mechanism has functioned at certain times, particularly in the early 1930's. There is no doubt that inadequate functioning of this mechanism has been an important factor in economic instability since 1914, but *the difficulties have been due to the management*, rather than to the "inherent" characteristics, of this phase of the monetary machinery. (emphasis added, 1952, 336)

*Fed policy and the Great Depression.* To substantiate his argument that poor management had been the cause of economic instability, Warburton focused on the Great Depression.

First, he argued that the Fed had deepened the Depression in the early 1930s with tight policy, an argument that he had also made in his 1951 correspondence with Friedman. In his 1952 paper, Warburton wrote:

> In the early 1930's the Federal Reserve Banks virtually stopped rediscounting or otherwise acquiring "eligible" paper. This was not due to lack of eligible

paper.... [This] virtual stoppage of the rediscounting process ... was due directly
to a combination of lines of action which must have been *deliberately* pursued
by the Federal Reserve authorities, for they could not have been adopted in any
other way. These lines of action included strenuous discouragement of continuous discounting by any member bank, "direct pressure" so strong as to amount
to virtual prohibition of rediscounting for banks which were making loans for
security speculation, and a hard-boiled attitude toward banks in special need of
rediscounts because of deposit withdrawals. (emphasis added, 1952, 339)

Warburton noted that, had the Fed undertaken expansionary operations
in the early 1930s, it "might have run up against [its] own gold reserve
requirements," which, as mentioned, at that time required 40 percent gold
backing for the issuance of Federal Reserve notes (1952, 341). He pointed
out, however, that "the Federal Reserve Act provided a safeguard by giving the Federal Reserve Board power to suspend Federal Reserve [gold]
requirements" (1952, 341).

Second, Warburton criticized the Fed for its policies in 1928 and 1929.
He argued that "in 1928 and 1929 the Federal Reserve Board became
deeply concerned with the problem of excessive speculation in corporate
stocks and use of bank credit for speculative purposes.... The obsession ...
became so great that they [the authorities] abandoned the attention they
had formerly given to important economic variables such as the price level
[and] the amount of employment" (1952, 347). This shift reflected "a lack
of understanding" since "no evidence was produced at that time, nor since,
that in 1928 and the first half of 1929, when the Federal Reserve Board
acted [to tighten policy], stock values were out of line" (1952, 347).[69]

Warburton concluded that these policies had been "disastrously wrong"
(1952, 343). The Fed had been created so that it would provide an elastic
currency. In the early 1930s, however, it failed to do so. Warburton wrote:
"The necessity of keeping this principle [i.e., provision of an elastic cur-
rency] in mind in the operations of the Federal Reserve System is so obvious ... that the failure of the Federal Reserve officials to handle the System
in conformity with it in the 1930s warrants a charge of lack of adherence to
the intent of the law" (1952, 339).

Why did the Fed fail to provide an "elastic currency"? Warburton argued that, since its inception, the Fed had operated under a "discarded"
principle—that of the "real-bills" doctrine (1952, 331). Under that principle, it was assumed "that banks would provide an appropriate quantity of circulating medium if their obligations were issued on the basis of

self-liquidating commercial paper" (1952, 331). Warburton argued, however, that "the problem of providing a monetary system which promotes economic stability is *not* a problem of what *type of assets* is held by the monetary system. . . . There is no reason to assume that the quantity of any kind of asset that might be acquired by the monetary system is likely to change with the quantity of circulating medium needed for full output and price stability" (emphasis added, 1952, 330). A key requirement for economic stability, he argued, was an adequate growth rate of the money supply to meet the needs of a growing economy, as real income expanded over time, and to meet secular declines in the velocity of circulation of money.

*Monetary rule.* Noting that "during much of the period since the establishment of the Federal Reserve System, particularly in the 1930's, there has been an almost complete lack of recognition by Federal Reserve authorities of the need for growth in the money supply," Warburton argued that changes in "monetary velocity associated with inflation and depression are generally the result, respectively, of excessive increase or of contraction or absence of growth in the quantity of money" (1952, 344–45). Referring to the statistical work of Carl Snyder during the 1920s and 1930s, Warburton noted that Snyder had held the view that a growth rate of the money supply of approximately 4 percent growth per year is needed to help maintain economic stability (1952, 344).[70] In his 1952 article, Warburton did not, however, explicitly argue in favor of a constant-money-growth rule.

*The 1953 article.* In the 1953 *JF* article, Warburton focused on the problems of implementation of Friedman's proposal (1951d) to use fiscal policy to generate changes in the money supply to stabilize output at full employment.

*Price-level stabilization.* Warburton thought that price-level stabilization is an appropriate goal for monetary policy. Still, it should be pursued indirectly by focusing on a constant growth rate of the money supply, which would avoid the problem of having to specify a particular price index. He argued that there were four key problems associated with direct price-level targeting. First, there was the problem of selecting the appropriate price index. Second, no (then-existing) price index was "sufficiently comprehensive" to reflect changes in the cost of living[71] or to account for quality changes accurately (1953, 374). Third, Warburton argued that monetary policy operates by affecting business expectations. Therefore, "if we are to attain economic stability it is the basis for business men's

expectations, rather than the prices they offer . . . which needs stabilization" (1953, 375). Fourth, monetary policy operates, he believed, with a
lag. As a result, "use of any price index as a criterion for the day-to-day
decisions of a monetary authority would necessarily mean that changes in
the direction of monetary policy are always late—always in the nature of
correction of its own past errors" (1953, 375).

*Complexity of Friedman's framework.* Warburton thought that Friedman's proposal to use fiscal policy to generate changes in the money
supply was embedded with "stupendous practical difficulty" (1953, 381).
Specifically, the proposal "would necessitate, in order to operate with adequate speed and with enough but not excessive force, a tax system with
sufficient precision as to yield, shortly after depression or inflation begins,
a change in the amount of the government deficit which is identical (or
nearly) with the additional or reduced quantity of money needed for restoration of business activity to a state of full employment without price
inflation, and to accomplish this within a time short enough to prevent too
great a departure from full employment equilibrium to be borne" (1953,
381). To illustrate the practical difficulties, Warburton pointed out that,
should the tax system "fail to produce the correct size of deficit under
the condition of 'full employment,' then it would *generate* business disturbances by providing either an excessive or insufficient monetary expansion" (emphasis added, 1953, 381). As a result, the proposal would keep
the quantity of money "perpetually uncertain and perpetually productive
of serious economic disturbances" (1953, 382).

*Political manipulation.* Warburton believed that, by combining fiscal
policy with monetary policy, Friedman's proposal invited political interference in monetary decision-making. In particular, it would encourage
politicians to use the supply of money as a means of financing fiscal deficits:

> automatic issue of money as a result of a government deficit would result in
> more temptation than at present to use currency expansion as a means of
> financing government expenditures. Friedman is aware of this danger, and ar-
> gues, correctly, that avoidance of this result, in any case, depends on a willingness
> of government legislators and administrators to abide by previously accepted
> rules and development of an overwhelmingly strong tradition in favor of doing
> so. However, he does not seem to recognize that development of, and adherence
> to, such a tradition, which is hard to accomplish when the monetary system is rel-
> atively independent of government financing, would be incredibly difficult when
> the monetary system and the revenue system are completely amalgamated. His

proposal enhances the opportunity for the government to indulge for trivial reasons in sprees of currency expansion as serious as those which have resulted in the past from government financing in wartime. (1953, 382)

Moreover:

if the temptation to use currency expansion in lieu of taxes is resisted, and the government cannot borrow from non-banking investors, the government would be placing itself in a financial strait jacket. It would be impossible, for example, for the government to borrow to meet new duties or any emergency situation pending an overhauling of the tax structure or curtailment of other phases of government activity. (1953, 382)

*Constant-money-growth rule.* Warburton argued that a monetary rule should be selected on the basis of its ability to achieve as closely as possible "full output and stability of prices of final products" (1953, 377). To this end, he stated: "Pursuit of this line of thinking leads to the conclusion that the most appropriate rule of action for the monetary authorities is that of maintaining a rate of growth in the quantity of the circulating medium which will compare with the general rate of growth in the total output of final products . . . in order to maintain stability of prices of final products" (1953, 377). He added: "My statistical studies published elsewhere have suggested about 5 per cent per year as the needed rate of growth in the quantity of money in the United States" (1953, 377n8).

Warburton concluded his critique of Friedman's proposal with the following, sharp wording: "It seems to me inevitable that successful operation of the system Friedman proposes would involve such a complicated and yet such a delicately balanced set of plans and controls of government expenditures and government revenues that it could be achieved only by a totalitarian government" (1953, 382).

## Discussion

In both his 1951 correspondence with Friedman and his two *JF* reviews of Friedman's monetary framework, Warburton struck at core elements of that framework, including the Simons-Mints-Friedman view that the US economy was inherently unstable. Whereas Mints and Friedman blamed the Fed for deepening the Great Depression, Warburton blamed the Fed for initiating, as well as deepening, the Depression, and he furnished data on the Fed's asset holdings to support his view. Warburton criticized Friedman's fiscal-monetary proposal as being overly complex and subject to political interference. Whereas Simons and Mints had (for the most part) supported a price-stabilization rule, and Friedman supported a rule that balanced the budget at full employment, Warburton advocated a 3 to 5 percent money-growth rule.

Friedman's views in each of the above areas would change in the 1950s. Indeed, his analytic views had already begun to change in 1951 as he had come to consider the possibility that changes in the money supply generated by the Federal Reserve, and not autonomous changes in velocity, were the primary mover of the business cycle. Friedman's references in the late 1940s and early 1950s to Warburton's empirical findings on money-supply changes and velocity, along with Friedman's correspondence with Warburton in 1951 and Warburton's detailed published criticisms in 1952 and 1953 (completed in October 1951) of Friedman's work , indicate that Warburton directly influenced Friedman. In each of the areas of Friedman's framework that Warburton singled out for criticism, Friedman moved to Warburton's position. Friedman came to share the view that the economy is inherently stable but had been knocked off course by changes in the money supply. He came to believe that the Fed could offset destabilizing shifts from deposits to currency by using open-market operations to counter those shifts. He concluded that the Fed both initiated and deepened the Great Depression. He abandoned the idea that monetary policy should be carried out through fiscal arrangements. Finally, Friedman adopted a rule under which the money supply should grow at an annual rate of 3 to 5 percent to maintain approximate price-level stability.

Why did Friedman abandon his earlier proposal under which fiscal policy would be used to bring about changes in the money supply? By the late 1950s Friedman had become convinced that "government interference in monetary matters . . . has proved a potent source of instability" (Friedman 1960, 23).[72] Moreover, Friedman stated the following concerning his earlier proposal:

> In [the late 1940s and early 1950s], I was at the point where I would say money is important but the quantity of money should vary countercyclically—increase when there was a recession and, the opposite, decrease when there was an expansion. Rules for taxes and spending that would give budget balance on average but have deficits and surpluses over the cycle that could automatically impart the right movement to the quantity of money. Then I got involved in the

statistical analysis of the role of money, and the relation between money and money income. I came to the conclusion that *this policy rule was more complicated than necessary* and that you really didn't need to worry too much about what was happening on the fiscal end, that you should concentrate on just keeping the money supply rising at a constant rate. That conclusion was, I'm sure, the result of the empirical evidence. (emphasis added, cited in Taylor 2001, 119)[73]

Three additional points are important to mention. First, as I have stressed, Friedman was also influenced by, and, in turn, influenced, Mints's thinking on money. As we saw, Warburton's empirical findings contributed to a change in Mints's views in the early 1950s. Thus, the channels of influence among Mints, Warburton, and Friedman were marked by feedback effects. Second, although Warburton clearly influenced Friedman's views, apart from *A Monetary History* (1963) Friedman did not cite Warburton very often. For example, Friedman's 1953 book *Essays in Positive Economics* contained only a single reference to Warburton; that reference, to which I previously referred, was in Friedman's 1951 *JPE* paper "Commodity-Reserve Currency." Similarly, Friedman's 1969 book *The Optimum Quantity of Money*, which was a collection of thirteen essays, most of which had been previously published in the 1950s and 1960s, also contained only a single reference to Warburton. Third, Friedman treated the ideas that (1) the money supply is the primary mover in the business cycle, (2) the demand for money, or velocity, is stable, and (3) the Fed both initiated and deepened the Great Depression as hypotheses that needed to be subjected to empirical testing. His views on these issues would not change until the empirical testing had been completed.

### Mints, Warburton, Viner, and the Real Bills Doctrine

We have seen that in his 1952 paper in the *Journal of Finance*, Warburton laid the blame for the Federal Reserve's inept policies during the Great Depression with that institution's reliance on the real bills doctrine. Warburton first referred to the real bills doctrine in a 1946 paper, "Monetary Control under the Federal Reserve Act," published in *Political Science Quarterly*. Referring to the real bills doctrine as the "convertibility theory" of monetary control, he stated: "According to this theory the quantity of money will be adequately controlled by the actions of individuals and business enterprises, and action by a government agency designed to influence the quantity of money is unnecessary" (1946b, 292). To ensure

that the quantity of money is adequately controlled, the following condition was needed: that "the assets of banks with deposit liabilities or
circulating notes serving as money are predominantly short-term loans
based on commodities in the course of production or marketing—that
is, working-capital loans to business enterprises" (1946b, 294). In a footnote on the "convertibility theory" of monetary control, Warburton acknowledged the precedence of Mints. Warburton wrote: "Logically, limitation of bank assets to 'commercial paper' (or the 'real-bills doctrine')
and convertibility into specie are, as pointed out by Lloyd W. Mints (see
these items in the index to *A History of Banking Theory*), alternative techniques assumed to provide a suitable limitation on the quantity of money
(circulating media)" (1946b, 294n4).

As we will see in chapter 8, Friedman and Schwartz (1963) expressed
the view that reliance on the real bills doctrine was one factor—among
several factors—that explained the Federal Reserve's misguided policies
during the Great Depression. As we shall also see in that chapter, in their
discussions of the real bills doctrine, Friedman and Schwartz acknowledged the earlier work of both Mints and Warburton on the role played
by that doctrine in the Fed's policies.

Thus, there is a link between the work of Mints and Warburton on the
role played by the real bills doctrine in the Great Depression and the
Friedman and Schwartz monetary hypothesis of the Great Depression.
Moreover, we have seen that Mints's argument about the role played by
the real bills doctrine preceded that of Warburton. How, then, did Mints
come upon that idea? As I now discuss, Mints likely got the idea from
Viner.

Mints's 1945 book *A History of Banking Theory* contained twelve citations to Viner's 1937 *Studies in the Theory of International Trade*. As
I documented in chapter 3, Viner's book included a discussion of the
eighteenth-century debates surrounding the Bank of England's policies
during the time of the Bullionist Controversy; Viner pointed out that bullionist writers criticized the Bank of England's directors for following a
policy based on the commercial loan theory of money, or the real bills
doctrine. As noted in that chapter, in his 1932 lecture "International Aspects of the Gold Standard" at the Chicago conference Viner compared
the inept performance of the Federal Reserve System during the Great
Depression to the performance of the Bank of England in the first half
of the nineteenth century, leaving open the possibility that Viner attributed the Fed's inept policies to its reliance on the same policy framework

followed by the Bank of England in the early nineteenth century—that is, to the real bills doctrine.[74]

Concerning the influence of Viner on Mints's 1945 book, three points are important. First, Mints was a participant at the 1932 conference at which Viner presented his lecture. Second, in his book, Mints referred to the factual background surrounding the Bank of England's policies at the beginning of the nineteenth century. In that connection, he described the writers who agreed with the Bank of England's policies as follows: "there were those [i.e., the antibullionists] who held that restriction of bank discounts to real bills would prevent overexpansion and who, therefore, defended the Bank of England from its critics" (1945a, 42). Mints's brief discussion of the background to the Bullionist Controversy included a note (1945a, 42n1) reading in part, "On this question and on the factual background of the period see Jacob Viner, *Studies in the Theory of International Trade*." Third, as noted in chapter 6, in Mints's preface to his 1945 book, Viner was one of four people whom Mints thanked for having "read the manuscript in its entirety" (1945a, 5). Therefore, it can be conjectured that Mints's articulation of the real bills interpretation of the Fed's policies during the Great Depression had been influenced by Viner. In turn, Mints's articulation influenced Warburton and, as we will see in chapter 8, Friedman and Schwartz (1963).[75]

## 7.6 The Case for Flexible Exchange Rates

The year 1953 saw the publication of Friedman's edited book *Essays in Positive Economics*. Most of the essays had been previously published, including the 1948 *AER* paper "A Monetary and Fiscal Framework for Economic Stability"; the 1951 *JPE* paper "Commodity-Reserve Currency"; and Friedman's contribution, "Comments on Monetary Policy," to the 1951 *REStat* symposium.[76] Two of the essays were new: (1) "The Methodology of Positive Economics," in which Friedman argued that the veracity of a hypothesis should be judged based on its predictive power rather than on the "realism" of the hypothesis itself;[77] and (2) the "The Case for Flexible Rates." Reviewers of the book continued to identify Friedman as part of a Chicago cohort that was distinctive, and eccentric. Kenneth Boulding reviewed the book for *Political Science Quarterly*. He characterized Friedman's monetary views as part of a "Chicago tradition" that "has no place on the conventional political spectrum—it is hard to classify as either right or left. It is 'radical' in the Benthamite sense though not liberal in the twentieth-century sense" (Boulding 1954, 132). Henry Oliver, who reviewed the book for *Ethics*, wrote that Friedman's views "may be termed the 'neo-traditional liberalism' of Frank Knight and the late Henry Simons" (Oliver 1954, 71). In a clear sign that the profession considered that Chicago's leadership baton had been passed on to Friedman, Peter Newman, who reviewed the book for *Economica*, wrote: "Professor Friedman is perhaps the most able living representative of that school of Chicago economists associated with the name of Henry Simons" (Newman 1954, 259). In what follows, I focus on "The Case for Flexible Exchange Rates," Friedman's first paper on international macroeconomics.[78]

As mentioned, that paper included the arguments that (1) high exchange-rate volatility is a function of the volatility of the underlying macroeconomic fundamentals—it is not an inherent characteristic of flexible-exchange-rate systems; (2) flexible exchange rates encourage the formation of forward markets in which exchange-rate risk can be hedged; (3) speculation in the foreign-exchange market is stabilizing; and (4) because exchange-rate risk can be hedged, flexible exchange rates do not increase uncertainty and, hence, do not hamper international trade. Friedman also argued that, by promoting adjustment in the balance of payments, flexible exchange rates reduce the need for direct controls on trade. These arguments had been made by Mints and Simons. Friedman (1953b), however, made original contributions to the exchange-rate-regime literature. He introduced the concepts of an optimum currency area and exchange-rate overshooting into that literature. Moreover, he conceived the daylight-saving-time argument for flexible exchange rates. Finally, he anticipated the literature on what has become known as exchange-rate corner-solution hypothesis.

*Optimum currency areas.* The concept of an optimum currency area was developed by Robert Mundell (1961).[79] Mundell addressed the question: Under what conditions should countries adopt a common currency and follow a common monetary policy? Mundell identified the degree of factor mobility as the relevant criterion. Countries or regions between which there is a high degree of factor mobility are better candidates for a monetary union because factor mobility provides a substitute for exchange-rate flexibility in promoting external adjustment. Subsequently, Peter Kenen (1969) introduced the idea that fiscal integration between two areas is a relevant criterion to employ in judging whether the areas should form a monetary union. The higher the level of fiscal integration between two countries, the greater their ability to smooth diverse shocks through fiscal transfers.

Friedman — and, as we shall see, Director — anticipated these arguments. In a discussion of the sterling area, Friedman considered the possibility of fixed exchange rates among members of that area and freely flexible exchange rates between that area and other currencies. He pointed out that there were two important differences among the states of the United States, which share the US dollar as a common currency, and the members of the sterling area: "the former [the US states] have, while the latter [the members of the sterling area] have not, effectively surrendered the right to impose restrictions on the movements of goods, people, or capital between one another" (1953b, 193n16). Thus, Friedman believed that there was what he called "a key difference" between the United States and the sterling area; the former possessed factor mobility while the latter did not. Additionally, he argued that a system of permanently fixed exchange rates required monetary *and* fiscal harmonization.

> The problem of maintaining fixed exchange rates within the sterling area without restrictions on trade differs only in degree from the corresponding problem for the world as a whole. In both cases the area includes a number of sovereign political units with independent final monetary and fiscal authority. In consequence, in both cases, the permanent maintenance of a system of fixed rates without trade restrictions requires the harmonization of internal monetary and fiscal policies and a willingness and ability to meet at least substantial changes in external conditions by adjustments in the internal price and wage structure. (Friedman 1953b, 193–94)

> Many of these differences are, of course, themselves the product of the prior existence of fixed and stable exchange rates. Whatever their cause, there can, I think, be little doubt that on balance they mean that a system of fixed exchange rates has more chance of surviving without trade restrictions in the sterling area than in the world as a whole. But, granted that the prospects are better for the sterling area than for the world as a whole, it does not follow that they are very good. (Friedman 1953b, 193–94)

*Exchange-rate overshooting.* Rudiger Dornbusch (1976) is widely credited as having been the first author to set down the idea that, in a model with sticky prices in the short run, the exchange rate will initially react to a greater extent to a shock to bring about an equilibrium in the balance of payments than it would have if prices were flexible. Over time, goods prices will respond so that the exchange-rate overshooting is dissipated. Similarly, Friedman (1953b, 183) wrote:

> It is clear that the initial change in exchange rates will be greater than the ulti-
> mate change required, for, to begin with, all the adjustment will have to be borne
> in those directions in which prompt adjustment is possible and relatively easy.
> As time passes, the slower-moving adjustments will take over part of the burden,
> permitting exchange rates to rebound toward a final position which is between
> the position prior to the external change and the position shortly thereafter. This
> is, of course, a highly oversimplified picture: the actual path of adjustment may
> involve repeated overshooting and undershooting of the final position, giving rise
> to a series of cycles around it or to a variety of other patterns. We are here enter-
> ing into an area of economics about which we know very little, so it is fortunate
> that a precise discussion of the path is not essential for our purposes.[80]

*The daylight-saving-time argument.* Friedman (1953b, 173) expressed the view that the argument for floating exchange rates is analogous to the argument for daylight saving time. Specifically, just as it is easier to change the clock than to have everyone change their reaction to the clock, it is similarly "far simpler to allow one price to change, namely, the price of foreign exchange, than to rely upon changes in the multiple of prices that together constitute the internal price structure."[81]

*The corner-solution hypothesis.* Barry Eichengreen (1994) is generally regarded as having been the first author to present the notion that, in a world of highly mobile capital, intermediate exchange-rate regimes are susceptible to speculative attacks so that the only viable options are the corner solutions of floating rates and hard pegs. In his 1953 essay, Fried-man considered three exchange-rate regimes—adjustable pegs (tempo-rarily rigid rates), floating rates, and hard pegs (genuinely rigid rates). He argued that, unlike the latter two regimes, adjustable pegs encourage spec-ulative attacks:

> Because the exchange rate is changed infrequently and only to meet substan-
> tial difficulties, a change tends to come well after the onset of difficulty, to be
> postponed as long as possible, and to be made only after substantial pressure on
> the exchange rate has accumulated. In consequence, there is seldom any doubt
> about the direction in which an exchange rate will be changed, if it is changed.
> (Friedman 1953b, 164)

Therefore,

> the system of occasional changes in temporarily rigid exchange rates seems to
> me the worst of two worlds: it provides neither the stability of expectations that
> a genuinely rigid and stable exchange rate could provide in a world of unre-
> stricted trade and willingness and ability to adjust the internal price structure
> to external conditions nor the continuous sensitivity of a flexible exchange rate.
> (Friedman 1953b, 164)

In addition to the above contributions, Douglas Irwin (2012, 35) pointed
out that the published version of Friedman's 1953 essay omitted important material that was contained in the original unpublished draft. In that
later version, the term "trilemma" was used to describe the incompatibility among fixed exchange rates, stable internal prices (that is, domestically oriented monetary policy), and unrestricted multilateral trade. In the
modern literature on exchange rates, the term "trilemma" is used to describe the incompatibility among fixed exchange rates, free capital movements, and monetary policy autonomy.[82] Thus, Friedman anticipated the
modern literature that emphasizes an open economy's monetary policy
constraints under fixed exchange rates and free capital mobility.

## Friedman versus the Economist

Before we take leave of the year 1953, there is one additional published
writing by Friedman on the exchange-rate regime issue to take into account.
The background to the writing in question was the so-called dollar shortage
of the late 1940s and 1950s. During those years, the US dollar emerged as
the predominant reserve currency. It was expected that the United States
would continually have "an export surplus greater than [what] the rest of
the world could find the dollars to finance" (Solomon 1977, 18). Specifically,
it was believed that technical progress in the United States would outstrip
that in European countries and Japan so that American products would
easily outcompete the products of those countries in their own markets,
in the markets of other countries, and in the United States (Kindleberger
1950, 24). As Robert Solomon (1977, 18) put it: "the United States would
continually tend to have an export surplus greater than the rest of the world
could find the dollars to finance. Hence the dollar shortage."

Britain was hit especially hard by the "dollar shortage." The country
experienced large current account deficits for most of the late 1940s and

the early 1950 despite a 30.5 percent devaluation of the pound sterling against the dollar in September 1949.[83] In an article, "Living with the Dollar," published in the November 22, 1952, issue of the *Economist*, the editors of that periodical recommended the continuation of discriminatory restrictions by Britain against US imports, subsidies on British exports, and the inconvertibility of the pound sterling, among other measures, to deal with Britain's dollar shortage. The article noted that another depreciation of sterling would be necessary but cautioned that "there is no reason to suppose that it can, by itself, blast the way clear for a major dash to convertibility and unrestricted trade. . . . The conclusion that in the absence of special currency arrangements, the world may face an irremediable shortage of dollars is not one that should surprise the trained economist." Regarding floating exchange rates, the article stated: "It is silly to suppose that any British or European government could allow rates to fluctuate to [the] extent" needed to bring about balance of payments equilibrium (*Economist* 1952, 592).

The January 3, 1953, issue of the *Economist* published a letter under the title "Living with the Dollar" by Friedman in which Friedman took issue with the *Economist*'s position. Friedman wrote: "If the exchange value of the pound is left to be determined primarily by private dealings in a free market without government support or intervention, Britain can at one blow remove all import restrictions and export subsidies, all restrictions on capital flows, and all discriminatory measures, without fear of any violent repercussions on the internal economy and without any large exchange reserves" (Friedman 1953f, 16).[84] Additionally, Friedman made the following arguments in favor of flexible exchange rates: (1) they would "allow Britain's international payments . . . [to] balance, without government control over exchange transactions"; (2) they would provide protection from "the monetary mistakes of others, without requiring any intervention into the internal affairs on one country by other countries or by an international agency"; and, (3) they would prevent the "easy to predict . . . break down" of the fixed-exchange-rate regime (1953f, 16).

*Postscript.* In the event, Britain remained on fixed exchange rates until the breakdown of the Bretton Woods system in 1973. During the 1960s, Britain experienced a succession of balance-of-payments crises. The crises culminated in a 14.3 percent devaluation of the pound sterling against the US dollar in November 1967. Nevertheless, the pound remained under pressure during the following year. In the November 30, 1968, issue of the *Economist*, that periodical ran the cover story "It's Better to Float." The editors at the *Economist* referred to "the economically obvious fact that the only maintainable exchange rate for sterling was the rate which the markets of the world were unconstrainedly willing to pay for it" (1968, 15–16).[85] In support of their view that flexible exchange rates should be adopted, the editors cited Milton Friedman as among "the majority of . . . American professional economists" who were "known to be ardently opposed to rigidly fixed exchange rates" (1968, 16).

## 7.7 Conclusions

In early 1952, Friedman exchanged letters with Lionel Robbins on the issue of alternative exchange-rate regimes. Friedman took the position that a flexible-exchange-rate regime would, in most instances, be preferable to other regimes. Robbins thought a system of permanently fixed rates, based on a common commodity, was the ideal regime. In a letter to Friedman, dated February 6, 1952, Robbins wrote that "in the completely liberal world, I am pretty sure that there would only be one kind of money," and that money would be "whatever commodity [people] thought most likely to be reasonably stable in value."[86] Friedman disagreed. In a letter to Robbins, dated February 22, 1952, Friedman presented the case for flexible exchange rates although he noted that the most suitable exchange-rate regime for each country or region depended on its characteristics. In his letter, Friedman stated that his view on exchange-rate regimes had been formulated jointly with Director. Friedman wrote: "If we [Friedman and Director] have given the impression that a free exchange rate is, and a fixed exchange rate is not, a liberal solution, it must have been in the heat of the argument, and is not a position that either of us would now want to defend." In anticipation of the 1960s and 1970s literature on optimum currency areas, Friedman went on to explain that he and Director believed that each country's exchange-rate regime should be decided on the basis of the country's characteristics:

> You may well be right that the end-result in a completely liberal world would be a single currency, though I am less clear that it would be a commodity standard. Whether you are [right] seems to me to depend on whether there would be sufficient mobility of men and capital in such a world to prevent [the need of] independent monetary policies. Our [Friedman and Director's] rejection of flexible exchange rates covering the several states of the United States brings

out that flexible exchange rates are not a necessary component of a rigorously liberal position and what seems to me the fundamental consideration—*the appropriate area for a single currency* (i.e., rigid exchange rates) is that over which a single authority controls monetary policy and within which there is reasonably free movement of men, goods, and capital. (emphasis added, letter, Friedman to Robbins, February 22, 1952)

The above quotation makes clear that, in the early 1950s, Friedman and Director had jointly worked out the core of what subsequently emerged as optimum-currency-area analysis.

The year 1953 marked a critical juncture in the development of monetarism. As mentioned, Mints retired that year, moved to Colorado, and terminated any involvement with academic research. Warburton also terminated his involvement with academic research but for a different reason from that of Mints. In light of his harsh criticisms of the Fed's performance during the Great Depression, in 1953 Warburton's employer, the FDIC, ordered him to cease publishing.[87] He would not resume his publishing efforts until ten years later, by which time his research capabilities had been rendered out of date in comparison to the sophistication of professional output at that time. The year 1953 also saw the institutionalization of the University of Chicago's Workshop in Money and Banking, supervised by Friedman.[88] Papers produced in that workshop, including those published in *Studies in the Quantity Theory of Money* (1956), edited by Friedman, were empirically oriented and had a substantial impact on the economics profession's views on the importance of money in the economy.

After 1953, Friedman and Director were the remaining standard bearers of the 1930s and 1940s Chicago monetary tradition. As we shall see, both continued to pay homage to Simons. After 1953, both Director and Friedman cultivated the notion of a Chicago monetary tradition while contributing— Friedman, of course, far more than Director—to modifications in the Chicago monetary framework. Director, as usual, worked behind the scenes. Friedman, as usual, led the charge against the Keynesian orthodoxy and, in doing so, provided the scientific gunfire. A substantial part of Friedman's work from 1954 to 1960 was consisted of statistical analysis to confirm specific hypotheses about the role of money in the economy and, in the process, to build the monetarist architecture, brick by brick.

## CHAPTER EIGHT

# The Monetarists

The years 1954 to 1960 saw the completion of Milton Friedman's transformation of the 1930s and 1940s Chicago monetary framework into what became known as monetarism.[1] Empirical research by Friedman, both on his own and with his associates, especially Anna Schwartz, in the mid- and late 1950s emphasized the role of changes in the quantity of money in causing changes in output and prices in the short run—and, therefore, the short-run non-neutrality of money—and the secular stability of the velocity of circulation of money and the long-run neutrality of money. Those findings established the empirical basis for a policy rule of monetary expansion (Nobay and Johnson 1977, 477). To be sure, Friedman would continue producing influential works in the 1960s and after, including his and Schwartz's 1963 book *A Monetary History*, and his famous December 1967 Presidential Address before the American Economic Association, in which he argued that the Phillips curve trade-off between inflation and unemployment disappears at the natural rate of unemployment when inflation is fully anticipated.[2] However, as will be discussed in this chapter, the central findings of *A Monetary History* had already been published in the latter half of the 1950s. Meanwhile, the natural-rate hypothesis, although highly influential (to this day), appeared at a time when the profession had begun referring to the body of research that emphasized the role of money in the economy as monetarism—without referring to the natural-rate hypothesis.[3] Friedman's influential paper "The Relative Stability of Monetary Velocity and the Investment Multiplier in the United States, 1897–1958," co-authored with David Meiselman, was also published in 1963. As discussed below, the main findings of the paper were available in the mid-1950s although with a truncated sample period.

This chapter describes Friedman's monetary research from 1954 to 1960, culminating in his monetarist structure.[4] In particular, I show how

Friedman's views about the role of monetary forces in the Great Depression, the relative effectiveness of monetary policy and fiscal policy, monetary rules, and 100 percent reserves evolved. Along the way, we will encounter some familiar personalities. In Chicago's Law School, Aaron Director continued to interact with Friedman and carried Henry Simons's message to the Chicago of the mid-1950s. I discuss several published and unpublished works by Director. Jacob Viner and Paul Douglas will also make reappearances—Viner in light of written correspondence with Friedman in the mid-1950s in which the two economists sparred over the efficacy of floating exchange rates; and Douglas, who had become chair of Congress's Joint Economic Committee, via exchanges with Friedman before that committee in which Douglas praised Friedman's 1956 essay "The Quantity Theory of Money: A Restatement." In his appearance before Douglas's committee, Friedman referred to his work reestablishing the important role of money as forming part of a "counterrevolution."

An important part of Friedman's empirical research in the second half of the 1950s was to show that the velocity of circulation of money was a well-behaved variable. In line with this research, Friedman provided results showing that an empirical specification in which the demand for real money balances is a function of permanent income explained both the cyclical and the secular behavior of velocity. Although Friedman's work on money in the 1950s gained increasing attention within the profession, he was nonetheless viewed by much of the profession as an oddball.[5] Friedman's view that velocity was well behaved clashed with the view of much of the economics profession in the late 1950s. For example, Alvin Hansen, in his 1957 book *The American Economy*, wrote:

> I think we should do well to eliminate, once and for all, the phrase "velocity of circulation" from our vocabulary. Instead, we should simply speak of the ratio of money to aggregate spending. The phrase "velocity of circulation" is, I feel unfortunate because those who employ it tend to make an independent entity out of it and imbue it with a soul. This little manikin is placed on the stage, and the audience is led to believe that it is endowed with the power of making decisions directing and controlling the flow of aggregate spending. In fact, it is nothing of the sort. It is mere residual. We should get on much better if we substituted the word "ratio." The little manikin would then be forced back into oblivion, where it properly belongs. (Hansen 1957, 50)

On the other side of the Atlantic, the view about velocity was, if anything, even more dismissive. In 1957, the Committee on the Working of the Monetary System, known as the Radcliffe Committee, was appointed by the chancellor of the exchequer, to examine the working of monetary policy and Britain's financial system.[6] The committee's report, published in August 1959, had the following to say about the velocity of circulation of money:

> We have not made more use of this concept [i.e., velocity] because we cannot find any reason for supposing, or any experience in monetary history indicating, that there is any limit to the velocity of circulation; *it is a statistical concept that tells us nothing directly of the motivation that influences the level of total demand.* (emphasis added, Committee on the Working of the Monetary System 1959, 133)

Such was the intellectual backdrop in which Friedman pursued his research in the second half of the 1950s.

In my description of Friedman's emerging monetarism in this chapter, I consider the monetary-growth rule to be a core policy outgrowth of his monetarism. Clearly, the monetary-growth rule need not be part of a monetarist framework although it fits into that framework very well (Mayer 1978, 33–34). Thus, in specifying eleven propositions that he believed characterized monetarism, Friedman (1970a, 22–26) focused on empirical relationships and did not mention the monetary-growth rule.[7] Nevertheless, the monetary-growth rule became so closely connected to Friedman's monetary framework that I treat it as a key ramification of Friedman's monetarism. This treatment has substantial precedence. Niels Thygesen (1977, 79) argued: "One may regard [the monetary-growth] rule as the core proposition of monetarism." Friedman's former student Phillip Cagan (1978, 88) wrote that "a policy of constant growth in the money stock [is] the bête noire of the opponents of monetarism." Paul Samuelson (1971), one such opponent, listed the quantity theory and the monetary-growth rule as the two basic propositions of monetarism. Friedman, himself, stated (1983, 3): "The idea that monetary growth should be steady and predictable is the core of the monetarist policy view."[8]

## 8.1 The Road to Monetarism 2

*Friedman, 1954*

As discussed in chapter 7, in the early 1950s, Friedman began highlighting the apparent role played by the Federal Reserve in deepening the Great Depression. Specifically, in his unpublished 1951 paper "The Role of the Monetary and Banking System in the Business Cycle," Friedman put forward the hypothesis that the Fed exacerbated the Depression with its policy tightening in the autumn of 1931. He cautioned, however, that the hypothesis was "exceedingly tentative," adding that it needed to be tested. Another feature that marked the unpublished 1951 paper was the absence of any mention of the role played by the fractional-reserve banking system in the business cycle, despite both the title of the paper and Friedman's emphasis on that role in his previous work. In this section, I provide evidence on Friedman's evolving views on the banking structure, the Great Depression, and the automatic fiscal stabilizers from a lecture, "Why the American Economy Is Depression-Proof," delivered in Sweden in April 1954.[9]

Friedman no longer considered a fractional-reserve banking system to be a potent force in the business cycle. Three changes had occurred, he believed, since the early 1930s that strengthened the resilience of the banking system. First, the establishment of the Federal Deposit Insurance Corporation in 1934 effectively "converted all deposit liabilities of private banks into a Federal liability. It has thus eliminated the basic cause for runs on banks of the kind that occurred in 1931 and 1933" (Friedman 1954, 60).[10] Second, the share of government obligations on banks' balance sheets, which Friedman estimated to be about 15 percent of banks' deposit liabilities in 1929, had risen to more than 50 percent. As a result, deposits (like currency) had increasingly become a direct liability of the government. Friedman argued that a "consequence [of this development is] that it greatly reduces the potential effects of changes in private demand and supply for credit on the quantity of money. The private lending activities of banks are no longer the dog; they are threatening to become the tail" (Friedman 1954, 60). Third, the removal of gold from domestic circulation in 1934 loosened the link "between gold and the internal supply of money" (Friedman 1954, 61). The combined effect of the three changes was to "eliminate as a practical possibility anything approaching a collapse of the American banking structure" (Friedman 1954, 61).

Friedman's position on the Great Depression had also evolved. First, the evidence had convinced him that by the summer of 1931 there had been signs of an economic revival. "But the decline," he argued, "did not come to an end." Fed officials took "strong deflationary measures, putting up the bank rate more sharply and suddenly than at any previous time in their history—and this after two years of economic contraction" (Friedman 1954, 64–65).[11] Thus, the Fed deepened the Great Depression in the early 1930s. Second, Friedman had also begun to assess the Fed's policies beginning in 1929 (but not 1928 as he would do subsequently). While he did not argue that the Fed had initiated the Great Depression, he did argue that its policies, beginning in 1929, worsened the Great Depression in its early stages: "From 1929 to 1931 the Reserve System was largely passive. It allowed the stock of money to decline by about 10 per cent and banks to fail in a steady if not spectacular stream" (Friedman 1954, 64).

In sum, by 1954, Friedman had changed his view about the inherent in-stability of a fractional-reserve banking system and the Federal Reserve's role in the Great Depression. As had Lloyd Mints in the early 1950s, Fried-man had come around to the view that federal deposit insurance and the large share of government securities on banks' balance sheets eliminated the possibility of runs on banks. As had Warburton, Friedman came to believe that the removal of the domestic gold constraint loosened the link between that commodity (as a reserve asset) and bank runs. Meanwhile, the evidence amassed in his work with Schwartz had convinced Friedman that the Fed (1) deepened the Great Depression in the early 1930s, and (2) was largely passive in the initial stages of the Depression.

Friedman pointed out, however, that, although the historical evidence had convinced him that the Fed had played a pernicious role in the Great Depression, the evidence that he had accumulated at that point was in-sufficient to generalize about the role played by money in business cycles:

> To avoid misunderstanding, let me say explicitly that I do not mean to assert that all cyclical fluctuations are monetary in origin. Far from it. The usual run of cyclical fluctuations have occurred under a wide variety of monetary insti-tutions and conditions, and have been accompanied by no standard behavior of the stock of money or other monetary indexes. Monetary factors doubtless play a role in such fluctuations but I believe that we do not yet know what role. Nor do we as yet in my view have any alternative explanation of such fluctuations: we are here in an area where we simply do not know the answers. My proposition is much more limited. It is that we must distinguish between mi-nor recessions and major depressions and that it takes a monetary contraction or collapse—a monetary mistake—to covert a minor recession into a major depression. Though not directly connected with my present theme, a similar proposition seems to me valid for expansions: it takes monetary measures to convert minor expansions into inflationary booms. (1954, 66)

Why, as stated in the title of the lecture, did Friedman consider the US economy to be depression proof? The answer had to do with changes in the *fiscal* structure of the economy. On the expenditure side, the effects of programs such as social security and unemployment insurance were to raise government expenditures in periods of weakening economic activity. Likewise, on the income side, the progressive income tax and the corporation tax increased the sensitivity of tax receipts to changes in economic conditions in a countercyclical way. Friedman concluded that "the fiscal structure is now an exceedingly important and powerful 'built-in stabilizer'" (1954, 68).[12] Thus, Friedman considered automatic fiscal stabilizers to be a potent countercyclical tool. An implication of this conclusion, though not stated explicitly by Friedman, was that the US economy was inherently *stable* and, thus, was not dependent on discretionary policies in the event of a shock.

One additional point about the 1954 Swedish presentation merits comment. Friedman employed, for the first time, a historical, monetary narrative about the US economy. The starting point for the narrative was the major depression that began in the late 1830s following the political dispute over the Second Bank of the United States. The narrative continued with descriptions of the depressions of the 1870s, the 1890s, the early 1920s, and the early 1930s. The narrative also covered the banking panics of 1837, 1873, 1893, 1907, and the early 1930s. The narrative's objective was to bring to light the causal role played by monetary factors in major cyclical fluctuations. The historical-narrative approach became a recurring— and effective—feature of Friedman's approach to monetary economics into the 1990s, with *A Monetary History* being the classic example of the effectiveness of the approach.[13]

### Friedman and Schwartz, 1956

As mentioned in chapter 6, Friedman began his collaboration with Schwartz on *A Monetary History* in 1948.[14] At the time, he estimated that the research project would take three years to complete (Hammond 1996); it ultimately took fifteen years as the scope of the data to be constructed, assembled, and evaluated increased over time. Their collaboration—she in New York and he in Chicago—took the form of exchanges of drafts through the mail. As Schwartz put it, "In those days you didn't pick up the telephone the way you do nowadays—it had to be something very urgent to make a phone call! I would simply write a letter to him, and he would answer it. It took a number of years before we had a final money series" (Schwartz, quoted in Nelson 2004, 401). But once they had their money series, and had begun to compare movements in that series with movements in other key macroeconomic variables, "the whole thing seemed to come alive" (Schwartz, quoted in Nelson 2004, 401).

What was finally published in 1963 was a historical narrative evaluating ninety-three years of annual data and more than fifty years of monthly data pertaining to many economic time series, including the money supply and its determinants, credit, real output, velocity (several measures), prices, Federal Reserve credit outstanding, interest rates, reserves, share prices, personal income, industrial production, capital flows, gold flows, and estimates of the purchasing-power price of gold. Friedman and Schwartz defined money as currency held by the public plus adjusted demand deposits and time deposits in commercial banks.[15]

The origins and development of A Monetary History have been dealt with by Hammond (1996), Rockoff (2010), Bordo and Rockoff (2013b), and Nelson (2020). Here, I want to highlight two points. The first point has to do with Friedman's role. From the beginning of the project, he was the lead investigator, inquiring about both the availability of data and the possibility of constructing data. Once certain data sets received Friedman's approval, he would sometimes write papers using inferences drawn from these data. Schwartz's role, especially during the early years of her collaboration with Friedman, was to investigate the availability of the data and, if data were not available, to construct the data.[16] In her correspondence with Friedman, she would often question the reasons that Friedman had requested specific data; Friedman would typically write back, explaining his motivations, and Schwartz would then recognize the reasons underlying Friedman's inquiry. A typical exchange took place at the beginning of their collaboration, in March 1948, when, in a letter to Schwartz, Friedman wrote about the possibility of constructing a time series on government obligations held by individuals, business firms, and banks. In a letter, dated April 5, 1948, Schwartz wrote to Friedman as follows: "With regard to your contemplated series of government obligations ... I have been troubled by a variety of considerations that I note below. They will indicate to you how far I am from comprehending what you have in mind." Friedman wrote back on April 22, 1948, as follows: "I apparently did a very poor job of explaining myself." He then provided a detailed explanation of the reasons underlying his interest in a series on government obligations, to which, on May 12, 1948, Schwartz replied, "light has dawned. . . . I now see the point of the series you have in mind."[17]

By April 1956, Friedman and Schwartz had constructed annual money-supply data for the period 1879 to 1954 and monthly money-supply data for the period June 1917 to December 1954. At that time, they wrote two draft chapters for their *A Monetary History*. The chapters were titled "The Estimates" (chapter 1) and "Cyclical Behavior" (chapter 2) and were mainly descriptions of the components of their money-supply series and the methods used to compile those components.[18] However, in the chapter "Cyclical Behavior," Friedman and Schwartz also compared cyclical peaks and troughs in both the level and the rate of change[19] in their money supply series with peaks and troughs (as determined by the NBER's methodology) in economic activity. For economic activity, they used two measures. The first was an index comprising the average of three indices of "general business activity" compiled by Geoffrey Moore, a pioneer in the development of leading economic indicators and a director at the NBER during the 1950s.[20] Friedman and Schwartz called this index "the Moore index." The second was an index of bank clearings and debits outside of New York, which Friedman and Schwartz called "the clearings index."

The main findings included the following: (1) "both indicators [of economic activity] agree that the five contractions since 1879 with the largest percentage decline in activity are 1893–94, 1907–08, 1920–21, 1929–33, and 1937–38" (Friedman and Schwartz 1956, chap. 2, 4);[21] (2) both indices of economic activity ranked the 1929–33 contraction as the most severe of the five major contractions; (3) each of the five major contractions had been preceded by declines in both the level of the money-supply series and the rate of change in that series in the same direction—that is, the peaks in those series had occurred prior to the peaks in the two series for economic activity; (4) between June 1929—the month of the cyclical peak in the level of the money-supply series—and March 1933 (the trough in the series), the level of the (monthly) money supply fell by 35.9 percent, by far the largest decline in that series registered for any of the five major contractions—the second largest decline in that series was 5½ percent, registered between June 1920 and July 1921;[22] and (5) based on two methods[23] for identifying peaks, the peak in the change in the money-supply series occurred well before the beginning of the Great Depression. Concerning the Great Depression, Friedman and Schwartz dated the cyclical peak in economic activity as having occurred in June 1929. They also identified the two peaks in the rate of change in the money supply as having occurred in April 1928 (for the so-called step peak) and in November 1927 (for the so-called specific cycle peak), that is, fourteen months and nineteen months, respectively, before the peak in economic activity. With those data, Friedman was equipped with findings to attribute *both* the initiation and the deepening of the Great Depression to monetary forces.

Friedman and Schwartz assessed the behavior of the income velocity of money, both cyclically and secularly. They found that, over the long run, the income velocity exhibited a well-behaved decline: "real cash balances per capita tended to increase by almost 1.75 percent for every one percent increase in real per capita income" (Friedman and Schwartz 1956, chap. 2, 48). During the business cycle, movements in income velocity were "fairly clearly marked," conforming "in general, though not precisely, to the movements in general business," rising during cyclical expansions and declining during cyclical contractions (Friedman and Schwartz 1956, chap. 2, 5).

In chapter 2 of their draft, Friedman and Schwartz referred to three alternative monetary rules: "a rule of maintaining the stock of money constant; or of increasing it at a constant rate of 6 per cent a year . . . or . . . of maintaining the stock of money at whatever level was required to keep a given price index stable" (Friedman and Schwartz, 1956, chap. 2, 19). These three rules, apart from the numerical value attached to the monetary-growth rule, were those favored by Mints in his 1950 book *Monetary Policy for a Competitive Society* and were among the five domestic-policy rules evaluated by Simons et al. in the November 1933 memorandum. Friedman and Schwartz, however, did not provide a comparative analysis of the three rules; nor did they express a preference for a particular rule.

In a letter to Schwartz dated August 12, 1956, Friedman summarized what he believed to be the main implications of their work:

I do not think we ought or can in this place and context outline a full-blown or comprehensive theory. What it seems to me we want to do is to make a number of major points suggested pretty directly by the empirical evidence; (1) there are long swings in the money series that correspond in time to the previously noted long swings in the output series; (2) these long swings are reflected most directly and clearly in prices and money national income; (3) we have reasonably straight-forward explanations of a historical or episodic character for most of the major swings in the money series; (4) if the swings in money are the primary mover—and the wider amplitude in them and in prices than in output makes this plausible—then an episodic explanation seems to be consistent with the evidence rather than a cyclical one; (5) whether this be right or not, no study of these supposed long cycles can afford to neglect the swings in money.

Two issues merit comments regarding the above summary points. First, points (1) and (2) imply that long swings in the money supply do not seem to affect the economy's long-run real growth rate. This conclusion follows from the observation that long swings in money are "reflected most directly and clearly in" long swings in nominal income, with the latter swings predominantly being price-level changes. Consequently, changes in the quantity of money do not affect real economic growth in the long run. It also follows that monetary policy should be based on a rule that aims to achieve price-level stability (either directly, via price-level targeting, or indirectly, via a monetary-growth rule) since (1) discretionary policy can be harmful, as evidenced by the experience of the Great Depression, and (2) monetary policy influences nominal, but not real, values in the long term. Second, the five episodes of deep contractions identified by Friedman and Schwartz occurred under different monetary regimes—for example, the contractions of 1893–94 and 1907–8 took place under a gold standard and in the absence of a central bank, while the contractions of 1920–21 and 1929–33 took place under the gold exchange standard and in the presence of a central bank. The fact that the deep contractions of money took place under different institutional arrangements and were followed by large contractions in nominal income allowed Friedman and Schwartz to argue in their *A Monetary History* that the stock of money changed for reasons that were independent of contemporaneous changes in real income or prices. As discussed below, Friedman would stress this latter point in his 1958 submission to Congress's Joint Economic Committee.

## Wabash Lectures, 1956

In June 1956, Friedman delivered a series of five lectures at Wabash College, located in Indiana. The lectures drew a picture of the free-market economy as a collection of unequally endowed individuals who were interconnected by a system of voluntary cooperation—the competitive market. In that free-market system, prices played a coordinating role in transmitting information, allocating resources, and distributing income.[24] Friedman maintained that the effect of a social organization on individual freedom is the overriding criterion according to which social organizations should be evaluated. In a lecture, "The Basic Principles of Liberalism," Friedman asserted that, because it is impersonal, the free market is the economic structure most consistent with freedom: "an impersonal market separates economic activities from political views and protects men from being discriminated against in their economic activities for reasons that are irrelevant to their productivity, whether these reasons are associated with their views or their color" (1956g, 5). A free-market system, he argued, "gives people what they want instead of what a particular group thinks they ought to want" (1956g, 7).

In a lecture titled "Monetary Policy, Domestic and International," Friedman linked the notion that the Fed both initiated and deepened the Great Depression with his advocacy of a money-growth rule—though the first part of that notion was introduced as a testable hypothesis while the second part, he now believed, had been confirmed by the data. Regarding the Great Depression, Friedman argued: "It may well be that earlier phases of this depression can be traced to unwise monetary policies. Be that as it may, there can be little question that the secondary decline from 1931 to 1933 was produced almost entirely by the Federal Reserve System's reaction in the fall of 1931 to England's going off the gold standard" (Friedman 1956c, 3). Friedman used the historical-narrative approach to drive home the view that major episodes of economic distress were attributable to discretionary policies. The historical record, he argued, demonstrated that "the private enterprise economy is a highly stable system if it is permitted to work. Indeed, what surprises me as I go back over our historical experience . . . is the extraordinary shocks and disturbances introduced from outside the system to which it has been able to adapt itself" (1956c, 9). The "major problem" facing the economy was "to establish a system . . . that makes it harder for monetary authorities to make big mistakes" (1956c, 9). In light of the Federal Reserve's inept historical performance, Friedman concluded: "it seems clear that an appropriate monetary policy, a monetary policy that can provide stability for a free enterprise society, should largely eliminate discretionary action on the part of the monetary authority and substitute some kind of a less erratic and more dependable monetary system" (1956c, 3). What was needed was a monetary rule.

Regarding the choice of monetary rules, Friedman stated: "I must confess that I am myself somewhat in a state of flux about the best answer" (Friedman 1956c, 5). He considered his earlier proposal that the federal budget should be used to control the money supply to be "more sophisticated than is necessary" (Friedman 1956c, 5). In its place, he proposed—for the first time—a money-growth rule:

> Consider the very simple rule: the monetary authorities do nothing whatsoever except see to it that the stock of money increases by simply 4% per year. . . . I think that almost any student of monetary experience and policy who compares month by month what the Federal Reserve actually did with what they would

have done under the 4% rule will conclude that in perhaps as many as 90% of the months, they would have done better if they had followed this simple-minded rule. . . . It seems to me we might at least try this simple-minded rule for a time and see how well it works before we introduce further complications. (Friedman 1956c, 6–7)[25]

Friedman also discussed his 100 percent reserve proposal. Although he continued to advocate the proposal, he believed that it had become less necessary because "unnoticed by anyone, we have in effect moved something like half or two-thirds of the way toward the essence of a hundred per cent reserve system since the 1930s, when the proposal first received much attention" (Friedman 1956c, 8). What accounted for this "unnoticed" change toward a 100 percent reserve system? Friedman singled out the factors that he had cited in his 1954 lecture in Sweden—the establishment of the Federal Deposit Insurance Corporation, the increased share of government financial instruments on banks' balance sheets, and the departure of the United States from the gold standard.

*Free market system.* As discussed in chapter 5, Henry Simons's agenda for a simple, unregulated market system for allocating resources to competing uses consisted of four main elements: (1) the elimination of private monopolies, especially, as of the 1940s, labor unions; (2) the establishment of monetary rules; (3) a restructuring of the tax system, under which the progressive income tax would play an important role for achieving greater equality and as a mainstay of federal revenue; and (4) the elimination of tariffs, to promote free international trade.[26] As noted in chapters 6 and 7, Simons's agenda was carried forward by Mints although Mints mainly focused on the need of monetary-policy rules.

In the late 1940s and early 1950s, Friedman's views on the functioning of the free-market system—like his views on monetary economics—had been influenced by Simons's writings. Simons's influence was reflected in Friedman's article "Neo-liberalism and Its Prospects," published in the February 17, 1951, issue of *Farmand*. In that article, Friedman singled out two problems with nineteenth-century liberalism: (1) it assigned essentially no role to the state other than the maintenance of order and the enforcement of contracts; and, (2) it underestimated the danger that "private individuals could through agreement and combination usurp power and effectively limit the freedom of other individuals" (1951a, 3). The liberal doctrine, Friedman argued, needed to be redefined: "it must explicitly recognize that there are important positive functions that must be performed by the state" (1951a, 3). The way forward, he asserted, "is associated particularly with the name of Henry Simons" (1951a, 3).

In his *Farmand* article, Friedman, following Simons, identified three areas in need of state intervention. The first "would require the avoidance of state regulation of entry, the establishment of rules for the operation of business enterprises that would make it difficult or impossible for an enterprise to keep out competitors by any means other than selling a better product at a lower price, and the prohibition of combinations of enterprises or actions by enterprises in restraint of trade" (1951a, 3). Friedman expressed the view that the Sherman antitrust laws had provided a competitive economic environment. In another 1951 article, "Free Enterprise in the United States," Friedman cited Warren Nutter's 1951 study *The Extent of Enterprise Monopoly in the United States, 1899–1939* as evidence that, despite several areas in which there was "explicit collusion"—Friedman mentioned medicine, law, and the labor unions—the US economy was marked by competition (1951b, 2–3).[27]

The other two areas in need of state intervention that Friedman had identified in his 1951 article "Neo-liberalism and Its Prospects" were the provision of both monetary stability and welfare. Regarding monetary stability, he followed Simons in calling for a reform of the banking system and the institution of a monetary rule although he did not identify a specific rule. Regarding welfare, he again followed Simons, calling on the government to take a major responsibility: "Our world has become too complicated and intertwined, and we have become too sensitive, to leave this function entirely to private charity or local responsibility" (1951a, 4). He concluded: "There is justification for subsidizing people because they are poor. . . . There is justification in trying to achieve minimum income for all; there is no justification for setting a minimum wage and thereby increasing the number of people without income" (1951a, 4).

By 1956, Friedman's position on welfare had changed. In a Wabash lecture, "The Distribution of Income and the Welfare Activities of Government," Friedman broke ranks with Simons on the issue of the government's role in fostering greater income equality. Capitalism, Friedman argued, had greatly lessened income inequality, both over time and compared with other economic systems (1956e, 5).[28] Concerning, progress in reducing inequality over time, Friedman argued: "The chief characteristic of progress and development over the past century has been to free the masses from back-breaking toil and to make available to them products and services that were formerly the monopoly of the [upper] classes" (1956e, 5).

Concerning the comparison among economic systems, Friedman maintained that the available evidence indicated that "inequality is less in capitalist than in Communist countries" and less in countries that were more capitalist, such as the United States, than in less capitalist countries, such as France (1956e, 5).[29] The fact that capitalism had achieved greater equality was "a desirable by-product of a free society, not its major justification" (1956e, 12). However, the progressive income tax was not an effective way to bring about greater equality for two main reasons. First, part of the effect of progressive tax measures, Friedman stated, had been "simply to make pre-tax distribution more unequal. This is the usual incidence effect of taxation; by discouraging entry into activities highly taxed—in this case activities with large risk and nonpecuniary disadvantages—they raise returns in those lines" (1956e, 6). Second, the progressive income taxes had "stimulated both legislative and other provisions to evade the tax . . . so-called 'loopholes' in the law" (1956e, 6). Parting ways with Simons on this issue, Friedman (1956e, 7) argued: "I find it hard, as a liberal, to see any justification for progressive taxation solely to redistribute income. This seems to be a clear case of using coercion to take from some in order to give to others and thus to conflict head-on with individual freedom." Friedman argued that inequality derived from imperfections, such as special monopoly privileges granted by the government, tariffs, and other legal enactments that benefited specific groups. Thus, there was "every reason to adjust the rules of the game so as to eliminate these sources of inequality" (1956e, 7).

In the same lecture, Friedman supported the notion of a negative income tax, under which wage earners below a certain income level would receive a cash subsidy.[30] The rates of the subsidy could be progressive, just as the rates of tax above the exemption level were progressive (1956e, 11). Friedman (1956e, 11) maintained that the arrangement included the following advantages:

> it is directed specifically at the problem of poverty; it gives help in the form most useful to the individual, namely, cash; it is general and could be substituted for the host of special measures now in effect; it makes explicit the cost borne by society; it operates outside the market; while it, like any other measures to alleviate poverty, reduces the incentives of those helped to help themselves, it does not eliminate that incentive entirely, as a system of supplementing incomes up to some fixed minimum would, since an extra dollar earned always means more money available for expenditure.

In his lecture "The Role of Government in a Liberal Society," Friedman dealt with the problems posed by monopolies. He distinguished between two types of monopolies: (1) those that arise from "governmental support or from collusive agreements among individuals," and (2) those that arise because technical conditions make a monopoly the natural outcome of competitive market forces—that is, natural monopolies (1956f, 4). The way to deal with the former type was "to keep the government from permitting monopoly or to stimulate the effective enforcement of rules such as those embodied in our anti-trust laws to prevent monopoly from arising" (1956f, 4). He had come to believe that the emergence of competitors under the market system would erode the position of monopolies unless the government—as, for example, under the Roosevelt administration—supported monopoly power.[31] Unlike Simons and Knight, Friedman did not single out labor unions as a particular problem.[32]

In the same lecture, Friedman also took a different position from that of Simons for dealing with natural monopolies. Simons (1934a) had identified three ways of dealing with a natural monopoly: (1) private ownership; (2) government ownership; and (3) public regulation. Friedman (1956f, 4) pointed out that, while Simons thought that none of these solutions was good, Simons concluded that government ownership was the least of the evils. Friedman's view was the following:

> I am inclined to believe that, if tolerable, private monopoly may be the least of the evils.... My main reason for favoring it is because in a rapidly-changing society what at one time may need to be a monopoly may not need to be at another, and I suspect that both public regulation and public monopoly are likely to be less responsive to such changes in conditions, to be less readily capable of elimination, than private monopoly. Railroads in the United States are an excellent example. A large degree of monopoly in railroads was perhaps inevitable on technical grounds in the 19th century. This was the justification for the Interstate Commerce Commission. But conditions have changed. The emergence of road and air transport has reduced the monopoly element in railroads to negligible proportions. Yet we have not as a result eliminated the ICC. (1956f, 4)

Friedman argued that the ICC, which had started out as an agency to protect the public from exploitation by the railroads, had become an agency to protect the railroads from other means of transport, like the trucking industry.

*Quantity theory versus income-expenditure theory.* In another June 1956 Wabash lecture, "The Keynesian Revolution and Economic Liberalism," Friedman presented empirical results from the Chicago Workshop in Money and Banking that compared two competing theories of nominal income determination: (1) the Keynesian income-expenditure model, in which nominal income is determined by autonomous expenditures; and (2) the quantity-theory model, in which nominal income is determined by the stock of money. The basic modeling strategy was to estimate and compare the following two equations:

$$Y = \alpha_0 + \alpha_1 M \qquad \qquad \textbf{(8.1)}$$

$$Y = \beta_0 + \beta_1 A \qquad \qquad \textbf{(8.2)}$$

The first equation expresses the level of nominal income, $Y$, as a linear function of the stock of money, $M$. The coefficient $\alpha_1$ is the income velocity. The second equation expresses income as linear function of autonomous expenditures, $A$. The coefficient $\beta_1$ is the expenditure multiplier. Friedman reported results in which personal consumption was used in place of nominal income as the dependent variable in most regressions because of potential statistical problems created by correlations between aggregate income and autonomous expenditures.[33] The main issue studied was the relative in-sample forecast accuracy, as measured by the unadjusted $R^2$, of consumption produced by the two hypotheses. Autonomous expenditures were defined as net private domestic investment plus the net government deficit on income and product account plus the net foreign balance. The measure of the money stock was currency outside banks plus adjusted demand deposits plus time deposits in commercial banks (i.e., M2). Friedman stated:

> In a research group at the University of Chicago called the Workshop in Money and Banking, we have been making a fairly intensive comparison of the two theories for the United States from 1896 to 1953 [not from 1896 to 1958 as in Friedman and Meiselman (1963)] and for a number of foreign countries. Our procedure is limited to the two equations cited earlier [that is, the Keynesian income-expenditure model, under which income is determined by autonomous expenditure, and the quantity theory, under which income is determined by the money stock]. The aim is to see which equation fits historical experience during a particular series of years the better. (1956d, 7)

The variables were expressed in nominal terms. To account for price changes, separate regressions were estimated in which a price index was entered into both the quantity theory and income-expenditure-theory equations.[34] The estimation period was 1897 to 1953—and not 1896 to 1953 as Friedman misstated in the above quotation. Ordinary-least-squares (OLS) regressions were estimated for each model on annual data over the entire sample period and eight subperiods, except for the subperiod 1946 to 1953, for which quarterly data were used.

Friedman attached two tables to the presentation. Table 1 consisted of three parts. The first part presented the coefficient of determination (unadjusted $R^2$) and estimated coefficients for twenty-six regressions using nominal values of the variables. The second part presented the corresponding results for twenty-six specifications in which the price level was included as a separate variable. The third part presented correlations between the variables expressed in real terms. Table 2 presented results for Germany, Chile, and India. In his discussion, Friedman (1956d, 10) stated that results had also been obtained for Czechoslovakia and France although results for the latter two counties were not presented.

What did the results show? First, for the period as a whole, the $R^2$ between consumption and money was .948; for the relationship between consumption and autonomous expenditures, the $R^2$ was .448. Second, results for various subperiods were similar. The $R^2$ for the relationship between consumption and money was stable among the periods; it ranged between .826 and .987. The relationship between consumption and autonomous expenditures ranged from .043 to .960, with the latter, estimated for the subperiod 1933–38, being by far the highest value obtained. Friedman called the results "striking, and surprisingly clear cut" in favor of the quantity theory (1956d, 9). In a footnote, Friedman singled out ten of the participants in the Chicago Workshop for having contributed to the findings. One of those participants was Friedman's student David Meiselman.[35]

An expanded version of Friedman's June 1956 presentation on the quantity theory versus the income-expenditure theory was presented on October 27, 1959, in the Chicago Workshop under the title "Judging the Predictive Abilities of the Quantity and Income-Expenditure Theories." The 1959 paper listed Meiselman as a co-author. The results presented in the tables of the 1959 paper were identical to those appended to Friedman's 1956 presentation, except that the 1959 paper included results for France (as well as for Germany, Chile, and India). Much of the narrative dealing with the interpretation of the results in the 1959 paper was a duplication of that contained in the 1956 Wabash lecture. As mentioned in the introduction to this chapter, Friedman and Meiselman published a revised version of the paper, with an extended data sample, but without non-US countries, in 1963 under the title "The Relative Stability of Monetary Velocity and the Investment Multiplier in the United States, 1897–1958." The results contained in the Friedman-Meiselman (1963) study were very similar to those in Friedman's 1956 presentation.

To provide an indication of the similarity between the 1956 Friedman results and the Friedman and Meiselman (1963) results, table 8.1 reproduces findings from *selected* estimation periods for equations (8.1) and (8.2) (with nominal consumption, C, the dependent variable instead of nominal income) from both the 1956 and 1963 works. (Not reported is the subperiod 1933–38, for which the relationship between consumption and autonomous expenditure was the highest.) Part A of the table reports the coefficients on money and autonomous expenditures and the $R^2$ of the regressions over the entire estimation periods (1897 to 1953 for the 1956 study; 1897 to 1958 for the 1963 study) and *selected* subperiods using annual data. Part B of the table reproduces results for equations (8.1) and (8.2) estimated on quarterly data (1946:Q1–1953:Q4 for the 1956 study; 1946:Q3–1958:Q4 for the 1963 study). Part C of the table reproduces the results from the 1963 study for a multiple regression with both money and autonomous expenditures used as regressors over the full estimation period.

The basic message from the table is that the results changed very little for common specifications from the 1956 study to the 1963 study. The 1963 provided results for many more regressions than the 1956 study — 215 regressions in the 1963 study versus 85 regressions (of which 57 regressions pertained to data for the United States) in the 1956 study.[36] Moreover, the narrative in the 1963 was much longer, richer, and deeper than in the earlier study.[37] Friedman's 1956 presentation (including tables) was eleven pages in length; the Friedman-Meiselman paper (including tables) was 104 pages in length.

As Nelson (2020, 2:91) observed, in the 1960s the Friedman and Meiselman 1963 article "produced a sensation." The finding that the money variable was highly correlated with consumption, and in a stable way, whereas the variable representing autonomous expenditures was not, generated a prolonged and heated debate in the literature: numerous articles were published in which counter-results and rebuttals (by Friedman and Meiselman) were presented. The September 1965 issue of the *AER* included critical appraisals by Ando and Modigliani (1965) and DePrano and Mayer (1965), with a response by Friedman and Meiselman (1965).[38] The Federal

TABLE 8.1. **Friedman (1956d) and Friedman and Meiselman (1963): Selected Regression Results**

Part A: Annual Data

| | Specification | | | | Period |
|---|---|---|---|---|---|
| | $C = \alpha_0 + \alpha_1 M$ | | $C = \beta_0 + \beta_1 A$ | | |
| | $\alpha_1$ | $R^2$ | $\beta_1$ | $R^2$ | |
| Friedman (1956d) | 1.52 | .986 | 1.70 | .248 | 1897–1908 |
| Friedman and Meiselman (1963) | 1.64 | .992 | 2.56 | .587 | 1897–1908 |
| Friedman (1956d) | 1.88 | .826 | 1.56 | .856 | 1921–33 |
| Friedman and Meiselman (1963) | 1.66 | .804 | 1.38 | .711 | 1921–33 |
| Friedman (1956d) | 1.65 | .848 | 2.30 | .783 | 1929–39 |
| Friedman and Meiselman (1963) | 1.53 | .832 | 2.50 | .878 | 1929–39 |
| Friedman (1956d) | 1.19 | .890 | 0.74 | .043 | 1938–53 |
| Friedman and Meiselman (1963) | 1.26 | .918 | 1.86 | .157 | 1938–53 |
| Friedman (1956d) | 1.10 | .948 | 2.77 | .448 | 1897–1953 |
| Friedman and Meiselman (1963) | 1.32 | .970 | 5.16 | .571 | 1897–1958 |

Part B: Quarterly Data

| | Specification | | | | Period |
|---|---|---|---|---|---|
| | $C = \alpha_0 + \alpha_1 M$ | | $C = \beta_0 + \beta_1 A$ | | |
| | $\alpha_1$ | $R^2$ | $\beta_1$ | $R^2$ | |
| Friedman (1956d) | 2.63 | .903 | 3.87 | .356 | 1946:Q1–1953:Q4 |
| Friedman and Meiselman (1963) | 2.42 | .970 | 3.70 | .261 | 1946:Q3–1958:Q4 |

Part C: Annual Data

| | Specification* | | | Period |
|---|---|---|---|---|
| | $C = \gamma_0 + \gamma_1 A + \gamma_2 M$ | | | |
| | $\gamma_1$ | $\gamma_2$ | $R^2$ | |
| Friedman and Meiselman (1963) | −.425 | 1.38 | .986 | 1897–1958 |

*Sources*: Data from Friedman (1956d) and Friedman and Meiselman (1963).
* Friedman (1956d) did not provide results for this specification.

Reserve Bank of St. Louis entered the debate with a paper by Andersen and Jordan (1968), which expanded the Friedman and Meiselman single-equation approach in response to criticisms of that approach.[39] Although the empirical methodology employed by Friedman and Meiselman would, with the passage of time, not stand up to developments in econometric estimation, Thygesen was able to argue as late as 1977 that "in retrospect . . .

this [the Friedman-Meiselman study] is the single most influential study among Friedman's many publications" (Thygesen 1977, 75).[40]

Nelson (2020, 1:319) pointed out that "after 1948 Friedman became skeptical about the idea that fiscal policy actually had much of a distinct impact [apart from monetary policy] on aggregate demand." Nelson cited two studies by Friedman as having provided the empirical basis for Friedman's post-1948 skepticism about the effectiveness of fiscal policy: (1) Friedman's 1952 *AER* article on the wartime impacts of fiscal and monetary magnitudes on inflation, and (2) the Friedman-Meiselman 1963 study. As documented above, the basic results of the Friedman-Meiselman study had already been generated in 1956. This circumstance helps explain a fundamental shift that took place in Friedman's fiscal-policy position between the early 1950s and the late 1950s (that is, before 1963). Whereas in the early 1950s Friedman had argued that, if monetary policy were to be successful in controlling inflation, fiscal policy needed to behave in a circumscribed manner, in the late 1950s, as we shall see, Friedman came to believe that monetary policy alone was capable of controlling inflation, irrespective of the budgetary settings.

## 8.2 Director in the Mid-1950s

*Money*

As I have emphasized, Friedman's monetarist views in the 1950s emerged in light of his empirical work, including that produced in his NBER project with Schwartz and in the Chicago Workshop in Money and Banking. There is also evidence that Director played a role—most likely as a counselor—for the changes in Friedman's views. In what follows, I discuss the contents of three works on the subject of money by Director: two unpublished 1955 memoranda and a 1956 lecture. In those works, Director emphasized the role of money in the economy and assessed alternative monetary rules, giving credit to Simons for having established the case in favor of rules. I show that Director advocated a constant money-supply growth-rate rule in 1955, a year before Friedman first proposed such a rule in a public forum, with the implication that there had been cross-fertilization between Friedman's formulation of a monetary-growth rule and that of Director. Director also blamed the Fed for causing the Great Depression. Finally, I show that Director supported the 100 percent reserves scheme in the mid-1950s, although he did not view the scheme as essential for stabilizing the economy.

## *1955 Memoranda*

In July 1955, Director wrote two memoranda on monetary policy, both of which were sent to John Davenport—a four-page memorandum, dated July 11, and a three-and-a-half-page memorandum, dated July 29. Davenport was a financial journalist who graduated from Yale in 1926, two years after Director graduated. Along with Director, Friedman, Frank Knight, and George Stigler, Davenport was one of the original thirty-nine members of the Mont Pèlerin Society, having attended the first meeting of the society in 1947 (Milton Friedman, from Friedman and Friedman 1998, 160). Davenport had been with *Barron's Weekly* from 1949 to 1954 before becoming an assistant managing editor of *Fortune* in 1954. He was the author of the book *The US Economy*, published in 1964. Director's memoranda were written in response to questions addressed to Director by Davenport.

The economic backdrop to the July 1955 memoranda is relevant. The money stock ($M2$) rose at a fairly steady rate: 2.8. percent from June 1953 to June 1954, and 3.9 percent from June 1954 to June 1955 (Friedman and Schwartz 1963, 614). A recession ended in May 1954, and a robust recovery followed (Meltzer 2009, 112–14). Consumer-price inflation was mildly negative in the year through August 1955. At the beginning of 1955, the Fed raised margin requirements on stock purchases and short sales from 50 percent to 60 percent "to prevent the recovery from being hampered by excess speculative activity" (Federal Reserve Board, *Annual Report* 1955, 84; quoted from Meltzer 2009, 114). Evidently, the state of the economy, including the Fed's action to raise margin requirements, prompted Davenport to ask for Director's assessment of monetary policy. That assessment was provided in the July 11 memorandum.

Director's appraisal of the Fed's policy stance was generally positive, although critical of the measure aimed at reducing speculative activity in the stock market. Director pointed to the steady growth in the money supply: "If the monetary authorities are now committed to a policy of increasing the supply of money by 2 to 3 percent per year, it marks a decided improvement in monetary management. Providing, of course, they adhere to this commitment and quit worrying about particular sectors of the economy" (July 11, 1955a, 1). Concerning the Fed's attempt to curb stock-market speculation, Director queried: "How does one know that [stock] prices are too high?" (July 11, 1955a, 1). He expressed the view that the Fed's concern with stock-market speculation could trigger an unwarranted "general monetary contraction" (July 11, 1955a, 2). He continued:

"Facing the [contractionary] consequences of such action on the general level of activity, [the Fed] will [then] go out of [its] way to foster monetary expansion," bringing about "a general inflation" (July 11, 1955a, 2).

Director then considered the appropriate framework for monetary policy. He asked: "What standards or rules shall it [the monetary authority] use?" (July 11, 1955a, 3). He wrote:

> [The Fed] has these alternatives.
> a) Regulate the supply of money to prevent substantial changes in the level of economic activity.
> b) Regulate the supply of money to prevent significant changes in the general level of prices.
> c) Increase the supply of money by some given percentage per year. (July 11, 1955a, 3)

"Rule (a)," he argued, "provides more discretion than we should provide any government agency" (July 11, 1955a, 3). While he thought that there was "little difference between rule (b) and rule (c)," rule (c), he noted, "requires no forecasting, and no discretion" (July 11, 1955a, 4).[41]

Director concluded his appraisal of the Fed's monetary-policy framework with a call for a monetary-growth rule and a comment on the fixed-quantity-of-money rule (*cum* falling price level) as contained in the November 1933 memorandum:[42]

> A steady increase in the supply of money is required to prevent a decline of prices resulting from the growth of output due to the growth of the labor force and capital equipment, even in the absence of increases in productivity. While we could adjust ourselves to a falling price level, this would entail unnecessary strain on the economy. (July 11, 1955a, 4)

Director followed his advocacy of a monetary-growth rule with criticism of Friedrich Hayek's position on such a rule, noting that, all else equal, an increase in the supply of money would keep prices stable if productivity increases. He continued: "Some people call this inflation. And Hayek and others have talked about resulting structural maladjustments with disastrous consequences. I wish I knew what they are saying" (July 11, 1955a, 4).

The July 29 memorandum evidently represented an initiative by Director to answer queries about monetary policy that Davenport had addressed to Hayek. A handwritten note by Director to Davenport was attached to the memorandum. It read, in part, as follows:

Dear John:

I am enclosing some brief additional notes on your questions. I doubt whether Hayek will answer your questions. He has gone to Aspen for the month. . . . Monetary policy has been one of the bright spots of the Eisenhower administration. So you better be cautious in undermining it.

The July 29 memorandum was mainly a critique of Hayek's monetary framework. Director stated: "[Hayek] still adheres to the conclusion that inflation—including an increase in the supply of money which because of an increase in productivity keeps general prices stable—creates maladjustments. . . . But he cannot set out the mechanism which leads to his conclusion" (1955b, 1).[43]

The memorandum contained an important argument about the origins of the Great Depression directly related to Friedman's emerging monetarism of the 1950s, indicating that discussions between Director and Friedman on the causes of the Great Depression had been taking place. In the July 29 memorandum, Director stated: "There was nothing wrong with the 20's except that they did not last long enough. What I just outlined is not an inaccurate account of what happened when the Board became concerned with overspeculation and brought on the depression" (1955b, 4).

### 1956 Lecture on Full Employment Policies

In June 1956, Director gave a series of eight lectures at the Institute of Humane Studies. Seven of the lectures dealt with issues related to (1) the ideas of classical economists and (2) monopolies. However, one of the lectures, titled "Full Employment Policies," focused on the role of money in the economy. The lecture was delivered in two parts on June 20; each part lasted for approximately forty-five minutes. From the question-and-answer session toward the end of the lecture, it is clear that Hayek was in attendance. I describe the views on money expressed by Director in that lecture, and I compare them with Friedman's views in the 1950s.[44]

Director began the lecture by expressing the view that the Keynesian emphasis on the role of the government's income and expenditure policies in stabilizing economic activity—a role that he considered incompatible with the liberal emphasis on the minimization of the government's in-volvement in the economy—was giving way to a revival of interest in the role of monetary factors in the determination of short-run variations in income (1956, 2). This revival of interest, he argued, directed attention to an examination of the appropriate monetary system (1956, 2–3). That system was an exception to the liberal emphasis on reducing the role of government. Director stated that "the issuance of fiduciary currency is a natural monopoly" and should not be left unregulated: "Monetary ar-rangements are a necessary function of government" (1956, 2). Once it is determined that the government has a role in the monetary system, Director maintained, then "the only problem that remains is the [choice of monetary] standard that should be adopted." The liberal position, he stated, is that "discretionary authorities should be eliminated or at least minimized" (1956, 3).[45]

Director argued that discretionary policies cannot successfully stabi-lize the economy for two main reasons. First, to be successful, such poli-cies need to have access to accurate forecasts, but there is an "inherent difficulty—some would say, the impossibility—of forecasting short run changes in the economy" (1956, 3). Second, echoing the argumentation made in the November 1933 memorandum, Director stated that a basic component of successful policies is to "provide some certainty in the way of [policy] expectations," which "[discretionary policies] cannot provide" (1956, 3–4). Such certainty can be provided only by a monetary rule. What is important, he argued, is not the particular rule followed, but that the rule be complied with. At this point, Director referred to Simons.

> I would point out that the late Professor Simons's original emphasis was pri-marily on the role of stable rules [rather] than on the character of the rules themselves. There were occasions when he was inclined to argue that it really didn't make a difference what kind of monetary system you establish—one that led to rising prices or falling prices, and so on—but what was important was that the rules should be fixed and known in advance so that the community could rely upon them. (1956, 4)

Director then considered the following alternative monetary standards.

*Gold standard.* Its main advantages, Director stated, are "the fact that it provides a check to governmental irresponsibility," and "it removes dis-cretion or authority." However, it contains the following problems. (1) It is costly since it entails devoting "a fraction of [the community's] resources to produce the gold necessary" to operate a monetary standard (1956, 4). (2) While it eliminates discretionary authority, it does not stabilize expectations, which would have to be based on prospective changes in gold production. (3) It is subject to destabilizing shifts from deposits to currency—unless there is a system of insurance on deposits or the aboli-tion of the fractional-reserve system: "But if fractional reserves were abol-ished, then the cost of producing the necessary gold to continue opera-tions on the present level of prices might not be a minor factor anymore." (4) Its successful operation depends on not only the adherence of any particular country, "but it mainly requires the adherence of other coun-tries" (1956, 4–5).

Director's overall evaluation of the gold standard was the following: "My own conclusion is that the conditions for assuring adherence to the system are now lacking. Consequently, we can no longer say that it will provide a check to government irresponsibility" (1956, 5). What is needed, he argued, is "a new religion" to replace the gold standard (1956, 5). Here, the influence of Simons on Director's thinking deserves mention. In his 1936 paper "Rules versus Authorities in Monetary Policy," Simons wrote:

> In a free-enterprise system we obviously need highly definite and stable rules of the game, especially as to money. . . . To put our present problem as a para-dox—we need to design and establish with the greatest intelligence a monetary system good enough so that, hereafter, we may hold to it unrationally—on faith—*as a religion*, if you please. The utter inadequacy of the old gold standard, either as a definite system of rules or as the basis of a *monetary religion*, seems beyond intelligent dispute. (emphasis added, 1936, 169)

*Price-level stability.* Director argued that the main advantage of a rule that aims to stabilize the price level is that it is easy to comprehend. Its dis-advantages are (1) that it introduces "a considerable amount of discretion with respect to the timing and magnitude of the operations of the mon-etary authority" and (2) that "it introduces the problem of the definition of the price level" (1956, 6).

*Fixed quantity of money.* Director stated that a rule that fixes the quan-tity of money was "the original position of the so-called Chicago view or Chicago School, which is essentially the work of Henry Simons" (1956, 6). A "great advantage" of such a rule is that it is easily understood. The early 1930s Chicagoans, he noted, combined their advocacy of a policy rule with the 100 percent reserves proposal:

In the original formulation of the fixed-quantity-of-money rule or the stable-level-of-prices rule, great importance was attached to the reorganization of the banking structure, which is really a different thing from the rule adopted. This is the part of the formulation which has received most criticism. If it had not been incorporated in the original scheme, the scheme [i.e., policy rule] itself might have received a lot more support. Why this should be I have never known except the fact that we seem to believe that everything we have must be the result of natural forces and any drastic change [such as] that embodied in the 100 percent reserve banking scheme [must be] suspect. (1956, 6–7)

Director then discussed the rationale underlying the 100 percent scheme. In common with the argument made in the November 1933 memorandum, he argued that the scheme aimed to prevent the "possible loss of confidence in banks [during] unfavorable conditions which would lead to striking changes in the supply of money" (1956, 7). One key development had taken place, however, after November 1933 that reduced the possibility of a loss in confidence in banks: "At the time [that] this proposal was first made we didn't have an insurance system for banking. Now [with deposit insurance] this [reason for the 100 percent scheme] has been largely eliminated" (1956, 7–8).

Director also provided an argument in favor of the 100 percent reserves scheme not contained in the November 1933 memorandum—"the choice between fractional reserves and 100 percent reserves depends on the extent to which we want to rely on discretionary authorities" (1956, 8). The argument ran as follows. Suppose, as Director did, that monetary policy followed a growth-rate rule: "With 100 percent reserve banking, all the authorities would have to do is to make certain that they, themselves, created the necessary addition, say, to the quantity of money." Under a fractional-reserve system, in contrast, the authorities would have to "create that amount of reserves which they thought would carry with it the necessary increase in the quantity of money." Therefore, "if the fractional-reserve system responded in different ways over [different] periods of time to the level of reserves, then the monetary authorities would have to be given some discretion in determining the increase in the level of reserves in order to accomplish the final increase in the total quantity of money" (1956, 8). Director concluded his assessment of the 100 percent reserves scheme as follows: "there is still a great deal to be said for working in the direction of a banking system with 100 percent reserves; but, it is not nearly as crucial a factor as we once considered it" (1956, 8).

During the question-and-answer session toward the end of the presentation, a member from the audience, whom Director identified as "Professor Hayek," asked the following question: "What would happen under a 4 percent annual money-growth rule if the level of prices suddenly went up, by 10 percent or 15 percent? Then the monetary authorities are no longer in there" (i.e., are not able to act in a discretionary way to reduce inflation). Director's response was: "But our position [is that] these things will not happen in such a [rules-based] system. But this is an empirical issue" (1956, 12).

Three additional arguments made by Director are important. First, Director expressed the view that the emerging empirical evidence indicated that the "primary source of instability [in the economy] has not been . . . changes in preferences [with regard to consumption and investment], but the primary source has been changes in the quantity of money" (1956, 10). With Friedman and his collaborators having been the main producers of that evidence, Director's view on the role of money in the economy had clearly been influenced by Friedman's work. Second, in expressing his preference for rules over discretion, Director stated: "a necessary implication of an independent national monetary policy is for free, flexible exchange rates" (1956, 6). Third, in response to the question, "How would you modify the Fed?," Director replied: "the first thing to do is abolish it and substitute a rule under which the money supply would increase by 2 percent or 3 percent per year" (1956, 12).

## Discussion

As mentioned in chapter 2, along with Simons, Director was the main co-drafter of the Chicago November 1933 memorandum (Simons et al. 1933). Director's close personal relationships with Simons and Friedman provided a bridge from the Chicago monetary tradition of the 1930s and 1940s to Friedman's emerging monetarism of the 1950s. Although Director did not engage in empirical research in the 1950s—as noted in previous chapters, he produced little in the way of published research throughout his career—he was firmly grounded in statistical methods; as noted in chapter 1, in the early 1930s, Director taught the course Introduction to Statistics (Econ 211) at Chicago. Thus, he was in a position to appraise Friedman's empirical work on money.

Director's amalgamation of the Chicago monetary tradition with Friedman's emerging monetarist framework is evident in several areas.

- As had Simons, Director favored 100 percent reserve requirements. As had Friedman, he thought that they were not essential in light of the establishment of the FDIC.
- As had Simons, Director strongly advocated monetary rules. In 1955, Director favored a money-supply-growth rule. As we shall see, Friedman first publicly advocated that rule in 1956.
- As had Simons and Friedman, Director believed that a libertarian order involved government intervention in the area of money.
- In the mid-1950s, Director criticized discretion in light of its reliance on accurate forecasts. As discussed in chapter 6, Friedman put forward that argument in the late 1940s.
- As had Simons and Friedman, Director advocated flexible exchange rates.
- As had Friedman in his January 1952 congressional testimony, Director advocated the abolishment of the Federal Reserve.
- In the mid-1950s, Friedman had become convinced that the Fed deepened the Great Depression and was assessing the hypothesis that the Fed had brought on the Depression with its policy tightening in the late 1920s. In his July 29, 1955, memorandum, Director blamed the Fed for causing the Great Depression.

What is relevant is that in essentially *each* of the above areas—the advocacy of monetary rules, 100 percent reserves, and flexible exchange rates; the Fed's role in the Great Depression; the call for the abolishment of the Fed; the dismissal of discretionary policies on account of difficulties with forecasting—the views of Director and Friedman were part of a *very* small minority of professional economists in the mid-1950s. These views were also expressed by Mints before he retired in 1953 although Mints did not go so far as to call for the abolishment of the Fed. The fact that Director, Mints (before his retirement), and Friedman held essentially identical views in *all* the areas suggests that the Chicagoans had been in regular consultation and influenced each other's thinking on monetary issues.

### The Monopoly Issue

As discussed in chapter 6, during his presentation at the 1947 Mont Pèlerin Society gathering, Director, as had Simons in the 1930s, believed that the existence of monopolistic firms posed a major obstacle to the functioning of a free-market system. As had Simons in the 1930s, Director favored the application of antitrust laws to break up industrial monopolies although Director considered the application of those laws to be a stopgap measure.[46] It was the government's responsibility, Director argued, to disperse concentrated market power through vigorous antitrust enforcement.

During the first half of the 1950s, Director's view on the issue of industrial monopolies changed. Like Simons in the 1940s, Director no longer considered industrial monopolies to be a major problem. Director came to the view that monopoly, in all its forms, was almost always undone by the forces of competition.[47] Therefore, he believed that a relatively sanguine attitude toward the existence of both monopoly and large corporations should be adopted (Van Horn 2009, 207–8). In a 1950 review of Charles Lindblom's book *Unions and Capitalism*, Director maintained that competitive forces emanating from the supply side of the market had the "effective tendency" to "destroy all types of monopoly" (Director 1950, 165, 166). Consequently, competitive forces worked to undermine monopoly unless the government intervened to prevent those forces from working (Van Horn 2009, 218).

In a 1956 article, "Law and the Future: Trade Regulation," co-authored with Edward Levi, those authors argued that "the conclusions of economics do not justify the application of the antitrust laws in many situations in which the laws are now being applied" (Director and Levi 1956, 282). In support of that argument, Director and Levi (1956, 284) pointed out that the degree of industrial concentration had declined markedly since the early part of the twentieth century.[48] They argued:

> Today the industrial pattern is far different than it was at the beginning of the century. It is much less common than it was to have an industry in which one firm has seventy or more percent control over productive capacity or sales. There are likely to be at least three or four units of considerable relative size in an industry. . . . And there is an additional change. The role of combination appears to be different. Whatever the ultimate conclusion may be, it has not yet been shown that such industrial concentration as exists is due in any widespread way to recent mergers or acquisitions. (Director and Levi 1956, 284)

Thus, Director's work in the 1950s extended Simons's view in the 1940s that industrial monopolies did not need to be broken up through the enforcement of antitrust laws.[49]

## 8.3 Friedman versus Viner on Exchange-Rate Regimes

As we have seen, Viner was a supporter of fixed-exchange-rate regimes, including the gold standard, throughout the 1930s and 1940s. Friedman, in contrast, was an advocate of flexible-exchange-rate regimes and, as we have also seen, in 1953, published the paper "The Case for Flexible Exchange Rates," which became a classic in the literature on exchange-rate regimes. In the mid-1950s, the two economists exchanged letters in which they sparred over the issue of exchange-rate regimes.

The background to the exchange was a 1955 conference titled "The State of the Social Sciences," held at the University of Chicago, in which Viner presented the paper "Some International Aspects of Economic Stabilization." In that paper, Viner criticized arguments that Friedman had made in his 1953 paper on flexible exchange rates. Specifically, Viner took exception to Friedman's view that flexible exchange rates foster balance-of-payments adjustment while providing the policy authorities the independence to pursue domestic economic stabilization. Viner stated that "it is widely, and perhaps authoritatively, held that speculation tends to stabilize the price of the commodity which is the subject of speculation" (Viner 1956, 290). This position, Viner maintained, was based "on the common assumptions that an exchange rate is a market price having a common characteristic with other market prices and that in free-market competitive economies which enjoy good monetary management changes in relative market prices in general perform socially useful stabilizing functions" (Viner 1956, 289). Viner disagreed. He argued that the "currently fashionable treatment of exchange flexibility as something approaching a cure all" for international and domestic economic problems needed to "be regarded with suspicion" (Viner 1956, 289). Like other asset markets, the foreign-exchange market could be subject to destabilizing speculation. Referring to past periods of high exchange-rate instability, he argued that those periods were marked by flexible rates, providing evidence that flexible exchanges had encouraged destabilizing speculation.

Friedman did not attend the Chicago conference. However, he replied to Viner's criticisms through personal correspondence.[50] In a letter dated December 2, 1955, he wrote:

> I have read your paper with very great interest and admiration but you will not be surprised that I too am unconverted. It seems to me that your historical references to allegedly destabilizing speculation fail to distinguish between cases in which the exchange rate was held temporarily rigid but subject to change without notice—a situation that is certain to produce a maximum of destabilizing speculation—and truly floating exchange rates, when I doubt that there is much historical evidence of destabilizing speculation. The big hot money

movements of the 30's were largely under regimes of pegged exchange rates. In any event, with respect to this period, does it not seem in retrospect that the flight from the mark and other European currencies was a correct anticipation of the future and hence to be regarded as stabilizing rather than destabilizing speculation?

Friedman also argued that exchange-rate changes under flexible rates were more likely than fixed rates to impose discipline on governments. During the 1950s, proponents of fixed-but-adjustable exchange rates argued that pegged exchange rates impose discipline on the authorities for two primary reasons.[51] First, under pegged rates a country's foreign-exchange reserves are put on the line so that the country needed to maintain disciplined policies to protect its reserves. Second, the authorities who devalued were considered to have failed in their macroeconomic management, a situation that imposed political costs on the authorities. The need to protect reserves and to avoid the political costs of devaluation was thought to impart discipline to pegged rates. Friedman challenged that argument. He questioned the assertion that changes in foreign-exchange reserves "should be more effective in stiffening the backbone of the monetary authorities to follow on tough monetary policy than more immediate and obvious declines in the exchange rate." Friedman continued: "It seems to me [the] only effect [of declines in official reserves] is to make direct controls a more attractive measure."

In a letter dated January 16, 1956, Viner responded to Friedman.[52] He expressed the view that the extent of exchange-rate changes during the interwar period had been in excess of what was warranted by the economic fundamentals, with the implication that the changes had been destabilizing. Second, Viner disputed Friedman's contention that changes in exchange rates under floating rates can impose discipline: "you are arguing that for a government *greatly concerned about the level of the exchange value of its currency* actual declines in that level will be a more effective pressure than declines in reserves under a pegged exchange. But my interpretation of the whole exchange propaganda is that any concern about the level of the exchange rate is foolish and should be dropped" (emphasis in the original). Viner concluded his letter with the following remark: "I don't think, therefore, that our minds have met, and I leave it open whose fault it is."

In the 1960s, a series of balance-of-payments crises under the Bretton Woods fixed-but-adjustable regime converted increasing numbers of economists to favor flexible exchange rates. With the collapse of the Bretton Woods regime in the early 1970s and the successful move to flexible exchange rates by the large industrial countries, Friedman's 1950s view on exchange-rate regimes turned out to be the prescient one.[53]

## 8.4 The Road to Monetarism 3

As indicated, the timing of Friedman's adoption of a constant-money-growth rule corresponded with his empirical confirmation of the hypotheses that the Federal Reserve had initiated the Great Depression with its policy tightening in 1928 and 1929 and deepened the Depression with its policies in the early 1930s. In this connection, I have documented that Friedman worked on the confirmation of both hypotheses over several years. In the previous chapter, it was shown that, in the early 1950s, Friedman described the Fed's role in deepening the Depression as a tentative hypothesis. In this chapter, I documented the following. (1) In his 1954 lecture in Sweden, Friedman confirmed the Fed's role in deepening the Great Depression; he also had begun examining the Fed's policies in the initial stages of the Depression. (2) By 1956, Friedman and Schwartz had produced evidence showing that peaks in their money-supply series in the late 1920s preceded peaks in two measures of economic activity by fourteen months and nineteen months, depending on the measure of economic activity used. (3) In a 1956 Wabash lecture, Friedman reaffirmed that the Fed deepened the Great Depression and considered it likely that the Fed had initiated the Great Depression, although he was not ready to confirm the latter hypothesis. In that lecture, he proposed, for the first time, a 4 percent money-growth rule. Until the time of that proposal, Friedman's preferred, publicly stated rule had been his 1948 proposal that the government's fiscal position should underpin changes in the money supply to smooth the business cycle. Finally, in 1955, Director blamed the Fed for initiating the Great Depression and advocated a money-growth rule.

This section moves us forward in time to the years 1957 to 1959. Friedman's ongoing work with Schwartz allowed those scholars to pin down the role played by money in business cycles, including the Great Depression, more conclusively. As we will see, by 1958 Friedman believed that he had confirmed that the Fed had both initiated and deepened the Great Depression, and he published his *numerical* monetary-growth rule for the first time in that year. The following works are discussed in this section:

(1) the paper "Consumer Credit Control as an Instrument of Stabilization Policy," prepared for a conference held at the Federal Reserve Board on October 12–13, 1956—the paper was published in 1957; (2) the 1958 paper "The Supply of Money and Changes in Prices and Output," submitted to the Joint Economic Committee (JEC); (3) Friedman's May 1959 appearance before the JEC, chaired at that time by Paul Douglas, in which Friedman discussed his 1956 essay "The Quantity Theory of Money: A Restatement"; (4) the 1959 paper "The Demand for Money: Some Theoretical and Empirical Results"; and (5) Friedman's October 1959 appearance before the JEC in which he presented his monetarist policy framework.

### Friedman, 1957

As in his 1954 lecture in Sweden, in his 1957 paper "Consumer Credit Control as an Instrument of Stabilization Policy," Friedman presented a historical narrative of the role of money in US business cycles.[54] The objective was to show that the tools available to the Fed permitted a far better performance than had been realized. What accounted for the economy's subpar performance? Friedman argued: "The instability that this country has experienced has unquestionably been accentuated and perhaps even produced by the improper use of available tools. These mistakes resulted . . . from unavoidable ignorance or from the difficulty of the task or the presence of alternative objectives, rather than from incompetence" (Friedman 1957a, 95). Friedman laid the blame for the poor performance on lags inherent in discretionary policies: "Measures taken operate only with a lag and we know all too little about the length and variability of the lag" (Friedman 1957a, 76).

Federal Reserve policy in the Great Depression again took on the role of the big, bad actor in the narrative. Friedman's assessment of the Fed's policy, however, had evolved. Following a description of the Fed's actions, Friedman had this to say about the Fed's role in deepening the Depression: "If this analysis is right, the Federal Reserve's action in the fall of 1931 must bear primary responsibility for the length and severity of the Great Depression" (Friedman 1957a, 98). What about the Fed's role in initiating the Depression? Friedman was more critical of the Fed than he had been to that point in time, but he was somewhat equivocal: "it seems likely, in retrospect, that money was tightened unduly from 1928 to the end of 1929—the final rise in the rediscount rate from 5 to 6 percent at the New York Federal Reserve Bank took place in August 1929, whereas the

National Bureau dates the onset of the contraction in June. But this mistake, if mistake it was, was less clear and serious than those that followed" (Friedman 1957a, 96–97).[55]

In light of his criticism of discretionary monetary policy, Friedman argued in favor of a policy rule. In a footnote, he published for the first time a money-growth rule that aimed to limit the harm that could be inflicted by discretionary monetary policy. In contrast to his 1956 Wabash lecture, Friedman did not propose a specific numerical rule. After referring to his 1948 paper "A Monetary and Fiscal Framework for Economic Stability," in which he proposed a fiscal-based rule, Friedman wrote:

> Subsequent research on monetary experience leads me to go even farther than I did in that paper. On the one hand, this research has strengthened my confidence in the efficacy of the policies there proposed; on the other, it has led me to believe that even a much less sophisticated monetary policy—namely, simply providing for a steady increase in the stock of money year by year—would be consistent with a high degree of stability and might therefore be preferable on grounds of ease of public understanding and administrative operation. (1957a, 76n1)

As in his lecture in Sweden, Friedman argued that the automatic fiscal stabilizers and federal deposit insurance had solved the problem of the inherent instability of the economy. Regarding the former, he stated: "Our Federal tax and expenditure structure now has a decidedly larger measure of built-in countercyclical flexibility than it had in the past." Regarding the latter, Friedman argued: "The banking system is now largely proof against the kinds of panics that have so often in the past made it a prime source of instability, thanks primarily to Federal deposit insurance, the enactment of which in my view constituted a more important change in our banking structure than the establishment of the Federal Reserve System" (Friedman 1957a, 75–76). The combination of the "built-in flexibility in the Federal tax and expenditure structure plus a largely automatic monetary policy," he maintained, "would yield a satisfactory degree of economic stability" (Friedman 1957a, 76).

## JEC Statement, 1958

On March 31, 1958, Friedman submitted a statement, "The Supply of Money and Changes in Prices and Output," to the congressional Joint Economic Committee (JEC). Friedman (1958a, 172n1) wrote that the evidence discussed in the statement was "based partly on the preliminary results of an extensive study by Anna J. Schwartz and myself—[and] partly on a series of studies done in the workshop in money and banking in the University of Chicago." The data sample covered 1865 to 1957 and included both annual and quarterly data.[56] Friedman summarized the evidence about the role played by money in the economy and described the implications of that evidence for monetary policy. He structured his discussion so that it distinguished between empirical regularities over long periods and regularities within the business cycle.

*Long periods.* Friedman stated that, over long periods, there is "perhaps no empirical regularity among economic phenomena that is based on so much evidence for so wide a range of circumstances as the connection between substantial changes in the stock of money and in the level of prices. To the best of my knowledge there is no instance in which a substantial change in the stock of money per unit of output has occurred without a substantial change in the level of prices in the same direction" (Friedman 1958a, 172–73).[57] In light of the variety of monetary arrangements for which that regularity held, Friedman concluded that changes in the money supply were largely responsible for changes in prices, and not the other way around. Thus, over the long run "substantial changes in the stock of money are both a necessary and a sufficient condition for substantial changes in the general level of prices" (Friedman 1958a, 173).

Friedman (1958a, 174) asserted that the "relationship between changes in the stock of money and changes in prices, while close, is not of course precise or mechanically rigid." Changes in the ratio that people desired to maintain between their cash balances and their income could "introduce a discrepancy between movements in money and prices" (Friedman 1958a, 175). In turn, that ratio was affected by two sets of factors. The first, and the more substantial, factor was a secular rise in the demand for real money balances. Friedman argued that the holding of cash balances was regarded as a luxury good, like education and recreation. Consequently, the amount of money that the public desired to hold increased more than in proportion to increases in real income: "Judging by evidence for the past 75 years in the United States, a 1 percent rise in real income per capita tends to be accompanied by nearly a 2 percent increase in the real amount of money held" (Friedman 1958a, 175).

As discussed in chapter 7, Warburton, in his 1949 article "The Secular Trend in Monetary Velocity," reported that the income velocity of money declined by about 1½ percent per year from the late eighteenth century to the late 1940s. In accounting for that trend, Warburton presented an analogous argument to that of Friedman. Warburton argued: "There is probably a general tendency for people to hold larger cash balances, as time goes by and their average income increases, relative to their expenditures for goods and services. This is in line with the tendency to hold larger stocks of other types of goods, such as the number of shoes, or suits of clothing relative to the number in use at a particular moment" (1949, 90). As mentioned in chapter 7, Friedman cited Warburton's paper in his (Friedman's) 1951 article "Commodity-Reserve Currency." Hence, Friedman may have acquired the idea that money is a luxury good from Warburton. Regardless, Warburton's thesis anticipated Friedman's.[58]

The second set of factors that Friedman identified as affecting the relationship between cash balances and income in the longer term related to the opportunity costs of holding cash balances against financial assets and goods, respectively. These factors were the rate of interest, for financial assets; and the rate of change in prices, for goods. Friedman considered the effect of interest rates on the demand for money to be "rather small" while he posited that "the second factor, the rate of change of prices [or inflation], has no discernible effect in ordinary times when price changes are small" (Friedman 1958a, 176). However, that factor had "a clearly discernible and major effect when price change is rapid and long continued as during extreme inflations or deflations" (Friedman 1958a, 176).

*The business cycle.* Friedman reported that "there is a close link" between monetary changes and prices within the business cycle. However, "the direction of influence between the money stock and income and prices is less clear-cut and more complex for the business cycle than for longer movements." Three important considerations loosened the link. First, during the cycle, the "character of our monetary and banking system means that an expansion of income contributes to expansion in the money stock," partly through reductions in banks' cash-reserve positions and "partly through a tendency for currency in public hands to decline relative to deposits" (Friedman 1958a, 179). The second consideration that loosened the link, Friedman argued, is the fact that monetary changes worked with long and variable lags. The third consideration is that "there are some other factors at work" during the business cycle that lead to variations in prices and income (Friedman 1958a, 180–81).[59]

Friedman (1958a, 181–82) stated that the evidence showed that money was non-neutral during the business cycle. Both output and prices rose during expansions and fell during contractions. A monetary change, he argued, that promoted a vigorous expansion was likely to promote rises in *both* output and prices. Once a change in the money supply set off a change in nominal economic activity, velocity behaved procyclically (1958a, 179). Friedman maintained that the fractional-reserve banking system imbued a self-perpetuating character to the business cycle: "Thus changes in the money stock are a consequence as well as an independent cause of income and prices, though once they occur they will in their turn produce still further effects on income and prices. This consideration blurs the relation between money and prices but does not reverse it" (Friedman 1958a, 179). This self-aggravating role of fractional-reserve banking during the business cycle was similar to that of the early 1930s Chicagoans, with the difference that Friedman (as did Mints in the early 1950s) believed that there was a limit to the decline in the money supply and, thus, in economic activity during recessions in light of deposit insurance whereas the earlier Chicagoans (writing before the advent of deposit insurance) thought that there was no downward limit.

Over the longer period, however, the evidence showed that money was neutral: "What happens to a nation's output over longer periods of time depends in the first instance on such basic factors as resources available, the industrial organization of society, the growth of knowledge and technical skills, the growth of population, the accumulation of capital and so on. This is the stage on which money and price changes play their parts as supporting cast" (Friedman 1958a, 182).

As an example of the role played by long lags, Friedman described monetary policy during the Great Depression. In doing so, he made it clear that he had become convinced that the Fed had both precipitated and deepened the Depression:

A ... dramatic example [of the effects of monetary policy] is the tight monetary policy from early 1928 on and the associated lack of growth in the money supply which coexisted with economic expansion [in 1928 and early 1929] but contributed *both to the occurrence and the severity* of the 1929 downturn. The fact that these policies had a delayed effect in turn misled the monetary authorities ... [who] were induced to believe that still stronger [tightening] measures were required and so tended to overdo a repressive policy. On other occasions, notably in 1932 as well as earlier in that major catastrophe, the failure of tentative movements toward easy money to have an immediate effect led them to regard their actions as ineffective and to permit and contribute to the sharp decline in the stock of money which occurred and which played so crucial a role in that episode. (emphasis added, Friedman 1958a, 181)

Notice that, in contrast to his 1954 lecture in Sweden, when Friedman dated the Fed's initial tightening as having occurred in 1929, in the above statement he dated the initial tightening as having taken place in early 1928. Thus, Friedman reached the conclusion that the Fed's policy tightening had preceded the initial stage of the Great Depression.

Friedman (1958a, 185) concluded that the historical evidence demonstrated that a highly fluctuating price level "is as disturbing to economic growth as to economic stability." A "direct and immediate" implication of this evidence was the need "for the price level to be reasonably stable" (1958a, 184). To attain that objective, Friedman set down, for the first time in published form, a *numerical* version of the monetary-growth rule:

> An essential requirement for the avoidance of either substantial inflation or substantial deflation over the coming decades is the avoidance of a substantially more rapid or a substantially less rapid increase in the stock of money than the 3 to 5 per cent a year required for price stability. A substantially more rapid rate of growth in the money supply will inevitably mean inflation; conversely, continued inflation of substantial magnitude cannot occur without such a large rate of growth in the money supply. A substantial slower rate of growth in the money supply, let alone an absolute decline, will inevitably mean deflation; conversely, continued deflation of substantial magnitude cannot occur without a small negative rate of growth in the money supply. (Friedman 1958a, 185)

Several months later, in September 1958, Friedman reiterated his call for a 3 to 5 percent monetary-growth rule in a paper titled "Inflation," delivered at a meeting of the Mont Pèlerin Society in Princeton.[60]

Thus, as of 1958, Friedman's monetary framework included the following elements: (1) the long-run neutrality of money; (2) the long-run (functional) stability of the demand for money or the velocity of circulation of money, with real money balances increasing more than in proportion to increases in real income; (3) the non-neutrality of money during the business cycle, with the velocity of circulation of money and the quantity of money behaving in a procyclical way; (4) the confirmation of the dual hypotheses that the Federal Reserve brought on and deepened the Great Depression; and (5) advocacy of a specific, numerical monetary-growth rule.

*Joint Economic Committee, May 1959: Friedman and Douglas*

Friedman appeared before the Joint Economic Committee (JEC) on May 25, 1959, at which time Douglas was the JEC's chair. In introducing Friedman, Douglas praised his former Chicago colleague: "We are very glad to welcome as the initial witness an old colleague of mine, one of the most brilliant American economists" (JEC 1959a, 605).

In beginning his testimony, Friedman identified the Great Depression as a key event in the shaping of intellectual history:

> The great depression spawned a revolution in views. Though on a retrospective examination the depression is a tragic testimonial to the potency of monetary factors—the stock of money fell by a third from 1929 to 1933—the failure of the monetary authorities to stem the depression was taken as evidence that they could not have done so. And in any event, the obvious disorders in the economy and the urgent need for a remedy made the world in general and the economic profession in particular receptive to new ideas. (JEC 1959a, 606)

Friedman pointed out that "John Maynard Keynes was the architect of the subsequent intellectual revolution." Keynes, Friedman stated, shifted emphasis from the relation between the stock of money and the flow of income, which had been "at the heart of the quantity theory," to the relations among various flows, especially between the flow of investment expenditure and the flow of income. The Keynesian revolution promoted the notion that "'money does not matter,' that the stock of money was a purely passive concomitant of economic change and played no independent part except as it might affect interest rates, and that hence the only role for monetary policy was the minor one of keeping interest rates so as to avoid interfering with the investment regarded as needed to offset the secular stagnation that was confidently expected to be the major problem for the future" (JEC 1959a, 606–7).

Friedman asserted that the intellectual environment in the 1950s had been changing. In light of the neoclassical synthesis, Keynes's proposition "that, for a given stock of money, there might, even in principle, exist no price and wage level consistent with full employment" had been shown to be erroneous. Keynes neglected to consider different levels of prices on the real value of wealth and the effect of changes in wealth on expenditures. In addition, Friedman maintained that "the brute force of events" following the end of World War II showed that countries that followed "cheap-money policies" experienced either "open inflation or a network of partly effective, partly ineffective, controls designed to suppress the inflationary pressure." These developments produced a rebirth of research on the subject of money, with the result that "it is by now clear and widely accepted that money does matter and matters very much." Friedman referred to this rehabilitation of the role of money as "a counterrevolution that is still incomplete but promises to be no less sweeping [than the Keynesian revolution]" (JEC 1959a, 606–7).

Friedman summarized the empirical evidence that he and his collaborators had produced. He emphasized two points. The first was the "closeness, regularity, and predictability of the relation among the stock of money, the level of price, and the level of output over any considerable period of years." The second was the "inability to predict at all accurately this same relation over very short periods, from month to month, quarter to quarter, even year to year" (JEC 1959a, 611). The implication of the second point, he argued, was that "in the present state of our knowledge" discretionary monetary and fiscal policies should not be used as countercyclical instruments. Fiscal policy should comprise solely the automatic stabilizers. Monetary policy should consist of "keeping the stock of money growing at a regular and steady rate, month in and month out" (JEC 1959a, 611). Douglas, who had proposed such a rule in the 1930s, led Friedman through a series of questions about that rule—for example, the particular series on money that would be used—but did not express a view on the merits of the rule.

Toward the end of Friedman's testimony, Douglas stated that, in preparation for Friedman's appearance before the JEC, he had read the essays in the 1956 book *Studies in the Quantity Theory of Money*, which Friedman had edited. Douglas singled out Friedman's "The Quantity Theory of Money: A Restatement" for comment. As noted, Friedman first broached the idea of a Chicago quantity-theory tradition in that essay. Douglas asserted that the essay "contained a rather bewildering type of equations, and I realize that things have moved a long way since the days of Irving Fisher, but the equation that I studied [i.e., the Fisherine equation of exchange] was very similar" to Friedman's presentation of the demand for money (JEC 1959a, 633). Friedman then led the JEC members through a brief discussion of the several equations in his 1956 essay. The following exchange between Douglas and Friedman took place.

THE CHAIRMAN. Mr. Friedman, the Federal Reserve Board loves to brief Senators and Congressmen on economic affairs in order to diminish our economic ignorance, and so does the Council of Economic Advisers. I wonder if we could arrange a seminar in which you could brief these gentlemen on these equations [in Friedman's "The Quantity Theory of Money: A Restatement"]. I will be glad to invite them and have you brief them on these equations, if you would be willing to come, and of course we will pay you an honorarium for it. I think an advanced course for the Federal Reserve and possibly even the Council of Economic Advisers would be very good. Could you do that possibly?

MR. FRIEDMAN. A professor is always ready to profess. (JEC 1959a, 634)

I am not aware whether such a briefing took place. Friedman's 1956 essay on the quantity theory was, however, reprinted as an attachment to his JEC testimony.

Thus, by 1959 Friedman had begun to refer to the challenge to the Keynesian view that fiscal policy should be the primary instrument for stabilizing the economy, with monetary policy playing a subsidiary role, as a "counter-revolution." Moreover, he believed that the economy was inherently stable. Discretionary fiscal and monetary policies, he had concluded, were both destabilizing.

### Friedman, 1959: The Behavior of Velocity

Friedman's empirical work with Schwartz showed that, over long periods, real income per capita and income velocity tended to move in opposite directions: income velocity declined as income rose. During the business cycle, however, the data showed that income velocity rose as real income rose, and fell as real income fell—the reverse of the secular relation between income and velocity. Friedman's 1959 study "The Demand for Money: Some Theoretical and Empirical Results," published in the JPE, investigated these apparent contradictions. The study covered the period 1869 to 1957. Friedman used reference-cycle averages as his basic units of observation: instead of relying on time series observations to generate data, Friedman used cyclical swings in economic activity, or reference cycles, as defined by the National Bureau of Economic Research. Thus, he was able to focus on positions of long-run equilibrium and get around both the problem of monetary endogeneity and the partially related econometric problems inherent in modeling short-run monetary adjustment.[61]

Friedman's analysis included the following assumptions. First, the nominal stock of money is determined, in the first instance, by the monetary authorities and cannot be altered by non-bank holders of money.

Second "the real stock of money is determined in the first instance by the holders of money" (1959a, 116). Third, money can be viewed as a durable consumer good, held for services that it provides and yielding a flow of services proportional to the stock (1959a, 119).

As mentioned in chapter 1, Friedman viewed the demand for money as an exercise in capital theory. In a letter dated August 21, 1956, addressed to Schwartz, Friedman explained his approach as follows:

> the important point is the comparability of the services of money to consumer "services," whether like haircuts or the services of maids, or the services from food. Fundamentally, all consumption can most usefully be viewed as the consumption of services (after all the law of conservation of energy tells us we never consume "goods" as matter). The services are rendered by some capital source which may vary in durability from food to houses etc. The notion I was trying to get at was that money was a source of services and what was consumed was the flow of services. Unlike, however, haircuts and like owner-occupied houses and washing machines, the consumer typically buys the source rather than directly the service—though he may do the latter when he borrows to hold a cash balance. This is the only respect in which durable consumer goods seemed to me a particularly relevant comparison. (Milton Friedman Papers, Hoover Institution Library and Archives, Stanford University)

A way to explain the difference in the cyclical and secular behavior of income velocity was suggested in Friedman's 1957 study *A Theory of the Consumption Function*, in which Friedman presented his permanent income hypothesis.[62] Friedman's point of departure in that study was his rejection of the usual concept of income, what is typically called "measured" income, and its replacement with "permanent" income—what Friedman interpreted as the "the mean income regarded by the consumer unit in question, which in turn depends on its horizon and foresightedness" (1957b, 93). Friedman divided the consumer unit's measured income in a given time period into permanent and transitory components so that its measured income could be larger or smaller than its permanent income. Under the permanent income hypothesis, transitory rises in income— for example, if a wage earner receives an unexpected bonus in a certain year—raise measured income above permanent income. This transitory element is added to assets, perhaps in the form of durable goods, or is used to reduce the consumer unit's liabilities, rather than to increase consumption. Conversely, if the consumer unit experiences an unexpected decline in income—for example, due to a temporary firm shutdown—this income element is regarded as negative transitory income. The transitory element reduces measured income but not permanent income. In this case, the consumer unit adjusts consumption to permanent income, financing any excess of consumption over measured income by drawing down its assets or increasing its liabilities.

In his 1959 study on the demand for money, Friedman used the idea of permanent income to reconcile the difference in the behavior of velocity in the business cycle, during which velocity moved in the same direction as measured income, with the behavior of velocity secularly, which showed a decline in velocity. He posited that if permanent income rose less than measured income during cyclical expansions, and fell less than measured income during cyclical expansions, and if real money balances adapted to permanent income, those balances "might rise and fall more than in proportion to permanent income, as is required by our secular results, yet less than in proportion to measured income, as required by our cyclical results" (1959a, 119). For example, suppose that during a cyclical expansion measured income rises, but permanent income rises by proportionally less. If real money balances depend on permanent income, they, too, will rise by less than measured income. Thus, during the cycle, the velocity of circulation, the reciprocal of the demand for money, is procyclical.

Friedman fitted a logarithmic function in which he regressed permanent real money balances per capita on permanent real income per capita. In place of the measured concept of prices, he used permanent prices.[63] He obtained a permanent income elasticity of real money balances of 1.8. Using the estimated relationship, Friedman calculated annual within-cycle projections of velocity and found that his specification captured velocity's procyclical pattern. He argued: "These results give strong support to the view that cyclical movements in velocity largely reflect movements along a stable demand curve for money and that the apparent discrepancy between the secular and the cyclical results reflects a divergence between measures of income and of prices constructed by statisticians for short periods and the magnitudes to which holders of money adjust their cash balances" (1959a, 130). Friedman also found that the errors from his predictions were almost completely unrelated to the level of interest rates. Thus, in a summary in the *AER* of his 1959 *JPE* paper "The Demand for Money: Some Theoretical and Empirical Results," Friedman drew the following inference: the results "render it highly dubious that the amount of cash balances held is highly sensitive to 'the' or 'a' rate of interest" (1959b, 527).[64]

*JEC, October 1959*

On October 26, 1959, Friedman made his second appearance before the JEC, chaired by Douglas, within six months. On that occasion, he presented an agenda for monetary reform. The presentation was an abbreviated version of Friedman's lectures given at Fordham University, also in October 1959.[65] Friedman's proposals for reform ranged over several areas, including monetary policy, fiscal policy, and international trade and finance.

Friedman made it clear that monetary history was a major factor that shaped his views, with the Great Depression playing the lead role. The Depression, he maintained, "did more perhaps than any other single event to instill and reinforce [the view in the economics profession] that a private market economy is inherently unstable" (JEC 1959b, 3020). This view, he argued, was "fundamentally mistaken." The historical record showed that the major inflations and depressions, including the Great Depression, had "in almost every instance been produced, or at the very least, strongly reinforced, by the failure of government to discharge properly the tasks assigned to it, in particular of providing a stable monetary framework" (JEC 1959b, 3020–21).

Regarding monetary policy, Friedman again called for a required rate of increase in the money supply of 3 to 5 percent annually to produce an approximately constant price level. Open-market operations would be the tool to effectuate changes in the money supply. The Fed's powers to rediscount and to vary reserve requirements would be eliminated (JEC 1959a, 3022).

Friedman stated that he would reform the banking system by requiring depository institutions to have reserves of 100 percent, thereby eliminating the need of deposit insurance. The 100 percent scheme would provide three benefits: it would (1) "eliminate present government controls over lending and investing activities"; (2) "eliminate instability arising out of shifts in the fraction of its money income the public wishes to hold in the form of currency and in the fraction of their assets banks want to hold in the form of cash or Federal Reserve deposits"; and (3) "establish a closer link between Federal Reserve action and the money supply" (JEC 1959b, 3023). Each of these properties had been earlier identified by Knight, Simons, Douglas, Cox, Mints, and Director as advantages of the 100 percent scheme. Friedman also proposed that interest be paid on banks' reserves with the Federal Reserve since those deposits are a form of lending by private citizens to the government. Finally, he favored the removal of limitations on the interest rates that banks were allowed to pay to depositors (JEC 1959b, 3023).

Regarding fiscal policy, Friedman thought that it would be desirable to avoid discretionary measures that aimed to smooth the business cycle. Such measures typically had the effect of exacerbating the cycle: "Increases in governmental expenditures designed to offset the recessions have taken so much time that they have come into play in important measure only after the economic tide has turned and recovery has resumed, thus reinforcing rather than offsetting cyclical fluctuations" (JEC 1959b, 3021). Friedman advocated a stable program of government expenditures and a stable tax structure although he thought that the latter required a fundamental reform. As did Simons, Friedman favored the elimination of the corporate income tax. He also proposed that income tax rates be "drastically" reduced and that certain exemptions, including the percentage depletion on oil and other raw materials, and the tax exemption of interest on certain governmental securities, be eliminated (JEC 1959b, 3027). Unlike Simons, Friedman did not view the progressive income tax as an instrument for promoting income equality. Over the course of the business cycle, the budget would be balanced (JEC 1959b, 3035).

On debt management, Friedman favored the simplification of the debt structure. He proposed that only two kinds of government debt (other than money) be issued—a short-term bill and an intermediate security— say, an eight-year or ten-year maturity. Both issues would be sold at public auction. Simons, it will be recalled, favored a simplification of the government debt structure in such a way that it would include only cash and consols. Concerning trade policy, Friedman advocated the complete elimination of trade barriers. He continued to advocate a system of flexible exchange rates.

Douglas reacted very favorably to Friedman's reform agenda. Douglas said: "It is reassuring to have my economic and fiscal views upheld by so eminent an economic authority that I am basking in the light of your approval" (JEC 1959b, 3030). In closing the session, Douglas stated: "I want to thank the witness for his brilliant, honest, and rigorous analysis and to express the personal pleasure that he comes from the university that was formerly my own" (JEC 1959b, 3052).

Thus, in 1959, Friedman pushed forward the Simons-Mints policy agenda although Friedman's particular views differed in some areas from those of his Chicago predecessors. As had his predecessors, Friedman favored a monetary rule, free trade, and flexible exchange rates. Although Friedman believed that federal deposit insurance sharply reduced the likelihood of banking panics, he favored the 100 percent scheme instead of deposit insurance. As had Simons and Mints, Friedman advocated simplifying the government's debt structure and balancing the government's fiscal position over the business cycle. Friedman's views differed from those of his Chicago predecessors in three fundamental ways: (1) Friedman believed that, in the absence of discretionary policies, the economic system is inherently stable, an attribute produced by federal deposit insurance and the automatic fiscal stabilizers; (2) Friedman favored open-market operations, and not changes in the government's fiscal position, as the instrument to be used to generate changes in the money supply; and (3) while favoring the simplification of the tax structure and a stable level of government expenditures—as Simons and Mints had—Friedman did not advance the progressive income tax as an instrument for the promotion of equality.

## 8.5 The Fordham Lectures

As mentioned, Friedman's 1960 book *A Program for Monetary Stability* was a revised and expanded version of lectures given at Fordham University in October 1959. In the "Prefatory Note" to the book, Friedman stated that his suggestions for monetary reform were "largely a by-product" of his research in the field of money—notably his study with Schwartz, "now nearly complete, of the secular and cyclical behavior of the money supply in the United States," and the research projects conducted in the Chicago Workshop in Money and Banking. Among those whom Friedman acknowledged for providing comments were Schwartz, Director, and Meiselman.

I discuss the following issues in Friedman's lecture: the role of government in economic affairs; the use of the historical narrative; the rationale for 100 percent reserves despite the existence of deposit insurance; and Friedman's assessment of alternative policy rules.

*Role of government.* Following the precedents of his Chicago predecessors, Friedman maintained that the market is the only means of enabling individuals to coordinate their activities without coercion. Economic freedom, he maintained, had produced an unprecedented development in the capacity and productivity of individuals. Friedman stated that he was "suspicious" of assigning to the government any functions that could be performed through the market (1960, 4). The state had a limited role to play in economic affairs. One such role was in the provision of a stable legal framework. Another such role was in the provision of a stable monetary framework (1960, 8).[66]

Friedman expressed the view that several features of money justified government intervention in its provision: (1) the resource cost of maintaining a pure commodity standard and, hence, its tendency to become partly fiduciary—that is, the maintenance of a commodity standard requires the use of real resources to produce additional amounts of the monetary commodity; (2) the difficulty of enforcing contracts involving promises to pay that serve as a medium of exchange—including the difficulty of preventing counterfeiting in those contracts;[67] (3) the technical monopoly character of a pure fiduciary currency, which makes the setting of some limit on its amount essential—competition among competing issuers does not provide an effective limit; and (4) the pervasive character of money, which means that its issuance has important effects on parties other than those directly involved (1960, 5–8). In light of these factors, the setting of monetary arrangements cannot be left to the market. The government, Friedman argued, has a responsibility for providing a stable monetary framework "on a par with the provision of a stable legal framework" (1960, 8).

*Historical narrative.* Twenty-five pages of the book consist of a historical narrative about (1) the role played by money in major contractions before the establishment of the Federal Reserve and (2) the Federal Reserve's performance from 1913 to the late 1950s.[68] The narrative approach provided an important complement to Friedman's statistical work on money. Specifically, the narrative approach allowed Friedman the added flexibility of examining data within the context of historical and political dimensions that could not easily be distilled from statistical analyses. Romer and Romer (1989, 122) wrote the following about the narrative approach: "its central element is the identification of 'monetary shocks' through non-statistical procedures." Those authors went on to state: "Both this casual analysis and the more systematic analysis of Friedman and Schwartz have probably been more persuasive than purely statistical studies because the isolation of shocks from the historical record can overcome the reverse causation problem that plagues any regression of output on money" (Romer and Romer 1989, 122).

Once again, the Great Depression figured prominently in the narrative. Friedman stated: "The Great Depression did much to instill and reinforce the now widely held view that inherent instability of a private market economy has been responsible for the major periods of economic distress experienced by the United States" (1960, 9). This view underpinned the idea that "only a vigilant government" could offset the "vagaries of the private economy" (1960, 9). Friedman's reading of the historical record was very different from the standard narrative: "In almost every instance, major instability in the United States has been produced or, at the very least, greatly intensified by monetary instability" (1960, 9). After describing the Fed's policies during the Great Depression, Friedman stated:

> I have described this episode in some detail because it has played such an important role in forming—or should I say deforming—opinions about monetary policy. It was interpreted to mean that monetary policy is an ineffective instrument for stemming deflation. In fact it is a tragic testament to the harm that an inappropriate monetary policy can do. (1960, 19–20)

Friedman blamed the Federal Reserve for allowing the money supply to contract during the initial phase of the Great Depression and subsequently. The Fed was misled, he argued, because it looked at the absolute level of the discount rate rather than the relation of that rate to market rates, or to the behavior of the money supply.

There were two new elements in Friedman's historical narrative. First, whereas he had previously identified the Fed's policy tightening in October 1931 as having initiated the deepening phase of the Great Depression, in his 1960 book Friedman stated: "The serious fault of the Federal Reserve dates from the end of 1930, when a series of bank failures, including the notable failure of the Bank of the [sic] United States in New York, changed the monetary character of the contraction" (1960, 18).[69] Although Friedman did not describe the significance of the failure of Bank of United States in detail in his Fordham lecture, the failure figured prominently in his and Schwartz's A Monetary History. That bank, a private bank—with over four hundred thousand depositors, more than any other bank in the country—faced a liquidity crisis, as opposed to a solvency crisis, in late 1930. Friedman and Schwartz judged it a sound bank; its difficulties stemmed from rumors that produced a run on it. Friedman and Schwartz (1963, 310) believed that in a financial crisis the monetary authorities should follow a well-established rule: if a bank was sound, but was facing a run on deposits, the monetary authorities needed to act as a lender of last resort, lending freely to the bank to quench the panic.[70] New York State banking officials, however, refused to provide liquidity to the financial institution, and in December 1930, the bank was forced to close. That single event, Friedman and Schwartz argued, dramatically changed the character of the downturn.

Friedman and Schwartz (1963) asserted that there were two reasons for this turn of events: (1) the Bank of United States was the largest US commercial bank ever to have failed up to that time, and (2), although it was an ordinary commercial bank, its name had led many at home and abroad to regard it as an official, government-owned bank. Hence, its failure undermined confidence more than the fall of a bank with a less distinctive name would have done. Friedman and Schwartz also hinted that anti-Semitism might have played a role in the failure to provide liquidity to the bank; its stakeholders and officers were mainly Jewish.[71]

The second new element in Friedman's narrative was his identification of the real bills doctrine as a key factor underlying the Federal Reserve's misguided policies in the past. Citing Mints's book *A History of Banking Theory*, Friedman stated that eligibility requirements for borrowing by banks from the Fed "date from the origin of the Federal Reserve System, which was set up by men mostly wedded to that ubiquitous fallacy, the real bills doctrine" (1960, 26). In line with the Fed's emphasis on eligibility requirements, Friedman (1960, 27) stated: "In 1928 and 1929, the System's concern with the stock market led it to follow a general credit policy that was too tight for general business and too easy to stop the stock market boom."

Friedman and Schwartz (1963) cited the real bills doctrine (or the needs-of-trade view) as a factor—although not the most important factor—underlying the climate of opinion under which the Federal Reserve System operated during the Great Depression:

> The System was operating in a climate of opinion that in the main regarded recessions and depressions as curative episodes, necessary in order to purge the body economic of the aftereffects of its earlier excesses. The prevailing opinion also confused money and credit; confused the elasticity of one component of the money stock relative to another with the elasticity of the total stock; regarded it as desirable that the stock of money should respond to the "needs of trade," rising in expansions and falling in contractions; and attached much greater importance to the maintenance of the gold standard and the stability of exchanges than to the maintenance of internal stability. (1963, 691)

The reference to the needs of trade, although not the most significant factor in Friedman and Schwartz's account of the Great Depression, provided a link with Mints's criticisms of the real bills doctrine. Although the climate of opinion under which the system operated was a necessary condition for the system's inept policies, Friedman and Schwartz (1963, 692) believed that the main factors underlying those policies were the death of New York Fed governor Benjamin Strong in October 1928 and the fragmented nature of the Federal Reserve System, which thwarted centralized decision-making.

In their account of the intellectual climate under which the Federal Reserve System was created, Friedman and Schwartz (1963, 169) stated: "There was a widespread feeling that the money stock should conform to the 'needs of trade.' . . . That view was partly [the result of the] . . . failure to recognize fully the significance of deposits as money, partly a particular manifestation of the ubiquitous 'real bills' doctrine." In their presentations of the real bills doctrine, Friedman and Schwartz referred the reader to Mints's discussion of the real bills origins of the Federal Reserve Act in the latter's 1945 book *A History of Banking Theory*, and to Warburton's discussion in his 1952 *Journal of Finance* article "Monetary Difficulties and the Structure of the Monetary System," in which that economist criticized the Federal Reserve's policies during the Great Depression based on the Fed's adherence to the real bills doctrine.[72] The upshot of the citations to Mints's negative assessment of the role played by the real bills doctrine in the Fed's policies is that they provide evidence that Friedman's reliance of what he called the real bills fallacy (1960, 26, 43) had been influenced not only by Mints, to whom Friedman gave credit, but, indirectly, through Mints, by Viner, to whom Friedman did not gave credit in the late 1950s and early 1960s.

In his later years, Friedman came to believe that he and Schwartz should have accorded more emphasis to the role played by the real bills doctrine in contributing to the Fed's inept policies during the Great Depression. In personal correspondence, dated December 14, 2004, addressed to Richard Timberlake, in which Friedman commented on a draft of Timberlake's paper "Gold Standards and the Real Bills Doctrine in US Monetary Policy," Friedman wrote: "We [i.e., Friedman and Schwartz (1963)] stressed and discussed at great length the shift of power in the System. We did not emphasize, as in hindsight we should have, the widespread belief in the real bills doctrine on the part of those to whom power shifted."[73]

*100 percent reserves.* Friedman (1960, 65) stated: "As a student of Henry Simons and Lloyd Mints . . . I shall follow them also in recommending that the present system be replaced by one in which 100% reserves are required."[74] Friedman singled out two "major defects" of fractional-reserve banking. First, it involves extensive intervention of the government in lending and investing activities. Second, changes by holders of money about the form in which they choose to hold money and by banks about the structure of their assets "affect the amount available to be held. This has often been referred to as the 'inherent instability' of a fractional reserve system" (1960, 66). While deposit insurance had ameliorated this defect, Friedman argued that it had done so at the cost of "a substantial increase in governmental intervention into the lending and investing process" (1960, 68).[75] Thus, although deposit insurance had, in Friedman's view, ameliorated banking crises, Friedman believed that the 100 percent reserves scheme would be preferable: "while federal deposit insurance has performed a signal service in rendering the banking system panic-proof, it does not seem to me the most desirable method of achieving this" (1960, 38).

As in his October 26, 1959, appearance before the *JEC*, in *A Program for Monetary Stability* Friedman proposed that the Federal Reserve pay interest on banks' reserves. Three reasons underpinned that proposal. First, if the interest rate on reserves is below the interest on competing assets, as it was when the interest rate on reserves was set at zero, banks would not hold the optimum quantity of reserves.[76] Second, it would reduce the incentive by banks to evade the 100 percent reserve scheme. Third, it would eliminate the discrimination inherent under a situation in which the government pays resources to one group of creditors—those who hold interest-bearing government securities—and pays nothing to another group of creditors—the holders of money (1960, 72–74). In proposing that interest be paid on banks' reserves, Friedman (1960, 109n12) credited Mints for originating the idea.[77]

*The instrument of monetary policy.* Friedman maintained that open-market operations should be the instrument of choice. Although the Federal Reserve could not directly control the money supply, open-market operations affected the amount of high-powered of money (i.e., the monetary base). By changing the stock of high-powered money, open-market operations could be used to offset changes in the ratios underlying the money multiplier, and, thus, control the stock of money (1960, 30–32).[78] In contrast to the use of the government's fiscal position to effectuate changes in the money supply, open-market operations were flexible: they "could be used continuously, from day to day, and in amounts varying by fine gradations" (1960, 50). Discounting operations and variable reserve requirements should be abolished (1960, 50). Both the adoption of the 100 percent reserves scheme and the abolition of discounting operations would allow the monetary authorities to control the money supply better.

*Monetary-policy transmission.* As mentioned in chapter 1, beginning in the 1950s Friedman shifted away from the view that changes in the money supply exert their influence on the economy via a wealth channel. In *A Program for Monetary Stability*, Friedman espoused a transmission process under which changes in the money supply affected a broad spectrum of interest rates:

> It is analytically possible to treat all effects of changes in the quantity of money as taking place via changes in interest rates and their effects in turn on flows of spending. But to do so in a comprehensive way requires taking account of a much broader range of rates of interest than "recorded market" rates, for example, implicit rates entering into consumer decisions about stocks of durable goods to hold. (1960, 43)

*Monetary rules.* Under what kind of framework should internal monetary policy be conducted? Friedman (1960) noted that Simons had posed this question. As did Simons, Friedman (1960, 86) believed that a rule would eliminate "the danger of instability and uncertainty of policy."[79] Additionally, like Simons, Friedman (1960, 85) argued that discretion "is highly objectionable on political grounds in a free society." Moreover, Friedman believed that discretion absolves the policy makers of any criteria by which to judge their performance and leaves them vulnerable to political pressures (1960, 85).[80] Finally, relying on the evidence of his work with Schwartz on short-term relationships, Friedman (1960, 85) argued that, in the past, discretion had led to "continual and unpredictable shifts in policy and in the content of policy as the persons and attitudes dominating the authorities had changed." A money-growth rule, he believed, would have avoided the "excessive" mistakes of the past, including the collapse of money from 1929 to 1933, the discount-rate increases of 1931, and the resulting depression (1960, 93). It would not rule out mild cyclical fluctuations, but it "would almost certainly rule out . . . rapid and sizeable fluctuations" (1960, 92). Importantly, the rule "might be expected to correspond with a roughly stable price level" (1960, 91).

Similarly to Simons and Mints, Friedman thought that a benefit of his particular proposal was that it would be easy to understand (1960, 90). However, in contrast to the proposal of Simons and Mints, and his own earlier proposal, Friedman argued that the money supply should be controlled by the Fed instead of being connected to the government's fiscal operations. In marked contrast to the Simons and Mints proposal, and his own earlier proposal, Friedman (1960, 90) argued that his monetary-growth proposal has the following advantage; "it would largely separate the monetary problem from the fiscal [problem]."

Why not a rule that directly targets the price level? A price-level target, he argued, has two major problems. First, it is not evident which particular price index should be targeted (1960, 87). Second, as his work with Schwartz had shown, "the link between price changes and monetary changes *over short periods* is too loose and too imperfectly known to make price stability an objective and unambiguous guide to policy" (emphasis added, 1960, 87). What caused Friedman to switch from his earlier Simons-type framework under which fiscal policy would be used to generate changes in the money supply to smooth the business cycle? In his May 1958 congressional testimony, Friedman (emphasis added, 1958, 186) provided the answer: "[The] *evidence* has persuaded me that the major problem [of that earlier rule] is to prevent monetary changes from themselves contributing to instability rather than to use monetary changes to offset other forces." Friedman, however, stated that he was open to rules other than the monetary-growth rule: "But I should hope that as we operated under it we would accumulate more evidence and learn to understand more fully the workings of the monetary mechanism. As we did so, we could perhaps devise still better rules for controlling the stock of money that could command widespread professional support and public understanding" (1960, 99).

In his *A Program for Monetary Stability*, Friedman (1960, 52–65) argued that debt management and monetary policy were tightly connected. This circumstance reflects the fact that control of the money supply becomes infeasible if the monetary authorities are obligated to peg the secondary price of government securities within a limited range, as under the pre-accord regime, or if they are compelled to purchase government securities on an unlimited basis (Nelson 2020, 1:321). What was absent from the book, however, was any mention of a role for fiscal policy—that is, of changes in government expenditures and taxes. Thus, Friedman had come to believe that monetary policy on its own was sufficient to "assure long-run stability in the purchasing power of the dollar" (1960, 98–99). As mentioned, in the late 1940s and early 1950s, Friedman had argued that, for monetary policy to be successful in controlling inflation, fiscal policy needed to act in a circumscribed way. What caused Friedman to change his view? The evidence that he had accumulated, including in his 1952 study on wartime inflations and in his ongoing projects with both Meiselman and Schwartz, played key roles in helping Friedman conclude that monetary policy on its own could produce an approximately stable price level.

## 8.6 Conclusions

As we have seen, in 1948, when Friedman embraced monetary economics as his primary field of interest, his monetary framework had been that of his Chicago mentors. The equation of exchange was the vehicle used to attribute the source of business cycles to exogenous shifts in the velocity of circulation of money; the severity of those cycles was attributed to the perverse behavior of the fractional-reserve banking system and the effects of changes in price expectations on velocity. Economic stability during the cycle required countercyclical changes in money produced through the government's fiscal position. Long-term economic stability required a monetary rule and 100 percent reserves. Domestic-policy space required flexible exchange rates.

By the time of his 1959 Fordham lecture, the basic components of Friedman's revision of the Chicago tradition's framework and the construction of his monetarist framework had been completed. Between the late 1940s and the mid-1950s, Friedman's empirical validation of the dual hypotheses that constituted the monetary interpretation of the Great Depression, based on his work with Schwartz, corresponded with his adoption of a monetary-growth rule. In contrast to the view of the Chicago tradition, which saw the economy consistently being buffeted by velocity shocks, Friedman came around to the view that the automatic fiscal stabilizers and federal deposit insurance delivered an inherently stable economy. The economy, Friedman's empirical evidence showed, was constantly knocked off course by changes in the money supply produced by discretionary monetary policies; from its creation in 1913, the Federal Reserve was the big, bad actor on the economic stage. His empirical work on the demand for money showed that velocity was well behaved secularly and also explained the procyclicality of velocity during short periods. In keeping with the Chicago tradition, Friedman believed that the fractional-reserve banking system contributed to the procyclicality of both the volume and the velocity of deposits; in contrast to the belief of that tradition, federal deposit insurance, and the large amounts of government securities held by banks on their balance sheets, put a limit on velocity movements during the cycle.[81] To exploit the economy's inherent stability, Friedman called for the elimination of discretionary fiscal and monetary policies. Fiscal policy should comprise solely automatic stabilizers. In light of the long-run stability of velocity, monetary policy should follow a simple and definite rule under which the money supply grows by 3 to 5 percent annually. With the termination of the Fed's pegging of the prices of government securities in the early 1950s, base money and government securities had become differentiated assets, rendering open-market operations effective. Thus, open-market operations, the most flexible of monetary policy instruments, would be used to implement the secular money-supply increases and to offset short-run changes to the currency-deposit ratio. Although federal deposit insurance had helped stabilize the deposit-to-currency ratio, Friedman viewed the 100 percent reserves scheme as the superior alternative to deposit insurance.

By the late 1950s, Friedman viewed his work on monetary economics, both that undertaken on his own and that with his collaborators, as having formed part of a counter-revolution in the field of money. His empirical work comprised both state-of-the-art statistical analysis and historical narratives about the role of money. Director performed the role of confidant, typically acting behind the scenes. Director, as Friedman, brought Simons's views about the importance of money and the need of government intervention in monetary affairs to Chicago in the 1950s; and Director came to share Friedman's empirically based views about the Federal Reserve's culpability in the Great Depression and the need of a monetary-growth rule. The other collaborators were Schwartz, whose work provided the necessary inputs for Friedman's empirical studies and monetary narratives, and Friedman's students in the Chicago Workshop in Money and Banking.

In addition to reshaping the monetary framework that he had taken over from his Chicago predecessors, Friedman, along with Director, moved away from Simons's view about the role of the government in the economy. Simons, writing during a time in which many American intellectuals favored a greatly expanded role for government in economic activity, supported a larger role for government in providing socialized consumption services (e.g., medical services, education) and for extending the range of social welfare services. Although he was an ardent supporter of the free-enterprise system, Simons thought that the actual market was far from ideal (Miller 1962, 67). He had become less concerned about industrial monopolies in the 1940s, but throughout his career, he thought that labor unions had the potential to destroy capitalism. Friedman and Director, in contrast, did not express concerns about the power of labor unions. Director believed that competitive forces, emanating from the supply side of the market, worked to destroy all types of monopoly. Whereas Simons favored government takeover of natural monopolies, Friedman favored private ownership of such monopolies. Simons advocated the use of the progressive income tax to help advance equality. Friedman argued that the progressive income tax could be regressive. He thought that the way to reduce inequality was to reduce government-produced distortions in the market. Friedman worked to advance the Chicago tradition's money-cum-free-market framework but, in doing so, he focused on reducing government participation in the market.

## CHAPTER NINE

# Summary and Conclusions

This study has chronicled the development of the Chicago monetary tradition from its initial sprouts in 1927 to its transformation into monetarism in 1960. The year 1927 saw Paul Douglas present his ideas on the desirability of monetary rules and money-financed fiscal deficits, and Frank Knight publish his misgivings about fractional-reserve banking, each of which would become distinguishing characteristics of the Chicago tradition. The year 1927 also saw the arrival of Knight, Henry Simons, and Aaron Director at Chicago. The year 1960 saw Milton Friedman publish his monetarist-policy framework, including the monetary-growth rule. The main conclusions of this study are the following.

*What the Chicago tradition was.* In the early 1930s, Chicago economists, who referred to themselves collectively as The Group, developed an original and distinctive approach to the quantity theory of money. Using the Fisherine equation of exchange as their analytical framework and writing in the midst of the Great Depression, the Chicagoans emphasized the inherent instability of the velocity of circulation of money in the absence of a rule for long-term money management. Changes in velocity were considered to be the primary mover of the business cycle and a contributor to the cumulative character of the cycle through the effect of changing price expectations on profits and output. The Chicagoans believed that the cumulative character of the cycle was greatly aggravated by the "perverse" nature of a fractional-reserve banking system, which rendered the economic system "inherently unstable." The cumulative process of economic contraction had no natural limit.

The Chicago tradition was policy centric and policy activist. It emphasized the need of changes in the money supply to counteract the business cycle. Building on the policy framework of the English Bank Act of 1844 (or Peel Act), in the 1920s Knight and Simons originated the idea of 100 percent reserve requirements against demand deposits although the idea did not make it into their writings during that decade. The requirement that demand deposits be backed with 100 percent reserves, the Chicagoans argued, would (1) protect depositors from bank failures, making banking crises less frequent, (2) allow the monetary authorities to better control the money supply, (3) reduce the frequency and amplitude of the business cycle, and (4) make seigniorage from the creation of money the exclusive privilege of the government. The idea was introduced into American policy discussions in the March 1933 Chicago memorandum. That memorandum also advocated money-financed fiscal deficits, the abandonment of the gold standard in favor of flexible exchange rates, balancing the government's fiscal position over the business cycle, and monetary-policy rules. Those policies were pushed forward in the November 1933 memorandum, which contained detailed presentations of the Chicagoans' views of the business cycle and policy rules. Earlier, in an April 1932 memorandum, the Chicagoans had advocated an identical set of policy proposals with the exception of flexible exchange rates and the 100 percent reserves scheme. In their early 1930s memoranda, the Chicagoans (with the exception of Viner) argued that monetary policies that operate through the banking system are ineffective in combating depressions.

The November 1933 memorandum marked the genesis of the long-running (to this day) discussion in the literature about rules versus discretion. Although other economists, including Irving Fisher, had advocated a policy of price-level stabilization in the 1920s and 1930s, the Chicagoans were the first economists to (1) make the case for rules within the context of an assessment of rules versus discretion, (2) provide criteria (e.g., simplicity, definiteness, ease of communication) to evaluate rules, (3) assess the advantages and disadvantages of alternative rules, and (4) advocate rules because they tie the hands of the authorities, thereby reducing potential policy mistakes, political manipulation of monetary policy, and policy uncertainty. The orientation of policy rules in terms of the reduction of policy uncertainty helped distinguish the views of Simons and Lloyd Mints from those of other advocates of price-level stabilization, including Irving Fisher, and helps resolve the so-called puzzle as to why Simons did not give credit to Fisher for the latter's proposal of a stable price level.

In my discussion of the origins of the rules-versus-discretion debate, I showed that the nineteenth-century debate in Britain between the banking school and the currency school was not about rules versus discretion, contrary to the present consensus among doctrinal historians. In particular, I showed that the nineteenth-century debate was about the "optimal" degree of activism in a rule. Both sides of the debate were hostile to discretionary policies. Both sides favored an automatic mechanism to regulate the quantity of money in order to stabilize the economy, but the banking school, unlike the currency school, favored an activistic, interest-rate rule. I also show that my interpretation of the currency school–banking school debate coincides with that of historians of economic thought prior to the 1970s.

The Chicagoans' approach to advancing their policy agenda was distinctive in terms of its originality, the combination of policies proposed, and the assertiveness with which it was put forward. In the early 1930s, the Chicagoans held two major conferences on the causes of—and policy responses to—the Great Depression, featuring some of the most distinguished economists of the day, including John Maynard Keynes, and they sent a series of policy memoranda to Washington policy makers, a pattern that would be repeated in the late 1940s and early 1950s in the contexts of the post–World War II inflation and the inflation associated with the Korean War.

*Perseverance.* In the 1930s and 1940s, a period that saw the American intellectual community overwhelmingly endorse increased government intervention in economic affairs, Chicagoans Knight, Simons, Director, Lloyd Mints, and Garfield Cox defended the free-market system.

- Knight and Simons published sharply critical reviews of Keynes's *General Theory*, viewing it as a platform for government control over economic life.
- Knight stressed the idea that markets perform an essential function as a social mechanism for achieving voluntary cooperation among diverse economic units. Only such a system, he believed, provides the freedom of choice required to allow individuals to set and pursue their own objectives.
- Simons pushed forward an agenda for a market system comprising (1) the elimination of private monopolies, (2) monetary rules, (3) the restructuring of the tax system, with the progressive income tax playing an important role in achieving equality and underpinning the generation of revenue, and (4) the elimination of tariffs on international trade.
- At a time that the Keynesian income-expenditure model swept through the economics profession, the Chicagoans continued to use the quantity theory of money to analyze the business cycle and to stress the importance of money. Simons, Mints, Director, and Friedman engaged the leading Keynesians of the 1940s and 1950s, including Alvin Hansen, Michal Kalecki, Abba Lerner, Seymour Harris, Paul Samuelson, and James Tobin, in debate, defending the quantity theory.

- At a time that the economics profession overwhelmingly endorsed secular fiscal deficits and paid essentially no attention to the means of financing the deficits, the Chicagoans favored money-financed fiscal deficits with the provision that the budget should be balanced over the business cycle. The Chicagoans' use of the quantity theory to justify fiscal deficits in the early 1930s left them well placed to rebuff the central policy message of Keynes's *General Theory*, a main purpose of which was to provide a theory to rationalize fiscal deficits (Patinkin 1987, 24). Neither Director, Douglas, Knight, Mints, nor Simons abandoned the quantity theory for the Keynesian theoretical framework.

- In the late 1940s and early 1950s, a period during which the economics profession downplayed the role of money in the economy and supported the Fed's interest-rate-pegging policy, a policy that subordinated the Fed to the Treasury, Chicagoans, including Director, Friedman, Knight, and Mints, fought for the termination of that policy. In his capacity as a US Senator, Douglas was the leading figure in achieving the 1951 "accord" between the Fed and the Treasury, which provided the Fed with independence. The accord was the first example of the postwar influence of the Chicago tradition on monetary policy.

- In the mid- and late 1940s, when a large majority of the economics profession endorsed the Bretton Woods fixed-but-adjustable exchange-rate system, Mints, building on the arguments of the November 1933 memorandum and Simons's work in the mid-1930s, criticized that exchange-rate regime and put forth original insights about the benefits of flexible rates. Mints's work on exchange-rate regimes was subsequently extended by Friedman, who, together with Director, conceived the notion that a group of countries could form an optimum currency area if the characteristics of their economies fulfilled certain criteria.

Thus, a conclusion that emerges from this study is the following: in the midst of the Keynesian revolution, which both greatly downplayed the role of money in the economy and advocated a much-expanded role for government engagement in economic affairs, the University of Chicago Economics Department was a stronghold in which the allegiances to the importance of money and free markets were defended and preserved. Not only does this conclusion emerge from the doctrinal evidence presented in the preceding chapters, but it is observable in the contemporaneous literature following the publication of the *General Theory*. In a 1950 article, "The Economists," published in *Fortune*, business historian John McDonald provided a survey of the then state of economics.[1] Regarding the influence of Keynes, McDonald (1950, 128) wrote that, throughout the Keynesian revolution, a "fortress of [monetary and free-market] orthodoxy was maintained at Chicago. . . . The effect of Keynes . . . was not localized. He swept the profession, excepting Chicago." A similar view was expressed by Francis X. Sutton at the peak of Keynesian influence on US policy making. In a 1963 review of Friedman's book *Capitalism and Freedom*, Sutton stated: "For more than a generation, the University of Chicago has been a citadel of resistance to economic doctrines that have become orthodoxy in our time." After noting that Knight, Simons, and Friedman had "given Chicago a name for brilliant critiques that usually get called 'conservative,' but which Friedman insists are 'liberal,'" Sutton added: "Friedman has long been known as a formidable knight in the Chicago citadel" (1963, 491).[2]

Upon his move into monetary economics as his primary field of interest in 1948, Friedman embraced the conceptual and policy frameworks of the Chicago monetary tradition. Using the Fisherine equation of exchange, he considered velocity shocks to be the primary mover of the business cycle. The cycle, he believed, was exacerbated by the "perverse" character of the fractional-reserve banking system, rendering the economy "inherently unstable." Friedman thought that there was no bottom to a depression. He called for a policy rule under which the federal government's budget position would be used to generate changes in the money supply automatically. He believed that the budget should be balanced over the business cycle, and he advocated 100 percent reserves and flexible exchange rates. In the late 1940s Friedman called for the abolition of open-market operations.

*What the Chicago tradition was not.* Doctrinal historians have long incorrectly maintained that the Chicago tradition was characterized by (1) the belief in the efficacy of open-market operations and (2) the view that the Great Depression was caused and deepened by a failure of monetary policy. Those attributes did *not* characterize the Chicago tradition. The 1930s and 1940s Chicagoans believed that open-market operations were ineffective during depressions because banks did not want to lend and businesses did not want to borrow during such episodes. The January 1932 Hoover telegram—signed by twenty-four economists, including twelve Chicagoans, calling for expansionary measures that worked through the banking system—has been cited by Friedman (and others) as representative of Chicago thinking. It was not. It was a compromise document representing the heterogeneous views of its signatories. The policy measures espoused in that document did not reappear in the strictly Chicago memoranda, nor in the writings of the individual Chicagoans (with the exception of Viner). In the 1930s, the members of The Group did not attribute the origins of the Great Depression to Federal Reserve policies.

*Jacob Viner.* In contrast to the other Chicagoans, in the early 1930s, Viner criticized the Fed for its policies during the Depression and believed in the efficacy of open-market operations. Viner's views were not, however, representative of the Chicago monetary tradition. In contrast to the other Chicagoans, Viner (1) favored retention of the gold standard and opposed flexible exchange rates, (2) favored branch banking and opposed the 100 percent reserves scheme, (3) thought that cost cutting was an appropriate response to the Depression, (4) opposed money-financed fiscal deficits, (5) favored monetary-policy discretion and opposed policy rules, and (6) was not averse to increased government intervention in the economic system. Viner refused to identify himself as a member of the Chicago tradition.

During the Great Depression, Viner criticized the Federal Reserve System's policies, arguing that those policies were based on the real bills doctrine.[3] Moreover, in the early 1930s, Harvard economist Lauchlin Currie— whose views had been influenced at Harvard by Ralph Hawtrey and Allyn Young (the former while a visitor at Harvard)—blamed the Great Depression on the Fed's real bills orientation. The criticisms of the Federal Reserve's policies by Viner likely influenced Mints's development of the monetary hypothesis of the Great Depression in the 1940s; through Mints, the criticisms by Viner were transmitted to Clark Warburton's thinking. Ultimately, the criticisms of the Fed's policies based on the real bills orientation of those policies made their way into Friedman and Schwartz's *A Monetary History.* Friedman and Schwartz presented the real bills doctrine as one factor, among several factors, that helped explain the Federal Reserve's calamitous policies during the Great Depression.

*Paul Douglas.* In the late 1920s and early 1930s, Douglas was among those American intellectuals who had been attracted to the Soviet Union's planning system. Douglas was a political activist who increasingly became involved in local politics in Chicago. His political views and his opposition to Director's and Simons's faculty appointments became sources of friction with Knight. In the 1930s, Douglas increasingly distanced himself from the Economics Department and, in the first half of the 1940s, went off to engage in combat in World War II. With his increased involvement in politics, Douglas, in contrast to Knight, did not establish a cohort of disciples to perpetuate his research agenda (in labor economics) or his political philosophy. From the mid-1930s to the mid-1940s, work on monetary economics at Chicago was increasingly spearheaded by a small group of free-market economists—Knight, Simons, and Mints. Beginning in 1946, a group of former Knight students and protégés returned to Chicago in teaching positions to carry forward free-market views. The group included Friedman (Economics Department), Director (Law School), and W. Allen Wallis (Graduate School of Business), all of whom returned in 1946. They were joined by George Stigler, who began teaching in the School of Business in 1958. The critical mass, in quality and numbers, necessary for the intergenerational transmission of ideological attitudes formed around what was known as "Knight's affinity group" (Reder 1982, 7).

Despite sharp differences with the other members of The Group over politics, Douglas shared their views on monetary issues. He was a quantity theorist who drew on underconsumptionist analytics to bring the idea of using the government's fiscal position to change the money supply to Chicago. He advocated monetary rules, initially a 3 to 4 percent money-growth rule and, subsequently, a price-level-stabilization rule, 100 percent reserves, and flexible exchange rates. In addition to spearheading the Treasury–Federal Reserve accord in 1951, in congressional hearings in the late 1950s, he gave tacit approval to Friedman's monetarist policy agenda.

*Lloyd Mints.* Mints's entry into the monetary debates in the mid-1940s produced changes in the Chicago quantity-theory framework. As Knight (1937; 1941a) had done earlier, Mints (1945a; 1950) incorporated elements of portfolio theory in an analysis of the demand for money. However, the money-demand frameworks of Knight and Mints differed fundamentally from those of Keynes (in the *General Theory*) and Friedman (in his 1956 "Restatement" of the quantity theory). That difference was reflected in their respective treatments of stocks and flows. In particular, for Keynes and Friedman, wealth was the variable that constituted the total budget constraint on the holdings of assets, including money—so that an increase in wealth generally resulted in increased holdings of all assets—whereas an increase in income increased the demand for money at the expense of other assets. Knight and Mints, in contrast, did not distinguish between the effects of income and wealth on the demand for money. Thus, Patinkin's (1969) argument that Friedman's (1956a) model of the demand for money owed more to Keynes than to Chicago was correct, an argument that Friedman (1972) subsequently accepted.

In his *A History of Banking Theory in Great Britain and the United States*, Mints introduced the historical-narrative technique into the Chicago literature to criticize the Federal Reserve's discretionary policies. In doing so, he used the real bills doctrine, a name that he originated, to describe the Fed's policies since that institution's inception, thus providing a cohesive thread that tied his historical critiques of the Fed's policies together. Mints criticized the role of the Federal Reserve in deepening the Great Depression, arguing that the severity of that episode would have been prevented had the Fed followed a policy rule, instead of adhering to the real bills doctrine. While expressing a preference for 100 percent reserves, he recognized that federal deposit insurance helped eliminate the "inherent instability" of fractional-reserve banking. Influenced by Clark Warburton's work, in the early 1950s he accepted the idea that the economy is inherently stable but is thrown off course by discretionary monetary policies, and not, as he had earlier argued, by autonomous shifts in velocity. In contrast to the Chicago tradition's view that there is no natural limit to the decline in economic activity during a depression, he came to believe that, regardless of the kinds of shocks that generated business cycles, the real balance effect provided a limit to the downside of a depression. Mints developed the notion that, if the central bank attempted to bring unemployment below its frictional level, serious inflation would result. He put forward the idea that the effectiveness of discretionary policies is dependent on accurate forecasting, a view shared by Friedman and Director.

*Milton Friedman.* After adopting key elements of the 1930s and 1940s Chicago monetary framework, Friedman methodically reconstructed that framework, brick by brick, into his particular monetarist structure. Friedman brought to the table a skill set that his Chicago predecessors working in the field of money did not have—a cutting-edge knowledge of applied and theoretical statistics. He applied that skill set to his work, and to his collaborations with Anna Schwartz and his students in the Chicago Workshop in Money and Banking, to demonstrate the following: (1) the damage that discretionary policies could inflict in the presence of long and variable lags; (2) the neutrality of money in the long run; (3) the secular stability of the demand for money or the velocity of circulation of money, with velocity declining over the long run; (4) the non-neutrality of money during the business cycle, with velocity behaving in a procyclical way, its intensity dependent on the magnitude of the prior change in the money supply; (5) the robust explanatory power of a money-demand function that incorporates permanent income and permanent prices for predicting both secular velocity and cyclical velocity; (6) the complete dominance of money per unit of output compared to other variables, including the government's fiscal position, in explaining prices during wartime episodes— that is, episodes marked by very high inflation; (7) the destructive role played by the Fed in both initiating and deepening the Great Depression; (8) the superior empirical performance of the money supply, as compared with autonomous expenditures, in explaining personal consumption expenditures, thus providing evidence in favor of the quantity theory over the Keynesian income-expenditure model. To support his critiques of discretionary policies, Friedman supplemented statistical analyses with the historical-monetary narrative; the latter provided the added flexibility of examining data within the context of historical and political dimensions that could not be easily distilled from statistical analyses.

Friedman modified the free-market element of the Chicago monetary-cum-free-market agenda, especially as put forward by Simons. Unlike Simons, Friedman (1) did not single out labor unions as a major problem, (2) thought that the progressive income tax had a negligible effect on inequality and could even be regressive, and (3) thought that natural monopolies should be put in private hands rather than socialized. Friedman believed that the capitalistic system worked to reduce inequality. He favored a negative income tax to help deal with poverty. Like Simons (in the 1940s), Friedman did not believe that industrial monopolies were a major problem. In cases in which such monopolies existed, like Simons, Friedman favored the use of antitrust legislation. Director's work, showing that competitive forces from the supply side of the market had the effective tendency to destroy all types of monopoly, contributed to the Chicagoan deemphasis of the monopoly issue in the 1950s. In sum, Friedman and Director moved the Chicago framework in the direction of less government involvement in economic affairs than had been the case under Simons.

Clark Warburton provided criticisms of Friedman's initial monetary framework, which helped Friedman redirect his research efforts—notably in assessing the role of the Fed in the Great Depression, the long-run behavior of velocity, the efficacy of open-market operations in a monetary system in which the monetary unit consists solely of the government's fiat liability, and the 3 to 5 percent monetary-growth rule. Friedman did not give Warburton sufficient credit for shaping his views at a critical juncture in the development of his (Friedman's) monetary economics. More generally, Friedman had a tendency to not give sufficient consideration to the intellectual origins of his ideas despite the fact that he cited the influences of his Chicago predecessors, especially Simons and Mints, on numerous occasions.[4]

Director worked behind the scenes as a confidant to Friedman. In the mid-1950s, Director shared Friedman's views on monetary policy, including the Fed's role in causing the Great Depression, the advocacy of a monetary-growth rule, and the benefits of both flexible exchange rates and 100 percent reserves. Apart from Warburton, very few economists held these views at the time.

What about the claim that Friedman made in his 1956 "Restatement" of the quantity theory that his formulation "convey[ed] the flavor of the [Chicago] oral tradition"? The following points are important.

- Friedman was not the first person to refer to a "Chicago tradition" or to a "Chicago school." By the mid-1940s, members of the economics profession had begun to refer to the Chicago monetary-policy framework and free-market orientation as the "Mints-Simons program," indicating that the profession viewed the Chicagoans as unconventional and intractable. By the early 1950s, the Chicago singular advocacy of flexible exchange rates was called the "Friedman-Mints scheme" (Kindleberger 1953, 302), and referral to a Chicago tradition was standard nomenclature among economists, including Harry Johnson, who subsequently accused Friedman of having invented the notion of a Chicago monetary tradition. By the early 1950s, the Chicagoans publicly referred to their views on money and free markets as those of the "Chicago tradition."
- In 1956, when Friedman published his "Restatement," the Chicago monetary tradition had undergone a thorough revision. To be sure, core elements remained in place—including the emphasis on money and the advocacies of monetary-policy rules, 100 percent reserves, and flexible exchange rates. Friedman's empirical studies had, as emphasized, produced substantial changes to the Chicago tradition. The end of the Federal Reserve's policy of pegging the prices of Treasury securities in the early 1950s allowed Friedman to consider those securities and money to be differentiated assets. That factor, combined with his empirical studies showing monetary dominance, contributed to the view that open-market operations were an effective instrument for generating changes in the money supply. By changing the stock of high-powered money, Friedman had come to believe that open-market operations could be used in a flexible way to offset changes in the ratios underlying the money multiplier and, thus, control the money stock. Federal deposit insurance and the automatic fiscal stabilizers, he believed, rendered the economy inherently stable. Major business cycles were caused by discretionary monetary policies in his view.
- As Friedman (1956a, 3) wrote in his "Restatement," "the Chicago tradition was not a rigid system, an unchangeable orthodoxy, but a way of looking at things. It was a theoretical approach that insisted that money does matter." Friedman's research underpinned the changing character of the Chicago tradition while maintaining the belief that money matters.

Why did Friedman (in his 1956 "Restatement" of the quantity theory) choose to convey the flavor of the Chicago tradition in terms of a

Keynesian portfolio-demand function for money? There were at least two possible reasons. First, as mentioned, there were post–*General Theory* antecedents for the portfolio approach in the works of Mints and Knight that likely influenced Friedman's thinking. Second, to mount an effective theoretical challenge to the Keynesian orthodoxy, Friedman might have thought that it would be most effective to meet that orthodoxy on its own terms, with its own model. Whereas Keynesians posited that the demand for money is unstable and highly interest elastic, Friedman (1956a) argued that the demand for money is a stable function of a few variables. His empirical work provided support of a stable demand-for-money function in which real per capita income, rather than an interest rate variable, was the important factor in explaining variations in real money balances.

Why, in the defense of his claim that his monetary economics was an outgrowth of a Chicago tradition, did Friedman (1972) rely on (1) the January 1932 Hoover telegram that emphasized the need of policies that operate through the banking system and (2) Viner's critiques of Fed policies in the early 1930s? As demonstrated, neither the Hoover telegram nor Viner's views on Fed policies in the early 1930s characterized the Chicago monetary tradition. The Chicagoans considered open-market and discounting operations to be ineffective. Mints was the only member of The Group to criticize the Fed's policies during the Depression, and he did not do so until the late 1930s—in his classroom lectures—and in the mid-1940s—in his published work. The answer to the question posed at the beginning of this paragraph is that—as noted in chapter 1—Friedman was not a doctrinal historian. He could not have been expected to have had a rigorous knowledge of the evolution of the Chicago tradition. Consequently, in his debate with Patinkin, and, to some extent, Johnson, Friedman was at a distinct disadvantage since Johnson and (especially) Patinkin had a thoroughgoing knowledge of monetary doctrine. A more relevant question, in my view, is why doctrinal historians, who should have had knowledge of the full picture of the monetary literature of the 1930s and 1940s, let the Patinkin-Johnson side of the story go unchallenged and untarnished for so long.

*Postscript.* In May 1967, Friedman delivered the third Henry Simons Lecture, at the University of Chicago Law School. The title of the lecture was "The Monetary Theory and Policy of Henry Simons." Friedman described Simons as "my teacher and my friend—and above all, a shaper of my ideas" (1967, 82).[5] Friedman characterized Simons's theory—the quantity theory of money—as "sophisticated and correct." Friedman noted that during a period "when, thanks to the Keynesian Revolution, the economics profession came to regard money . . . as an unimportant and uninteresting subject," Simons maintained the view that "the quantity of money and its behavior play a central role in affecting the course of prices and of economic activity; that monetary stability is an essential prerequisite for economic stability" (1967, 82).

Regarding monetary *policy*, Friedman put some distance between his views and those of Simons. Friedman noted that Simons placed priority on the reform of the financial system, including the 100 percent reserves scheme, limitations on the borrowing powers of corporations (i.e., corporations would be allowed to issue equities but not debt), and the simplification of the government debt structure (i.e., government debt would be limited to money and consols). Friedman thought that Simons's financial reforms "went in the wrong direction." Friedman argued: "Why should we not have variety and diversity in the market for borrowing and lending as in other markets? . . . Is it not a sign of the ingenuity and efficiency of the free market that financial intermediaries develop which reconcile the needs of borrowers and lenders—providing funds on terms desired by borrowers and borrowing on terms desired by lenders?" (1967, 83). On the issue of 100 percent reserves, Friedman stated that he agreed with Simons on its desirability but regarded it as less important than Simons. For Simons, the 100 percent reserves scheme was a step toward making effective the legislative limitations he favored on the terms on which people could borrow and lend. For Friedman, the scheme was "a step toward reducing government interference with lending and borrowing in order to permit a greater degree of freedom and variety in the arrangements for borrowing and lending" (1967, 83). Finally, Friedman noted that, whereas he favored a monetary-growth rule, Simons favored a price-level-stabilization rule.

Friedman then queried: "What explains this contrast [in policy views]?" (1967, 84). The answer, Friedman explained, had to do with Simons's interpretation of the Great Depression. Simons's policy views, like those of Keynes, had been shaped by that episode. Both Simons and Keynes, Friedman argued, thought that the Great Depression had been caused by a collapse in the velocity of circulation of money. As did Keynes, Simons "implicitly regarded the Great Depression as occurring despite not because of governmental monetary policy" (1967, 86).

Friedman proceeded to provide a historical narrative of the Great Depression's key episodes, beginning with the Federal Reserve's initial tightening in mid-1928 to quell stock-market speculation, and continuing with the "dramatic failure" of the Bank of United States in New York in December 1930, and the Fed's policy tightening in the fall of 1931 after Britain left the gold standard (1967, 89–93). At the conclusion of his narrative, Friedman summarized the empirical evidence that he and Schwartz had produced as follows:

> It turns out that the rate of growth of the quantity of money has systematically tapered off well before the economy in general slows down and has speeded up well before the economy speeds up. The movements in velocity—which Simons took as an independent source of instability—come later than the movements in the quantity of money and are mild when the movements in the quantity of money are mild. They have been sharp only when there have been sharp movements in the quantity of money. (1967, 92)

Friedman (1967, 91) concluded his essay by stating that he had "stressed the Great Depression because this climactic episode clearly played a key role in leading Simons—and also Keynes—to believe that the orthodox powers of the monetary authorities were too weak to cope with disorders arising in private financial markets."

The introduction to Friedman's 1967 Henry Simons Lecture was given by Director. In his (unpublished) introduction, Director made a statement that affirmed *his* belief in the existence of a Chicago monetary tradition: "One of the fields which Henry Simons cultivated was that of monetary theory and policy. That he did so accounts in no small measure for the continued interest in, and cultivation of, this subject at the University of Chicago, while it languished elsewhere" (Director 1967, 3). That Director, and especially Friedman, *also* cultivated that field accounts in no small measure for the continued interest in monetary theory and policy at the University of Chicago in the 1950s and 1960s and for the continuity in stressing the importance of money between the framework of Chicago of the early 1930s and that of Chicago of the 1950s and after—Director, as always, working behind the scenes, making sure that the candle to the old-time Chicago religion remained lit, and Friedman, as always, at the frontlines of the intellectual battlefield, leading the counter-revolutionary charge against the Keynesian orthodoxy.

# Notes

## Chapter One

1. There were four essays by Friedman's students. The essays were by Cagan (1956), J. Klein (1956), E. Lerner (1956), and Selden (1956). The authors of the essays constructed aggregate time series on measures of the money supply and prices to study the effects on inflation during and after the world wars and in the US. Lucas (2017, 1831) judged the dissertations as "stunning examples of economics at its best."

2. Blaug (1985, 689) stated that "monetarism began with Friedman's 1956 formulation of what he understood to be the quantity theory." The view that monetarism began with Friedman's "Restatement" was also expressed by Johnson (1972, 60), Gordon (1981, 504), Snowdon, Vane, and Wynarczyk (1994, 138), and Desai (2004, 166). As will be discussed in what follows, Friedman's work on restoring the quantity theory began in the late 1940s.

3. Friedman earned an MA (master of arts) degree from Chicago in 1933. Upon his return to Chicago during the 1934–35 academic year, he took additional course work. Between his stints at Chicago in the 1930s, Friedman earned a master's degree from Columbia University. See Nelson (2020, 1:28–29). Friedman satisfied the requirements for a PhD, other than the dissertation, at both the University of Chicago and Columbia University but decided to complete his PhD at Columbia "for purely practical reasons" (Friedman and Friedman 1998, 51).

4. Friedman then assumed that the money-demand function is homogenous of degree one in $P$ and $Y$, thereby converting the function into a demand for real money balances, with $M/P$ replacing $M$ as the dependent variable and $Y/P$ replacing $Y$ as an explanatory variable.

5. A similar point was made by Tavlas (1998, 217–18). Meltzer (1977) observed that Friedman (1956a) allowed for the possibility of a spread between the real yields on bonds and equities so that, in contrast to Keynesian theory, the yields on financial instruments could not be reduced to a single rate of return under Friedman's framework. Fand (1969, 563) noted that by treating the demand for money as a problem in capital theory, focusing on the composition of the balance sheet and

the selection of assets, Friedman's formulation of the quantity theory was distinguishable from the earlier Fisherine and Cambridge versions of the quantity theory, which emphasized payments relations and store-of-value relations, respectively.

6. Patinkin was a research associate at the Cowles Commission. The work of the Cowles Commission is explained later in this chapter.

7. According to the University of Chicago 1946–47 *Catalogue* (which in all cases actually refers to the following academic year), for the academic year 1946–47 Patinkin taught the following courses: Introduction to Statistics (Econ 201), Introduction to Mathematics for Economists (Econ 213), and Statistical Inference (Econ 312).

8. Leeson (1998, 437) reported, that during the late 1940s and the 1950s, Patinkin often asked for and received advice from Friedman.

9. The correspondence could be highly personal and poignant. Patinkin, who was born in Chicago in 1922 to a family of Jewish emigrants from Poland, accepted a position at the Hebrew University of Jerusalem in 1949. In a letter dated November 21, 1950, Patinkin wrote to Friedman in response to a letter Friedman had sent in which he (Friedman) wrote about a visit he had made to postwar Germany. Patinkin responded: "I found your reaction to your visit to Germany very interesting. Under ordinary circumstances, I would probably react the same way. It is hard to continue hating when the acts which have instigated that hatred have become only memories, and all one sees in front of him is a human being with normal human reactions. But in my case—and in the case of most people living in Israel—the memory is still a reality. I had the experience a few weeks ago of counseling a student and suddenly noticing his Nazi concentration camp number burnt into his arm. That is not an experience one can forget. And here it is not an isolated experience" (Milton Friedman Papers, Hoover Institution Library and Archives, Stanford University).

10. In a 1948 paper, Patinkin argued that Keynes's "fundamental error" was in focusing exclusively on the relationship between real cash balances and interest rates through the liquidity-preference function, thus, failing to take into account of the relationship between real cash balances and consumption (Patinkin 1948, 555).

11. Patinkin's book (*Money, Interest, and Prices*) was used as a text for graduate courses in macroeconomics in the 1960s. A second edition was published in 1965, and an abridged second edition was published in 1989. Patinkin (1965, 21) claimed that "the real balance effect in the commodity markets is the *sine qua non* of monetary theory," a claim that generated considerable discussion. See, for example, Archibald and Lipsey (1958) and Ball and Bodkin (1960). As pointed out by Aschheim and Tavlas (1991, 506), in the second, abridged edition, Patinkin (1989) turned to the special circumstance of the immediate aftermath of World War II (massive accumulation of excess liquidity and suppressed demands of households and firms suddenly released by the outbreak of peace) for empirical validation of the real balance effect. Patinkin (1989, xxiii) reported that various empirical studies had shown that the real balance effect was statistically significant.

12. A major impetus for the change in focus was Friedman's (1968a) work on the Phillips curve. According to Nelson (2020, 1:219), in the late 1940s Friedman

attached considerable importance to real balance effects on aggregate demand. Subsequently, however, Friedman did not believe that the real balance effect was important for output fluctuations.

13. In his 1968 entry, Friedman interpreted the expected rate of change of the prices of goods, $(1/P)(dP/dt)$, as the rate of return on real assets, whereas in his 1956 essay he had interpreted it as the cost of holding money. In his 1968 entry, he introduced an additional variable, $r_w$, to capture the cost of holding money. Conceptually, there is no distinction between the rate of return on real assets and the cost of holding money, provided that the latter means the cost of holding an alternative to money (i.e., an opportunity cost). Friedman (1982, 274) used the two concepts interchangeably in his book *Monetary Trends*, co-authored with Anna Schwartz.

14. Friedman had earlier made a similar concession in a 1963 paper. See Friedman (1963, 1).

15. Patinkin's statement suggests that he believed that Friedman took courses with Simons, Mints, Knight, and Viner in the early 1930s. The inference that Friedman took courses from those four individuals can be drawn—incorrectly—from his 1956 "Restatement" of the quantity theory in which he wrote that those four Chicagoans "taught and developed a more subtle and relevant version" of the quantity theory (Friedman 1956a, 3). In fact, although Friedman took courses with Mints, Knight, and Viner, he did not take a course with Simons. See, for example, Kitch (1983, 179), where Friedman is quoted as stating: "I never took a course from him" [i.e., Simons]. Nevertheless, Friedman had been heavily influenced by Simons's writings—see chapter 6 below.

16. Patinkin's formal presentation of the Fisherine equation omitted the term $M'V'$. It was clear, however, from his written depiction of the earlier Chicago framework that $M'V'$ played a key role in his understanding of the working of the business cycle in that framework, as evidenced in Patinkin's third "summary proposition," described below.

17. See also Patinkin (1972b; 1972c).

18. The lecture was delivered in December 1970 and published in the May 1971 issue of the *American Economic Review*.

19. The specific purpose of Johnson's lecture was to draw attention to some striking similarities between the conditions that contributed to the Keynesian revolution and those that contributed to the monetarist counter-revolution.

20. See Friedman (1970b; 1971a).

21. The other reviewers were Karl Brunner and Allan Meltzer (jointly), James Tobin, and Paul Davidson.

22. I list the signatories in chapter 2. Credit for the discovery of the telegram belongs to J. R. Davis (1968).

23. Viner's views on the Federal Reserve's role in the Great Depression are discussed in some detail in chapters 2 and 3.

24. The 1972 *JPE* symposium was published as a book, edited by Gordon (1974). Some of the contributors made minor changes to their papers. In the case of Patinkin's paper, the changes were in the form of additional footnotes.

25. In a 1990 *JPE* publication, Steindl mistakenly wrote that "Patinkin . . . disputes the existence" of a Chicago quantity-theory tradition (Steindl 1990, 430). In a draft reply to Steindl's publication, submitted to the *JPE*, Patinkin wrote: "far from denying the existence of such a tradition (as Steindl . . . alleges) . . . I devoted section III of my 1969 paper . . . to document a Chicago oral tradition of monetary theory . . . which differs fundamentally from the picture that Friedman presents of it in his 1956 essay" (Patinkin 1991, 381). Leeson (2003b) reported that Patinkin's submission was rejected by George Stigler, who, at the time, was a coeditor of the *JPE*.

26. Leeson (2000, 238) stated: "From the late 1960s both (Patinkin and Johnson) were highly agitated about a one-page section in a 1956 essay: this can only adequately be explained by Friedman's increasing influence over policy, their jealousy, the competition for Nobel Prizes, and their sense of being oppressed by the shadow of Friedman." A similar argument about Patinkin's motives was made by Forder (2019, 225–26).

27. This possibility was brought to my attention by David Laidler in personal correspondence with me dated August 16, 2021. Laidler added that Patinkin "was working in relative isolation in Jerusalem, with heavy local teaching and administrative commitments" and that in the mid-1960s Patinkin had become involved with the emerging literature on money and growth, which, in many ways, was a natural extension of the analysis in *Money, Interest, and Prices*. In these circumstances, Laidler conjectured that Patinkin had not focused on providing a paper on the Chicago monetary tradition, but when Patinkin received an invitation to contribute to the inaugural issue of the *JMCB*, "he [Patinkin] saw an opportunity to place an article that he had long contemplated but never written."

28. Johnson taught at Chicago from 1959 until his death in 1977. Moggridge (2008) reported that Johnson was generally unhappy at Chicago and from time to time considered the possibility of moving to another academic institution. In 1966 Johnson accepted a joint appointment (with Chicago) at the London School of Economics, where he taught until 1974. In 1976–77 he held a joint appointment at Chicago and the Graduate Institute of International Studies in Geneva. What apparently displeased Johnson about Chicago was the "rough and tough of discussions in the economics department" and the right-wing, almost theological, character of those discussions. See Moggridge (2008, 203–9).

29. Evidently, Johnson's view was motivated by the following remark made by Keynes (1911, 393) in the latter's review of Irving Fisher's 1911 book *The Purchasing Power of Money*: "the theory of money, as it has been ordinarily understood and taught by academic economists in England [i.e., at Cambridge] for some time past, is considerably in advance of any published account of it. It is hardly an exaggeration to say that monetary theory, in its most accurate form, has become in England a matter of oral tradition."

30. Patinkin's PhD dissertation, completed in 1947, was titled "On the Inconsistency of Economic Models: A Theory of Involuntary Unemployment." As the title suggests, the thesis was a theoretical tract. It consisted of two parts. One part aimed

to demonstrate how general equilibrium models failed to incorporate money in a consistent manner. The second part provided microfoundations for the existence of involuntary unemployment. The thesis was inspired by Patinkin's course work with Oskar Lange, who taught theory at Chicago from 1939 to 1945 (see below). The thesis chair was Jacob Marschak. For discussions on the contents of Patinkin's thesis, see Boianovsky (2002) and Rubin (2012).

31. In personal correspondence with me, dated August 16, 2021, David Laidler recalled Patinkin's reaction to Laidler's having referred to Friedman's money-demand equation (equation [1.1]) as "the modern quantity theory" in Laidler's book *The Demand for Money: Theories and Evidence* (1969, chap. 5). Laidler wrote: "he [Patinkin] told me that by referring to Milton's equation as 'the modern quantity theory' ... I was acting like one of the editors of the Soviet Encyclopedia!" In his personal correspondence with me, Laidler emphasized Patinkin's reputation for impeccable personal integrity.

32. Forder (2019, 221) expressed the view that "Patinkin did not seem to be willing to let go of the issue," the implication being that Patinkin was motivated by personal factors.

33. In a letter from Friedman to Lionel Robbins, dated July 12, 1951, Friedman described himself as "a tyro in the history of thought" (quoted from Leeson 2003d, 513). In an interview that he conducted with Friedman's former student and collaborator David Meiselman on July 16, 2014, Nelson (2020, 2:207) reported that Meiselman stated: "Friedman was never very interested in the history of thought. . . . He just wasn't involved in the intellectual battles of who said what first." Friedman did display a selective knowledge of doctrinal monetary history. See, for example, Friedman (1975b), where he discussed Irving Fisher's view on the short-term trade-off between inflation and unemployment, and Friedman (1992b), where he briefly discussed the quantity-theory views of Fisher, David Hume, J. S. Mill, Simon Newcomb, and A. C. Pigou.

34. Nevertheless, Colander and Freedman (2019, 198n20) erroneously claimed: "Friedman relentlessly battled Don Patinkin over a fair stretch of years in his quest to construct a bridge tying his formulated quantity theory of money with some ersatz oral tradition that mysteriously thrived in Chicago during the 1930s."

35. In an article that was not directly related to the relationship between Friedman's 1956 "Restatement" and the earlier Chicago monetary tradition, Hammond (1999) showed that the roots of the "Restatement" could be traced to Friedman's pre-1956 use of National Bureau of Economic Research business-cycle methods, Marshallian methodology and value theory, and the Cambridge cash-balances version of the quantity theory. Hammond documented that these elements were used by Friedman beginning in the 1940s.

36. Although Snyder anticipated Friedman's monetary-growth rule, Tavlas (1982) documented that Snyder's rendition of the quantity theory was uncompromising and inflexible. In addition, Snyder opposed the use of fiscal deficits to combat depressions.

37. In a study of the development of Keynes's theory of a monetary economy, Dimand (1988) showed that a large number of economists in the 1930s were supporters of the UK "Treasury view" that higher fiscal spending has no effect on total economic activity. Dimand also showed that many academic supporters of higher public-works spending advocated theoretical views from which their policy advice could not be derived. For similar views, see Patinkin (1972c, 141–42) and Dimand (2002, 319).

38. Alternatively, Mints's views on the Fed's policies could have been shaped by his Chicago colleague Viner, who, as mentioned, had criticized the Fed's policies in the early 1930s.

39. As discussed in chapter 7, going into an April 1951 conference sponsored by the University of Chicago Law School, the Chicagoans indeed regarded Viner to be a "qualified" member of the Chicago school. Heading out of the conference, they did not.

40. Mints's course was titled Graduate Study of Money and Banking.

41. Laidler (1993) did not deny that Friedman's monetary economics was related to ideas that were current at Chicago in the 1930s. What Laidler claimed was that Friedman's monetary economics placed him closer to the work of Hawtrey, Young, and Currie than to the work of the 1930s Chicagoans, thereby casting doubt about the "uniqueness" of the earlier Chicago monetary tradition. The view that the ideas of the earlier Chicago monetary tradition were not unique has been a consistent theme in Laidler's work. See, for example, Laidler (1998a; 1998b; 1999, chap. 9; 2010).

42. As in the above quotation, Craig Freedman's writings have been characterized by their heavy use of metaphors and a lack of supporting evidence to substantiate the metaphors. In a review of Freedman's 2016 book *In Search of the Two-Handed Economist: Ideology, Methodology and Marketing in Economics*, Backhouse (2019a, 129) wrote: "Freedman's extravagant use of metaphor . . . can make it harder for the reader to assess the evidence [presented by Freedman]." Nelson (2020, vol. 1) contained four citations to Freedman's writings; in each instance, Nelson cited a statement by Freedman (sometimes with co-authors) that was misleading or not supported with evidence or both. See Nelson (2020, 1:215, 355, 503n174, 494n91).

43. See, also, Skidelsky (1992, 579), who, in his biography of Keynes, wrote that the "recollections of Friedman [with respect to the Chicago monetary tradition] should be taken with a 'pinch of salt'" and Blaug (1985, 652), who, in his highly regarded study on the history of economic doctrine, stated that Friedman's claim that "his restatement [of the quantity theory] was nothing more than the University of Chicago 'oral' tradition . . . was effectively destroyed by D. Patinkin." More recently, Backhouse and Tribe (2018, 369–70), in their book *The History of Economics*, wrote the following of Friedman's claim that "there was a long-standing tradition of work on the quantity theory" at Chicago: "subsequent work checking

syllabi and lists of doctoral theses [i.e., Patinkin's work] challenged the existence of any such tradition." Freedman et al. (2017, 618) stated that Patinkin had exposed the "flaw" in Friedman's account of a Chicago monetary tradition.

44. As mentioned, Patinkin stated that the Chicagoans were indifferent with regard to the sources changes in the quantity of money: the banking system or the government's fiscal position.

45. In a review of Johan Van Overtveldt's book *The Chicago School: How the University of Chicago Assembled Thinkers Who Revolutionized Economics and Business*, Laidler (2009, 413) downplayed the originality of the contributions of the early 1930s Chicagoans to 100 percent reserves and monetary rules as follows: "The 1933 Chicago plan for 100 percent money is rightly praised [by Van Overtveldt], but no hint is given that others were developing similar schemes at that time. One was [by] Lauchlin Currie. . . . Henry Simons is hailed as a key contributor to the analysis of rule-constrained monetary policy; so he was, but there is no mention that Irving Fisher had been visiting the same territory since the founding of the Fed."

46. In terms of policy preferences, as discussed in the next chapter, Viner was an outlier among the Chicagoans. Yet, Viner was such a major figure in the economics profession that the other Chicagoans sought to include him in what Director called the "Chicago tradition." See chapter 7.

47. The social gatherings typically took place on Sunday afternoons at Knight's home (see Tavlas 2019). In 1988, Mints recalled that, being single, he had a standing invitation for Sunday dinner at Knight's home and that other departmental members arrived for coffee and dessert (Peterson and Phillips 1991, 80).

48. The following material draws on University of Chicago catalogs for various academic years contained in the University's Special Collections Research Center. Additional biographical material is presented in subsequent chapters.

49. Mints taught the course in the second semester.

50. See Peterson (1980).

51. At Yale, Director and Rothko published a left-leaning newspaper called the *Saturday Evening Pest*.

52. Burgin (2012, 171) incorrectly stated that Director received a PhD.

53. In his autobiography *In the Fullness of Time*, Douglas recounted an aspect of the US academic environment of the early part of the twentieth century that warrants mentioning. Douglas (1972, 34) wrote: "There was one feature of Harvard life that I did not like. . . . Though the University had given up rating students in the catalogue with numbers indicating their social standing, informally the practice was still followed. The poor were regarded with disdain by all but a few, while an air of effortless superiority exuded from the others."

54. Douglas joined the Quaker Society of Friends in 1920.

55. See Cobb and Douglas (1928) and Douglas (1934). Biddle (2012) showed that the main innovation made by Cobb and Douglas was the use of their production

function as the basis of a least-squares regression for estimating the relationships between inputs and outputs.

56. Young moved to Harvard in 1920. For a discussion of Young's work on monetary economics, see Laidler (1993). See also chapter 3 below.

57. See Blaug (1985, 462–63) and G. Stigler (1987).

58. In his 2013 Nobel Prize lecture, Lars Peter Hansen quoted the above passage by Knight, noting that it posed a direct challenge to time series econometrics (Hansen 2014, 973). Research by Hansen has explored ways to take uncertainty into account in econometric estimation by, for example, using a range of models that, in turn, allows for a range of uncertainties, and assigning probabilities to each model. The probabilities can then be updated (for example, by Bayesian learning) as new information becomes available. See, for example, Hansen (2007) and Hansen and Sargent (2010).

59. In a survey of the Chicago school, Reder (1982, 6) wrote: "[Knight's] contribution to the Chicago tradition was that of sage and oracle, rather than initiator of research programs. It was mainly through his personal impact on a few influential students that Knight affected the subsequent course of Chicago economics." See also chapter 3.

60. The Francis A. Walker Medal was instituted in 1947 by the American Economic Association (AEA) and was awarded every five years "to the living American economist who in the judgement of the awarding body has during his career made the greatest contribution to economics" (American Economic Association website, https://www.aeaweb.org/about-aea/honors-awards/walker-medalists). Upon the creation of the Nobel Memorial Prize, the Walker Medal was discontinued. Francis Walker was the first president of the AEA.

61. This circumstance reflected the shortage of teachers in light of the large increase in student enrolment stemming from returning veterans from World War I.

62. The numberings assigned to these courses occasionally varied over the years.

63. In a paper on the teaching of economics at Chicago during the interwar period, Fiorito and Nerozzi (2018) mistakenly claimed that Mints: (1) arrived at the University of Chicago in 1922 (instead of 1919); (2) completed his PhD at Chicago (his highest degree was a master's); and (3) became a full professor in 1929 (Mints never attained full professorship).

64. In a letter, dated June 19, 1946, from George Stigler to W. Allen Wallis, Stigler wrote: "Milton [Friedman] reported a week ago that Henry was psychologically a very sick man, and [Milton said] that Henry had threatened, or mentioned, suicide" (quoted from Van Horn 2014, 531). The evidence presented by Van Horn (2014) is not conclusive. (1) There was no suicide note. (2) Since Simons had been depressed and had been taking sleeping pills, he may accidently have taken an overdose. (3) In a letter (which Van Horn quoted) from Mints to Director, dated June 19, 1946, Mints wrote: "there is no presumption whatever that it was suicide."

The aim of Van Horn's (2014) article was to provide evidence in support of a *claim* made by Van Horn and Mirowski (2009). The latter authors had been criticized by Caldwell (2011, 306) for exercising "poor taste" in calling Simons's death a suicide in the absence of evidence. In my view, Caldwell's characterization of "poor taste" was valid before the publication of Van Horn's 2014 article and remains valid after its publication.

65. Bloomfield (1992, 2081) stated that Viner "was the first to apply to trade theory the diagram . . . that combines a strictly concave production-possibility curve with community-indifference curves." This statement is incorrect. As documented by Humphrey (1988a), in 1907 Irving Fisher was the first economist to combine indifference and transformation curves with market price lines in a single diagram, and to use it to illustrate the gains from *intertemporal* trade. Specifically, Fisher used the diagram to depict an individual's optimum investment decision over time rather than a country's foreign trade equilibrium. In 1908, Enrico Barone extended Fisher's diagram to *international* trade. As Humphrey also documented, subsequent contributions were made by Allyn Young (1928b) and Gottfried Haberler (1930), before Viner's initial use of the diagram in a lecture delivered at the London School of Economics in 1931.

66. Viner was editor of the *JPE* from 1925 to 1927. Knight and Viner coedited the *JPE* from 1928 to 1945.

67. The University of Chicago was founded in 1890 and held its first classes on October 1, 1892.

68. For an account of the initial years of the Department of Political Economy, see Coats (1963). For an excellent assessment of recent scholarship on Chicago economics, see Irwin (2018).

69. Laughlin (1903, 317) argued that increases in the price level were caused by increases in the costs of production, which, in turn, were caused by monopolistic practices of firms and labor unions. Irving Fisher's work *The Purchasing Power of Money* (1911b), was likely a rebuttal to Laughlin's anti-quantity-theory views. At the 1910 American Economic Association meetings, Fisher (1911a) responded to Laughlin in the following manner: "I find myself unable to agree with most of the positions taken by Professor Laughlin in his able paper. In my opinion, the old quantity theory is in essence correct. What it needs is to be restated not rejected. I have attempted to make what I believe to be the needed restatement in a forthcoming book on *The Purchasing Power of Money*." For a discussion of the Fisher-Laughlin debate, see Girton and Roper (1978).

70. Before moving to Chicago, Laughlin taught at Cornell University, where one of his students was Thorstein Veblen. Laughlin brought Veblen to Chicago, where Veblen established a reputation as social critic. Veblen taught at Chicago from 1892 to 1906 and helped edit the *JPE*.

71. However, the composition of the economics faculty changed slightly. In the 1934–35 academic year, Albert Hart joined the faculty as an assistant in economics

(as opposed to assistant professor), replacing Director. Hart did his undergraduate work at Harvard. He began his graduate studies at Harvard, but completed his PhD at Chicago. He left Chicago for Columbia in 1946. His views on monetary policy were not representative of the Chicago monetary tradition. Hart was a supporter of price controls to stem the inflationary pressures emanating from the military spending associated with World War II, in contrast to the Chicago monetary tradition's view that monetary policy was sufficient to control wartime inflation. See the discussion between Hart and Friedman in the transcript (Friedman, Hart, and Jacoby 1946) of a January 1946 radio address (NBC 1946), *What Can Be Done about Inflation?* In a letter dated July 29, 1947, addressed to Friedman, Hart commented on Friedman's support for the 100 percent reserves proposal in a draft of Friedman (1948a): "you seem to show what I often suspected poor Henry [Simons] of—a need to be defeated, so deep that proposals have to be made to look unattainable. The 100% money plank that you start with, being pictured as essential, and as all-or-none, will seem to most readers to say that if you aren't conceded the impossible you won't play" (Milton Friedman Papers, Hoover Institution Library and Archives, Stanford University). In a 1946 paper, "Lord Keynes and the General Theory," Samuelson (1946, 188) put Hart in a group, including Alvin Hansen and Abba Lerner, whose views had been "unmistakably" tainted by Keynes's *General Theory*.

72. See Nelson (2020, 1:34–35). In an interview conducted by Hammond (1992, 98), Friedman stated: "His [Schultz's] book on *The Theory and Measurement of Demand* is a great book—even the parts I didn't write."

73. As discussed in chapter 2, Schultz signed the key early 1930s Chicago policy memoranda and co-led a session, "Are Wage Cuts a Remedy for Unemployment," at the June/July 1931 Chicago conference "Unemployment as a World Problem" (Harris Foundation 1931). I do not, however, treat Schultz as a member of The Group because, to my knowledge, Schultz never wrote anything, published or unpublished, on macroeconomic issues. His presentation at the 1931 Chicago conference consisted of setting out a series of microeconomic conditions under which reductions in wages would increase profits. He had nothing to say about policy, concluding with regard to the policy implications of his presentation: "Please note that I am passing the buck" (Harris Foundation 1931, 1:197).

74. The committee's objective is to foster interdisciplinary research. The other cofounders wee Knight, Robert Hutchins, who was president of the University of Chicago from 1929 to 1945 and chancellor of the university from 1945 to 1951, and Robert Redfield, who taught anthropology at Chicago from 1927 to 1958.

75. Lange was hired to continue the work in mathematical economics that had been started by Schultz. Patinkin (1981a, 8–9) described Lange as an excellent teacher—"clear, systematic, and thorough, with the wonderful ability of getting to the essence of a problem." However, Patinkin painted a picture of Lange as a person whose activities as a researcher became increasingly diverted by Lange's

involvement with Polish socialist party politics. In light of Lange's involvement with Polish politics to the detriment of his academic work, Patinkin's (1981a, 9) assessment of Lange was the following: "I have thought of Lange as a tragic figure."

76. Minsky was a professor at Washington University in St. Louis from 1965 to 1990. He believed that financial instability was a characteristic feature of capitalist economies. His theory of financial crises, which linked financial market fragility to the changing way that investment was financed during the upswing of the business cycle, received considerable attention in the aftermath of the 2007–8 financial crisis. On his theory of financial crises, see Minsky (1975).

77. For example, Jacob Marschak, Tjalling Koopmans, and Clifford Hildreth, all associated with the Cowles Commission, were listed as faculty members in the Economics Department in the 1950–51 University of Chicago *Catalogue*. Koopmans was director of research at Cowles. Marschak and Hildreth were research associates at Cowles. The faculty members listed in the 1951–52 *Catalogue* numbered twenty-one.

78. Lawrence Klein was with the Cowles Commission from 1944 to 1947. He was awarded the Nobel Prize in 1980 mainly for his work on large-scale macroeconometric models. Klein's work on macroeconometric modeling was discussed by Pinzón-Fuchs (2019). In the 1980s, I worked under Klein's guidance on the construction and simulation of those models. See, for example, Elliott, Kwack, and Tavlas (1986).

79. See Cicarelli and Cicarelli (2003).

80. Ebenstein (2015, 23) reported that close to one-third of Chicago undergraduates during the 1930s were Jewish. According to McNeill (1991, 53), the large percentage of Jewish undergraduate students at Chicago in the 1930s, a time when many other academic centers discriminated against Jews, was "the sociological fact that made the College of the University of Chicago unique in the country."

81. See Friedman and Friedman (1998, 100). See also Lipkes (2019, 221–22). In a 2003 interview, Samuelson stated: "Anti-Semitism was omni-present in pre–World War II academic life" (Samuelson, quoted in Barnett 2004, 531). Franco Modigliani stated that he turned down an offer from the Economics Department at Harvard in the 1940s because of anti-Semitism in that department (Modigliani, quoted in Barnett and Solow 2000, 226–27). Arthur Marget, one of the most prolific writers on monetary economics during the late 1920s and the 1930s, taught at Harvard from 1923 to 1927, before leaving for the University of Minnesota. Marget was likely denied tenure at Harvard because he was Jewish. This information was independently provided to me by two sources: Morris Marget Goldings, nephew of Arthur Marget and, before he retired, a leading US First Amendment attorney, as well as the trustee of his uncle's professional writings; and the late Edward Bernstein, who did his graduate work in economics at Harvard during 1927–31.

82. The origination of the term "monetarism" is often credited to Karl Brunner, who in a July 1968 paper, "The Role of Money and Monetary Policy," repeatedly

used the word "monetarist." Brunner (1968a) defined monetarism to include the following, empirically supported propositions: (1) Federal Reserve actions dominate movements in the monetary base over time; (2) movements of the monetary base dominate movements of the money supply over the business cycle; and (3) accelerations or decelerations of the money supply are closely followed by accelerations or decelerations in economic activity. As Nelson (2020, 2:164–65) showed, however, the terms "monetarist" and "monetarism" had appeared in debates about the causes of the Latin American inflation of the early to mid-1960s. Nelson also showed that the term "monetarist" was introduced into the US economics literature by Bronfenbrenner and Holzman (1963, 602) and Dewald (1966, 509). To my knowledge, the first economist to attribute (in print) the origination of the word "monetarism" to Brunner's 1968 article was Mayer, who did so in a 1975 paper "The Structure of Monetarism (I)." See Mayer (1975, 190; reprinted in Mayer 1978, 1). Others who also attributed the coining of the term "monetarism" to Brunner include J. Stein (1976, 1); Cagan (1987, 493); and Snowdon, Vane, and Wynarczyk (1994, 56).

83. Mayer (1978) noted that monetarism can be defined both in a broad way, as above, and in a way in which the term *monetarism* comprises a set of specific propositions. For the latter, Mayer presented a list of twelve propositions, beginning with the quantity theory of money, to characterize monetarism. The list included the long-run neutrality of money, the stability of the demand for money, and the monetary-growth rule. Kevin Hoover (1988, 10), who noted that the definition of monetarism had become an "intellectual parlour game," defined monetarism to include two propositions: (1) money causally dominates prices and nominal income; and (2) the long-run supply curve is vertical—thus money is neutral in the long run. For other characterizations of monetarism, see Friedman (1970a), J. Stein (1976), De Long (2000), and Mayer and Minford (2004). Friedman (1970a, 7–8) wrote the following about the monetarist counter-revolution: "The counter-revolution also needs a name, and perhaps the one most widely used in referring to it is 'the Chicago School.' More recently, it has been given a name which is less lovely but which has become so attached to it that I find it hard to avoid using it. That name is 'monetarism' because of the renewed emphasis on the role of the quantity of money."

84. As discussed in chapter 3, Douglas did not adhere to a free-market philosophy.

85. The advocacy of a private-enterprise economy reflects, in part, the view that "people react to incentives, and that incentives are important." This point was made by Heckman. See "Interview with James Heckman" (Cassidy 2010).

86. See Miller (1962, 67) in his article "On the 'Chicago School' of Economics."

87. Beginning in the 1950s, Friedman's emphasis on the use of simple theoretical models to derive testable hypotheses came to be viewed as a characteristic of the Chicago school (Hetzel 2013, 200). As Heckman pointed out, the Chicago school subsequently came to be identified with the efficient-market hypothesis. See "Interview with James Heckman" (Cassidy 2010).

88. Friedman continued to make important contributions after 1960. See Nelson (2020) for a careful and comprehensive assessment of Friedman's economics from the early 1930s to the early 1970s.

89. As will be discussed in chapter 6, the nomenclature "the Mints-Simons program" was bestowed on the views of Mints and Simons by Alvin Hansen, the leading American Keynesian economist of the 1940s.

**Chapter Two**

1. Unconventional measures became the staple of monetary policies during and following the 2007–8 financial crisis. A main difference is that the use of quantitative-easing policies during the 2007–8 crisis, instead of open-market operations, was attributed to the fact that interest rates were close to the zero lower bound rather to the Chicagoan's view that open-market operations are ineffective during depressions, regardless of the level of interest rates.

2. I am not aware of any other occurrence in which a university economics department circulated a jointly signed *departmental* memorandum during the Great Depression advocating a common view about the causes of, and policy responses to, the Great Depression.

3. A review of the "Plan" by Albert Hart (1935) was titled "The 'Chicago Plan' of Banking Reform: A Proposal for Making Monetary Management Effective in the United States." In the editor's introduction to Simons's 1934 *A Positive Program for Laissez Faire*, Harry Gideonse referred to the 100 percent reserve proposal as "this so-called 'Chicago' or '100 Per Cent Reserve' plan" (Simons 1934a, iii).

4. Simons's first substantive (i.e., apart from book reviews) publication that dealt with money was the pamphlet *A Positive Program for Laissez Faire*, which, as mentioned, was published in 1934. Frank Knight's first paper devoted entirely to money was published in 1937. These works are discussed in chapter 4. For reasons that will become apparent, I treat Jacob Viner's publications on money in the early 1930s separately, in chapter 3.

5. Don Patinkin referred to a similar interpretation of the quantity equation, as described in Mints's lecture notes, and observed: "[this] has always represented for me 'the flavor of the Chicago tradition'" (1969, 250).

6. See, for example, Foster and Catchings's 1923 book *Money*. Foster was the founding president of Reed College, where Douglas had taught in the late 1910s. Catchings was a businessman. Together, in the 1920s Foster and Catchings established the Pollak Foundation for Economic Research, which published several highly regarded books, including Fisher's *The Making of Index Numbers* (Fisher 1922b) and Douglas's *Real Wages in the United States, 1890–1926* (Douglas 1930), on economics. Patinkin (1973a) credited Foster and Catchings for originating the concept of income velocity of money. In July 1929, Foster and Catchings predicted

that the Fed's monetary tightening in 1928 and 1929 would lead to depression—see Tavlas (2011). For a critical view of their work, see Laidler (1999, 206–11). For a sympathetic treatment of their work, see Dorfman (1959, 4:339–52). For a discussion of the underconsumption literature, see Bleaney (1976).

7. See Laidler (1998a; 1998b; 1999, chap. 9) and Laidler and Sandilands (2002a).

8. To support the view that underconsumptionism dominated Douglas's thinking, Laidler cited the book *The Problem of Unemployment*, by Douglas and Director (1931), which did *not* include underconsumptionist theory. Laidler (1999, 222) speculated that "Director might have had some influence on the absence of underconsumptionism from that book." As discussed below, however, *several* of Douglas's works during the early 1930s omitted any discussion of underconsumptionism. Moreover, while underconsumption was present in Douglas's 1935 *Controlling Depressions*, it took a backseat to the view that depressions are caused by overly high profits rather than depleted profits as posited by underconsumptionism (see the discussion in chapter 5).

9. Friedman wrote: "Re Douglas, I must confess that my main impressions of his [Douglas's] views on money are based on my postwar contacts with him when he was in the Senate. There is no doubt whatsoever that he was then a quantity theorist. Also, while underconsumptionism does not require the quantity theory, there is no incompatibility between a person being an underconsumptionist and a quantity theorist just as there is no incompatibility between communism and quantity theory as evidenced by both Marx and, some years back, the head of the Chinese central bank" (letter, Friedman to Laidler, April 3, 1998, Milton Friedman Papers, Hoover Institution Library and Archives, Stanford University).

10. In written correspondence, dated July 7, 2017, with the author, David Laidler offered to me an interesting reconciliation between our respective views, as follows. In the conditions of the early 1930s, quantity theorists wanted, above all, monetary expansion. In the extremely depressed conditions of the time, some quantity theorists viewed public works, financed by money creation, as the only realistic means of increasing the money supply. But such measures were the standard prescription of underconsumptionists under any depressed circumstances, which they considered typical of a capitalistic economy. Consequently, some quantity theorists and underconsumptionists were able to forge a common policy stance to combat the Great Depression.

11. Douglas (1927, 37) characterized Foster and Catchings's writings as "brilliant and suggestive."

12. The aim of Douglas's policy proposal in his 1927 paper was not to advocate the use of money-financed fiscal deficits to combat a cyclical downturn. Instead, it was to put money into the hands of consumers to enable them to increase their expenditure and, hence, alleviate the chronic underconsumption that Douglas believed to be an inherent characteristic of a market economy. This point was stressed by Laidler (1999, 222–28).

13. In using the word "credit," Douglas meant bank money, in the form of checking deposits. He referred to the Fisherine $M'$ as "credit" instead of "bank deposits." Douglas's use of the word "credit" was common among economists in the 1930s and 1940s. For documentation, see the discussions in Laidler (1999, 133, 188n6, 192). The modern use of credit is different. Strictly speaking, "bank credit" refers to the loans and discounts on the asset side of banks' balance sheets. Bank credit should be sharply distinguished from the "bank money" or the "deposits" account on the liability side of those balance sheets.

14. The signatories included Irving Fisher (Yale) and Frank Taussig (Harvard). For details about the 1930 Wagner Bill, see J. R. Davis (1971, 14–15).

15. In April 1932, however, Senator Wagner sent a letter to a number of individuals, including Knight, soliciting their views on deficit spending. Knight responded with a letter, which included the following: "As far as I know, economists are completely agreed that the Government should spend as much and tax as little as possible, at a time such as this—using the expenditure in the way to do the most good in itself and also to point toward relieving the depression" (*Congressional Record* 1932b, 10323). Credit for the discovery of this letter belongs to J. R. Davis (1971, 15–16).

16. As discussed in chapter 3, the characterization of Douglas as a "man of action" was made by Knight.

17. The work by Douglas and Director on the book was financed by Swarthmore College in conjunction with the Steering Committee of the Swarthmore Unemployment Study.

18. Friedman communicated the information to Laidler in a letter dated October 9, 1996 (Milton Friedman Papers, Hoover Institution Library and Archives, Stanford University).

19. As mentioned, the notion that it is not possible to isolate a single cause of the business cycle was expressed by Douglas in his book *Know America* (1933a, 49).

20. Douglas and Director argued: "And while business men will be attracted by the lower rate of interest which results from the abundance of credit, they will also be deterred by the general shrinkage of prices and the declining volume of sales" (1931, 243).

21. See chapter 4 for a discussion of Fisher's proposal.

22. Laidler (1999, 224) noted that, in Tavlas (1997), I had treated the book by Douglas and Director as an important building block in the development of the Chicago monetary tradition.

23. The first Russian Five-Year Plan commenced in October 1928.

24. I conjecture that the monograph was completed at the very end of 1932 or the beginning of 1933. The conjecture is based in the following: (1) the latest citation in the monograph is to an article published in the *Nation* on December 27, 1932, and (2) the monograph was published under the University of Chicago's Public Policy Pamphlets series, then edited by Harry Gideonse; Gideonse's "Introduction" to the pamphlet was dated February 2, 1933.

25. I discuss Mints's criticism of the "real bills doctrine" in chapter 6.

26. The conferences were sponsored by the Norman Wait Harris Memorial Foundation.

27. See Meltzer (2003, 333–34).

28. Keynes's keynote lecture was delivered in three separate presentations.

29. The single roundtable attended by Knight was the one that was led by Keynes. Knight's intervention was in the form of a question to a conference participant who had objected to a policy aimed at raising the price level to its 1929 level (Harris Foundation 1931, 2:481).

30. As mentioned in chapter 1, Schultz did not address policy issues in his presentation. J. R. Davis (1971, 107–15) provided a detailed discussion of the presentation by Schultz and Goodrich.

31. Quincy Wright, who chaired all the roundtables, pointed out that Gideonse was serving as a "pinch-hitter" on very short notice since the person who had been originally designated to be the roundtable leader on international capital movements was not able to attend (Harris Foundation 1931, 2:356).

32. Patinkin (1979, 216) stated that Keynes's lecture "was essentially a song of praise to his *Treatise*."

33. In an interesting paper, Cate (1981) pointed out that the *Treatise* proposed three major policies, each of which aimed to stabilize the general level of prices: (1) For an economy, such as that of the United States, that was relatively closed to international trade, price stabilization could be achieved by having the central bank bring the market rate of interest into equality with the natural rate of interest (in the Wicksellian sense). (2) For an economy with a relatively large trade sector, the central bank would adopt a tripartite system of control centered on the bank rate, the forward exchange rate, and the buying and selling points of gold. The tripartite system would allow the bank to set different short-term rates for domestic and foreign funds, allowing it to achieve price stabilization without having a balance-of-payments crisis short-circuit price stability. And (3) in cases in which capital outflows were viewed as sensitive to a decline in the market rate, the country in question would adopt a program of loan-financed domestic investment.

34. In the *Treatise*, Keynes referred to an empirical study of US interest rates over the period 1919 to 1929 by Fed economist Winfield Riefler to show that the long-term rate—defined by "the average of sixty high-grade bonds"—followed the variations of the average of short-term rates (1930, 2:315). Credit for this source belongs to Brillant (2019), who provided a detailed assessment of Keynes's term-structure theory.

35. The Nathan-led roundtable discussion took place on June 29, 1930. Keynes's roundtable presentation took place on July 1, 1930. With the rise of Hitler to power, Nathan, who was Jewish, fled to the United States in 1933, where he taught at Princeton University and later at New York University. Nathan served as the executor of Albert Einstein's estate after the latter's death in 1955.

36. Keynes stated: "We had a Round Table on public works, which I think covered a great deal of the ground of what governments could do, and, I propose that I pass over that, and I concentrate on Central Bank action" (Harris Foundation 1931, 2:446).

37. The presentation was made on June 24, 1931. The intervention in question was Director's only intervention during the conference.

38. What exactly did Viner mean in comparing the Fed's inept policies to those of "the Bank of England during its worst period'? I discuss this issue in chapter 5.

39. I discuss the contents of that lecture in chapter 3.

40. The twelve Chicagoans were: Aaron Director, John Cover, Garfield Cox, Harry Gideonse, Frank Knight, Harry Millis, Lloyd Mints, Henry Schultz, Henry Simons, Jacob Viner, Chester Wright, and Theodore Yntema. The twelve non-Chicagoans were James Angell, Irving Fisher, Max Handman, Alvin Hansen, Charles Hardy, Arthur Marget, Harold Moulton, Ernest Patterson, Chester Phillips, Charles Tippetts, John H. Williams, and Ivan Wright.

41. The first Glass Steagall Act, passed by the US Congress on February 27, 1932, permitted the Federal Reserve to issue banknotes backed by government securities if there was a shortage of eligible paper. Regardless of the composition of the backing of the notes by either government securities or eligible paper, the notes required 40 percent backing in gold. The 1913 Federal Reserve Act had prohibited government securities as backing for note issue. See Meltzer (2003, 70n7).

42. The bill establishing the RFC was signed into law on January 22, 1932. By July 1932, the RFC had loaned more than one billion dollars to banks, railroads, credit unions, and mortgage loan companies. By mid-1935, the RFC owned more than one-third of the outstanding capital of the banking system. See R. Phillips (1995, 85–88).

43. Friedman's claim that the Harris Foundation telegram was signed by twelve University of Chicago *economists* was not strictly correct. One of the Chicago signatories was John H. Cover, who taught statistics in the University of Chicago Business School.

44. Laidler (1999, 228) correctly included two additional characteristics of the earlier Chicago monetary tradition in his list—the advocacy of monetary rules and the commitment to 100 percent reserves, both of which were missing in Patinkin's (1969) description of that tradition.

45. As of early 1932, France was the last of the major (i.e., big three) European economies still on the gold exchange standard. In 1931, Britain allowed sterling to float while Germany introduced capital controls, effectively abandoning its adherence to the rules of the gold standard. In September 1936 France, along with the Netherlands and Switzerland, devalued their currencies, marking the end of the interwar gold standard.

46. The legislation that granted the certificates was enacted in May 1924.

47. The signatories were the same as those who signed the Hoover telegram with two exceptions—Douglas, who signed, and John H. Cover, who did not sign, the April memorandum.

48. The term "sticky" prices (or costs) referred to the prices charged by public utilities. The Chicagoans believed that public-utility companies were monopolies, the policies of which "impeded" price adjustment (Pettengill Memorandum 1932, 524).

49. The sale of Treasury bonds to the Federal Reserve in exchange for Federal Reserve notes would entail increases in both the asset and the liability sides of the Fed's balance sheet by equivalent amounts. Under this method, the Treasury would finance the deficit by borrowing from the Fed, which is equivalent to printing money to finance the deficit.

50. The Chicagoans focused on the roles of low confidence and bank deleveraging in inhibiting the effectiveness of open-market and discounting operations. A major justification for the Fed's quantitative-easing program following the 2007–8 financial crisis was the view that conventional open-market operations, working through the portfolio-adjustment channel, would be ineffective at the zero (lowerbound) interest rate. To maintain control of the federal funds rate, even in situations where the quantity of reserves in the banking system is very large, in October 2008 the Fed introduced interest payments on reserves. A side effect of that policy was to cushion commercial banks' loss of income during the financial crisis. To *discourage* banks from holding reserves, in June 2014 the European Central Bank introduced negative interest rates on reserves.

51. The data in this paragraph are from Friedman and Schwartz (1963, chap. 7) and Walton and Rockoff (2005, chap. 23).

52. The bank holiday was a success, supported during Roosevelt's first week in office by the passage of the Emergency Banking Act, which, among other things, extended the president's powers to close, liquidate, license, and reopen financially sound banks, and empowered the secretary of the Treasury to order all domestic gold holders to sell their holdings to the Treasury (Meltzer 2003, 384). Silber (2009) showed that Roosevelt's first "fireside chat," on Sunday, March 12, and the Emergency Banking Act, combined with the Federal Reserve's commitment to supply unlimited amounts of currency to banks, creating de facto 100 percent deposit insurance, were instrumental in making the bank holiday a success. Edwards (2018) provided a first-rate narrative of the events leading up to, and following, Roosevelt's announcement. These events included the temporary departure from the gold standard by the United States in 1933.

53. The budget program was presented to the US Congress on December 8, 1932. The 1933–34 fiscal year ran from July 1, 1933 to June 30, 1934.

54. The other signatories were department chair Harry Millis; Simeon Leland; Donald Slesinger, who taught in Chicago's Law School; L. D. White, a professor of history at Chicago; and four local-government officials (Frank Bane, Paul Betters, Carl Chatters, and Clarence Ridley). Van Overtveldt (2007, 83) incorrectly stated that the pamphlet "was signed by 11 Chicago economists." The pamphlet was the first issued as part of the University of Chicago's Public Policy Pamphlets series. The publication date is listed as 1933. I deduce that the pamphlet was written

before Roosevelt's inauguration on March 4, 1933 since there is no reference to Roosevelt's assumption of the presidency or to his specific budget action on March 10, 1933, that aimed to cut an additional $500 million from the fiscal year 1933–34 budget.

55. The other signatories were Hart and Schultz.

56. According to R. Phillips (1995, 216), who described the March 16, 1933 version, that version was titled "Memorandum on Banking Reform." In fact, the two March versions of the memorandum—the March 15, 1933, and the March 16, 1933, versions—were untitled. The April 1933 version (also untitled), which is discussed by Phillips, is not available at the Special Collections Section of the University of Chicago Library. I have corresponded with Phillips about the availability of the April 1933 version, but he has not retained a copy. In my discussion (below) of the April 1933 version, I rely on Phillips's (1995) reproduction of several parts of that version.

57. On March 23, 1933, Wallace wrote to Roosevelt as follows: "The memorandum from the Chicago economists, which I gave you at [the] Cabinet meeting Tuesday, is really awfully good and I hope that you or [Treasury] Secretary [William] Woodin will have the time and energy to study it. Of course, the plan outlined is quite a complete break with our present banking history. It would be an even more decisive break than the founding of the Federal Reserve System" (quoted from R. Phillips 1995, 49). Wallace served as secretary of agriculture from 1933 to 1940. He then served as vice president of the United States from 1941 to 1945. He was the Progressive Party's nominee for president in 1948, winning 2.4 percent of the popular vote.

58. For other discussions of the proposals, see Fisher (1935a), Hart (1935), Friedman (1967), and R. Phillips (1995). For a recent analysis, see Demeulemeester (2018). The banking proposals in the two March versions and the April version were identical.

59. Apart from R. Phillips (1995), who provided a brief description of the macroeconomic-policy proposals, previous writers have downplayed those proposals. For example, Allen (1993, 705) stated: "The memorandum [was] directed almost entirely to banking and supervisory institutional and procedural concerns, with little attention to policy objectives and criteria." In fact, almost one-half of the memorandum was devoted to macroeconomic policy objectives.

60. This policy would have led to an expansion of the Fed's balance sheet. The Fed's liabilities (i.e., reserves and, to a lesser extent, banknotes) would rise, and its assets (i.e., government bonds) would rise by an equal amount. This particular policy was carried out by the Fed in the aftermath of the 2007–8 financial crisis as part of its quantitative-easing program.

61. On April 20, 1933, President Roosevelt signed an executive order requiring all US residents to exchange their holdings of gold coin, bullion, and gold certificates for Federal Reserve notes and token coins at the then-official rate of

$20.67 per troy ounce, effectively suspending participation of the United States in the gold standard. See Edwards (2017).

62. Ruml was dean of the University of Chicago's Division of Social Sciences.

63. The recommendation of the March–April 1933 memorandum was that the gold standard should be abandoned regardless of the domestic objectives of monetary policy. As mentioned, the Pettengill memorandum was not adamant about the need to abandon the gold standard.

64. See, for example, Simons (1934a, 57).

65. I deduce that the monograph was completed during this period in light of the following. (1) On page 16 of the monograph Douglas referred to "the action of March 5 and April 19, 1933," because of which the United States "was already off gold." On the former date, Roosevelt announced the bank holiday. On April 20, 1933, Roosevelt issued a proclamation prohibiting both exporting gold and financial institutions converting deposits and fiat currency into gold coins, effectively taking the United States off the gold standard. (2) On page 17 Douglas referred to the World Economic Conference in the future tense. The conference convened in London on June 10, 1933.

66. Simons's emphasis on the need to avoid uncontrolled inflation was an outgrowth of his concern that the hyperinflation, financed by money creation, experienced by some countries during and following the first World War, should not be repeated.

67. In his 1933 book *Know America*, Douglas estimated that wholesale prices had fallen by 40 percent since 1929. Therefore, he argued: "In order to relieve society from this greatly increased pressure of fixed debts, it would seem but just to raise the American price level to a point somewhere reaching that of 1929 and then stabilize it" (1933a, 25). Recall, Fisher had also estimated that wholesale prices had fallen by 40 percent, but Fisher used the year 1926 as the base. Between 1926 and 1929 the US wholesale price index fell by about 5 percent.

68. The November 1933 memorandum underwent wider circulation than the March 1933 memorandum (letter, Simons to Douglas, October 2, 1934, Henry C. Simons Papers, Special Collections Research Center, Joseph Regenstein Library, University of Chicago).

69. I refer to the November 1933 memorandum under the co-authorship of Simons et al. Ronnie Phillips (1995, 64) wrote that the November 1933 memorandum was signed by the same group of economists that signed the March memorandum. In fact, the November memorandum was unsigned.

70. However, quarterly real GNP growth declined at an annual rate of 24 percent in the fourth quarter. That collapse was followed by another spurt of growth in early 1934. See Friedman and Schwartz (1963, 495) and Meltzer (2003, 462–63).

71. The 1933 Banking Act is also known as the Glass-Steagall Act of 1933, to distinguish it from the Glass-Steagall Act of 1932. As mentioned, the latter act widened the collateral pool of the Reserve Banks, allowing those banks to use government securities, in addition to commercial paper and gold, as collateral against Federal Reserve notes; the 1932 act also established the Reconstruction Finance Corporation.

72. Both the March and the November memoranda presumed that during a transition period demand deposits of private financial institutions would be replaced with notes and deposits of the Federal Reserve Banks. This process would include the purchases of the government bonds held by private banks by the Federal Reserve as the private banks were liquidated. The November memorandum also made explicit what the March memorandum did not, namely, that, under this procedure "the entire burden of the federal debt might thus be eliminated" (Simons et al. 1933, 4).

73. Essentially, the business-cycle theory in the absence of a fractional-reserve banking system was identical to that put forward by Douglas and Director (1931) and by those authors in their individual publications in the early 1930s.

74. The identical wording appeared in the March and the April versions.

75. Ebenstein (2015, 72) incorrectly stated that, in 1933, the Chicagoans favored "a fixed expansion of the money supply according to a rule each year."

76. Friedman (1960, 81) expressed a similar view about the gold standard: "it seems dubious that such a monetary system is stable."

77. The parallels with Friedman (1953b) are evident: "flexible exchange rates [are conducive to] the promotion of unrestricted multilateral trade" (Friedman 1953b, 196). In contrast, "control over foreign trade . . . is therefore almost certain to be the primary technique adopted to meet substantial movement in conditions of international trade so long as exchange rates remain rigid" (Friedman 1953b, 197).

78. Under method (a), if the Federal Reserve bought the federal debt in the secondary market, the procedure would be a straightforward open-market operation. If the debt were bought on the primary market, the procedure would be the monetary financing of fiscal expansion. The November memorandum did not identify the particular market, primary or secondary, from which the bonds would be purchased. Method (b), under which the Fed would purchase non-government securities, is part of what is considered to be quantitative easing.

79. Simons's letter was a response to a September 22, 1934, letter (Paul Douglas Papers, Special Collections Research Center, Joseph Regenstein Library, University of Chicago) from Douglas in which the latter wrote that he was preparing a manuscript in which he wanted to refer to the memorandum. The manuscript on which Douglas was working was his book *Controlling Depressions* (1935b).

80. The debate about the renewal of Simons's appointment had emerged in 1932.

81. I exclude the 1932 Hoover memorandum since it was a joint product of non-Chicagoans and Chicagoans.

## Chapter Three

1. As mentioned in chapter 2, the March 1933 memorandum was untitled. It was signed by the following core members of The Group: Cox, Director, Douglas, Knight, Mints, and Simons. It was also signed by Hart and Schultz.

2. This section draws on Tavlas (2022b).

3. The Harvard-trained economists included Lauchlin Currie, Harry Dexter White, and John H. Williams.

4. As Laidler (1993) pointed-out, many of the views expressed in the telegram were similar to views held by John H. Williams, who also co-drafted the telegram.

5. As discussed in chapter 2, the pamphlet, *Balancing the Budget* (Bane et al. 1933), which Viner co-authored with a group of Chicagoans and local public officials, dealt exclusively with President Hoover's 1933–34 fiscal year budget.

6. What is available is *Report of the Round Tables*, which provides quotes from Viner's lecture and comments from attendees of the lecture.

7. The lecture was published in April 1933.

8. Flanders (1989, 227–29) provided a discussion of Viner's dissertation.

9. Capital would flow quickly between countries to eliminate interest-rate differentials. See Bordo (1992) and Bordo and Schwartz (1999). Viner (1937, 405) noted that short-term capital flows allowed necessary adjustments in national gold stocks to be spread over longer periods, helping to avoid internal crises. For example, a country with a trade deficit could borrow short term abroad so that bank credit in that country could be gradually—instead of abruptly—contracted. Adam Smith had identified the equilibrating role played by short-term capital—in the form of bank money—in external adjustment. See Laidler (1981, 189–90).

10. Under the gold exchange standard of the 1920s, key currencies, including the pound sterling and the US dollar, were used, along with gold, as foreign-exchange reserves.

11. In the late nineteenth century, a follow-the-leader convention with regard to interest rates emerged among central banks. If there was a need to act on interest rates, the Bank of England often took the lead, changing its discount rate, and other central banks followed. Keynes (1930, 2:306–7) referred to the Bank of England under the classical gold standard as "the conductor of the international orchestra." During crises, central banks took exceptional steps to support one another—for example, by lending gold to the monetary authorities of a central bank facing an attack on its gold reserves. See Eichengreen (1996, 33–34).

12. Following the (temporary) abandonment of the gold standard by the United States in April 1933, Viner favored a return to the gold standard (Meltzer 2003, 451n69, 544). In 1942, he wrote: "what we should hope for, and work for, in the field of post-war monetary structure, is a return to the international gold standard, but with regulation through international action of either or both the rate of production of gold and the world monetary value of gold, and with provision for modification through international agreement of the gold value of particular national currencies when conditions peculiar to such countries seem to call for such modification" (1942b, 130; quoted from Irwin 2016, 765).

13. The quotation below is from a six-page, double-spaced text. A copy of the draft is in the Henry C. Simons Papers in the Special Collections Section of the Regenstein Library of the University of Chicago. The earlier quotations are from a three-page, single-spaced text of the final memorandum.

14. Viner (1931b, 183) argued that government spending "financed from taxation" could also exert an expansionary effect on economic activity provided that the taxable funds would have otherwise been "hoarded and saved." The suggestion of financing government spending through taxation would seem inconsistent with Viner's call for "taxing lightly" during depressions.

15. Viner has been incorrectly characterized as a proponent of (fiat) money-financed fiscal deficits. Thus, Steindl (1995, 84) contended that Viner called for "the monetization of budget deficits created as a conscious matter of policy" to generate increases in the money supply.

16. The Williamstown conference report did not provide the numerical data.

17. Strong died in October 1928. Friedman and Schwartz (1963, 413) stated: "Once he [Strong] was removed from the scene, neither the Board nor the other Reserve Banks . . . were prepared to accept the leadership of the New York Bank." For a similar view, see Fisher (1934, 228). For a contrary view, see Wheelock (1992).

18. See Humphrey (1971) and Sandilands (1990) for discussions of Currie's views.

19. For similar views, see Director (1933, 24–25), Douglas (1935b, 19–24), and Mints (1945a, 270).

20. Subsequent research has supported Viner's view about the damage inflicted by limitations on branch banking. In a series of studies, Eugene White (1981; 1984; 1986) provided evidence supporting the view that the strict limitations on branch banking produced a rural banking system in the early 1930s that was unable to absorb shocks. Referring to White's findings, Walton and Rockoff (2005, 444) noted that the high number of bank failures in the early 1930s was a consequence of "legislation that prohibited branch banking. Small unit banks were unable to diversify their loan portfolios and had no resources to draw on during periods of temporary illiquidity. . . . Eventually, most states began to eliminate crippling prohibitions against branch banking, but by then the damage had been done, and it was too late to build a system that could withstand the deflation of the 1930s."

21. The argument is not logically correct since banks could impose negative interest rates on deposits.

22. The term "inherent instability" to characterize the Chicago monetary tradition's view of a fractional-reserve banking system has long been in usage. For example, in his discussion of Simons's theory of the business cycle, Friedman (1967, 6) described Simons's view as follows: "the inherent instability of the financial structure . . . is the source of cumulative maladjustments." Simons (1944c, 107), in describing criticisms of the free-market system, stated that one such criticism was that the free-market system is "inherently and intolerably unstable." In classroom lectures delivered in 1936 at the University of California, Berkeley, Knight (1936c, 84) was quoted as saying: "A business cycle represents an inherently unstable situation." I discuss the lectures in question in chapter 5. See also chapters 7 and 8 for additional examples of the use of this term by Friedman.

23. Similarly, Steindl (1995, 84n7) argued that "Viner's refusal to publicly endorse the Chicago economists' Memorandum on Banking Reform" reflected

Viner's "judgement on the political feasibility of [the] policies." As I pointed out, and contrary to what Steindl wrote, the March 1933 memorandum was untitled.

24. The Chicago conference took place in January 1932. The publication year of the book *Gold and Monetary Stabilization*, containing the lecture, was 1932. See Wright (1932).

25. This argument is consistent with the view expressed by Nelson (2020, 2:40): "there is evidence that Friedman was not someone who kept close tabs on Viner's monetary writings. Only in retrospect did Friedman appreciate the strength of the links between Viner's arguments in the 1930s and those in Friedman-Schwartz's *Monetary History* of 1963."

26. Laidler (1993) pointed out that the earlier Chicago monetary tradition was also characterized by a preference for rules.

27. The following presentation briefly summarizes the evidence presented in Laidler (1993; 1999, chap. 9).

28. During the 1920s, Hawtrey originated the "Treasury view" of fiscal policy, according to which fiscal policy does not affect economic activity in the absence of money financing. After World War I, Hawtrey advocated drastic budgetary and monetary restraint to achieve price stability. See E. G. Davis (1981) and Mattei (2018).

29. Young wrote the chapter "Business Cycles" for the 1923 edition of Richard Ely's widely used textbook *Outlines of Economics*. Laidler (1993, 1080) stated that "there is strong circumstantial evidence of Hawtrey's influence" on that chapter. For a discussion of Young's monetary economics, see Mehrling (1996).

30. This point was made by Laidler (1993). Currie's thesis was titled "Bank Assets and Banking Theory." It was submitted at Harvard in January 1931. See Currie (1931).

31. Williams's thesis examined balance-of-payments adjustment in Argentina from 1880 to 1900, a period featuring a flexible-exchange-rate regime and a paper currency. As in the case of Viner's thesis, Williams's thesis was supervised by Taussig. See Laidler (1998a, 9). For a discussion of Williams's thesis, see Flanders (1989, 225–27).

32. Williams's paper was titled "Monetary Stability and the Gold Standard." See Williams (1932).

33. See Laidler and Sandilands (2000). The memorandum did not contain a specific date. Harry D. White would go on to work at the US Treasury, where he became, along with Keynes, one of the two principal architects of the Bretton Woods system. To my knowledge, the memorandum was first cited in the secondary literature in a biography of White by Rees (1973, 37). Laidler and Sandilands cited Rees's book in the context of referring to biographical material on White. They did not mention Rees's citation of the memorandum.

34. See Laidler and Sandilands (2002b). Laidler and Sandilands found the memorandum in the Harry D. White Papers at Princeton University Library.

35. Friedman's letter was a reaction to the memorandum published in the 2000 working paper by Laidler and Sandilands.

36. Friedman and Schwartz (1963, chap. 3, 98–99n15) cited Williams with regard to the US trade balance in the late nineteenth century; they also cited Williams's view that reserve requirements needed to be raised in 1937. See Friedman and Schwartz (1963, 525). At the time of the latter occasion, Williams was vice president of the New York Fed.

37. As we will see in subsequent chapters, Viner was knowledgeable about Currie's views on the Great Depression, and Mints was knowledgeable about Viner's views.

38. As mentioned in chapter 1, Knight completed his PhD in 1916.

39. I have previously noted that Hart was not part of the Chicago monetary tradition.

40. There is no date attached to the reading list. There is a total of forty-seven items on the list, the latest being Mints's 1950 book *Monetary Policy for a Competitive Society*. The reading list in question is contained under the title "Reading Lists" in the Milton Friedman Papers at the Hoover Institution at Stanford University.

41. This circumstance was noted by Douglas in a letter, dated January 8, 1935, to Knight (Paul Douglas Papers, Special Collections Research Center, Joseph Regenstein Library, University of Chicago). In that letter, Douglas recalled that he had brought Director to Chicago as his personal assistant. Douglas continued: "Beginning in 1932, Director increasingly fell under your [Knight's] influence, and this in itself neither pained me nor gave me any regrets, since I have always felt that one's intellectual life should be free and that past favors should not bind one's thought in the future."

42. In his article "Chicago Economics: Permanence and Change," Reder (1982, 4) provided a similar assessment of Knight's influence: "Knight was a man of insight and reflection, above all a critic." Homer Jones had studied under Knight at the University of Iowa and followed Knight to Chicago to do graduate work. In the late 1920s and the 1930s, Jones taught at Rutgers University; at Rutgers, one of his undergraduate students was Friedman. Later in his career Jones served as research director and senior vice president at the Federal Reserve Bank of St. Louis.

43. Fetter taught at Cornell and Princeton. He was an advocate of the Austrian school of economics.

44. This circumstance was noted by Reder (1982, 6): "[Knight] could—and did—vigorously support Henry Simons's retention in the Economics Department against strong opposition, but it is doubtful that he could have approved *A Positive Program for Laissez Faire* (1934) or any other of Simons's policy tracts." In an accompanying footnote to the foregoing quotation, Reder (1982, 6) stated that the opposition to Simons's retention came "particularly from Douglas."

45. In a letter to Knight, dated January 6, 1934, department chair Millis wrote: "I do wish that you and Paul could be the good friends that you were. Perhaps this is wishing entirely too much, but I do think that you fellows would understand each

other better if you were to have a perfectly frank talk" (Frank H. Knight Papers, Special Collections Research Center, Joseph Regenstein Library, University of Chicago). In a letter to Knight, dated January 5, 1935, Douglas referred to the years immediately following Knight's appointment to the Chicago faculty in 1927 as "the time when I regarded you as one of my best friends" (Paul Douglas Papers, Special Collections Research Center, Joseph Regenstein Library, University of Chicago).

46. At the time of the visit, the US government did not recognize the Soviet Union diplomatically.

47. Shlaes (2007, chap. 2) provided an account of the delegation's experience. See, also Douglas (1972, 49–54).

48. Douglas authored chapters titled "Labor Legislation and Social Insurance," "Wages and the Material Condition of the Industrial Workers," and "The Consumers' Cooperative Movement." The chapter co-authored with Dunn was titled "The Trade Union Movement." The latter chapter comprised nine sections, each of which was attributed to either one of the two co-authors.

49. In 1932, Tugwell was a member of Franklin Roosevelt's "Brains Trust," an informal group of individuals who advised Roosevelt on economic issues. After Roosevelt assumed the presidency in March 1933, Tugwell was appointed assistant secretary at the Department of Agriculture. In the late 1940s, Robert Hutchins, then president of the University of Chicago, tried to bring Tugwell to that institution. The Economics Department, however, refused to appoint Tugwell to its faculty. Consequently, Hutchins set up a Department of Planning, and he made Tugwell a professor in that department. See Friedman's remarks in Kitch (1983, 188–89).

50. In 1933, Tugwell published the book *The Industrial Discipline and the Government Arts*, in which he again argued that laissez-faire should be abandoned in favor of government planning. The book was reviewed favorably by Douglas, who wrote: "Tugwell paints with vivid and yet thoughtful strokes, which stamp the author as an artist in his technique as well as an economist" (Douglas 1933d, 703).

51. Proponents of the "Newer Economics" in the early 1930s called for the adoption of large-scale government planning.

52. Slichter's book was first published in 1926 and went through a total of five editions. The edition reviewed by Knight was the second; it was published in 1931. The book was used as a standard introductory economics textbook in the 1930s and 1940s. Following teaching stints at Cornwell and Princeton, Slichter moved to Harvard in 1930. He was president of the American Economic Association in 1941.

53. Reder (1982, 6) wrote the following about Knight: "Knight's . . . expository style made few concessions to listeners or readers."

54. The above discussion is based on H. Stein (1987). The specific proposals provided by Simons are discussed in chapter 5.

55. Johnson, a retired military officer, assumed the leadership of the NRA amid considerable fanfare. He was named *Time* magazine's Man of the Year of 1933. In 1935, the US Supreme Court unanimously ruled that the law that established the NRA was unconstitutional.

56. In an August 3, 1938, letter to Arthur Dahlberg, Simons wrote that "the main direction of New Deal policies is toward authoritarian collectivism" (quoted from Burgin 2012, 39).

57. The article was treated by the editors of the *Tribune* with considerable hype. It was published as the lead article on the front page of the business section and it included a photo of Simons. A similar assessment of the New Deal was made by Garfield Cox in a lecture, "The New Deal and Business Recovery," delivered in Fairmont, Indiana, on November 15, 1933. Cox (1933, 1) stated that "those elements of the New Deal which create uncertainty concerning future profits are a serious bar to sustained expansion of employment." Cox also stated: "Arbitrarily imposed increases in wage raises, for example, although giving the employed more purchasing power, are likely to decrease the volume of employment in more directions than they increase it." Finally, Cox criticized the Roosevelt administration's gold policy. He argued that it overlooked "the quantity and frequency of bank credit," the implication being that banks' ability to create and destroy deposits needed to be dealt with. Cox's lecture was reported in the November 16, 1933 issue of the *Fairmont News*, from which these quotations are taken.

58. Many years later, Chicagoan James Heckman, who was awarded the Nobel Prize in Economics in 2000 for his contributions to selection bias and self-selection analysis, echoed Knight's remarks: "Economists have gone public. Economists are making bold and often unsupported statements. The amazing thing is that the public listens to some of these people. In truth, they really don't have much to say. . . . I am not a party to that" (quoted from Ginther 2010, 571). Heckman's Nobel Prize was shared with Daniel McFadden, the latter for his work in discrete choice.

59. Douglas was supported by department chair Millis and by Gideonse, Leland, Schultz, Viner, and Wright (letter, Douglas to Knight, dated January 5, 1935, Paul Douglas Papers, Special Collections Research Center, Joseph Regenstein Library, University of Chicago).

60. This information is contained in a letter, dated January 8, 1935, from Millis to Knight (Frank H. Knight Papers, Special Collections Research Center, Joseph Regenstein Library, University of Chicago).

61. In fact, Simons had, as previously stated, moved to the University of Chicago in 1927.

62. Concerning Simons, George Stigler (1988, 184) expressed the following view: "Simons's credentials did not fit the former half of a 'publish or perish' policy in 1935."

63. Neither Simons nor Director would ever obtain a PhD.

64. As mentioned in chapter 1, Simons was promoted to full professor in 1945.

65. See chapter 5.

66. A major exception was H. Gregg Lewis, who was Douglas's research assistant in the 1930s. Lewis taught at Chicago from 1939 to 1975 and carried on the tradition of empirical labor economics founded by Douglas.

67. Wallis, who was both a statistician and an economist, served as dean of Chicago's Graduate School of Business from 1956 to 1962. In 1962 he became

president of the University of Rochester. He was chancellor at Rochester from 1970 to 1982. From 1982 until 1988, Wallis was under secretary of state for economic, business and agricultural affairs in the Reagan administration. Under the leadership of Secretary of State George Shultz, Wallis spearheaded an enlarged role for economic analysis at the State Department, a process that had been initiated by Under Secretary of State Richard Cooper in the Carter administration. As a member of the economic analysis group at the State Department from 1977 to 1985, I worked under the direction of both Cooper and Wallis. During the tenure of James Baker as secretary of state from 1989 to 1992, the economic analysis group at the State Department was disbanded.

68. Reder (1982, 8) stated: "the younger members of the group (Friedman, Stigler, and Wallis), were extremely good expositors and very effective advocates, qualities which Knight did not share."

## Chapter Four

1. The idea that the 100 percent reserves scheme and the policy proposal that the monetary authorities follow a rule were not inexorably linked was stressed by Demeulemeester (2021).

2. The act of 1742 conferred on the bank a monopoly on the issuance of notes in England. The only banks not affected by the monopoly were those with fewer than six partners. See Andreades (1966, 171).

3. The country banks' promissory notes were issued in the process of the banks' discounting of commercial bills.

4. This point was made by Laidler (1992, 257).

5. Richard Cantillon's *An Essay on Economic Theory* was published (in French) in 1755 but written in 1730. Bordo (1983) discussed Cantillon's contributions to economics.

6. An alternative to the Humean mechanism was developed by Adam Smith in his *An Inquiry into the Nature and Causes of the Wealth of Nations* (1776). For a discussion of Smith's theory, see Humphrey (1981).

7. The bank's holdings of gold, which had amounted to about £7 million in 1794, fell to £1.27 million in February 1797 (Viner 1937, 122; Kynaston 2017, 82).

8. Price indices had not been constructed during these years. Following the end of the Napoleonic Wars, prices fell. In 1819, David Ricardo provided several estimates before parliamentary committees of the fall in the price level that had occurred. Viner (1937, 174–75) commented on these estimates: "In the absence of any index numbers, [Ricardo] could have had only a vague idea as the extent of the fall in the price level which had occurred."

9. I follow the convention of classifying the protagonists in the controversy as "bullionists" and "antibullionists." However, as Laidler (1992, 255) cautioned:

"Such labels are useful as organizing devices, but it is dangerous to apply them rigidly. The bullionist controversy was a series of debates about a variety of issues, and those debates involved a shifting cast of participants, whose views sometimes changed as controversy continued."

10. Schumpeter (1954, 688) noted that "most of [the participants] were men of practical affairs and primarily interested in practical measures."

11. Viner (1937) characterized this argument as the "extreme bullionist position." It was the position taken by Ricardo and John Wheatley. According to Viner (1937, 127–28) "[other] bullionists were prepared to make several qualifications to this reasoning and to concede that the existence of a premium of bullion over paper, or of a discount of sterling exchange from metallic parity was not an absolute proof of excess issue, and was strong presumptive evidence of excess issue only if it was substantial and prevailed for a considerable period of time."

12. The bullionists believed that country banks tended to keep a constant percentage of Bank of England notes as reserves against their liabilities. Any overissue of country banknotes would drain Bank of England notes from country banks' reserves to London via a regional Humean adjustment mechanism, forcing the country banks to contract their notes. In this way, the Bank of England could determine the money supply through the issuance of its notes, which served as the monetary base of the country banks. This point was made by Humphrey (1974, 7).

13. Mill eventually converted to the bullionist position, and Torrens became a proponent of the currency school, the successor to the bullionist position.

14. Sargent and Wallace (1982) attempted to rehabilitate the real bills doctrine by showing that what they called a "free-banking or real bills regime" (1982, 1214) would lead to a fluctuating and perhaps indeterminate price level along with a Pareto-optimal allocation of resources. In a comment on the Sargent and Wallace paper, Laidler (1984) showed that those authors mistakenly interpreted the real bills doctrine because the advocates of that doctrine believed that bank lending "confined to loans made on the security of short-term bills of exchange issued by reputable merchants or manufacturers to finance the production and distribution of real goods" would guarantee price-level stability (Laidler 1984, 153). I provide an in-depth discussion of the real bills doctrine in chapter 6.

15. Closely associated with this point of view is the notion that the restriction of lending to commercial loans ensures that the currency has a desirable elasticity so that banks will be in a liquid position at all times (Mints 1945a, 9).

16. Mints (1945a, 50) stated: "Apparently the management of the Bank of England leaned heavily in the direction of the real-bills doctrine." See also Viner (1937, 168).

17. The following arguments were contained in a report in 1810 by the Bullion Committee, a parliamentary committee that included Thornton as a member. Key arguments in the report had been made earlier by Thornton in his 1802 book *Paper Credit*.

18. The Bank of England's lending rate, called "Bank rate," was set by law at a maximum of 5 percent until 1833. The English Bank Charter Act of 1833 exempted the discounting of bills maturing within three months from the 5 percent ceiling.

19. This argument had been made by Thornton (1802).

20. The pamphlet was published posthumously; Ricardo died in 1823. Ricardo's pamphlet was discussed by R. Phillips (1995, 67–68) and Demeulemeester (2019, 26–27). It was not mentioned in such classic studies as Viner (1937) and Mints (1945a).

21. In his *Plan for the Establishment of a National Bank* (1824), Ricardo argued that the central bank could issue notes against gold and government securities. In his 1810 *High Price of Bullion*, Ricardo proposed that the Bank of England notes be convertible into gold ingots, rather than gold coins.

22. I am grateful to Samuel Demeulemeester for bringing to my attention Ricardo's letter to Malthus. In correspondence with me, Demeulemeester wrote that Ricardo got the idea of separating the Bank of England's functions from an unpublished 1814 paper by Jean-Baptiste Say. Demeulemeester pointed out that this circumstance was noted by Sraffa (1951, 4:272).

23. The initial years of the deflation featured an economic slowdown associated with the restoration of sterling to its prewar parity.

24. As in the case of the debate between the "bullionists" and "antibullionists," the labels need to be viewed as organizing devices. Schumpeter (1954, 726) wrote the following about the banking and currency schools: "Neither group was a school in our sense of the word. Within both, there were considerable differences of opinion." Currency school member George W. Norman was the paternal grandfather of Montagu Norman, who was governor of the Bank of England from 1920 to 1944. As we saw in chapter 2, in July 1931 Montagu Norman predicted that, unless drastic measures were taken, the capitalist system throughout the world would collapse within a year.

25. Although the currency school is often considered to have been the successor of the bullionist position, the banking school authors, like the bullionist writers, insisted that the currency should remain convertible into gold.

26. Meltzer (2003, 36) pointed out that Ricardo had made a similar argument in parliamentary testimony.

27. Banking school advocates put considerable weight on the equilibrating role of the law of reflux. Fullarton argued: "It is the *reflux* that is the great regulating principle of the internal currency" (emphasis in original, 1845, 68). Similarly, Tooke (1848, 194) stated that "if the loans or discounts are advanced on proper securities, for short periods, the reflux of the notes, if any have been issued, will be equal to the efflux, leaving the circulation unaltered."

28. Humphrey (1976; 1979) showed that members of the banking school developed cost-push theories of inflation under which inflation was attributed to nonmonetary factors such as production bottlenecks and supply-side inelasticities.

29. Palmer expressed the view that when the exchanges were at par, the "currency" was "full."

30. Loyd (1837) presented an assessment of the Bank of England's gold holdings and its deposit and note liabilities in the mid-1830s; Loyd concluded that the Palmer rule was not followed.

31. This description of the Bank Act of 1844 has benefitted from very helpful comments from Samuel Demeulemeester.

32. This point was stressed by Demeulemeester (2019), but it has typically been overlooked in studies on the Bank Act of 1844 (e.g., Whale 1944; Cameron 1992; O'Brien 1998). The omission is significant. Unlike Ricardo's objective, seigniorage remained in private hands.

33. The amount was set considerably below the actual circulation so that there would be a safe margin backed by gold.

34. The Banking Department competed with other banks in providing lending services, but it maintained higher shares of reserves relative to its total liabilities than those banks. Bagehot (1873, 18–19) reported that, in the middle of the nineteenth century, the Banking Department's reserves in banknotes and coin averaged between 30 and 50 percent of its total liabilities, compared with between 11 and 13 percent for other banks.

35. The modules of the Bank Act of 1844 were applied to Scotland and Wales under separate acts in 1845.

36. The following discussion on the origination of the rules-versus-discretion debate is based on Dellas and Tavlas (2022).

37. This point was made by Daugherty (1943). That author reported that when the Peel Act came into effect in August 1844, the Bank of England's reserves amounted to fourteen million pounds, an unprecedentedly large amount.

38. In his paper "Thomas Tooke on Monetary Reform," Laidler (1972, 213) stated that Tooke's objective was to provide the Bank of England with sufficient time to ride out temporary disequilibria without causing serious domestic repercussions. In this way, the bank would be able to distinguish between temporary and permanent shocks. Laidler (1972, 211) referred to Tooke as "the leading member of the banking school."

39. See, also, O'Brien (1992, 564). Earlier, O'Brien (1975) did not connect the debate between the currency school and the banking school with the rules-versus-discretion literature.

40. In his 1972 paper "Thomas Tooke on Monetary Reform," Laidler (1972) did not describe Tooke's views within the context of rules versus discretion.

41. Blaug's book went through five editions, the last of which was published in 1997. Each edition after the first involved substantial revisions. The quotation above was left unaltered.

42. Not all contemporary historians have identified the banking school with discretionary policies. In a paper on the history of rules, Asso and Leeson (2012,

8) stated: "both the Currency School and the Banking School provided cases for subjecting the Bank of England to some preconceived rules of conduct." In a paper on Fullarton's views, Skaggs (1991, 478) stated: "To Fullarton . . . constraining discretion with firm principles [e.g., maintain the reflux of bills, do not reduce the discount rate below the market rate] can prevent major errors in credit policy. Seen in this light, Fullarton's attitude toward central bank policy is strikingly similar to that of the currency school, who sought to prevent major errors by imposing the currency principle on the Bank of England."

43. This section draws on Tavlas (forthcoming).

44. Graham (1936, 428), an advocate of the proposal, pointed out that "few suggestions for monetary reform have commanded such immediate and widespread interest as that which has attended the proposal to require 100 percent cash reserves against bank demand deposit liabilities."

45. In contrast to the Chicago proposal, Fisher did not advocate a reform of the banking structure. Under his proposal, the 100 percent reserve requirements would be applied to demand deposits, but banks would be able to lend funds obtained from savings and time deposits under the fractional-reserve principle. See Fisher (1935). A similar scheme was advocated by Lauchlin Currie in 1934. Demeulemeester (2019) compared the Chicago proposal with those of Fisher and Currie.

46. Dimand (1993b), R. Phillips (1995), and Demeulemeester (2019) reviewed the 1930s academic literature on the 100 percent reserve scheme. Phillips (1995) also reviewed the congressional debate on the issue.

47. Soddy (1877–1956) taught chemistry at the University of Oxford from 1919 until 1937. He won the Nobel Prize in Chemistry for his work showing that radioactivity is due to the transmutation of elements. He predicted the existence of, and coined the term for, isotopes.

48. Fisher's books *Stable Money* and *100% Money*, published in 1934 and 1935, respectively, cited Soddy's 1926 book. Fisher also cited other forerunners, including Thomas Joplin (1823) and Ludwig von Mises (1912), of the 100 percent reserves scheme. Thus, while Fisher gave credit to Soddy, Fisher did not consider Soddy the originator of the idea.

49. In fact, the idea of 100 percent reserves against checking deposits—as opposed to reserves against currency—can be found in the mid-nineteenth-century work of Charles H. Carroll (see Carroll 1860), although neither Soddy nor the Chicagoans seemed to have been aware of Carroll's work as of the mid-1930s. Consequently, the debate between Soddy and Knight and Simons about origination was actually about the rediscovery of the 100 percent reserves idea in the context of the 1920s depression in the United Kingdom and the 1930s depression in the United States. Subsequently, Mints (1945a) provided an assessment of Carroll's work.

50. See also Alrifai (2015, 202) and Dittmer (2015, 9). Not all modern writers take the view that the Chicago economists got the idea of 100 percent reserves

from Soddy. Dimand (1993b) noted that Soddy formulated the idea in 1926, but he left open the possibility that the Chicagoans came up with the idea independently of Soddy. Credit to Soddy for originating the 100 percent reserves proposal has been long-standing in the literature. See, for example, Graham (1936), Watkins (1938), and Reed (1942).

51. As mentioned, Daly (1980) assessed Soddy's views on economics. Daly did not, however, discuss Soddy's view of the trade cycle, which is the subject of the following few pages.

52. Knight (1927b, 732) stated that "[Soddy's] effort to establish a conception of physical wealth . . . must be briefly dismissed."

53. Knight's review was published in April 1927. In a paper published in the March 1927 issue of the *American Economic Review* he stated: "as the loans made by commercial banks in connection with created deposits form an important fraction of the total supply of capital in the world of trade and industry, the payment received by the banks for this alleged service of economizing gold and increasing the supply of exchange-medium (and I say advisedly 'alleged' service, as a further suggestion, without stopping to develop that idea either) the payment for this alleged service to the community takes the form of interest. . . . It seems to me that the whole problem of the relation of commercial banking to the capital market is crying loudly for thorough examination" (Knight 1927a, 121).

54. The other two books were *The Money Revolution* (1934), authored by Charles Morgan-Webb, and *Moneyless Government* (1934), authored by Henry McCowen.

55. Simons (1939, 275) expressed the view that "[Hansen's] monetary theory, like that of Mr. Keynes, may not unjustly be characterized as a theory which attains to magnificent generality by being about nothing at all."

56. Credit for directing me to the following exchange between Hansen and Simons belongs to Rockoff (2015).

57. The other two writers cited by Hansen were James W. Angell and Fritz Lehmann. As mentioned, Angell was a proponent of the 100 percent reserves scheme. Lehmann was not an advocate of the 100 percent reserves idea.

58. The following exchange between Fisher and Knight was reproduced in Barber (1997, 4, fn. b).

59. The exact teaching assignments varied from year to year. The information in the above paragraph is from the *Bulletin of the State University of Iowa* (various years).

60. Schumpeter (1954, 1116) called Chester Phillips's *Bank Credit* "a great stride" in the banking literature. Humphrey (1987) and Timberlake (1988) discussed Phillips's contributions.

61. Knight and Simons evidently maintained a friendly relationship with Phillips after they left Iowa. This observation is based on the fact that Phillips was one of the non-Chicagoans who was invited to participate in the January 1932 Chicago conference. Phillips was one of the twelve non-Chicagoans who signed the Hoover memorandum.

62. Friedman and Schwartz (1963, 235) also stated that "the [1920–21] contraction was accompanied by a sharp curtailment in customer loans by member banks . . . [and] a sharp increase in bank failures."

63. The origin of the distinction between the effects of deposit creation by an individual bank and those of deposit creation by the banking system as a whole traces back to the work of English economist James Pennington in the 1820s. For a discussion of Pennington's works, see Humphrey (1987).

64. Fisher had a different view. In a letter, dated December 14, 1934, to Simons, Fisher wrote: "It seems to me quite preposterous to consider savings deposits as on all fours, or very similar to, deposits subject to check. I feel sure that a statistical study will convince you of this if you will take the trouble to make it" (quoted from R. Phillips 1995, 92).

65. Cochrane (2014) proposed a version of the 100 percent reserve scheme updated for modern banking, communication, and financial markets. Under his proposal, 100 percent reserves would be short-term interest-bearing government debt, including interest-paying reserves at the Fed; banks would be able to fund risky investments without the need to issue large amounts of deposits. Other recent advocates of 100 percent reserves include Benes and Kumhof (2012) and Wolf (2014).

66. This section draws on Tavlas (2021b).

67. See Dorn (2018) for an excellent discussion of the rationale for monetary rules.

68. For a discussion of Fisher's views on price stabilization in the 1920s, see Hetzel (1985).

69. Laidler (2010, 72) added that Chicagoan Aaron Director also came to share those views.

70. In his survey of the literature on rules, Fischer (1990, 1163) called a rule that aims to stabilize the price level "the Fisher-Simons rule." Humphrey (1990) drew a connection between the policy rules of Fisher and Mints.

71. For expressions of this view, see Asso and Leeson (2012) and Taylor (2017). Dimand (1998, 196) argued that there were many parallels between the views of Fisher and those of Friedman, including in the area of "rules rather than monetary policy discretion."

72. Shortly before the stock-market crash in October 1929, Fisher (1929, 8) expressed the view that stock prices had "reached what looks like a permanently high plateau." For months after the crash, he continued to assure investors that a recovery was just around the corner. See Barber (1999, 14–15). In his 1933 Presidential Address to the American Statistical Association, Fisher attempted to change the public record concerning his widely inaccurate predictions. He contended: "It is true that in September, 1929, I publicly stated my belief that we were 'then at the top of the stock market' and that there would be a recession. . . . And this proved true" (Fisher 1933a, 10). Dimand (2015, 202) described Fisher's attempt to revise the historical record as "comparable to Napoleon's insistence in his memoirs that he won the battle of Waterloo."

73. Discussions of Fisher's business-cycle and policy views include Tobin (1987), Dimand (1993a; 2020), Barber (1998), Laidler (1999; 2013), and Bordo and Rockoff (2013a).

74. Dimand (1999a, 49–50) discussed the possible role played by Brown in the making of *The Purchasing Power of Money*. Dimand indicated that Brown's views on the role of the banking system in economic crises may have influenced Fisher's theory of the cycle in that book, but that Brown's precise contribution to the writing of the book is not possible to determine.

75. Fisher's formulation has more in common with modern targeting rules, such as that of Svensson (2003), that allow the use of judgement and extra model information to formulate precise *objectives* for monetary policy. For a comparison of instrument rules and targeting rules, see McCallum and Nelson (2005).

76. As Howitt (1992, 123–24) pointed out, the linear approximation is derived from the formula $1 + r = (1 + i)/(1 + \pi)$. For low rates of inflation, $r$ is well approximated by $r = i - \pi$. The formula is exactly correct if $i, r$, and $\pi$ are calculated on the basis of continuous compounding. In the steady state, Fisher believed that expected inflation would equal actual inflation. Fisher first expressed what is now called the Fisher relation as an equation in his 1896 monograph *Appreciation and Interest*. The idea that the nominal rate is equal to the sum of the real rate and inflation rate was put forward, if not systematically analyzed, in the literature before Fisher's work (Howitt 1992, 123). In an interesting paper, Dimand and Betancourt (2012, 193) showed that Fisher was aware of, and drew attention to, earlier statements made by Marshall ([1890] 1920), de Haas (1889), J. B. Clark (1896), and Douglass ([1740] 1897). Dimand and Betancourt (2012, 193) also showed that, in addition to expressing the Fisher relation, Fisher "undertook a substantial verification of the theory, and extended the analysis from real and nominal interest to interest rates in two currencies (uncovered interest parity), interest rates over different durations of loans (the expectations theory of the term structure of interest rates), and interest rates in pairs of commodities (own rates of interest)." See also Dimand (1999b).

77. Fisher subsequently investigated the impact of past price changes on nominal interest rates, the volume of real economic activity, and unemployment using distributed lags, an estimation procedure that he originated. See Dimand (1993a).

78. Fisher was concerned that social unrest could underpin revolutionary forces. A continuation of unstable prices could, he argued, "perpetuate a chief source of social injustice, discontent, violence, and Bolshevism" (1920, xxviii).

79. Tobin (1987, 375) called this theory a "Schumpeterian" theory of the business cycle.

80. In his 1933 article "The Debt-Deflation Theory of Great Depressions," Fisher relegated his discussion of the role of the lag between real and nominal interest rates to a footnote (1933b, 350n4).

81. This point was made by Boianovsky (2011) and Laidler (2013). Boianovsky put forward the idea that Fisher lost confidence in the compensated dollar during the 1920s. In the second edition of *The Purchasing Power of Money*, published in

1913, Fisher added an appendix, "Standardizing the Dollar," that spelled out his plan in more detail than did the first edition.

82. Index numbers for prices were published in the United States beginning in 1890. See Patinkin (1993, 17).

83. To my knowledge of Fisher's works, this was one of the only two occasions in which the use of the word "rule" entered his lexicon during the period from 1911 until the early 1930s. The other occasion was in 1913. Referring to a scheme under which prices would not be permitted to fall, Fisher stated: "many people would not object to this limitation which permits prices to fall below the present level, but does not permit them to rise further. Yet it is a poor rule that will not work both ways" (Fisher 1913b, 25).

84. In an appendix titled "Technical Details" in *Stabilizing the Dollar*, Fisher (1920, 213) stated: "The Federal Reserve Board could assist in the prompt and efficient operation of the new system by having due regard to the rise and fall of the Index Number.... This would help its adjustment of the rate of discount and its general loan policy to be such as to keep the volume of individual deposits subject to check approximately proportional both to bank reserves and to Government gold reserve against gold bullion dollar certificates."

85. Throughout his career, Fisher emphasized the effects of a changing price level on distributive justice.

86. When Fisher first proposed his compensated-dollar plan in 1911, the Fed had not yet come into existence. Therefore, policies such as central-bank open-market operations and rediscounting operations were not available.

87. Laidler (2013) stressed the link between Fisher's support for a variety of policy proposals and an apparent loss of Fisher's ability to think creatively. In this connection, Laidler (2013, 194) stated: "The slippage in his [Fisher's] innovative powers as a thinker and commentator on monetary policy issues that had already begun to be apparent in the mid-1920s thus became ever more evident in the 1930s even as the pace of his activities as an advocate seemed to accelerate."

88. As mentioned in chapter 2, Fisher's aim in raising the price level during the Great Depression was to bring wholesale prices back to their 1926 level.

89. Stamped money was a scheme to stimulate the velocity of money by providing what effectively was an interest-free loan to all citizens. Under the scheme, a specially issued money, say $100, would be provided to all citizens (or a subset of citizens). To spend the money, individuals would have to buy, say, a $1 stamp and affix it to the money at, for example, monthly intervals. At the end of one hundred months, the entire principal of what was effectively an interest-free loan would have been repaid. Fisher wrote a book (1933d) on the stamped-money idea. The stamped-money idea was originated by Silvio Gesell, a German businessman, in the late nineteenth century. See Fisher (1934, 43–44) and Keynes (1936a, chap. 23).

90. Fisher (1933c, 136) expressed his unabashed support for Roosevelt's discretionary changes in the price of the dollar as follows: "the words given out by

the President, under his discretionary control of the currency, constitute thus far the climax to the most basic reform movement in economic history." Fisher's book *Stable Money* (1934) was dedicated to Roosevelt. See also the discussion in the subsection "Simons, Mints, and Fisher" below. The policy of changing the exchange rate of the dollar had the effect of providing the monetary authorities with greater scope to pursue domestic policy objectives, which was Fisher's aim.

91. The specifics of Fisher's policy proposals underwent variations over time. See Barber (1998).

92. These reforms included 100 percent reserve requirements.

93. The preface to the book was written in November 1933.

94. The article, "Finds New Deal Queer Jumble; Aims Conflict," was discussed in chapter 3.

95. The argument that Simons advocated a policy rule to effectuate a liberal policy agenda was emphasized by Laidler (1993).

96. Cox was also one of the twelve Chicago signatories of the January 1932 telegram sent to President Hoover. See chapter 2.

97. Cox constructed an elaborate metric to compare the performances of several forecasters, including those of Roger Babson—who successfully predicted the 1929 stock-market crash and also founded Babson College—and the Harvard Economic Service. See Cox's *An Appraisal of American Business Forecasts* (1929) and *Forecasting Business Conditions* (1928); the latter book was co-authored with Charles O. Hardy. See Hardy and Cox (1928). Both books went through several editions. For a brief discussion of Cox's technique of forecasting appraisal, see Walter Friedman's 2014 book *Fortune Tellers: The Story of America's First Economic Forecasters*.

98. See, for example, "Evaluation of Economic Forecasts" (Cox 1930) and "Some Distinguishing Characteristics of the Current Recovery" (Cox 1936a). In a 1928 review of Cox's book, with Hardy, *Forecasting Business Conditions*, the reviewer, F. E. Richter, wrote: "one is left with a sense not only of lack of finality [about the authors' preference among business-cycle theories] ... but even a lack of pointing up to anything in particular. Given the audience to which the book was addressed, this is unfortunate" (Richter 1928, 341).

## Chapter Five

1. As mentioned in chapter 2, the word "credit" was used to represent bank money in the form of checking deposits on the liability side of banks' balance sheets instead of the present-day terminology under which credit refers to the loans and discounts on the asset side of banks' balance sheets.

2. As we shall see in the next chapter, in the late 1940s and early 1950s, Director, Knight, and Mints, along with Friedman, cosigned joint policy memoranda that stressed the important role of money in the economy.

3. Ellis was a professor of economics at the University of California, Berkeley. He served as president of the American Economic Association in 1949.

4. Villard was a professor of economics at Hofstra College.

5. Villard did not identify either the 1930 text or the 1947 text to which he referred. Evidently, the 1947 "new elementary text" to which Villard referred was *The Elements of Economics* (1947) by Lorie Tarshis.

6. This point was made by H. Stein (1987). In an obituary on Simons, Davenport (1946, 5) wrote: "Simons took up that fight [in support of free markets] early when the majority of the American intelligentsia had lost faith in American tradition and were looking to Moscow if not to Berlin to point the way of the future."

7. Herbert Stein was chairman of the Council of Economic Advisers from January 1972 until August 1974. He completed his graduate coursework in economics at the University of Chicago in 1938 although he did not finish his dissertation and earn his doctorate until 1958.

8. The Beveridge Report, drafted by British economist and social reformer William Beveridge, was published in 1942. The report formed the basis of the United Kingdom's post–World War II welfare state.

9. Director stated: "I never took a course from him, but I was greatly influenced by him" (Kitch 1983, 179). Mints (n.d.) wrote: "for sheer analytical ability few of his contemporaries equaled Henry Simons; and yet his chief interest lay not in this direction, but in the problem of evolving a program of public policy for the promotion of public welfare." George Stigler (1974, 1), who *was* a student of Simons, described his teacher as "the Crown Prince of that hypothetical Kingdom, the Chicago school of economics." On Simons's influence, see also Friedman (1967) and Wallis (in Kitch 1983, 179).

10. In his 1944 paper "Some Reflections on Syndicalism," Simons wrote: "The essence of [traditional economic liberalism] is a distrust of all concentrations of power" (1944b, 124).

11. As pointed out by Van Horn (2009), in the 1950s Director came to the view that industrial monopolies were almost always undone by the forces of competition and that, consequently, a relatively sanguine attitude should be adopted toward both industrial monopolies and large corporations. Van Horn (2009, 228–29) argued, "In a period of just ten years (1946–56), the contents of liberalism at Chicago underwent a radical transformation. Director and other neoliberal advocates and converts no longer regarded monopoly as the great enemy of democracy [as did Simons]." Van Horn's statement that a "radical transformation" in Chicagoan views about industrial monopolies had taken place is incorrect as evidenced in the above quotations from Simons's works in the mid-1940s. By the mid-1940s, Simons no longer regarded industrial monopolies as "the great enemy of democracy." Hence, Director's views about industrial monopolies in the 1950s were not very different from Simons's views in the mid-1940s.

12. Herbert Stein (1987, 334) maintained that Simons's increased concern about labor unions in the 1940s reflected the quadrupling of labor-union membership

in the decade after 1934. Davenport (1946, 10) expressed the view that Simons had been reluctant to criticize labor unions, citing Simons's 1944 paper "Some Reflections on Syndicalism" as an example. The opening sentence of that paper reads: "Questioning the virtues of the organized labor movement is like attacking religion, monogamy, motherhood, or the home" (1944b, 121). Davenport (1946) reported that the paper was completed in 1941, but that Simons held up its publication until 1944. We will encounter Davenport again in chapter 7.

13. Simons's 1942 paper "Hansen on Fiscal Policy" was a review of Alvin Hansen's book *Fiscal Policy and Business Cycles* (1941). I discuss Hansen's book, and Simons's review of the book, below. In a 1942 review of the document *The Structure of the American Economy*, Simons (1942b, 45–46) wrote: "I believe that our great monopoly problem for the future, and the great barrier to new investment, lies in the spread of militant and aggressive labor organizations, and in their inevitable effort to appropriate as much as possible of what would otherwise be the productivity of investment assets."

14. For a discussion, see Tavlas (2015).

15. Simons's call for 100 percent reserves on demand deposits would provide the authorities with improved control over the supply of money by making the money supply equivalent to the monetary base.

16. In his book *Chicagonomics: The Evolution of Chicago Free Market Economics*, Ebenstein (2015, 84) mischaracterized the views of the pre–World War II Chicago tradition as follows: "There was not the focus on monetary policy that became the hallmark of the later Chicago school of economics." Contrary to Ebenstein's characterization, monetary policy was a hallmark of the 1930s and 1940s Chicago tradition.

17. The November 1933 memorandum (Simons et al. 1933) was unclear on the institution that would be responsible for implementing monetary policy: page 5 of that memorandum stated that the Federal Reserve Board should be "charged with carrying out the rule," but page 14 stated that "a government agency" should carry out the rule.

18. In maintaining that the Treasury should be the primary administrative agency for monetary-policy implementation, Simons noted that the US Congress would have oversight of the Treasury. In a 1945 review of the book (published in 1944) *World Commodities and World Currency* by Benjamin Graham, Simons wrote: "Powers over the quantity of money (and money substitutes, from bank deposits to corporate bonds) and responsibility for the value of money should not be further dispersed but concentrated as closely as possible in the Treasury and in (and within) Congress as the ultimate fiscal authority" (1945c, 280).

19. During the early 1920s, Hawtrey was a strong proponent of the view that Britain should return to the gold standard. See Bigg (1987).

20. As noted in chapter 2, in the early 1930s the Chicagoans did not support the use of open-market operations because they believed that those operations were

too slow to take effect during depressions. Simons's argument that open-market operations were ineffective because of the close substitutability between money and government bonds is different from the argument that such operations are slow to take effect. This point was stressed by Rockoff (2015).

21. A slightly revised version of the paper, with the title "Money, Tariffs, and the Peace," was published in 1948. See Simons (1948a).

22. This point was made by Hettich (1979, 3), who provided a detailed account of Simons's work on taxation. See also Director (1946) for an overview of Simons's contributions to the tax literature.

23. Simons (1934a, 65) maintained that a "drastic reduction in inequality" could be attained without a significant loss to the higher income groups and a large loss of efficiency.

24. For that reason, Simons (1942a, 212) advocated a "continuous and ultimately drastic reduction" in government spending.

25. This measure of income has come to be called the Haig-Simons definition of income. See Haig (1921). Simons wrote two books—both were on taxation. His book *Personal Income Taxation* was written in the early 1930s, but not published until 1938. It was his doctoral dissertation. The second book, *Federal Tax Reform*, was completed in 1943 and published posthumously in 1950. Viner, who was a member of Simons's dissertation committee and who had a poor relationship with Simons, evidently held up the acceptance of the dissertation. In a letter addressed to Kenneth A. Lohf, dated February 8, 1985, Albert Hart wrote that Viner had "blighted" Simons's career by "blocking acceptance of his [Simons's] thesis" (quoted from Cristiano and Fiorito [2016, 69n4]). According to Emmett (2006, 781), Simons never received a PhD because he (Simons) refused to participate in the oral examination.

26. Simons's proposal for tax reform included a simplification of the tax system. In this connection, Simons called for the "abolition of all excises on commodities of wide and general consumption and ultimately of the innumerable miscellaneous levies which have no justification in terms of broad considerations of policy" (1934a, 68).

27. It will be recalled from chapter 3 that a similar argument was made in the November 1933 Chicago memorandum. Following the collapse of the Bretton Woods system in 1973, an extensive empirical and theoretical literature emerged that examined the relationship between exchange-rate volatility and export performance. By and large, this literature rejected the hypothesis that exchange-rate volatility hampers exports. See, for example, Bailey, Tavlas, and Ulan (1986; 1987).

28. Similarly, in his review of Benjamin Graham's book *World Commodities and World Currency*, Simons wrote that "the dollar promises to be the dominant world currency" (1945c, 280).

29. The reprint of the article in Simons (1948b), like the 1942 *JPE* version, was also thirty-six pages.

30. Hansen was elected president of the American Economic Association in 1938. In 1967, he was awarded the Francis A. Walker Medal. Hansen came from a modest background. He was reared in a small rural community in South Dakota, and he attended school in a one-room schoolhouse (Musgrave 1987, 591).

31. Barber (1987, 198) reported that Hansen first met Keynes in June 1934 in New York, but "Hansen was no stranger to Keynes's ideas at the time of his encounter." This statement is inaccurate. As discussed in chapter 2, both Keynes and Hansen participated in the Chicago June/July 1931 conference, "Unemployment as a World Problem." Both presented papers at the conference—Hansen on June 24 and Keynes on July 1. Both intervened at each other's presentation.

32. Credit for discovery of this citation belongs to Nelson (2020, 1:109).

33. See Barber (1987, 193).

34. In a discussion of Hansen's 1949 book *Monetary Theory and Fiscal Policy*, Nelson (2020, 1:113) pointed out that, although Hansen's formulation of income-expenditure mechanics might suggest otherwise, Hansen's formulation "was not really an account centered on an endogenous-money story. For Hansen contended that even, if money were held constant when the multiplier process was in motion, the same nominal spending path would be the outcome: a constant money stock would simply raise the amount of income variation that could be attributed to velocity."

35. According to Nelson (2020, 1:108): "After the 1940s ... indeed right into the 1980s and 1990s—Friedman would cite Hansen repeatedly as an example of the extreme nature of Keynesian economics."

36. In an interview with J. Ronnie Davis, conducted in 1966 but not published until 1974, Knight was quoted as saying that he thought that "Simons's review of the *General Theory* was, in some respects, the best one." See J. R. Davis (1974, 25).

37. The paper was published as a "white paper" on April 7, 1943. See Keynes (1943). For discussion of Keynes's contributions to the blueprint that established the Bretton Woods system, see Steil (2013).

38. The preface to the book was dated January 31, 1935.

39. See Douglas (1935a).

40. Douglas (1935b, 10) noted that "instead of one ever-recurring 'cause' of depressions, there may be a very considerable number of such 'causes.'"

41. Other "cumulative causes" cited by Douglas were an excess of saving over investment, as stressed by Keynes in his *Treatise on Money* (1930), and the dependency of the demand for capital goods on both the level of consumer demand and the rate of change in the demand for consumer products (i.e., the accelerator principle).

42. As mentioned in chapter 2, Douglas (1935b, 26) explicitly wrote out the Fisherine equation in *Controlling Depressions*.

43. It may be recalled (from chapter 3) that Simons (1934a, 54) stated: "It is no exaggeration to say that the major proximate factor in the present crisis is commercial banking."

44. As discussed in the next chapter, during the mid- and late 1940s, Mints's views were very similar to those held by his colleagues Simons, Director, and Knight in the 1930s and the early 1940s.

45. This research was summarized in Douglas's presidential address "Are There Laws of Production," delivered at the Sixtieth Annual Meeting of the American Economic Association on December 29, 1947. See Douglas (1948).

46. On March 4, 1938, Douglas issued a statement before the Senate Committee on Unemployment in which he argued that "monopoly fixation of prices" was "a major cause" of the Great Depression and the 1937–38 depression. See Douglas (1938, 1).

47. This information is based on Allen (1993, 714). Unfortunately, not all the doctrinal literature has reported the facts accurately. A case in point is the book *The Economic Thought of Henry Calvert Simons* (2018), authored by G. R. Steele. The book relies exclusively on secondary accounts of Simons's work and contains numerous factual inaccuracies. Here are two examples. (1) As mentioned, in Knight's cover letter to the March 1933 memorandum, Knight wrote that the memorandum had been circulated to some "forty odd" individuals. In Steele's presentation of the March 1933 memorandum, the author wrote: "With an initial circulation limited to some forty individuals, the memorandum brought a total of 320 responses from 157 universities. Over seventy percent of those responding gave general agreement to the proposals with fewer than fifteen percent registering disapproval" (Steele 2018, 69). The corresponding numbers cited for the above 1939 memorandum were 318 (235 + 40 + 43) responses from 157 universities, with 74 percent approving. Thus, Steele incorrectly referred to the responses to the 1939 memorandum as pertaining to the March 1933 memorandum. (2) On page 50 of his book, Steele wrote that the same group of twenty-four economists (twelve Chicagoans and twelve non-Chicagoans) who signed the January 1932 Harris Foundation memorandum (sent to President Hoover) "quickly followed" that document with a second memorandum. A similar statement had been made by Ronnie Phillips in his book *The Chicago Plan and New Deal Banking Reform* (1995, 29). In fact, there was no second statement by those economists. Backhouse (2019b) provided a good review of Steele's book although Backhouse did not report the factual errors in the book.

48. The *JPE* article to which Simons referred was his 1936 "Rules versus Authorities in Monetary Policy."

49. See Patinkin (1973b) and Baumol (1983).

50. This point about Knight's work was made by Baumol (1983, 1081).

51. A major part of Knight's writings on economics in the 1930s focused on capital theory in which Knight criticized the Austrian theory of capital. That theory claimed that labor and natural resources (i.e., "primary" factors) join together to produce capital goods, a process that is time-consuming. The Austrians claimed that the process of producing such goods could be characterized by an economy-wide

average period of production, which could be measured. They also believed that the average period of production could be included in a production function characterized by diminishing productivity. In a series of articles, Knight (1934a; 1935a; 1936a; 1936b) denied the existence of any primary factors of production that do not contain capital; he believed that diminishing marginal returns for capital did not exist because the long-run substitution possibilities of capital for labor were extremely large. He also denied the possibility of measuring the period of production (G. Stigler 1987, 57). Blaug (1985, chap. 12) provided a detailed discussion of Austrian capital theory while Laidler (1999, 33–34) provided a succinct account of the theory.

52. Knight's brother, Melvin Moses Knight, apparently played a role in arranging a visiting position at Berkeley for his brother. Melvin Knight taught economic history in UC-Berkeley's economics department from 1928 to 1954. Melvin Knight, who never attended high school—at age thirteen he found himself responsible for running his family's farm near Bloomington, Illinois—was self-taught. After passing the entrance exams, he was admitted into Milligan College, in Tennessee. He eventually earned a PhD in sociology from Clark University, with a thesis titled "Taboo and Genetics." Melvin Knight apparently shared some of Frank's idiosyncratic characteristics. An obituary published by the University of California, Berkeley, called him a "salty individualist."

53. In a paper, "Frank Knight as Teacher," Patinkin used the words "rambling" and "disjointed" to describe his initial impression of Knight's teaching style (1973b, 24) in the latter's course Price and Distribution Theory (Econ 301).

54. The lectures are contained in the Frank H. Knight Papers at the Special Collections Research Center of the University of Chicago's Regenstein Library.

55. As will be detailed in notes that follow, there are several minor errors in the transcription from the original lecture notes to those published by Cristiano and Fiorito.

56. The transcription by Cristiano and Fiorito (2016, 80) substituted the word "done" in place of the word "made" in the above quotation.

57. To the extent that the transcripts accurately reflect what Knight said in the course, this statement is in error. See, for example, Humphrey (1984) and Laidler (1991, 20–26) for discussions of the classical theory of what was called the trade cycle.

58. The emphasis attached to the word "failed" was missing in the transcription by Cristiano and Fiorito (2016, 83).

59. Cristiano and Fiorito (2016, 84) mistakenly replaced the term "self-aggravating" with "self-aggregating."

60. The emphasis on the word "credit" in the original notes was missing in the transcription by Cristiano and Fiorito (2016).

61. The view that the *General Theory* was heavily shaped by the British economic experience of the 1920s was echoed by Johnson (1978, 206).

62. Keynes (1936a, 207) stated: "But whilst this limiting case might become practically important in the future, I know of no example of it hitherto."

63. In a letter dated February 12, 1937, Albert Hart, who completed his PhD at Chicago in 1936, wrote to Knight about the review as follows: "I am sorry to say I think your review of Keynes is the worst thing you've written for some time; though fortunately what ails it is largely fairly early, so that it doesn't leave a bad taste. Broadly, I think that the tone suggests that you are 'out to get' Keynes" (quoted from Cristiano and Fiorito 2016, 69).

64. In an introductory footnote, Knight stated: "In view of the late date of this review, and particularly of the number of extensive reviews already published, some familiarity with the content of the book may be assumed" (1937, 100n1).

65. In his review of the *General Theory*, Knight did not mention that he had been identified by Keynes as an author who had argued that the interest rate is determined by the equation of saving and investment.

66. Knight's 1934 *Economica* article triggered a debate between Knight and Friedrich von Hayek and Fritz Machlup on the nature of capital and the theory of interest. For a review of the debate and references to the literature, see Kaldor (1937). Concerning Knight's contributions to the debate, Kaldor (1937, 202–3) wrote the following: "[Knight] makes so many points that one is apt to get lost among them, not knowing how to distinguish between the primary and the secondary, the important and the unimportant; while the conclusions are frequently clothed in paradoxical sentences which are intended to challenge the mind but without a sufficient indication of where to turn in order to uncover those mental processes which must have led up to them."

67. This point was made by Patinkin (1979, 299).

68. In his 1936 course Business Cycles, Knight mainly focused on the business-cycle theories of early twentieth-century economists, including those of William Foster and Waddill Catchings, Arthur Pigou, Ralph Hawtrey, and Wesley C. Mitchell. The lack of attention to the nineteenth-century literature suggests that Knight did not think that the classical economists had formulated an adequate business-cycle theory.

69. The use of the analogy from mechanics to explain the business cycle was a consistent theme of Knight's writings. In the March 1927 issue of the *AER* he was quoted as saying: "the fundamental theory of the business cycle is to be found in a general mechanical principle of a tendency to oscillation whenever there is a time lag between a cause and its effect" (Knight 1927c, 19–20).

70. Knight (1941a, 213) wrote: "Wages are notoriously sticky, especially with respect to any downward changes in hourly wage-rates."

71. In the *General Theory*, Keynes (1936a, 143) expressed skepticism about Fisher's distinction between nominal and real interest rates.

72. Knight's paper was mainly concerned with the *theory* of the business cycle. Consequently, in discussing countercyclical policy, Knight (1941a, 223) noted that he would give "a very brief consideration to the [policy] problem."

73. Kiekhofer was a professor of economics at the University of Wisconsin at Madison.

74. Knight (1923, 52) wrote: "The workings of competition educate men progressively for monopoly, which is being achieved not merely by the 'capitalist' producers of more and more commodities, but by labour in many fields, and in many branches of agriculture, while the producers of even the fundamental crops are already aspiring to the goal."

75. Knight's view that government policies, rather than market competition, encourage monopolies presaged the views of Director and Friedman in the 1950s. See chapter 8.

76. See also Knight (1923, 51).

77. This point was made by Buchanan (1991) and Burgin (2009, 520–28).

78. See Buchanan (1991, 249). Kasper (1993) argued that Knight's support for laissez-faire also rested on efficiency grounds: socialist managers show a tendency to "play safe," whereas, under private ownership, entrepreneurs are willing to take risks. Kasper (1993, 424) wrote: "because economic activity takes place in a world of uncertainty, Knight argued that an economic system organized on the basis of laissez faire was more efficient" than a system based on economic control of economic activity. To support her argument, Kasper relied on Knight's writings of the early 1920s. To my knowledge, Knight did not use the economic-efficiency argument to support his advocacy of laissez-faire in the 1930s and after.

79. As mentioned in chapter 3, in a 1932 *JPE* article, "The Newer Economics and the Control of Economic Activity," Knight (1932a) critically reviewed Slichter's book *Modern Economic Society*. Slichter replied with a comment in the *JPE* (see Slichter 1932), and Knight provided a rejoinder (see Knight 1932b), from which the above quotation in the text is taken.

80. Knight (1951, 252) added: "but of late this wave of the future has happily been passing." In adding that qualification, Knight might have been influenced by the work of his colleague and former student Milton Friedman. He might also have been influenced by work on the real balance effect by Pigou (1943) and Patinkin (1948).

81. The other contributors to the symposium were Wassily W. Leontief (1936) and Dennis H. Robertson (1936).

82. Viner (1936b, 157) pointed out that Dennis Robertson had made a similar argument in his contribution to the *QJE* symposium. See Robertson (1936). The word "tho" is a dated construction for the word "though." The word "rôles" is a dated spelling of the word "roles."

83. In a 1963 retrospective on his review of the *General Theory* for the *QJE*, Viner stated that Frank Taussig, the editor of the *QJE* in 1936, had asked him to focus on the short-term determinants of changes in employment. Viner wrote: "I consequently refrained from any attempt to assess the contribution of the *General Theory* to policy formulation or to long-run analysis" (1963, 417).

84. I briefly referred to Viner's 1937 study in chapter 4 in the section of my discussion on rules versus discretion in the currency school–banking school debates.

85. The context of the above statements on velocity by Viner was the Bullionist Controversy. As discussed in chapter 4, that controversy centered around the
reasons for the depreciation of the pound against gold and other currencies in the
early part of the nineteenth century.

86. Viner's position on this point was noted by Irwin (2016, 765).

87. See Viner (1937, 254–80).

88. Laidler (2000, 14–16) and Humphrey and Timberlake (2019, 12–14) provided documentation showing that the Bank of England operated under the
influence of the real bills doctrine in the first decade of the nineteenth century.

89. This interpretation was suggested to me by David Laidler.

90. As discussed in chapter 6, Humphrey and Timberlake (2019) provided a
comprehensive criticism of the Fed's policies during the Great Depression based
on that institution's reliance on the real bills doctrine.

91. Concerning organized labor, Viner (1942a, 686) wrote: "The customary lag
of wages after prices has probably been reduced to minor proportions, or even
reversed, by the combined effects of the growth of collective bargaining and the
rise of governments sensitive to the claims of organized labor." Thus, "the unequal
distribution of gains and burdens would be most marked as between different cat-
egories of labor—organized labor versus the salaried class and unorganized labor
in general" (1942a, 687).

92. As mentioned, Director never completed his PhD thesis.

93. Director presented the paper on December 29, 1939, at a session called
"Economics of War," chaired by Charles O. Hardy (Brookings Institution). While
Director was at Brookings, he assisted Hardy on the latter's book *Wartime Control
of Prices* (1940).

94. Director, however, occasionally published book reviews.

95. It should be recalled that Director presented his paper two years before the
entry of the United States into World War II (in December 1941).

96. Director (1940, 351) added—without explaining—that the criteria of price-
level stabilization and a fixed quantity of money would be "subject to serious limitation" as permanent policies.

97. As discussed in section 4.1, Peel's Act was another name for the English
Bank Charter Act of 1844, which imposed 100 percent marginal gold-reserve requirements on Bank of England notes.

98. Patinkin (1987, 25) argued that the main novel feature of the *General Theory* and its central message was to provide a theory of effective demand as a theory
that depends on the equilibrating effect of the decline in output itself to explain
why the economic system may find itself in stable equilibrium with unemployment
below full employment. Tobin (1981, 205–6) expressed a similar view: "[Keynes's]
strong conviction and his true message are that the automatic self-rightening
mechanism of whole economies are slow, weak, and unreliable. Excess supply can
persist for long periods, whether one calls the situation equilibrium or not."

99. This argument was made by Tavlas (1976, 688–89). The identical argument was subsequently made by Patinkin (1979, 302–3) without attribution to the earlier source.

100. As documented earlier in this chapter, Douglas was not sympathetic to the *General Theory*.

101. There has long been a debate in the literature about the extent to which Keynes held such views about the ineffectiveness of monetary policy. What is not a source of debate is that, by the mid-1940s, the *General Theory* had been interpreted as conveying those views.

102. Simons used identical language in an October 5, 1937, letter to Walter Lippmann. In that letter, Simons called Keynes "irresponsible and untrustworthy" to those who held liberal beliefs and warned that the *General Theory* had the potential to become the "economic bible of a fascist movement" (quoted from Burgin 2012, 62).

103. In the German-language forward to the *General Theory*, penned on September 7, 1936, Keynes acknowledged the adaptability of his theory of aggregate demand to the totalitarian state. Keynes wrote: "The theory of aggregate output which constitutes the object of the following book, can nevertheless be much more easily adapted to the conditions of a totalitarian state than would the theory of production and distribution of a given output produced under conditions of free competition and a large measure of *laissez-faire*" (Keynes 1936b, ix). The translation from the German language to English was made by Joseph Aschheim; it appeared in Aschheim and Tavlas (1984).

## Chapter Six

1. In an undated memorandum, likely written in the 1940s, Simons wrote that Knight was "increasingly preoccupied with philosophy and philosophies, not to mention historians, theologians, and anthropologists, *et al.*, and is not deeply interested in concrete problems of economic policy" (quoted from Van Horn and Mirowski 2009, 145).

2. Samuelson (1946, 187) wrote: "The *General Theory* caught most economists under the age of 35 with the unexpected virulence of a disease first attacking and decimating an isolated tribe of South Sea islanders."

3. Referring to the late 1940s and early 1950s, Meltzer (2003, 581) stated: "The dominant view of professional economists at the time was that the task of monetary policy was to promote budgetary finance. Fiscal or budgetary policy was believed to have much more powerful effects on prices and economic activity than changes in the quantity of money or interest rates."

4. Arnold Harberger, who was Mints's student in the late 1940s, stated: "Lloyd Mints is very underappreciated. I went back to his notes, and he taught monetary

economics from the fact that prices of international goods, as he called them, were determined in international markets. And the doings in this country didn't have to do with that. They had to do with the exchange rate, and the balance of payments and things like that. He was far more subtle, far better than what he was given credit for" (quoted in Harberger and Edwards 2021, 6).

5. As noted, Mints published occasional book reviews in the years from 1931 to 1944. Two possible reasons for Mints's absence from substantive academic publishing from 1931 to 1944 are the following. First, Mints's 1945 book *A History of Banking Theory* entailed an enormous amount of doctrinal research and, therefore, time to produce. Second, according to the rumor mill at Chicago in the 1940s and early 1950s, Mints had experienced difficulties in his personal life because of a failed marriage from which he never fully recovered.

6. The point that Friedman's 1953 article on flexible exchange rates played an influential role in the debate about exchange-rate regimes was made by Bordo (1993, 30–31) in his definitive study of the Bretton Woods system.

7. Lutz was a German economist who was affiliated with Princeton University — initially under a Rockefeller Foundation fellowship and then as a faculty member — from 1938 to 1951. Lutz contributed to the literature on the theory of the term structure of interest rates. His 1940 paper "The Structure of Interest Rates" provided a synthesis of the neoclassical view that long-term interest rates are, in equilibrium, an average of short-term rates (Niehans 1987, 253).

8. Knight taught consecutively at Chicago from 1927 until his retirement in 1952. After he formally retired, Knight remained active in Chicago until he died in 1972. His activities in retirement included occasional teaching.

9. Friedman took Mints's two-semester course on money and banking during the 1932–33 academic year. Friedman's lecture notes from that course were the focus of papers by Leeson (2003b; 2003c). Leeson used the lecture notes—in particular, their emphasis on Keynes's 1930 *Treatise on Money*, with that book's use of money-demand analytics—to draw a connection between the early 1930s Chicago tradition and Friedman's (1956a) money-demand framework. Nelson (2020, 1:31) reached a different view: "[Mints's] course must be discounted as a decisive influence on Friedman's monetary views: for the emphasis on the quantity theory in Mints's course was not sufficient to stop Friedman from taking . . . a strongly negative perspective on the quantity theory in his writings in the early 1940s."

10. Rockoff (2015), however, was an exception to this view. Rockoff (2015, 28) stated: "To judge from the public record, it appears that Mints was the transition figure between Simons and Friedman."

11. The neglect of Mints's work is evidenced by the fact that there is no biographical information on him on any economics (including the history of economic thought) website; likewise, no institution houses a collection of his writings or correspondence. A book on the Chicago school edited by Emmett (2010) contained biographical articles on nineteen early Chicagoans, including Director, Douglas,

Knight, Simons, and Viner, but not on Mints. This neglect occurred even though Friedman (1956a, 3; 1960, 65; 1972, 937) credited Mints with having influenced his monetary economics. Recent work by Dellas and Tavlas (2021) and Demeule-meester (forthcoming) has helped remedy this circumstance.

12. These studies include Tavlas (1977b), McIvor (1983), Steindl (1995), and Rockoff (2010). Rockoff (2010, 97) noted that "it is possible that Mints's views on the role of the Federal Reserve in the Great Depression formed part of the background that shaped the narrative in *Monetary History*, but his views . . . are not cited explicitly." Steindl concluded that, while there were similarities between the views of Mints and those of Friedman and Schwartz concerning the monetary origins of the Great Depression, Mints, unlike Friedman and Schwartz, did not express the view that open-market purchases could have raised the money stock from 1929 to 1933. The evidence presented below is not consistent with Steindl's argument.

13. Dellas and Tavlas (2021) is an exception.

14. Because the article was a pristine critique of the real bills doctrine, it fore-shadowed Mints's (1945a) and Friedman and Schwartz's (1963) critiques of the Fed's reliance on that doctrine.

15. The book's bibliography contains references to over four hundred authors and over six hundred works. In a generally critical review of the book, Horsefield (1946, 136) wrote: "The first impression of this book is one of incredible industry." Morgan (1946, 291), who also critically appraised the book, wrote: "The monumental industry which has gone into the collection of this material is the great merit of the book." In another generally critical review, Woosley (1946, 389) wrote: "In a brief review it is difficult to depict the detailed scope of this study. Meticulous research is evidenced in the critical appraisal of the ideas of several hundred writers." Overall, the book received mixed reviews. Demeulemeester (forthcoming) discussed the receptions of the book by the academic community.

16. Patinkin, who took Mints's graduate course Banking Theory and Monetary Policy in the 1944–45 academic year, reported that Mints lectured from a draft of the book. Patinkin (1981a, 9) added: "By means of repeated arithmetical examples . . . he also gave us a life-time inoculation against the fallacies of the real-bills doctrine."

17. Charles Raymond Whittlesey taught economics at the Wharton School at the University of Pennsylvania from 1944 until 1967. As discussed in chapter 5, Whittlesey was a co-drafter of the memorandum *A Program for Monetary Reform* (Douglas et al. 1939). Mints also thanked Garfield Cox and Simeon Leland for having read parts of the manuscript. The acknowledgment to Director is evidence that Director continued to interact with his former Chicago colleagues in the first half of the 1940s even though he worked in Washington, DC, during that period.

18. According to Ritter and Silber (1974, 400), the ideal asset under the real bills framework would have a maximum maturity of three months. Humphrey and Timberlake (2019, 1–2) made a similar point about the real bills doctrine: "So long

as bankers lend only at short term on goods that will become finished and mar-
keted in 30, 60, or 90 days, the money stock will be secured by and will vary with
real production, so that real output will be matched by just enough money to purchase it at existing prices."

19. Meltzer (2003) noted that the real bills "principle" was accepted as "basic at the start of the Federal Reserve System" because the law that created the
Fed specified that only certain types of collateral were eligible for discount at the
Fed. That principle, he observed, "prevented purchases of government securities,
mortgages, other long-term debt and the use of those instruments or equities as
collateral for borrowing from the central bank" (2003, 22).

20. This argument was emphasized by Humphrey and Timberlake (2019, 15).

21. As pointed out in chapter 4, a similar argument had been made by Thornton
in his 1802 book *Paper Credit*, during the Bullionist Controversy. Mints (1945a, 43)
appraised Thornton's contributions as follows: "Thornton's analysis was excellent
and, indeed, has hardly been surpassed to the present day." It was noted in chapter 4 that Thornton had argued that if the loan rate were set below the expected
profit rate, the supply of bills offered for discount (and, thus, the money supply) could
expand without limit. Humphrey has been the most effective modern critic of the
real bills doctrine. See Humphrey (1982) and Humphrey and Timberlake (2019).

22. Mints (1945a, 219n87) wrote: "we do not need to inquire into the question of
precisely how these shifts (changes in velocity or in liquidity preferences or in the
propensity to hoard or in hoarding, whatever terminology one might prefer) work
their influence on business activity."

23. Mints (1945a, 281n51) cited several proponents of expansionary fiscal policies during depressions, including Keynes (1936a), Simons (1936a), and the authors
of the 1933 pamphlet *Balancing the Budget* (Bane et al. 1933); as discussed in chapter 2, the latter publication was co-authored by a group of Chicagoans, including
Douglas, Simons, and Viner, and local government officials.

24. Mints cited, among others, the studies by Soddy (1926) and Simons (1934a).

25. As we shall see, both Friedman and Director would make a similar argument.

26. The thesis that the Federal Reserve's reliance on the real bills principle triggered the Great Depression was pushed forward by Currie (1934b). Meltzer (2003)
argued that the Fed's tight policy in 1928 and 1929, based on the real bills principle,
triggered a recession in 1929; the Fed's inability to stem the banking panics that
followed in the early 1930s converted an otherwise ordinary recession into the
Great Depression. Humphrey and Timberlake (2019) argued that supporters of
the doctrine had gained control of the Fed in 1929. As a result, the Fed "treated any
bank lending for stock market 'gambling' as a vice." In these circumstances, banks
stopped using the discount window. Hence, the Fed "stopped 'speculation' by a
policy of 'direct pressure' on commercial bank lending and in so doing unleashed
an avalanche of bank failures much beyond anything preceding it in the history of
banking" (2019, 171). See, also, Bordo (2008).

27. McIvor had been Mints's student at Chicago in the late 1930s.

28. Viner, however, shared the prevailing view at Chicago that the Depression had been caused by an autonomous fall in velocity. Both Viner (1931b, 174) and Simons (1948a, 272) attributed the fall in velocity to the decline in confidence stemming from the 1929 stock-market crash. Friedman and Schwartz (1963, 306–9) argued that the stock-market crash *exacerbated* the initial decline in output by increasing uncertainty, thus reducing the willingness of consumers and business enterprises to spend. Romer (1992) provided evidence that the 1929 stock-market crash generated uncertainty, resulting in sharp falls in spending on consumer durables and semidurables immediately following the crash.

29. See Schwarzer (2018).

30. Nurkse's book (1944) appeared under the authorship of the League of Nations. Apart from William A. Brown, who wrote chapter 6, "Exchange Stabilization Funds," the rest of the book was written by Nurkse.

31. Bordo (1993, 31n16) wrote that "Nurkse's (1944) interpretation of the lessons of the interwar period should be viewed as largely reflecting the collective views of [John Maynard] Keynes, [Harry Dexter] White and others."

32. Ellis (1946b, 378) called the book "international monetary analysis at its best." Salera (1945, 129) stated that the book "is perhaps the best available study of international monetary developments during the interwar period." See also Knox (1945) and Nichols (1945). One of the areas to which *International Currency Experience* contributed was that of equilibrium exchange rates. Nurkse (1944, 184–85) argued that the conditions underlying a nation's equilibrium exchange rate are continually subject to change. Therefore, equilibrium exchange rates needed to be viewed in a dynamic context. In 1945, Nurkse published *Conditions of International Monetary Equilibrium*, which expanded on his earlier discussion of equilibrium exchange rates. In the 1950s and 1960s, Nurkse's work in the area of equilibrium exchange rates achieved classic status. For example, in his 1969 book *Balance-of-Payments Policy*, Cohen (1969, 95) referred to Nurkse's 1945 study as a "classic essay on international monetary equilibrium."

33. We encountered Ellis and Hansen in earlier chapters. Kalecki (1899–1970), who was born in Poland, made contributions in the areas of the business cycle, growth, and income distribution (among others). He worked at the United Nations from 1946 until 1955. During his career, he taught at Cambridge, the London School of Economics, Oxford, and the Warsaw School of Economics. Patinkin (1982) assessed the relationship between Kalecki's pre-1936 work on aggregate demand and Keynes's theory of effective demand presented in the *General Theory*. Lerner (1903–82) was born in Russia and studied in England. Among his contributions, he originated the theory of functional finance, which postulated that taxing and spending decisions by the government should be manipulated to bring the overall economy into balance—regardless of the size of the fiscal deficit and the government debt. Lerner taught at various academic institutions, never remaining at any one

institution for very long. Lerner's development of the theory of functional finance was discussed by Colander (2005). The theory of functional finance forms a core principle of recent discussions on modern monetary theory (MMT). See Kelton (2020, 60–64). For a critique of functional finance under MMT, see Tavlas (2021a).

34. Mints did not take a position on tariffs in his 1946 paper since the objective of the paper was to assess domestic economic policies.

35. Mints's argument that a policy rule would limit the downside of a depression represented a departure from the views of Simons (1938, 222; 1942a, 188) and Knight (1941a, 211) that there is no natural limit to a depression. Unlike Mints, however, neither Simons nor Knight analyzed the mechanics of a depression under a policy rule. Given that a policy rule aimed to reduce uncertainty, had Simons and Knight done so they may well have reached a similar conclusion as that drawn by Mints.

36. Thus, Steindl's (1995, 92) argument that Mints's "conception of the money supply mechanism was that even if the Federal Reserve acted appropriately during the 1929–33 period, the money stock would not have increased sufficiently to combat the deflationary pressures of that time" is incorrect. Mints believed that expansionary open-market operations would be less effective than money-financed fiscal deficits during depressions, but he believed that such operations should nevertheless be employed. It was for that reason that Mints criticized the Fed in his 1946 paper. Under normal circumstances, open-market operations would be the primary policy instrument.

37. As pointed out by Rockoff (2010, 93), Friedman and Schwartz (1963) emphasized a direct monetary-transmission channel running from a temporary excess of money holdings to increased spending.

38. In a letter addressed to Friedrich Hayek, dated December 1, 1944, Ludwig von Mises wrote that the "Veblen-Hansen [anti-free-market] ideology dominates public opinion in this country [i.e., the United States]"; von Mises added that the Veblen-Hansen ideology had pervaded the entire generation of economists under the age of forty (quoted from Burgin 2012, 80).

39. See Oxford Institute of Statistics (1944).

40. In Hansen's 1949 book *Monetary Theory and Fiscal Policy*, that economist assigned a supplementary role to monetary policy as an aid to fiscal policy. In the concluding chapter of the book, Hansen (1949, 202) summarized the preceding part of the book as follows: "Money, as we have noted in previous chapters, cannot alone ensure the expansion of income."

41. See Kalecki (1941).

42. The FMS Project was primarily the product of the persistent efforts of Hayek. The project was financed by the William Volker Fund, which promoted free-market research. See Van Horn (2014).

43. Cherrier (2011) argued that the FMS had a predetermined agenda of confirming the status quo, that is, to prove that the US economy was competitive and did not require policy interventions to make it more competitive.

44. Levi became dean of the Law School in 1950, replacing Katz. In 1968, Levi became president of the University of Chicago, serving until 1975, when he was appointed US attorney general. We will encounter Levi again, via his work with Director, in chapter 8.

45. As an example of the work supported by the FMS, Van Horn (2020, 224) cited Warren Nutter's 1951 study *The Extent of Enterprise Monopoly in the United States, 1899–1939*. In his study, Nutter challenged the then widely held view that US industry was becoming increasingly concentrated except when government regulation was employed to counter concentration. Nutter showed that government intervention could increase concentration. Nutter's study was an extension of his 1949 PhD dissertation at Chicago. Nutter's dissertation was supervised by Friedman—it was the first PhD dissertation written under Friedman's supervision.

46. The proposal by Hayek and Simons to offer Director a position in the Law School to head the FMS Project was initially turned down by the Law School's administration.

47. Hayek's aspiration that Director continue the tradition created by Simons was fulfilled. Twenty years later, Edward Levi (1966, 4) wrote: "The Director influence has been to keep strong at one law school the interest in economic theory which was developed by Henry Simons." Director joined forces with Mints to publish a collection of Simons's essays following the latter's death. Van Horn (2014, 526) reported the following: "With Director and Mints doing the lion's share of the work, they compiled *Economic Policy for a Free Society* (Simons 1948b) and negotiated with the University of Chicago Press to publish it."

48. The following discussion on Director draws on Tavlas (2022a).

49. A press release issued by the University of Chicago upon Director's death in 2004 referred to him as "founder of the field of Law and Economics" (University of Chicago News Office 2004, 1). Ronald Coase, who became coeditor with Director of the *Journal of Law and Economics* in 1964, expressed the view that "Director played an important, perhaps crucial, role in the emergence of that new subject, law and economics, in the United States" (Coase 1998, 601).

50. See Coase (1998). In an essay on the development of Chicago economics, Reder (1982, 7) wrote: "In preparing this essay, I have been struck by the many strong expressions of intellectual indebtedness both of Chicago economists and legal scholars (such as Edward Levi and Robert Bork) to Aaron Director.... Director appears to have exercised a great deal of influence upon the principal figures in Chicago economics from the 1930s to the present."

51. As will be discussed below, Director cosigned, with six Chicago colleagues (including Friedman and Mints), a 1948 letter on monetary policy. He also edited the conference volume *Defense, Controls and Inflation*, published in 1952, and wrote the introduction to that volume, which dealt with monetary policy. I discuss that volume in chapter 7.

52. George Stigler stated the following about Friedman's reaction to Director's lack of published output: "Milton Friedman was always chiding—to use a mild word—his brother-in-law for not writing his ideas up. 'It belongs in the public domain,' he said, and 'if you don't write anything, you've got it coming.' If quality is an increasing function of time, this was a method by which you create pearls, but it didn't work in this case" (quoted in Kitch 1983, 203).

53. For discussions of the origins of the Mont Pèlerin Society, see Van Horn and Mirowski (2009), Caldwell (2011), and Burgin (2012).

54. The participants included George Stigler, then at Brown University, who (after a stint at Columbia) began teaching at Chicago's School of Business in 1958. In addition, Harry Gideonse participated in the first meeting of the Mont Pèlerin Society. As mentioned in chapter 1, Gideonse taught in Chicago's Economics Department in the 1930s. According to his son Stephen Stigler (2005), George Stigler and Aaron Director became best of friends after being introduced at the first Mont Pèlerin meeting.

55. I am grateful to Bruce Caldwell for making Director's presentation available to me.

56. Director did not elaborate on what he meant by "certain economic functions."

57. It will be recalled that the Bank Act of 1844 established 100 percent gold backing for the issuance of Bank of England notes above a certain fiduciary issuance; as discussed in chapter 4, the Bank Act of 1844 was the doctrinal antecedent of the 1933 Chicago proposal for 100 percent reserves on demand deposits.

58. Director asserted that inequalities in income and wealth reflected, in part, the monopoly power of industry.

59. For a comprehensive discussion of Friedman's career in the 1930s and 1940s, see Nelson (2020, vol. 1).

60. As David Laidler pointed out to me in personal correspondence, the Keynesian perspective was not that of the *General Theory*, but that of Keynes's 1940 work *How to Pay for the War*. As Keynes had done in the latter work, Friedman, in a 1943 book co-authored with Carl Shoup and Ruth Mack, used the "inflationary gap" to assess the amount of fiscal adjustment that would be needed to contain inflation. See Shoup, Friedman, and Mack (1943). Freedman et al. (2016, 609) claimed that, in the 1930s, Friedman "resisted" the Keynesian revolution, but they provided *no* evidence to support that claim. I know of no such evidence.

61. Friedman attended congressional hearings on inflation and taxation in 1942. See Nelson (2020, 1:84). This paragraph and the following two paragraphs draw on Lothian and Tavlas (2018).

62. Friedman's Keynesian perspective in the early 1940s was reflected in his view that, to control inflation, it would be necessary to raise tax rates or impose controls or both, with monetary policy playing no role. Forder (2019, 113) expressed a different view, arguing that Friedman's statement (quoted above) in Friedman

and Friedman (1998) "really does nothing to show that Friedman had previously been under any kind of Keynesian influence." Forder (2019, 114) concluded: "So the remarks in Friedman and Friedman (1998) about his being a Keynesian in the 1940s are probably best regarded as just a cheap shot for the readers of that book." Forder does not provide any documentation to support his argument.

63. Friedman's original comment (1942a) on the Salant article was titled "The Inflationary Gap: II. Discussion of the Inflationary Gap." It was published in the *AER*. See Friedman and Friedman (1998, 113) for a discussion of the Salant comment and its subsequent reincarnation. Apropos of the price-control issue, Friedman wrote in the original: "The price system seems the least undesirable method of allocating the limited resources that will be available for the production of civilian goods." The statement is completely consistent with the view that Friedman's 1942 congressional testimony was heavily influenced by his being a government employee at that time.

64. See Friedman (1944).

65. Friedman filled the faculty spot vacated by the departure of Viner for Princeton. Viner's position was that of professor. Friedman was promoted to professor in 1948. Mitch (2016) provided evidence showing that Friedman's appointment reflected a compromise between Knight and his followers and those faculty members associated with the Cowles Commission. In the 1945–46 academic year, Friedman taught at the University of Minnesota, where held the position of associate professor.

66. Freedman et al. (2016, 608) asserted that Friedman returned to Chicago in 1946 with "an ideological blueprint mapping a defined strategy to impede and reverse any shift to Keynesianism that might appear within the faculty." Freedman et al. (2016) provided no evidence to support that assertion.

67. See the papers by Friedman and Savage (1948; 1952), the aim of which was to show that choices involving risk could be represented as a simple process in a framework in which households maximized expected utility. Nelson (2020, 1:130–38) provided a discussion of those papers, as well as of Friedman's work (1949b) in the late 1940s on the Marshallian demand curve.

68. Friedman stated: "At Columbia, where I spent my second year of graduate study[,] . . . Harold Hotelling gave me the same kind of feeling for mathematical statistics that Viner had for economic theory" (Friedman and Friedman 1998, 43).

69. As noted in chapter 1, the book, *The Theory and Measurement of Demand*, was published in 1938, shortly before Schultz's untimely death.

70. This argument was made by Walters (1987, 423), who conjectured that had Friedman chosen a career in the area of statistics, "he would have achieved a stature probably as great as that of his most influential teacher, Harold Hotelling." In 1937 Friedman published a paper in which he developed the use of rank order statistics to avoid making the assumption of normality in the analysis of variance. See Friedman (1937). The paper became a classic in the area of statistical theory.

71. This paragraph is based, in part, on Lothian and Tavlas (2018).

72. The following quote from Friedman and Schwartz on the choice of a monetary definition is illustrative: "The problem is one that is common in scientific work. A preliminary decision . . . must be made. Yet the decision can be made properly only on the basis of the research in which the preliminary decision is to be used. Strictly speaking, the 'best' way to define money depends on the conclusions that we reach about how various monetary assets are related to one another and to other economic variables; yet we need to define 'money' to proceed with our research. The solution, also common in scientific work, is successive approximations" (Friedman and Schwartz 1970, 91).

73. Friedman's main method of testing hypotheses involved the assessment of the ability of hypotheses to predict over alternative data samples. A description of his statistical methodology, and a criticism of formal econometric methods, is provided in Friedman and Schwartz (1991). For discussions of Friedman's empirical approach, see Hammond (1996, 192–207), Lothian (2009), Rockoff (2010), and Heckman (2012).

74. Hansen and Sargent (2015) noted that model uncertainty helped underpin Friedman's case against discretionary policies. Those authors referred to Friedman's (1951f) formal demonstration that discretionary policies can be destabilizing as "Friedman's Bayesian decision rule" (Hansen and Sargent 2015, 99).

75. Nelson (2020, 1:143) wrote: "The key significance of the 1948 [*AER*] paper is that it fixed monetary economics as a permanent area of specialty for Friedman and tied him to the advocacy of monetary policy rules." I view the initiation of Friedman's project with Schwarz as an equally significant marking of his move into monetary economics.

76. Friedman (1948a, 131) wrote the following about the views in the paper: "I feel at one and at the same time as if I were preaching in the wilderness and belaboring the obvious." An earlier version of the paper had been presented at the Econometric Society meeting on September 17, 1947, in Washington, DC. Freedman et al. (2016, 618) mistakenly claimed that Friedman's 1956 "Restatement" of the quantity theory was his "first monetary broadside."

77. Nevertheless, the fact that Friedman proposed that open-market operations should be abolished does not mean that Friedman believed that those operations would not be effective in altering the money stock in regimes that made use of open-market operations. As we will see, in 1948 Friedman cosigned a letter with his Chicago colleagues that was underpinned by the belief in the power of open-market operations.

78. The adoption of the 100 percent reserves scheme would also reduce the discretionary powers of the Fed by eliminating rediscounting.

79. Simons, however, favored reducing government spending over time.

80. Simons and Mints supported changing exemption levels during recessions; Friedman did not express a view on that issue.

81. This point about Friedman's position was made by Nelson (2020, 1:139).

82. Simons's position was motivated by his belief that short-term private debt instruments are close substitutes for money.

83. On this point, see Nelson (2020, 1:139).

84. This point was made by Nelson (2020, 1:139).

85. Friedman noted that his analysis of the real balance effect was based on Pigou (1943) and Patinkin (1948).

86. As discussed earlier in this chapter, Mints had noted that a problem associated with lags was the difficulty of forecasting the lags.

87. Orphanides (2003a, 636; 2003b) noted that Friedman had criticized the reliance on unrealistic informational assumptions for Keynesian prescriptions to maintain "full employment." Orphanides also noted that interest-rate rules that emulate money-growth targeting should be specified in terms of differences. Nelson (2020, 1:141) conjectured—in my view, plausibly—that Friedman's proposal that full-employment income could be determined every five or ten years corresponded to the use of a long-term concept of income, which would reduce the estimation problem.

88. Thus, Forder's (2019, 227) argument—that Friedman's claim in his 1956 "Restatement" of the quantity theory that his monetary economics reflected the views of an earlier Chicago quantity-theory tradition "suggest[ed] that [Friedman] had little in the way of real information about what had been said or thought in Chicago before the *General Theory*"—is inaccurate.

89. Nelson (2020, 2:89) wrote that, while at the Treasury, Friedman had "embraced the [*General Theory*'s] negative perspective regarding the power of monetary policy as well as its emphasis on fiscal policy."

90. In the spring of 1947, Director, Friedman, and Knight spent six weeks together as part of their trip to Mont Pèlerin for the first meeting of the Mont Pèlerin Society.

91. Friedman also acknowledged comments from Arthur Burns, Albert Hart, H. Gregg Lewis, Don Patinkin, and George Stigler.

92. In an interview conducted in 2002, Friedman stated that he had read Simons's work despite not having taken a course with Simons. Friedman also mentioned that he and Simons had become personal friends. See Friedman, quoted in Goldin (2002). Friedman's frequent acknowledgments of the influence of Simons on his views have led to the misperception that he took a course taught by Simons. See, for example, Van Overtveldt (2007, 92) and Forder (2019, 17).

93. In a 1975 retrospective on the development of monetary economics during the previous twenty-five years, Friedman declared himself to be a follower of Simons on the issue of monetary rules (Friedman 1975a).

94. The other signatories were Abram Harris, H. Gregg Lewis, Russell Nichols, and W. Allen Wallis. I thank Ed Nelson for bringing this letter to my attention.

95. In a 1945 paper, "Stability and Expansion," Hansen provided an additional reason for the Fed's policy of pegging interest rates. He argued that, in light of the

threat posed by secular stagnation, the policy of maintaining a low long-term interest rate could make a small contribution to supporting domestic demand (1945, 250–51). Credit for the discovery of Hansen's 1945 article belongs to Nelson (2020, 1:158–59).

96. In 1945 inflation averaged 2.2 percent. Consumer prices rose 16.6 percent between the fourth quarters of 1945 and 1946, reflecting, in part, the removal of wartime price controls (Meltzer 2003, 631).

97. In response to the increase in inflation, the government imposed wage and price controls in January 1951. Additionally, the Revenue Act of 1950, enacted in September of that year, provided for higher personal and corporate tax rates (Walton and Rockoff 2005, 547).

98. Douglas served three (six-year) terms in the Senate. As a Senator, Douglas established a reputation as someone concerned with fiscal discipline. He earned a reputation as a passionate crusader for civil rights.

99. The other members of the committee were Senator Ralph Flanders (Vermont) and Congressmen Wright Patman (Texas), Frank Buchanan (Pennsylvania), and Jessie Wolcott (Michigan).

100. Meltzer (2003, 685) wrote: "Paul Douglas was a distinguished economist who had been an economics professor at the University of Chicago before his election to the Senate. As is often the case, senators who had little understanding of the technical issues relied on a colleague's expertise, so Douglas's opposition to pegged rates carried considerable weight."

101. Eccles was on the Fed's Board of Governors from 1934 to 1951. He was chairman of the Board from 1934 to 1948.

102. Douglas did not provide a reference for the document.

103. Allan Sproul, president of the Federal Reserve Bank of New York, appeared before the Subcommittee on December 2, 1949. Unlike Eccles and McCabe, Sproul was critical of the Fed's policy of pegging interest rates during periods of inflation. Unlike Eccles, Sproul argued that changes in reserve requirements were not an effective tool in restraining inflation. The effectiveness of reserve requirements, he maintained, had been "'oversold,' being offered as powerful remedies for problems than can better be solved in other ways" (Subcommittee Hearings 1950, 433). In his opening statement, he stated: "The country cannot afford to keep money cheap at all times and in all circumstances if the counterpart of that action is inflation" (Subcommittee Hearings 1950, 432).

104. As mentioned in chapter 5, Ellis edited the American Economic Association's 1948 volume *A Survey of Contemporary Economics.*

105. The other signatories were Howard Bowen (University of Illinois), James Hall (University of Washington), Clarence Heer (University of North Carolina), E. A. Kincaid (University of Virginia), Simeon Leland (Northwestern University), Lawrence Seltzer (Wayne University), Tipton Snavely (University of Virginia), H. Christian Sonne (National Planning Association), and Donald Wallace (Princeton University).

106. The Employment Act of 1946 charged the federal government with re-sponsibility for maintaining "maximum employment, production, and purchasing power." The Employment Act created the Council of Economic Advisers and re-quired the president to submit the *Economic Report of the President*. It also cre-ated the Joint Economic Committee on the Economic Report, on which Douglas served. See (Meltzer 2003, 610–11).

107. As noted, Ellis was also one of the signatories of the joint statement of sixteen economists discussed above.

108. The US economy entered a recession in November 1948. The recession lasted until October 1949, with the consequence that, from November 1948 to October 1949, real GDP fell by 7.9 percent. Friedman and Schwartz (1963, 605) reported that the Fed sold over $3 billion of government bonds in the first half of 1949.

109. Simons also criticized the policy of pegging interest rates. In his 1946 paper "Debt Policy and Banking Policy," Simons argued: "Most current talk about fixing or controlling interest rates has, for me, simply no meaning, save as talk about varying the 'moneyness' of governmental obligations. . . . Low rates deriving from liquidity that only government with issue powers can give to securities may stimu-late *governmental* investment by making it seem irresistibly cheap in terms of quite misleading interest-burden calculations. How they promote private investment, save by creating expectations of inflation, I cannot see" (emphasis in original, 1946, 339–40n3).

110. Hetzel and Leach (2001a) provided a behind-the-scenes account of de-velopments at the Fed and the Treasury in late 1950 and early 1951 leading up the accord. Leach joined the Fed's Board of Governors in June 1950 as chief of the Government Finance Section. Hetzel and Leach did not, however, provide an ac-count of Congress's role in bringing about the accord.

111. The other signatories were Frederick H. Harrison, Lloyd Metzler, D. Gale Johnson, Theodore Schultz, and H. Gregg Lewis.

112. Douglas's picture was on the cover of the January 22, 1951, issue of *Time* magazine.

113. One of Douglas's Senate colleagues, Eugene Millikin (Wyoming), inter-rupted Douglas at one point to characterize Douglas's lecture as "the Senator's seminar." At another point, Millikin stated: "I am a humble student; I am a sopho-more, listening to the Senator's academics" (*Congressional Record* 1951, 1478, 1477, respectively). Douglas's lecture, including occasional interventions by other Sena-tors during the lecture, took up more than nine pages of the *Congressional Record*.

114. The Chicago memorandum stated: "adjusted demand deposits" rose by "over 8 percent" (*Congressional Record* 1951, 1482).

115. In an August 1951 article, "The Controversy over Monetary, Policy: In-troductory Remarks," Seymour Harris (1951a, 180) wrote: "it was in early 1951, when Senator Douglas made his famous speech." (I discuss Harris's article in the next chapter.) Similarly, Eichengreen and Garber's (1991, 184) account of the key

developments leading to the accord included the following: "In February [1951], Senator Paul H. Douglas made a famous speech critical of the Treasury. The specter of an inflationary crisis prompted a series of staff-level conferences between the Treasury and the Fed. On the last day of February, [Treasury] Secretary Snyder gave in."

116. In light of what I consider the historical importance of this letter and the fact that it has never been previously cited in the literature, I reproduce it in its entirety (the letter is in the Milton Friedman Papers, Hoover Institution Library and Archives, Stanford University).

117. The Federal Reserve extracted itself from its agreement to peg interest rates only gradually. Nelson (2020, 1:378) reported that the Fed continued to exert some maintenance of the prices of US Treasury securities "into about 1953."

118. In addition to the two sources of outside pressure cited above, Friedman referred to pressure from the Eisenhower administration.

**Chapter Seven**

1. In a review of Friedman's 1953 book *Essays in Positive Economics*, Peter Newman wrote: "While Friedman is not a mathematical economist in the sense that, say, Samuelson is, some of his work has a quite distinctive mathematical flavor. He often applies *statistical* theory to problems of economic theory, with fascinating results" (emphasis in original, 1954, 259).

2. In Aaron Director's "Prefatory Note," written in March 1947, for Simons's 1948 book *Economic Policy for a Free Society*, Director (1947a) stated: "Through his writings and more especially through his teaching at the University of Chicago, [Simons] was slowly establishing himself as the head of a 'school'" (quoted from Simons 1948b, v). In a 1950 article, "The Economists," published in *Fortune*, John McDonald referred to the "Chicago school." I will have occasion to refer to MacDonald's article again in chapter 9. Earlier, in a 1940 Chicago PhD dissertation, "Price Level Stabilization: Some Theoretical and Practical Considerations," George Bach stated that the theoretical part of the dissertation, which dealt with the impact of changes in price expectations on hoarding in the face of sticky costs, "has been in the nature of an 'oral tradition'" at Chicago. Quoted from Patinkin (1969, 98).

3. Bronfenbrenner's article was reprinted in the July 1950 issue of the *American Journal of Economics and Sociology*. Bronfenbrenner earned a PhD in 1939 at Chicago, where he studied under Paul Douglas. He taught at several universities, including at Duke from 1971 to 1984.

4. Barro was a graduate student at Harvard in the late 1960s. Meghnad Desai (1981, 2) stated that, prior to the early 1960s, in the United Kingdom Friedman's monetary economics was regarded as "a peculiar Chicago madness, indulgently mocked."

5. Philbrook earned his PhD in economics at Chicago in 1947. He taught at the University of North Carolina from 1947 until 1975. From 1959 to 1969 he was treasurer of the Mont Pèlerin Society. Mints also acknowledged his indebtedness to Director in his book's discussion of a policy that would stabilize the price of a basket of commodities. See Mints (1950, 159n1).

6. The 1950–51 University of Chicago *Catalogue* lists Friedman as teaching the course in the fall semester and Mints as teaching the course in the winter semester.

7. After Mints retired, he moved to Fort Collins, Colorado (Peterson and Phillips 1991). During the first decade of his retirement, he and Friedman occasionally corresponded. For example, Friedman sent drafts of *A Monetary History* to Mints, and Mints provided comments. In a letter from Mints to Friedman, dated February 12, 1962, Mints provided the following assessment of a draft of *A Monetary History*: "it represents an appalling amount of work, and that it is so very good that it ought easily to become the definitive work on the subject" (Milton Friedman Papers, Hoover Institution Library and Archives, Stanford University).

8. Mints kept tabs on Warburton's work in the 1940s. For example, in Warburton's 1945 article "Monetary Theory, Full Production and the Great Depression," Warburton noted that "Lloyd W. Mints . . . has read this paper [and provided comments]" (Warburton 1945, 115n10).

9. Taylor (1998, 36–44) argued that a short-run trade-off exists between inflation *variability* and output *variability*. Under Taylor's argument, suppose a positive demand shock hits an economy in which real output equals potential output. Also, suppose that the shock cannot be avoided or immediately offset by monetary policy. After the shock has hit and impacted on the economy, the monetary authorities are left with the following choice: (1) tighten policy sharply to reduce inflation and slow down the economy, or (2) tighten policy modestly, producing a smaller impact on both inflation and real GDP. The first outcome produces more inflation stability but less real output stability; the second outcome produces more output stability but less inflation stability. This trade-off is known as the Taylor Curve—as opposed to the Taylor Rule. Under the latter, the monetary authority would set the federal funds rate based on the gap between targeted inflation and actual inflation, and the gap between actual output and potential output. See Taylor (1993; 2012).

10. Friedman and Schwartz (1963, 300) used similar language; they asserted that the Great Depression "is in fact a tragic testimonial to the importance of monetary forces."

11. Mints criticized the Fed's policy during the period 1929–32 repeatedly in his 1950 book (1950, 8, 36–39, 44–49, 128–32, 179–80). As mentioned, Mints had been critical of the Fed's policies during the Great Depression in his classroom lectures in the late 1930s.

12. In a footnote, Mints (1950, 116) also cited Woodlief Thomas and Ralph Young as advocates of discretionary policy. In particular, Mints cited their 1947 study "Problems of Postwar Monetary Policy." Both Thomas and Young worked for the Federal Reserve Board.

13. As mentioned in chapter 6, in his 1946 article "Monetary Policy," Mints had also proposed a general retail-sales subsidy to increase the deficit. That proposal was not part of the 1950 framework. In his review of Mints's book, Tobin (1951a, 233) wrote: "One powerful weapon in Mints's 1946 arsenal, a general retail sales subsidy, has now unaccountably been discarded." Tobin (1951a, 234) also noted that "[Mints] expresses skepticism concerning the effectiveness of open-market operations."

14. In an appendix (amounting to eighteen pages) to chapter 3 of his book, Mints provided a detailed critique of Keynes's *General Theory*. The appendix was titled "Some Aspects of the Theories of J. M. Keynes."

15. Mints's 1950 book devoted two chapters (chapters 6 and 7), amounting to fifty-eight pages, to an evaluation of alternative rules. Several other chapters also contained discussions of rules.

16. For additional discussion, see Dellas and Tavlas (2021).

17. Friedman (1953b, 174) argued: "Under flexible exchange rates traders can almost always protect themselves against changes in the rate by hedging in a futures market. Such futures markets in foreign currency readily develop when exchange rates are flexible."

18. Friedman (1953b, 174) argued: "The substitution of flexible for rigid exchange rates changes the form in which uncertainty in the foreign-exchange market is manifested; it may not change the extent of uncertainty at all and, indeed, may even decrease uncertainty."

19. See Friedman (1953b, 157).

20. The others were Aaron Director, James Meade, and Lionel Robbins.

21. Sixteen years following the publication of Friedman's 1953 paper on exchange rates, Johnson published the paper "The Case for Flexible Exchange Rates, 1969." In his paper, Johnson (1969, 12) paid homage to Friedman's work as follows: "The title acknowledges the indebtedness of all serious writers on this subject to Milton Friedman's modern classic essay, 'The Case for Flexible Exchange Rates,' written in 1950, and published in 1953!!" Johnson's paper, in turn, is the subject of Maurice Obstfeld's recent paper "Harry Johnson's 'Case for Flexible Exchange Rates'—50 Years Later." Obstfeld (2020, 87) stated that Johnson's essay "drew inspiration" from Friedman's 1953 paper. I would argue that Johnson's arguments in favor of flexible exchange rates were heavily influenced by Friedman's 1953 essay.

22. Robertson's overall appraisal was positive. He called the book "thoughtful and vigorously argued" (1951, 465).

23. As noted in chapter 6, Mints (1945a) had earlier identified the stabilizing role played by banks' government bond holdings. The rise in the share of government securities held by banks on their balance sheets reflected the large purchases of those securities by banks during World War II.

24. Credit for the discovery of this source belongs to Ed Nelson (2020, 478n150).

25. In the event, President Harry Truman chose to finance the war out of current revenue (mainly large increases in corporate and personal tax rates). After

registering a (fiscal year) deficit of 1.1 percent of GDP in 1950, the government balance moved into a surplus of 1.9 percent of GDP in 1951. Meltzer (2003, 684) characterized the rise of inflation during the Korean War as follows: "The Korean War inflation is one of the few examples of expectationally driven price increases. Concerns about demand shortages and possible rationing increased demand, and an anticipated reallocation of resources from civilian to military uses reduced expected supply."

26. The anti-inflation program worked well. Consumer prices rose at an annual rate of 2.1 percent from the start of the price and wage freeze in January 1951 to the termination of the controls in February 1953 (Walton and Rockoff 2005, 548).

27. Market participants were not sure how the Fed would use its newfound independence. In the event, the Fed used its independence to follow a noninflationary policy.

28. Financial support was provided by the William Volker Fund. As mentioned in chapter 6, the William Volker Fund sponsored Director's position in the Law School.

29. Hayek held that position from 1950 to 1962. As mentioned, Cox had become dean of the School of Business. Wallis taught in the School of Business. The Chicagoans also included seven faculty members from the Law School.

30. Director was the chair of the six-member committee in charge of the conference. The other members of the committee were Friedman, Wallis, and three Law School professors—Walter J. Blum, Wilber G. Katz, and Edward H. Levi.

31. As mentioned, in his 1951 *AER* paper "Monetary Policy and Stabilization," Mints had identified six episodes containing large movements in the price level. For his conference presentation, Mints prepared a background paper that updated his 1951 *AER* paper. See the discussion below.

32. Twelve speakers—all non-Chicagoans—expressed sympathy with that view. None of the Chicagoans (apart from Mints and Friedman) expressed a view on monetary policy versus controls during this session. They did so, however, in subsequent sessions.

33. In the 1930s, Burgess had been a vice president of the New York Fed.

34. Harrod pointed to what he called the "large liquid imbalances, which we inherited from the last war" as a major factor contributing to excess demand (Director 1952, 88).

35. The Mints-Friedman argument that the government's fiscal position should be balanced or in a "minor" deficit reflected their view that changes in the fiscal position entail changes in the quantity of money. Large fiscal deficits would, therefore, entail large increases in the money supply, necessitating tighter open-market operations.

36. This argument was made by DiSalle and Ackley. From 1964 to 1968, Ackley served as the chair of the Council of Economic Advisers under President Lyndon Johnson. In 1982, Ackley was president of the American Economic Association.

37. In his only intervention during the conference, department chair Schultz stated that he wanted to correct "the impression that Mr. Director may have left when he perhaps inadvertently implied that there was only one point of view in economics at the University of Chicago" (Director 1952, 191). Schultz went on to argue that the wage and price controls "have, in fact, done little or no harm" although he did not explicitly come out in favor of those controls (Director 1952, 192).

38. Friedman's comments at the conference were based on the findings in his 1952 paper although he did not refer to the paper. The paper is discussed below.

39. Heflebower was a professor of economics at Northwestern University.

40. I located the paper at the University of Chicago's Regenstein Library's Special Collections Center. The paper was located in box 56 of the Frank H. Knight Papers. The title of the paper was preceded with the words "Prepared for the University of Chicago Law School Conference on 'The Economics of Mobilization.'" The material presented in the paper, including the identification of six specific episodes in which the Fed's policies exacerbated price movements, exactly match what Mints presented at the conference.

41. The issue was based on papers presented at the annual meeting of the American Economic Association held in Chicago during December 27–29, 1952.

42. As noted in chapter 6, recent studies by Dellas and Tavlas (2021) and Demeulemeester (forthcoming) have helped remedy the lack of recognition of Mints's contributions.

43. *REStat* was the outlet for the 1946 symposium on monetary policy, featuring contributions from Mints, Hansen, Howard Ellis, Michal Kalecki, and Abba Lerner. That symposium was discussed in chapter 6.

44. Harris's paper contained data published in June 1951, indicating that the papers in the symposium had been finalized in early summer. We encountered Harris in chapter 6 in association with Douglas's Senate hearings. Harris taught at Harvard from 1922 until his retirement in 1964. His career at Harvard was illustrative of the anti-Semitism at that institution. According to the History of Economics Society website: "Allegedly as a result of Harvard's unsavory quota policy, Seymour E. Harris was the only Jewish member of . . . Harvard's [economics] department [in the 1930s] and had to wait eighteen years before earning tenure, becoming full professor only in 1945." See History of Economic Thought (2021). Harris's name, before it was changed, was Cohen. I thank Morris Marget Goldings, a Harvard Law School graduate, for providing me with this information. As mentioned in chapter 1, Goldings is the nephew of Arthur Marget, who experienced anti-Semitism at Harvard in the 1920s.

45. Chandler taught at Princeton. In the early 1950s he was an economic adviser for Congress's Joint Economic Committee, on which Paul Douglas served. Among Chandler's books was *Benjamin Strong: Central Banker* (Chandler 1958). Chandler was president of the American Economic Association in 1958. Tobin taught at Yale. He was awarded the American Economic Association's John Bates Clark

Medal in 1955 and the Nobel Prize in Economics in 1981. He was president of the American Economic Association in 1971.

46. As mentioned, Friedman introduced the term "long and variable lags" in his 1948 *AER* paper. In a 1951 paper, "The Effects of a Full-Employment Policy on Economic Stability: A Formal Analysis," originally published in French, he formalized the idea that long and variable lags can render discretionary policy destabilizing. Using the formula that the variance of outcomes equals the variance of the policy intervention plus the variance without policy intervention plus twice their covariance, Friedman showed that policy intervention will be destabilizing if the covariance is positive. If there were no lags in the system, it would be straightforward to stabilize the system if the authorities knew the variances and the covariance. However, if policies operate with variable lags, it becomes very difficult to obtain the policy objective. A slightly revised version of the paper (Friedman 1953c) was published in English in Friedman's 1953 book *Essays in Positive Economics*. The paper became highly influential in the debate about rules versus discretion.

47. Friedman did not cite a specific study by Warburton.

48. Warburton called the income velocity of money the "circuit" velocity, by which he meant "transfers of money from one person to another . . . associated with the production and marketing of the current products of the economy" (1949, 194).

49. In modern terminology, the trend was either trend stationary or was a unit root with drift. Warburton's interpretation of the trend was in line with the view that the decline in velocity was trend stationary.

50. Additionally, as Nelson (2020, 1:155) pointed out, in a February 1949 radio address Friedman cited the 1931 discount rate hike as a reason the Federal Reserve "must take a large share of the responsibility for making the depression as deep as it was."

51. The document did not provide a specific month in 1951 in which it was written.

52. The two subhypotheses are jointly known as the monetary hypothesis of the Great Depression. See Tavlas (2011).

53. Friedman showed that prices approximately doubled from the outbreak to the end of each of three wartime episodes, although the duration of the episodes differed.

54. Friedman (1952, 165n9) defined the money supply as "currency outside banks and the Treasury plus adjusted demand deposits plus time deposits," that is, the M2 measure of the money supply.

55. The appearance was before the Joint Committee on the Economic Report.

56. The appearance was before the Subcommittee on the General Credit Control and Debt Management of the Joint Committee on the Economic Report.

57. Friedman and Samuelson were among a group of five economists who appeared jointly before the Subcommittee. The other economists were Howard Ellis and Charles Whittlesey, both of whom we previously encountered, and Raymond Mikesell, who was then at the University of Virginia. In 1944, Mikesell represented

the US Treasury at the Bretton Woods conference, at which he produced five formulas used to calculate quotas, or voting power, for IMF members. Those five formulas were officially adopted by the IMF. The formulas included such variables as national income and trade openness as determinants of quotas. In the early 1990s, while I was with the IMF, I was in charge of producing a report on the history of the IMF's quota formulas. In that capacity, I interviewed Mikesell (over the phone). The formulas, he stated, had been produced so that they provided a specific order desired by the US Treasury of the quotas of the major countries. He said that the quota formulas had no scientific basis. At the time of the interview, Mikesell, who was then in his eighties, had just returned from a mountain-climbing expedition.

58. Mints (1950, 46n5) stated that his critique of discretionary policies was not aimed at "any particular group of men" but at discretionary policies.

59. For earlier discussions of Warburton's contributions, see Selden (1962), Humphrey (1971), Patinkin (1973a), Bordo and Schwartz (1979; 1983), Cargill (1979; 1981; 2006), Yeager (1981; 1987), and Steindl (1995, chap. 9). For recent discussions of Warburton's views and their influence on Friedman's work, see Lothian and Tavlas (2018) and Tavlas (2019b).

60. In the 1960s, Warburton advocated a 2 percent annual rate of growth in the money stock. The shift in emphasis in the 1960s to a lower proposed growth rate for money incorporated the assumption that the reversal in the trend of velocity in the 1950s—from negative to positive—would continue. See Bordo and Schwartz (1983).

61. In a 1946 paper, "Quantity and Frequency of Use of Money in the United States, 1919–45," Warburton, using quarterly data, estimated that the M2 measure of the money supply (currency plus demand deposits plus time deposits) fell by 26 percent between the third quarter of 1929 and the second quarter of 1933. Using monthly data and a similar measure of the money supply (i.e., M2), Friedman and Schwartz (1963, 299) estimated that the money supply fell by about a third from the cyclical peak in August 1929 to the cyclical trough in March 1933.

62. Steindl (1995, 160) wrote that "Warburton's monetary analysis of the Great Depression . . . anticipates in *all* fundamental respects the analytical core of Friedman and Schwartz" (emphasis in the original). Cargill (1979, 428) argued that Warburton stood out from other precursors of monetarism in terms of the breadth and depth of his contributions.

63. Correspondence, in the form of exchanges of reprints of articles, between Warburton and Friedman, dates back to 1939. The existing letters between Warburton and Friedman are available in the Clark E. Warburton Papers in the Special Collections Research Center, Library Collections, George Mason University.

64. Apparently, Warburton had submitted the initial draft to the *JPE*. Such an inference can be drawn from Warburton's letters. In a letter from Warburton to Friedman dated November 21, 1951, Warburton wrote: "I want to thank you for going over my manuscript, 'Rules and Implements for Monetary Policy,' so carefully and giving me so many critical comments." In an earlier letter, dated October 5, 1951, Warburton wrote to Friedman as follows: "The enclosed article is being

submitted to the *Journal of Political Economy* for consideration for publication. I am sending you a copy because I would like to be certain that I have not in any way misinterpreted your opinions and point of view. Any comments or suggestions you may have will be most welcome." Warburton's paper was apparently rejected by the *JPE*. Since the *JPE* was (and is) an in-house Chicago journal, it is likely that Friedman, or Mints, or both, would have been asked to referee a paper that was a critique of their monetary framework.

65. My discussion is based, in part, on material presented in Lothian and Tavlas (2018) and Tavlas (2019b).

66. However, in his correspondence with Friedman, Warburton did not attribute the onset of the Depression *directly* to that policy tightening. He would do so subsequently in his *JF* articles.

67. For a discussion of the "free-gold problem," see Friedman and Schwartz (1963, 400–406).

68. The Glass-Steagall Act of 1932 and the Banking Acts of 1933 and 1935 included provisions that expanded the types of collateral that could be used for rediscounting and for undertaking open-market operations.

69. Subsequently, studies by Bierman (1991) and Cecchetti (1992) indicated that share prices were not overvalued before October 1929.

70. Snyder was an economist at the New York Fed during the 1920s and 1930s. As mentioned in chapter 1, Snyder has been credited as a forerunner of monetarism.

71. Warburton estimated that the then-available consumer price index "is reasonably representative of roughly one-half of the final products of the economy" (1953, 374).

72. Friedman was opposed to central-bank independence because he believed that it gave too much power to the individuals in charge of the central bank and subjected those individuals to political pressures even if the central banks were supposedly independent. See Friedman (1962b). For a discussion of Friedman's views on central-bank independence, see Dellas and Tavlas (2018).

73. For a similar statement concerning the complexity of his earlier fiscal-monetary proposal, see Friedman (1958a, 186). In contrast, in Friedman's October 1951 letter to Warburton commenting on the latter's draft for the *JF*, Friedman wrote the following about Warburton's criticism that the proposal to use fiscal operations to change the money supply was overly complicated: "This is simply nonsense. Further, it seems to me an irresponsible statement. There is nothing complicated or delicately balanced about my scheme" (letter, Friedman to Warburton, October 19).

74. As David Laidler has pointed out to me in personal correspondence, Viner was cognizant before 1932 of the damage that could be inflicted by adherence to the real bills doctrine. Viner's PhD thesis (1924) is generally credited as being the first twentieth-century study to do justice to Henry Thornton, whose demolition of the real bills doctrine in his 1802 book *Paper Credit* is regarded, even today, as a classic refutation.

75. There is no evidence that Friedman in the 1950s and early 1960s was aware of Currie's work on the Great Depression, whereas he was highly cognizant of, and influenced by, the work of Warburton and Mints. I know of no evidence that Warburton was influenced by Currie's work on the monetary origins of the Great Depression. Mints, however, was aware of Currie's book: as mentioned in chapter 3, Mints assigned Currie's 1934 book *The Supply and Control of Money in the United States* in a graduate course in the early 1950s.

76. The book consisted of eleven essays: six on monetary theory and policy, three on methodology, and two on price theory. In addition to the three above-mentioned essays, the essays on monetary theory included "The Effects of a Full-Employment Policy on Economic Stability: A Formal Analysis," which, as mentioned earlier, was published in 1951 in French, and the amended version of Friedman's 1942 *AER* paper "Discussion of the Inflationary Gap."

77. Friedman's essay on methodology gave rise to a large literature, including Boland (1979), K. Hoover (1984; 2009), Hirsch and de Marchi (1990), and Hammond (1991), that critically assessed Friedman's methodology.

78. For a discussion of Friedman's views on exchange rate regimes for economies in general, see Dellas and Tavlas (2018). For a discussion of Friedman's views on exchange rate regimes in the particular case of emerging market economies, see Edwards (forthcoming).

79. For reviews of the literature, see Tavlas (1993; 1994) and Dellas and Tavlas (2005; 2009).

80. In his seminal paper on exchange-rate overshooting, Dornbusch (1976) did not refer to Friedman's 1953 article. Dornbusch did his graduate studies at the University of Chicago and is likely to have read Friedman's paper.

81. The same metaphor had been used by Fisher in his 1920 book *Stabilizing the Dollar* in the context of Fisher's "compensated dollar" proposal: "So if prices tend to rise or fall, we can correct this tendency by loading or unloading the gold in our dollar, employing an index number of prices as the guide for such adjustments. The process for doing this is as simple as clock shifting for daylight saving and would produce its effects as unobtrusively" (Fisher 1920, xvii–xviii).

82. The "trilemma" is also known as the "impossible trinity."

83. Following the devaluation, the UK's current moved into surplus in 1950 before swinging back into a deficit (Bordo 1993, 44).

84. To my knowledge, Friedman's letter has never been cited in the literature dealing with Friedman's views on exchange rates.

85. The *Economist* devoted several articles to the cover story, "It's Much Better to Float." One of those articles was titled "It's Better to Float," from which the above quotation is taken.

86. The 1952 correspondence between Friedman and Robbins is located in the Milton Friedman Papers, Hoover Institution Library and Archives, Stanford University.

87. See Tavlas (2019) for evidence that Warburton's criticisms of the Fed led the FDIC, under pressure from the US Treasury, to instruct Warburton to cease publishing.

88. As Hammond (1999, 462) and Nelson (2020, 1:398) pointed out, Friedman had supervised a version of the workshop beginning in 1951. The workshop was initially given as a graduate seminar in monetary dynamics. Van Overtveldt (2007, 165) erroneously reported that Friedman began the workshop in 1954. Evidently, at one point, Director played a role in overseeing the workshop. In an email sent to me on December 20, 2019, Richard Timberlake, who was a graduate student at Chicago in the early 1950s and who participated in the workshop, wrote: "I also knew Aaron Director and respected him. He co-taught a graduate seminar in Monetary Theory and Policy that Friedman put together."

## Chapter Eight

1. Tooze (2021, 9) wrote: "In 1963 Friedman and his collaborator Anna Schwartz launched the revival of the defunct quantity theory of money with the publication of *A Monetary History of the United States, 1867–1960*." Tooze, a historian, was off by some fifteen years. As demonstrated in previous chapters, Friedman began his counterattack against the Keynesian revolution in the late 1940s and early 1950s.

2. The paper was published in the March 1968 issue of the *AER*. See Friedman (1968a).

3. As noted in chapter 1, the origination of the term "monetarism" is often mistakenly credited to Brunner in his 1968 paper "The Role of Money and Monetary Policy." In that paper, Brunner (1968a) did not refer to Friedman's 1968 *AER* paper on the natural-rate hypothesis, nor did Brunner discuss the inflation-unemployment rate trade-off under the Phillips curve. Whelan (2021, 8) drew a clear distinction between Friedman's work on monetarism and his work on the natural-rate hypothesis.

4. Nelson (2020, vols. 1 and 2) provides a thorough examination of all aspects of Friedman's research in the 1950s and 1960s.

5. This point, as mentioned in chapter 7, was made by Lucas (1984) and Barro (1998).

6. The committee was composed of Cyril Radcliffe, who was a lawyer, and two businessmen, two bankers, two trade union leaders, and two academic economists, the latter two being A. K. Cairncross and R. S. Sayers.

7. Friedman (1970a, 27) stated, however, that the empirical relationships led him to advocate "a quasi-automatic monetary policy under which the quantity of money would grow at a steady rate of 4 or 5 per cent per year, month-in, month-out."

8. Similarly, in a retrospective on monetarism at the Federal Reserve Bank of St. Louis, which was a bastion of monetarist research from the 1960s to the 1980s,

Hafer and Wheelock (2001, 1) referred to the monetary-growth rule as "Friedman's 'monetarist' policy rule."

9. The lecture was initially published in *Nationalekonomiska Föreningens Förhandlingar* and was later made more widely available in Friedman's *Dollars and Deficits: Inflation, Monetary Policy and the Balance of Payments* (Friedman 1968b). Page citations are from the original.

10. As mentioned in chapter 6, Friedman and Schwartz (1963, 441) expressed the view that, had the FDIC been in place in 1930, the severity of the banking crises of the early 1930s would have been sharply reduced. Friedman and Schwartz (1963, 434) also expressed the view that "federal insurance of bank deposits was the most important structural change in the banking system to result from the 1933 panic, and, indeed in our view, the structural change most conducive to monetary stability since state bank note issues were taxed out of existence immediately after the Civil War."

11. As mentioned, the Fed's tightening occurred after the United Kingdom's departure from the gold standard in September 1931.

12. Friedman (1949a, 952–53) contained a similar argument.

13. Friedman's 1992 book *Monetary Mischief: Episodes in Monetary History* used historical events to describe the problems that can arise from the misunderstanding of the monetary system.

14. This section draws on Lothian and Tavlas (2018). The correspondence between Friedman and Schwartz described in this section is from the Milton Friedman Papers, Hoover Institution Library and Archives, Stanford University.

15. This particular measure of money—known as M2—was chosen both because of its close empirical relationship to income and other economic magnitudes and because it was impossible to separate demand and time deposits before 1914. As mentioned in chapter 7, it was also used by Friedman in his 1952 article "Price, Income and Monetary Changes in Three Wartime Periods." Nelson (2007) showed that Friedman's choice of a monetary aggregate would change in the 1980s.

16. Schwartz received assistance from research staff at the NBER.

17. This pattern would persist at least until the late 1950s. Often, Schwartz's questions would deal with issues of economic substance, for example, the rationale for viewing money demand as the demand for the services that money provides or the effects of changes in the gold stock on the exchange-rate premium under the gold standard. In a 2004 interview, Schwartz stated: "I didn't think that my education in economics was really attended to until I started working with Friedman. And it was as if he were my real instructor in economics" (Schwartz, quoted in Nelson 2004, 595). In personal correspondence dated September 14, 2021, David Laidler, who worked with Schwartz at the NBER in 1961, wrote: "It is true, she started out as very much the secondary researcher, following Milton's instructions. But . . . she learned as she went along, and by the summer of 1961 when I worked for her at the Bureau—a time when major revisions to the book were still being made—she was completely on top of the project in her own right, and talked and acted as a

full co-author as she assigned tasks to me and explained their significance for the project. I've always thought that the profession underestimated (a) the extent of her intellectual growth as the project progressed and (b), as a corollary, the extent of her independent contribution to the final product." For a similar view about the profession's underestimation of Schwartz's contributions, see Tavlas (2013).

18. Chapter 1 was ten pages in length, and chapter 2 was sixty-eight pages in length. Many of the draft pages have faded and are difficult, if not impossible, to read. The drafts are located in the Milton Friedman Papers, Hoover Institution Library and Archives, Stanford University.

19. To compute rates of change, Friedman and Schwartz used the first differences of logarithms, effectively eliminating deterministic trends from the data.

20. Moore, who earned a PhD from Harvard in 1947, joined the NBER staff in 1939. From the beginning of the Friedman and Schwartz project, Moore was concerned that those researchers did not give sufficient emphasis to the role of credit quality in the business cycle. See Hammond (1996, 78–79).

21. These findings would not change. Thus, in their *A Monetary History*, Friedman and Schwartz (1963, 677) found that "In 93 years, there have been six periods of severe economic contractions. . . . The most severe contraction was the one from 1929 to 1933. The others were 1873–79 [a period not evaluated in the 1956 draft chapters], 1893–94 . . . , 1907–08, 1920–21, and 1937–38. Each of those periods was accompanied by an appreciable decline in the stock of money, the most severe accompanying the 1929–33 contraction."

22. Friedman and Schwartz (1963, 74) dated the peak in the level of the money supply as August 1929.

23. The methods were "the step approach" and the "specific cycle method."

24. This argument was made earlier in Friedman (1947).

25. Freedman et al. (2016, 613) mistakenly contended that Friedman advocated a monetary-growth rule throughout his career.

26. The initial agenda included a fifth element, the limitation of resources used for advertising, but, as I mentioned in chapter 5, that element was eventually dropped from the list.

27. As mentioned in chapter 6, Nutter's study was an extension of his 1949 PhD dissertation at Chicago. Friedman's paper "Free Enterprise in the United States" was published in late 1951 in the *Bulletin of the Société Belge d'Etudes et d'Expansion*. The page citations given above are from the May 1951 draft.

28. Friedman's discussions of capitalism at Wabash were extensive elaborations of a 1955 article, "Liberalism, Old Style," published in *Collier's Year Book*. See Friedman (1955). In turn, the Wabash lectures served as the basis for Friedman's 1962 book *Capitalism and Freedom*.

29. Friedman (1956e, 5) noted that the empirical evidence on these issues was "hard to come by, though such studies as have been made . . . confirm the broad conclusions just outlined."

30. Nelson (2020, 2:130) pointed out that the notion of a negative income tax had been raised by Kenneth Boulding in his 1945 book *The Economics of Peace*. Nelson (2020, 2:131) also pointed out that Friedman had indirectly supported the negative income tax in 1948 with the following statement: "It may be hoped that the present complex structure of transfer payments will be integrated into a single scheme coordinated with the income tax and designed to provide a universal floor for personal incomes" (Friedman 1948a, 137n6).

31. This point was made by Nelson (2020, 1:147), who noted that Friedman reached this view by the early 1950s. As we will see below, Director put this view forward in a 1950 paper.

32. In the article "On the 'Chicago School of Economics,'" Miller (1962, 65) stated: "Whereas Simons attacked monopoly and unions as vigorously as he attacked government, Friedman and other modern Chicagoans concentrate their attack almost entirely on government intervention."

33. Friedman presented several sets of results in which nominal income was regressed on the money stock. Reflecting his concern with endogeneity, Friedman did not present comparable results for equations in which autonomous expenditures were the sole independent variable.

34. Friedman argued that deflating all variables by the same price index to obtain real values would introduce common errors of measurement and, thus, spurious correlation into the regressions.

35. The other participants named were Gary Becker, Phillip Cagan, Raymond Zelder, John Klein, Divurri Ramana, Boris Pesek, John Deaver, Roy Elliot, and Robert Snyder.

36. Friedman and Meiselman (1963) reported results only for the United States. A planned follow-up study with results for a large number of additional countries was never completed for reasons explained in Tavlas (2022c).

37. For example, unlike the 1956 presentation, the 1963 study included a description of the monetary transmission mechanism.

38. Edge (1967) provided a survey of the initial stages of the debate between Friedman and Meiselman and their critics.

39. The Andersen and Jordan specification became known as the St. Louis equation. Silber (1971) expressed the view that the empirical findings in the debate often conformed to the political persuasions of the researchers. Silber's paper was aptly titled "The St. Louis Equation: 'Democratic' and 'Republican' Versions and Other Experiments." Bias (2014) provided a chronological ordering of many of the papers published in the debate, mainly from 1963 to the mid-1980s. Bias (2014, 2) called the Friedman and Meiselman paper "the seminal empirical" study of monetary and fiscal policy comparisons.

40. Thygesen's 1977 paper "The Scientific Contributions of Milton Friedman" was published in the *Scandinavian Journal of Economics* in conjunction with Friedman's having been awarded the Nobel Prize in Economics in 1976. Meigs (1972, 19)

expressed the view that the Friedman and Meiselman article was "one of the most devastating critiques of the conventional Keynesian faith." More recently, Desai (2015, 156) expressed the view that the paper "had dented, if not shaken, a pillar of the Keynesian edifice." Nelson (2020, 2:91) correctly pointed out that citations of the Friedman-Meiselman paper in the recent literature have become infrequent. Exceptions include Walsh (2017, 12), who called the paper "one of the earliest times-series econometric attempts to estimate the impact of money"; McCallum (2016, 56–57), who described the Friedman-Meiselman results as "striking" and added that "the Friedman-Meiselman study was highly influential in generating a reconsideration by the profession of the importance of monetary policy, with the outcome assigning a greatly enhanced role to the latter"; and Sims, who, in his Nobel Prize lecture (Sims 2011), gave the paper a prominent place in his description of the evolution of the profession's understanding of monetary policy. See also Auerbach (2016, 418–19), Boskin (2016, 413), and Lucas (2016, 15). For a recent discussion of the debate, see Belongia and Ireland (2021). Credit for the Thygesen (1977), Meigs (1972), and Sims (2012) sources cited in the present paper belongs to Nelson (2020, 2:12).

41. Director did not state that rule (b), price-level targeting, involves some discretion. He was certainly aware, however, from Simons's work (1936a), that price-level targeting involves discretion in the choice of a specific price index and the use of policy instruments. Director made this point in his 1956 lecture, discussed below.

42. With output rising over time, the fixed-quantity-of-money rule would entail a falling price level.

43. In the mid-1930s and again in 1960, in *The Constitution of Liberty*, Hayek argued that monetary policy should follow a "productivity norm," under which changes in the money supply would not respond to increases in real output; the money supply would respond to changes in the income velocity of money. Under this norm, increases in overall productivity, everything else remaining the same, would be accompanied by declines in the price level. This policy implication follows directly from Austrian business-cycle theory, according to which any net creation of credit (and hence money) by the banking system would generate forced saving and hence increasingly distort the time structure of production for as long as it continued. See Laidler (1999), Selgin (1999), and L. White (1999). Hayek published essentially nothing on monetary policy in the 1940s and 1950s.

44. The lecture is available at the Hoover Institution Archives as a sound recording. I have transcribed the lecture (word for word) into written form. It is available on my webpage: https://sites.google.com/site/georgetavlasresearch/home. The typed-up version of my transcription is twelve pages in length. The page numbers below refer to the typed-up version. Based on the information provided by the staff of the Hoover Archives, the lectures apparently were supported by the William Volker Fund.

45. Friedman provided a similar argument: "The production of a fiduciary currency is, at it were, a technical monopoly" (Friedman 1960, 7). After enumerating

"the features of money that justify government intervention" in the issuance of currency—including the resource cost of a pure commodity currency, the need to enforce contracts involving promises to pay in the medium of exchange designated to be money, and the need to set limits on the amount of money issued—Friedman argued: "Something like a moderately stable [monetary] framework seems an essential prerequisite for the effective operation of a private market economy" (1960, 8). See also Friedman (1951d).

46. As discussed in chapter 5, by the 1940s Simons no longer considered industrial monopolies to be a major problem. The hard monopoly problem, he came to believe, was labor organization.

47. For discussions of Director's view about monopolistic, firms, see Peltzman (2005), Van Horn (2009), Van Horn and Mirowski (2009), and Van Horn and Emmett (2015).

48. This conclusion was likely based, at least in part, on Warren Nutter's 1951 study *The Extent of Enterprise Monopoly in the United States, 1899–1939*, which criticized the view that US industry had become more concentrated since the beginning of the twentieth century. Director and Levi, however, did not cite Nutter's study.

49. My view differs from that expressed by Peltzman (2005), Van Horn (2009), and Van Horn and Mirowski (2009), all of whom argued that Director's hands-off approach of industrial monopolies represented a break with Simons's approach. Director's approach differed from Simons's approach in the latter's 1934 *A Positive Program for Laissez Faire* but not with Simons's view in his works in the 1940s.

50. See Irwin (2016, 767). The following correspondence between Friedman and Viner is located in the Milton Friedman Papers, Hoover Institution Library and Archives, Stanford University.

51. For a discussion, see Dellas, Swamy, and Tavlas (2002).

52. In their respective letters, Friedman and Viner conformed to their early 1930s roles of student and teacher, respectively. Friedman addressed Viner as "Dear Professor Viner"; the latter addressed Friedman as "Dear Milton."

53. The theoretical and empirical literature on alternate exchange-rate regimes finds that economies that follow flexible exchange-rate arrangements perform better in terms of real growth and inflation than economies with other exchange-rate arrangements, including hard pegs and adjustable pegs. The literature was critically reviewed in Tavlas, Dellas, and Stockman (2008).

54. In contrast to the 1954 lecture, in which Friedman began the narrative with the 1830s, the narrative in the 1957 paper began with 1913, the year of the establishment of the Federal Reserve.

55. The Federal Reserve Bank of New York had earlier raised its discount rate in 1928, from 3.5 percent to 5 percent.

56. Annual data were available for the entire period. Friedman did not specify the time period covered by the quarterly data.

57. For movements spanning long periods, Friedman used the qualification "per unit of output" on the money series to cover those periods involving a long-term decline in prices, such as the decline in US prices in the late nineteenth century. See Friedman (1958a, 176n3).

58. A similar argument was made by Friedman and Schwartz (1963, 639): "We are inclined to attribute the secular decline [in velocity] to the associated rise in per capita real income, that is, to view the services rendered by money balances as a 'luxury' of which the amount demanded rises more than in proportion to the rise in real income." Gould and Nelson (1974) studied the stochastic properties of the Friedman and Schwartz data and found that velocity was empirically indistinguishable from a random walk: successive changes in velocity were found to be essentially uncorrelated. Gould and Nelson (1974, 405) stated: "This [finding] would imply that of the past history available at any given date only the current observation is relevant for prediction. We also find that the apparent downward historical 'drift' in velocity [i.e., the secular downward trend found by Friedman] is not statistically significant." Stewart (2005, 693–96) provided a good discussion of the econometric issues involved in distinguishing between treating velocity as a random walk, as in Gould and Nelson, and as a trend stationary process, as in Friedman and Schwartz.

59. Friedman did not provide examples of the "other factors."

60. In the paper delivered at the Mont Pèlerin meeting, Friedman (1958b, 8) stated, "The rate of growth that would be consistent with a reasonable stable secular price level is, on the basis of past experience, somewhere in the range of 3 to 5 per cent. It makes less difference which particular rate, or what specific definition of the money supply, is adopted than that some rate and some definition be accepted and adhered to." Van Overtveldt (2007, 166) mistakenly stated that Friedman's "first clear statement" of the money-growth rule was made in 1960.

61. This point was made by Lothian (2009, 1089). Friedman had the correct intuition that the long run needs to be distinguished from the short run, but the tools to make that distinction had not been developed at the time that he began working on money-demand estimation. In commenting on money-demand functions estimated by Friedman and Schwartz in their 1982 study *Monetary Trends in the United States and United Kingdom*, Hendry and Ericsson (1991) and Ericsson, Hendry, and Hood (2016) made the valid point that the use of phase averaging comes at the cost of a considerable loss of information. Modern work on cointegration distinguishes between the long run and the short run, and specifies the process of moving from the short run to the long run. Swamy and Tavlas (1995; 2001; 2007) used time-varying estimation to eliminate specifications errors, including those due to phase averaging. Work by Hall, Swamy, and Tavlas (2012) on money-demand estimation showed that the long run and the short run can be integrated into one model and can be separately identified.

62. Friedman (1957b) sought to reconcile the disparity between the findings of time series regressions fitted over short periods, which showed that the average

propensity to consume exceeded the marginal propensity to consume, with the findings of consumption schedules using data assembled by Simon Kuznets (1946) over the period 1869–1938, which showed that the average propensity to consume equaled the marginal propensity to consume. For a discussion, see Sargent (1979, 298–323).

63. Friedman (1959a, 120–21) explained: "the distinction between measured and permanent income implies a corresponding distinction for prices. . . . [The] analysis suggests that holders of cash balances determine the amount to hold in light of their longer-term income position rather than their monetary receipts— this is the justification for distinguishing measured from permanent income. By the same token, they may be expected to determine the amount of cash balances to hold in light of longer-term price movements—permanent prices, as it were— rather than current or measured prices." Both permanent income and permanent prices were constructed as weighted averages of past values of those variables, respectively, with the weights declining exponentially.

64. A similar test to Friedman's was carried out by Laidler (1966) with the rate of interest included in the cycle average regressions. The inclusion of the interest rate was found to increase the predictive power of the function, showing the importance of the interest rate as a determinant of the demand for money. Although Friedman did not find a significant role for interest rates in explaining the behavior of real money balances in his 1959 article, he did not maintain that the interest elasticity of real money balances is zero. In a 1966 paper, "Interest Rates and the Demand for Money," he wrote: "Neither in that article [i.e., Friedman 1959b], nor, to the best of my knowledge, elsewhere, have I ever asserted that interest rates have no effect on the quantity of money demanded or on velocity, only that (a) they appear to be less important as a determinant of quantity demanded than real per capita income and as a determinant of measured velocity than the ratio of measured to permanent income; and (b) that the interest elasticity is not very high" (Friedman 1966, 72n1).

65. The lectures were published in 1960 as a book, *A Program for Monetary Stability*. See the following section.

66. Similarly, in his October 1959 appearance before the JEC, Friedman argued that the state had an essential role in providing a legal framework that ensured free markets and prevented physical coercion of one individual of another (JEC 1959b, 3020).

67. Friedman (1960, 6) stated: "What is involved is essentially the enforcement of contracts, if the failure of an issuer to fulfill his promise is in good faith, or the prevention of fraud, essentially of counterfeiting, if it is not."

68. The length of the text was ninety-nine pages.

69. The bank's name was Bank of United States, not Bank of *the* United States as stated in Friedman's 1960 book.

70. Rockoff (forthcoming) provides an excellent assessment of the evolution of Friedman's views on bailouts of banks, shadow banks, manufacturing firms, and governments.

71. Subsequently, Friedman (1974) confirmed that he believed that anti-Semitism among some New York State officials played a role in the closing of the bank.

72. For the citation to Mints, see Friedman and Schwartz (1963, 169n56). For the citation to Warburton, see Friedman and Schwartz (1963, 408n163).

73. Timberlake's paper was subsequently published in the *Independent Review*. See Timberlake (2007). I am grateful to Thomas Humphrey for calling my attention to Friedman's letter to Timberlake and making it available to me. As noted in chapter 6, Humphrey and Timberlake (2019) emphasized the role played by the Fed's reliance on the real bills doctrine in the Great Depression.

74. In contrast to Simons, who proposed 100 percent reserves against demand deposits, Friedman's 1960 proposal would apply 100 percent reserves against both demand and time deposits.

75. In the 1960s, Friedman, while continuing to favor 100 percent reserves on demand deposits, would reduce the emphasis that he attached to that reform. See Friedman (1967).

76. This argument was an early version of the "Friedman rule," under which monetary policy should be conducted in a way that drives the nominal interest rate on money substitutes to zero. Friedman argued that the opportunity cost faced by private agents should equal the social cost of creating additional money, which, under a fiat standard, is approximately zero. See Friedman (1969a). This rule, of course, is different from Friedman's money-growth rule.

77. See Mints (1950, 186).

78. Although Friedman thought that federal deposit insurance had stabilized the deposit-currency ratio, he believed that the Federal Reserve had the power to offset variations in the deposit-currency ratio even in the absence of deposit insurance. For example, Friedman argued that the Fed could have expanded the amount of high-powered money sufficiently to prevent the bank failures arising out of initial attempts by the public to convert deposits into currency in the early 1930s (1960, 31).

79. Recent research has emphasized policy prescriptions that reduce uncertainty. Taylor (2015) argued that the major advantage of following a rule is that it makes monetary policy transparent and predictable; the better that people can predict the way the monetary authority will act, the better they can plan their consumption and investment decisions, and the more likely they will act the way the monetary authority desires them to act. Orphanides and Williams (2002), showed that policy rules that are optimal for a high degree of uncertainty in the estimation of the natural rate of unemployment are robust, while rules that do not account for uncertainty in the estimation of the natural rate are fragile. The authors proposed that monetary policy should follow a strategy involving difference rules in which the short-term nominal interest rate is raised or lowered in response to inflation and changes in economic activity. Orphanides (2015) proposed that the Fed adopt a simple rule that is subject to periodic review to account for, and occasionally

adapt to, the evolving understanding of the economy. See also Orphanides (2003), Hansen and Sargent (2010), and Taylor (2017). Dellas and Tavlas (2022) reviewed the origins of the literature on policy rules.

80. Taylor (2012, 1024) argued that "[rules] help policymakers avoid pressures from special interest groups and instead take actions consistent with long-run goals."

81. As noted, in his 1950 book *Monetary Policy for a Competitive Society*, Mints had come round to the views that changes in the money supply might initiate business cycles and that federal deposit insurance and the large holdings of government securities held by banks lessened the procyclicality of velocity.

**Chapter Nine**

1. McDonald discussed the views of a large number of economists, several of whom we encountered in this study. In addition to Chicagoans Knight, Simons, and Friedman, among those whose views McDonald discussed were Edward Chamberlin (Harvard), John Maurice Clark (Columbia), Simon Kuznets (Pennsylvania), Abba Lerner (Roosevelt College), Wassily Leontief (Harvard), Edward Mason (Harvard), Oskar Morgenstern (Princeton), Paul Samuelson (MIT), Sumner Slitcher (Harvard), George Stigler (Columbia), Jacob Viner (Princeton), and John H. Williams (Harvard).

2. Sutton was a social scientist with the Ford Foundation. As mentioned in chapter 8, *Capitalism and Freedom* was an elaboration of Friedman's 1956 Wabash lectures.

3. As noted in chapter 5, Viner's use of the real bills doctrine to criticize the Fed's policies was implicit in his 1932 Chicago lecture (Viner 1932a).

4. In an interview conducted with Friedman by Claudia Goldin on August 16, 2002, Friedman was asked how Simons and Mints influenced *A Monetary History*. After responding that those economists, along with Viner, provided the theoretical background for *A Monetary History*, Friedman stated: "I have to admit that I am not very much given to introspection" (see Goldin 2002, minutes 39–41). Similarly, in an earlier interview with George Martin, Friedman described himself as "not being very introspective" (Martin 1983, 50).

5. Friedman used the word "teacher" in the allegorical since he had not taken a course with Simons. As mentioned, however, Friedman had studied Simons's works.

# References

Ahamed, Liaquat. 2010. *Lords of Finance*. London: Windmill Books.

Alacevich, Michael, Pier F. Asso, and Sebastiano Nerozzi. 2015. "Harvard Meets the Crisis: The Monetary Theory and Policy of Lauchlin B. Currie, Jacob Viner, John H. Williams, and Harry D. White." *Journal of the History of Economic Thought* 37, no. 3 (August): 387–410.

Allen, William R. 1993. "Irving Fisher and the 100 Percent Reserve Proposal." *Journal of Law and Economics* 36, no. 2 (October): 703–17.

Alrifai, Tariq. 2015. *Islamic Finance and the New Financial System: An Ethical Approach to Preventing Future Financial Crises*. Singapore: John Wiley and Sons Singapore.

Andersen, Leonall C., and Jerry L. Jordan. 1968. "Monetary and Fiscal Actions: A Test of their Relative Importance in Economic Stabilization." *Federal Reserve Bank of St. Louis Review* 50 (November): 11–23.

Ando, Albert, and Franco Modigliani. 1965. "The Relative Stability of Monetary Velocity and the Investment Multiplier." *American Economic Review* 55, no. 4 (September): 693–728.

Andreades, Andreas. 1966. *History of the Bank of England, 1640 to 1903*. London: Frank Cass.

Angell, James W. 1927. "Book Review: *Wealth, Virtual Wealth and Debt*, by Frederick Soddy." *Political Science Quarterly* 42, no. 4 (December): 621–24.

Archibald, George C., and Richard G. Lipsey. 1958. "Monetary and Value Theory: A Critique of Lange and Patinkin." *Review of Economic Studies* 26, no. 1 (October): 1–22.

Arnon, Arie. 1991. *Thomas Tooke: Pioneer of Monetary Theory*. Ann Arbor: University of Michigan Press.

———. 2010. *Monetary Theory and Policy from Hume and Smith to Wicksell: Money, Credit, and the Economy*. New York: Cambridge University Press.

Aschheim, Joseph, and George S. Tavlas. 1984. "The Monetary-Ideology Nexus: Keynes versus Simons." *Banca Nazionale del Lavoro Quarterly Review*, no. 149 (June): 177–96.

——. 1991. "Doctrinal Foundations of Monetary Economics: A Review Essay." *Journal of Monetary Economics* 28, no. 3 (December): 501–10.

Asso, Pier F., and Robert Leeson. 2012. "Monetary Policy Rules: From Adam Smith to John Taylor." In Evan F. Koenig, Robert Leeson, and George A. Kahn, eds., *The Taylor Rule and the Transformation of Monetary Policy*. Stanford, CA: Hoover Institution Press. 3–62.

Auerbach, Robert D. 2016. "Friedman and the Income Effects of Financing Government Deficits." In Robert A. Cord and J. Daniel Hammond, eds., *Milton Friedman: Contributions to Economics and Public Policy*. Oxford: Oxford University Press, 417–35.

Bach, George. 1940. "Price Level Stabilization: Some Theoretical and Practical Considerations." PhD diss., University of Chicago.

Backhouse, Roger E. 2013. "Book Review: *The Elgar Companion to the Chicago School of Economics*, edited by Ross B. Emmett." *History of Political Economy* 45, no. 2 (Fall): 345–49.

——. 2019a. "Book Review: *In Search of the Two-Handed Economist: Ideology, Methodology and Marketing in Economics*, by Craig Freedman." *Journal of the History of Economic Thought* 41, no. 1 (March): 129–30.

——. 2019b. "Book Review: *The Economic Thought of Henry Calvert Simons, Crown Prince of the Chicago School*, by Gerald R. Steele." *Journal of the History of Economic Thought* 41, no. 4 (December): 645–47.

Backhouse, Roger E., and Keith Tribe. 2018. *The History of Economics: A Course for Students and Teachers*. New Castle upon Tyne: Agenda.

Bagehot, Walter. 1873. *Lombard Street: A Description of the Money Market*. Reprinted with a new introduction by Frank C. Genovese. Homewood, IL: Richard D. Irwin, 1962.

Bailey, Martin J., George S. Tavlas, and Michael Ulan. 1986. "Exchange-Rate Variability and Trade Performance: Evidence for the Big Seven Industrial Countries." *Review of World Economics* 122, no. 3:466–77.

——. 1987. "The Impact of Exchange-Rate Volatility on Export Growth: Some Theoretical Considerations and Empirical Results." *Journal of Policy Modeling* 9, no. 1 (Spring): 225–43.

Ball, R. J., and Ronald Bodkin. 1960. "A Symposium on Monetary Theory: The Real Balance Effect and Orthodox Demand Theory: A Critique of Archibald and Lipsey." *Review of Economic Studies* 28, no. 1 (October): 44–49.

Bane, Frank, Paul Betters, Carl Chatters, Paul Douglas, Simeon Leland, Harry Millis, Clarence Ridley, Henry Simons, Donald Slesinger, Jacob Viner, and Leonard D. White 1933. *Balancing the Budget*. Chicago Public Policy Pamphlet 1. Chicago: University of Chicago Press.

Barber, William J. 1985. *From New Era to New Deal: Herbert Hoover, the Economists, and American Economic Policy, 1921–33*. Cambridge: Cambridge University Press.

———. 1987. "The Career of Alvin H. Hansen in the 1920s and 1930s: A Study in Intellectual Transformation." *History of Political Economy* 19, no. 2 (Summer): 191–205.

———. 1996. *Designs within Disorder: Franklin D. Roosevelt, the Economists, and the Shaping of American Economic Policy, 1933–1945.* Cambridge: Cambridge University Press.

———. 1997. "Introduction." In William J. Barber, James Tobin, Robert W. Dimand, and Kevin Foster, eds., *The Works of Irving Fisher.* Vol. 11. London: Pickering and Chatto. 1–8.

———. 1998. "Irving Fisher as a Policy Advocate." In Malcolm Rutherford, ed., *The Economic Mind in America: Essays in the History of American Economics.* London: Routledge. 31–42.

———. 1999. "Irving Fisher (1867–1947): Career Highlights and Formative Influences." In Hans-E. Loef and Hans G. Monissen, eds., *The Economics of Irving Fisher.* Cheltenham, UK: Edward Elgar. 3–21.

Barber, William, James Tobin, Robert W. Dimand, and Kevin Foster, eds. 1997. *The Works of Irving Fisher.* Vol. 11. London: Routledge.

Barnett, William A. 2004. "An Interview with Paul A. Samuelson." *Macroeconomic Dynamics* 8, no. 4 (September): 519–42.

Barnett, William A., and Robert Solow. 2000. "An Interview with Franco Modigliani." *Macroeconomic Dynamics* 4, no. 2 (June): 222–56.

Barone, Enrico. 1908. *Principi di economia politica.* Roma: Tipografia Nazionale di G. Bertero.

Barro, Robert J. 1998. "Tribute on the Quad." *Hoover Digest* 4 (October 30): 1–9.

Baumol, William J. 1983. "Book Review: *Essays On and In the Chicago Tradition*, by Don Patinkin." *Journal of Political Economy* 91, no. 6 (December): 1080–82.

Belongia, Michael T., and Peter N. Ireland. 2021. "A Missing Stop on the Road from Warburton to Friedman—Meiselman and St. Louis." Unpublished manuscript.

Benes, Jaromir, and Michael Kumhof. 2012. "The Chicago Plan Revisited." IMF Working Paper 12/202, August.

Beveridge, Sir William. 1942. *Social Insurance and Allied Services.* London: His Majesty's Stationery Office.

Bias, Peter V. 2014. "A Chronological Survey of the Friedman-Meiselman / Andersen-Jordan Single Equation Debate." *Research in Business and Economics Journal* 10 (October): 1–21.

Biddle, Jeff. 2012. "Retrospectives: The Introduction of the Cobb-Douglas Regression." *Journal of Economic Perspectives* 26, no. 2 (Spring): 223–36.

Bierman, Harrold, Jr. 1991. *The Great Myths of 1929 and the Lessons to Be Learned.* New York: Greenwood.

Bigg, R. J. 1987. "Hawtrey, Ralph George (1879–1975)." In John Eatwell, Murray Milgate, and Peter Newman, eds., *The New Palgrave: A Dictionary of Economics.* Vol. 2. London: Macmillan. 605–9.

Blaug, Mark. 1962. *Economic Theory in Retrospect*. Cambridge: Cambridge University Press.

——. 1985. *Economic Theory in Retrospect*. 4th ed. Cambridge: Cambridge University Press.

Bleaney, Michael. 1976. *Underconsumption Theories: A History and Critical Analysis*. New York: International.

Bloomfield, Arthur I. 1992. "On the Centenary of Jacob Viner's Birth: A Retrospective View of the Man and His Work." *Journal of Economic Literature* 30, no. 4 (December): 2052–85.

Boianovsky, Mauro. 2002. "Patinkin, the Cowles Commission, and the Theory of Unemployment and Aggregate Supply." *European Journal of the History of Economic Thought* 9, no. 2:226–59.

——. 2011. "Fisher and Wicksell on Money: A Reconstructed Conversation." *European Journal of the History of Economic Thought* 20, no. 2:206–37.

Boland, Lawrence A. 1979. "A Critique of Friedman's Critics." *Journal of Economic Literature* 17 (June): 503–22.

Bordo, Michael D. 1983. "Some Aspects of the Monetary Economics of Richard Cantillon." *Journal of Monetary Economics* 12, no. 2 (August): 235–58.

——. 1992. "Gold Standard: Theory." In Peter Newman, Murray Milgate, and John Eatwell, eds., *The New Palgrave: Dictionary of Money and Finance*. Vol. 1. London: Macmillan. 267–70.

——. 1993. "The Bretton Woods International Monetary System: A Historical Overview." In Michael Bordo and Barry Eichengreen, eds., *A Retrospective on the Bretton Woods System: Lessons for International Monetary Reform*. Chicago: University of Chicago Press. 3–108.

——. 2008. "The History of Monetary Policy." In Steven Durlauf and Lawrence E. Blume, eds., *The New Palgrave: A Dictionary of Economics*. New York: Palgrave Macmillan. 205–15.

——. 2019. "Rules versus Discretion: A Perennial Theme in Monetary Economics." In Michael Bordo, ed., *The Historical Performance of the Federal Reserve: The Importance of Rules*. Stanford, CA: Hoover Institution Press. 3–27.

Bordo, Michael, D., and Hugh Rockoff. 2013a. "The Influence of Irving Fisher on Milton Friedman's Monetary Economics." *Journal of the History of Economic Thought* 35, no. 2 (June): 153–77.

——. 2013b. "Not Just the Great Contraction: Friedman and Schwartz's *A Monetary History of the United States, 1867 to 1960*." *American Economic Review* 103, no. 3 (Papers and Proceedings of the One Hundred Twenty-Fifth Annual Meeting of the American Economic Association): 61–65.

Bordo, Michael D., and Anna J. Schwartz. 1979. "Clark Warburton: Pioneer Monetarist." *Journal of Monetary Economics* 5, no. 1 (January): 43–65.

——. 1983. "The Importance of Stable Money: Theory and Evidence." *Cato Journal* 3, no. 1 (Spring): 63–91.

———. 1999. "Monetary Policy Regimes and Economic Performance: The Historical Record." In John Taylor and Michael Woodford, eds., *Handbook of Macroeconomics*. Vol. 1. New York: North Holland. 149–234. Reprinted in Michael D. Bordo, ed., *The Historical Performance of the Federal Reserve: The Importance of Rules*. Stanford, CA: Hoover Institution Press, 2019. 53–166.

Boskin, Michael J. 2016. "Milton Friedman's Contributions to Fiscal Economics." In Robert A. Cord and J. Daniel Hammond, eds., *Milton Friedman: Contributions to Economics and Public Policy*. Oxford: Oxford University Press, 401–16.

Boulding, Kenneth E. 1945. *The Economics of Peace*. New York: Prentice-Hall.

———. 1954. "Book Review: *Essays in Positive Economics*, by Milton Friedman." *Political Science Quarterly* 69, no. 1 (March): 132–33.

Breit, William, and Barry T. Hirsch, eds. 2009. *Lives of the Laureates: Twenty-Three Nobel Economists*. 5th ed. Cambridge, MA: MIT Press.

Brillant, Lucy. 2019. "Hicks's Theory of the Short-Term Rate of Interest and Thornton and Hawtrey's Influences." *Journal of the History of Economic Thought* 41, no. 3 (June): 393–410.

Bronfenbrenner, Martin. 1950. "Contemporary American Economic Thought." *Doshisha University Economic Review* 1, no. 3:1–18. Reprinted in *American Journal of Economics and Sociology* 9, no. 4 (July): 483–96.

Bronfenbrenner, Martin, and Franklyn D. Holzman. 1963. "Survey of Inflation Theory." *American Economic Review* 53, no. 4 (September): 593–661.

Brown, Cary E. 1989. "Alvin H. Hansen's Contributions to Business Cycle Analysis." MIT, Department of Economics, Working Paper 515, March.

Brunner, Karl. 1968a. "The Role of Money and Monetary Policy." *Federal Reserve Bank of St. Louis Review* 50 (July): 8–24.

———. 1968b. "Introduction." In Lauchlin Currie, ed., *The Supply and Control of Money in the United States*. New York: Russell and Russell. ix–xxxv.

Buchanan, James M. 1991. "Frank H. Knight." In Edward Shils, ed., *Remembering the University of Chicago: Teachers, Scientists, and Scholars*. Chicago: University of Chicago Press. 244–52.

Burgin, Angus. 2009. "The Radical Conservatism of Frank Knight." *Modern Intellectual History* 6, no. 3 (November): 513–38.

———. 2012. *The Great Persuasion: Reinventing Free Markets since the Depression*. Cambridge, MA: Harvard University Press.

Cagan, Phillip. 1956. "The Monetary Dynamics of Hyperinflation." In *Studies in the Quantity Theory of Money*, edited by Milton Friedman. Chicago: University of Chicago Press. 25–120.

———. 1978. "Monetarism in Historical Perspective." In Thomas Mayer, ed., *The Structure of Monetarism*. New York: W. W. Norton. 85–93.

———. 1987. "Monetarism." In John Eatwell, Murray Milgate, and Peter Newman, eds., *The New Palgrave: A Dictionary of Economics*. Vol. 3. London: Macmillan. 492–97.

Caldwell, Bruce. 2011. "The Chicago School, Hayek and Neoliberalism." In Robert Van Horn, Philip Mirowski, and Thomas Stapleford, eds., *Building Chicago Economics: New Perspectives on the History of America's Most Powerful Economics Program*. Cambridge: Cambridge University Press. 301–34.

Cameron, Rondo. 1992. "Bank Charter Act of 1844." In Peter Newman, Murray Milgate, and John Eatwell, eds., *The New Palgrave: Dictionary of Money and Finance*. Vol. 1. London: Macmillan. 124–25.

Cantillon, Richard. 1755. *Essai sur la nature du commerce en general (An Essay on Economic Theory)*, edited by Henry Higgs, with an English translation and other material. London: Macmillan, 1931; New York: Augustus M. Kelley, 1964.

Cargill, Thomas F. 1979. "Clark Warburton and the Development of Monetarism since the Great Depression." *History of Political Economy* 11, no. 3 (Fall): 425–49.

———. 1981. "A Tribute to Clark Warburton, 1896–1979: Note" *Journal of Money, Credit and Banking* 13, no. 1 (February): 89–93.

———. 2006. "Warburton, Clark." In Ross Emmett, ed., *The Biographical Dictionary of American Economists*. London: Thoemmes. 889–92.

Carlson, John B. 1988. "Rules versus Discretion: Making a Monetary Rule Operational." *Federal Reserve Bank of Cleveland Economic Review* 24, no. 3 (Quarter 3): 2–13.

Carroll, Charles H. 1860. "Mr. Lowell vs. Mr. Hooper on Banking and Currency." *Hunts Merchants' Magazine and Commercial Review* 42 (May): 576–83.

Cassidy, John. 2010. "Interview with James Heckman." *New Yorker*, January 14. https://www.newyorker.com/news/john-cassidy/interview-with-james-heckman.

Cate, Tom. 1981. "Keynes on Monetary Theory and Policy: Comment." *Southern Economic Journal* 47, no. 4 (April): 1132–36.

Cecchetti, Stephen G. 1992. "Stock Market Crash of October 1929." In Peter Newman, Murray Milgate, and John Eatwell, eds., *The New Palgrave: Dictionary of Money and Finance*. Vol. 3. London: Macmillan. 573–77.

Chandler, Lester V. 1951. "The Place of Monetary Policy in the Stabilization Program." *Review of Economics and Statistics* 33, no. 3 (August): 184–86.

———. *1958. Benjamin Strong: Central Banker*. Washington, DC: Brookings Institution.

Chase, Stuart, Robert Dunn, and Rexford Guy Tugwell, eds. 1928. *Soviet Russia in the Second Decade: A Joint Survey by the Technical Staff of the First American Trade Union Delegation*. New York: John Day.

Cherrier, Beatrice. 2011. "The Suspicious Consistency of Milton Friedman's Science and Politics, 1933–1963." Paper presented at the First Annual Conference on the History of Recent Economics (HISRECO). Reprinted as "The Lucky Consistency of Milton Friedman's Science and Politics, 1933–1963." In Robert Van Horn, Philip Mirowski, and Thomas Stapleford, eds., *Building Chicago Economics: New Perspectives on the History of America's Most Powerful Economics Program*. Cambridge: Cambridge University Press. 335–67.

Cicarelli, James, and Julianne Cicarelli. 2003. *Distinguished Women Economists*. Westport, CT: Greenwood.

Clark, John Bates. 1896. "Review of *Appreciation and Interest* by Irving Fisher." *Economic Journal* 6 (December): 567–70. Reprinted in Robert W. Dimand, ed., *Irving Fisher: Critical Responses*. Vol. 1. Abingdon: Taylor and Francis, 2006.

Clark, John M. 1934. *Strategic Factors in Business Cycles*. New York: National Bureau of Economic Research.

Coase, Ronald. 1998. "Director, Aaron." In Peter Newman, ed., *The New Palgrave Dictionary of Economics and the Law*. Vol. 1. London: Macmillan. 601–5.

Coats, A. W. 1963. "The Origins of the 'Chicago School(s)'?" *Journal of Political Economy* 71, no. 5 (October): 487–93.

Cobb, Charles W., and Paul H. Douglas. 1928. "A Theory of Production." *American Economic Review* 18, no. 1 (Supplement, Papers and Proceedings of the Fortieth Annual Meeting of the American Economic Association) (March): 139–65.

Cochrane, John. 2014. "Toward a Run-Free Financial System." In *Across the Great Divide: New Perspectives on the Financial Crisis*, edited by Martin Neil Baily and John B. Taylor. Stanford, CA: Hoover Institution Press. 197–249.

Cohen, Benjamin J. 1969. *Balance-of-Payments Policy*. Middlesex, England: Penguin Books.

Colander, David. 2005. "From Mudding Through to the Economics of Control: Views of Applied Policy from J. N. Keynes to Abba Lerner." *History of Political Economy* 37 (supplement 1): 277–91.

Colander, David, and Craig Freedman. 2019. *Where Economics Went Wrong: Chicago's Abandonment of Classical Liberalism*. Princeton, NJ: Princeton University Press.

Committee on the Working of the Monetary System. 1959. *Radcliffe Report*. London: Her Majesty's Stationery Office.

*Congressional Record*. 1932a. "Report of 31 Scientific Economists on Programs for Relief of Jobless and Business by $5,000,000 US Bond Issue." 72nd Cong., 1st sess., 75:1655–57.

———. 1932b. Senate. 72nd Cong., 1st sess., 75, part 9:10323.

———. 1951. 82nd Cong., 1st sess., 97 *Congressional Record* Bound, pt. 2:1468–82.

Cox, Garfield V. 1929. *An Appraisal of American Business Forecasts*. Studies in Business Administration 1, no. 2. Chicago: University of Chicago, School of Commerce and Administration.

———. 1930. "Evaluation of Economic Forecasts." *Journal of the American Statistical Association* 25, no. 169 (March): 31–35.

———. 1933. "Garfield Cox Urges Sound Money Stand." *Fairmont News*, November 16, 1.

———. 1936a. "Some Distinguishing Characteristics of the Current Recovery." *American Economic Review* 26, no. 1 (Supplement, Papers and Proceedings of the

Forty-Eighth Annual Meeting of the American Economic Association) (March): 1–10.

———. 1936b. "Book Review: *The Supply and Control of Money in the United States*, by Lauchlin Currie." *Journal of Business of the University of Chicago* 9, no. 1 (January): 93–94.

———. 1936c. "Forums Conducted by Dr. Garfield V. Cox: General Theme; Business Cycles, Booms and Depressions; Can We Manage Money and Credit?" Unpublished document, Colorado Springs Board of Education, Forum, September 21–25.

———. 1947. "Free Enterprise *vs.* Authoritarian Planning." *Journal of Business* 2, no. 2 (April): 59–66.

Cristiano, Carlo, and Luca Fiorito. 2016. "Two Minds That Never Met: Frank H. Knight on John M. Keynes Once Again—A Documentary Note." *Review of Keynesian Economics* 4, no. 1 (January): 67–98.

Currie, Lauchlin. 1931. "Bank Assets and Banking Theory." PhD diss., Harvard University.

———. 1933. "Treatment of Credit in Contemporary Monetary Theory." *Journal of Political Economy* 41, no. 1 (February): 58–79.

———. 1934a. "The Failure of Monetary Policy to Prevent the Depression of 1929–32." *Journal of Political Economy* 42, no. 2 (April): 145–77.

———. 1934b. *The Supply and Control of Money in the United States*. Cambridge, MA: Harvard University Press.

Currie, Lauchlin, Paul J. Ellsworth, and Harry D. White. 1932. Untitled memorandum. Harvard University, January. Published in *History of Political Economy* 34, no. 3 (Fall): 515–32.

Daly, Herman E. 1980. "The Economic Thought of Frederick Soddy." *History of Political Economy* 12, no. 4 (Winter): 469–88.

———. 2016. "Negative Interest Rates or 100% Reserves: Alchemy vs Chemistry." *Real-World Economics Review* 76:2–4. http://www.paecon.net/PAEReview/issue 76/Daly76.pdf/.

Daugherty, Marion R. 1942. "The Currency-Banking Controversy: Part 1." *Southern Economic Journal* 9, no. 2 (October): 140–55.

———. 1943. "The Currency-Banking Controversy: Part 2." *Southern Economic Journal* 9, no. 3 (January): 241–50.

Davenport, John. 1946. "The Testament of Henry Simons." *University of Chicago Law Review* 14, no. 1:5–14.

———. 1964. *The US Economy*. Washington, DC: H. Regnery.

Davis, E. G. 1981. "R. G. Hawtrey, 1879–1975." In D. P. O'Brien and John R. Presley, eds., *Pioneers of Modern Economics in Britain*. London: Palgrave Macmillan. 203–33.

Davis, J. Ronnie. 1968. "Chicago Economists, Deficit Budgets and the Early 1930s." *American Economic Review* 58, no. 3 (Part 1) (June): 476–82.

———. 1971. *The New Economics and the Old Economists*. Iowa City: Iowa State University Press.

———. 1974. "Three Days with Knight: A Personal Reminiscence." *Nebraska Journal of Economics and Business* 13, no. 1 (Winter): 17–29.

de Haas, Jacob A., Jr. 1889. "A Third Element in the Rate of Interest." *Journal of the Royal Statistical Society*, ser. A, 52, no. 1:99–116.

Dellas, Harris, P. A. V. B. Swamy, and George S. Tavlas. 2002. "The Collapse of Exchange Rate Pegs." *Annals of the American Academy of Political and Social Science* 579 (January): 53–72.

Dellas, Harris, and George S. Tavlas. 2005. "Wage Rigidity and Monetary Union." *Economic Journal* 115, no. 506 (October): 907–27.

———. 2009. "An Optimum-Currency-Area Odyssey." *Journal of International Money and Finance* 28, no. 7 (November): 1117–37.

———. 2018. "Milton Friedman and the Case for Flexible Exchange Rates and Monetary Rules." *Cato Journal* 38, no. 2 (Spring/Summer): 361–77.

———. 2021. "The Dog That Didn't Bark: The Curious Case of Lloyd Mints, Milton Friedman and the Emergence of Monetarism." *History of Political Economy* 53, no. 4 (August): 633–72.

———. 2022. "On the Evolution of the Rules versus Discretion Debate in Monetary Policy." *Journal of Economic Perspectives* 36, no. 3 (Summer): 245–60.

De Long, Bradford J. 2000. "The Triumph of Monetarism?" *Journal of Economic Perspectives* 14, no. 1 (Winter): 83–94.

Demeulemeester, Samuel. 2018. "The 100% Money Proposal and Its Implications for Banking: The Currie-Fisher Approach versus the Chicago Plan Approach." *European Journal of the History of Economic Thought* 25, no. 2 (May): 357–87.

———. 2019. "The 100% Money Proposal of the 1930s: Conceptual Clarification and Theoretical Analysis." PhD diss., Université de Lyon, December.

———. 2021. "The 100% Money Proposal of the 1930s: An Avatar of the Currency School's Reform Ideas?" *European Journal of the History of Economic Thought* 28, no. 4 (August): 577–98.

———. Forthcoming. "Lloyd W. Mints (1888–1989)." In Robert A. Cord, ed., *The Palgrave Companion to Chicago Economics*. London: Palgrave Macmillan.

DePrano, Michael, and Thomas Mayer. 1965. "Tests of the Relative Importance of Autonomous Expenditures and Money." *American Economic Review* 55, no. 4 (September): 729–52.

Desai, Meghnad. 1981. *Testing Monetarism*. London: Frances Pinter.

———. 2004. "Monetarism: A Response." *World Economics* 5, no. 3 (July–September): 165–70.

———. 2015. *Hubris: Why Economists Failed to Predict the Crisis and How to Avoid the Next One*. New Haven: Yale University Press.

Dewald, William G. 1966. "Money Supply versus Interest Rates as Proximate Objectives of Monetary Policy." *National Banking Review* 3, no. 4 (June): 509–22.

Dimand, Robert W. 1988. *The Origins of the Keynesian Revolution: The Development of Keynes's Theory of Employment and Output*. Hants, England: Edward Elgar.

———. 1993a. "The Dance of the Dollar: Irving Fisher's Monetary Theory of Economic Fluctuations." *History of Economics Review* 20, no. 1 (Summer): 161–72.

———. 1993b. "100 Percent Money: Irving Fisher and Banking Reform in the 1930s." *History of Economic Ideas* 1, no. 2:59–76.

———. 1998. "The Fall and Rise of Irving Fisher's Macroeconomics." *Journal of the History of Economic Thought* 20, no. 2 (June): 191–201.

———. 1999a. "Irving Fisher's Macroeconomics." In Hans-E. Loef and Hans G. Monissen, eds., *The Economics of Irving Fisher*. Cheltenham, UK: Edward Elgar. 35–58.

———. 1999b. "Irving Fisher and the Fisher Relation: Setting the Record Straight." *Canadian Journal of Economics* 32, no. 3 (May): 744–50.

———. 2002. "Patinkin on Irving Fisher's Monetary Economics." *European Journal of the History of Economic Thought* 9, no. 2 (October): 308–26.

———. 2010. "David Laidler's Contributions to the History of Monetary Economics." In Robert Leeson, ed., *David Laidler's Contributions to Economics*. London: Palgrave Macmillan. 60–84.

———. 2015. "Book Review: *Fortune Tellers: The Story of America's First Economic Forecasters*, by Walter A. Friedman." *History of Political Economy* 47, no. 1, 201–3.

———. 2020. "J. Laurence Laughlin versus Irving Fisher on the Quantity Theory of Money, 1894 to 1913." *Oxford Economic Papers* 72, no. 4:1032–49.

Dimand, Robert W., and Rebeca Gomez Betancourt. 2012. "Retrospectives: Irving Fisher's *Appreciation and Interest* (1896) and the Fisher Relation." *Journal of Economic Perspectives* 26, no. 4 (Fall): 185–96.

Director, Aaron. 1930. "Making Use of Public Works." *Survey* 64 (August 15): 427–28.

———. 1932. *Unemployment*. Chicago: American Library Association.

———. 1933. *The Economics of Technocracy*. Chicago Public Policy Pamphlet 2. Chicago: University of Chicago Press.

———. 1940. "Does Inflation Change the Economic Effects of War?" *American Economic Review* 30, no. 1 (Part 2, Supplement, Papers and Proceedings of the Fifty-Second Annual Meeting of the American Economic Association) (March): 351–61.

———. 1946. "Simons on Taxation." *University of Chicago Law Review* 14, no. 1: 15–19.

———. 1947a. "Prefatory Note." In Henry C. Simons, ed., *Economic Policy for a Free Society*. Chicago: University of Chicago Press, 1948. v–vii.

———, ed. 1947b. Mont Pèlerin Conference. Unpublished presentation.

———. 1950. "Book Review: *Unions and Capitalism*, by Charles E. Lindblom." *University of Chicago Law Review* 18, no. 1:164–67.

———, ed. 1952. *Defense, Controls, and Inflation: A Conference Sponsored by the University of Chicago Law School*. Chicago: University of Chicago Press.

———. 1955a. Memorandum on Monetary Policy to John Davenport 1, July 11. John Davenport Papers, Hoover Institution Library and Archives, Stanford University.

———. 1955b. Memorandum on Monetary Policy to John Davenport 2, July 29. John Davenport Papers, Hoover Institution Library and Archives, Stanford University.

———. 1956. "Full Employment Policies." Lecture, Institute of Humane Studies, June 20. Aaron Director Collection, Hoover Institution Library and Archives, Stanford University.

———. 1967. "Introduction for the Henry Simons Lecture." Unpublished, May 5. Aaron Director Papers, Hoover Institution Library and Archives, Stanford University.

Director, Aaron, Milton Friedman, Abram L. Harris, Frank H. Knight, Gregg Lewis, Lloyd W. Mints, Russell T. Nichols, and W. Allen Wallis. 1948. "Control of Prices: Regulation of Money Supply to Halt Inflation Advocated." *New York Times*, Letters to the Times, January 11, E8.

Director, Aaron, and Edward Hirsch Levi. 1956. "Law and the Future: Trade Regulation." *Northwestern University Law Review* 51:281–96.

Dittmer, Kristofer. 2015. "100 Percent Reserve Banking: A Critical Review of Green Perspectives." *Ecological Economics* 109 (January): 9–16.

Dorfman, Joseph. 1959. *The Economic Mind in American Civilization*. Vols. 4 and 5. New York: Viking.

Dorn, Jim. 2018. "Monetary Policy in an Uncertain World: The Case for Rules." *Cato Journal* 38, no. 1 (Winter): 81–108.

Dornbusch, Rudiger. 1976. "Expectations and Exchange Rate Dynamics." *Journal of Political Economy* 84, no. 6 (December): 1161–76.

Douglas, Paul H. 1927. "The Modern Technique of Mass Production and Its Relation to Wages." *Proceedings of the Academy of Political Science in the City of New York* 12, no. 3 (July): 17–42.

———. 1928. "Labor Legislation and Social Insurance." In Stuart Chase, Robert Dunn, and Rexford Guy Tugwell, eds., *Soviet Russia in the Second Decade: A Joint Survey by the Technical Staff of the First American Trade Union Delegation*. New York: John Day. 216–52.

———. 1930. *Real Wages in the United States 1890–1926*. Boston: Houghton Mifflin.

———. 1932a. "Money, Credit and the Depression." *World Tomorrow* 15:78–80.

———. 1932b. *The Coming of the New Party*. New York: McGraw-Hill.

———. 1933a. *Know America: Its Ills and Cures*. Chicago: Buti-Lami.

———. 1933b. "Karl Marx the Prophet." *World Tomorrow* 16, no. 11 (March 15): 255–57.

———. 1933c. "The New Deal after Ten Weeks." *World Tomorrow* 16 (June): 419.

———. 1933d. "Rooseveltian Liberalism." *Nation* (June 21): 702–3.

———. 1933e. *Collapse or Cycle.* Chicago: American Library Association.

———. 1934. *The Theory of Wages.* New York: Macmillan.

———. 1935a. "Purchasing Power of the Masses and Business Depressions." In Wesley C. Mitchell, ed., *Economic Essays in Honor of Wesley Clair Mitchell: Presented to Him by His Former Students on the Occasion of His Sixtieth Birthday.* New York: Columbia University Press. 105–30.

———. 1935b. *Controlling Depressions.* New York: Norton.

———. 1938. Statement before the Senate Committee on Unemployment, March 4.

———. 1948. "Are There Laws of Production." *American Economic Review* 38, no. 1 (March): i–ii and 1–41.

———. 1972. *In the Fullness of Time: The Memoirs of Paul H. Douglas.* New York: Harcourt Brace Jovanovich.

Douglas, Paul H., and Aaron Director. 1931. *The Problem of Unemployment.* New York: Macmillan.

Douglas, Paul H., Irving Fisher, Frank D. Graham, Earl J. Hamilton, Willford I. King, and Charles R. Whittlesey. 1939. *A Program for Monetary Reform.* Mimeograph. http://www.muratopia.org/Yamaguchi/doc/revisedAProgramforMonetary Reform0713101.pdf.

Douglass, William. (1740) 1897. "A Discourse concerning the Currencies of the British Plantations in America." Reprinted with introduction by Charles J. Bullock, *Publications of the American Economic Association,* 2nd ser., 2, no. 5: 1–228.

Dwyer, Gerald P. 2016. "Milton Friedman: A Bayesian?" In Robert A. Cord and J. Daniel Hammond, eds., *Milton Friedman: Contributions to Economics and Public Policy.* Oxford: Oxford University Press. 575–84.

Ebenstein, Lanny. 2015. *Chicagonomics: The Evolution of Chicago Free Market Economics.* London: St. Martin's.

*Economist.* 1952. "Living with the Dollar." 165 (November 22): 579–96.

———. 1968. "It's Better to Float." 229 (November 30): 15–17.

Edge, Stephanie K. 1967. "The Relative Stability of Monetary Velocity and the Investment Multiplier." *Australian Economic Papers* 6, no. 9 (December): 192–207.

Edwards, Sebastian. 2017. "Gold, the Brains Trust, and Roosevelt." *History of Political Economy* 49, no. 1 (March): 1–30.

———. 2018. *American Default: The Untold Story of FDR, the Supreme Court, and the Battle over Gold.* Princeton, NJ: Princeton University Press.

———. Forthcoming. "Milton Friedman and Exchange Rates: History and Controversies." *History of Political Economy.*

Eichengreen, Barry. 1994. *International Monetary Arrangements for the 21st Century.* Washington, DC: Brookings Institution.

———. 1996. *Globalizing Capital: A History of the International Monetary System.* Princeton, NJ: Princeton University Press.

———. 2008. *Globalizing Capital: A History of the International Monetary System.* 2nd ed. Princeton, NJ: Princeton University Press.

Eichengreen, Barry, and Peter M. Garber. 1991. "Before the Accord: US Monetary-Financial Policy, 1945–51." In R. Glenn Hubbard, ed., *Financial Markets and Financial Crises.* Chicago: University of Chicago Press. 175–206.

Elliott, James, Sung Y. Kwack, and George S. Tavlas. 1986. "An Econometric Model of the Kenyan Economy." *Economic Modelling* 3, no. 1 (January): 2–30.

Ellis, Howard S. 1946a. "Comments on the Mints and Hansen Papers." *Review of Economics and Statistics* 28, no. 2 (May): 74–77.

———. 1946b. "Book Review: *International Currency Experience: Lessons of the Inter-war Period*, by Ragnar Nurkse." *Journal of Political Economy* 54, no. 4 (August): 378–80.

———, ed. 1948. *A Survey of Contemporary Economics.* Philadelphia: published on behalf of the American Economic Association by Blakiston.

Ely, Richard, T., ed. 1923. *Outlines of Economics.* 4th ed. New York: Macmillan.

Emmett, Ross B. 2006. "Simons, Henry Calvert." In Ross B. Emmett, ed., *The Biographical Dictionary of American Economists.* Vol. 2. Thoemmes: London. 781–82.

———, ed. 2010. *The Elgar Companion to the Chicago School of Economics.* Cheltenham, UK: Edward Elgar.

Ericsson, Neil R., David F. Hendry, and Stedman B. Hood. 2016. "Milton Friedman as an Empirical Modeler." In Robert A. Cord and J. Daniel Hammond, eds., *Milton Friedman: Contributions to Economics and Public Policy.* Oxford: Oxford University Press. 91–142.

Fand, David. 1969. "Keynesian Monetary Theories, Stabilization Policy, and the Recent Inflation." *Journal of Money, Credit and Banking* 1, no. 3:556–87.

Federal Reserve Board. 1955. *Annual Report.* Washington, DC: Federal Reserve System.

Fergusson, Donald A. 1951. "Book Review: *Monetary Policy for a Competitive Society*, by Lloyd W. Mints." *Accounting Review* 26, no. 3 (July): 438–40.

Fiorito, Luca, and Sebastiano Nerozzi. 2018. "Chicago Economics in the Making, 1926–1940: A Further Look at United States Interwar Pluralism." In Robert Leeson, ed., *Hayek: A Collaborative Biography, Part XV: The Chicago School of Economics, Hayek's "Luck" and the 1974 Nobel Prize for Economic Science.* Switzerland: Palgrave Macmillan. 373–418.

Fischer, Stanley. 1990. "Rules versus Discretion in Monetary Policy." In B. M. Friedman and F. H. Hahn, eds., *Handbook of Monetary Economics.* Vol. 2. Amsterdam: North Holland / Elsevier. 1156–84.

Fisher, Irving. 1896. *Appreciation and Interest.* New York: Macmillan.

———. 1907. *The Rate of Interest.* New York: Macmillan.

———. 1911a. "Recent Changes in Price Levels and Their Causes." *American Economic Review* 1, no. 2 (Papers and Discussions of the Twenty-Third Annual Meeting of the American Economic Association) (April): 37–45.

——. 1911b. *The Purchasing Power of Money: Its Determination and Relation to Credit, Interest, and Crisis*. New York: Macmillan.

——. 1913a. *The Purchasing Power of Money*. 2nd ed. New York: Macmillan.

——. 1913b. "A Remedy for the Rising Cost of Living: Standardizing the Dollar." *American Economic Review* 3, no. 1 (Supplement, Papers and Proceedings of the Twenty-Fifth Annual Meeting of the American Economic Association) (March): 20–28.

——. 1919. "Stabilizing the Dollar." *American Economic Review* 19, no. 1 (Supplement, Papers and Proceedings of the Thirty-First Annual Meeting of the American Economic Association) (March): 156–60.

——. 1920. *Stabilizing the Dollar: A Plan to Stabilize the General Price Level without Fixing Individual Prices*. New York: Macmillan.

——. 1922a. *Stabilization of Purchasing Power of Money*. Hearings before the Committee on Banking and Currency of the House of Representatives, 67th Cong., 4th sess., on H.R. 11788, to stabilize the purchasing power of money. December 18, 19, 20, and 21. Washington, DC: US Governing Printing Office. https://fraser.stlouisfed.org/title/3940.

——. 1922b. *The Making of Index Numbers*. Boston: Houghton Mifflin.

——. 1928. *The Money Illusion*. New York: Adelphi.

——. 1929. "Fisher Sees Stocks Permanently High." *New York Times*, October 16, 8.

——. 1932. *Booms and Depressions*. London: George Allen and Unwin.

——. 1933a. "Statistics in the Service of Economics." *Journal of the American Statistical Association* 28, no. 181 (March): 1–13.

——. 1933b. "The Debt-Deflation Theory of Great Depressions." *Econometrica* 1, no. 4 (October): 337–57.

——. 1933c. *Mastering the Crisis*. New York: Adelphi.

——. 1933d. *Stamp Scrip*. New York: Adelphi.

——. 1934. *Stable Money: A History of the Movement*. New York: Adelphi.

——. 1935a. *100% Money*. New York: Adelphi.

——. 1935b. *Banking Act of 1935*. Hearings before the Committee on Banking and Currency of the House of Representatives, 74th Cong., 1st sess., on H.R. 5357, to provide for the sound, effective, and uninterrupted operation of the banking system, February 21 to April 8. Washington, DC: US Governing Printing Office. https://fraser.stlouisfed.org/title/5309.

——. 1936. *100% Money*. 2nd ed. New York: Adelphi.

Flanders, June M. 1989. *International Monetary Economics, 1870–1960: Between the Classical and the New Classical*. New York: Cambridge University Press.

Forder, James. 2019. *Milton Friedman*. London: Palgrave Macmillan.

Foster, William T., and Waddill Catchings. 1923. *Money*. Boston: Houghton Mifflin.

Freedman, Craig. 2006. "Not for Love nor Money: Milton Friedman's Counter-Revolution." *History of Economics Review* 44, no. 1 (March): 87–119.

———. 2016. *In Search of the Two-Handed Economist: Ideology, Methodology and Marketing in Economics.* London: Palgrave Macmillan.

Freedman, Craig, G. C. Harcourt, Peter Kriesler, and J. W. Nevile. 2016. "How Friedman Became the Anti-Keynes." In Robert A. Cord and J. Daniel Hammond, eds., *Milton Friedman: Contributions to Economics and Public Policy.* Oxford: Oxford University Press. 607–30.

Friedman, Milton. 1937. "The Use of Ranks to Avoid the Assumption of Normality Implicit in the Analysis of Variance." *Journal of the American Statistical Association* 32, no. 200 (December): 675–701.

———. 1942a. "The Inflationary Gap: II. Discussion of the Inflationary Gap." *American Economic Review* 32, no. 2 (Part 1) (February): 314–20.

———. 1942b. "Exhibit 66: Statement by Milton Friedman, May 7, 1942, on the Relation of Taxation to Inflation." In Treasury Department and the Staff of the Joint Committee on Internal Revenue Taxation, *Data on Proposed Revenue Bill of 1942, Submitted to the Committee on Ways and Means, House of Representatives.* Washington, DC: US Government Printing Office.

———. 1944. "Review of *Saving, Investment, and National Income*, by Oscar L. Altman." *Review of Economics and Statistics* 26, no. 2 (May): 101–2.

———. 1946. "OPA Alone Cannot Prevent Inflation." *Congressional Record*, Statement to the House of Representatives, April 16, A2336.

———. 1947. "Lerner on the Economics of Control." *Journal of Political Economy* 55, no. 5 (October): 405–16.

———. 1948a. "A Monetary and Fiscal Framework for Economic Stability." *American Economic Review* 38, no. 3 (June): 245–64. Reprinted in Milton Friedman, ed., *Essays in Positive Economics.* Chicago: University of Chicago Press, 1953. 133–56.

———. 1948b. "Preliminary Plan for Completion of Data for Study of Monetary Factors in Business Cycles." Unpublished manuscript. Milton Friedman Papers, Hoover Institution Library and Archives, Stanford University.

———. 1949a. "Professor Friedman's Proposal: Rejoinder." *American Economic Review* 39, no. 5 (September): 949–55.

———. 1949b. "The Marshallian Demand Curve." *Journal of Political Economy* 57, no. 6 (December): 463–95.

———. 1949c. "Outline of Work in the First Phase of the Banking Study: Cyclical Behavior of the Quantity and Rate of Use of Circulating Media." Unpublished manuscript. Milton Friedman Papers, Hoover Institution Library and Archives, Stanford University.

———. 1951a. "Neo-liberalism and Its Prospects." *Farmand*, February 17. Available on Hoover Institution website. https://miltonfriedman.hoover.org.

———. 1951b. "Free Enterprise in the United States." Draft manuscript, May 21. Milton Friedman Papers, Hoover Institution, Library and Archives, Stanford University. Published in *Bulletin Bimestriel de la Société Belge d'Etudes et d'Expansion*, no. 148 (November–December 1951): 783–88.

———. 1951c. "Comments on Monetary Policy." *Review of Economics and Statistics* 33, no. 3 (August): 186–91.

———. 1951d. "Commodity-Reserve Currency." *Journal of Political Economy* 59, no. 3 (June): 203–32. Reprinted in Milton Friedman, ed., *Essays in Positive Economics*. Chicago: University of Chicago Press, 1953. 204–50.

———. 1951e. "The Role of the Monetary and Banking System in the Business Cycle." Unpublished manuscript. Milton Friedman Papers, Hoover Institution Library and Archives, Stanford University.

———. 1951f. "The Effects of a Full-Employment Policy on Economic Stability: A Formal Analysis" / "Les effets d'une politique de plein emploi sur la stabilité économique: Analyse formelle." *Économie Appliquée* 4 (July–December): 441–56. Reprinted in Milton Friedman, ed., *Essays in Positive Economics*. Chicago: University of Chicago Press, 1953. 117–32.

———. 1952. "Price, Income and Monetary Changes in Three Wartime Periods." *American Economic Review* 42, no. 2 (Papers and Proceedings of the Sixty-Fourth Annual Meeting of the American Economic Association) (May): 612–25. Reprinted in Milton Friedman, ed., *The Optimum Quantity of Money, and Other Essays*. Chicago: University of Chicago Press, 1969. 157–70.

———. 1953a. *Essays in Positive Economics*. Chicago: University of Chicago Press.

———. 1953b. "The Case for Flexible Exchange Rates." In Milton Friedman, ed., *Essays in Positive Economics*. Chicago: University of Chicago Press. 157–203.

———. 1953c. "The Effects of a Full Employment Policy on Economic Stability: A Formal Analysis." In Milton Friedman, ed., *Essays in Positive Economics*. Chicago: University of Chicago Press. 117–32.

———. 1953d. "The Methodology of Positive Economics." In Milton Friedman, ed., *Essays in Positive Economics*. Chicago: University of Chicago Press. 3–43.

———. 1953e. "Discussion of the Inflationary Gap." Revised Version. In Milton Friedman, ed., *Essays in Positive Economics*. Chicago: University of Chicago Press. 251–62.

———. 1953f. "Living With the Dollar." *The Economist* 166 (January 3): 16.

———. 1954. "Why the American Economy Is Depression Proof." *Nationalekonomiska Föreningens Förhandlingar*, no. 3:58–77. Reprinted in Milton Friedman, ed., *Dollars and Deficits: Inflation, Monetary Policy and the Balance of Payments*. Englewood Cliffs, NJ: Prentice Hall, 1968. 72–96.

———. 1955. "Liberalism, Old Style." In William T. Couch, ed., *Collier's 1955 Year Book: Covering National and International Events of the Year 1954*. New York: P. F. Collier and Son. 360–63.

———. 1956a. "The Quantity Theory of Money: A Restatement." In Milton Friedman, ed., *Studies in the Quantity Theory of Money*. Chicago: University of Chicago Press. 3–21.

———, ed. 1956b. *Studies in the Quantity Theory of Money*. Chicago: University of Chicago Press.

———. 1956c. "Monetary Policy, Domestic and International." Lecture, Wabash College, June. Available on Hoover Institution website. https://miltonfriedman .hoover.org.

———. 1956d. "The Keynesian Revolution and Economic Liberalism." Lecture, Wabash College, June. Available on Hoover Institution website. https://milton friedman.hoover.org.

———. 1956e. "The Distribution of Income and the Welfare Activities of Government." Lecture, Wabash College, June. Available on Hoover Institution website. https://miltonfriedman.hoover.org.

———. 1956f. "The Role of Government in a Liberal Society." Lecture, Wabash College, June. Available on Hoover Institution website. https://miltonfriedman .hoover.org.

———. 1956g. "The Basic Principles of Liberalism." Lecture, Wabash College, June. Available on Hoover Institution website. https://miltonfriedman.hoover.org.

———. 1957a. "Consumer Credit Control as an Instrument of Stabilization Policy." In Federal Reserve Board, ed., *Consumer Instalment Credit, Part 2*. Vol. 2, *Conference on Regulation*. Washington, DC: Federal Reserve Board. 73–103.

———. 1957b. *A Theory of the Consumption Function*. Princeton, NJ: Princeton University Press.

———. 1958a. "The Supply of Money and Changes in Prices and Output." In Joint Economic Committee, *The Relationship of Prices to Economic Stability and Growth*, 85th Cong., 2nd sess. Washington, DC: US Government Printing Office. Reprinted in Milton Friedman, ed., *The Optimum Quantity of Money, and Other Essays*. Chicago: Aldine, 1969. 171–87.

———. 1958b. "Inflation." Paper delivered at the Ninth Meeting of the Mont Pèlerin Society, Princeton, NJ, September 3–8.

———. 1959a. "The Demand for Money: Some Theoretical and Empirical Results." *Journal of Political Economy* 67, no. 4 (August): 327–51. Reprinted in Milton Friedman, ed., *The Optimum Quantity of Money, and Other Essays*. Chicago: Aldine, 1969. 111–39.

———. 1959b. "The Demand for Money: Some Theoretical and Empirical Results." *American Economic Review* 49, no. 2 (May): 525–27.

———. 1960. *A Program for Monetary Stability*. Fordham, NY: Fordham University Press.

———. 1962a. *Capitalism and Freedom*. Chicago: University of Chicago Press.

———. 1962b. "Should There Be an Independent Monetary Authority?" In Leland B. Yeager, ed., *In Search of a Monetary Constitution*. Cambridge, MA: Harvard University Press. 219–43.

———. 1963. "The Present State of Monetary Theory." *Bank of Japan Economic Studies Quarterly* 14, no 1 (September): 1–15.

———. 1965. "Economics 331: Final Exam. Autumn 1965." December 15, 1965. Mimeograph, Milton Friedman Papers, Hoover Institution Library and Archives, Stanford University.

———. 1966. "Interest Rates and the Demand for Money." *Journal of Law and Economics* 9 (October): 71–85.

———. 1967. "The Monetary Theory and Policy of Henry Simons." *Journal of Law and Economics* 10, no. 1 (October): 1–13. Reprinted in Milton Friedman, ed., *The Optimum Quantity of Money, and Other Essays.* Chicago: Adeline, 1969. 82–93.

———. 1968a. "The Role of Monetary Policy." *American Economic Review* 58, no. 1 (March): 1–17.

———. 1968b. *Dollars and Deficits: Inflation, Monetary Policy and the Balance of Payments.* Englewood Cliffs, NJ: Prentice Hall.

———. 1968c. "Money: Quantity Theory." In David L. Sills, ed., *International Encyclopaedia of the Social Sciences.* Vol. 10. New York: Macmillan. 432–47.

———. 1969a. "The Optimum Quantity of Money." In Milton Friedman, ed., *The Optimum Quantity of Money, and Other Essays.* Chicago: Aldine. 1–50.

———. 1969b. *The Optimum Quantity of Money, and Other Essays.* Chicago: Aldine.

———. 1970a. *The Counter-Revolution in Monetary Theory.* Institute of Economic Affairs Occasional Paper 33. London: Institute of Economic Affairs.

———. 1970b. "A Theoretical Framework for Monetary Analysis." *Journal of Political Economy* 78, no. 2:193–238.

———. 1970c. "Comment on Tobin." *Quarterly Journal of Economics* 84, no. 2 (May): 318–27.

———. 1971a. "A Monetary Theory of Nominal Income." *Journal of Political Economy* 79, no. 2 (March/April): 323–37.

———. 1971b. "Comments on the Critics." Draft, unpublished. Milton Friedman Papers, Hoover Institution Library and Archives, Stanford University.

———. 1972. "Comments on the Critics." *Journal of Political Economy* 80, no. 5 (September/October): 906–50.

———. 1974. "A Dramatic Experiment." *Newsweek,* April 1, 65.

———. 1975a. "Twenty-Five Years after the Rediscovery of Money: What Have We Learned? Discussion." *American Economic Review* 65, no. 2 (Papers and Proceedings of the Eighty-Seventh Annual Meeting of the American Economic Association) (May): 176–79.

———. 1975b. *Unemployment versus Inflation? An Evaluation of the Phillips Curve.* IEA Lecture 2. London: Institute of Economic Affairs.

———. 1977. "Nobel Lecture: Inflation and Unemployment." *Journal of Political Economy* 85, no. 3 (June): 451–72.

———. 1982. "Monetary Policy: Theory and Practice." *Journal of Money, Credit and Banking* 14, no. 1 (February): 98–118.

———. 1983. "Monetarism in Rhetoric and Practice." *Bank of Japan Monetary and Economic Studies* 1, no. 2 (October): 1–14.

———. 1987. "Laughlin, James Laurence." In John Eatwell, Murray Milgate, and Peter Newman, eds., *The New Palgrave: A Dictionary of Economics.* Vol. 3. London: Macmillan. 139–40.

———. 1992a. *Money Mischief: Episodes in Monetary History*. New York: Harcourt Brace Jovanovich.

———. 1992b. "Quantity Theory of Money." In Peter Newman, Murray Milgate, and John Eatwell, eds., *The New Palgrave: Dictionary of Money and Finance*. Vol. 3. London: Macmillan. 247–64.

———. 2001. Preface. In Robert Leeson, ed., *Keynes, Chicago and Friedman*. London: Pickering and Chatto, 2003. ix–x.

Friedman, Milton, and Rose D. Friedman. 1998. *Two Lucky People: Memoirs*. Chicago: University of Chicago Press.

Friedman, Milton, Albert G. Hart, and Neil H. Jacoby. 1946. *What Can Be Done about Inflation? A Radio Discussion*. Chicago: University Chicago Press.

Friedman, Milton, and David Meiselman. 1959. "Judging the Predictive Abilities of the Quantity and Income-Expenditure Theories." Manuscript, for discussion at Workshop on Money and Banking session of October 27, 1959. Milton Friedman Papers, Hoover Institution Library and Archives, Stanford University.

———. 1963. "The Relative Stability of Monetary Velocity and the Investment Multiplier in the United States, 1897–1958." In Commission on Money and Credit, ed., *Stabilization Policies*. Englewood Cliffs, NJ: Prentice Hall. 165–268.

———. 1965. "Reply to Ando and Modigliani and to DePrano and Mayer." *American Economic Review* 55, no. 4 (September): 753–85.

Friedman, Milton, Lloyd A. Metzler, Frederick H. Harbison, Lloyd W. Mints, D. Gale Johnson, Theodore W. Schultz, and H. G. Lewis. 1951. "The Failure of the Present Monetary Policy." In Joint Committee on the Economic Report, US Congress, January 1951, *Economic Report of the President: Hearings*. Washington, DC: US Government Printing Office. 458–60.

Friedman, Milton, and Leonard J. Savage. 1948. "The Utility Analysis of Choices Involving Risk." *Journal of Political Economy* 56, no. 4 (August): 279–304.

———. 1952. "The Expected-Utility Hypothesis and the Measurability of Utility." *Journal of Political Economy* 60, no. 6 (December): 463–74.

Friedman, Milton, and Anna J. Schwartz. 1956. Draft chapters, "The Estimates" and "Cyclical Behavior," April. Milton Friedman Papers, Hoover Institution Library and Archives, Stanford University.

———. 1963. *A Monetary History of the United States, 1867–1960*. Princeton, NJ: Princeton University Press.

———. 1970. *Monetary Statistics of the United States: Estimates, Sources, Methods*. New York: Columbia University Press for the NBER.

———. 1982. *Monetary Trends in the United States and the United Kingdom: Their Relation to Income, Prices, and Interest Rates, 1867–1975*. Chicago: University of Chicago Press.

———. 1991. "Alternative Approaches to Analyzing Economic Data." *American Economic Review* 81, no. 1 (March): 39–49.

Friedman, Milton, and George J. Stigler. 1946. *Roofs or Ceilings? The Current Housing Problem*. Irvington-on-Hudson, NY: Foundation for Economic Education.

Friedman, Walter A. 2014. *Fortune Tellers: The Story of America's First Economic Forecasters*. Princeton, NJ: Princeton University Press.

Fullarton, John. 1845. *On the Regulation of Currencies*. 2nd ed. London: J. Murray.

Garvey, George. 1978. "Carl Snyder, Pioneer Economic Statistician and Monetarist." *History of Political Economy* 10, no. 3:454–90.

Ginther, Donna K. 2010. "An Interview with James J. Heckman." *Macroeconomic Dynamics* 14, no. 4 (September): 548–84.

Girton, Lance, and Don Roper. 1978. "J. Laurence Laughlin and the Quantity Theory of Money." *Journal of Political Economy* 86, no. 4 (August): 599–625.

Goldin, Claudia. 2002. "Milton Friedman Oral History Interview with Claudia Goldin." National Bureau of Economic Research, August 16. https://www.nber .org/historical-video/milton-friedman-oral-history-interview-claudia-goldin.

Goodhart, Charles A. E., and Meinhart A. Jensen. 2015. "Currency School versus Banking School: An Ongoing Confrontation." *Economic Thought* 4, no. 2:20–31.

Gordon, Robert J., ed. 1974. *Milton Friedman's Monetary Framework: A Debate with His Critics*. Chicago: University of Chicago Press.

———. 1981. "Output Fluctuations and Gradual Price Adjustment." *Journal of Economic Literature* 19, no. 2 (June): 493–530.

Gould, John, and Charles Nelson. 1974. "The Stochastic Structure of the Velocity of Money." *American Economic Review* 64, no. 3 (June): 405–18.

Graham, Frank D. 1936. "Partial Reserve Money and the 100 Percent Proposal." *American Economic Review* 26, no. 3 (September): 428–40.

Haberler, Gottfried. 1930. "The Theory of Comparative Costs and Its Use in the Defense of Free Trade." *Weltwirtschaftliches Archiv* 32 (July 1930): 349–70. Reprinted in A. Y. C. Koo, ed., *Selected Essays of Gottfried Haberler*. Cambridge, MA: MIT Press, 1985. 1–19.

Hafer, Rik, and David C. Wheelock. 2001. "The Rise and Fall of a Policy Rule: Monetarism at the St. Louis Fed, 1968–1986." *Federal Reserve Bank of St. Louis Review* 83:1–24.

Haig, Robert M. 1921. "The Concept of Income—Economic and Legal Aspects." In Robert H. Murray, ed., *The Federal Income Tax*. New York: Columbia University Press. 1–28.

Hall, Stephen G., P. A. V. B. Swamy, and George S. Tavlas. 2012. "Milton Friedman, the Demand for Money, and the ECB's Monetary Policy Strategy." *Federal Reserve Bank of St. Louis Review* 94, no. 3 (May/June): 153–85.

Hammond, Daniel J. 1991. "Book Review: *Milton Friedman: Economics in Theory and Practice*, by Abraham Hirsch and Neil de Marchi." *History of Political Economy* 23, no. 4, 769–72.

———. 1992. "An Interview with Milton Friedman on Methodology." *Research in History of Economic Thought and Methodology* 10, no. 1:91–118.

———. 1996. *Theory and Measurement: Causality Issues in Milton Friedman's Monetary Economics*. Cambridge: Cambridge University Press.

———. 1999. "Labels and Substance: Friedman's Restatement of the Quantity Theory." *History of Political Economy* 31, no. 3, 449–71.

Hansen, Alvin H. 1932. *Economic Stabilization in an Unbalanced World*. New York: Harcourt Brace.

———. 1936a. "Under-employment Equilibrium." *Yale Review* 35:828–30.

———. 1936b. "Mr. Keynes and Underemployment Equilibrium." *Journal of Political Economy* 44, no. 5 (October): 667–86.

———. 1938. *Full Recovery or Stagnation?* New York: W. W. Norton.

———. 1941. *Fiscal Policy and Business Cycles*. Berkeley, CA: W. W. Norton.

———. 1945. "Stability and Expansion." In Paul T. Homan and Fritz Machlup, eds., *Financing American Prosperity: A Symposium of Economists*. New York: Twentieth-Century Fund. 199–265.

———. 1946. "Notes on Mints' Paper on Monetary Policy." *Review of Economics and Statistics* 28, no. 2 (May): 69–74.

———. 1947. "*The General Theory (2)*." In Seymour E. Harris, ed., *The New Economics: Keynes' Influence on Theory and Public Policy*. New York: Alfred A. Knopf. 133–44.

———. 1949. *Monetary Theory and Fiscal Policy*. New York: McGraw-Hill.

———. 1951. "Monetary Policy and the Control of Inflation." *Review of Economics and Statistics* 33, no. 3 (August): 191–94.

———. 1957. *The American Economy*. New York: McGraw-Hill.

Hansen, Lars P. 2007. "Beliefs, Doubts and Learning: Valuing Macroeconomic Risk." *American Economic Review* 97, no. 2:1–30.

———. 2014. "Nobel Lecture: Uncertainty Outside and Inside Economic Models." *Journal of Political Economy* 122, no. 5:945–87.

Hansen, Lars P., and Thomas J. Sargent. 2010. "Fragile Beliefs and the Price of Uncertainty." *Quantitative Economics* 1, no. 1:129–62.

———. 2015. "Four Types of Ignorance." *Journal of Monetary Economics* 69, C: 97–113.

Harberger, Arnold C., and Sebastian Edwards. 2021. "The Department of Economics at the University of Chicago, 1947–1982." Draft manuscript. Forthcoming in Robert A. Cord, ed., *The Palgrave Companion to Chicago Economics*. London: Palgrave Macmillan.

Hardy, Charles O. 1940. *Wartime Control of Prices*. Washington, DC: Brookings Institution.

———. 1948. "Liberalism in the Modern State: The Philosophy of Henry Simons." *Journal of Political Economy* 56, no. 4 (August): 305–14.

Hardy, Charles O., and Garfield V. Cox. 1928. *Forecasting Business Conditions*. New York: Macmillan.

Harris Foundation. 1931. *Unemployment as a World Problem*. Chicago: University of Chicago Press.

———. 1932. *Gold and Monetary Stabilization*, edited by Quincy Wright. Chicago: University Chicago Press.

Harris, Seymour E. 1951a. "The Controversy over Monetary Policy: Introductory Remarks." *Review of Economics and Statistics* 33, no. 3 (August): 179–84.

———. 1951b. "Summary and Comments." *Review of Economics and Statistics* 33, no. 3 (August): 198–200.

Harrod, Roy F. 1927. "Book Review: *Wealth, Virtual Wealth and Debt*, by Frederick Soddy." *Economic Journal* 37, no. 146:271–73.

———. 1934. "Doctrines of Imperfect Competition." *Quarterly Journal of Economics* 48, no. 3:442–70.

Hart, Albert G. 1935. "The 'Chicago Plan' of Banking Reform: A Proposal for Making Monetary Management Effective in the United States." *Review of Economic Studies* 2, no. 2 (February): 104–16.

———. 1945. "Postwar Effects to be Expected from Wartime Liquid Accumulations." *American Economic Review* 35, no. 2 (Papers and Proceedings of the Fifty-Seventh Annual Meeting of the American Economic Association): 341–51.

Hawtrey, Ralph G. 1913. *Good and Bad Trade: An Inquiry into the Causes of Trade Fluctuations*. London: Constable.

———. 1919. *Currency and Credit*. London: Longmans, Green.

———. 1938. *A Century of Bank Rate*. London: Longmans, Green.

Hayek, Friedrich A. 1960. *The Constitution of Liberty*. Chicago: University of Chicago Press.

Heckman, James. 2012. "The Power of Ideas: Milton Friedman's Empirical Methodology." Revised unpublished notes to a talk delivered at the conference "Milton Friedman and the Power of Ideas: Celebrating the Friedman Centennial," Becker Friedman Institute, Chicago, November 12.

Heflebower, Richard B. 1953. "Review of *Defense, Controls and Inflation*, by Aaron Director." *American Economic Review* 43, no. 3 (June): 456–59.

Hendry, David F., and Neil R. Ericsson. 1991. "An Econometric Analysis of UK Money Demand in *Monetary Trends in the United States and the United Kingdom* by Milton Friedman and Anna Schwartz." *American Economic Review* 81, no. 1:8–38.

Hettich, Walter. 1979. "Henry Simons on Taxation and the Economic System." *National Tax Journal* 32, no. 1 (March): 1–9.

Hetzel, Robert L. 1985. "The Rules versus Discretion Debate over Monetary Policy in the 1920s." *Federal Reserve Bank of Richmond Economic Review* 71 (November/December): 3–14.

———. 2007. "The Contributions of Milton Friedman to Economics." *Federal Reserve Bank of Richmond Economic Quarterly* 93, no. 1 (Winter): 1–30.

———. 2013. "Friedman, Milton." In Thomas Cate, ed., *An Encyclopedia of Keynesian Economics*. 2nd ed. Cheltenham, UK: Edward Elgar. 200–203.

Hetzel, Robert L., and Ralph F. Leach. 2001a. "The Treasury-Fed Accord: A New Narrative Account." *Federal Reserve Bank of Richmond Economic Quarterly* 87, no. 1 (Winter): 33–55.

——. 2001b. "After the Accord: Reminiscences on the Birth of the Modern Fed." *Federal Reserve Bank of Richmond Economic Quarterly* 87, no. 1 (Winter): 57–64.

Hirsch, Abraham, and Neil de Marchi. 1990. *Milton Friedman: Economics in Theory and Practice*. Ann Arbor: University of Michigan Press.

History of Economic Thought. 2021. "Seymour Edwin Harris, 1897–1975." Last modified February 23, 2021. https://www.hetwebsite.net/het/profiles/seharris.htm.

Hoover, Herbert C. 1932. *Message of the President: Budget, Fiscal Year Ending June 30, 1934* (December 5). Washington, DC: United States Government.

Hoover, Kevin D. 1984. "Two Types of Monetarism." *Journal of Economic Literature* 22, no. 1 (March): 58–76.

——. 1988. *The New Classical Macroeconomics: A Sceptical Inquiry*. Oxford, UK: Basil Blackwell.

——. 2009. "Milton Friedman's Stance: The Methodology of Causal Realism." In Uskali Maki, ed., *The Methodology of Positive Economics: Reflections on the Milton Friedman Legacy*. Cambridge: Cambridge University Press. 303–20.

Horsefield, J. K. 1946. "Review of *A History of Banking Theory*, by Lloyd W. Mints." *Economica* 13, no. 50 (May): 138–40.

Howitt, Peter. 1992. "Fisher Effect." In Peter Newman, Murray Milgate, and John Eatwell, eds., *The New Palgrave: Dictionary of Money and Finance*. Vol. 2. London: Macmillan. 123–24.

Howson, Susan. 2005. "Keynes, Chicago, and Friedman." *History of Political Economy* 37, no. 2 (Summer): 386–91.

Hume, David. 1752. "Of the Balance of Trade." First published in *Political Discourses* (London). Reprinted in David Hume, ed., *Essays: Moral, Political and Literary*. London: Oxford University Press, 1963.

Humphrey, Thomas M. 1971. "Role of Non-Chicago Economists in the Evolution of the Quantity Theory in America 1930–1950." *Southern Economic Journal* 38, no. 1 (July): 12–18.

——. 1973. "On the Monetary Economics of Chicagoans and Non-Chicagoans: Reply." *Southern Economic Journal* 39, no. 3 (January): 460–63.

——. 1974. "The Quantity Theory of Money: Its Historical Evolution and Role in Policy Debates." *Federal Reserve Bank of Richmond Economic Review* 60 (May): 2–19. Reprinted in Thomas Humphrey, ed., *Essays on Inflation*. 3rd ed. Richmond, VA: Federal Reserve Bank of Richmond, 1982. 1–18.

——. 1976. "On Cost-Push Theories of Inflation in the Pre-war Monetary Literature." *Banca Nazional del Lavoro Quarterly Review*, no. 118 (March): 77–89. Reprinted in *Federal Reserve Bank of Richmond Economic Review* (May/June 1977): 3–9.

——. 1979. "The Interest Cost-Push Controversy." *Federal Reserve Bank of Richmond Economic Review* (January/February): 3–10.

——. 1981. "Adam Smith and the Monetary Approach to the Balance of Payments." *Federal Reserve Bank of Richmond Economic Review* 67, no. 6 (November/December): 3–10.

———. 1982. "The Real-Bills Doctrine." *Federal Reserve Bank of Richmond Economic Review* 68, no. 5 (September/October): 3–13.

———. 1984. "On Nonneutral Relative Price Effects in Monetarist Thought: Some Austrian Misconceptions." *Federal Reserve Bank of Richmond Economic Review* 70, no. 3 (May/June):13–19.

———. 1987. "The Theory of Multiple Expansion of Deposits: What It Is and Whence It Came." *Federal Reserve Bank of Richmond Economic Review* 73, no. 2 (March/April): 3–11.

———. 1988a. "The Trade Theorist's Sacred Diagram: Its Origin and Early Development." *Federal Reserve Bank of Richmond Economic Review* 74, no. 1 (January/February): 3–15.

———. 1988b. "Rival Notions of Money." *Federal Reserve Bank of Richmond Economic Review* 74, no. 5 (September/October): 3–9.

———. 1990. "Fisherian and Wicksellian Price-Stabilization Models in the History of Monetary Thought." *Federal Reserve Bank of Richmond Economic Review* 76, no. 3 (May/June): 3–19.

———. 2013. "Chicago School of Economics." In Thomas Cate, ed., *An Encyclopedia of Keynesian Economics*. 2nd ed. Cheltenham, UK: Edward Elgar. 94–98.

Humphrey, Thomas M., and Richard H. Timberlake. 2019. *Gold, the Real Bills Doctrine, and the Fed: Sources of Monetary Disorder 1922–1938*. Washington, DC: Cato Institute.

Irwin, Douglas A. 2012. *Trade Policy Disaster: Lessons from the 1930s*. Cambridge, MA: MIT Press.

———. 2016. "Friedman and Viner." In Robert A. Cord and J. Daniel Hammond, eds., *Milton Friedman: Contributions to Economics and Public Policy*. Oxford: Oxford University Press. 757–73.

———. 2018. "The Midway and Beyond: Recent Work on Economics at Chicago." *History of Political Economy* 50, no. 4 (December): 735–75.

Johnson, Harry G. 1951. "Book Review: *Monetary Policy for a Competitive Society*, by Lloyd W. Mints." *Economic Journal* 61, no. 242:382–84.

———. 1969. "The Case for Flexible Exchange Rates, 1969." *Federal Reserve Bank of St. Louis Review* 51 (June): 12–24.

———. 1970. "Recent Developments in Monetary Theory—A Commentary." In D. R. Croome and H. G. Johnson, eds., *Money in Britain 1959–1969*. London: Oxford University Press. 83–114.

———. 1971. "The Keynesian Revolution and the Monetarist Counter-Revolution." *American Economic Review* 61, no. 2 (Papers and Proceedings of the Eighty-Third Annual Meeting of the American Economic Association) (May): 1–14.

———. 1972. *Inflation and the Monetarist Controversy*. Amsterdam: North Holland.

———. 1978. "Keynes and British Economics." In Elizabeth S. Johnson and Harry G. Johnson, eds., *The Shadow of Keynes: Understanding Keynes, Cambridge and Keynesian Economics*. Oxford: Basil Blackwell. 203–20.

Joint Committee on the Economic Report. 1952. *Monetary Policy and the Management of the Public Debt: Their Role in Achieving Price Stability and High-Level Employment*. Vol. 2. Washington, DC: US Government Printing Office.

Joint Economic Committee. 1959a. *Employment, Growth, and Price Levels*. Hearings before the Joint Economic Committee, Congress of the United States, 86th Cong., 1st sess. Pt. 4—the Influence on Prices of Changes in the Effective Supply of Money. Washington, DC: US Government Printing Office.

———. 1959b. *Employment, Growth, and Price Levels*. Hearings before the Joint Economic Committee, Congress of the United States, 86th Cong., 1st sess. Pt. 9A—Constructive Suggestions for Reconciling and Simultaneously Obtaining the Three Objectives of Maximum Employment, and Adequate Rate of Growth, and Substantial Stability of the Price Level. Washington, DC: US Government Printing Office.

Joplin, Thomas. 1823. *Outlines of a System of Political Economy . . . to Suggest a Plan for the Management of the Currency*. London: Baldwin, Cradock, and Joy.

Kaldor, Nicholas. 1937. "Annual Survey of Economic Theory: The Recent Controversy on the Theory of Capital." *Econometrica* 5, no. 3:201–33.

Kalecki, Michal. 1941. "General Rationing." *Oxford Institute of Statistics* 3, no. 1: 1–6.

———. 1946. "A Comment on 'Monetary Policy.'" *Review of Economics and Statistics* 28, no. 2 (May): 81–84.

Kasper, Sherryl D. 1993. "Frank Knight's Case for Laissez Faire: The Patrimony of the Social Philosophy of the Chicago School." *History of Political Economy* 25, no. 3 (Fall): 413–33.

Kelton, Stephanie. 2020. *The Deficit Myth: Modern Monetary Theory and the Birth of the People's Economy*. New York: Public Affairs.

Kemmerer, Edwin W. 1938. *The ABC of the Federal Reserve System: Why the Federal Reserve System Was Called into Being, the Main Features of Its Organization, and How It Works*. 11th revised ed. Princeton, NJ: Princeton University Press.

Kenen, Peter B. 1969. "The Theory of Optimum Currency Areas: An Eclectic View." In Robert A. Mundell and Alexander K. Swoboda, eds., *Monetary Problems of the International Economy*. Chicago: University of Chicago Press. 41–60.

Keynes, John M. 1911. "Review of *The Purchasing Power of Money: In Its Determination and Relation to Credit, Interest, and Crisis*, by Irving Fisher." *Economic Journal* 21, no. 83 (September): 393–98.

———. 1930. *A Treatise on Money*. 2 vols. London: Macmillan.

———. 1931. "An Economic Analysis of Unemployment." In Quincy Wright, ed., *Unemployment as a World-Problem*. Chicago: University of Chicago Press.

———. 1936a. *The General Theory of Employment, Interest and Money*. New York: Harcourt, Brace.

———. 1936b. *Allgemeine Theorie des Beschaftigung, des Zinses und des Geldes*. Berlin: Duncker and Humblot.

———. 1939. "Democracy and Efficiency." *New Statesman and the Nation*, August 11, 121–23.

———. 1940. *How to Pay for the War: A Radical Plan for the Chancellor of the Exchequer*. London: Macmillan.

———. 1943. "Proposals for an International Clearing Union." British Government Publication British White Paper Cmd. 6437.

Kindleberger, Charles P. 1950. *The Dollar Shortage*. Cambridge, MA: MIT Press.

———. 1953. *International Economics*. Homewood, IL: Richard D. Irwin.

Kitch, Edmund W. 1983. "The Fire of Truth: A Remembrance of Law and Economics at Chicago, 1932–1970." *Journal of Law and Economics* 26, no. 1 (April): 163–234.

Klein, John J. 1956. "German Money and Prices, 1932–44." In Milton Friedman, ed., *Studies in the Quantity Theory of Money*. Chicago: University of Chicago Press. 121–62.

Klein, Lawrence R. 1947. *The Keynesian Revolution*. New York: Macmillan.

Knight, Frank H. 1921. *Risk, Uncertainty and Profit*. Boston: Houghton Mifflin.

———. 1923. "The Ethics of Competition." *Quarterly Journal of Economics* 37, no. 4 (August): 579–624. Reprinted in Frank H. Knight, *The Ethics of Competition, and Other Essays*. New York: Harper and Brothers, 1935. 41–75.

———. 1924. "Some Fallacies in the Interpretation of Social Cost." *Quarterly Journal of Economics* 38, no. 4 (August): 582–606.

———. 1927a. "Interest Theory and Price Movements—Discussion." *American Economic Review* 17, no. 1 (Supplement, Papers and Proceedings of the Thirty-Ninth Annual Meeting of the American Economic Association) (March): 106–22.

———. 1927b. "Book Review: *Wealth, Virtual Wealth and Debt*, by Frederick Soddy." *Saturday Review of Literature* 16 (April): 732.

———. 1927c. "The Use of the Quantitative Method in the Study of Economic Theory: Round Table" (chaired by Holbrook Working). *American Economic Review* 17, no. 1 (Supplement, Papers and Proceedings of the Thirty-Ninth Annual Meeting of the American Economic Association) (March): 18–24.

———. 1932a. "The Newer Economics and the Control of Economic Activity." *Journal of Political Economy* 40, no. 4 (August): 433–76.

———. 1932b. "Comment on Mr. Slichter's Comment and on the Issues." *Journal of Political Economy* 40, no. 6 (December): 820–25.

———. 1933a. "Can We Vote Ourselves Out of the Fix We Are In?" *Christian Century*, April, 151–54.

———. 1933b. "Book Review: *Economic Stabilization in an Unbalanced World*, by Alvin Hansen." *Journal of Political Economy* 41, no. 2 (April): 242–45.

———. 1934a. "Capital, Time and the Interest Rate." *Economica*, n.s., 1, no. 3 (August): 257–86.

———. 1934b. "Social Science and the Political Trend." *University of Toronto Quarterly* 3, no. 4 (July): 407–27.

————. 1935a. "Professor Hayek and the Theory of Investment." *Economic Journal* 45, no. 177 (March): 77–94.

————. 1935b. *The Ethics of Competition, and Other Essays.* New York: Harper and Brothers.

————. 1936a. "The Quantity of Capital and the Rate of Interest. I." *Journal of Political Economy* 44, no. 4 (August): 433–63.

————. 1936b. "The Quantity of Capital and the Rate of Interest. II." *Journal of Political Economy* 44, no. 5 (October): 612–42.

————. 1936c. "Business Cycles: Lecture Notes." Frank H. Knight Papers, Special Collections Research Center, Joseph Regenstein Library, University of Chicago. Reprinted in Carlo Cristiano and Luca Fiorito, "Two Minds that Never Met: Frank H. Knight on John M. Keynes Once Again—a Documentary Note." *Review of Keynesian Economics* 4, no. 1 (2016): 67–98.

————. 1937. "Unemployment: And Mr. Keynes's Revolution in Economic Theory." *Canadian Journal of Economics and Political Science* 3, no. 1 (February): 100–23.

————. 1941a. "The Business Cycle, Interest, and Money: A Methodological Approach." *Review of Economics and Statistics* 23, no. 2 (May): 53–67. Reprinted in Frank H. Knight, ed., *On the History and Method of Economics.* Chicago: University of Chicago Press, 1956. 202–26.

————. 1941b. "The Meaning of Freedom." *Ethics* 52, no. 1 (October): 86–109.

————. 1951. "The Role of Principles in Economics and Politics." *American Economic Review* 41, no. 1 (March): 1–29. Reprinted in Frank H. Knight, ed., *On the History and Method of Economics.* Chicago: University of Chicago Press, 1956. 251–81.

————. 1956. *On the History and Method of Economics.* Chicago: University of Chicago Press.

Knight, Frank H., G. V. Cox, Aaron Director, Paul Douglas, A. G. Hart, L. W. Mints, Henry Schultz, and Henry C. Simons. 1933a. Untitled memorandum. March 15.

————. 1933b. Untitled memorandum. March 16.

————. 1933c. Untitled memorandum. April.

Knox, F. A. 1945. "Book Review: *International Currency Experience: Lessons of the Inter-war Period,* by Ragnar Nurkse." *Canadian Journal of Economics and Political Science / Revue canadienne d'economique et de science politique* 11, no. 2:294–96.

Kuznets, Simon. 1946. *National Product since 1869.* New York: National Bureau of Economic Research.

Kynaston, David. 2017. *Till Time's Last Sand: A History of the Bank of England 1694–2013.* London: Bloomsbury.

Laidler, David E. W. 1966. "The Rate of Interest and the Demand for Money—Some Empirical Evidence." *Journal of Political Economy* 74, no. 6 (December): 543–55.

———. 1969. *The Demand for Money: Theories and Evidence*. Scranton, PA: International Textbook.

———. 1972. "Thomas Tooke on Monetary Reform." In Maurice Peston and Bernard Corry, eds., *Essays in Honour of Lord Robbins*. London: Weidenfeld and Nicolson. 163–85. Reprinted in David E. W. Laidler, *Essays on Money and Inflation*. Manchester: Manchester University Press, 1975. 211–22.

———. 1973. "Book Review: *Studies in Monetary Economics*, edited by D. Patinkin." *Economic Journal* 83, no. 329:262–64.

———. 1981. "Adam Smith as a Monetary Economist." *Canadian Journal of Economics* 14, no. 2 (May): 185–200.

———. 1984. "Misconceptions about the Real-Bills Doctrine: A Comment on Sargent and Wallace." *Journal of Political Economy* 92, no. 1 (February): 149–55.

———. 1991. *The Golden Age of the Quantity Theory: The Development of Neoclassical Monetary Economics 1870–1914*. New York: Harvester Wheatsheaf.

———. 1992. "Bullionist Controversy." In Peter Newman, Murray Milgate, and John Eatwell, eds., *The New Palgrave: Dictionary of Money and Finance*. Vol. 1. London: Macmillan. 255–61.

———. 1993. "Hawtrey, Harvard, and the Origins of the Chicago Tradition." *Journal of Political Economy* 101, no. 6 (December): 1068–103.

———. 1998a. "More on Hawtrey, Harvard and Chicago." *Journal of Economic Studies* 25, no. 1 (February): 4–21.

———. 1998b. "Hawtrey, Harvard and Chicago: A Final Comment." *Journal of Economic Studies* 25, no. 1 (February): 22–24.

———. 1999. *Fabricating the Keynesian Revolution: Studies of the Inter-war Literature on Money, the Cycle, and Unemployment*. Cambridge: Cambridge University Press.

———. 2000. "Highlights of the Bullionist Controversy." Department of Economics Research Reports 2. London, ON: University of Western Ontario.

———. 2002. "Rules, Discretion, and Financial Crises in Classical and Neoclassical Economics." *Economic Issues* 7, no. 2 (September): 11–34.

———. 2009. "Book Review: *The Chicago School: How the University of Chicago Assembled Thinkers Who Revolutionized Economics and Business*, by Johan Van Overtveldt." *History of Political Economy* 41, no. 2:411–14.

———. 2010. "Chicago Monetary Traditions." In Ross B. Emmett, ed., *The Elgar Companion to the Chicago School of Economics*. London: Edward Elgar. 70–80.

———. 2013. "Professor Fisher and the Quantity Theory—a Significant Encounter." *European Journal of the History of Economic Thought* 20, no. 2 (April): 174–205.

Laidler, David E. W., and Roger Sandilands. 2000. "An Early Harvard Memorandum on Anti-depression Policies—an Introductory Note." University of Western Ontario, Departmental Research Report Series 20004, Department of Economics.

———. 2002a. "An Early Harvard Memorandum on Anti-depression Policies: An Introductory Note." *History of Political Economy* 34, no. 3 (Fall): 515–32.

———. 2002b. "Memorandum Prepared by L. B. Currie, P. T. Ellsworth, and H. D. White (Cambridge, Mass., January 1932)." *History of Political Economy* 34, no. 3 (Fall): 533–52.

Laughlin, James L. 1903. *Principles of Money*. New York: Charles Scribner's Sons.

Layman, Richard, ed. 1994. *American Decades: 1950–1959*. Detroit: Gale Research.

Lee, Joong-Koon, and Donald C. Wellington. 1984. "Angell and the Stable Money Rule." *Journal of Political Economy* 92, no. 5 (October): 972–78.

Leeson, Robert. 1998. "The Early Patinkin-Friedman Correspondence." *Journal of the History of Economic Thought* 20, no. 4 (June): 433–48.

———. 2000. "Patinkin, Johnson, and the Shadow of Friedman." *History of Political Economy* 32, no. 4 (Winter): 733–64.

———. 2003a. "The Initial Controversy." In Robert Leeson, ed., *Keynes, Chicago and Friedman*. Vol. 1. London: Pickering and Chatto. 1–30.

———. 2003b. "The Debate Widens: Introduction." In Robert Leeson, ed., *Keynes, Chicago and Friedman*. Vol. 1. London: Pickering and Chatto. 283–309.

———. 2003c. "Toward a Resolution of the Dispute: Introduction." In Robert Leeson, ed., *Keynes, Chicago and Friedman*. Vol. 2. London: Pickering and Chatto. 293–314.

———. 2003d. "From Keynes to Friedman via Mints: A Resolution of the Dispute." In Robert Leeson, ed., *Keynes, Chicago and Friedman*. Vol. 2. London: Pickering and Chatto. 481–525.

———, ed. 2003e. *Keynes, Chicago and Friedman*. 2 vols. London: Pickering and Chatto.

Leontief, Wassily W. 1936. "The Fundamental Assumption of Mr. Keynes' Monetary Theory of Unemployment." *Quarterly Journal of Economics* 51, no. 1 (November): 192–97.

Lerner, Abba P. 1944. *The Economics of Control: Principles of Welfare Economics*. New York: Macmillan.

———. 1946. "Monetary Policy and Fiscal Policy." *Review of Economics and Statistics* 28, no. 2:77–81.

———. 1951. "Fighting Inflation." *Review of Economics and Statistics* 33, no. 3, 194–96.

Lerner, Eugene M. 1956. "Inflation in the Confederacy, 1861–65." In Milton Friedman, ed., *Studies in the Quantity Theory of Money*. Chicago: University of Chicago Press. 163–78.

Levi, Edward H. 1966. "Aaron Director and the Study of Law and Economics." *Journal of Law and Economics* 9 (October): 3–4.

Lewis, Gregg. 1946. "Henry Calvert Simons." *American Economic Review* 36, no. 4 (September): 668–69.

Lindblom, Charles E. 1949. *Unions and Capitalism*. New Haven, CT: Yale University Press.

Lipkes, Jeff. 2019. "'Capitalism and the Jews': Milton Friedman and His Critics." *History of Political Economy* 51, no. 2 (April): 193–236.

Loef, Hans-E., and Hans G. Monissen. 1999. "Irving Fisher's Contributions to Monetary Macroeconomics." In Hans-E. Loef and Hans G. Monissen, eds., *The Economics of Irving Fisher: Reviewing the Scientific Work of a Great Economist*. Cheltenham, UK: Edward Elgar. 81–108.

*London Times, Times Literary Supplement*. 1926. "Book Review: Wealth, Virtual Wealth and Debt, by Frederick Soddy." August 26.

Lothian, James R. 2009. "Milton Friedman's Monetary Economics and the Quantity-Theory Tradition." *Journal of International Money and Finance* 28, no. 7 (November): 1086–96.

Lothian, James R., and George S. Tavlas. 2018. "How Friedman and Schwartz Became Monetarists." *Journal of Money, Credit and Banking* 50, no. 4 (June): 757–87.

Loyd, Samuel J. 1837. *Reflections Suggested by a Perusal of Mr. J. Horsley Palmer's Pamphlet: On the Causes and Consequences of the Pressure on the Money Market*. London: Palhan Richardson.

Lucas, Robert E., Jr. 1984. "Conversations with New Classical Economists." In A. Klamer, ed., *Conversations with Economists*. Totowa, NJ: Rowman and Allanheld. 29–57.

———. 2016. "Milton Friedman as Teacher and Scholar." In Robert A. Cord and J. Daniel Hammond, eds., *Milton Friedman: Contributions to Economics and Public Policy*. Oxford: Oxford University Press. 7–17.

———. 2017. "Memories of Friedman and Patinkin." *Journal of Political Economy* 125, no. 6:1831–34.

Lutz, Friedrich A., and Lloyd Mints, eds., on behalf of the American Economic Association. 1951. *Readings in Monetary Theory*. New York: Blakiston.

Marshall, Alfred. (1890) 1920. *Principles of Economics*. 8th ed. London: Macmillan. Variorum (9th) ed., edited by C. W. Guillebaud, published by Macmillan for the Royal Economic Society, 1961.

Martin, George R. 1983. *Thread of Excellence*. Chicago: Martin Hughes.

Mattei, Clara E. 2018. "Hawtrey, Austerity, and the 'Treasury View,' 1918 to 1925." *Journal of the History of Economic Thought* 40, no. 4 (December): 471–92.

Mayer, Thomas. 1975. "The Structure of Monetarism," parts 1 and 2. *Kredit und Kapital* 8, no. 2/3:190–218 and 293–316. Reprinted in Thomas Mayer, ed., *The Structure of Monetarism*. New York: W. W. Norton, 1978. 1–46.

Mayer, Thomas, and Patrick Minford. 2004. "Monetarism." *World Economics* 5, no. 2 (April): 147–85.

McCallum, Bennett. 2016 "The Place of Milton Friedman in the History of Economic Thought." In Robert A. Cord and J. Daniel Hammond, eds., *Milton Friedman: Contributions to Economics and Public Policy*. Oxford: Oxford University Press, 49–71.

McCallum, Bennett, and Edward Nelson. 2005. "Targeting versus Instrument Rules for Monetary Policy." *Federal Reserve Bank of St. Louis Review* 87, no. 5 (September/October): 597–611.

McCowen, Henry. 1934. *Moneyless Government*. Los Angeles: Wetzel.

McDonald, John. 1950. "The Economists." *Fortune*, December, 109–13, 126, 128, 131–32, 134–35, 136, 138.

McIvor, Graig R. 1983. "A Note on the University of Chicago's 'Academic Scribblers.'" *Journal of Political Economy* 91, no. 5 (October): 888–93.

McNeill, William H. 1991. *Hutchins' University: A Memoir of the University of Chicago, 1929–1950*. Chicago: University of Chicago Press.

Mehrling, Perry G. 1996. "The Monetary Thought of Allyn Abbott Young." *History of Political Economy* 28, no. 4 (Winter): 607–32.

Meigs, James A. 1972. *Money Matters: Economics, Markets, Politics*. New York: Harper and Row.

Meltzer, Allan H. 1977. "Monetarist, Keynesian and Quantity Theories." *Kredit und Kapital* 10, no. 2 (June): 149–82. Reprinted in Thomas Mayer, ed., *The Structure of Monetarism*. New York: W. W. Norton, 1978. 145–75.

———. 1998. "Monetarism: The Issues and the Outcome." *Atlantic Economic Journal* 26 (March): 8–31.

———. 2003. *A History of the Federal Reserve, Volume 1: 1913–1951*. Chicago: University of Chicago Press.

———. 2009. *A History of the Federal Reserve, Volume 2, Book 1: 1951–1969*. Chicago: University of Chicago Press.

Miller, H. Laurence, Jr. 1962. "On the 'Chicago School of Economics.'" *Journal of Political Economy* 70, no. 1 (February): 64–69.

Minsky, Hyman P. 1975. *John Maynard Keynes*. New York: McGraw-Hill.

———. 1985. "Beginnings." *Banca Nazionale del Lavoro Quarterly Review* 38, no. 154:211–21.

Mints, Lloyd W. N.d. "The Work of Henry Simons." In Henry C. Simons Papers, Special Collections Research Center, Joseph Regenstein Library, University of Chicago.

———. 1923a. "Open Market Borrowing to Finance the Production of Goods Sold for Future Delivery." *Journal of Political Economy* 31, no. 1 (February): 128–38.

———. 1923b. "Expansion of Fixed and Working Capital by Open Market Borrowing." *Journal of Political Economy* 31, no. 2 (April): 299–302.

———. 1925. "Financing a Promotion by Selling Receivables." *University Journal of Business* 3, no. 2 (March): 198–202.

———. 1930. "The Elasticity of Bank Notes." *Journal of Political Economy* 38, no. 4 (August): 458–71.

———. 1940. "Book Review: *The ABC of the Federal Reserve System: Why the Federal Reserve System Was Called into Being, the Main Features of Its Organization, and How It Works*, by Edwin W. Kemmerer." *Journal of Political Economy* 48, no. 4 (August): 602.

———. 1945a. *A History of Banking Theory in Great Britain and the United States.* Chicago: University of Chicago Press.

———. 1945b. "Book Review: *International Currency Experience: Lessons of the Inter-war Period*, by Ragnar Nurkse." *American Economic Review* 35, no. 1 (March): 192–95.

———. 1946. "Monetary Policy." *Review of Economic Statistics* 28, no. 2 (May): 60–69.

———. 1950. *Monetary Policy for a Competitive Society.* New York: McGraw-Hill.

———. 1951a. "The Role of Monetary Policy in Mobilization." Paper presented for the University of Chicago Law School Conference on the Economics of Mobilization. Located in box 56, Frank H. Knight, Papers, Special Collections Research Center, Joseph Regenstein Library, University of Chicago.

———. 1951b. "Monetary Policy and Stabilization." *American Economic Review* 41, no. 2 (Papers and Proceedings of the Sixty-Third Annual Meeting of the American Economic Association) (May): 188–93.

———. 1953. "Monetary Policy: Discussion." *American Economic Review* 43, no. 2 (Papers and Proceedings of the Sixty-Fifth Annual Meeting of the American Economic Association) (May): 54–56.

Mishkin, Frederic S. 2018. "Improving the Use of Discretion in Monetary Policy." *International Finance* 21, no. 3 (December): 224–38.

Mitch, David. 2016. "A Year of Transition: Faculty Recruiting at Chicago in 1946." *Journal of Political Economy* 124, no. 6 (December): 1714–34.

Mitchell, Wesley C. 1927. *Business Cycles: The Problem and Its Setting.* New York: National Bureau of Economic Research.

Moggridge, Donald E. 1992. *Maynard Keynes: An Economist's Biography.* London: Routledge.

———. 2008. *Harry Johnson: A Life in Economics.* New York: Cambridge University Press.

Moggridge, Donald, and Susan Howson. 1974. "Keynes on Monetary Policy, 1910–1946." *Oxford Economic Papers* 26, no. 2 (July): 226–47.

Morgan, Victor E. 1946. "Book Review: *A History of Banking Theory in Great Britain and the United States*, by Lloyd W. Mints." *Economic Journal* 56, no. 222 (June): 290–92.

Morgan-Webb, Charles. 1934. *The Money Revolution.* Introduction by Frank A. Vanderlip. New York: Economic Forum.

Mundell, Robert A. 1961. "A Theory of Optimum Currency Areas." *American Economic Review* 51, no. 4 (September): 657–65.

Musgrave, Richard M. 1987. "Hansen, Alvin (1887–1975)." In John Eatwell, Murray Milgate, and Peter Newman, eds., *The New Palgrave: A Dictionary of Economics.* Vol. 2. London: Macmillan. 591–92.

NBC. 1946. *What Can Be Done about Inflation?* University of Chicago Radio Round Table 420, April 7.

Nelson, Edward. 2004. "An Interview with Anna J. Schwartz." *Macroeconomic Dynamics* 8, no. 3 (June): 395–417.

———. 2007. "Milton Friedman and US Monetary History: 1961–2006." *Federal Reserve Bank of St. Louis Review* 89, no. 3 (May/June): 153–82.

———. 2020. *Milton Friedman and Economic Debate in the United States, 1932–1972.* 2 vols. Chicago: University of Chicago Press.

Nerozzi, Sebastiano. 2009. "Jacob Viner and the Chicago Monetary Tradition." *History of Political Economy* 41, no. 3 (Fall): 575–604.

Newman, Peter. 1954. "Book Review: *Essays in Positive Economics*, edited by Milton Friedman." *Economica* 21, no. 83:259–60.

*New York Times.* 1932. "Economists Advise Credit 'Expansion': Deflation Has Gone Far Enough Says Advisory Board in Offering Recovery Program." January 16, 30.

Nichols, Jeannette P. 1945. "Book Review: *International Currency Experience: Lessons of the Inter-war Period*, by Ragnar Nurkse." *Journal of Economic History* 5, no. 2 (November): 255–56.

Niehans, Jurg. 1987. "Lutz, Friedrich August (1901–1975)." In John Eatwell, Murray Milgate, and Peter Newman, eds., *The New Palgrave: A Dictionary of Economics.* Vol. 3. London: Macmillan. 252–53.

Nobay, A. Robert, and Harry G. Johnson. 1977. "Monetarism: A Historic-Theoretic Perspective." *Journal of Economic Literature* 15, no. 2 (June): 470–85.

Nurkse, Ragnar. 1944. *International Currency Experience: Lessons of the Inter-war Period.* Princeton, NJ: Princeton University Press.

———. 1945. *Conditions of International Monetary Equilibrium.* Essays in International Finance 4. Princeton, NJ: Princeton University Press.

Nutter, Warren G. 1951. *The Extent of Enterprise Monopoly in the United States, 1899–1939: A Quantitative Study of Some Aspects of Monopoly.* Chicago: University of Chicago Press.

O'Brien, Denis P. 1975. *The Classical Economists.* Oxford: Clarendon.

———. 1992. "Currency Principle." In Peter Newman, Murray Milgate, and John Eatwell, eds., *The New Palgrave: Dictionary of Money and Finance.* Vol. 1. London: Macmillan. 564–65.

———. 1998. "Monetary Base Control and the Bank Charter Act of 1844." *History of Political Economy* 29, no. 4 (November): 593–633.

———. 2007. *The Development of Monetary Economics: A Modern Perspective on Monetary Controversies.* Cheltenham, UK: Edward Elgar.

Obstfeld, Maurice. 2020. "Harry Johnson's 'Case for Flexible Exchange Rates'—50 Years Later." *Manchester School* 88 (July): 86–113.

Oliver, Henry M. 1954. "Book Review: *Essays in Positive Economics*, by Milton Friedman." *Ethics* 65, no. 1 (October): 71–72.

Orphanides, Athanasios. 2003a. "The Quest for Prosperity without Inflation." *Journal of Monetary Economics* 50, no. 3 (April): 633–63.

———. 2003b. "Historical Monetary Policy Analysis and the Taylor Rule." *Journal of Monetary Economics* 50, no. 5 (July): 983–1022.

———. 2015. "Fear of Liftoff: Uncertainty, Rules, and Discretion in Monetary Policy Normalization." *Federal Reserve Bank of St. Louis Review* 97, no. 3, 173–96.

Orphanides, Athanasios, and John C. Williams. 2002. "Robust Monetary Policy with Unknown Natural Rates." *Brookings Papers and Economic Activity* 33, no. 2:63–118.

Oxford Institute of Statistics. 1944. *The Economics of Full Employment.* Oxford: Basil Blackwell.

Palmer, Horsley J. 1832. *Report of the Bank of England Charter.* London: Bank of England.

Parkin, Michael. 1986. "Book Review: *Essays On and In the Chicago Tradition*, by Don Patinkin." *Journal of Money, Credit and Banking* 18, no. 1 (February): 104–16.

Parliamentary Committee on Banks of Issue. 1840. *Report from the Select Committee on Banks of Issue.* London: Parliament, House of Commons.

Patinkin, Don. 1948. "Price Flexibility and Full Employment." *American Economic Review* 38, no. 4 (September): 543–64. Reprinted in F. A. Lutz and L. W. Mints, eds., *Readings in Monetary Theory.* New York: Blakiston, 1952. 252–83.

———. 1956. *Money, Interest, and Prices.* New York: Harper and Row.

———. 1965. *Money, Interest, and Prices.* 2nd ed. New York: Harper and Row.

———. 1969. "The Chicago Tradition, the Quantity Theory, and Friedman." *Journal of Money, Credit and Banking* 1, no. 1 (February): 46–70. Reprinted with minor modifications and additions in Don Patinkin, ed., *Essays On and In the Chicago Tradition.* Durham, NC: Duke University Press, 1981. 241–74.

———. 1972a. "Friedman on the Quantity Theory and Keynesian Economics." *Journal of Political Economy* 80, no. 5 (September/October): 883–905.

———. 1972b. "On the Short-Run Non-neutrality of Money in the Quantity Theory." *Banca Nazionale del Lavoro Quarterly Review* 25, no. 100 (March): 3–22.

———. 1972c. "Keynesian Monetary Theory and the Cambridge School." *Banca Nazionale del Lavoro Quarterly* 25, no. 101 (June): 38–58.

———. 1972d. *Studies in Monetary Economics.* New York: Harper and Row.

———. 1973a. "On the Monetary Economics of Chicagoans and Non-Chicagoans: Comment." *Southern Economic Journal* 39, no. 3 (January): 454–59. Reprinted in Robert Leeson, ed., *Keynes, Chicago and Friedman.* Vol. 1. London: Pickering and Chatto, 2003. 329–39.

———. 1973b. "Frank Knight as Teacher." *American Economic Review* 63, no. 5 (December): 787–810. Reprinted in Don Patinkin, ed., *Essays On and In the Chicago Tradition.* Durham, NC: Duke University Press. 23–51.

———. 1979. "Keynes and Chicago." *Journal of Law and Economics* 22, no. 2 (October): 213–32. Reprinted in Don Patinkin, ed., *Essays On and In the Chicago Tradition.* Durham, NC: Duke University Press, 1981. 289–308.

———. 1981a. "Introduction: Reminiscences of Chicago, 1941–1947." In Don Patinkin, ed., *Essays On and In the Chicago Tradition*. Durham, NC: Duke University Press. 3–20.

———. 1981b. *Essays On and In the Chicago Tradition*. Durham, NC: Duke University Press.

———. 1982. "Anticipations of the General Theory? Michal Kalecki." In Don Patinkin, ed., *Anticipation of the General Theory, and Other Essays on Keynes*. Chicago: University of Chicago Press. 58–78.

———. 1986. "*Essays On and In the Chicago Tradition* by Don Patinkin—a Review Essay: A Reply." *Journal of Money, Credit and Banking* 18, no. 1 (February): 116–21.

———. 1987. "Keynes, John Maynard." In John Eatwell, Murray Milgate, and Peter Newman, eds., *The New Palgrave: A Dictionary of Economics*. Vol. 3. London: Macmillan. 19–41.

———. 1989. *Money, Interest, and Prices: An Integration of Monetary and Value Theory*. 2nd ed., abridged with a new introduction. Cambridge, MA: MIT Press.

———. 1991. "The Chicago Tradition: A Comment." In Robert Leeson, ed., *Keynes, Chicago and Friedman*. Vol. 2. London: Pickering and Chatto. 379–81.

———. 1993. "Irving Fisher and His Compensated Dollar Plan." *Federal Reserve Bank of Richmond Economic Quarterly* 79, no. 3 (Summer): 1–34.

Peltzman, Sam. 2005. "Aaron Director's Influence on Antitrust Policy." *Journal of Law and Economics* 48, no. 2 (October): 313–30.

Peterson, Rodney D. 1980. Unpublished notes, visit with Lloyd Mints, March 20.

Peterson, Rodney D., and Ronnie J. Phillips. 1991. "In Memoriam: Lloyd W. Mints, 1888–1989; Pioneer Monetary Economist." *American Economist* 35, no. 1 (March): 79–81.

Pettengill Memorandum. 1932. "Payment of Adjusted-Compensation Certificates." Henry C. Simons Papers, Special Collections Research Center, Joseph Regenstein Library, University of Chicago.

Pettengill Memorandum: Draft. 1932. "Payment of Adjusted-Compensation Certificates." Hearings before the Committee on Ways and Means, House of Representatives, April. Washington, DC: United States Government.

Phillips, Chester A. 1920. *Bank Credit*. New York: Macmillan.

Phillips, Ronnie J. 1995. *The Chicago Plan and New Deal Banking Reform*. New York: M. E. Sharpe.

Pigou, Arthur Cecil. 1927. *Industrial Fluctuations*. London: Macmillan.

———. 1943. "The Classical Stationary State." *Economic Journal* 53, no. 212 (December): 343–51.

Pinzón-Fuchs, Erich. 2019. "Lawrence R. Klein and the Making of Large-Scale Macroeconometric Modeling, 1938–55." *History of Political Economy* 51, no. 3 (June): 401–23.

Reder, Melvin W. 1982. "Chicago Economics: Permanence and Change." *Journal of Economic Literature* 20, no. 1 (March): 1–38.

Reed, H. L. 1942. *Money, Currency and Banking*. New York: McGraw-Hill.

Rees, David. 1973. *Harry Dexter White: A Study in Paradox*. New York: Coward, McCann, and Geoghegan.

Reeve, Joseph E. 1943. *Monetary Reform Movements: A Survey of Recent Plans and Panaceas*. Washington, DC: American Council on Public Affairs.

Ricardo, David. 1810. *The High Price of Bullion, a Proof of the Depreciation of Bank Notes*. London: John Murray.

———. 1824. *Plan for the Establishment of a National Bank*. London: John Murray.

———. 1851. "Letters." In Piero Sraffa, ed., *The Works and Correspondence of David Ricardo*. Vol. 6. Cambridge: Cambridge University Press.

Richter, F. E. 1928. "Book Review: *Forecasting Business Conditions*, by Charles O. Hardy and Garfield V. Cox." *Journal of the American Statistical Association* 23, no. 163 (September): 339–42.

Ritter, Lawrence S., and William L. Silber. 1974. *Principles of Money, Banking, and Financial Markets*. New York: Basic Books.

Robbins, Lionel. 1958. *Robert Torrens and the Evolution of Classical Economics*. London: Macmillan.

———. 1970. *Jacob Viner, 1892–1970*. Princeton, NJ: Princeton University Press.

Robertson, Dennis H. 1936. "Some Notes on Mr. Keynes' General Theory of Employment." *Quarterly Journal of Economics* 51, no. 1 (November): 168–91.

———. 1951. "Book Review: *Monetary Policy for a Competitive Society*, by Lloyd W. Mints." *American Economic Review* 41, no. 3 (June): 465–69.

Robinson, Joan. 1933. *The Economics of Imperfect Competition*. New York: Macmillan.

———. 1972. *Economic Heresies*. London: Macmillan.

Rockoff, Hugh. 2010. "On the Origins of a Monetary History." In Ross B. Emmett, ed., *The Elgar Companion to the Chicago School of Economics*. Cheltenham, UK: Edward Elgar. 81–113.

———. 2015. "Henry Simons and the Quantity Theory of Money." Paper presented at the conference on the Legacy of Chicago Economics, Becker Friedman Institute, University of Chicago, October 5.

———. Forthcoming. "Milton Friedman on Bailouts." *Journal of Financial Stability*.

Romer, Christina D. 1992. "What Ended the Great Depression?" *Journal of Economic History* 52, no. 4 (December): 757–84.

Romer, Christina D., and David H. Romer. 1989. "Does Monetary Policy Matter? A New Test in the Spirit of Friedman and Schwartz." *NBER Macroeconomics Annual* 4, no. 1:121–84.

Rotwein, Eugene. 1983. "Jacob Viner and the Chicago Tradition." *History of Political Economy* 15, no. 2 (Summer): 265–80.

Rubin, Goulven. 2012. "Don Patinkin's PhD Dissertation as the Prehistory of Disequilibrium Theories." *History of Political Economy* 44, no. 2:235–76.

Salera, Virgil. 1945. "Book Review: *International Currency Experience: Lessons of the Inter-war Period*, by Ragnar Nurkse." *Journal of the American Statistical Association* 40, no. 229 (March): 129–30.

Samuelson, Paul A. 1946. "Lord Keynes and the General Theory." *Econometrica* 14, no. 3 (July): 187–200.

———. 1971. "Reflections on the Merits and Demerits of Monetarism." In James J. Diamond, ed., *Issues in Fiscal and Monetary Policy: The Eclectic Economist Views the Controversy.* Chicago: DePaul University. 7–21.

———. 1972. "Jacob Viner, 1892–1970." *Journal of Political Economy* 80, no. 1 (January/February): 5–11.

———. 1979. "Paul Douglas's Measurement of Production Functions and Marginal Productivities." *Journal of Political Economy* 87, no. 5 (October): 923–39.

———. 1991. "Jacob Viner (1892–1970)." In Edward Shils, ed., *Remembering the University of Chicago: Teachers, Scientists, and Scholars.* Chicago: University of Chicago Press. 533–47.

Sandilands, Roger. 1990. *The Life and Political Economy of Lauchlin Currie: New Dealer, Presidential Adviser, and Development Economist.* Durham, NC: Duke University Press.

Sargent, Thomas J. 1979. *Macroeconomic Theory.* New York: Academic.

Sargent, Thomas J., and Neil Wallace. 1982. "The Real-Bills Doctrine versus the Quantity Theory: A Reconsideration." *Journal of Political Economy* 90, no. 2 (December): 1212–36.

Schultz, Henry. 1938. *The Theory and Measurement of Demand.* Chicago: University of Chicago Press.

Schumpeter, Joseph A. 1954. *History of Economic Analysis.* New York: Oxford University Press.

Schwartz, Anna J. 1992. "Banking School, Currency School, Free Banking School." In Peter Newman, Murray Milgate, and John Eatwell, eds., *The New Palgrave: Dictionary of Money and Finance.* Vol. 1. London: Macmillan. 148–51.

Schwarzer, Johannes A. 2018. "Cost-Push and Demand-Pull Inflation: Milton Friedman and the 'Cruel Dilemma.'" *Journal of Economic Perspectives* 32, no. 1 (Winter): 195–210.

Selden, Richard T. 1956. "Monetary Velocity in the United States." In *Studies in the Quantity Theory of Money,* edited by Milton Friedman, 179–260. Chicago: University of Chicago Press.

———. 1962. "Stable Money Growth." In Leland B. Yeager, ed., *In Search of a Monetary Constitution.* Cambridge, MA: Harvard University Press. 322–56.

Selgin, George. 1999. "Hayek versus Keynes on How the Price Level Ought to Behave." *History of Political Economy* 31, no. 4 (Winter): 699–721.

Shils, Edward. 1991. *Remembering the University of Chicago: Teachers, Scientists, and Scholars.* Chicago: University of Chicago Press.

Shlaes, Amity. 2007. *The Forgotten Man: A New History of the Great Depression.* New York: Harper Collins.

Shoup, Carl S., Milton Friedman, and Ruth P. Mack. 1943. *Taxing to Prevent Inflation: Techniques for Estimating Revenue Requirements.* New York: Columbia University Press.

Silber, William. 1971. "The St. Louis Equation: 'Democratic' and 'Republican' Versions and Other Experiments." *Review of Economics and Statistics* 53, no. 4 (November): 362–67.

———. 2009. "Why Did FDR's Bank Holiday Succeed?" *Federal Reserve Bank of New York Economic Policy Review* 15 (July): 19–30.

Silverman, A. G. 1927. "Book Review: *Wealth, Virtual Wealth and Debt*, by Frederick Soddy." *American Economic Review* 17, no. 2:275–78.

Simons, Henry C. 1934a. *A Positive Program for Laissez Faire: Some Proposals for a Liberal Economic Policy*. Public Policy Pamphlet 15. Chicago: University of Chicago Press. Reprinted in Henry C. Simons, ed., *Economic Policy for a Free Society*. Chicago: University of Chicago Press, 1948. 40–77 and 325–35.

———. 1934b. "Finds New Deal Queer Jumble; Aims Conflict." *Chicago Tribune*, Finance and Business Section, March 12.

———. 1934c. "Currency Systems and Commercial Policy." In International Economic Relations, *Commission of Inquiry into National Policy in International Economic Relations*. Minneapolis: University of Minnesota Press. 344–49. Reprinted in Ross B. Emmett, ed., *The Chicago Tradition in Economics 1892–1945*. London: Routledge, 2002. 111–16.

———. 1935a. "Book Review: *The Supply and Control of Money in the United States*, by Lauchlin Currie." *Journal of Political Economy* 63 (August): 555–58.

———. 1935b. "Depression Economics." *Christian Century*, November 6, 1421.

———. 1936a. "Rules versus Authorities in Monetary Policy." *Journal of Political Economy* 44, no. 1 (February): 1–30. Reprinted in Henry C. Simons, ed., *Economic Policy for a Free Society*. Chicago: University of Chicago Press, 1948. 160–83 and 325–35.

———. 1936b. "Keynes's Comments on Money." *Christian Century* 53 (July): 1016–17.

———. 1938. *Personal Income Taxation*. Chicago: University of Chicago Press.

———. 1939. "Book Review: *Full Recovery or Stagnation?*, by Alvin Hansen." *Journal of Political Economy* 4, no. 2 (April): 272–76.

———. 1941. "For a Free-Market Liberalism." *University of Chicago Law Review* 8, no. 2 (February): 202–14. Reprinted in Henry C. Simons, ed., *Economic Policy for a Free Society*. Chicago: University of Chicago Press, 1948. 90–106.

———. 1942a. "Hansen on Fiscal Policy." *Journal of Political Economy* 50, no. 2 (February): 161–96. Reprinted in Henry C. Simons, ed., *Economic Policy for a Free Society*. Chicago: University of Chicago Press, 1948. 184–219.

———. 1942b. "Review of *The Structure of the American Economy: Part II. Toward Full Use of Resources*, by Gardiner C. Means, D. E. Montgomery, J. M. Clark, Alvin H. Hansen, and Mordecai Ezeliel." *Review of Economics and Statistics* 24, no. 1 (February): 44–47.

———. 1943. "Postwar Economic Policy: Some Traditional Liberal Proposals." *American Economic Review* 33, no. 1 (Part 2, Supplement, Papers and Proceedings of the Fifty-Fifth Annual Meeting of the American Economic Association)

(March): 431–45. Reprinted in Henry C. Simons, ed., *Economic Policy for a Free Society*. Chicago: University of Chicago Press, 1948. 240–59.

———. 1944a. "On Debt Policy." *Journal of Political Economy* 70:356–61. Reprinted in Henry C. Simons, ed., *Economic Policy for a Free Society*. Chicago: University of Chicago Press, 1948. 220–30.

———. 1944b. "Some Reflections on Syndicalism." *Journal of Political Economy* 52, no. 1 (March): 1–25. Reprinted in Henry C. Simons, ed., *Economic Policy for a Free Society*. Chicago: University of Chicago Press, 1948. 121–59.

———. 1944c. "Economic Stability and Antitrust Policy." *University of Chicago Law Review* 11, no. 4 (June): 338–48. Reprinted in Henry C. Simons, ed., *Economic Policy for a Free Society*. Chicago: University of Chicago Press, 1948. 107–20.

———. 1944d. "The US Holds the Cards." *Fortune*, September, 157–59 and 196–200.

———. 1945a. "The Beveridge Program: An Unsympathetic Interpretation." *Journal of Political Economy* 53, no. 3 (September): 212–33. Reprinted in Henry C. Simons, ed., *Economic Policy for a Free Society*. Chicago: University of Chicago Press, 1948. 277–312.

———. 1945b. "Introduction: A Political Credo." In Henry C. Simons, ed., *Economic Policy for a Free Society*. Chicago: University of Chicago Press, 1948. 1–39.

———. 1945c. "Book Review: *World Commodities and World Currency*, by Benjamin Graham." *Journal of Political Economy* 53, no. 3:279–81.

———. 1946. "Debt Policy and Banking Policy." *Review of Economic Statistics* 28, no. 2 (May): 85–89. Reprinted in Henry C. Simons, ed., *Economic Policy for a Free Society*. Chicago: University of Chicago Press, 1948. 231–39.

———. 1948a. "Money, Tariffs, and the Peace." In Henry C. Simons, ed., *Economic Policy for a Free Society*. Chicago: University of Chicago Press, 1948. 260–76.

———. 1948b. *Economic Policy for a Free Society*. Chicago: University of Chicago Press.

———. 1950. *Federal Tax Reform*. Chicago: University of Chicago Press.

Simons, Henry C., et al. 1933. "Banking and Currency Reform," including appendix, "Banking and Business Cycles," and a supplementary memorandum, "Long-Time Objectives of Monetary Management." Unsigned mimeograph. Department of Economics, University of Chicago.

Sims, Christopher A. 2011. "Statistical Modeling of Monetary Policy and Its Effects." 2011 Nobel Prize Lecture, published in *American Economic Review* 102, no. 4 (June): 1187–205.

Skaggs, Neil T. 1991. "John Fullarton's Law of Reflux and Central Bank Policy." *History of Political Economy* 23, no. 3:457–80.

Skidelsky, Robert. 1992. *John Maynard Keynes*. Vol. 2, *The Economist as Saviour, 1920–1937*. London: Macmillan.

Slichter, Sumner. 1931. *Modern Economic Society*. 2nd ed. New York: Holt.

———. 1932. "Comments on Mr. Knight's Review." *Journal of Political Economy* 40, no. 6 (December): 814–20.

Smith, Adam. 1776. *An Inquiry into the Nature and Causes of the Wealth of Nations*. Reprinted in 1937. New York: Random House.

Snowdon, Brian, Howard Vane, and Peter Wynarczyk. 1994. *A Modern Guide to Macroeconomics: An Introduction to Competing Schools of Thought*. Aldershot: Edward Elgar.

Soddy, Frederick. 1926. *Wealth, Virtual Wealth and Debt: The Solution of the Economic Paradox*. New York: E. P. Dutton.

———. 1934. *The Role of Money: What It Should Be, Contrasted with What It Has Become*. London: George Rutledge and Sons.

Solomon, Robert. 1977. *The International Monetary System, 1945–1976*. New York: Harper and Row.

Solow, Robert M., and John B. Taylor, eds. 1998. *Inflation, Unemployment, and Monetary Policy*. Cambridge, MA: MIT Press.

Sraffa, Piero, ed. 1951. *The Works and Correspondence of David Ricardo*. Vol. 6, *Letters 1810–1815*. Indianapolis: Liberty Fund.

Steele, Gerald R. 2018. *The Economic Thought of Henry Calvert Simons, Crown Prince of the Chicago School*. London: Routledge.

Steil, Benn. 2013. *The Battle of Bretton Woods: John Maynard Keynes, Harry Dexter White, and the Making of a New World Order*. Princeton, NJ: Princeton University Press.

Stein, Herbert. 1987. "Simons, Henry Calvert (1899–1946)." In John Eatwell, Murray Milgate, and Peter Newman, eds., *The New Palgrave: A Dictionary of Economics*. Vol. 4. London: Palgrave Macmillan. 333–35.

Stein, Jerome. 1976. "Introduction: The Monetarist Critique of the New Economics." In Jerome Stein, ed., *Monetarism*. Amsterdam: North Holland. 1–16.

Steindl, Frank G. 1990. "The 'Oral Tradition' at Chicago in the 1930s: Confirmations and Contradictions." *Journal of Political Economy* 98, no. 2 (April): 430–32.

———. 1995. *Monetary Interpretations of the Great Depression*. Ann Arbor: University of Michigan Press.

———. 2004. "Friedman and Money in the 1930s." *History of Political Economy* 36, no. 3:521–31.

Stewart, Kenneth G. 2005. *Introduction to Applied Econometrics*. Belmont, CA: Brooks / Cole Thomson Learning.

Stigler, George J. 1974. "Henry Calvert Simons." *Journal of Law and Economics* 17, no. 1 (April): 1–5.

———. 1987. "Knight, Frank Hyneman." In John Eatwell, Murray Milgate, and Peter Newman, eds., *The New Palgrave: A Dictionary of Economics*. Vol. 3. New York: Stockman. 55–59.

———. 1988. *Memoirs of an Unregulated Economist*. New York: Basic Books.

Stigler, Stephen. 2005. "Aaron Director Remembered." *Journal of Law and Economics* 48, no. 2:307–11.

Subcommittee Hearings. 1950. "Monetary, Credit, and Fiscal Policies." Hearings before the Subcommittee on Monetary, Credit, and Fiscal Policies of the Joint

Committee on the Economic Report Congress of the United States. 81st Cong., 1st sess. Washington, DC: US Government Printing Office.

Subcommittee on General Credit Control and Debt Management of the Joint Committee on the Economic Report: Congress of the United States. 1952. *Monetary Policy and the Management of the Public Debt: Hearings, March 10, 11, 12, 13, 14, 17, 18, 19, 20, 21, 24, 25, 26, 27, 28, and 31, 1952.* 82nd Cong., 2nd sess. Washington, DC: US Government Printing Office.

Subcommittee Report. 1950. "Monetary, Credit, and Fiscal Policies." Report of the Subcommittee on Monetary, Credit, and Fiscal Policies of the Joint Committee on the Economic Report Congress of the United States. 81st Cong., 2nd sess. Document no. 129. Washington, DC: US Government Printing Office.

Subcommittee Statements. 1949. "Monetary, Credit, and Fiscal Policies." A Collection of Statements Submitted to the Subcommittee on Monetary, Credit, and Fiscal Policies by Government Officials, Bankers, Economists, and Others, Joint Committee on the Economic Report. 81st Cong., 1st sess. Washington, DC: US Government Printing Office.

Sutton, Francis X. 1963. "Book Review: *Capitalism and Freedom*, by Milton Friedman." *American Sociological Review* 28, no. 3:491–92.

Svensson, Lars. 2003. "What Is Wrong with Taylor Rules? Using Judgement in Monetary Policy through Targeting Rules." *Journal of Economic Literature* 41, no. 2:426–77.

Swamy, P. A. V. B., and George S. Tavlas. 1995. "Random Coefficient Models: Theory and Applications." *Journal of Economic Surveys* 9, no. 2 (June): 165–96.

———. 2001. "Random Coefficient Models." In *A Companion to Theoretical Econometrics*, edited by Badi H. Baltagi, 410–28. Malden, MA: Wiley-Blackwell.

———. 2007. "The New Keynesian Phillips Curve and Inflation Expectations: Respecification and Interpretation." *Economic Theory*, 31, no. 2 (May): 293–306.

Tarshis, Lorie. 1947. *The Elements of Economics: An Introduction to the Theory of Price and Employment.* Boston: Houghton Mifflin.

Tavlas, George S. 1976. "Some Further Observations on the Monetary Economics of Chicagoans and Non-Chicagoans." *Southern Economic Journal* 42, no. 4 (April): 685–92.

———. 1977a. "The Chicago Tradition Revisited: Some Neglected Monetary Contributions; Senator Paul Douglas (1892–1976)." *Journal of Money, Credit and Banking* 9, no. 4 (November): 529–35.

———. 1977b. "Chicago Schools Old and New on the Efficacy of Monetary Policy." *Banca Nazionale del Lavoro Quarterly Review* 30, no. 120 (March): 51–73.

———. 1981. "Keynesian and Monetarist Theories of the Monetary Transmission Process." *Journal of Monetary Economics* 7, no. 3:317–38.

———. 1982. "Notes on Garvy, Snyder, and the Doctrinal Foundations of Monetarism." *History of Political Economy* 14, no. 1 (March): 89–100.

———. 1993. "The 'New' Theory of Optimum Currency Areas." *World Economy* 16, no. 6:1–16.

———. 1994. "The Theory of Monetary Integration." *Open Economies Review* 5, no. 2:211–30.

———. 1997. "Chicago, Harvard, and the Doctrinal Foundations of Monetary Economics." *Journal of Political Economy* 105, no. 1 (February): 153–77.

———. 1998. "Was the Monetarist Tradition Invented?" *Journal of Economic Perspectives* 12, no. 4 (Fall): 211–22.

———. 1999. "Was the Monetarist Tradition Invented? Response." *Journal of Economic Perspectives* 13, no. 3 (Summer): 241–42.

———. 2011. "Two Who Called the Great Depression: An Initial Formulation of the Monetary-Origins View." *Journal of Money, Credit and Banking* 43, no. 2/3 (March/April): 565–74.

———. 2013. "Anna Jacobson Schwartz: In Memoriam." *Cato Journal* 33, no. 3 (Fall): 321–32.

———. 2015. "In Old Chicago: Simons, Friedman, and the Development of Monetary-Policy Rules." *Journal of Money, Credit and Banking* 47, no. 1 (February): 99–121.

———. 2019a. "'The Group': The Making of the Chicago Monetary Tradition, 1927–36." *History of Political Economy* 51, no. 2 (April): 259–96.

———. 2019b. "The Intellectual Origins of the Monetarist Counter-Revolution Reconsidered: How Clark Warburton Influenced Milton Friedman's Monetary Thinking." *Oxford Economic Papers* 71, no. 3 (July): 645–65.

———. 2021a. "Modern Monetary Theory Meets Greece and Chicago." *Cato Journal* 41, no. 1:1–23.

———. 2021b. "A Reconsideration of the Doctrinal Foundations of Monetary-Policy Rules: Fisher versus Chicago." *Journal of the History of Economic Thought* 43, no. 1 (March): 55–82.

———. 2022a. "'The Initiated': Aaron Director and the Chicago Monetary Tradition." *Journal of the History of Economic Thought* 44, no. 1 (March): 1–23.

———. 2022b. "Jacob Viner, Milton Friedman, and the Chicago Monetary Tradition: A Reconsideration." *History of Political Economy* 54, no. 2, 251–89.

———. 2022c. "The Long and Unfinished Road to Friedman and Meiselman's 'The Relative Stability of Monetary Velocity and the Investment Multiplier.'" Draft manuscript.

———. Forthcoming. "On the Controversy over the Origins of the Chicago Plan for 100 Percent Reserves: Sorry, Frederick Soddy, It Was Knight and (Most Probably) Simons!" *Journal of Money, Credit and Banking.*

Tavlas, George S., Harris Dellas, and Alan C. Stockman. 2008. "The Classification and Performance of Alternative Exchange-Rate Systems." *European Economic Review* 52, no. 6 (August): 941–63.

Taylor, John B. 1993. "Discretion versus Policy Rules in Practice." *Carnegie-Rochester Conference Series on Public Policy* 39, no. 1:195–214.

———. 1998. "Monetary Policy Guidelines for Employment and Inflation Stability."

In Robert M. Solow and John B. Taylor, eds., *Inflation, Unemployment, and Monetary Policy*. Cambridge, MA: MIT Press. 29–54.

———. 2001. "An Interview with Milton Friedman." *Macroeconomic Dynamics* 5, no. 1 (February): 101–31.

———. 2012. "Monetary Policy Rules Work and Discretion Doesn't: A Tale of Two Eras." *Journal of Money, Credit and Banking* 44, no. 6:1017–32.

———. 2015. "A Monetary Policy for the Future." *Economics One*, April 16. http://economicsone.com/2015/04/16/a-monetarypolicy-for-the-future.

———. 2017. "Rules versus Discretion: Assessing the Debate over the Conduct of Monetary Policy." National Bureau of Economic Research Working Paper 24149.

Teigen, Ronald L. 1972. "A Critical Look at Monetarist Economics." *Federal Reserve Bank of St. Louis Review* 54 (January): 10–25.

Thomas, Woodlief, and Ralph A. Young. 1947. "Problems of Postwar Monetary Policy." In Karl R. Bopp, Robert V. Rosa, Carl E. Parry, Woodlief Thomas, and Ralph A. Young, eds., *Federal Reserve Policy*. Postwar Economic Studies 8, November. Washington, DC: Board of Governors of the Federal Reserve System. 88–119.

Thornton, Henry. 1802. *An Enquiry into the Nature and Effects of the Paper Credit of Great Britain*. Reprint, New York: Augustus M. Kelley, 1969.

Thygesen, Niels. 1977. "The Scientific Contributions of Milton Friedman." *Scandinavian Journal of Economics* 79, no. 1:56–98.

Timberlake, Richard H. 1988. "A Reassessment of C. A. Phillips's Theory of Bank Credit." *History of Political Economy* 20, no. 2:299–308.

———. 2007. "Gold Standards and the Real Bills Doctrine in US Monetary Policy." *Independent Review* 11, no. 3 (Winter): 325–54.

Tobin, James. 1951a. "Book Review: *Monetary Policy for a Competitive Society*, by Lloyd W. Mints." *Journal of Business of the University of Chicago* 24, no. 3, 233–34.

———. 1951b. "Monetary Restriction and Direct Controls." *Review of Economics and Statistics* 33, no. 3 (August): 196–98.

———. 1981. "Book Review: *Keynes' Monetary Thought: A Study of Its Development*, by Don Patinkin." *Journal of Political Economy* 89, no. 1 (February): 204–7.

———. 1987. "Irving Fisher (1867–1947)." In John Eatwell, Murray Milgate, and Peter Newman, eds., *The New Palgrave: A Dictionary of Economics*. Vol. 2. London: Palgrave Macmillan. 369–76.

Tooke, Thomas. 1844. *An Inquiry into the Currency Principle: The Connection of the Currency with Prices, and the Expediency of a Separation of Issue from Banking*. London: Longman, Brown, Green, and Longmans.

———. 1848. *A History of Prices and of the State of the Circulation from 1839 to 1847*. Vol. 4. London: Longman, Brown, Green, and Longmans.

Tooze, Adam. 2021. "Battle of the Giants." *Financial Times Weekend*, October 16–17.

Tugwell, Rexford G. 1932. "The Principle of Planning and the Institution of Laissez Faire." *American Economic Review* 22, no. 1 (Supplement, Papers and Proceedings of the Forty-Fourth Annual Meeting of the American Economic Association) (March): 75–92.

———. 1933. *The Industrial Discipline and the Government Arts*. New York: Columbia University Press.

University of Chicago News Office. 2004. "Aaron Director, Founder of the Field of Law and Economics." http://www-news.uchicago.edu/releases/04/040913.direc tor.shtml.

Van Horn, Robert. 2009. "Reinventing Monopoly and the Role of Corporations: The Roots of Chicago Law and Economics." In Philip Mirowski and Dieter Plehwe, eds., *The Road from Mont Pèlerin: The Making of the Neoliberal Thought Collective*. Cambridge, MA: Harvard University Press. 204–37.

———. 2010a. "Aaron Director." In Ross B. Emmett, ed., *The Elgar Companion to the Chicago School of Economics*. London: Edward Elgar. 265–69.

———. 2010b. "Harry Aaron Director: The Coming of Age of a Reformer Skeptic (1914–24)." *History of Political Economy* 42, no. 4:601–30.

———. 2014. "Henry Simons's Death." *History of Political Economy* 46, no. 3:525–35.

———. 2020. "Corporations and the Rise of the Chicago Law and Economics Movement." ProMarket, Chicago Booth, Stigler Center for the Study of the Economy and the State, January 15. https://promarket.org/2020/01/15/corpora tions-and-the-rise-of-the-chicago-law-and-economics-movement/.

Van Horn, Robert, and Ross B. Emmett. 2015. "Two Trajectories of Democratic Capitalism in the Post-war Chicago School: Frank Knight versus Aaron Director." *Cambridge Journal of Economics* 39, no. 5 (September): 1443–55.

Van Horn, Robert, and Philip Mirowski. 2009. "The Rise of the Chicago School of Economics and the Birth of Neoliberalism." In Philip Mirowski and Dieter Plehwe, eds., *The Road from Mont Pèlerin*. Cambridge, MA: Harvard University Press. 139–81.

Van Overtveldt, Johan. 2007. *The Chicago School: How the University of Chicago Assembled Thinkers Who Revolutionized Economics and Business*. Chicago: Agate.

Villard, Henry H. 1948. "Monetary Theory." In Howard S. Ellis, ed., *A Survey of Contemporary Economics*. Philadelphia: published on behalf of the American Economic Association by Blakiston. 314–51.

Viner, Jacob. 1924. *Canada's Balance of International Indebtedness, 1900–1913: An Inductive Study in the Theory of International Trade*. Cambridge, MA: Harvard University Press.

———. 1931a. "Cost Curves and Supply Curves." *Zeitschrift für Nationalokonome* 3, no. 1:23–46.

———. 1931b. "Problems of International Commercial and Financial Policy." In A. H. Buffington, ed., *Report of the Round Tables and General Conferences at the Eleventh Session.* Williamstown, MA: Institute of Politics. 165–93.

———. 1932a. "International Aspects of the Gold Standard." In Quincy Wright, ed., *Gold and Monetary Stabilization.* Chicago: University of Chicago Press. 3–42.

———. 1932b. "Book Review: *The Problem of Maintaining Purchasing Power,* by P. W. Martin." *Journal of Political Economy* 40, no. 3 (June): 418–19.

———. 1933a. "Balanced Deflation, Inflation, or More Depression." *Day and Hour Series of the University of Minnesota* 3 (Minneapolis: University of Minnesota Press): 5–30.

———. 1933b. "Inflation as a Possible Remedy for the Depression." In *Proceedings of the Institute of Public Affairs, University of Georgia.* Athens: University of Georgia Press. 120–35.

———. 1936a. "Recent Legislation and the Banking Situation." *American Economic Review* 26, no. 1 (Supplement, Papers and Proceedings of the Forty-Eighth Annual Meeting of the American Economic Association) (March): 106–19.

———. 1936b. "Mr. Keynes on the Causes of Unemployment." *Quarterly Journal of Economics* 51, no. 1 (November): 147–67.

———. 1937. *Studies in the Theory of International Trade.* New York: Harper and Brothers.

———. 1940. "The Short View and the Long View in Economic Policy." *American Economic Review* 30, no. 1 (March): 1–15.

———. 1942a. "Inflation: Menace or Bogey?" *Yale Review* 31 (June): 684–702.

———. 1942b. "The International Economic Organization of the Future." In *Toward International Organization.* Oberlin College Lectures. New York: Harper and Brothers. 110–37.

———. 1947. "Can We Check Inflation?" *Yale Review* 37 (Winter): 209–10.

———. 1953. "Interview." Jacob Viner Papers. Princeton University.

———. 1956. "Some International Aspects of Economic Stabilization." In Leonard D. White, ed., *The State of the Social Sciences.* Chicago: University of Chicago Press. 283–98.

———. 1963. "Comment on My 1936 Review of Keynes's *General Theory.*" In Robert Lekachman, ed., *Keynes' General Theory: Reports of Three Decades.* New York: St. Martin's, 1964. 265–66.

von Mises, Ludwig. 1912. *Theorie des Geldes und der Umlaufsmittel.* Munich: Duncker and Humblot. 2nd ed., Frank H. Knight, 1924. English translation by H. E. Batson, *The Theory of Money and Credit.* Indianapolis: Liberty Classics, 1980.

Walsh, Carl E. 2017. *Monetary Theory and Policy.* 4th ed. Cambridge, MA: MIT Press.

Walters, Alan. 1987. "Friedman, Milton." In J. Eatwell, M. Milgate, and P. Newman, eds., *The New Palgrave: A Dictionary of Economics.* Vol. 2. London: Macmillan. 422–27.

Walton, Gary M., and Hugh Rockoff. 2005. *History of the American Economy*. Mason, OH: South-Western.

Warburton, Clark. 1945. "Monetary Theory, Full Production, and the Great Depression." *Econometrica* 13, no. 2 (April): 114–28.

———. 1946a. "Quantity and Frequency of Use of Money in the United States, 1919–45." *Journal of Political Economy* 54, no. 5 (October): 436–50. Reprinted in Clark Warburton, ed., *Depression, Inflation, and Monetary Policy: Selected Papers, 1945–1953*. Baltimore: Johns Hopkins University Press, 1966. 144–61.

———. 1946b. "Monetary Control under the Federal Reserve Act." *Political Science Quarterly* 61, no. 4 (December): 505–34. Reprinted in Clark Warburton, ed., *Depression, Inflation, and Monetary Policy: Selected Papers, 1945–1953*. Baltimore: Johns Hopkins University Press, 1966. 291–316.

———. 1949. "The Secular Trend in Monetary Velocity." *Quarterly Journal of Economics* 63, no. 1 (February): 68–91. Reprinted in Clark Warburton, ed., *Depression, Inflation, and Monetary Policy: Selected Papers, 1945–53*. Baltimore: Johns Hopkins University Press, 1966. 192–213.

———. 1950. "Monetary Theory and the Price Level in the Future." In *Five Monographs on Business Income*. Study Group on Business Income. New York: American Institute of Accountants. 161–93.

———. 1952. "Monetary Difficulties and the Structure of the Monetary System." *Journal of Finance* 7, no. 4 (December): 523–45. Reprinted in Clark Warburton, ed., *Depression, Inflation, and Monetary Policy: Selected Papers, 1945–53*. Baltimore: Johns Hopkins University Press, 1966. 327–49.

———. 1953. "Rules and Implements for Monetary Policy." *Journal of Finance* 8, no. 1 (March): 1–21. Reprinted in Clark Warburton, ed., *Depression, Inflation, and Monetary Policy: Selected Papers, 1945–53*. Baltimore: Johns Hopkins University Press, 1966. 371–91.

Watkins, Leonard. L. 1938. *Commercial Banking Reform in the United States: With Especial Reference to the 100 Per Cent Plan and the Regulation of Interest Rates on Bank Deposits*. Ann Arbor: University of Michigan.

Weber, Warren E. 1980. "The Effect of Real and Monetary Disturbances on the Price Level under Alternative Commodity Reserve Standards." *International Economic Review* 21, no. 3:673–90.

Whale, Barret. 1944. "A Retrospective View of the Bank Charter Act of 1844." *Economica* 11, no. 43:109–11.

Wheelock, David C. 1992. "Monetary Policy in the Great Depression: What the Fed Did and Why." *Federal Reserve Bank of St. Louis Review*, March, 3–28.

Whelan, Karl. 2021. "Central Banks and Inflation: Where Do We Stand and How Did We Get Here?" CEPR Discussion Paper 16557.

White, Eugene N. 1981. "State-Sponsored Insurance of Bank Deposits in the United States." *Journal of Economic History* 41, no. 3 (September): 537–57.

———. 1984. "A Reinterpretation of the Banking Crisis of 1930." *Journal of Economic History* 44, no. 1 (March): 119–38.

———. 1986. "Before the Glass-Steagall Act: An Analysis of the Investment Banking Activities of National Banks." *Explorations in Economic History* 23, no. 1: 33–55.

White, Lawrence H. 1999. "Hayek's Monetary Theory and Policy: A Critical Reconstruction." *Journal of Money, Credit and Banking* 31, no. 1 (February): 109–20.

Williams, John H. 1932. "Monetary Stability and the Gold Standard." In Quincy Wright, ed., *Gold and Monetary Stabilization*. Chicago: University of Chicago Press. 133–58.

Wolf, Martin. 2014. "Strip Private Banks of Their Power to Create Money." *Financial Times*, April 24.

Woodford, Michael. 1999. "Revolution and Evolution in Twentieth-Century Macroeconomics." Prepared for the conference "Frontiers of the Mind in the Twenty-First Century," Library of Congress, Washington, DC, June 14–18.

Woosley, John B. 1946. "Book Review: *A History of Banking Theory in Great Britain and the United States*, by Lloyd W. Mints." *Southern Economic Journal* 12, no. 4 (April): 388–90.

Wright, Quincy, ed. 1932. *Gold and Monetary Stabilization*. Chicago: University of Chicago Press.

Yeager, Leland B. 1981. "Clark Warburton, 1896–1979." *History of Political Economy* 13, no. 2 (Summer): 279–84.

———. 1987. "Warburton, Clark (1896–1979)." In J. Eatwell, M. Miligate, and P. Newman, eds., *The New Palgrave: A Dictionary of Economics*. Vol. 4. London: Macmillan. 874.

Young, Allyn A. 1928a. *An Analysis of Bank Statistics for the United States*. Cambridge, MA: Harvard University Press.

———. 1928b. "Increasing Returns and Economic Progress." *Economic Journal* 38, no. 152 (December): 527–42.

# Index